IT'S HERE!

PRENTICE HALL
SCIENCE

FINALLY. THE PERFECT FIT.

NOW YOU CAN CHOOSE THE PERFECT FIT FOR ALL YOUR CURRICULUM NEEDS.

The new Prentice Hall Science program consists of 19 hardcover books, each of which covers a particular area of science. All of the sciences are represented in the program so you can choose the perfect fit to *your* particular curriculum needs.

The flexibility of this program will allow you to teach those topics you want to teach, and to teach them *in-depth*. Virtually any approach to science—general, integrated, coordinated, thematic, etc.—is possible with Prentice Hall Science.

Above all, the program is designed to make your teaching experience easier and more fun.

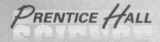

ELECTRICITY AND MAGNETISM

Ch. 1. Electric Charges and Currents
Ch. 2. Magnetism
Ch. 3. Electromagnetism
Ch. 4. Electronics and Computers

HEREDITY: THE CODE OF LIFE

Ch. 1. What is Genetics?
Ch. 2. How Chromosomes Work
Ch. 3. Human Genetics
Ch. 4. Applied Genetics

ECOLOGY: EARTH'S LIVING RESOURCES

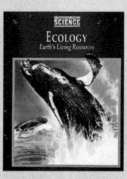

Ch. 1. Interactions Among Living Things
Ch. 2. Cycles in Nature
Ch. 3. Exploring Earth's Biomes
Ch. 4. Wildlife Conservation

PARADE OF LIFE: MONERANS, PROTISTS, FUNGI, AND PLANTS

Ch. 1. Classification of Living Things
Ch. 2. Viruses and Monerans
Ch. 3. Protists
Ch. 4. Fungi
Ch. 5. Plants Without Seeds
Ch. 6. Plants With Seeds

EXPLORING THE UNIVERSE

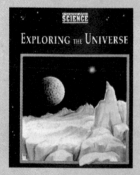

Ch. 1. Stars and Galaxies
Ch. 2. The Solar System
Ch. 3. Earth and Its Moon

EVOLUTION: CHANGE OVER TIME

Ch. 1. Earth's History in Fossils
Ch. 2. Changes in Living Things Over Time
Ch. 3. The Path to Modern Humans

EXPLORING EARTH'S WEATHER

Ch. 1. What Is Weather?
Ch. 2. What Is Climate?
Ch. 3. Climate in the United States

THE NATURE OF SCIENCE

Ch. 1. What is Science?
Ch. 2. Measurement and the Sciences
Ch. 3. Tools and the Sciences

**ECOLOGY:
EARTH'S NATURAL RESOURCES**

Ch. 1. Energy Resources
Ch. 2. Earth's Nonliving
Resources
Ch. 3. Pollution
Ch. 4. Conserving Earth's
Resources

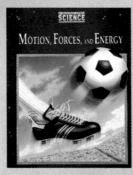

**MOTION, FORCES,
AND ENERGY**

Ch. 1. What Is Motion?
Ch. 2. The Nature of Forces
Ch. 3. Forces in Fluids
Ch. 4. Work, Power, and
Simple Machines
Ch. 5. Energy: Forms
and Changes

PARADE OF LIFE: ANIMALS

Ch. 1. Sponges, Cnidarians,
Worms, and Mollusks
Ch. 2. Arthropods and
Echinoderms
Ch. 3. Fish and Amphibians
Ch. 4. Reptiles and Birds
Ch. 5. Mammals

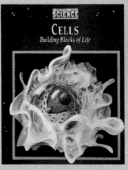

**CELLS:
BUILDING BLOCKS OF LIFE**

Ch. 1. The Nature of LIfe
Ch. 2. Cell Structure and
Function
Ch. 3. Cell Processes
Ch. 4. Cell Energy

DYNAMIC EARTH

Ch. 1. Movement of the
Earth's Crust
Ch. 2. Earthquakes and
Volcanoes
Ch. 3. Plate Tectonics
Ch. 4. Rocks and Minerals
Ch. 5. Weathering and
Soil Formation
Ch. 6. Erosion and Deposition

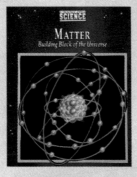

**MATTER: BUILDING BLOCK OF
THE UNIVERSE**

Ch. 1. General Properties
of Matter
Ch. 2. Physical and Chemical
Changes
Ch. 3. Mixtures, Elements, and
Compounds
Ch. 4. Atoms: Building Blocks
of Matter
Ch. 5. Classification of Elements:
The Periodic Table

CHEMISTRY OF MATTER

Ch. 1. Atoms and Bonding
Ch. 2. Chemical Reactions
Ch. 3. Families of Chemical
Compounds
Ch. 4. Chemical Technology
Ch. 5. Radioactive Elements

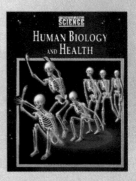

**HUMAN BIOLOGY AND
HEALTH**

Ch. 1. The Human Body
Ch. 2. Skeletal and Muscular
Systems
Ch. 3. Digestive System
Ch. 4. Circulatory System
Ch. 5. Respiratory and
Excretory Systems
Ch. 6. Nervous and Endocrine
Systems
Ch. 7. Reproduction and
Development
Ch. 8. Immune System
Ch. 9. Alcohol, Tobacco,
and Drugs

EXPLORING PLANET EARTH

Ch. 1. Earth's Atmosphere
Ch. 2. Earth's Oceans
Ch. 3. Earth's Fresh Water
Ch. 4. Earth's Landmasses
Ch. 5. Earth's Interior

HEAT ENERGY

Ch. 1. What Is Heat?
Ch. 2. Uses of Heat

SOUND AND LIGHT

Ch. 1. Characteristics of Waves
Ch. 2. Sound and Its Uses
Ch. 3. Light and the Electro-
magnetic Spectrum
Ch. 4. Light and Its Uses

A COMPLETELY INTEGRATED LEARNING SYSTEM...

The Prentice Hall Science program is an *integrated* learning system with a variety of print materials and multimedia components. All are designed to meet the needs of diverse learning styles and your technology needs.

THE STUDENT BOOK

Each book is a model of **excellent writing and dynamic visuals**— designed to be exciting and motivating to the student *and* the teacher, with relevant examples integrated throughout, and more opportunities for many different activities which apply to everyday life.

Problem-solving activities emphasize the thinking process, so problems may be more open-ended.

"Discovery Activities" throughout the book foster active learning.

Different sciences, and other disciplines, are integrated throughout the text and reinforced in the "Connections" features (the connections between computers and viruses is one example).

TEACHER'S RESOURCE PACKAGE

In addition to the student book, the complete teaching package contains:

ANNOTATED TEACHER'S EDITION

Designed to provide **"teacher-friendly"** support regardless of instructional approach:

■ **Help is readily available** if you choose to teach thematically, to integrate the sciences, and/or to integrate the sciences with other curriculum areas.

■ **Activity-based learning** is easy to implement through the use of Discovery Strategies, Activity Suggestions, and Teacher Demonstrations.

■ Integration of all components is part of the teaching strategies.

■ For instant accessibility, all of the teaching suggestions are wrapped around the student pages to which they refer.

ACTIVITY BOOK

Includes a **discovery activity for each chapter**, plus other activities including problem-solving and cooperative-learning activities.

THE REVIEW AND REINFORCEMENT GUIDE

Addresses **students' different learning styles** in a clear and comprehensive format:

■ Highly visual for visual learners.

TEACHER'S RESOURCE PACKAGE

FOR THE PERFECT FIT TO YOUR TEACHING NEEDS.

■ Can be used in conjunction with the program's audiotapes for auditory and language learners.

■ More than a study guide, it's a guide to comprehension, with activities, key concepts, and vocabulary.

ENGLISH AND SPANISH AUDIOTAPES
Correlate with the Review and Reinforcement Guide to aid auditory learners.

LABORATORY MANUAL ANNOTATED TEACHER'S EDITION
Offers **at least one additional hands-on opportunity per chapter** with

answers and teaching suggestions on lab preparation and safety.

TEST BOOK
Contains **traditional and up-to-the-minute strategies for student assessment.** Choose from performance-based tests in addition to traditional chapter tests and computer test bank questions.

STUDENT LABORATORY MANUAL
Each of the 19 books also comes with its own Student Lab Manual.

ALSO INCLUDED IN THE INTEGRATED LEARNING SYSTEM:

■ Teacher's Desk Reference

■ English Guide for Language Learners

■ Spanish Guide for Language Learners

■ Product Testing Activities

■ Transparencies

■ Computer Test Bank (IBM, Apple, or MAC)

■ VHS Videos

■ Videodiscs

■ Interactive Videodiscs (Level III)

■ Courseware

All components are integrated in the teaching strategies in the Annotated Teacher's Edition, where they directly relate to the science content.

THE PRENTICE HALL SCIENCE
INTEGRATED LEARNING SYSTEM

The following components are integrated in the teaching strategies for
HUMAN BIOLOGY AND HEALTH.

- **Spanish Audiotape English Audiotape**
- **Activity Book**
- **Review and Reinforcement Guide**
- **Testing Program—** including Performance-Based Tests
- **Laboratory Manual, Annotated Teacher's Edition**
- **Product-Testing Activities:**

Testing Bandages
Testing Cereals
Testing Orange Juice
Testing Sports Drinks
Testing Yogurts
Testing Antacids

- **Laboratory Manual**
- **English Guide for Language Learners**
- **Spanish Guide for Language Learners**
- **Transparencies:**

Joints
Circulatory System
The Heart
Respiratory System
Urinary System
Three Types of Neurons
The Skin
The Eye
The Ear
Male Reproductive System
Female Reproductive System

- **Videos/Videodiscs:**

Systems Working Together

- **Videos:**

Skeletal System
Muscular System
The Bones and Muscles Get Rhythm
Digestive System
Circulatory System
Respiratory System
The Heart and the Lungs Play Ball
Excretory System
Nervous System
The Brain and Nervous System Think Science
Endocrine System

INTEGRATING OTHER SCIENCES

Many of the other 18 Prentice Hall Science books can be integrated into **HUMAN BIOLOGY AND HEALTH.** The books you will find suggested most often in the Annotated Teacher's Edition are: CELLS: BUILDING BLOCKS OF LIFE; CHEMISTRY OF MATTER; MOTION, FORCES, AND ENERGY; PARADE OF LIFE: ANIMALS; DYNAMIC EARTH; ELECTRICITY AND MAGNETISM; HEAT ENERGY; ECOLOGY: EARTH'S NATURAL RESOURCES; EXPLORING PLANET EARTH; SOUND AND LIGHT; EXPLORING THE UNIVERSE; PARADE OF LIFE: MONERANS, PROTISTS, FUNGI, AND PLANTS; ECOLOGY: EARTH'S LIVING RESOURCES and HEREDITY; THE CODE OF LIFE.

INTEGRATING THEMES

Many themes can be integrated into **HUMAN BIOLOGY AND HEALTH.**
Following are the ones most commonly suggested in the Annotated Teacher's Edition: ENERGY, SYSTEMS AND INTERACTIONS, STABILITY, and SCALE AND STRUCTURE.

For more detailed information on teaching thematically and integrating the sciences, see the Teacher's Desk Reference and teaching strategies throughout the Annotated Teacher's Edition.

For more information, call 1-800-848-9500 or write:

 P R E N T I C E   H A L L

Simon & Schuster Education Group
113 Sylvan Avenue Route 9W
Englewood Cliffs, New Jersey 07632
Simon & Schuster A Paramount Communications Company

Annotated Teacher's Edition

Prentice Hall Science
Human Biology and Health

Anthea Maton
Former NSTA National Coordinator
Project Scope, Sequence,
   Coordination
Washington, DC

Jean Hopkins
Science Instructor and Department
   Chairperson
John H. Wood Middle School
San Antonio, Texas

Susan Johnson
Professor of Biology
Ball State University
Muncie, Indiana

David LaHart
Senior Instructor
Florida Solar Energy Center
Cape Canaveral, Florida

Charles William McLaughlin
Science Instructor and Department
   Chairperson
Central High School
St. Joseph, Missouri

Maryanna Quon Warner
Science Instructor
Del Dios Middle School
Escondido, California

Jill D. Wright
Professor of Science Education
Director of International Field
   Programs
University of Pittsburgh
Pittsburgh, Pennsylvania

Prentice Hall
A Division of Simon & Schuster
Englewood Cliffs, New Jersey

ISBN 0-13-986787-2

   3 4 5 6 7 8 9 10   96 95 94 93

Contents of Annotated Teacher's Edition

To the Teacher   T–3

About the Teacher's Desk Reference   T–3

Integrating the Sciences   T–4

Thematic Overview   T–4

Thematic Matrices   T–5

Comprehensive List of Laboratory Materials   T–14

To the Teacher

Welcome to the *Prentice Hall Science* program. *Prentice Hall Science* has been designed as a complete program for use with middle school or junior high school science students. The program covers all relevant areas of science and has been developed with the flexibility to meet virtually all your curriculum needs. In addition, the program has been designed to better enable you—the classroom teacher—to integrate various disciplines of science into your daily lessons, as well as to enhance the thematic teaching of science.

The *Prentice Hall Science* program consists of nineteen books, each of which covers a particular topic area. The nineteen books in the *Prentice Hall Science* program are

The Nature of Science
Parade of Life: Monerans, Protists, Fungi, and Plants
Parade of Life: Animals
Cells: Building Blocks of Life
Heredity: The Code of Life
Evolution: Change Over Time

Ecology: Earth's Living Resources
Human Biology and Health
Exploring Planet Earth
Dynamic Earth
Exploring Earth's Weather
Ecology: Earth's Natural Resources
Exploring the Universe
Matter: Building Block of the Universe
Chemistry of Matter
Electricity and Magnetism
Heat Energy
Sound and Light
Motion, Forces, and Energy

Each of the student editions listed above also comes with a complete set of teaching materials and student ancillary materials. Furthermore, videos, interactive videos and science courseware are available for the *Prentice Hall Science* program. This combination of student texts and ancillaries, teacher materials, and multimedia products makes up your complete *Prentice Hall Science* Learning System.

About the Teacher's Desk Reference

When you purchase a textbook in the *Prentice Hall Science* program, you also receive a copy of the *Teacher's Desk Reference*. The *Teacher's Desk Reference* includes all the standard information you need to know about *Prentice Hall Science*.

The *Teacher's Desk Reference* presents an overview of the program, including a full description of each ancillary available in the program. It gives a brief summary of each of the student textbooks available in the *Prentice Hall Science* Learning System. The *Teacher's Desk Reference* also demonstrates how the seven science themes incorporated into *Prentice Hall Science* are woven throughout the entire program.

In addition, the *Teacher's Desk Reference* presents a detailed discussion of the features of the Student Edition and the features of the Annotated Teacher's Edition, as well as an overview section that summarizes issues in science education and offers a message about teaching special students. Selected instructional essays in the *Teacher's Desk Reference* include English as a Second Language (ESL), Multicultural Teaching, Cooperative-Learning Strategies, and Integrated Science Teaching, in addition to other relevant topics. Further, a discussion of the Multimedia components that are part of *Prentice Hall Science*, as well as how they can be integrated with the textbooks, is included in the *Teacher's Desk Reference*.

The *Teacher's Desk Reference* also contains in blackline master form a booklet on Teaching Graphing Skills, which may be reproduced for student use.

Integrating the Sciences

The *Prentice Hall Science* Learning System has been designed to allow you to teach science from an integrated point of view. Great care has been taken to integrate other science disciplines, where appropriate, into the chapter content and visuals. In addition, the integration of other disciplines such as social studies and literature has been incorporated into each textbook.

On the reduced student pages throughout your Annotated Teacher's Edition you will find numbers within blue bullets beside selected passages and visuals. An Annotation Key in the wraparound margins indicates the particular branch of science or other discipline that has been integrated into the student text. In addition, where appropriate, the name of the textbook and the chapter number in which the particular topic is discussed in greater detail is provided. This enables you to further integrate a particular science topic by using the complete *Prentice Hall Science* Learning System.

Thematic Overview

When teaching any science topic, you may want to focus your lessons around the underlying themes that pertain to all areas of science. These underlying themes are the framework from which all science can be constructed and taught. The seven underlying themes incorporated into *Prentice Hall Science* are

Energy
Evolution
Patterns of Change
Scale and Structure
Systems and Interactions
Unity and Diversity
Stability

A detailed discussion of each of these themes and how they are incorporated into the *Prentice Hall Science* program are included in your *Teacher's Desk Reference.* In addition, the *Teacher's Desk Reference* includes thematic matrices for the *Prentice Hall Science* program.

A thematic matrix for each chapter in this textbook follows. Each thematic matrix is designed with the list of themes along the left-hand column and in the right-hand column a big idea, or overarching concept statement, as to how that particular theme is taught in the chapter.

The primary themes in this textbook are Energy, Scale and Structure, Systems and Interactions, and Stability. Primary themes throughout *Prentice Hall Science* are denoted by an asterisk.

CHAPTER 1

The Human Body

*ENERGY	• Like all living things, humans need energy to perform their life activities.
EVOLUTION	
PATTERNS OF CHANGE	• The human body is organized into organ systems that enable it to maintain homeostasis despite changes in its internal and external environment.
*SCALE AND STRUCTURE	• The human body consists of trillions of cells that are organized into tissues, organs, and organ systems.
*SYSTEMS AND INTERACTIONS	• In multicellular living things, such as humans, cells, tissues, organs, and organ systems interact with one another, enabling the living things to function smoothly.
UNITY AND DIVERSITY	• Although human organ systems are composed of organs containing different tissues, the organ systems work together so that humans can survive.
*STABILITY	• All human organ systems work together to maintain a stable internal environment (homeostasis).

CHAPTER 2

Skeletal and Muscular Systems

*ENERGY	• The skeletal and muscular systems obtain and use energy in order to perform their functions.
EVOLUTION	
PATTERNS OF CHANGE	• Many of the body's bones develop from a type of connective tissue called cartilage. • The three types of muscle tissues are specialized to perform specific voluntary and involuntary functions.
*SCALE AND STRUCTURE	• The skeletal system consists of bones, ligaments, tendons, and joints. • The muscular system consists of muscle cells that are specialized for contraction.
*SYSTEMS AND INTERACTIONS	• The skeletal system shapes, supports, allows for movement, protects, stores certain materials, and produces blood cells for the body. • Of the three types of muscles, skeletal muscle permits voluntary movement; smooth and cardiac muscles permit involuntary movement.
UNITY AND DIVERSITY	• The structure of bones, muscles, and related organs and tissues are different, yet they work together to enable the body to move.
* STABILITY	• The combined action of skeletal and muscular systems enables the human body to maintain a stable internal environment.

CHAPTER 3

Digestive System

*ENERGY	• The digestive system breaks down food into simpler substances that provide the body with energy and raw materials for its proper functioning and growth.
EVOLUTION	
PATTERNS OF CHANGE	• The digestive system transforms food into simpler substances that can be absorbed and used by the cells.
*SCALE AND STRUCTURE	• As food moves through the digestive system, various organs function in breaking down large food particles into smaller ones that the cells can use.
*SYSTEMS AND INTERACTIONS	• Although the enzymes secreted by digestive organs are specific, they work together to complete the process of digestion.
UNITY AND DIVERSITY	• The many different organs of the digestive system work together to break down food into a usable form.
*STABILITY	• The digestive system breaks down food so that the energy it provides can be used to maintain homeostasis.

CHAPTER 4

Circulatory System

*ENERGY	• The circulatory system delivers to the cells raw materials for the production of energy and carries away the waste products of energy production.
EVOLUTION	
PATTERNS OF CHANGE	• The circulatory system delivers digested food and oxygen to cells and carries wastes away from cells.
*SCALE AND STRUCTURE	• The circulatory system, consisting of the heart, blood vessels, and blood, carries materials to and from the cells.
*SYSTEMS AND INTERACTIONS	• The circulatory system delivers food and oxygen to body cells and carries carbon dioxide and other wastes away from body cells.
UNITY AND DIVERSITY	• Although arteries, capillaries, and veins are all blood vessels, they each have a unique structure that helps them perform their function.
*STABILITY	• By delivering food and oxygen to the cells and carrying wastes away from the cells, the circulatory system maintains homeostasis.

CHAPTER 5

Respiratory and Excretory Systems

*ENERGY	• The respiratory system provides body cells with the oxygen they need and combines it with nutrients to produce energy. • The excretory system removes from the cells the waste products of energy production and metabolism.
EVOLUTION	
PATTERNS OF CHANGE	• The respiratory system brings about the exchange of gases (O_2 and CO_2) with the environment. • The excretory system carries various waste products out of the body into the environment.
*SCALE AND STRUCTURE	• The respiratory system consists of lungs that are composed of structures called alveoli, in which the exchange of gases occurs. • The excretory system consists of kidneys that contain structures called nephrons, which remove wastes from the blood.
*SYSTEMS AND INTERACTIONS	• The respiratory system permits the exchange of gases between the body cells and the environment. • The excretory system removes wastes from the body.
UNITY AND DIVERSITY	• The structures of the respiratory and excretory systems are different, yet they work together in transporting materials either to or from the blood.
*STABILITY	• By delivering oxygen to the blood and by removing wastes from the blood, the respiratory and excretory systems maintain homeostasis.

CHAPTER 6

Nervous and Endocrine Systems

*ENERGY	• The nervous and endocrine systems require the use of energy to control the activities of the body.
EVOLUTION	
PATTERNS OF CHANGE	• Through the constant monitoring of changes inside and outside the body, the nervous and endocrine systems regulate the activities of the body.
*SCALE AND STRUCTURE	• The nervous system consists of the brain, spinal cord, sense organs, and nerves, which are made of specialized cells called neurons. • The endocrine system consists of glands that secrete hormones.
*SYSTEMS AND INTERACTIONS	• The nervous and endocrine systems receive and process information from the body's internal and external environment.
UNITY AND DIVERSITY	• Although the nervous and endocrine systems regulate activities in the body, they perform their functions in different ways. • The nervous system sends its electrochemical signals through neurons; the endocrine system sends its chemical messengers (hormones) through the blood.
*STABILITY	• By regulating and coordinating the activities of the body, the nervous and endocrine system maintain homeostasis.

CHAPTER 7

Reproduction and Development

*ENERGY	• The processes of reproduction and development require the use of energy for the production of new cells.
EVOLUTION	• Reproduction is the process that ensures the survival of the species.
PATTERNS OF CHANGE	• Human development begins with the fertilization of the egg and continues throughout the entire life of a human.
*SCALE AND STRUCTURE	• The male and female reproductive systems contain structures that produce sex cells. • When these sex cells join, they produce new humans.
*SYSTEMS AND INTERACTIONS	• The function of the male and female reproductive systems is to produce sex cells that are needed for reproduction and to produce hormones that regulate certain body activities.
UNITY AND DIVERSITY	• The male and female reproductive systems differ in structure, but they each produce sex cells that are needed for reproduction as well as hormones that are needed for the proper functioning of the body.
*STABILITY	• The hormones produced by the male and female reproductive systems maintain a chemical stability within the body.

CHAPTER 8

Immune System

*ENERGY	• In order to defend the body against invaders, energy is needed.
EVOLUTION	
PATTERNS OF CHANGE	• When an antibody encounters its specific antigen, it changes shape, converting from its inactive T shape to its active Y shape.
*SCALE AND STRUCTURE	• The human body's lines of defense consist of the skin, mucus, cilia, special white blood cells, and antibodies.
*SYSTEMS AND INTERACTIONS	• The body's three lines of defense protect it by attacking and destroying organisms that may harm the body.
UNITY AND DIVERSITY	• Although the structures that make up the body's lines of defense are different, they all work together in defending the body against invaders. • There are two types of immunity: active immunity and passive immunity.
*STABILITY	• The body's lines of defense maintain homeostasis by keeping out foreign invaders.

CHAPTER 9

Alcohol, Tobacco, and Drugs

*ENERGY	• Alcohol, tobacco, and drugs have different effects on the body. They may either speed up or slow down certain activities of the body.
EVOLUTION	
PATTERNS OF CHANGE	• Alcohol, tobacco, and drugs are substances that cause changes to occur in the body.
*SCALE AND STRUCTURE	
*SYSTEMS AND INTERACTIONS	• Each drug has a particular effect on a certain body system.
UNITY AND DIVERSITY	• Although all drugs affect the body, they do so in different ways.
*STABILITY	• Alcohol, tobacco, and drugs cause changes in the body and therefore upset the body's stable internal environment.

Comprehensive List of Laboratory Materials

Item	Quantities per Group	Chapter
Alcohol	1 bottle	8
Beaker, 100 mL	1	8
Beef, small lean raw piece	2	1
Blindfold	1	6
Cardboard, 6 cm x 10 cm	1	6
Chicken leg with meat removed	2	2
Clock with second hand	1	4
Coverslip	1	1, 2
Glass slide	1	1
	2	2
Graduated cylinder	1	5, 8
Jar with lid	2	2
Knife	2	1
Magazines	3	9
Medicine dropper	1	1, 2
Methylene blue	1 small bottle	1, 2
Metric ruler	1	6
Microscope	1	1, 2
Needle, dissecting	2	2
Paper, graph, 20 cm x 28 cm	1	4,7
Paper clips	2	8
Paper towel	1	1, 2, 5
Pencil		
colored	1 set	7
glass marking	1	5, 8
Pennies	2	8
Petri dish with sterile nutrient agar	2	8
Pins, straight	9	6
Scale	1 (per class)	3
Scissors	1	6
Spirometer	1	5
Tape, transparent	1 roll	8
Thumbtacks	2	8
Toothpick	1	1
Vegetable coloring, red	1 small bottle	5
Vinegar	1 small bottle	2

HUMAN BIOLOGY AND HEALTH

Anthea Maton
Former NSTA National Coordinator
Project Scope, Sequence, Coordination
Washington, DC

Jean Hopkins
Science Instructor and Department Chairperson
John H. Wood Middle School
San Antonio, Texas

Susan Johnson
Professor of Biology
Ball State University
Muncie, Indiana

David LaHart
Senior Instructor
Florida Solar Energy Center
Cape Canaveral, Florida

Charles William McLaughlin
Science Instructor and Department Chairperson
Central High School
St. Joseph, Missouri

Maryanna Quon Warner
Science Instructor
Del Dios Middle School
Escondido, California

Jill D. Wright
Professor of Science Education
Director of International Field Programs
University of Pittsburgh
Pittsburgh, Pennsylvania

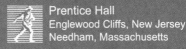

Prentice Hall
Englewood Cliffs, New Jersey
Needham, Massachusetts

Prentice Hall Science
Human Biology and Health

Student Text and Annotated Teacher's Edition
Laboratory Manual
Teacher's Resource Package
Teacher's Desk Reference
Computer Test Bank
Teaching Transparencies
Science Reader
Product Testing Activities
Computer Courseware
Video and Interactive Video

The illustration on the cover, rendered by Keith Kasnot, shows the human skeletal system in motion.

Credits begin on page 257.

FIRST EDITION

ISBN 0-13-981176-1

3 4 5 6 7 8 9 10   96 95 94 93

 Prentice Hall
A Division of Simon & Schuster
Englewood Cliffs, New Jersey 07632

STAFF CREDITS

Editorial:	Harry Bakalian, Pamela E. Hirschfeld, Maureen Grassi, Robert P. Letendre, Elisa Mui Eiger, Lorraine Smith-Phelan, Christine A. Caputo
Design:	AnnMarie Roselli, Carmela Pereira, Susan Walrath, Leslie Osher, Art Soares
Production:	Suse Cioffi, Joan McCulley, Elizabeth Torjussen, Christina Burghard, Marlys Lehmann
Photo Research:	Libby Forsyth, Emily Rose, Martha Conway
Publishing Technology:	Andrew Grey Bommarito, Gwendollynn Waldron, Deborah Jones, Monduane Harris, Michael Colucci, Gregory Myers, Cleasta Wilburn
Marketing:	Andy Socha, Victoria Willows
Pre-Press Production:	Laura Sanderson, Denise Herckenrath
Manufacturing:	Rhett Conklin, Gertrude Szyferblatt

Consultants

Kathy French	National Science Consultant
William Royalty	National Science Consultant

CONTENTS

HUMAN BIOLOGY AND HEALTH

CHAPTER 1 The Human Body 12

1–1 The Body as a Whole 14
1–2 Levels of Organization 15

CHAPTER 2 Skeletal and Muscular Systems 28

2–1 The Skeletal System................................30
2–2 The Muscular System 37
2–3 Injuries to the Skeletal and Muscular
Systems 42

CHAPTER 3 Digestive System 50

3–1 The Importance of Food 52
3–2 Digestion of Food 61
3–3 Absorption of Food 69
3–4 Maintaining Good Health 71

CHAPTER 4 Circulatory System....................................78

4–1 The Body's Transportation System...........80
4–2 Circulation in the Body.............................82
4–3 Blood—The River of Life 88
4–4 Cardiovascular Diseases..........................96

CHAPTER 5 Respiratory and Excretory Systems...106

5–1 The Respiratory System 108
5–2 The Excretory System 118

THIS IS A

SMOKE-FREE
BUILDING

CHAPTER 6

Nervous and Endocrine Systems 130

6–1 The Nervous System 132
6–2 Divisions of the Nervous System...........137
6–3 The Senses 144
6–4 The Endocrine System 155

CHAPTER 7

Reproduction and Development 166

7–1 The Reproductive System 168
7–2 Stages of Development 177

CHAPTER 8

Immune System 190

8–1 Body Defenses 192
8–2 Immunity 197
8–3 Diseases..203

CHAPTER 9

Alcohol, Tobacco, and Drugs..............214

9–1 What Are Drugs? 216
9–2 Alcohol...219
9–3 Tobacco 223
9–4 Commonly Abused Drugs......................226

SCIENCE GAZETTE

Claire Veronica Broome: Disease Detective....236
Are Americans Overexercising? 238
The Bionic Boy 241

Reference Section

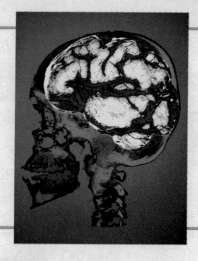

For Further Reading 244
Appendix A: The Metric System 245
Appendix B: Laboratory Safety: Rules and Symbols 246
Appendix C: Science Safety Rules 247
Glossary 249
Index 253

Features

Laboratory Investigations
Looking at Human Cheek Cells 24
Observing Bones and Muscles 46
Measuring Calories Used 74
Measuring Your Pulse Rate 102
Measuring the Volume of Exhaled Air 126
Locating Touch Receptors 162
How Many Offspring? 186
Observing the Action of Alcohol
  on Microorganisms 210
Analyzing Smoking Advertisements 232

Find Out by Doing
The Skin 18
Bones as Levers 30
Examining a Bone 33
Voluntary or Involuntary? 39
Muscle Action 42
How Sweet It Is 63
Simulating Peristalsis 65
Enzymes 67
Do Oil and Water Mix? 68
Catch the Beat 83
Circulation 86
What Is in Exhaled Air? 109
Close at Hand 122
A Reflex Reaction 137
Fight or Flight? 143
Reaction Time 149
Multiple Births 180
How Antibodies Work 199
Drugs and *Daphnia* 218
Up in Smoke 224

Find Out by Calculating
How Many Cells? 16
Determining Your Metabolic Rate 54
Pumping Power 97
A Speedy Message 133
How Much Is Enough? 160
Cigarette Smoking 225

Find Out by Writing
Organs and Organ Systems 22
Vitamin-Deficiency Diseases 58
Blood Donating Center 93
Blood Pressure 100
Bacterially Produced Hormones 156
The Developing Embryo 177
You Only Look as Old as You Feel 184
Antiseptics and Disinfectants 194
Vaccines 198
What Are Generic Drugs? 216
What Is DWI? 220

Find Out by Reading
Reading Poetry 118
A Master Sleuth 144

Problem Solving
What Kind of Joint Is This? 37
Reading Food Labels 60
Are Heart Attacks Influenced
  by the Time of Day? 98
How Do I Explain This? 125
I Can See Clearly Now 148

Connections
Artificial Body Parts 23
Turning on Bone Growth 45
What's Cooking? 73
It's All in a Heartbeat 101
How a Lie Detector Gives Its Verdict 117
With or Without Pepperoni? 154
Electronic Reproduction 185
A Cure for Us or Yews? 209
"Bad Breath?" 222

Careers
Athletic Trainer 35
Nurse 72
Biomedical Engineer 99
Respiratory Therapy Technician 121
Optometric Assistant 145
School Social Worker 172
Emergency Medical Technician 230

CONCEPT MAPPING

hroughout your study of science, you will learn a variety of terms, facts, figures, and concepts. Each new topic you encounter will provide its own collection of words and ideas—which, at times, you may think seem endless. But each of the ideas within a particular topic is related in some way to the others. No concept in science is isolated. Thus it will help you to understand the topic if you see the whole picture; that is, the interconnectedness of all the individual terms and ideas. This is a much more effective and satisfying way of learning than memorizing separate facts.

Actually, this should be a rather familiar process for you. Although you may not think about it in this way, you analyze many of the elements in your daily life by looking for relationships or connections. For example, when you look at a collection of flowers, you may divide them into groups: roses, carnations, and daisies. You may then associate colors with these flowers: red, pink, and white. The general topic is flowers. The subtopic is types of flowers. And the colors are specific terms that describe flowers. A topic makes more sense and is more easily understood if you understand how it is broken down into individual ideas and how these ideas are related to one another and to the entire topic.

It is often helpful to organize information visually so that you can see how it all fits together. One technique for describing related ideas is called a **concept map**. In a concept map, an idea is represented by a word or phrase enclosed in a box. There are several ideas in any concept map. A connection between two ideas is made with a line. A word or two that describes the connection is written on or near the line. The general topic is located at the top of the map. That topic is then broken down into subtopics, or more specific ideas, by branching lines. The most specific topics are located at the bottom of the map.

To construct a concept map, first identify the important ideas or key terms in the chapter or section. Do not try to include too much information. Use your judgment as to what is really important. Write the general topic at the top of your map. Let's use an example to help illustrate this process. Suppose you decide that the key terms in a section you are reading are School, Living Things, Language Arts, Subtraction, Grammar, Mathematics, Experiments, Papers, Science, Addition, Novels. The general topic is School. Write and enclose this word in a box at the top of your map.

SCHOOL

Now choose the subtopics—Language Arts, Science, Mathematics. Figure out how they are related to the topic. Add these words to your map. Continue this procedure until you have included all the important ideas and terms. Then use lines to make the appropriate connections between ideas and terms. Don't forget to write a word or two on or near the connecting line to describe the nature of the connection.

Do not be concerned if you have to redraw your map (perhaps several times!) before you show all the important connections clearly. If, for example, you write papers for Science as well as for Language Arts, you may want to place these two subjects next to each other so that the lines do not overlap.

One more thing you should know about concept mapping: Concepts can be correctly mapped in many different ways. In fact, it is unlikely that any two people will draw identical concept maps for a complex topic. Thus there is no one correct concept map for any topic! Even though your concept map may not match those of your classmates, it will be correct as long as it shows the most important concepts and the clear relationships among them. Your concept map will also be correct if it has meaning to you and if it helps you understand the material you are reading. A concept map should be so clear that if some of the terms are erased, the missing terms could easily be filled in by following the logic of the concept map.

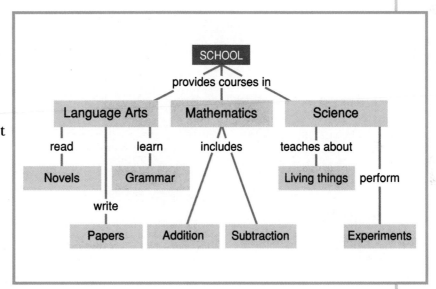

Human Biology and Health

TEXT OVERVIEW

In this textbook students are introduced to the anatomy, physiology, and development of humans. They learn first about the multicellular organization of the human body. They then study the various systems of the human body. These are the skeletal and muscular systems, the digestive system, the circulatory system, the respiratory and excretory systems, and the nervous and endocrine systems. Students go on to study the male and female reproductive systems and human reproduction and development. They also read about the immune system and diseases. Finally, they learn about the effects of the use of drugs, alcohol, and tobacco.

TEXT OBJECTIVES

1. Classify the four basic types of tissues.
2. Describe the features and functions of the skeletal, muscular, digestive, circulatory, respiratory, excretory, nervous, and endocrine systems.
3. Describe human reproduction and development.
4. Identify the immune system and its function.
5. Explain the effects of the use of drugs, alcohol, and tobacco.

CHAPTER DESCRIPTIONS

1 The Human Body Chapter 1 describes the process by which the human body's internal environment is kept stable. The human body is described as a multicellular structure with four levels of organization. The cells, tissues, organs, and organ systems are discussed.

2 Skeletal and Muscular Systems In Chapter 2 the characteristics and functions of the skeletal system and of specific bones and joints are discussed. The functions and types of muscles are also described.

HUMAN BIOLOGY AND HEALTH

 To play soccer, all parts of the bodies of these young soccer players must work together in perfect harmony.

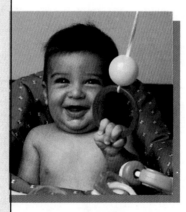
A smiling child reaching for a toy illustrates how different parts of the body—even a very young body—work together.

The day for the championship soccer game has finally arrived. The stadium is filled to capacity. The game is about to begin. The crowd quiets down as a soccer player on the attacking team prepares to kick off. The defending team members anxiously await the ball on their half of the field so that they can advance the ball into the attacking team's territory. The players on both sides have spent many years of training for this moment.

As the kicker begins to kick off, nerves carry messages to her brain, telling her body exactly what movements it must make. Her muscles move, pulling on her bones so that she kicks the ball out of the center circle. At the same time, chemicals flow through her blood, informing certain parts of her body to speed up and others to slow down.

INTRODUCING HUMAN BIOLOGY AND HEALTH

USING THE TEXTBOOK

Begin your introduction of the textbook by having students examine the textbook-opening photographs and captions.
• **What is happening in the top photograph on page H10?** (A group of young people are playing soccer.)

• **What is taking place in the bottom photograph on the page?** (A baby is reaching for a toy.)
• **What is happening in the photograph on page H11?** (An adult is running.)
• **How are the pictures all alike?** (Responses may include all show people in activities, all depict some form of action.)
• **How are the pictures different?** (Responses may include the ages of people, the type of activity, individual and group efforts.)

CHAPTERS

1 The Human Body
2 Skeletal and Muscular Systems
3 Digestive System
4 Circulatory System
5 Respiratory and Excretory Systems
6 Nervous and Endocrine Systems
7 Reproduction and Development
8 Immune System
9 Alcohol, Tobacco, and Drugs

Now comes the kickoff. She moves toward the ball, keeping her nonkicking foot next to the ball, her head down, and her eyes on the ball. Then she swings her kicking leg with the toes pointed downward and kicks the ball squarely with her instep. It's out of the center circle. The game has begun!

To help her team win the championship, all parts of the soccer player's body have to work in perfect harmony. And even though you may never compete in a championship soccer game, your body parts are also working in their own perfect harmony at this very moment. In this textbook you will discover how the different parts of your body work and how they all work together as one.

▲ Exercise, such as running, helps to keep the body in good working condition.

Discovery Activity

Yesterday, Today, and Tomorrow

1. Take a look at your classmates or a group of people who are about your age. Make a mental note of the features that you share with them.

2. Complete the same exercise with a group of adults and a group of young children.
   - In what ways are people of all ages the same?
   - What changes occur in people as they grow from children to adults?
   - Are all changes that occur in people easily observed?

H ■ 11

3 Digestive System In Chapter 3 various basic nutrients are related to bodily functions. The digestive processes that occur in the mouth, stomach, and small intestine, and the roles of organs, such as the pancreas, are explained. The absorption process in the digestive system is then discussed. The chapter concludes with an analysis of general health practices in terms of weight and exercise.

4 Circulatory System In Chapter 4 the function and structure of the blood, blood vessels, and heart are treated. The four human blood groups are also described. Finally, cardiovascular diseases are discussed.

5 Respiratory and Excretory Systems The functions and structures of the respiratory system are explained first in Chapter 5. The flow of air during breathing is also traced. The chapter goes on to describe the functions and structures of the excretory system.

6 Nervous and Endocrine Systems Chapter 6 opens with a description of the structure and function of the nervous system. The functions of the various endocrine glands are explained next, as is the operation of the feedback mechanisms.

7 Reproduction and Development Chapter 7 first discusses fertilization and compares the male and female reproductive systems. The development of the embryo, the process of birth, and the stages of development after birth are also described.

8 Immune System In Chapter 8 the operation of the immune system is discussed, along with the uses of vaccines in preventing the spread of diseases. The nature and spread of infectious diseases are discussed, and examples of noninfectious diseases are presented.

9 Alcohol, Tobacco, and Drugs Chapter 9 opens with a discussion of the nature of drugs and the dangers of drug and alcohol abuse. Next, cigarette smoking is related to the occurrence of certain diseases. Finally, various depressants, stimulants, hallucinogens, and opiates are classified and compared.

Then have students read the copy on pages H10 and H11. Explain that the human body is a complex structure that includes a number of systems that enable people to function.

DISCOVERY ACTIVITY

Yesterday, Today, and Tomorrow

Begin your introduction of the textbook by having students perform the Discovery Activity. After completing the activity, students should be able to distinguish characteristics of young children, adolescents, and adults. They will also be able to see similarities among people of different ages. Explain that the human body changes as it grows and develops but that the basic operations of its systems remain the same throughout life. Tell students that in the textbook chapters, they will discover how the systems in the body operate and how healthful practices can help to keep the systems working properly. Students also will learn about the problems that substance abuse can cause.

Chapter 1 THE HUMAN BODY

SECTION	LABORATORY INVESTIGATIONS AND DEMONSTRATIONS
1–1 The Body as a Whole pages H14–H15	**Teacher Edition** Simple to Complex, p. H12d
1–2 Levels of Organization pages H15–H23	**Student Edition** Looking at Human Cheek Cells, p. H24 **Laboratory Manual** Investigating Tissues **Teacher Edition** Organization in Living Things, p. H12d
Chapter Review pages H24–H27	

*All materials in the Chapter Planning Guide Grid are available as part of the Prentice Hall Science Learning System.

OUTSIDE TEACHER RESOURCES

Books

ABC's of The Human Body, Reader's Digest General Books.

Anthony, Catherine, and Gary Thibodeau. *Structure and Function of the Body,* 8th ed., Mosby.

Elson, L. M. *It's Your Body,* McGraw-Hill.

Evans, W. *Anatomy and Physiology,* Prentice-Hall.

Harrison, R. J., and W. Montagna. *Man,* Prentice-Hall.

Nourse, A. E., et al. *The Body,* Time, Inc.

Tully, M., and M. A. Tully. *Facts About the Human Body,* Watts.

Audiovisuals

Cells, Tissues and Organs, film or video, Coronet

Inquiring Into Life, film or video, Coronet

Man: The Incredible Machine, film or video, National Geographic

Understanding Your Body, Series I and II, 15 filmstrips, EBE

OTHER ACTIVITIES	MULTIMEDIA

Activity Book
    Chapter Discovery: Discovering Levels of Organization
Review and Reinforcement Guide
    Section 1–1
	English/Spanish Audiotapes
	    Section 1–1

Activity Book
    ACTIVITY: What Is a Tissue?
    ACTIVITY: Medical Terminology Made Easy
    ACTIVITY: Describing the Skin
Student Edition
    Find Out by Calculating: How Many Cells? p. H16
    Find Out by Doing: The Skin, p. H18
    Find Out by Writing: Organs and Organ Systems, p. H22
Review and Reinforcement Guide
    Section 1–2
	Interactive Videodisc
	    BioExplorer
	Video/Videodisc
	    Systems Working Together
	English/Spanish Audiotapes
	    Section 1–2

Test Book
    Chapter Test
    Performance-Based Test
	Test Book
	    Computer Test Bank Test

Chapter 1 THE HUMAN BODY

CHAPTER OVERVIEW

The functions carried out by the human body are accomplished through a wide variety of different structures. These varied components must all work together in a coordinated fashion for the body to remain in a healthy state. The concept of internal balance or stability known as homeostasis is key to an understanding of the human body. In the same way that living and nonliving things in an environment must remain in a state of stability in order for the environment to survive, the human body uses internal mechanisms to adjust to changes in the external world and thus remain in a stable state.

Levels of organization can help us understand the structure and functions of the human body. On the first level is the cell, the basic unit of structure and function in all living organisms. In complex organisms such as the human body, however, there is a division of labor among cells. The cells exist in diverse sizes and shapes and specialize in different functions. Cells performing the same function are organized into tissues. The tissues combine to make the different organs, and the organs are organized into organ systems such as the nervous system, circulatory system, skeletal system, and so on. Various organizing schemes are possible because many organs have more than one function. In even the simplest human activities, the various organ systems function together. As each part of the human body does its job, a stability is maintained within the organism, which keeps it alive and healthy.

1–1 THE BODY AS A WHOLE

THEMATIC FOCUS

The purpose of this section is to explain homeostasis, an underlying concept that helps students begin to learn about the organization, structure, and functions in the human body. Homeostasis is the process by which the human body maintains a stable internal state, regardless of changes in the external environment.

One example of homeostasis is the level of glucose in the body. When glucose levels fall below a certain point, the liver breaks down a substance called glycogen so that glucose can be delivered by the circulatory system to the cells that need it.

The themes that can be focused on in this section are energy, stability, and systems and interactions.

*Energy: Like all living things, humans need energy to perform their life activities. Energy from food, as well as oxygen, is provided to all cells of the human body.

*Systems and interactions: In a multicellular living organism, such as the human body, cells, tissues, organs, and organ systems interact with one another, enabling the organism to function smoothly and remain in a stable state. The coordinated operation of all the organ systems enables the body to remain in a state of homeostasis during the majority of human activities.

*Stability: All human organ systems work together to maintain a stable internal environment (homeostasis). If the human body were unable to maintain homeostasis, its existence in an ever-changing external environment would be endangered.

PERFORMANCE OBJECTIVES 1–1

1. Explain the meaning of homeostasis and its importance for the human body.
2. Describe how the human body uses energy to carry out its functions.

SCIENCE TERMS 1–1
homeostasis p. H15

1–2 LEVELS OF ORGANIZATION

THEMATIC FOCUS

The purpose of this section is to show students the organization of the human body. Similar cells are organized into tissues. Different types of tissues are combined to form organs. And the organs are grouped into organ systems.

One example of an organ is the human hand. The hand consists of many different cells—bone, muscle, nerve, blood, epithelial (skin), and others—organized into different tissues in order to perform the functions of grasping and handling objects. Students will explore four kinds of tissue: muscle, connective, nerve, and epithelial. These four tissues work together in organs and organ systems to enable the body to perform many functions. Even though they perform functions that are remarkably distinctive, all the body's organs are made up of just these four kinds of tissue.

It is important for students to understand that the organ systems work together. Even in carrying out the simplest function, the body uses more than one system. The muscular system, for example, enables the body to move, but it can only do so by working in cooperation with the skeletal system. The muscles are stimulated to move by the nerves (nervous system); food and energy are provided to muscle cells by blood (circulatory system), and oxygen to the blood by the respiratory system. The excretory system removes waste from the muscle cells. In fact, all systems are functioning at any one time during the life of the body.

The themes that can be focused on in this section are patterns of change, scale and structure, and unity and diversity.

Patterns of change: The human body is organized into 11 different organ systems: skeletal, muscular, digestive, circulatory, respiratory, excretory, nervous, endocrine, reproductive, immune, and integumentary. The organ systems work together to enable the body to maintain homeostasis despite changes in its internal and external environment.

*Scale and structure: The human body consists of trillions of cells that are organized into tissues, organs, and organ systems. The cells have a wide variety of specializations. Some cells absorb food and convert it to usable products. Cells also are builders, breaking down food into simpler substances or producing hormones, bone tissue, and other needed material. The cells in the muscles are specialized for movement. Through the contractions of muscle cells, bones are moved, and the heart pumps blood through the body.

Unity and diversity: Although human organ systems are composed of organs containing different tissues, the organ systems work together so that humans can survive.

PERFORMANCE OBJECTIVES 1–2

1. **Describe four levels of organization in the human body.**
2. **Explain three functions of cells.**
3. **Describe four types of tissue.**
4. **List the organ systems in the human body.**

SCIENCE TERMS 1–2

cell p. H16
tissue p. H18
organ p. H21
organ system p. H21

Discovery *Learning*

TEACHER DEMONSTRATIONS MODELING

Simple to Complex

Obtain a photograph of a single-celled organism such as a bacterium, a paramecium, or an ameba.

• **How would you describe this organism?** (Accept all logical responses. Students should note that this is a single-celled organism.)

Then display a photograph of a human.

• **How would you describe this organism?** (Accept all logical responses.)

Now display both photographs.

• **How are these organisms alike?** (Both are living.)

• **How are they different?** (Accept all logical responses. Students should understand that whereas one of the organisms consists of a single cell, the other contains many cells.)

• **Which organism is more complex?** (The human.)

• **Which organism would be more difficult to study and to understand? Why?** (Accept all responses. Lead students to see that the human body is much more complex than a single-celled organism and that people devote many years to an understanding of human biology.)

Explain to students that in this chapter they will learn how the parts of the human body are able to work together for the benefit of the organism.

Organization in Living Things

Begin this demonstration by explaining that the highest level of organization of living things is the organism. Tell students that an organism is an entire living thing that carries out all its basic life functions.

• **What are some examples of organisms?** (Accept all logical answers.)

Write the phrase "Organism X" on the chalkboard and have students list the characteristics they think an organism (plant or animal) should have to be well suited for the area in which it is living. As students generate ideas, list them on the chalkboard. For example, in warm areas, students might list the need for little hair or fur, for an efficient body cooling system, and so forth.

Next, have students list the organ systems that contribute to the characteristics listed on the chalkboard. For example, the circulatory system, respiratory system, and excretory system all contribute to the cooling of an organism.

CHAPTER 1
The Human Body

INTEGRATING SCIENCE

This life science chapter provides you with numerous opportunities to integrate other areas of science, as well as other disciplines, into your curriculum. Blue numbered annotations on the student page and integration notes on the teacher wraparound pages alert you to areas of possible integration.

In this chapter you can integrate mathematics (p. 16), life science and cells (p. 16), language arts (p. 22), and physical science and chemical technology (p. 23).

SCIENCE, TECHNOLOGY, AND SOCIETY/COOPERATIVE LEARNING

Thousands of people are in need of new organs in order to survive. People can spend years waiting for "the call" informing them that they are not only on the top of the organ waiting list, but that an organ has been donated for them. These people are grateful to the many people who have made the decision to donate certain body organs and tissues when they die. Donors carry organ-donor cards, which indicate their wishes.

Among the tissues and organs used for research and transplants are bones, skin, corneas, pituitary glands, blood vessels, kidneys, livers, lungs, and hearts. Each of the 50 states has passed legislation that governs the donation of organs. Under this legislation, mentally competent people can donate any or all of their bodies' organs to hospitals, medical schools, dental schools, organ-storage facilities, or to sci-

INTRODUCING CHAPTER 1

DISCOVERY LEARNING

▶ *Activity Book*

Begin your teaching of the chapter by using the Chapter 1 Discovery Activity from the *Activity Book*. Using this activity, students will make a model showing the four levels of organization in the human body: cells, tissues, organs, and organ systems.

USING THE TEXTBOOK

Have students examine the photograph, which shows a thermogram of a young boy and his dog. A thermogram, also called a heat map, is essentially a color-coded infrared photograph. Almost any color coding can be used. In the photograph shown, the lowest temperature areas appear purple or black, and the highest-temperature areas appear white. After students have read the introduction, ask:

• **Exactly what exposes the photographic film that produces the thermogram?** (Invisible, low-frequency light called infrared light exposes the film.)
• **What is the relationship between the hotness of an object and the amount of infrared light it gives off?** (In general, the higher the temperature of the object, the more infrared light it gives off.)
• **Which parts of the photograph are coolest? Which parts are hottest?** (The black or purple areas are coolest; the white areas are hottest.)

The Human Body

Guide for Reading

After you read the following sections, you will be able to

1–1 The Body as a Whole
- ■ Define homeostasis.
- ■ Explain why energy is important to the human body.

1–2 Levels of Organization
- ■ Describe the levels of organization of multicellular living things.
- ■ Classify the four basic types of tissues.

All objects, including the human body, give off infrared rays. Infrared rays cannot be seen, but they can be felt as heat. You have felt infrared rays in the form of heat from the sun or a glowing light bulb. A thermograph, which looks like a small television camera, converts the body's invisible infrared rays into a visible picture called a thermogram. So an object that appears to be invisible in the dark becomes visible with the help of a thermograph.

As a thermograph converts the invisible heat rays given off by the body into thermograms, it creates heat maps. Look carefully at the thermogram, or heat map, of a young boy and his dog. Notice that different areas of the body show various colors. The warmest areas of the body appear white. The coolest areas appear purple or black. What does the color of the dog's nose tell you about its temperature?

Thermograms are useful in medicine because they help doctors "see" what is happening inside the body. In some cases, they help doctors diagnose certain illnesses. As you turn the pages that follow, you too will be able to "see" what is happening inside the human body. Why not take a look.

Journal *Activity*

You and Your World   In your journal, draw a picture of yourself performing your favorite activity. Below your drawing, describe what you are doing and what parts of your body are involved in the activity. Which actions occur automatically? Which actions do you have to think about?

◀ *In this thermogram, the warmest areas appear white and the coolest areas appear black.*

H ■ 13

Explain that the human body always gives off heat but that different parts are warmer than others. Paired parts of the body, such as shoulders, arms, hips, or legs, usually give off the same amount of heat.

• How might doctors use thermographs to diagnose disease or illness? (Accept all responses. If paired body parts are giving off different amounts of heat, something may be wrong. Also, cancerous tumors are hotter than normal body tissue and so can be located by the heat given off.)

• Can you think of any dangers or disad- **vantages connected with the use of thermograms?** (There are no obvious dangers. Students may point out the problem of possible error or misdiagnosis, however.)

• What nonmedical practical uses of thermogramlike infrared photography can you think of? (Answers will vary. Some students may suggest uses in detecting areas of heat loss in buildings or in determining characteristics of different areas of the Earth by means of aerial or satellite photography.)

---

entists engaged in research, therapy, transplantation, or education. The intention to donate an organ can be placed in a person's will or in a written statement signed in the presence of two witnesses. In most states, a person's driver's license also can give permission for an organ donation in case of a fatal accident. People under the age of 18 must have a parent or legal guardian countersign their donor card. Most laws also permit the next of kin to authorize donation unless it is shown that the person would have objected to the donation if he or she were alive. If a person changes his or her mind after obtaining a donor card, he or she can destroy it and/or notify the motor vehicle bureau.

Cooperative learning: Using preassigned groups or randomly selected teams, have groups complete one of the following assignments:
• Design a public-service message encouraging people to donate their organs. You can let groups determine the medium for their message or assign them one of the following: bill-board, 30-second TV or radio announcement, full-page newspaper or magazine ad, or a bumper sticker.
• React to the following scenario: Due to the tremendous shortage of organs available for transplants, the U.S. Congress is considering a bill that would require the donation of organs upon death. Groups should compose a letter to their representative in Congress expressing their opinion of this proposed new law. Encourage groups to consider social (equal access to organs, rights of individuals, rights of family members) as well as scientific aspects of this issue.

See Cooperative Learning in the *Teacher's Desk Reference.*

JOURNAL ACTIVITY

You may want to use the Journal Activity as the basis of class discussion. As students describe the parts of the body involved in the activity they have chosen, encourage them to classify similar parts together. For example, they might first describe which bones and muscles are involved and then include as many internal organs as they can think of. Organizing the journal entries by similar parts of the body can serve as an introduction to the classification systems described in this chapter. Students should be instructed to keep their Journal Activity in their portfolio.

1–1 The Body as a Whole

Guide for Reading

Focus on this question as you read.
▶ How does the body maintain a stable internal environment?

Figure 1–1 *No matter what the weather is outside, the human body is able to maintain homeostasis, or a stable internal environment.*

14 ■ H

1–1 The Body as a Whole

Every minute of the day, even when you are asleep, your body is busily at work. Blood is being pumped through blood vessels by your heart. Air is being pushed in and out of your body by your lungs. Your intestines are giving off chemicals that break down the food you have eaten into smaller parts. Your nerves are sending out signals from the brain to all parts of your body. Chemical messengers are regulating all kinds of processes.

To you these activities probably seem quite different—and in many ways they are. However, all these activities have the same purpose: to delicately control the body's internal environment. This internal environment must remain stable, or constant, even during extreme changes in the activities of the body or in its surroundings.

For example, you may eat a large amount of sweets (foods containing mainly sugar) on one day and none at all on the next day. The amount of sugar that goes into your body is quite different on the two days. But the amount of sugar in your blood remains remarkably stable, or unchanged. **The process by which the body's internal environment is kept stable in spite of changes in the external environment is called homeostasis** (hoh-mee-oh-STAY-sihs). Put another way, **homeostasis is the process by which the delicate balance between the activities occurring inside your body (amount of sugar in the blood) and those occurring outside your body (amount of sweets you eat) is maintained.**

In order to perform all the life activities, humans, like all living things, need energy. Even homeostasis needs energy. After all, the body works hard to keep its internal environment stable. Where does the body get the energy to do all of this work? Just as an engine uses gasoline as its energy source, living things use food as the source of energy for all their activities.

1–1 Section Review

1. What is homeostasis?
2. What is the body's source of energy?

Critical Thinking—*Applying Concepts*
3. Explain why it is important for all living things to maintain homeostasis.

1–2 Levels of Organization

Here's a riddle for you: What do you and an ameba have in common? The answer: Both of you are made of cells. Actually, the whole "body" of the ameba is made up of one cell. Your body, however, is made up of many cells. Living things that are composed of only one cell are called unicellular; those that are composed of many cells are called multicellular.

In multicellular living things—humans, birds, trees, turtles, and hamsters, to name just a few—the work of keeping the living thing alive is divided among the different parts of its body. Each part has

Guide for Reading

Focus on this question as you read.

▶ *What are the levels of organization in the human body?*

MULTICULTURAL OPPORTUNITY 1–2

Systems are composed of smaller units referred to as subsystems. In order for the system to operate, the subsystems must also operate in harmony.

Have students think of something that is familiar to them, such as a bicycle. What are some subsystems that make up the bicycle? (Gears, wheels, support frame, brakes, and so on.) How do these subsystems work together? What is the function of each?

Once students begin to see the relationship among the subsystems in a familiar object, they can begin to see how the human body is a system composed of interrelated subsystems. You may want to discuss how the failure of one subsystem (for example, the heart) affects the entire system.

ESL STRATEGY 1–2

Use the diagram shown below to illustrate four levels of organization in a multicellular living thing. Explain that the bottom stack represents the largest and most complicated part and that the top stack shows the smallest and least complicated part.

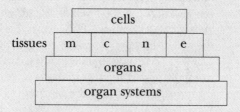

Have students identify the four different types of tissues in the human body by completing the term whose first letter appears on each block. (Answers are muscle, connective, nerve, and epithelial.)

INDEPENDENT PRACTICE

Section Review 1–1

1. The process by which the internal environment of the human body is kept stable despite changes in the external environment.
2. Food.
3. The external environment in which a living organism exists is constantly changing. Mechanisms for the organism to maintain internal stability are needed, or the organism would not be able to withstand any changes in its environment.

REINFORCEMENT/RETEACHING

Review students' responses to the Section Review questions. Reteach any material that is still unclear, based on students' responses.

CLOSURE

▶ *Review and Reinforcement Guide*

Have students complete Section 1–1 in the *Review and Reinforcment Guide.*

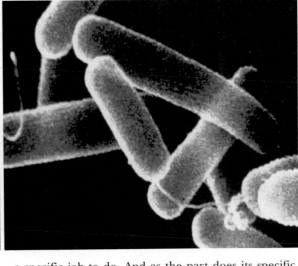

Figure 1–2 *All living things are made of cells. Bacteria are unicellular, whereas the giraffe is multicellular. Does the giraffe have bigger cells than a bacterium or just more of them?* ❶

a specific job to do. And as the part does its specific job, it works in harmony with all the other parts to keep the living thing healthy and alive.

The groupings of these specific parts within a living thing are called levels of organization. **The levels of organization in a multicellular living thing include cells, tissues, organs, and organ systems.**

Cells

Your body is made up of different **cells,** which are the building blocks of living things. Just as a house is made up of many bricks, so your body is made up of many cells—trillions of cells, in fact! And each of the trillions of cells in your body has its own special job. For example, some cells work to continuously provide fuel for your body. Other cells are involved in sensing external conditions for your body. And still other cells aid in the job of the organization and control of your entire body.

Cells come in all shapes and sizes. There are box-shaped cells, cells that resemble giant balls, and cells that look like tiny strands of wool. Regardless of its particular job or shape, a cell works in harmony with other cells to keep the body alive. Let's take a look at three different kinds of cells, each specialized for a particular job.

FIND OUT BY CALCULATING

How Many Cells?

❶ There are 5 million red blood cells in every milliliter of blood. How many red blood cells are there in 5 milliliters of blood? How many milliliters of blood will contain 7.5 million red blood cells? Ten million red blood cells?

16 ■ H

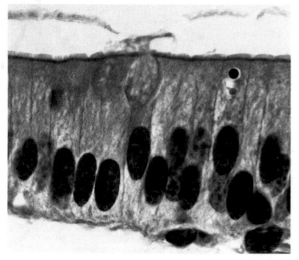

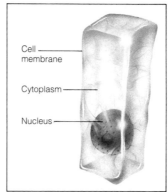

Figure 1–3 *The illustration shows some of the basic parts of a typical cell. Can you find the corresponding parts in the photograph of cells of the small intestine?* ❷

Cell membrane

Cytoplasm

Nucleus

ABSORBING CELLS The small intestine is a tube-like structure located below the liver and the stomach. The small intestine plays an important role in the process of digestion. Lining the inside of the small intestine are cells that absorb digested food and then transport it to the bloodstream. The blood-stream (also made of cells) delivers the digested food to all parts of the body. Remember, food provides the body with the energy it needs to stay alive. In order to do this, the food must come into contact with huge numbers of absorbing cells.

Figure 1–4 *Each of these "hills" in the small intestine contains blood vessels ready to carry digested food throughout the body. Why is a "hilly" small intestine better suited to absorbing digested food than a smooth small intestine would be?* ❸

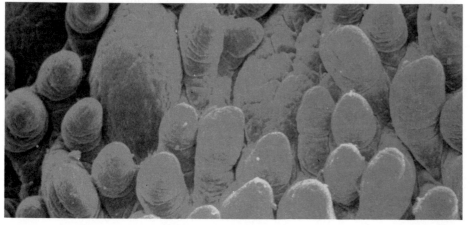

H ■ 17

els of organization, going from the smallest unit to the largest unit.

Cell	Person
Tissue	Family
Organ	Community
System	Nation

• **How many levels of organization are shown in the chart?** (Four.)
• **Illustrate four levels of organization in an automobile.** (Answers will vary: for ex-ample, battery cell, battery, ignition system, car; brake lever, hand brake, braking system, car.)

Using yourself or a specific student, illustrate the hierarchy shown in the right column. For example, Sally Martinez is one member of the Martinez family. Her family is part of the city of New York, which is part of the United States.

Use the circulatory system as one example of the left column. Muscle cells form muscle tissue. One type of muscle tissue is the heart. The heart is one organ

in the circulatory system, which also includes the blood vessels and blood.

● ● ● ● **Integration** ● ● ● ●

Use the discussion of cells to integrate concepts of cell biology into your lesson.

FOCUS/MOTIVATION

Write the figure 50,000,000,000,000 on the chalkboard.
• **Can you read this large number?** (Fifty trillion, or fifty thousand billion.)
Explain that there are approximately 50 trillion cells in the human body.

CONTENT DEVELOPMENT

Explain to students that 50 trillion body cells must be well organized in order for the body to function efficiently. Cells are specialized to provide different functions in the body. Groups of similar cells that perform a given function are called tissues.

INDEPENDENT PRACTICE

▶ *Activity Book*

Students can practice using Latin and Greek roots to decode scientific terms in the Chapter 1 activity called Medical Terminology Made Easy. Each root indicates a particular organ in the human body; for example, the prefix *cardio-* indicates the heart.

FIND OUT BY DOING

THE SKIN

Discovery Learning

Skills: Making observations, making inferences, making comparisons

Materials: cotton ball, rubbing alcohol

In this activity students explore some functions of the skin, the boundary that separates the human body from the outside world. The two functions shown in the three activities are sensory perception and temperature regulation.

Students will realize that water on the skin feels cool and that rubbing alcohol feels still cooler. This helps to illustrate how perspiration is used as a mechanism to cool the body and maintain a stable internal temperature.

The skin consists of two main layers. The top layer, the epidermis, is made up of epithelial cells, and the second layer, the dermis, is composed of connective tissue with glands, blood vessels, and nerves. The nerve endings of the sense of touch, temperature, and pressure are in the dermis; those of pain, in the epidermis.

FIND OUT BY DOING

The Skin

1. Wet your finger and blow on it. Describe how it feels. Wet a spot on your arm and blow on it. Describe this feeling.

2. Think about when you first get out of a shower or a bathtub. How do you feel when you are wet? Do you feel better after you are dry? Think about the times you perspire. How do you think perspiration helps the body?

3. Now touch a cotton ball that has been dipped in water and another cotton ball that has been dipped in isopropyl (rubbing) alcohol on two different areas of your arm. Compare the different feelings you experience in both areas.

■ Which functions of the skin are apparent in these activities?

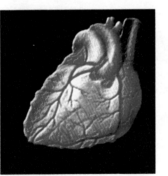

If you were to look at the lining inside the small intestine under a microscope, you would see that it is covered by structures resembling tiny and even tinier hills. See Figure 1–4 on page 17. In just 6.5 square centimeters of the small intestine, there are 20,000 tiny hills and 10 billion tinier hills!

Within each hill is a network of tiny blood vessels. As digested food passes through these hill-like structures, it is absorbed by these cells. Then it is passed on to the tiny blood vessels, which carry the digested food to all parts of the body.

ASSEMBLY CELLS The body contains millions of cells that are responsible for assembling, or putting together, important chemical substances. The pancreas, a fish-shaped structure located just behind the stomach, contains a variety of these assembly cells. Some of them are specialized to produce enzymes. Enzymes are chemicals that help to break down food into simpler substances. Others are specialized to produce hormones. Hormones are chemical messengers that help to regulate certain activities of the body.

CELLS FOR MOVEMENT Every move you make—from the twitch of an eyebrow to the powerful stride of running to the lifting of this textbook—depends on muscle cells. A muscle cell is like no other type of cell in the body because a muscle cell is able to contract, or shorten. In doing so, a muscle cell causes movement. You will read more about the different types of muscle cells in Chapter 2.

Tissues

Your body is a masterpiece of timing and organization. Its trillions of cells work together to keep you alive. To help you accomplish this task, the cells that make up your body are organized into **tissues**. A tissue is a group of similar cells that perform the same function. **There are four basic types of tissues in the human body: muscle, connective, nerve, and epithelial** (ehp-ih-THEE-lee-uhl). Observing these tissues under a microscope, you might be surprised to see how different they are from one another.

Figure 1–5 *The heart contains muscle tissue, epithelial tissue, connective tissue, and nerve tissue.*

1–2 (continued)

FOCUS/MOTIVATION

Have students think of something that they really do well and what special characteristic(s) they have that make it possible. You can make this activity as serious or as funny as you like, and they will still get the point. The students would probably enjoy sharing their "specializations." You might want to set the tone by giving the first example or two.

CONTENT DEVELOPMENT

In the same way that people often have different specializations, the cells in the human body perform different functions. Cells that perform the same function are grouped together into tissues.

Even though the human body contains many different parts and performs hundreds of different functions, there are only four basic kinds of tissue. List these four types of tissue on the chalkboard: muscle tissue, connective tissue, nerve tissue, and epithelial tissue.

• **What is the primary function of connective tissue?** (Provides support for the body.)

• **What kind of tissue carries messages from the brain to other parts of the body?** (Nerve tissue.)

• **What kind of tissue forms the outer surface of the body and also lines such body parts as the mouth and stomach?** (Epithelial tissue.)

MUSCLE TISSUE   The only kind of tissue in your body that has the ability to contract, or shorten, is muscle tissue. By contracting and thus pulling on bones, one type of muscle tissue makes your body move. Another type of muscle tissue lines the walls of structures inside your body. This muscle tissue does jobs such as moving food from your mouth to your stomach. A third type of muscle tissue is found only in the heart. This muscle tissue enables the heart to contract and pump blood.

CONNECTIVE TISSUE   The tissue that provides support for your body and connects all its parts is called connective tissue. Bone is an example of connective tissue. Are you surprised to learn that bone is a tissue? Not all tissues need to be soft. Without bone, your body would lack support and definite shape. In other words, without bone you would just be a blob of flesh! Blood is another example of connective tissue. One of the blood's most important jobs is to bring food and oxygen to body cells and carry away wastes. A third kind of connective tissue is fat. Fat keeps the body warm, cushions structures from the shock of a sudden blow, and stores food.

NERVE TISSUE   The third type of tissue is nerve tissue. Nerve tissue carries messages back and forth between the brain and spinal cord and every other part of your body. And it does so at incredible speeds. In the fraction of a second it takes for you to feel the cold of an ice cube you are touching, your nerve tissue has carried the message from your finger to your brain. Next time you have a chance to hold an ice cube, think about this.

H ■ 19

BACKGROUND INFORMATION
FAT CELLS

When a person eats more food than is needed, the body stores the extra energy by producing fat. This fat is deposited in a layer under the skin. When the body needs more energy than its glucose and glycogen can provide, it relies on the energy stored in that fat.

FACTS AND FIGURES
THE SKIN

The skin is the body's largest organ, covering an area of almost 2 square meters. About 6.5 square centimeters of skin may contain 20 blood vessels, 650 sweat glands, and more than 1000 nerve endings. Grooves and ridges formed by epidermal cells on the fingertips cause the fingerprint patterns unique to each individual.

7. Layer of tissue immediately beneath the skin (Connective)

GUIDED PRACTICE
▶ *Laboratory Manual*

Skills Development

Skills: Making observations, applying concepts, making inferences

At this point you may want to have students complete the Chapter 1 Laboratory Investigation in the *Laboratory Manual* called Investigating Tissues. In the investigation students will examine the tissues in a chicken wing and identify their functions.

• **To which group of tissue does bone belong?** (Connective tissue.) **Skin?** (Epithelial tissue.) **Blood?** (Connective tissue.) **Biceps?** (Muscle tissue.) **Spinal cord?** (Nerve tissue.)

REINFORCEMENT/RETEACHING
▶ *Activity Book*

Students who have difficulty understanding the concepts of this section should be provided with the Chapter 1 activity called What Is a Tissue?

ENRICHMENT

Challenge students to use reference books to identify the type of tissue found at each of the following locations:
1. Lining of the throat (Epithelial)
2. Tendons around muscles (Connective)
3. Air sacs in the lungs (Epithelial)
4. Surface layer of lining of stomach (Epithelial)
5. Outer part of ear (Connective)
6. Walls of the blood vessels (Muscle)

Unlike the four types of tissue found in humans and other animals, the tissues in the larger land plants (vascular plants) can be classified into just three types: dermal, vascular, and ground. As in animals, the specialized plant tissues represent a division of labor among the cells that contributes to the survival of the plant. Water and nutrients are circulated through the plant by the vascular tissues, dermal tissue forms a covering over the root system and shoot, and the remainder of the plant is ground tissue.

1–2 (continued)

REINFORCEMENT/RETEACHING

Review the four basic tissue types discussed in the chapter. Point out that tissues are made up of a group of similar cells that perform similar functions. Remind students that tissues can be further grouped into organs. An organ is made up of different types of tissues, all of which combine to perform the duties of that particular organ. Ask students to identify each of the following as a tissue or an organ:

1. Lungs (Organ)
2. Blood (Tissue)
3. Nerve (Tissue)
4. Brain (Organ)
5. Stomach (Organ)
6. Bone (Tissue)

FOCUS/MOTIVATION

Have students take a relatively simple task and describe all the movements that would be needed to accomplish the task. You might want to have students describe all the movements that are needed to get ready for school each morning. Have students list each task separately and describe the body parts that are needed to accomplish each task.

Students should realize that even a simple task, such as tying one's shoes, requires some complicated and sophisticated body movements. Write their responses on the chalkboard. Do not erase any of the responses. By the time the simple tasks performed daily to get ready for

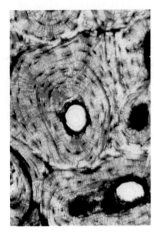
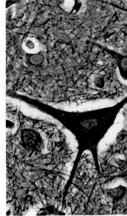

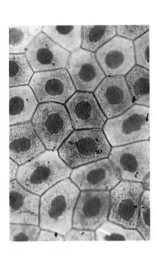
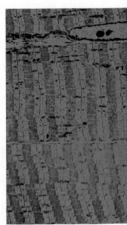
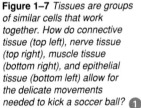

Figure 1–7 *Tissues are groups of similar cells that work together. How do connective tissue (top left), nerve tissue (top right), muscle tissue (bottom right), and epithelial tissue (bottom left) allow for the delicate movements needed to kick a soccer ball?* ❶

EPITHELIAL TISSUE The fourth type of tissue is epithelial tissue. Epithelial tissue forms a protective surface on the outside of your body. When you look in a mirror, you are looking at a special kind of epithelial tissue, one that makes up your outer covering—your skin! Another kind of epithelial tissue lines the cavities, or hollow spaces, of the mouth, throat, ears, stomach, and other body parts.

school have been described, the chalkboard will be really full.

Stress that even when performing these tasks, the body is also performing many other tasks. All the systems and organs of the body must coordinate their efforts. The heart continues to pump blood, the lungs continue to take in and give out gases, and so on.

CONTENT DEVELOPMENT

Explain that the human body is customarily divided into systems for the purpose of study and analysis. Tell students that the number of systems used varies in different books. For example, in a medieval Persian anatomy book, just four systems were used: nervous, venous (veins), arterial (arteries), and skeletal.

Have students examine Figure 1–8.
• **How does this diagram illustrate the four levels of organization in the human body?** (Cells form connective tissue. Connective tissue makes up bones. Bones compose the skeletal system.)

Organs

Just as cells join together to form tissues, different types of tissues combine to form **organs.** An organ is a group of different tissues with a specific job. The heart, stomach, and brain are familiar examples of organs. But did you know that the eye, skin, and tongue are also organs? The heart is an example of an organ made up of all four kinds of tissues. Although the heart consists mostly of muscle tissue, it is covered and protected by epithelial tissue and also contains connective and nerve tissues.

Organ Systems

Many times even a complicated organ is not adequate enough to perform a series of specialized jobs in the body. In these cases, an **organ system** is needed. An organ system is a group of organs that work together to perform a specific job. Your body can work as it does because it is made up of many organ systems. The organ systems and their functions are shown in Figure 1–9 on page 22. Although each system performs a special function for the body, no one system acts alone. Each organ system contributes to the constant "teamwork" that keeps you, and most multicellular living things, alive.

To help you better understand how organ systems, organs, tissues, and cells are related, try this: Think of an organ system as an automobile manufacturing company. The organs would be represented by the different company divisions that are responsible for a particular model of automobile. Within each division, there are many departments—for example, accounting, assembly, design, and sales. Each department would represent the tissues that form each organ. And the people that work in each of the various departments would represent the cells that make up each type of tissue.

So whether it's in the automobile manufacturing company or in the body, it should now be clear to you that each level has its own specialized job to do. Yet each level is dependent on the activities of the other levels to either build an automobile or keep a body alive.

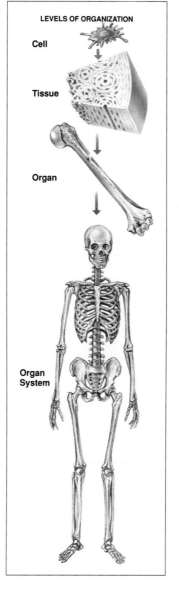

LEVELS OF ORGANIZATION

Cell

Tissue

Organ

Organ System

Figure 1–8 *Notice how bone cells are organized to form a tissue, an organ, and an organ system.*

HISTORICAL NOTE
ANDREAS VESALIUS

Many historians agree that the foundation of modern medicine can be traced to the work of the Belgian scientist Andreas Vesalius (1514–1564). Born in Brussels and appointed a professor at the University of Padua in his early twenties, Vesalius conducted the most accurate and thorough examinations of the human body that had ever been done.

Vesalius wrote a classic book on anatomy in which he described the systems of the human body; in particular, he was the first to give a correct description of the anatomy of the heart. Perhaps one reason for the popularity of Vesalius's book was that the anatomical drawings were probably the finest yet made. The drawings were done by Jan Stephan van Calcar, an artist who had been a student of Titian.

GUIDED PRACTICE

Skills Development

Skills: Making observations, making classifications, applying concepts, making inferences

At this point have students complete the in-text Chapter 1 Laboratory Investigation: Looking at Human Cheek Cells. In the investigation, students will identify the parts of a cell.

ENRICHMENT

▶ *Activity Book*

Students who have mastered the concepts in this section will be challenged by the Chapter 1 activity called Describing the Skin. In the activity students use a diagram to interpret structures found in a cross section of the skin.

• **How would the diagram differ if it showed the muscular system instead of the skeletal system?** (The tissue would be muscle tissue instead of connective tissue; the organ would be one of the muscles attached to a bone, or perhaps the heart; the bottom diagram would show all the muscles in the body.)

Before students look at Figure 1–9, ask them how many systems they think the human body should be divided into. Challenge them to give names to the systems. Write all responses on the chalkboard and then have them compare their list with that in Figure 1–9.

▶ *Multimedia* ◀

Students can now begin the Interactive Videodisc called BioExplorer. Students will become campers investigating the human body. Students should continue to explore body systems as they continue on to the following chapters. When they have completed the videodisc, have students choose a body system and describe how it is interrelated to other human body systems.

SYSTEMS OF THE HUMAN BODY

System	Functions
Skeletal	Protects, supports, allows movement, produces blood cells, and stores minerals
Muscular	Allows body movement and maintains posture
Digestive	Breaks down food and absorbs nutrients
Circulatory	Transports nutrients, wastes, and other materials and plays a role in the immune response
Respiratory	Exchanges oxygen and carbon dioxide between blood and air
Excretory	Removes solid and liquid wastes
Nervous	Detects sensation and controls most functions
Endocrine	Plays a part in the regulation of metabolism, reproduction, and many other functions
Reproductive	Performs reproduction and controls male and female functions and behaviors
Immune	Controls the immune response and fights disease
Integumentary (skin)	Protects, regulates temperature, prevents water loss

FIND OUT BY WRITING

ORGANS AND ORGAN SYSTEMS

Skills: Making classifications, using reference materials

In this activity students use their reference skills to match organs to the system of which they are a part. Remind students that the division of the human body into systems is arbitrary and that different books will have different categorizations. Sometimes an organ—the skin is one example—is considered to belong to more than one system. When students have prepared their lists, have them compare some of the different categorizations they have found. Some suggested answers are given below.

Organ	Organ System
lung	respiratory
small intestine	digestive
kidney	excretory
brain	nervous
rib	skeletal
heart	circulatory
thyroid gland	endocrine
biceps	muscular
skin	integumentary
pancreas	digestive

Integration: Use the Find Out by Writing feature to integrate language arts into your lesson.

FIND OUT BY WRITING

Organs and Organ Systems

On a sheet of paper, copy the following chart.

Organ	Organ System
lung	
small intestine	
kidney	
brain	
rib	
heart	
thyroid gland	
biceps	
skin	
pancreas	

Using books in the library, find out the name of the organ system to which each organ belongs. Write the name of the organ system next to the proper organ. Now expand this list by adding other organs you have heard of or read about. Find out to which organ system each of these organs belongs.

1

22 ■ H

1–2 Section Review

1. List the levels of organization in humans.
2. What are the four basic types of human tissues?
3. List the organ systems of the human body.

Connection—*You and Your World*

4. Using a bicycle or any type of machine as an example, explain how each part of the machine works with every other part so that the machine can do its job. Compare this with the way the systems of the body work together.

1–2 (continued)

CONTENT DEVELOPMENT

Have students read the information in Figure 1–9. Emphasize that the division of the human body into systems is for the convenience of study and that the systems do not work in isolation. In carrying out even the simplest function, the body uses more than one system.

Explain that some organs are considered to belong to more than one system.

• **The lungs are part of the excretory system because they expel the waste product carbon dioxide from the body. To what other system do you think the lungs belong?** (The respiratory system.)

• **Name some systems to which the skin could belong. Give a reason for each choice.** (Accept all logical answers. In addition to the integumentary system, possible answers are the excretory system because the skin gives off heat and water and the immune system because the skin helps to prevent disease.)

▶ *Multimedia* ◀

An introduction to the systems of the human body is provided in the video called Systems Working Together. The video illustrates the ways in which the organs and organ systems in the human body are interdependent. This is shown to be similar to the way in which people in any large community depend on one another for specialized services.

After students have seen the video, have them complete each of the following statements with the name of one organ system: **1.** In a community, the roads and highway systems function as the lines of communication and supply. In a similar way, the _____ system delivers food and oxygen to the cells in the body.

CONNECTIONS

Artificial Body Parts ❷

Thanks to *chemical technology*, many worn-out or damaged body parts can be replaced totally or in part by plastics. Plastics can be stronger than steel or lighter than a sheet of paper. Plastics are synthetic materials that can be shaped into any form, from a transparent bag to a football helmet. In fact, the word plastics comes from the Greek word *plastikos,* which means able to be molded.

Plastics are made from chemicals. These chemicals come from such raw materials as coal, petroleum, salt, water, and limestone. Because plastics have a variety of special properties, they can do some jobs better than other materials.

Two special properties—harmless to the human body and unaffected by chemicals in the body —make certain plastics useful in medicine. For example, if a hip, knee, elbow, or shoulder joint breaks because of an accident or wears out from a disease (such as arthritis), it can be replaced with an artificial joint made of plastics. Plastics have also been used to replace parts of the intestines and faulty valves in the heart. Whenever surgeons do these or other types of body repair, they use threads made of plastics to sew all the parts into place. Strong, lightweight plastics are also used to make artificial body parts. Some artificial hands have "skin" made of plastics, complete with fingerprints and a partial sense of touch!

As you might imagine, the list of uses for plastics in medicine is almost endless. In fact, the day of a bionic person— once a figment of the imagination of a television scriptwriter—may soon become a reality.

H ■ 23

CONNECTIONS
ARTIFICIAL BODY PARTS

Explain to students that the general name for an artificial body part is *prosthesis,* from a Greek word meaning "an addition." Years ago, artificial legs were made of willow wood. They were very heavy to lift and had limited mobility in the knee and ankle joints.

If you are teaching thematically, you may want to use the Connections feature to reinforce the themes of systems and interactions or stability.

Integration: Use the Connections feature to integrate chemical technology into your lesson.

2. Muscle, connective, nerve, and epithelial.

3. Skeletal, muscular, digestive, circulatory, respiratory, excretory, nervous, endocrine, reproductive, immune, integumentary.

4. Answers will vary depending on which machine students choose. Regardless of the choice, they should use more than one level of organization in their analysis.

REINFORCEMENT/RETEACHING

Review students' responses to the Section Review questions. Reteach any material that is still unclear, based on students' responses.

CLOSURE

▶ *Review and Reinforcement Guide*

Have students complete Section 1–2 in the *Review and Reinforcement Guide.*

2. In a community, waste disposal is accomplished through sewer systems and trash-removal companies. This function in the human body is the responsibility of the _____ system.

3. The legal and law-enforcement services regulate the behavior of people in a community and help to ensure balance. In the body, the balance of various substances as well as growth is regulated by the _____ system.
(Answers: circulatory, excretory, endocrine.)

Challenge students to devise other parallel statements comparing agencies in a community to human body systems. They might use the electric and power companies (respiratory system provides energy through oxygen), telephone company (nervous system provides communication), and so on.

INDEPENDENT PRACTICE

Section Review 1–2

1. Cells, tissues, organs, organ systems.

Laboratory Investigation

LOOKING AT HUMAN CHEEK CELLS

BEFORE THE LAB

1. Gather all equipment at least one day prior to the investigation. You should have as many sets of materials as you have microscopes.
2. Flat toothpicks work better than rounded ones for this investigation, but they may be harder to find.
3. Divide the class into groups of two to four students, depending on the number of microscopes available.
4. You may want to discuss the proper use of methylene blue one day prior to the lab. You may also want to caution students to wear old clothes for this investigation, even though they will use laboratory aprons.
5. Check the dilutions on the methylene blue. Too strong a solution makes it more difficult to see the cells.

SAFETY TIPS

Remind students that methylene blue is a stain, so they should be careful of spilling it on their clothing or on countertops where they might get it on their sleeves or skin.

Make sure students understand the proper procedure for handling a microscope. Caution them that glass microscope slides and coverslips are very fragile. Alert students to notify you immediately if they should break any glassware, particularly if they are cut by the broken glass.

Demonstrate the way that students are to scrape cheek cells without injuring themselves. Remind them that they will not be able to see any of the cells on the toothpick.

Laboratory Investigation

Looking at Human Cheek Cells

Problem

What are the characteristics of some typical human cells?

Materials (per pair of students)

microscope	medicine dropper
glass slide	methylene blue
coverslip	paper towel
toothpick	

Procedure 🧪📷 👁

1. Place a drop of water in the center of the slide.
2. Using the flat end of the toothpick, gently scrape the inside of your cheek. Although you will not see them, cells will come off the inside of your cheek and stick to the toothpick.
3. Stir the scrapings from the same end of the toothpick into the drop of water on the slide. Mix thoroughly and cover with the coverslip.
4. Place the slide on the stage of the microscope and focus under low power. Examine a few cells. Focus on one cell. Sketch and label the parts of the cell. (Refer to Figure 1–3 for the basic parts of the cell.)
5. Switch to high power. Sketch and label the cell and its parts.
6. Remove the slide from the stage of the microscope. With the medicine dropper, put one drop of methylene blue at the edge of the coverslip. **CAUTION**: *Be careful when using methylene blue because it may stain the skin and clothing*. Place a small piece of paper towel at the opposite edge of the coverslip. The stain will pass under the coverslip. Use another piece of paper towel to absorb any excess stain.

7. Place the slide on the stage of the microscope again and find an individual cell under low power. Sketch and label that cell and the cell parts that you see.
8. Switch to high power and sketch and label the cell and its parts.

Observation

How are cheek cells arranged with respect to one another?

Analysis and Conclusions

1. What is the advantage of staining the cheek cells?
2. Explain why the shape of cheek cells is suited to their function.
3. Based on your observations, to which tissue type do cheek cells belong?
4. **On Your Own** Examine some other types of human cells, such as muscle, blood, or nerve, under the microscope. Sketch and label the parts of the cell. How does this cell compare with the cheek cell?

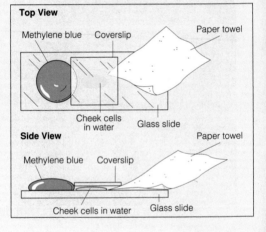

Top View
Methylene blue   Coverslip   Paper towel
Cheek cells in water   Glass slide
Side View
Methylene blue   Coverslip   Paper towel
Cheek cells in water   Glass slide

PRE-LAB DISCUSSION

Have students read the complete laboratory procedure and then reread it and follow it step-by-step. Discuss the procedure by asking questions similar to the following:

• **What is the purpose of this laboratory investigation?** (To use a microscope to discover the shape and arrangement of cells.)
• **Why is it necessary to place a coverslip over the material that is being observed?** (The coverslip protects the lens in the microscope from coming into contact with the specimen.)
• **When using a microscope with several levels of power, which level do you use first when focusing on an object?** (Always use the lowest level of power first.)
• **Why should you use only the fine-adjustment knob when focusing under high power?** (The coarse-adjustment knob moves the view much too quickly. Also, there is danger of crashing into the slide and causing damage to both the lens objective and the slide.)

Study Guide

Summarizing Key Concepts

1–1 The Body as a Whole

▲ The process by which the body's internal environment is kept stable in spite of changes in the external environment is called homeostasis.

▲ Humans, like all living things, need energy to do work.

1–2 Levels of Organization

▲ The levels of organization in a multicellular living thing include cells, tissues, organs, and organ systems.

▲ Cells come in all shapes and sizes. Regardless of its job or shape, a cell works in harmony with other cells to keep the body alive.

▲ Cells are the building blocks of living things.

▲ A tissue is a group of similar cells that perform the same function.

▲ There are four types of tissues in the human body: muscle, connective, nerve, and epithelial.

▲ Muscle tissue has the ability to contract, or shorten. By contracting and thus pulling on bones, one type of muscle tissue makes the body move. Another type of muscle tissue lines the walls of structures inside the body. A third type of muscle tissue enables the heart to contract and pump blood to all parts of the body.

▲ Connective tissue provides support for the body and connects all its parts.

▲ Nerve tissue carries messages back and forth between the brain and the spinal cord and every other part of the body.

▲ Epithelial tissue forms a protective surface on the outside of the body and lines its internal cavities.

▲ An organ is a group of different tissues with a specific function.

▲ An organ system is a group of organs that work together to perform a specific job.

Reviewing Key Terms

Define each term in a complete sentence.

1–1 The Body as a Whole
  homeostasis

1–2 Levels of Organization
  cell
  tissue
  organ
  organ system

see a single layer of cells instead of several layers—observing, predicting.)

• **What types of challenges do scientists encounter when using microscopes to investigate living tissues?** (Accept all responses. Point out that stains such as methylene blue are used to help make structures easier to see under a microscope—analyzing, relating.)

OBSERVATIONS

Cheek cells are arranged in a pattern like overlapping paving stones. Students will be looking at several layers of cells.

ANALYSIS AND CONCLUSIONS

1. Staining the cells makes it easier to see their shape and arrangement.
2. The shape of the cells allows them to be arranged in overlapping layers to form the covering tissue of the skin.
3. Cheek cells are epithelial tissue.
4. Answers will vary depending on the types of cells students choose.

GOING FURTHER: ENRICHMENT

Part 1

Have students examine a strand of human hair under the microscope. Tell them that the inside of the hair is made of keratin, a secretion of epidermal cells in the hair follicles of the scalp. The hair will appear to be covered with overlapping structures that look like shingles. The inside of the strand of hair is made up of parallel layers of uniform material. The cells observed will look similar to the cheek cells.

Part 2

Obtain hair from several common animals. Dogs, cats, rabbits, hamsters, gerbils, horses, and cows make good sources. Have students compare the various samples to the human hair and answer the following questions:

• **Do the hairs appear to be about the same thickness when you look at them with your eye? With the microscope?**
• **How do the cells that make up the hair shaft compare in size and shape?**
• **What other similarities or differences do you observe?** (Answers to all the questions will vary depending on the type of hair observed.)

TEACHING STRATEGY

1. You will probably want to circulate through the room, instructing students who are having trouble observing objects through the microscope. Some students may need assistance placing the cheek cells on the slides.
2. For the final activity, On Your Own, students may have difficulty making the comparisons between cheek cells and other types of cells. You might want one group of students to work with another group—one focusing on the cheek cells and the other on the cells being compared. Emphasize that they are to look for similarities and differences.

DISCOVERY STRATEGIES

Discuss how the investigation relates to the chapter ideas by asking open questions similar to the following:

• **What did you predict you would see when you examined the cheek cells under the microscope? How did your observations differ from your predictions?** (Accept all responses. Students might have expected to

Chapter Review

ALTERNATIVE ASSESSMENT

The *Prentice Hall Science* program includes a variety of testing components and methodologies. Aside from the Chapter Review questions, you may opt to use the Chapter Test or the Computer Test Bank Test in your *Test Book* for assessment of important facts and concepts. In addition, Performance-Based Tests are included in your *Test Book*. These Performance-Based Tests are designed to test science process skills, rather than factual content recall. Since they are not content dependent, Performance-Based Tests can be distributed after students complete a chapter or after they complete the entire textbook.

CONTENT REVIEW

Multiple Choice

1. b
2. c
3. a
4. a
5. b
6. c
7. d
8. d
9. a
10. d

True or False

1. T
2. T
3. T
4. F, Connective
5. T

Concept Mapping

Row 1: Stability
Row 2: Energy

CONCEPT MASTERY

1. The four types of tissue are muscle (used in motion and contraction), connective (used for support, transport, warmth, cushioning, and food storage), nerve (used to carry messages), and epithelial (used as protective surfaces and linings).

2. Cells are the simplest living parts of the human body. Cells that are similar in structure and function form tissues. Organs are groups of different tissues working together; for example, the heart and the eye are organs. Organ systems are

---

Content Review

Multiple Choice

Choose the letter of the answer that best completes each statement.

1. The term most closely associated with homeostasis is
   a. growth.   c. regulation.
   b. stability.   d. energy.
2. To do work, living things must have
   a. growth.   c. energy.
   b. green plants.   d. oxygen.
3. A group of similar cells that perform a similar function is called a(an)
   a. tissue.   c. organ system.
   b. organ.   d. living thing.
4. A tissue that has the ability to contract is
   a. muscle tissue.
   b. connective tissue.
   c. nerve tissue.
   d. epithelial tissue.
5. Which type of tissue is blood?
   a. muscle tissue
   b. connective tissue
   c. nerve tissue
   d. epithelial tissue
6. An organ made up of all four kinds of tissues is the
   a. brain.   c. heart.
   b. blood.   d. spinal cord.

7. A tissue that protects the surface of the body is
   a. muscle tissue.
   b. connective tissue.
   c. nerve tissue.
   d. epithelial tissue.
8. From smallest to largest, the levels of organization in a multicellular living thing are
   a. tissues, cells, organs, organ systems.
   b. cells, organs, tissues, organ systems.
   c. organ systems, organs, tissues, cells.
   d. cells, tissues, organs, organ systems.
9. Which is an example of a unicellular living thing?
   a. ameba   c. human
   b. tree   d. turtle
10. Which system removes wastes from the body?
   a. skeletal   c. digestive
   b. nervous   d. excretory

True or False

If the statement is true, write "true." If it is false, change the underlined word or words to make the statement true.

1. <u>Homeostasis</u> is the process by which the body's internal environment is kept stable in spite of changes in the external environment.
2. All living things need <u>energy</u> to do work.
3. A group of different tissues that have a specific function is called a (an) <u>organ</u>.
4. <u>Muscle</u> tissue provides support for the body and connects its parts.
5. Fat is an example of <u>connective</u> tissue.

Concept Mapping

Complete the following concept map for Section 1–1. Refer to pages H8–H9 to construct a concept map for the entire chapter.

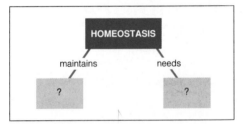

---

groups of organs that work together to perform certain functions.

3. Answers will vary. Students should choose three of the systems listed in Figure 1–9 on page H22. Descriptions of functions should match information given in the figure.

4. The external environment of a living thing is constantly changing. In order to survive in that environment, the organism needs a mechanism (homeostasis) to adjust its internal environment and keep it stable.

5. Energy is needed for the cells in the human body to live and perform their functions.

CRITICAL THINKING AND PROBLEM SOLVING

1. Homeostasis ensures that the internal environment of a living thing is kept stable regardless of changes in its external environment.

2. Wearing a heavy coat helps the body maintain a stable internal temperature by

Concept Mastery

Discuss each of the following in a brief paragraph.

1. List and describe the four types of tissues in the body.
2. Explain the relationship between cells, tissues, organs, and organ systems.
3. Name three systems of the body and give the function of each.
4. Why is homeostasis important to the survival of a living thing?
5. Explain why the human body needs energy.

Critical Thinking and Problem Solving

Use the skills you have developed in this chapter to answer each of the following.

1. **Making inferences** What role does homeostasis play in the existence of a living thing?
2. **Applying concepts** How does wearing a heavy coat in winter help to maintain homeostasis?
3. **Relating concepts** When exercising on a hot day, you begin to sweat a lot and you become thirsty. How do sweating and becoming thirsty illustrate homeostasis?

4. **Relating facts** Although the structures of the body are grouped into separate organ systems, they are not independent of one another. Explain how a bad cold, which affects the respiratory system, can keep you from playing a good game of softball.
5. **Developing a model** Design a new organ for the human body. The function of this organ will be storage of air for long periods during swimming and space travel. Which tissues might be needed? What will the function of each tissue be? What cells will make up each tissue? What will the cells look like? Include a sketch of this organ.
6. **Relating facts** Provide two examples of body activities in which two or more organ systems work together.
7. **Using the writing process** Develop an advertising campaign for the use of antacids. An antacid is a substance that helps to calm an upset stomach. In your campaign, show how an upset stomach affects not only the digestive system, of which the stomach is a part, but other organ systems as well.

ISSUES IN SCIENCE

The following issue can be used as a springboard for discussion or given as a writing assignment:

A great advance in medical science was the discovery of the X-ray by Wilhelm Roentgen (1845–1923) in 1895. Until X-rays could be used to show the workings of the inside of the human body, physicians had only their sense of touch to gain information about the location of both normal and diseased structures.

Although the safety and reliability of X-ray machines have been vastly improved since their early beginnings, some people believe that any unnecessary exposure to ionizing radiation should be avoided. Older X-ray equipment, which delivers radiation doses higher than necessary, is still in use. In particular, an annual chest X-ray for tuberculosis is now thought to be an unnecessary risk.

Have students do library research on the safety of X-rays ordered by physicians and dentists. What types of people should be particularly cautious about any extra exposure to X-rays? Which people should have annual X-rays to protect their health?

preventing heat loss to the colder environment.

3. Sweating helps to cool the body through evaporation and condensation. Becoming thirsty signals that the body needs more water. Both these actions help the body maintain a stable internal temperature.

4. Because the respiratory system provides oxygen needed by all cells in the body, the operations of the other systems are impeded when the respiratory system is not functioning properly

5. Answers will vary. Tissues will probably include connective tissue and epithelial tissue to line the inside of the organ.

6. Answers will vary. For example, breathing uses both the lungs (respiratory) and the muscles (muscular).

7. Answers will vary. Students should include diagrams or illustrations as well as written passages in their advertisements.

Chapter 2 SKELETAL AND MUSCULAR SYSTEMS

SECTION	LABORATORY INVESTIGATIONS AND DEMONSTRATIONS
2–1 The Skeletal System pages H30–H37	**Laboratory Manual** Examining Bones and Joints **Teacher Edition** Muscle Strength, p. H28d
2–2 The Muscular System pages H37–H42	**Student Edition** Observing Bones and Muscles, p. H46 **Laboratory Manual** Comparing Bones, Joints, and Muscles **Teacher Edition** Childproof Containers, p. H28d
2–3 Injuries to the Skeletal and Muscular Systems pages H42–H45	
Chapter Review pages H46–H49	

*All materials in the Chapter Planning Guide Grid are available as part of the Prentice Hall Science Learning System.

OUTSIDE TEACHER RESOURCES

Books

Curry, J. *The Mechanical Adaptations of Bones*, Princeton University Press.

Huxley, A. F. *Reflections on Muscle*, Princeton University Press.

Kittredge, Mary. *The Human Body: An Overview*, Chelsea House Publishers.

McMahon, Thomas A. *Muscles, Reflexes, and Locomotion*, Princeton University Press.

Shipman, Pat, et al. *The Human Skeleton*, Harvard University Press.

Steele, D. Gentry, and Claude A. Bramblett. *The Anatomy and Biology of the Human Skeleton*, Texas A & M University Press.

Audiovisuals

The Body Machine—Bone Structure, filmstrip, Denoyer-Geppert

The Body Machine—Muscular System, filmstrip, Denoyer-Geppert

Bones and Movement, film or video, Coronet

How the Body Moves, film, Time-Life

How Does Your Body Move? video, EBE

OTHER ACTIVITIES	MULTIMEDIA

Activity Book
    Chapter Discovery: Discovering Bones and Muscles
    ACTIVITY: Scrambled Bones
Student Edition
    Find Out by Doing: Bones As Levers, p. H30
    Find Out by Doing: Examining a Bone, p. H33
Review and Reinforcement Guide
    Section 2–1
	Video
	    Skeletal System
	Courseware
	    The Lever (Supplemental)
	Transparency Binder
	    Joints
	English/Spanish Audiotapes
	    Section 2–1

Activity Book
    ACTIVITY: Muscle Fatigue
    ACTIVITY: Making a Model of the Arm
Student Edition
    Find Out by Doing: Voluntary or Involuntary?, p. H39
    Find Out by Doing: Muscle Action, p. H42
Review and Reinforcement Guide
    Section 2–2
	Video
	    Muscular System
	English/Spanish Audiotapes
	    Section 2–2

Product Testing Activity
    Bandages
Review and Reinforcement Guide
    Section 2–3
	Video
	    The Bones and Muscles Get Rhythm
	English/Spanish Audiotapes
	    Section 2–3

Test Book
    Chapter Test
    Performance-Based Test
	Test Book
	    Computer Test Bank Test

Chapter 2 SKELETAL AND MUSCULAR SYSTEMS

CHAPTER OVERVIEW

The skeletal system performs five main functions for the body. It provides shape, allows for movement, protects certain organs, helps to produce some blood cells, and helps to store various chemical substances. As the human body develops within the mother, the structures that will become bone are first laid down as cartilage. Mature bones generally contain a hollow cavity filled with marrow and blood vessels. The solid bone that surrounds the marrow contains nerves and blood vessels. Thus, bone is living tissue.

The muscular system, along with the skeletal system, helps the body move. There are three different types of muscle tissue: skeletal, smooth, and cardiac. Skeletal muscle tissue is found mainly in muscles that are controlled voluntarily, whereas smooth muscle tissue is found in involuntary muscles. Cardiac muscle tissue is found only in the heart. Muscles always work in pairs, with muscle fibers contracting in an all-or-none fashion. Injuries to the skeletal and muscular systems include sprains, fractures, and dislocations.

2–1 THE SKELETAL SYSTEM
THEMATIC FOCUS

The purpose of this section is to introduce students to the bones and joints that make up the human skeletal system. In addition to movement, the skeletal system serves four other functions. It gives the body shape and support, protects the internal organs, stores important minerals, and produces blood cells.

Students will learn that the human skeleton contains about 206 bones that vary greatly in size and shape. The largest bones are found in the legs, whereas some of the smallest bones are found in the hands and feet. This section also describes different types of joints, the places where two bones meet.

The themes that can be focused on in this section are energy and scale and structure.

*Energy: The skeletal and muscular systems of the human body obtain and use energy in order to perform their functions. For example, the marrow contained in many bones uses food energy to produce the blood cells.

*Scale and structure: The human body can be organized in four levels: cells, tissues, organs, and organ systems. As each organ system is studied, it can be analyzed as a sum of smaller component parts. The skeletal system is made up of bones, ligaments, tendons, and cartilage.

PERFORMANCE OBJECTIVES 2–1

1. State the five basic functions of the skeletal system.
2. Explain the difference between ligaments and tendons.
3. Compare the structure and function of cartilage with those of bone.
4. Describe the structure of a typical bone.
5. Describe three types of joints and the kinds of movements each allows.

SCIENCE TERMS 2–1

bone p. H30
ligament p. H30
tendon p. H30
cartilage p. H32
marrow p. H34
joint p. H35

2–2 THE MUSCULAR SYSTEM
THEMATIC FOCUS

The purpose of this section is to describe three types of muscles found in the human body and to explain the ways muscles function. Muscles are first classified by their appearance and location: skeletal, or striated; smooth; and cardiac. Students learn that muscles move bones, pump blood through the body, and move food through the digestive system. Muscles working together in pairs move the bones in the body. One muscle contracts as its partner relaxes.

The themes that can be focused on in this section are systems and interactions and unity and diversity.

*Systems and interactions: Of the three types of muscles, skeletal muscle permits voluntary movement; smooth and cardiac muscles permit involuntary movement. The cells contained in the muscular system are specialized for contraction. In order for a bone to move, two muscles work together as a pair—one contracts, and the other relaxes.

Unity and diversity: The structure of bones, muscles, and related organs and tissues are different, yet they work together to enable the body to move. No one of the body's organ systems acts in isolation; they must function as a team in order to maintain the balances needed for good health.

PERFORMANCE OBJECTIVES 2–2

1. Compare the three types of muscles.
2. Describe how muscles work in pairs.

SCIENCE TERMS 2–2

skeletal muscle p. H38
smooth muscle p. H39
cardiac muscle p. H40

2–3 INJURIES TO THE SKELETAL AND MUSCULAR SYSTEMS

THEMATIC FOCUS

The purpose of this section is to introduce students to three types of injuries of the skeletal and muscular systems that occur quite frequently—especially among athletes. A sprain, or a tearing or twisting of a ligament or a tendon, usually occurs when a joint is forced beyond its normal range of motion. A fracture is a broken bone. It may be a crack or a complete breaking of the bone into two pieces. A bone that is forced out of its joint is known as a dislocation.

The themes that can be focused on in this section are stability and patterns of change.

*Stability: The combined action of the skeletal and muscular systems enables the human body to maintain a stable internal environment. Working together with the other systems of the body, the bones and muscles are contantly kept in a state of balance.

Patterns of change: Injuries occur to bones and muscles when the body undergoes conditions of extreme stress. However, the various tissues and organs that make up the skeletal and muscular systems contain mechanisms for repairing any injuries that may occur.

PERFORMANCE OBJECTIVES 2–3

1. Explain how a sprain occurs.
2. Define *fracture* and explain how it heals.
3. Describe the treatment for a dislocation.

SCIENCE TERMS 2–3

sprain p. H43
fracture p. H43
dislocation p. H43

Discovery *Learning*

TEACHER DEMONSTRATIONS MODELING

Muscle Strength

Have one of the stronger students come to the front of the class. Place a large book in the center of your desk. Have the student lift the book with the right hand.

• **Is this book heavy?** (Yes.)

Now have the student put the book back on the desk, relift it, and again place it on the desk. Have the student repeat this task as long as possible while the class records the number of times the book is lifted. Do not permit the student to become strained or overly fatigued.

Have the same student repeat this task each day for a week. Let the class count the number of times the book is lifted and have them record their daily observations. After the second day, ask this question:

• **Based on your observations, how many times do you predict the student will be able to lift the book after a week?** (Accept all answers, although some students should be able to infer that the number of times the book can be lifted before the person becomes tired should increase over time.)

Childproof Containers

Bring into class several different medicine containers. Do not have names or medications listed on the bottles.

• **Why do these bottles have caps that are difficult to open?** (The caps are designed to be difficult for children to open. A child's hands are not very strong, and a child's fingers are not able to perform sophisticated movements.)

Have a student try to remove the tops. After he or she has removed the tops successfully, explain that you are going to try an experiment to see how important the thumb was in removing the tops. Tape the student's thumb to the palm of the hand. Use medical adhesive tape. Do not tape the thumb tightly. In effect, you just want to move the thumb out of the way to prevent the student from using it. Now have the student try to open the medical containers again.

Repeat the demonstration with student volunteers.

• **Were you able to remove the caps without using your thumb?** (Students should have difficulty removing the tops. Do not let students use their teeth to pry the tops off; they should use only their hands.)

If you cannot get medicine containers, you might like to have students try to tie their shoes with their thumbs immobilized. Now pose a serious question to the class. Tell the class that many older people have difficulty with mobility. With age, disease sometimes makes it painful to move one's fingers.

• **How difficult do you think it is for an elderly person to remove the caps from medicine bottles or tie shoelaces without the full use of his or her fingers?** (Very difficult.)

CHAPTER 2
Skeletal and Muscular Systems

INTEGRATING SCIENCE

This life science chapter provides you with numerous opportunities to integrate other areas of science, as well as other disciplines, into your curriculum. Blue numbered annotations on the student page and integration notes on the teacher wraparound pages alert you to areas of possible integration.

In this chapter you can integrate physical science and mechanics (p. 30), life science and zoology (pp. 31, 38), earth science and geology (p. 33), physical education (p. 35), mathematics (p. 39), and physical science and electromagnetics (p. 45).

SCIENCE, TECHNOLOGY, AND SOCIETY/COOPERATIVE LEARNING

Anabolic steroids derived from the male hormone testosterone promote protein synthesis in many tissues of the body. As a result, the mass of skeletal muscle in the body can increase dramatically. By taking steroids, muscle development is enhanced.

Until recently, steroid use and abuse seemed limited to athletes who used these drugs to assist in recovery from injury or to enhance performance at the international and professional level of sports competition.

Now, teenagers are abusing steroids to get that "brawny" look, and they do not realize the dangerous side effects of their

INTRODUCING CHAPTER 2

DISCOVERY LEARNING

▶ *Activity Book*

Begin your teaching of the chapter by using the Chapter 2 Discovery Activity from the *Activity Book*. In this activity students will perform simple exercises to explore the properties of bones and muscles.

USING THE TEXTBOOK

• **What is the name of the type of circus act pictured on page H28?** (Trapeze or flying trapeze.)

Have students read the chapter introduction on page H29 to find out about one of the most incredible stunts ever performed by a trapeze artist.

• **What is this incredible stunt?** (A quadruple somersault.)

• **In order to perform this amazing feat, what body systems must work together?** (Muscular, skeletal, and nervous systems work together to carry out these intricate body movements.)

• **Which body system is most responsible for the strength needed to complete a quadruple somersault?** (Muscular system.)

• **Which body system coordinates the movements and carries the information to the other parts of the trapeze artist's body?** (Nervous system.)

• **What other circus acts or sports events require many hours of practice and a finely coordinated body?** (Answers will vary

Skeletal and Muscular Systems

Guide for Reading

After you read the following sections, you will be able to

2–1 The Skeletal System
- List the functions of each part of the skeletal system.
- Describe the characteristics and structure of bone.
- Describe three types of movable joints.

2–2 The Muscular System
- Classify the three types of muscle tissues.
- Explain how muscles cause movement.

2–3 Injuries to the Skeletal and Muscular Systems
- List the three most common injuries to the skeletal and muscular systems.

Slowly, the young man climbs up the ladder toward the top of the circus tent. The crowd grows quiet. You feel your heart beginning to beat faster. You tilt your head back. Your eyes follow the man in the glistening costume. As he grabs the trapeze, the muscles in his arms bulge. Suddenly, he leaps and is flying through space. Then he lets go of the trapeze and does a somersault in midair . . . once, twice, three times. You gasp and then gaze in disbelief as, incredibly, the man does another somersault—a quadruple! It has never been done before!

How, you wonder, has the trapeze artist been able to perform such a daring feat? Part of the answer lies in the hundreds of hours he has spent training and practicing. And part of the answer lies in the dedication he has brought to his work. But certainly he could never have performed this spectacular act if it were not for his finely coordinated body. Working together with many of his other organs, the trapeze artist's bones and muscles have made the "impossible" happen. In the pages that follow, you will discover how your skeletal and muscular systems work for you—making the ordinary to the almost impossible possible.

Journal *Activity*

You and Your World   Perform one type of movement with each of the following parts of your body: finger, wrist, arm, and neck. In your journal, describe the motion of each body part. What allows you to move these body parts? How is each motion different?

◀ *A trapeze artist performs a daring feat—a quadruple somersault!*

use. Steroid abuse can lead to serious medical problems, including high blood pressure, liver and kidney disorders, addiction, and heart damage. Young women who take steroids to enhance their athletic performance often experience problems with their menstrual cycle and may develop male sex characteristics—deep voice, facial hair, and enlarged muscles.

Perhaps the most frightening side effect of steroid abuse is the threat to the user's mental health. Users are prone to moodiness, irritability, depression, and what are called "roid rages."

Once they begin taking steroids, teenagers find it difficult to quit. The body that has been built by taking steroids quickly disappears when their use is stopped. What can be a deadly cycle that may continue for years has begun.

Cooperative learning: Using preassigned lab groups or randomly selected teams, have groups complete one of the following assignments:
• Assume that they are the editorial staff of a national daily newspaper. Using the issue of steroid use by athletes, have groups produce the editorial page for their newspaper. When completed, the page should contain the following components:
1. Background information—factual information about steroid use and abuse
2. Guest editorials supporting and opposing steroid use by athletes
3. Hypothetical quotes from "man-on-the-street" surveys
• Have groups design a cartoon or a cartoon strip that illustrates the effects of steroid use on the body.

See Cooperative Learning in the *Teacher's Desk Reference.*

JOURNAL ACTIVITY

You may want to use the Journal Activity as the basis of class discussion. Have students choose a practical movement for each body part; for example, "pressing a piano key" in preference to "bending a finger." For each movement, ask students to estimate the number of bones, joints, and muscles involved. Have them include diagrams to clarify their written descriptions of each movement. Students should be instructed to keep their Journal Activity in their portfolio.

but may include tightrope or high-wire act, tumbling, gymnastics, karate, basketball, soccer, pole vaulting, and so on.)
• **What movements do you carry out every day that require great harmony and coordination?** (Answers will vary.)

Explain to students that even such unconscious actions as walking, running, and writing require a great deal of coordination among the skeletal, muscular, and nervous systems. Remind them of the difficulty that babies experience in learning to walk or of the challenge that

persons with injured muscular, skeletal, or nervous systems must face in relearning to walk.

Explain to students that in this chapter they will learn more about how muscles and bones develop and work together to produce body movement.

2–1 The Skeletal System

MULTICULTURAL OPPORTUNITY 2–1

Discuss with students the importance of nutrition in the development of strong bone. Have students research the components of bone. What are some foods that would provide these needed nutrients? (Any foods high in calcium.)

ESL STRATEGY 2–1

Students who are learning English may be unfamiliar with some of the names of parts of the body used in this chapter. Make sure they can locate their ankles, back, chest, elbows, hips, knees, neck, shoulders, thighs, and wrists. Give these words as a spelling assignment. Then test for comprehension by providing a diagram for students to label.

Remind students that an *idiom* is an expression with a meaning that is different from its literal meaning. Explain these idioms that include the word *bone:*

- funny bone
- wet to the bone
- bone dry
- to bone up on

Ask students to write sentences using these idioms.

TEACHING STRATEGY 2–1

FOCUS/MOTIVATION

Have students brainstorm ways that the skeletal system works to help a person play a sport, such as basketball. Students should be able to suggest that the bones in the arms help the player move the ball down court; that bones in the legs help the player to jump; and that bones in the skull protect the brain from damage if the player is hit in the head with the ball. These bones also protect the player's eyes if a ball strikes him or her in the face. Other observations are also possible. Accept all reasonable answers.

- **What do you think would happen if all the bones in a basketball player's hand were fused into one bone?** (Students should be able to infer that the ability to control a basketball during a game is, in

---

FIND OUT BY DOING

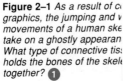

Bones as Levers

Using books in the library, find out about the three classes of levers. How do bones act as levers? On posterboard, draw one class of levers. Next to the drawing, draw an example of the bones that act like that lever. In the drawing, label the effort, load, and fulcrum. At the bottom of the posterboard, define effort, load, and fulcrum.

■ What are the two other classes of levers? Give an example for each of levers in the body.

Figure 2–1 *As a result of c... graphics, the jumping and v... movements of a human ske... take on a ghostly appearan... What type of connective tis... holds the bones of the skele... together?* ❶

---

part, dependent on the movements of the bones of the hand. If all the bones in the hand were fused, a basketball player would experience a great deal of trouble controlling the ball.)

▶ *Multimedia* ◀

An alternative way to begin this lesson is to have students use the video called Skeletal System. After students have viewed the video, have them make sketches of the joints in the skull, the pivot joint, the joint in the shoulder, and the joint in the elbow.

2–1 The Skeletal System

The skeletal system is the body's living framework. This complicated structure contains more than 200 **bones**—actually, about 206. The bones are held together by groups of stringy connective tissues called **ligaments.** Another group of connective tissues called **tendons** attach bones to muscles. Together, the bones, ligaments, and tendons make up most of the skeletal system.

Functions of the Skeletal System

The skeletal system has five important functions: It provides shape and support, allows movement, protects tissues and organs, stores certain materials, and produces blood cells. The first of these important functions—giving shape and support to the body—should be pretty clear to you. Imagine that you did not have a skeletal system. What would you look like? A formless mass? A blob of jelly? The answer is yes to both descriptions! In fact, if the skeletal system did not perform this vital role, it would be meaningless to consider any of its other functions.

The skeletal system helps the body move. Almost all your bones are attached to muscles. As the muscles contract (shorten), they pull on the bones,

CONTENT DEVELOPMENT

Refer students to Figure 2–2. Point out the way the vertebrae protect the spinal cord running through the vertebral column. Students should note that a cartilage disk is located between each vertebra.

- **What do you think the function of the cartilage disk is?** (To keep each vertebra from rubbing on the vertebrae above and below it.)
- **What might happen if the disk wore away?** (Bone would rub on bone, and the result would be pain and other back problems.)

causing the bones to move. By working together, the actions of the bones and muscles enable you to walk, sit, stand, and do a somersault.

Bones protect the tissues and organs of your body. If you move your fingers along the center of your back, you will feel your backbone, or vertebral column. Your backbone protects your spinal cord, which is the message "cable" between the brain and other body parts. As you may recall from Chapter 1, the spinal cord is made up of nerve tissue. Nerve tissue is extremely soft and delicate and, therefore, easily damaged. So you can see why it is important that the spinal cord is protected from injury.

Bones are storage areas for certain substances. Some of these substances give bones their stiffness. Others play a role in blood clotting, nerve function, and muscle activity. If the levels of these substances in the blood should fall below their normal ranges, the body will begin to remove them from where they are stored in the bones.

The long bones in your body (such as those in the arms and legs) produce many blood cells. One type of blood cell carries oxygen. Another type destroys harmful bacteria.

Parts of the Skeleton

Suppose you were asked to make a life-size model of the human skeleton. Where would you start? You might begin by thinking of the human skeleton as consisting of two parts. The first part covers the area that runs from the top of your head and down your body in a straight line to your hips. This part includes the skull, the ribs, the breastbone, and the vertebral column. The vertebral column contains 26 bones, which are called vertebrae (VER-tuh-bray; singular: vertebra, VER-tuh-bruh).

The second part of the skeletal system includes the bones of the arms, legs, hands, feet, hips, and shoulders. There is a total of 126 bones in this part of the skeletal system.

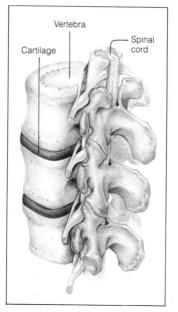

Figure 2–2 *The vertebral column consists of a series of small bones stacked one on top of the other. Together, these bones protect the delicate spinal cord and also form a strong support for the body. What are the individual bones of the vertebral column called?* ❷

Figure 2–3 *Unlike humans, the king crab has a hard external skeleton. What are some advantages of having an internal skeleton?* ❸

• **What do you think the term** *slipped disk* **means?** (The disk between two vertebrae has slipped out of position, possibly causing the vertebrae to rub together.)

● ● ● ● **Integration** ● ● ● ●

Use the photograph of the king crab to integrate concepts of zoology into your lesson.

FIND OUT BY DOING

BONES AS LEVERS

Discovery Learning

Skills: Applying concepts, relating concepts, making comparisons
Material: posterboard

In a first-class lever, the fulcrum is between the effort force and the resistance force. An example of a first-class lever is illustrated when the arm is bent at the elbow. The elbow is the fulcrum, the contraction of the triceps is the effort force, and the mass of the forearm bones is the resistance force.

In a second-class lever, the resistance force is between the effort force and the fulcrum. An example of this type of lever is shown when the foot is raised as if to stand on tiptoe. The fulcrums are the gliding joints at the tarsals. The pushing down of the tibia and fibula is the resistance effort, and the contraction of the soleus muscle in the leg is the effort force.

In a third-class lever, the effort force is between the fulcrum and the resistance force. When the biceps muscle acts to move the hand, it functions as a third-class lever. The fulcrum is the elbow, and the resistance force is the mass of the hand. In running or walking, the motions of the femur are also examples of third-class levers.

Integration: Use the Find Out by Doing feature to integrate mechanics into your lesson.

INTEGRATION

SPACE SCIENCE

Bone has a "grain," much like that of the wood of a tree, and the application of force causes the grain to align itself in such a way as to enable the bone to tolerate the constant stresses applied to it. But what happens when there is no force?

Studies of Soviet and American astronauts have shown that the absence of gravity in space causes, over a long period of time, severe loss of calcium from bones. Long-term space flight so weakens the skeleton that space scientists regard this loss as a major problem that future space explorers will face.

2–1 (continued)

FOCUS/MOTIVATION

Bend over and pick up a coin that you have previously placed on the floor. Have students describe your movements. They should observe that your vertebral column makes a slight arch when you bend over.

• **Why is my vertebral column able to bend slightly when I bend over?** (The vertebral column is made up of many small bones, or vertebrae, which permit slight movement.)

• **What would happen if I wanted to pick up a coin and my vertebral column were made up of only one bone?** (It would be very difficult for you to bend over and pick up a coin.)

Now dip down and pick up the coin by bending your knees and squatting.

• **What movements were involved this time?** (The bones in the legs were involved. The joints at the knees and hips permitted this kind of movement.)

CONTENT DEVELOPMENT

Have students list as many bones in the human skeletal system as they can. They may use common names or scientific names. Then have them compare their lists with the list presented in Figure 2–4. Have them locate each numbered bone on the diagram and then on a skeleton or on their own bodies.

• **What is the longest bone in your body?** (Femur.)

• **What is another name for clavicle?** (Collarbone.) **Scapula?** (Shoulder blade.) **Patella?** (Kneecap.)

• **What structures connect one bone to another?** (Ligaments.)

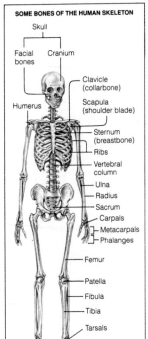

SOME BONES OF THE HUMAN SKELETON

Skull — Facial bones, Cranium
Clavicle (collarbone)
Humerus
Scapula (shoulder blade)
Sternum (breastbone)
Ribs
Vertebral column
Ulna
Radius
Sacrum
Carpals
Metacarpals
Phalanges
Femur
Patella
Fibula
Tibia
Tarsals
Metatarsals
Phalanges

Figure 2–4 There are approximately 206 bones in the human skeletal system. What is another name for the collarbone? **❶**

Development of Bones

Many bones are formed from a type of connective tissue called **cartilage** (KAHRT-'l-ihj). Cartilage is a dense material that contains fibers. Although cartilage is strong enough to support weight, it is also flexible enough to be bent and twisted. You can prove this to yourself by moving your nose back and forth and by flapping your ears. The tip of your nose and your ears are made of cartilage.

Many bones in the skeleton of a newborn baby are composed almost entirely of cartilage. The process of replacing cartilage with bone starts about seven months before birth and is not completed until a person reaches the age of about 25 years. At this time, a person "stops growing." However, some forming and reforming of bone still occurs even in adulthood, primarily where bone is under a great deal of stress.

Although most of your body's cartilage will eventually be replaced by bone, there are a few areas where the cartilage will remain unchanged, such as in the knee, ankle, and elbow. These areas are usually found where bone meets bone. Here the cartilage has two jobs. One job is to cushion the bones against sudden jolts, such as those that occur when you jump or run. The other job is to provide a slippery surface for the bones so that they can move without rubbing against one another. Because cartilage is three times more slippery than ice, it is the ideal material for this task.

Figure 2–5 X-rays of the hands of a 2-year-old (top left) and a 3-year-old (bottom left) show that the cartilage in the wrist has not yet been replaced by bone. In the X-ray of a 14-year-old's hand (center), the replacement of cartilage by bone is almost complete, as it is in the hand of a 60-year-old (right). What type of tissue is cartilage? **❷**

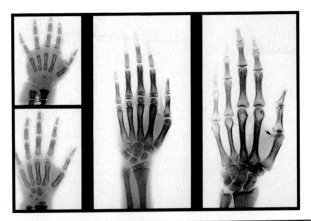

Structure of Bones

Bone is not only one of the toughest materials in the body, it is also one of the lightest. You may be surprised to learn that the 206 bones of your skeletal system make up barely 14 percent of your body's mass! Because of bone's strength, you may have thought of bone as nonliving. On the contrary, bones are alive. They contain living tissue—nerves, bone-forming cells, and blood vessels.

Bones, however, are similar in some ways to such nonliving things as rocks. Can you think of a few reasons why? Two obvious similarities are hardness and strength. Both bones and rocks owe their hardness and strength to chemical substances called minerals. Rocks contain a wide variety of minerals; bones are made up mainly of mineral compounds that contain the elements calcium and phosphorus. As you may already know, dairy products, such as milk and cheese, are good sources of calcium and phosphorus. So next time someone suggests that you drink lots of milk "to keep your bones strong and healthy," you will know why this suggestion makes sense.

Let's take a close look at the longest bone in the body to see what it (and other bones) is made of. This bone, called the femur (FEE-mer), links your hip to your knee. Probably the most obvious part of this bone is its long shaft, or column. The shaft, which is shaped something like a hollow cylinder, contains compact bone. Compact bone is dense and similar in texture to ivory. Within the shaft of a long bone are hollow cavities, or spaces. Inside these

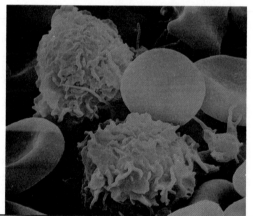

Figure 2–6 *The red marrow of bones such as the skull and ribs produces the body's red blood cells and white blood cells. As seen through an electron microscope, red blood cells are beret-shaped structures and white bloods cells are furry-looking structures. What does yellow marrow contain?* ❹

H ■ 33

OSTEOPOROSIS

Like most tissue, bone tissue declines in its rate of regeneration over time. A gradual decrease in bone mass is expected with advancing years. In some instances, however, bone loss is severe. This condition, known as osteoporosis, is especially common in women over the age of 55.

In osteoporosis, the bones become thin and porous and are easily susceptible to fractures. After the age of 35, women lose bone at an average rate of 0.5 percent per year. By age 75, a woman may have lost 20 to 30 percent of the bone in her arms and legs and 30 to 40 percent of the bone in her spine. The spine, hips, and wrists are most vulnerable to thinning and, hence, to fracturing. Fractures of the vertebrae may lead to severe back pain, loss of height, or a rounded upper back. Hip fractures are the most common indirect cause of death in older women.

Hormones, including estrogen, probably play a role in regulating the body's calcium balance. The most important reason for loss of bone calcium, however, appears to be nutritional. Most women's average calcium consumption of less than 500 mg per day falls substantially below the recommended daily allowance of 800 mg. Other substances and events that act as "calcium robbers" include childbearing, habitual dieting, lack of exercise, alcohol, caffeine, salt, smoking, and stress.

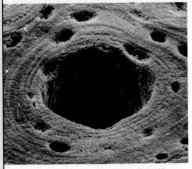

From *Tissues and Organs: A Text-Atlas of Scanning Electron Microscopy.* By Richard G. Kessel and Randy H. Kardon. Copyright © 1979 by W.H. Freeman and Company. Reprinted by permission.

Figure 2–7 *As the diagram illustrates, the most obvious feature of a long bone is its long shaft, or center, which contains dense, compact bone. Running through compact bone is a system of canals that bring materials to the living bone cells. One such canal is seen in the center of the photograph. What materials are carried through the canals?* ❶

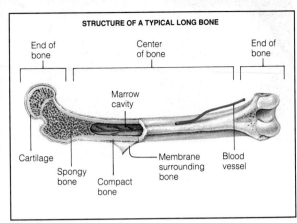

STRUCTURE OF A TYPICAL LONG BONE

cavities is a soft material called yellow **marrow.** Yellow marrow contains fat and blood vessels. Another type of marrow called red marrow produces the body's blood cells. Red marrow is found in the cavities of such places as the skull, ribs, breastbone, and vertebral column.

Surrounding the shaft of the femur is a tough membrane that contains bone-forming cells and blood vessels. This membrane aids in repairing injuries to the bone and also supplies food and oxygen to the bone's living tissue. Muscles are attached to this membrane's surface. At each end of the shaft is an enlarged knob. The knobs are made of a type of bone called spongy bone. Spongy bone is not soft and spongy, as its name implies, but is actually quite strong. Because spongy bone resembles the supporting girders of a bridge, its presence at the ends of long bones adds strength to bone without adding mass. Figure 2–7 shows these basic parts of a bone.

Running through the bone is a system of pipelike canals that bring food and oxygen to the living bone cells. These canals also contain nerves. The nerves send messages through the canals to living parts of the bone.

Skeletal Joints

Imagine that you are pitching your first baseball game of the season. The catcher signals you to throw a fast ball. You know that the batter is a powerful hitter, so you shake your head no. The catcher

---

2–1 (continued)

CONTENT DEVELOPMENT

Refer students to Figure 2–7. Have them find the major parts of this typical bone.

Ask a butcher to supply you with several different bones. You might be able to secure some of the leg bones of a calf or some chicken bones. Have students examine the bones. You might be able to show the class some marrow bones. These bones are often sold in a package of soup bones. Have students describe the marrow.

• **What is the function of marrow?** (Marrow is found in the long bones of the leg and the sternum. Blood cells are made in the marrow of these bones. The blood

cells are then moved through small holes in the bone and into the blood.)

FOCUS/MOTIVATION

If you are able to get a chicken leg with the thigh attached, you may be able to demonstrate the knee joint of the chicken. You should use a sharp knife to cut away the muscle tissue (meat) from the leg. If you are careful, you will be able to show the place where the bones of the leg meet. This joint also has a pad of cartilage at the place where the bones meet.

• **What is the function of this pad of cartilage?** (It cushions the two bones and prevents them from rubbing against each other.)

Tell students that they also have pads of cartilage at the places where bones come together in their body. In fact, the cartilage in the knee is often damaged while playing sports. Very sophisticated techniques of microsurgery are often used to repair damaged knee cartilage.

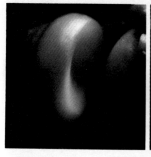
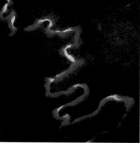

Figure 2–8 *Joints, or places where two bones meet, allow bones to move without damaging each other. The ball-and-socket joint in the shoulder (left) permits the greatest range of movement, whereas the joints in the skull (right) do not move at all. What type of joint is found at the elbow?* **2**

changes the signal to a curve ball. You agree and nod. And then you wind up and send your curve ball sailing over the plate. "Strike one!" the umpire shouts.

You could not make any of these simple movements—shaking and nodding your head or winding up and pitching the ball—if it were not for structures in your skeletal system called **joints.** A joint is any place where two bones come close together. Generally, a joint is responsible for keeping the bones far enough apart so that they do not rub against each other as they move. At the same time, a joint holds the bones in place.

There are several different kinds of joints. Some joints allow the bones they connect to move. Other joints permit little or no movement. Examples of joints that permit no movement are the joints found in the skull. Although these joints permit no movement, they enable the bones in the skull to fuse (join) as you grow. In the pitching example you just read about, the pivot joint, which is located between the first two vertebrae in your neck, enabled you to shake and nod your head in response to the catcher's signals. A pivot joint allows for rotation of one bone around another.

When you wound up to pitch your curve ball, the ball-and-socket joint of your shoulder allowed you to swing your arm in a circle. Ball-and-socket joints, which provide for the circular motion of bones, consist of a bone with a rounded head that fits into the cuplike pocket of another bone. Can you think of

two bones meet. Some joints, such as those in the top of the skull, are immovable. These joints are little more than cracks where several flat bones have grown together. Other joints, such as those where the ribs meet the vertebrae of the backbones, are partially movable. They allow the chest to expand and contract during breathing.

Demonstrate the movement permitted by the following joints;
1. Pivot joint—between first two vertebrae in neck: nod head up and down; move head from side to side.
2. Ball-and-socket joint—shoulder: swing arm in a circle.
3. Hinge joint—elbow: flex arm up and down, bending at elbow.

▶ *Multimedia* ◀

Use the transparency in the *Transparency Binder* called Joints to help students understand the different types of joints in the human skeleton.

CONTENT DEVELOPMENT

Ask the class to describe ways the body can be taught to perform a task such as pitching a baseball. Students should suggest that practice and repetition can be used to train the skeletal system to perform some very difficult and unfamiliar

movements. If you have access to a gymnastics class, you might be able to have some of these complicated moves demonstrated for the class. **CAUTION:** *Do not permit students who are untrained to perform any stunts. Without special training, serious injury can result.*

● ● ● ● **Integration** ● ● ● ●

Use the movements involved in pitching a baseball to integrate physical education into your lesson.

Explain that a joint is any place where

PROBLEM SOLVING

WHAT KIND OF JOINT IS THIS?

In this feature students explore three other joints that are part of the skeletal system: saddle joints, gliding joints, and ellipsoid joints.

In pushing open a door, you might use both the shoulder (ball and socket) and the elbow (hinge) joints. Lifting a book from a desk would involve the elbow (hinge), the joint at the base of the thumb (saddle), the gliding joint in the wrist, and the ellipsoid joints that connect the fingers with the palm of the hand. When kneeling, you would use the knee (hinge), the ankle (sliding), and the ellipsoid joints that connect the toes with the sole of the foot. Giving the "thumbs up" signal involves primarily the thumb joint (saddle). Waving the hand might use both the wrist (gliding) and the elbow (hinge). Shrugging the shoulders uses the collarbone (gliding), whereas shaking the head from side to side uses the pivot joint between the first two neck vertebrae.

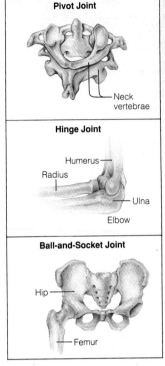

Figure 2–9 *The actions involved in pitching a ball require the use of many types of joints. What movement does the ball-and-socket joint allow for?* ❶

another location in your body where you would find a ball-and-socket joint? ❷

As you moved your arm forward, the bend at your elbow straightened out and you whipped the ball toward the batter. The elbow is a hinge joint. A hinge joint, which is also found at the knee, allows for movement in a forward and backward direction. However, it allows for little movement from side to side. Figure 2–9 shows where the hinge joint and the other joints you just read about are located in the body.

2–1 Section Review

1. What are the five functions of the skeletal system?
2. What is a ligament? A tendon?
3. List three places in the body where cartilage is found.
4. What is marrow?
5. Compare the movements of three types of movable joints.

Critical Thinking—*Relating Facts*

6. Suggest an advantage of having the ribs attached to the breastbone by cartilage.

PROBLEM Solving

What Kind of Joint Is This?

The pivot, ball-and-socket, and hinge joints that you have read about in the chapter are not the only types of movable joints in the body. There are several other movable joints.

The accompanying drawings illustrate six types of movable joints. Notice the motion that each joint is capable of producing. On a separate sheet of paper, copy the following list of activities.

- Pushing a door open
- Lifting a book from a desk

- Kneeling
- Giving the "thumbs up" signal
- Waving the hand
- Shrugging the shoulders
- Shaking the head from side to side

Applying Concepts

Now compare the motion of each joint with each activity. Determine which type of joint or joints is needed to perform each activity and write the name of the joint next to its appropriate activity.

SIX TYPES OF MOVABLE JOINTS

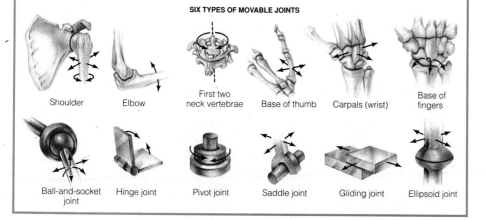

Shoulder · Elbow · First two neck vertebrae · Base of thumb · Carpals (wrist) · Base of fingers

Ball-and-socket joint · Hinge joint · Pivot joint · Saddle joint · Gliding joint · Ellipsoid joint

---

2–2 The Muscular System

It is three o'clock in the morning, and you have been asleep for several hours. All day you walked, ran, and played, using your muscles in a variety of ways. Now that you are asleep, all the muscles in your body are also at rest. Or are they?

Guide for Reading

Focus on this question as you read.

▶ *What are the three types of muscles?*

MULTICULTURAL OPPORTUNITY 2–2

Discuss with students the importance of exercise in the development of strong muscles. Have students compare different types of exercises (for example, isotonic versus isometric or low-impact versus high-impact aerobics). Which are most effective in developing muscles? Are some exercises more effective at different stages of students' growth and development?

ESL STRATEGY 2–2

Review the terms *antonym* and *synonym*. Explain that antonyms are words that are opposite in meaning; synonyms are words that have the same or nearly the same meaning. Ask students to give
1. The antonym for voluntary muscles. (Involuntary muscles.)
2. The synonyms for skeletal (striated and voluntary), smooth (involuntary), and heart (cardiac).

Working in cooperative groups, have students write three or four sentences describing
1. The appearance of each type of muscle tissue.
2. How each type of muscle functions.
Selectively check students' work by asking them to read aloud what they have written.

---

the ribs and the breastbone permits these movements.

REINFORCEMENT/RETEACHING

Review students' responses to the Section Review questions. Reteach any material that is still unclear, based on students' responses.

CLOSURE

▶ *Review and Reinforcement Guide*
Have students complete Section 2–1 in the *Review and Reinforcement Guide.*

TEACHING STRATEGY 2–2

FOCUS/MOTIVATION

• **Does the body have more bones than muscles or more muscles than bones?** (It has more muscles than bones. The human body has more than 600 muscles, compared to 206 bones.)
• **Can you name some of your body's muscles that continue to work while you are asleep?** (Examples: Heart muscles pump blood. Chest muscles and diaphragm help

you breathe. Muscles in the digestive tract continue to move food through the digestive system.)

CONTENT DEVELOPMENT

Explain to students that each muscle is composed of many long, thin fibers. These fibers run parallel to one another and are held together in bundles. Illustrate this parallel arrangement of fibers on the chalkboard.

BACKGROUND INFORMATION
MUSCLES

Muscles are capable of only one forceful action that involves movement: pulling, which they do by contracting or shortening. When muscles lengthen, they are relaxing. This process does not require energy, so actively, muscles can only pull and never push. Any pushing, such as sticking out the tongue, jutting the jaw forward, or moving a lawn mower, is the result of muscles pulling on bones or on each other.

HISTORICAL NOTE
WILLIAM HARVEY

The English scientist William Harvey (1578–1657) is well known for his discovery of the circulation of blood. Studies of the workings of the heart muscles had been made by Greek scientists as early as 400 BC, but until Harvey's experiments and writings, no one had a clear idea of how the blood entered and left the heart. Most scientists before Harvey believed that blood was constantly produced from food consumed. Harvey showed that the amount of blood leaving the heart in 30 minutes was far greater than the total weight of blood in the body. Thus, it would be impossible for such a volume of blood to be produced from the amount of food a person would be likely to eat.

Harvey theorized that the blood traveled away from the heart through the arteries, passed to the veins, and then returned to the heart. Although he was unable to find any connecting channels between the arteries and veins, his theory was verified within a few years of his death.

Without waking you, many of the more than 600 muscles in your body are still working to keep you alive. The muscles in your heart are contracting to pump blood throughout your body. Your chest muscles are working to help move air in and out of your lungs. Perhaps last night's dinner is still being moved through your digestive system by muscles.

Most muscles, or muscle tissue, are composed of muscle fibers that run beside, or parallel to, one another and are held together in bundles of connective tissue. Each muscle fiber is actually a single cylinder-shaped cell. Recall from Chapter 1 that a tissue is a group of similar cells that work together to perform a specific function. In the case of muscle tissue, that function is to contract, or shorten.

Types of Muscles

In the human body, there are three types of muscle tissue: skeletal muscle, smooth muscle, and cardiac muscle. Each type of muscle tissue has a characteristic structure and function. The muscle tissue that attaches to and moves bones is called **skeletal muscle.** This is an appropriate name for this type of muscle tissue because it is associated with the bones of the body, or the skeletal system. By contracting, skeletal muscle causes your arms, legs, head, and other body parts to move.

Figure 2–10 *Like an American toad and an impala, a human can perform many types of movements as a result of the actions of muscles pulling on bones.*

2–2 (continued)

FOCUS/MOTIVATION

Have students view slides of different kinds of muscle tissue.
• **How do these cells differ in appearance?** (Students should observe that skeletal muscles have stripes, or striations, on them. Students may also observe that these muscle cells have many nuclei in them. Smooth and cardiac muscle cells have only one nucleus per cell.)

• **Why are skeletal muscles also called striated muscles?** (Under the microscope, they appear to have stripes or bands. These stripes are also called striations.)

CONTENT DEVELOPMENT

Explain to students that skeletal muscles are voluntary; that is, they move only when you want them to. Smooth and cardiac muscles are involuntary; that is, they act without you telling them to do so.
• **What type of action involves voluntary, skeletal muscles?** (Answers will vary. Ex-

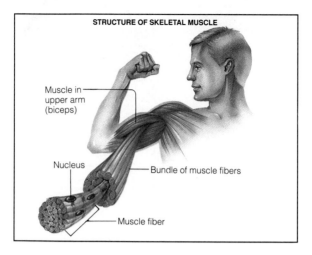

STRUCTURE OF SKELETAL MUSCLE

Muscle in upper arm (biceps)

Nucleus

Bundle of muscle fibers

Muscle fiber

Figure 2–11 *Muscle tissue is composed of muscle fibers that run parallel to one another and are held together in bundles of connective tissue. The biceps muscle, which is located in the upper arm, is an example of skeletal muscle tissue. Why is the biceps classified as a skeletal muscle?* **1**

If you were to look at skeletal muscle under a microscope, you would see that it is striated (STRIGH-ayt-ehd), or banded. For this reason, skeletal muscles are called striated muscles. Figure 2–12 on page 40 shows the bands associated with skeletal muscle. And because skeletal muscles move only when you want them to, they are also called voluntary muscles.

To appreciate how some of the voluntary (skeletal) muscles in your body work, think of the movements you make in order to write your name on a sheet of paper. The instant you want it to, your arm stretches out to pick up the paper and pencil. You grasp the pencil and lift it. Then you press the pencil down on the paper and move your hand to form the letters in your name. Your eyes move across the page as you write. To do all of this, you have to use more than 100 muscles. Now suppose you did this little task 100 times. Do you think the muscles in your hand would ache? Probably so. For although skeletal muscles react quickly when you want them to, they also tire quickly. Perhaps you might want to actually try this.

A second type of muscle tissue is called **smooth muscle.** Unlike skeletal muscle, smooth muscle does not have bands. Hence, its name is smooth. In general, smooth muscles can contract without your actively causing them to. Thus, smooth muscles are also called involuntary muscles. The involuntary

FIND OUT BY DOING

Voluntary or Involuntary?

1. Blink your eyes three times.

2. Then try not to blink. Time how long you are able to keep yourself from blinking. Record your data.

3. Repeat step 2. Determine the average time you can keep from blinking. **2**

How does your average time compare with that of your classmates? Are the eye muscles involved with blinking voluntary or involuntary muscles? Explain.

■ Using a mirror, observe what happens to your pupils in bright light and in dim light. Are the muscles that are involved in these actions voluntary or involuntary? How does the action of these muscles differ from those involved in blinking?

amples: shaking your head, waving your arm, pointing your finger, sitting down, and so on.)

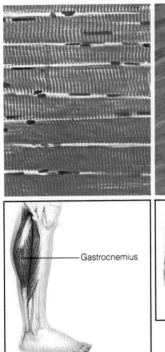
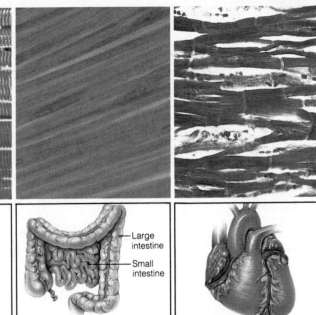
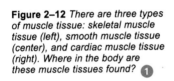

Figure 2–12 *There are three types of muscle tissue: skeletal muscle tissue (left), smooth muscle tissue (center), and cardiac muscle tissue (right). Where in the body are these muscle tissues found?* ❶

muscles of the body help to control breathing, blood pressure, and the movements of the digestive system. Unlike skeletal muscles, smooth muscles react slowly and tire slowly. How might this be an advantage for smooth muscles? ❷

A third type of muscle tissue, **cardiac muscle,** is found only in the heart. Branching out in many directions, cardiac muscle fibers weave a complex mesh. The contractions of these muscle fibers make the heart beat. Like smooth muscles, cardiac muscles are involuntary. Heart muscle, as you may have guessed, does not tire.

Action of Skeletal Muscles

As you have learned, muscles do work only by contracting, or shortening. In order for skeletal muscles to bring about any kind of movement, the action of two muscles or two groups of muscles is needed. Put another way, muscles always work in pairs.

FOCUS/MOTIVATION

Place a small rock on a corner of your desk. Have a volunteer come to the front of the room. Tell the student that this is a very small rock and easy to lift. Have the student lift the rock and tell the class if the rock is heavy. Tell the class that the muscles in their arms are strong enough to lift the rock. But the muscles of their arm can become tired when they work hard.

• **Was lifting this small rock hard work?** (Most of the class, including the student volunteer, will probably say no.)

• **What about lifting the rock many times?** (Students may suggest that it is easy to lift the rock and that they would have no trouble lifting it many times without stopping.) Now let the volunteer begin to lift the rock. Have the class count the number of times the person can lift the rock. Write the number on the chalkboard. If you have time, let other students perform the same lifting test. Keep a record of the number of times each volunteer was able to lift the small rock. Have each student

describe how the arm muscles felt when they could no longer lift the rock. Even though the rock was very small and easy to lift at the beginning of each trial, the rock became difficult to lift after repeated attempts.

• **Did the rock appear to become heavier after you lifted it a number of times?** (Students should suggest that the rock seemed to become heavier over time. The muscles in the arm, in fact, became tired over time.)

CONTENT DEVELOPMENT

Tell the class that the heart beats 24 hours a day, every day of the year.

• **How do you think the heart muscle differs from the muscles of your arm after you have lifted a rock a number of times?** (Students may infer that the heart does not tire as the muscles of the arm do.)

• **What do you think would happen if the muscle of your heart became tired as the muscles in your arm did?** (Students should infer some of the unpleasant consequences of such an action.)

For example, if you were to raise your lower arm at the elbow, you would notice that a bulge appears in the front of your upper arm. This bulge is caused by the contraction of a muscle called the biceps. At the same time the biceps contracts, a muscle called the triceps, which is located at the back of your upper arm, relaxes. Now suppose you wanted to straighten your arm. To perform this simple feat, your triceps would have to contract and your biceps would have to relax at the same time. Figure 2–13 shows how these two muscles (the biceps and the triceps) work together to help you bend and straighten your arm.

The mechanism by which muscles contract is actually a bit more complex than what you have just read. For it is not only muscles that are involved in this action. Nerve tissue is also involved. Skeletal

Figure 2–13 *When you "make a muscle," the biceps muscle and the triceps muscle work together. According to the diagram, which muscle relaxes when the arm is bent? When the arm is straightened?* ❸

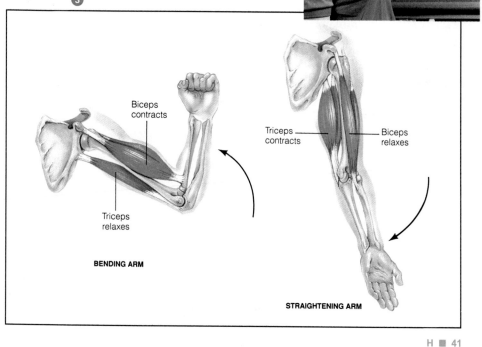

BENDING ARM

STRAIGHTENING ARM

H ■ 41

Tell the class that the heart muscle, unlike the muscles in your arm, does not become tired. It is able to continue beating without rest periods. Have one of the students who volunteered to lift the rock rest awhile after the arm muscles became tired. You might even let the volunteer's arm muscles rest overnight. Ask the person to begin to lift the rock again. Ask students to observe what happens. Students should observe that after a rest period the muscles in the arm can again pick up the small rock many times before tiring.

GUIDED PRACTICE

Skills Development

Skill: Interpreting illustrations

Use Figure 2–13 to develop the concept that muscles work in pairs. Point out that when one muscle in a team contracts, the other relaxes.

• **Suppose muscles did not come in pairs. What would happen when a muscle contracted?** (It would stay contracted and would not be of use ever again.)

ANNOTATION KEY

Answers

❶ Skeletal muscles are attached to the bones in the body that move, such as those in the arms and legs. Smooth muscles are found in internal organs such as the lungs and digestive system. Cardiac muscles are found only in the heart. (Applying concepts)

❷ Accept all logical answers. Possible answer is that the smooth muscles are used 24 hours a day, so it is important that they not become tired. (Making inferences)

❸ Biceps; triceps. (Interpreting diagrams)

INDEPENDENT PRACTICE

▶ *Activity Book*

Students who need further practice with the concepts of this section should be provided with the Chapter 2 activity called Making a Model of the Arm.

REINFORCEMENT/RETEACHING

▶ *Multimedia* ◀

Use the video called Muscular System to review the concepts presented in this section. After students have seen the video, have them choose one term from the box below to complete the sentences that follow. Each term is used only once.

striated	skeletal
voluntary	cardiac
smooth	involuntary

1. _____ muscle is responsible for motions that are not under conscious control.
2. Digestion is an example of _____ muscle function.
3. Another name for skeletal muscle is _____ muscle.
4. _____ muscles are attached to the bones of the skeleton and are stimulated to move by signals from the nerves.
5. The walls of the heart are made up of _____ muscle.
6. Some types of movements, such as blinking and breathing, can be considered both involuntary and _____.
(**Answers: 1.** Smooth **2.** involuntary **3.** striated **4.** Skeletal **5.** cardiac **6.** voluntary)

FIND OUT BY DOING

MUSCLE ACTION

Discovery Learning

Skills: Applying concepts, recording data, making comparisons

Materials: clothespin, timer

Students will be able to observe the fatigue that results from the exercise of voluntary muscles such as those in the hands. Students will also note that the hand they use more often will become less fatigued than does their other hand.

More advanced students or students with an interest in chemistry can be encouraged to do library research on the processes and substances involved in muscle fatigue and recovery.

2–2 (continued)

GUIDED PRACTICE

▶ *Laboratory Manual*

Skills Development

Skills: Making observations, applying concepts, making inferences

At this point you may want to have students complete the Chapter 2 Laboratory Investigation in the *Laboratory Manual* called Comparing Bones, Joints, and Muscles. In the investigation students will use a microscope to examine the internal structures of bone and muscle tissue.

FIND OUT BY DOING

Muscle Action

1. Obtain a spring-type clothespin.

2. Count how many times you can click the clothespin in two minutes using your right hand. Record the information.

3. Rest for one minute and repeat step 2. Then rest for another minute and repeat step 2 again. Determine the average number of clicks for the right hand.

4. Using your left hand, repeat steps 2 and 3.

Was there a difference in the number of clicks per minute between the right and the left hand? Explain.

▪ Why do you think you were able to click the clothespin faster at the beginning of the investigation than you were near the end?

Guide for Reading

Focus on this question as you read.

▶ What are the three most common injuries involving the skeletal and muscular systems?

muscles, you see, contract only when they receive a message from a nerve to do so. The nerves carry messages from the brain and spinal cord to the muscles, signaling them to contract.

You may be surprised to learn that there is no such thing as a weak or strong contraction of a muscle fiber. When a fiber receives a message to contract, it contracts completely or not at all. The strength of a muscle contraction is determined by the number of fibers that receive the message to contract at the same time. Strong muscle contractions, such as those that are involved in hitting a ball with a bat, require the contractions of more muscle fibers than would be needed to open a textbook.

2–2 Section Review

1. List the three types of muscle tissue.
2. Compare the structure of a voluntary muscle and an involuntary muscle.
3. Describe how muscles work in pairs.

Critical Thinking—*You and Your World*
4. If your biceps were paralyzed, what movement would you be unable to make?

2–3 Injuries to the Skeletal and Muscular Systems

Supported by bone and activated by muscle, your body can perform a wide range of movement—from hammering a nail to blinking an eye. The same foot that can stand on tiptoe can kick a soccer ball. The same hand that can pat a puppy's head can pound a desk. Based on these activities, you may be inclined to think that the bones and muscles—components of the skeletal and muscular systems—are invincible. But are they?

INDEPENDENT PRACTICE

Section Review 2–2

1. Skeletal (or striated), smooth, and cardiac.

2. A voluntary muscle is striated, or banded. An involuntary muscle is smooth.

3. As one muscle contracts, the other relaxes.

4. You would be unable to flex, or raise, your forearm at the elbow because the biceps muscle would be unable to contract.

REINFORCEMENT/RETEACHING

Review students' responses to the Section Review questions. Reteach any material that is still unclear, based on students' responses.

CLOSURE

▶ *Review and Reinforcement Guide*

Have students complete Section 2–2 in the *Review and Reinforcement Guide*.

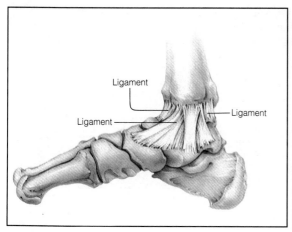

Ligament
Ligament
Ligament

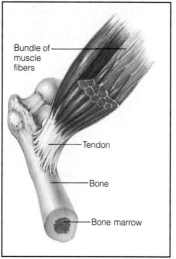

Bundle of muscle fibers
Tendon
Bone
Bone marrow

Although bones and muscles are able to withstand quite a bit of wear and tear, they are vulnerable to injuries. **Some injuries that affect the skeletal and muscular systems are sprains, fractures, and dislocations.** In a **sprain,** the ligaments or tendons, such as those in the ankle, get torn or pulled beyond their normal stretching range. Although a sprained ankle may be painful, you can move your ankle because the injured ligaments and tendons are still able to function.

The most common type of injury to the skeletal system is a **fracture.** A fracture is a break in a bone. Fortunately, because a bone is made up of living tissue, it begins to heal almost as soon as the fracture occurs. A bone's self-healing process takes place in an orderly sequence of events. First the broken blood vessels at the fracture area form a blood clot. In a few days, minerals from the sharp ends of the broken bone are absorbed into the bloodstream. At the same time, fibers of connective tissue grow out of the bone to hold the fractured ends together with a type of bone-making "glue." In as short a time as a few weeks, some bones have healed so well that even X-rays cannot show where the fracture occurred.

Sometimes a blow to the skeleton causes a bone to be forced out of its joint. This type of injury is called a **dislocation.** Dislocations can be serious, but fortunately they can be corrected easily in most cases.

Figure 2–14 *In a sprain, tendons or ligaments get torn or pulled beyond their normal reaching range. What structures are joined by tendons? Ligaments?* ❶

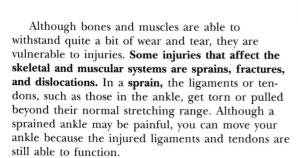

Figure 2–15 *Although the skeletal and muscular systems are able to withstand a lot of wear and tear, they are vulnerable to injuries. What injuries might this baseball player develop from swinging at the ball too hard?* ❷

H ■ 43

2–3 Injuries to the Skeletal and Muscular Systems

BACKGROUND INFORMATION
POSTURE

Proper posture has an important effect on the way people look and feel. Proper posture allows you to move with grace and efficiency and allows your body to adjust for the stretching of muscles and ligaments during movement. Poor posture is not only unattractive, it puts great strain on muscles and ligaments, often causing them to stretch abnormally.

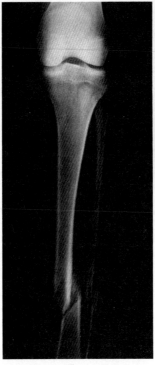

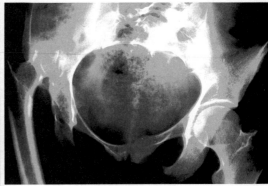

Figure 2–16 *In the X-ray of a lower leg (left), you can see breaks in the tibia and fibula. The X-ray of a hip (right) shows how a bone can be forced out of its joint in a dislocation. What is another name for a break in a bone?* ❶

The dislocated bone can be pushed back into position by a doctor.

As scientists learn more about the skeletal and muscular systems, they continue to develop new techniques for repairing or replacing damaged parts. One technique for healing fractures involves applying weak electrical currents to broken bones. In most cases, electricity causes the bones to heal more quickly. Sometimes badly damaged joints, such as the hip or the knee, can be replaced with artificial joints made of plastics or metal.

2–3 Section Review

1. List the three most common injuries to the skeletal and muscular systems.
2. Compare a sprain and a fracture.
3. Describe the repair of a broken bone.
4. Why do you think a sprained ankle is so painful?

Connection—*Chemistry*
5. Artificial hips are generally made of plastics and alloys (substances that are mixtures of metals or metals and other elements), which are lightweight and do not react with other materials. Explain why these characteristics make plastics and alloys useful in the replacement of human body parts.

2–3 (continued)

CONTENT DEVELOPMENT

Call attention to Figure 2–16. The left X-ray shows a fracture in both the tibia and fibula of the lower leg. Explain to students that a fracture may be just a small crack or a complete break in the bone.

Remind students that bones are living tissue. As such, they can heal a fracture by growing together again. Fibers of connective tissue grow out of the fractured ends to hold the bones together while new bones tissue is formed. Have students recall that one of the functions of bone is to store minerals. When a fracture occurs, some of these stored minerals are released into the blood and are used to help form the new bone.
• **Under what type of circumstance is it necessary to rebreak a bone?** (If a bone is not set properly, the pieces may grow together incorrectly. An incorrectly healed fracture may continue to cause pain or may impair movement. Therefore, a doctor may find it necessary to break the bone again so that it can be set properly and grow together correctly.)

REINFORCEMENT/RETEACHING

▶ *Multimedia* ◀
The video called The Bones and Muscles Get Rhythm may be used to review the basic concepts of this chapter.

After they view the video, have students work in groups to research the types of injuries that can occur while dancing. Have them interview teachers at local dance schools to collect safety suggestions to prevent dance-related injuries.

ENRICHMENT

Explain to students that even at rest, the skeletal muscles (such as biceps and triceps) are slightly contracted. This is called muscle tone. The more you exercise or use your muscles, the more tone they

CONNECTIONS

① Turning on Bone Growth

What has *electricity* got to do with the growth of bone? According to researchers Clinton Rubin and Kenneth McLeod at the State University of New York at Stony Brook, low, painless doses of electricity can prevent or treat osteoporosis. Osteoporosis is a disorder that causes a loss and a weakening of bone tissue. Affecting up to half of all women over the age of 45, osteoporosis can lead to spinal deformities and broken hips.

In one study, Rubin and McLeod experimented on turkeys because, like humans, turkeys lose bone tissue as they age. Rubin and McLeod sped up the loss of bone by immobilizing (preventing the movement of) one wing in each of about 40 turkeys. The immobilized bones in these turkeys wasted away significantly within a period of two months. Another group of turkeys wore small electric coils that set up electromagnetic (having to do with electricity and magnetism) fields that produced an electric current that traveled through the wing. The wing bones of these birds showed no wasting away. In fact, they actually showed an increase in

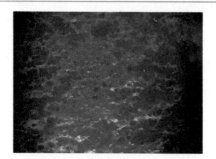

bone mass! In other studies, researchers have shown that cells zapped with electricity absorb greater amounts of calcium, which, as you may recall, is necessary for bone growth.

Although it may seem to you that scientists can turn on bone growth with the flip of a switch, it is not quite as simple as that. To begin with, scientists will have to prove that they are not causing one health problem while fixing another. At present, there is concern about the relationship between electromagnetic fields (which are produced by almost everything from high-power wires to household appliances) and the risk of cancer.

Scientists are now trying to find out just what the relationship and possible dangers are. Meanwhile, the bone researchers point out that they use electromagnetic waves that are different from those generated by power lines and electrical appliances. They also have proof that for the past 20 years, doctors have used currents of electricity to repair bone fractures.

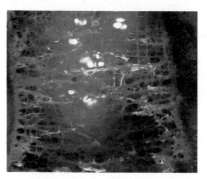

Notice that the bone tissue from an 80-year-old man with osteoporosis (bottom) has larger empty spaces than the bone tissue from a healthy 31-year-old man (top).

CONNECTIONS

TURNING ON BONE GROWTH

Before students read the Connections feature, explain the meaning of the condition known as osteoporosis. This decrease in bone density and mass is a common condition of many elderly people. Students may have relatives or older friends who have undergone surgery for hip replacement or knee replacement.

Explain that plastic or metal replacement joints, marvelous as they are, are short-term solutions. The joints often loosen and then must be reconstructed or replaced. If scientists could discover a way to prevent the bone problems often found in elderly people, this would be a much better situation than the replacement surgery done currently.

After students have read the Connections feature, have them discuss how the scientists might have thought of experimenting with electromagnetic fields. Point out that scientists often look for a way to counteract the effect of a condition or illness. If osteoporosis results in a loss of bone tissue, then finding a way to stimulate the body to create extra bone tissue might help to correct or prevent the condition.

If you are teaching thematically, you may want to use the Connections feature to reinforce the themes of systems and interactions or stability.

Integration: Use the Connections feature to integrate electromagnetics into your lesson.

---

have and the larger they get. Unused muscles become weak and flabby. They lose their tone and become smaller. This condition is called disuse atrophy.

INDEPENDENT PRACTICE

Section Review 2–3

1. Sprains, fractures, and dislocations.
2. In a sprain, ligaments or tendons are torn, pulled, or twisted. A fracture is a break in a bone.

3. Broken blood vessels form a blood clot, minerals from the broken bone are absorbed into the bloodstream, and connective tissue grows to hold the fractured ends of the bone together.
4. Accept all logical answers. One possible answer is that nerve tissue near the injured area is also affected.
5. Substances that are lightweight are easier for the muscles to move. Nonreactive substances present less danger of infection or rejection by the body.

REINFORCEMENT/RETEACHING

Review students' responses to the Section Review questions. Reteach any material that is still unclear, based on students' responses.

CLOSURE

▶ *Review and Reinforcement Guide*
Have students complete Section 2–3 in the *Review and Reinforcement Guide.*

BEFORE THE LAB

1. Gather all equipment at least one day prior to the investigation. You should have enough supplies to meet your class needs, assuming six students per group.
2. You may want to discuss the proper use of methylene blue one day prior to the lab. You may also want to caution students to wear old clothes for this investigation, even though they will use laboratory aprons.

PRE-LAB DISCUSSION

Have students read the complete laboratory procedure. Then review the basic structure of a typical bone.

• **What kind of bones will you be observing in this activity?** (Chicken leg bones.) Explain that chicken bones are very similar in structure and function to human bones. Review the five major functions of bones with students—shape and support, movement, protection for organs, mineral storage, and blood-cell production.

Remind students of the three main types of muscle tissue—skeletal, or striated; smooth; and cardiac.

• **What type of muscle cells will you be working with in this investigation?** (Skeletal, or striated.)

Demonstrate the proper technique for using methylene blue before allowing students to perform the investigation. Caution them that this stain will not come out of their clothes if they spill it. Review the methods of cleaning up such materials if they are spilled in the laboratory.

SAFETY TIPS

Again, caution students not to spill the methylene blue. Advise students that the glassware can be easily broken if not handled correctly, particularly coverslips if they are made of glass. Point out that the dissecting needles are sharp and must be handled with care.

Laboratory Investigation

Observing Bones and Muscles

Problem

What are the characteristics of bones and muscles?

Materials *(per group)*

2 chicken leg bones	vinegar
tiny piece of raw, lean beef	medicine dropper
	water
2 dissecting needles	2 glass slides
methylene blue	coverslip
2 jars with lids	microscope
knife	paper towel

Procedure 🧪 📷 👁 📼

Part A

1. Place one chicken leg bone in each of the two jars.
2. Fill one of the jars about two-thirds full with vinegar. Cover both jars.
3. After five days, remove the bones from the jars. Rinse each bone with water.
4. With the knife, carefully cut each of the bones in half. **CAUTION:** *Be careful when using a knife.* Examine the inside of each bone.

Part B

1. Place the tiny piece of raw beef on one of the glass slides. With a medicine dropper, place a drop of water on top of the beef.
2. With the dissecting needles, carefully separate, or tease apart, the fibers of the

beef. **CAUTION:** *Be careful when using dissecting needles.*

3. Transfer a few fibers to the second slide. Add a drop of methylene blue. **CAUTION:** *Be careful when using methylene blue because it may stain the skin and clothing.* Cover with a coverslip. Use the paper towel to absorb any excess stain.
4. Examine the slide under the microscope.

Observations

1. How do the two bones differ in texture and flexibility? Describe the appearance of the inside of each bone.
2. Describe the appearance of the beef under a microscope.

Analysis and Conclusions

1. What has happened to the minerals and the marrow within the bone that was put in vinegar? How do you know this?
2. Why was one bone put in an empty jar?
3. What type of muscle tissue did you observe under the microscope?
4. How does the structure of the muscle tissue aid in its function?
5. **On Your Own** Repeat this investigation using substances other than vinegar.

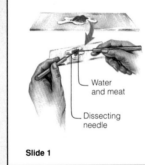
Water and meat — Dissecting needle — **Slide 1**

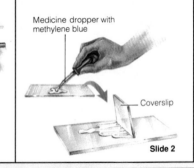
Medicine dropper with methylene blue — Coverslip — **Slide 2**

TEACHING STRATEGY

1. Part A of this investigation should be conducted in two sessions, five days apart.
2. The first session should be devoted to the pre-lab discussion and to setup of the jars. It should take approximately 20 minutes.
3. During the second session, students will need approximately 20 minutes to complete their observations and draw their conclusions for Part A. The remainder of the session may be used for Part B.
4. Have teams follow the directions carefully as they work in the laboratory.

DISCOVERY STRATEGIES

Discuss how the investigation relates to the chapter ideas by asking open questions similar to the following:

• **What is the purpose of Part A of the investigation?** (To observe some of the properties of bone—observing.)

• **What do you predict the effect of the vinegar will be on the chicken leg bone?** (Accept all logical responses—analyzing, predicting.)

• **What is the purpose of Part B of the investigation?** (To observe the structure of

Study Guide

Summarizing Key Concepts

2–1 The Skeletal System

▲ Bones are fastened together by connective tissues called ligaments. Tendons are connective tissues that connect muscles to bones.

▲ The skeletal system has five important functions: It provides shape and support, allows movement, protects tissues and organs, produces blood cells, and stores certain materials.

▲ The human skeleton is divided into two parts. One part consists of the skull, the ribs, the breastbone, and the vertebral column. The other part is made up of the bones of the arms, legs, hands, feet, shoulders, and hips.

▲ Cartilage is a flexible connective tissue that supports, acts as a shock absorber, and cushions other skeletal parts.

▲ A joint is a place where two bones come close together.

2–2 The Muscular System

▲ Muscle tissue is made of fibers bundled together by connective tissue. Muscle tissue moves only by contracting, or shortening.

▲ There are three types of muscle tissue: skeletal, smooth, and cardiac. Skeletal muscles permit voluntary movement and are connected to bone. Smooth muscles help control breathing, blood pressure, and movements of the digestive system. Cardiac muscles make the heart beat.

▲ All skeletal muscles work in pairs. When one contracts, the other relaxes.

2–3 Injuries to the Skeletal and Muscular Systems

▲ The most common injuries to the skeletal and muscular systems are sprains, fractures, and dislocations.

▲ A tearing or pulling of a ligament or a tendon beyond its normal stretching range is called a sprain.

▲ A fracture is a break in a bone.

▲ When a bone is forced out of its joint, the injury is called a dislocation.

Reviewing Key Terms

Define each term in a complete sentence.

2–1 The Skeletal System
    bone
    ligament
    tendon
    cartilage
    marrow
    joint

2–2 The Muscular System
    skeletal muscle
    smooth muscle
    cardiac muscle

2–3 Injuries to the Skeletal and Muscular Systems
    sprain
    fracture
    dislocation

substances students choose. Possible substances are vegetable oil, weak hydrochloric acid, and milk.

GOING FURTHER: ENRICHMENT

Part 1

Students may repeat Part A of the investigation using different types of bones such as fish, beef, or pork rib bones.

Part 2

Obtain several chicken necks. Boil them in salt water to make the meat (muscle tissue) easier to remove. Students can remove the muscle tissue and examine the different kinds of vertebrae and how they fit together.

Part 3

If you can obtain a sheep or cow heart, have students compare the muscle tissue in a heart to the tissue they observed in this investigation. Students should be able to draw as well as describe the two types of muscle tissue (skeletal and cardiac.)

muscle tissue under a microscope—observing.)

• **What do you predict you will see when you look at the beef muscle under the microscope?** (Accept all logical responses—observing, analyzing, predicting.)

OBSERVATIONS

1. The bone submerged in vinegar is more flexible and not as hard and solid as the bone in the empty jar. In comparison to the control, the bone submerged in vinegar has lost some of its hard, minerallike texture.

2. The beef should resemble long, fiberlike threads under the microscope.

ANALYSIS AND CONCLUSIONS

1. Some of the minerals and marrow dissolved in the vinegar. This can be determined by comparing the bone submerged in vinegar to the control.

2. This bone acts as a control.

3. Skeletal, or striated, muscle.

4. The fiberlike threads permit movement (contraction and relaxation) to occur.

5. Answers will vary, depending on the

Chapter Review

Chapter Review

ALTERNATIVE ASSESSMENT

The *Prentice Hall Science* program includes a variety of testing components and methodologies. Aside from the Chapter Review questions, you may opt to use the Chapter Test or the Computer Test Bank Test in your *Test Book* for assessment of important facts and concepts. In addition, Performance-Based Tests are included in your *Test Book*. These Performance-Based Tests are designed to test science process skills, rather than factual content recall. Since they are not content dependent, Performance-Based Tests can be distributed after students complete a chapter or after they complete the entire textbook.

CONTENT REVIEW

Multiple Choice
1. c
2. c
3. d
4. d
5. b
6. c
7. a
8. b
9. d
10. a

True or False
1. T
2. F, connective
3. F, connective
4. F, phosphorus
5. T
6. F, hinge
7. F, voluntary or striated
8. F, Cardiac

Concept Mapping
Row 1: functions
Row 2: Bones
Row 3: Protects tissues and organs
Row 4: Tendons
Row 5: Stores certain materials
Row 6: Produces blood cells
(**Note:** *The functions in rows 3, 5, and 6 may be listed in any order.*)

Content Review

Multiple Choice

On a separate sheet of paper, write the letter of the answer that best completes each statement.

1. Approximately how many bones are there in the skeletal system?
   a. 126   b. 26   c. 206   d. 96
2. Bones are held together by stringy connective tissue called
   a. cartilage.   c. ligaments.
   b. joints.   d. tendons.
3. The nose and ears contain a flexible connective tissue called
   a. marrow.   c. muscle.
   b. bone.   d. cartilage.
4. Two minerals that make up the nonliving part of bones are
   a. sodium and chlorine.
   b. calcium and iron.
   c. magnesium and phosphorus.
   d. calcium and phosphorus.
5. A place where two bones come close together is called a
   a. dislocation. c. tendon.
   b. joint.   d. ligament.
6. The longest bone in the body is the
   a. vertebra.   c. femur.
   b. collarbone.   d. breastbone.
7. An example of a ball-and-socket joint is the
   a. shoulder. b. neck. c. elbow. d. knee.
8. The elbow is an example of a
   a. ball-and-socket joint.
   b. hinge joint.
   c. pivot joint.
   d. bone.
9. Skeletal muscles are also known as
   a. involuntary muscles.
   b. smooth muscles.
   c. cardiac muscles.
   d. voluntary muscles.
10. Which of the following occurs when a bone is forced out of its joint?
    a. dislocation   c. fracture
    b. contraction   d. sprain

True or False

If the statement is true, write "true." If it is false, change the underlined word or words to make the statement true.

1. <u>Tendons</u> join muscles to bones.
2. Bone is an example of <u>nerve</u> tissue.
3. Cartilage is a flexible <u>muscle</u> tissue.
4. Bones contain the minerals calcium and <u>iron</u>.
5. A <u>joint</u> is a place where two bones come close together.
6. The elbow is an example of a <u>ball-and-socket</u> joint.
7. Skeletal muscle is also called <u>involuntary</u> muscle.
8. <u>Smooth</u> muscle tissue is found only in the heart.

Concept Mapping

Complete the following concept map for Section 2–1. Refer to pages H8–H9 to construct a concept map for the entire chapter.

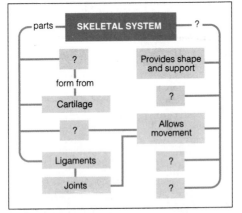

CONCEPT MASTERY

1. The first part runs from the top of the head and down the body in a straight line to the hips. It includes the skull, the ribs, the breastbone, and the vertebral column. The second part includes all the bones that branch off the central skeleton: the arms, the legs, the hands, the feet, the hips, and the shoulders.

2 **a.** femur **b.** phalange **c.** phalange **d.** patellas **e.** sternum **f.** scapula

3. Ligaments connect bones to bones. Tendons connect bones to muscles. Cartilage is a soft tissue that is usually changed to bone during ossification. All three are connective tissues.

4. Skeletal muscle is used in movement; smooth muscle is used to control breathing, blood pressure and movements in the digestive system; cardiac muscle is used to make the heart beat.

5. The femur links the hip to the knee. It is the longest bone in the human body.

6. Pivot joint located between the first two vertebrae in the neck allows you to shake or nod your head; ball-and-socket joint in

Concept Mastery

Discuss each of the following in a brief paragraph.

1. What are the two major parts of the human skeletal system? Which bones belong to each part?
2. Use Figure 2–4 on page 32 to identify the following bones with their scientific names.
   a. thigh
   b. finger
   c. toe
   d. kneecaps
   e. breastbone
   f. shoulder blade
3. Explain the differences among ligaments, tendons, and cartilage.
4. Name the three types of muscle tissue. Discuss their functions.
5. Describe the structure of the femur.
6. List three movable joints. Describe the actions of each joint.
7. Explain how the biceps and triceps enable you to bend and straighten your arm.
8. Compare a voluntary muscle and an involuntary muscle. Give an example of each type of muscle.

Critical Thinking and Problem Solving

Use the skills you have developed in this chapter to answer each of the following.

1. **Relating concepts** What is the advantage of having some joints, such as the knee and elbow, covered by a fluid-filled sac?
2. **Applying concepts** Bones heal faster in children than they do in adults. Why do you think this is so?
3. **Interpreting photographs** Because cartilage does not appear on X-ray film, it is seen as a clear area between the shaft and the knobs of individual bones. Examine the photographs showing the X-rays of two hands. Which hand belongs to the older person? Explain.

 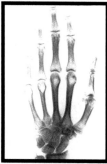

4. **Applying concepts** Suggest a reason why there are more joints in the feet and hands than in most other parts of the body.
5. **Relating concepts** What role does good posture play in maintaining healthy muscles and tendons?
6. **Relating facts** Explain why you feel pain when you fracture, or break, a bone.
7. **Relating cause and effect** Osteoporosis is a disease that usually occurs in older people. It involves a loss and a weakening of bone tissue. Doctors recommend that people over the age of 45 eat more foods that contain calcium. How is this helpful in preventing osteoporosis?
8. **Using the writing process** Choose a five-minute segment out of your day. In a journal, record all the activities that you performed during this time. Then try to identify all the muscles, bones, and joints you used. Use the figures in this chapter to help you, and don't forget those involuntary muscles, too!

---

shoulder or hip allows you to move those areas in a circle; and hinge joint in the knee or elbow allows you to bend or straighten those parts of your body.

7. To bend your arm, the biceps contracts, pulling the bones in your forearm toward your body. At the same time, the triceps relaxes. To straighten your arm, the triceps contracts, pulling your forearm bones away from your body. At the same time, the biceps relaxes.

8. A voluntary muscle is striated, or banded, and its action can be consciously controlled. Skeletal muscles are voluntary muscles. An involuntary muscle does not have striations; it is flat, and its action is automatic. Smooth and cardiac muscle are involuntary muscles.

CRITICAL THINKING AND PROBLEM SOLVING

1. The sac acts as a shock absorber and helps to relieve some of the pressure placed on the joint.
2. The bones of young children are still developing and will heal faster because they are in the formative stages. In adults, the bones have hardened and are less apt to heal because they are no longer growing.
3. The right photograph belongs to the older person because it shows less cartilage. As a person grows older, the cartilage in the hand is replaced by bone.
4. The hands and feet are the two parts of the body that require the most complex movements and movements that require fine motor coordination. To accomplish such diverse movement, a wide variety of bones and joints is necessary.
5. Poor posture puts more strain and stretching on muscles and tendons. Over long periods of time, these structures will no longer be taut and will not function well.
6. When you break a bone, you are almost certainly going to damage nearby pain receptors. Furthermore, severe breaks will also damage tissues in the area, again activating pain receptors.
7. Calcium is necessary for bone growth and to keep bones strong. The weakening of bones due to osteoporosis can be somewhat alleviated if the body has a plentiful supply of calcium, which can be used to make the bones harder.
8. Answers will vary depending on the activities students record in the journal.

KEEPING A PORTFOLIO

You might want to assign some of the Concept Mastery and Critical Thinking and Problem Solving questions as homework and have students include their responses to unassigned questions in their portfolio. Students should be encouraged to include both the question and the answer in their portfolio.

ISSUES IN SCIENCE

The following issue can be used as a springbroad for discussion or given as a writing assignment.

People who study yoga and biofeedback can be trained to control some muscles once considered involuntary. Yoga experts, for example, can raise and lower their blood pressure voluntarily. Can people be trained to control all involuntary actions of their muscular system? Would this be helpful or harmful to them?

SECTION	LABORATORY INVESTIGATIONS AND DEMONSTRATIONS
3–1 The Importance of Food pages H52–H61	**Student Edition** Measuring Calories Used, p. H74 **Laboratory Manual** Nutrient Identification Investigating Proteins How Much Vitamin C Is in Fruit Juice?
3–2 Digestion of Food pages H61–H68	**Laboratory Manual** Observing the Digestion of Starches
3–3 Absorption of Food pages H69–H71	**Teacher Edition** Finding Calorie Content, p. H50d Observing Digestion of Meat, p. H50d
3–4 Maintaining Good Health pages H71–H73	
Chapter Review pages H74–H77	

OUTSIDE TEACHER RESOURCES

Books

Calloway, D. H., and K. O. Carpenter. *Nutrition and Health*, Troy, MO: Saunders

College Publishing.

Elgin, K. *Digestive System*, New York: Watts.

Hightower, N. C., and H. D. Janowitz. *Digestion*, Melbourne, FL: Krieger.

OTHER ACTIVITIES	MULTIMEDIA

Activity Book
  Chapter Discovery: How Much Fat?
  ACTIVITY: Classifying Foods
  ACTIVITY: Nutrition Survey
  ACTIVITY: Snack Survey
  ACTIVITY: Identifying Nurtrients
Student Edition
  Find Out by Calculating: Determining Your Metaboic Rate, p. H54
  Find Out by Writing: Vitamin-Deficiency Diseases, p. H58
Product Testing Activity
  Cereals
  Orange Juice
  Sports Drinks
  Yogurts
Review and Reinforcement Guide
  Section 3–1
	English/Spanish Audiotapes
	  Section 3–1

Activity Book
  ACTIVITY: Categories of Digestion
  ACTIVITY: What Color Is Your Cracker?
  ACTIVITY: The Structure of Teeth
Student Edition
  Find Out by Doing: How Sweet It Is, p. H63
  Find Out by Doing: Simulating Peristalsis, p. H65
  Find Out by Doing: Enzymes, p. H67
  Find Out by Doing: Do Oil and Water Mix? p. H68
Product Testing Activity
  Antacid tablets
Review and Reinforcement Guide
  Section 3–2
	Courseware
	  Digestive System (Supplemental)
	English/Spanish Audiotapes
	  Section 3–2

Activity Book
  ACTIVITY: Digestive Trivia
Review and Reinforcement Guide
  Section 3–3
	Video
	  Digestive System
	English/Spanish Audiotapes
	  Section 3–3

Activity Book
  ACTIVITY: Calculating Your Nutritional Budget
Review and Reinforcement Guide
  Section 3–4
	English/Spanish Audiotapes
	  Section 3–4

Test Book
  Chapter Test
  Performance-Based Test
	Test Book
	  Computer Test Bank Test

*All materials in the Chapter Planning Guide Grid are available as part of the Prentice Hall Science Learning System.

Lukes, Bonnie L. *How to Be a Reasonably Thin Teen-Age Girl: Without Starving, Losing Your Friends or Running Away,* New York: Atheneum.

Nilsson, Lennart. *Behold Man,* Boston: Little, Brown, and Co.

Audiovisuals

Digestive System, film or video, National Geographic

Chapter 3 DIGESTIVE SYSTEM

CHAPTER OVERVIEW

Eating a balanced diet is important in maintaining a strong, healthy body. A balanced diet also provides energy for the body to function and grow. A balanced diet incorporates four basic food groups and six basic categories of nutrients. The four basic food groups include the milk group, the vegetable and fruit group, the meat and protein group, and the grain products group. The six basic categories of nutrients include proteins, carbohydrates, fats, vitamins, minerals, and water.

Most nutrients cannot be used directly by the human body. Nutrients are broken down by the digestive system into simpler substances. These simpler substances are then used by the body to maintain health, growth, and repair. The human body digests nutrients mechanically and chemically. Mechanical digestion—the physical action of breaking down food into smaller parts—occurs in the mouth and in the stomach. Chemical digestion—the digestion of food by chemical substances—occurs in the mouth, in the stomach, and in the small intestine. The mechanical and chemical digestion of food allows nutrients to be absorbed into the bloodstream in the small intestine.

A healthy diet supplies the digestive system with the materials needed for health, growth, and repair. In addition, regular exercise and weight control help to keep the human body in peak operating condition.

3–1 THE IMPORTANCE OF FOOD

THEMATIC FOCUS

The purpose of this section is to introduce students to the four basic food groups and the six basic types of nutrients (the usable portions of food). Generally speaking, many students realize the importance of a balanced diet. They will learn specifically that a balanced diet consists of nutrients from each of the four basic food groups: the milk group, the vegetable and fruit group, the meat and protein group, and the grain products group. The nutrients obtained from these groups include proteins, carbohydrates, fats, vitamins, minerals, and water.

The themes that can be focused on in this section are energy and unity and diversity.

*Energy: Stress that our bodies need energy and raw materials for proper health, growth, and repair. The energy and raw materials come from the food we eat. A balanced diet—food from the four basic food groups—is changed into simpler substances that are required by healthy bodies. These simpler substances include proteins, carbohydrates, fats, vitamins, minerals, and water. A balanced diet and a digestive system that is functioning properly are necessary to maintain a healthy body.

Unity and Diversity: Stress that many different nutrients are essential for proper health. Point out that by reading an ingredient label on a bottle of vitamins or on any food package, a person can see a sampling of the many nutrients needed by the human body. These nutrients are then put to work to help give our bodies energy and maintain health, growth, and tissue repair.

PERFORMANCE OBJECTIVES 3–1

1. Name the four basic food groups.
2. Identify the six basic types of nutrients.
3. Explain the term *Calorie.*

SCIENCE TERMS 3–1

nutrient p. H53
Calorie p. H53
protein p. H54
amino acid p. H54
carbohydrate p. H55
fat p. H56
vitamin p. H57
mineral p. H57

3–2 DIGESTION OF FOOD

THEMATIC FOCUS

The purpose of this section is to describe the structure and function of the digestive organs and to explain what happens to food during the process of digestion.

The themes that can be focused on in this section are scale and structure and systems and interactions.

*Scale and structure: Point out that as food moves through the digestive system, each organ functions to help break down large food particles into smaller particles. This is accomplished by mechnical digestion, chemical digestion, or both.

*Systems and interactions: Various organs in the digestive tract secrete different chemicals during the digestive process. Lead students to understand that although each one of these different chemicals has a specific role, they all work together to complete a task that none of them could accomplish individually.

PERFORMANCE OBJECTIVES 3–2

1. Name the organs of the human digestive system.
2. Describe the function of each digestive organ.

SCIENCE TERMS 3–2

ptyalin p. H62
enzyme p. H63
esophagus p. H65
peristalsis p. H65
stomach p. H66
pepsin p. H66
small intestine p. H67
liver p. H67
pancreas p. H67

3–3 ABSORPTION OF FOOD
THEMATIC FOCUS

The purpose of this section is to explain the process of absorption. Make sure students understand the differences between absorption in the small intestine and absorption in the large intestine. In the small intestine, absorption of nutrients into the blood stream occurs through villi. Villi are small fingerlike projections inside the intestine that increase the intestine's working surface area. In the large intestine, absorption of water and vitamins occurs from undigested material.

The themes that can be focused on in this section are stability and patterns of change.

*Stability: A balanced diet will give the digestive system enough material to provide the nutrients the body needs for a stable, healthy condition. Stress to students that the digestive system cannot produce nutrients from nothing—it must be provided with the correct materials.

Patterns of change: The digestive system transforms food into simpler substances that can be absorbed and used by cells. You might use the analogy that the digestive system is like an assembly line in reverse: Finished products (food) are input at the beginning, and raw materials (nutrients) are output at the end.

PERFORMANCE OBJECTIVES 3–3
1. Describe the process of absorption.
2. Name the materials absorbed in the small and the large intestines.

SCIENCE TERMS 3–3
villus p. H69
large intestine p. H70
rectum p. H70
anus p. H70

3–4 MAINTAINING GOOD HEALTH
THEMATIC FOCUS

The purpose of this section is to remind students that there is more to a healthy body than a balanced diet. Exercise and weight control are also important contributions to the overall health of an individual.

The themes that can be focused on in this section are stability and patterns of change.

*Stability: Point out that the human body will give its best performance if certain conditions are met. These conditions include balanced diet, proper exercise, and weight control. A lifetime of healthy habits will increase the probability of a lengthy life span.

Patterns of change: Remind students that a healthy body must be maintained if it is to remain healthy. A healthy body can be changed to an unhealthy one, and vice versa.

PERFORMANCE OBJECTIVES 3–4
1. Name two important factors in maintaining good health.
2. Explain how exercise benefits the human body.

Discovery *Learning*

TEACHER DEMONSTRATIONS MODELING

Finding Calorie Content

A simple calorimeter can be constructed by placing a small can inside a Styrofoam cup or container. Pour a measured amount of water into the area between the can and the cup so that the water level is about 2.5 cm from the top of the can. Insert a needle into a food substance to be burned. Then insert the other end of the needle into a cork. Place the cork inside the can.

Explain that a calorie is defined as the amount of energy needed to raise the temperature of 1 g of water 1 degree Celsius. One thousand calories equal one Calorie, or food calorie (kilocalorie).

Show students the calorimeter. Explain that you are going to burn a food and measure the amount of energy it releases by measuring the temperature change in the water that is being heated by the burning food.

Have a volunteer student measure the water temperature at the beginning of the experiment and record that measure on the chalkboard.

• **What else would we need to know in order to calculate the Calorie content of the food that is burned?** (We need to know the water temperature after burning and the mass of the water in the container. It is also helpful to know the mass of the food to be burned so that the Calorie content of larger amounts of the same food can be determined.)

Explain that the volume of water in milliliters can be used to determine the mass of water in grams because 1 mL of water has a mass of 1 g.

Have a volunteer student ready to measure the final temperature of the water; then ignite the food substance and allow it to burn completely. Measure the final water temperature and record it on the chalkboard.

On the chalkboard, multiply the change in temperature by the mass of water. Divide this result by 1000 to find the number of Calories in the food that was burned.

• **How much energy was released by the burning food?** (Answers will vary depending on the type of food.)

• **How do our results compare with established Calorie values for this food?** (Compare results with Calorie data from a cookbook, diet guide, or other source.)

Observing Digestion of Meat

Obtain four small pieces of cooked or uncooked meat. Finely chop two pieces. Place one half of the finely chopped meat into each of two small containers. Carefully add diluted hydrochloric acid to one container containing chopped meat and one container containing unchopped meat. Add water to the remaining two containers. Allow the containers to soak overnight.

On the next day, show the containers to students and compare the effects of chopping the meat (mechanical digestion) to the action of the hydrochloric acid (chemical digestion).

CHAPTER 3
Digestive System

INTEGRATING SCIENCE

This life science chapter provides you with numerous opportunities to integrate other areas of science, as well as other disciplines, into your curriculum. Blue numbered annotations on the student page and integrated notes on the teacher wraparound pages alert you to areas of possible integration.

In this chapter you can integrate physical science and heat energy (pp. 53, 73), mathematics (pp. 54, 60), language arts (p. 58), earth science and ecology (p. 59), physical science and solubility (p. 63), and physical science and acids and bases (p. 66).

SCIENCE, TECHNOLOGY, AND SOCIETY/COOPERATIVE LEARNING

The food a person eats provides raw materials needed by the body to produce energy, repair damaged tissues, and build new body parts. Some people "oversupply" their bodies with nutrients and gain weight. Being overweight can be an ego-threatening situation. Being overweight, however, can also be a medically life-threatening situation.

Quick-fix diets have been tried by more than 65 million Americans. These diets promise fast weight loss. The most recent diet fad is the liquid diet. Liquid diets can be medically administered or can be obtained over the counter.

Medically administered liquid diets require a complete physical examination and regular blood-pressure, heart-function, urine-content, and electrolyte-level checks. Behavior-modification programs are also included to help give patients strategies for dealing with their eating behaviors.

Many obesity specialists are concerned about the do-it-yourselfer who begins a liquid over-the-counter diet program. Many of these dieters do not consult a doctor, do not follow the directions, and, most important, are looking for a fast way to lose weight. Researchers are currently looking at other alternatives for helping people lose weight. Future diet aids may include powerful appetite suppressants,

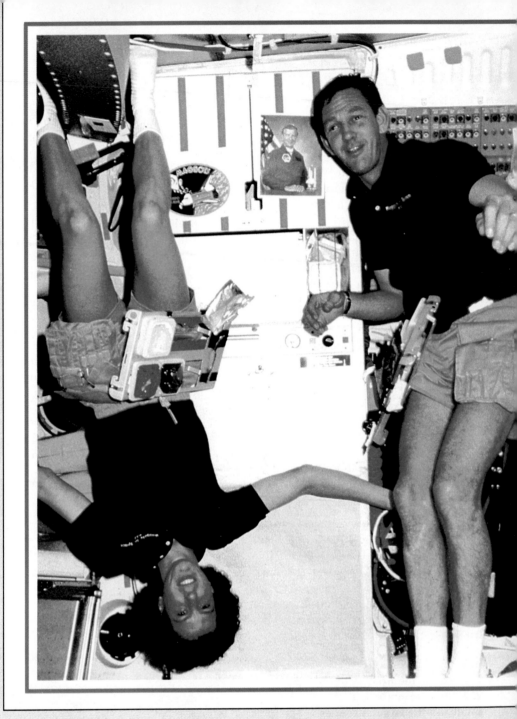

INTRODUCING CHAPTER 3

DISCOVERY LEARNING

▶ *Activity Book*

Begin your teaching of the chapter by using the Chapter 1 Discovery Activity from the *Activity Book*. Using this activity, students will determine the percentage of fat in various samples of ground beef.

Have students observe the photograph on page H50.

• **What are the astronauts doing?** (Eating a meal in space.)

Point out that there are differences between eating a meal on Earth and in space. Have students brainstorm with a partner and list as many differences as they can. After a few minutes, list some of the suggested differences on the chalkboard. Tell students that NASA provides the following information on the daily

Digestive System

Guide for Reading

After you read the following sections, you will be able to

3–1 The Importance of Food
- Define nutrients.

3–2 Digestion of Food
- Describe how food is digested in the mouth, stomach, and small intestine.
- Compare mechanical digestion and chemical digestion.

3–3 Absorption of Food
- Describe how nutrients are absorbed in the digestive system.

3–4 Maintaining Good Health
- Describe the roles weight control and proper exercise habits play in maintaining good health.

Eating a meal in space is no ordinary event! Mistakes can produce strange and funny scenes. A dropped fork may fall up instead of down. Spilled milk is just as likely to end up on the ceiling as on the floor. And a banana left unattended may float away from an open mouth—or toward one. These "tricks" produced by weightlessness are conditions of space travel to which all astronauts must adjust.

Would you like to live in space? Before you answer, take a moment to consider this: What must it be like to live in a place where every spoonful of pudding is in danger of escaping and lettuce leaves in a salad fly away like butterflies? Perhaps you have never thought seriously about the experience of eating and swallowing food in space. What happens to the food after it is swallowed? Without gravity, will it move up instead of down? And what about food that is already in the stomach? In the pages that follow, you will learn how your body digests and absorbs food—right here on Earth! Then you will be better able to answer the questions about eating in space.

Journal *Activity*

You and Your World What did you have for dinner last night? What did you eat for lunch today? Who was with you, and where did you eat these meals? In your journal, explore the thoughts and feelings you had during these mealtimes.

◀ *Astronauts eating a meal in space*

---

fat-absorption blockers, medicines to increase metabolism, or pills designed to block the pleasure receptors in the brain so that food will not taste as good. Researchers note that these diet aids are not designed for people who need a quick fix for their ego but are serious efforts to assist those who have a life-threatening need to lose weight.

Cooperative learning: Using preassigned groups or randomly selected teams, have groups complete one of the following assignments:
- Design a 30-second television commercial that correctly advertises the use of a liquid-diet product. Groups should give their product a name, be sure their commercial correctly identifies the type of dieter for whom their product is designed, include information about the proper use of the product, and include the general requirements for successful weight loss. Encourage groups to be creative, yet truthful, in their work.
- Design a one-week menu and exercise regime for a person who wants to lose 15 pounds. Remind students that their diet plan should consider the nutrients required by the body and include the four basic food groups.

See Cooperative Learning in the *Teacher's Desk Reference.*

JOURNAL ACTIVITY

You may want to use the Journal Activity as the basis of a class discussion. As students discuss the thoughts and feelings they have during mealtimes, lead them to understand that a person's thoughts and feelings during mealtime contribute toward general eating habits and that these habits sometimes contribute to people being underweight or overweight. Point out that they will understand this relationship better after they have completed the chapter and its activities. Students should be instructed to keep their Journal Activity in their portfolios.

---

needs of a Space Shuttle crew: (1) approximately 2800 Calories; (2) 15 minutes of exercise on the treadmill or its equivalent; (3) 8 hours of sleep.
- **Why do you think the astronauts need 2800 Calories of energy per day when drifting from compartment to compartment looks so easy?** (Accept all logical answers.)

Have students read the chapter opener on page H51.
- **Would you like to take a trip into space?** (Accept all responses.)

- **In addition to the problems in food preparation and eating that were mentioned, do you think there would be any problems swallowing and digesting food in space?** (Accept all suggestions. Keep a list of possible problems and unanswered questions to refer to at the completion of the chapter.)

Explain to students that they will learn in this chapter how swallowing and digestion work on Earth, and then they can better understand how these processes might be altered in space.

3-1 The Importance of Food

MULTICULTURAL OPPORTUNITY 3-1

If you have students in your class who represent various cultures, have them volunteer to make a list of three or four favorite foods of their culture. After the students have made their list, analyze the foods for their nutritional value. You will often find that the basic staple foods of many cultures (for example, rice) are high in many nutrients.

ESL STRATEGY 3-1

Students may be interested to know that about half of all English words are of Latin origin and that many scientific terms have Latin roots. Point out that *Calorie* is taken from a Latin word meaning "to be hot." Explain that when the original meaning of the word *Calorie* is known, it is easier to understand its scientific usage—the amount of energy needed to raise the temperature of 1 kilogram of water by 1 degree Celsius. Calorie units are measurements of the amount of energy we receive from the nutrients in foods we eat.

Have students make a chart using the four basic food groups as headings and have them list the type(s) of nutrient(s) found in each group. Then dictate the following sentences and have students complete them. Have volunteers read their answers to the class.
1. Nutrients that are the body's _____ of energy are _____, _____, and _____.
2. Nutrients that are used to build and repair parts of the body are _____.

Figure 3–1 *A balanced diet consists of nutrients from each of the four basic food groups. These groups are the milk group (top left), the vegetable and fruit group (top right), the meat and protein group (bottom left), and the grain and grain products group (bottom right). What foods other than meat are found in the meat and proteins group?* ❶

3-1 The Importance of Food

Throughout the world, more than 5 billion very special chemical factories are in operation both day and night. From basic raw materials, these factories produce a great variety of chemicals. What goes on in these factories could not occur anywhere else. These factories can discover and correct their own faulty work. They can reproduce and repair some of their parts. And they can also control their own growth. Have you already guessed what these factories are? If not, you can find out by simply looking in a mirror. Yes, you and all humans are, in a way, chemical factories.

Like any factory, you need raw materials to build new products, repair old parts, and produce the energy that keeps the factory going. Where do you get

TEACHING STRATEGY 3-1

FOCUS/MOTIVATION

• **What is your favorite food?** (List answers on chalkboard.)

Explain to students that a balanced diet contains food from four food groups: milk group; vegetable and fruit group; meat group; and bread and cereal group. List these as column headings on the chalkboard. Have students examine Figure 3–1 for examples of foods in each of these groups.

• **To which food group does your favorite food belong?** (Erase each food from the chalkboard list as you transfer it to the appropriate food-group column.)
• **Are your favorite foods distributed equally among the four basic food groups?** (Answers will depend on items chosen.)

If time permits, you might consider repeating the activity with students' least-liked foods.

CONTENT DEVELOPMENT

Remind students that a healthy diet contains a balance of foods from all four food groups.

INDEPENDENT PRACTICE

▶ *Product Testing Activity*

Have students perform the product test on cereals from the Product Testing Activity worksheets. Ask students to relate this activity to their favorite breakfast cereal.

these raw materials? The raw materials are provided by the **nutrients** (NOO-tree-ehnts) that are in the foods you eat. **Nutrients are the usable portions of food. Nutrients include proteins, carbohydrates, fats, vitamins, minerals, and water.**

You can get all the nutrients your body needs for proper functioning by drinking water and by eating the right amounts of foods from the four basic food groups. You are probably familiar with these groups. They are the milk group, the meat and proteins group, the fruits and vegetables group, and the grain and grain products group. Figure 3–1 contains some examples of the foods in each of the four basic food groups.

As you have just read, nutrients are the body's source of energy. The amount of energy that can be obtained from nutrients is measured in units known as **Calories**. A Calorie is the amount of energy needed to raise the temperature of 1 kilogram of water by 1 degree Celsius. Some foods are high in Calories, whereas others are quite low. For example,

Figure 3–2 *Nutrients provide the body with energy for studying, sledding, playing basketball, and raking leaves—to name just a few activities. In what unit is the amount of energy obtained from nutrients measured?* ❷

H ▪ 53

FACTS AND FIGURES
CALORIES

Approximately 3500 Calories of energy are stored in 0.45 kg of body fat. If a person wanted to lose weight and subtracted 500 Calories per day from his or her diet, the resulting weight loss should be about 0.45 kg per week. Many doctors consider this to be a safe rate of weight loss.

● ● ● ● **Integration** ● ● ● ●

Use the discussion of Calories to integrate the physical science concepts of heat energy into your lesson.

INDEPENDENT PRACTICE

▶ *Activity Book*

Students who need practice on the concept of the caloric content of foods should complete the chapter activity Snack Survey. In this activity students will explore the caloric content of various snack foods.

GUIDED PRACTICE

Skills Development

Skills: Making calculations, applying concepts

At this point have students complete the in-text Chapter 3 Laboratory Investigation: Measuring Calories Used. In this investigation students will explore caloric consumption in various situations.

CONTENT DEVELOPMENT

Food is important to people—important enough that people tend to think about it and talk about it several times a day. Although the average person may think of food in terms of enjoyment, appetite, or the need to count Calories, the most important role of food is to maintain the function and structure of the human body.

Emphasize to students that food must serve the body in two ways. First, it must provide energy in the form of Calories. Second, it must provide specific substances that are needed for body growth, maintenance, and repair. Point out that if the body needed Calories only for energy, it would not really matter if a person ate a chocolate bar or fish. Yet because the body requires various substances that are found in certain groups of foods, the type of food a person eats is of great importance. Therefore, when counting Calories, quality and quantity both count.

FIND OUT BY CALCULATING

Determining Your Metabolic Rate

1   Basal metabolic rate, or BMR, is the energy needed (in Calories) to keep your awake but restful body functioning.

To determine your BMR, multiply 1 Calorie by your weight in kilograms (2.2 lbs = 1 kg). Then multiply this number by 24 hours. You now have your basal metabolic rate in Cal/kg/day. What is your BMR? Would you need more or fewer Calories when you are doing some type of activity? Explain your answer.

Figure 3–3 *The photograph shows a hair penetrating the outer layer of skin. Both hair and skin are made mainly of proteins. What are the building blocks of proteins called?* **1**

54 ■ H

100 grams (4 ounces) of lettuce contain about 20 Calories. The same quantity of peanuts contains about 650 Calories. Notice that the amount of food is the same (100 grams), but the number of Calories is not. The number of Calories a person needs daily depends on the person's size, body build, occupation, and age.

Proteins

The nutrients that are used to build and repair body parts are called **proteins.** Proteins are made of chains of **amino** (uh-MEE-noh) **acids.** In fact, amino acids are sometimes called the building blocks of proteins. In order for your body to use proteins, they must first be broken down into their amino acid parts. Then they can enter the cells of your body, where they are reassembled into the proteins that make up your muscles, skin, and other organs inside your body.

Amazingly enough, the thousands of different proteins in your body are built from only 20 or so different amino acids. Your body can make 12 of these amino acids; the other 8 must be obtained from your diet (the foods you eat every day). These 8 amino acids are called essential amino acids because it is essential (necessary) that they are included in the foods you eat.

Foods that contain all 8 essential amino acids are red meat, fish, poultry, dairy products, and eggs. Because these foods contain all the essential amino acids, they are called complete proteins. Most plant proteins (rice, cereals, and vegetables), on the other hand, are missing one or more of the essential amino acids. Thus, these proteins are called incomplete proteins. If any essential amino acids are missing from the diet, the manufacture of important proteins stops completely. For this reason, people who are vegetarians must be sure that their diet includes different plant foods so that they obtain all the essential amino acids.

THE SIX BASIC NUTRIENTS		
Substances	**Sources**	**Needed For**
Proteins	Soybeans, milk, eggs, lean meats, fish, beans, peas, cheese	Growth, maintenance, and repair of tissues Manufacture of enzymes, hormones, and antibodies
Carbohydrates	Cereals, breads, fruits, vegetables	Energy source Fiber or bulk in diet
Fats	Nuts, butter, vegetable oils, fatty meats, bacon, cheese	Energy source
Vitamins	Milk, butter, lean meats, leafy vegetables, fruits	Prevention of deficiency diseases Regulation of body processes Growth Efficient biochemical reactions
Mineral salts		
Calcium and phosphorus compounds	Whole-grain cereals, meats, milk, green leafy vegetables, vegetables, table salt	Strong bones and teeth Blood and other tissues
Iron compounds	Meats, liver, nuts, cereals	Hemoglobin formation
Iodine	Iodized salt, seafoods	Secretion by thyroid gland
Water	All foods	Dissolving substances Blood Tissue fluid Biochemical reactions

Figure 3–4 *Nutrients are grouped into six categories in this chart. Which nutrient prevents vitamin-deficiency diseases?* 2

Carbohydrates

It is three o'clock in the afternoon, and you are beginning to feel tired and somewhat lazy. You really need to eat some type of food that will bring your body up to its working level again. Suddenly you remember the orange tucked neatly away in your knapsack. Like all fruits, oranges contain energy-rich substances called **carbohydrates.** Carbohydrates are also found in vegetables and grain products.

There are two types of carbohydrates: starches and sugars. A starch is made of a long chain of sugars. In order to digest a starch, the body must first break the connections between each of the sugars in the chain. Once this is done, the sugars can be used to provide much-needed fuel for the body. Sugars,

ANNOTATION KEY

Answers

1 Amino acids. (Relating facts)

2 Vitamins. (Interpreting charts)

Integration

1 Mathematics

FACTS AND FIGURES

CALORIES AND JOULES

One Calorie is equivalent to 4.1855 joules. The joule is the SI unit of heat and is often used in place of the Calorie.

compounds are needed for the formation of hemoglobin.)

• **Name some minerals that are needed for your body to grow and function properly.** (Calcium, phosphorus, iron, and iodine.)

INDEPENDENT PRACTICE

▶ *Activity Book*

Students who need practice on the concept of food groups and basic nutrients should complete the chapter activity Nutrition Survey. In this activity students will record and create a chart of all the carbohydrates, proteins, fats, and vitamins they eat in one week.

CONTENT DEVELOPMENT

Point out that Figure 3–4 lists two important functions of proteins: growth, maintenance, and repair of tissues and manufacture of enzymes, hormones, and antibodies. Explain that proteins are contained in every living part of the body. Proteins are large, complex molecules that are made up of smaller units called amino acids. For example, one molecule of hemoglobin contains 574 amino acids in a complicated chain.

When proteins are eaten, the digestive system breaks them down into amino acids. These amino acids can then be reassembled in different arrangements to form new kinds of proteins that the body needs.

GUIDED PRACTICE

▶ *Laboratory Manual*

Skills Development

Skill: Making observations

At this point you may want to have students complete the Chapter 3 Laboratory Investigation in the *Laboratory Manual* called Investigating Proteins. In this investigation students will observe the coagulation of protein molecules.

EARLY DIETS

Anthropologists and scientists have concluded that the earliest humans lived on a diet of fruits, seeds, and other plant materials. They knew nothing of the fats, sugars, and other food additives that are so much a part of the human diet in many parts of the world today. It is also interesting that modern efforts to eat a more healthful diet—with a greater emphasis on fiber, nonmeat products, and natural foods—have taken us right back to the eating habits of the earliest humans.

Figure 3–5 *Carbohydrates are substances that supply the body with its main source of energy. If you are a human, a muffin may be a good source of carbohydrates. If you are an iguana, however, a cactus leaf may be more to your liking as a source of carbohydrates.*

on the other hand, can be used for fuel almost immediately.

What happens if you eat more carbohydrates than your body can use for fuel? The excess carbohydrates are stored in your muscles and liver in the form of starch. Unfortunately, these stored carbohydrates add mass to the body. So a diet containing too many carbohydrates can cause a person to gain weight.

Fats

Figure 3–6 *Like carbohydrates, fats supply the body with energy. Any fat that is a liquid at room temperature is called an oil. Whether a fat is a solid or a liquid at room temperature, however, it is still a fat—and 100 percent fat! Which has more Calories: a gram of carbohydrates or a gram of fat?* ❶

Like carbohydrates, **fats** supply the body with energy. In fact, fats supply the body with twice as much energy (and twice as many Calories!) as do equal amounts of proteins and carbohydrates. In addition to providing energy for the body, fats help to support and cushion vital organs, protecting them from injury. Fats also insulate the body against heat loss.

Foods that are rich in fats come from both plants and animals. You may be surprised to learn that any plant or animal fat that is liquid at room temperature is called an oil. That is why the liquid fat in which you cook your French fries is called an oil and not a fat, even though it is 100 percent fat. The word fat, on the other hand, is used to describe any oil that is solid at room temperature. Some sources of fats are nuts, butter, and cheeses.

3–1 (continued)

GUIDED PRACTICE

Skills Development

Skill: Making predictions

Point out that there are two types of carbohydrates: sugars and starches. One method of testing for the presence of starch is to add several drops of iodine to the substance being tested. If starch is present, the iodine turns a dark purple-black color.

Have students collect small samples of several foods, such as crackers, bread, sugar, apples, bananas, and the like, from their lunches or from the cafeteria.

• **Which of these foods do you think will contain starch?** (Accept all predictions.)

Test the foods with iodine. Compare the results with the predictions. Have volunteer students summarize the results.

CONTENT DEVELOPMENT

Explain that starches are larger molecules than sugars. In fact, a starch is composed of a long chain of sugars. As a result, starches take longer to digest. They must be broken down into sugars first. Too much carbohydrate in a diet can make a person overweight. Excess carbohydrates are stored as starch in the liver and muscles. Once the storage capacity of the liver and muscles is filled, excess carbohydrates are then stored in other parts of the body.

• **Which would provide energy faster: eating a slice of bread (60 Calories) or a piece of candy (60 Calories?)** (The candy because sugars can be digested and used for fuel faster than starches can.)

Vitamins and Minerals

In addition to proteins, carbohydrates, and fats, your body also needs **vitamins** and **minerals.** Because they are required in only small amounts, vitamins and minerals are sometimes called micronutrients.

What role do vitamins and minerals have in the body? Vitamins help to regulate the growth and normal functioning of your body. There are two groups of vitamins—fat-soluble vitamins and water-soluble vitamins. The fat-soluble vitamins are so named because they can be stored in fat tissue. Vitamins A, D, E, and K are fat-soluble vitamins. The water-soluble

Figure 3–7 *According to this chart, which vitamin is important for proper vision? For blood clotting?* 2

VITAMINS

Vitamin	Source	Use
A (carotene)	Yellow and green vegetables, fish-liver oil, liver, butter, egg yolks	Important for growth of skin cells; important for vision
D (calciferol)	Fish oils, liver, made by body when exposed to sunlight, added to milk	Important for the formation of bones and teeth
E (tocopherol)	Green leafy vegetables, grains, liver	Proper red blood cell structure
K	Green leafy vegetables, made by bacteria that live in human intestine	Needed for normal blood clotting
B_1 (thiamine)	Whole grains, liver, kidney, heart	Normal metabolism of carbohydrates
B_2 (riboflavin)	Milk products, eggs, liver, whole grain cereal	Normal growth
Niacin	Yeast, liver, milk, whole grains	Important in energy metabolism
B_6 (pyridoxine)	Whole grains, meats, poultry, fish, seeds	Important for amino acid metabolism
Pantothenic acid	Many foods, yeast, liver, wheat germ, bran	Needed for energy release
Folic acid	Meats, leafy vegetables	Proper formation of red blood cells
B_{12} (cyanocobalamin)	Liver, meats, fish, made by bacteria in human intestine	Proper formation of red blood cells
C (ascorbic acid)	Citrus fruits, tomatoes, green leafy vegetables	Strength of blood vessels; important in the formation of connective tissue; important for healthy gums

ANNOTATION KEY

Answers

1 A gram of fat. (Applying concepts)

2 Vitamin A (carotene); Vitamin K. (Interpreting charts)

BACKGROUND INFORMATION

FATS

Fats are an important nutrient found in many foods. Most people, however, should restrict the amount, as well as the kinds, of fat they eat. Physicians recommend eating limited amounts of saturated, unsaturated, and/or polyunsaturated fats.

Fats and oils, a basic nutrient group, supply the body with twice as much energy as do equal amounts of carbohydrates and proteins.

GUIDED PRACTICE

▶ *Laboratory Manual*

Skills Development

Skill: Making observations

At this point you may want to have students complete the Chapter 3 Laboratory Investigation in the *Laboratory Manual* called Nutrient Identification. In this investigation students will perform tests for the presence of starches, sugars, proteins, and fats.

CONTENT DEVELOPMENT

Emphasize that fats and fatty acids are necessary in the human diet. A totally fat-free diet would be harmful. In one scientific study, young rats were placed on a diet containing no fat. Soon the rats began to grow abnormally, their hair fell off, their skin turned scaly, and eventually they died. When the same diet with small amounts of fatty acids were given to the rats, the animals grew normally, lived a full life span, and showed none of the problems with skin and hair.

INDEPENDENT PRACTICE

▶ *Product Testing Activity*

Have students perform the product test on sports drinks from the Product Testing Activity worksheets. In this activity students will investigate the nutritional value of different sports drinks.

ENRICHMENT

▶ *Activity Book*

Students will be challenged by the Chapter 3 activity in the *Activity Book* called Identifying Nutrients. In this activity students will learn to test for proteins and fats in various substances.

Check each report for scientific accuracy and that students have determined the cause(s), symptom(s), and method(s) of prevention for their chosen vitamin-deficiency disease. You may want to alert the language arts teacher of this assignment and have that teacher grade the reports as well.

Integration: Use the Find Out by Writing feature to integrate language arts skills into your science lesson.

MINERALS

Mineral	Source	Use
Calcium	Milk products, green leafy vegetables	Important component of bones and teeth; needed for normal blood clotting and for normal cell functioning
Chlorine	Table salt, many foods	Important for fluid balance
Magnesium	Milk products, meat, many foods	Needed for normal muscle and nerve functioning; metabolism of proteins and carbohydrates
Potassium	Grains, fruits, many foods	Normal muscle and nerve functioning
Phosphorus	Meats, nuts, whole grains, many foods	Component of DNA, RNA, ATP, and many proteins; part of bone tissue
Sodium	Many foods, table salt	Nerve and muscle functioning; water balance in body
Iron	Liver, red meats, grains, raisins, nuts	Important part of hemoglobin molecule
Fluorine	Water (natural and added)	Part of bones and teeth
Iodine	Seafood, iodized table salt	Part of hormones that regulate rate of metabolism

Figure 3–8 *Minerals help to keep the body functioning normally. Which minerals provide for normal nerve and muscle functioning?* ❶

FIND OUT BY
WRITING

Vitamin-Deficiency Diseases

❶ Use reference materials in the library to find out about a vitamin-deficiency disease, such as scurvy, pellagra, or rickets. Write a brief report on your findings. In your report, make sure that you answer the following questions: What causes the disease? What are the symptoms of the disease? How can the disease be prevented?

vitamins include vitamin C and vitamins B_1, B_2, B_6, and B_{12} (which are also known as the B complex). Water-soluble vitamins cannot be stored in fat tissue and are thus constantly washed out of the body. Therefore, water-soluble vitamins should be included in a balanced diet every day. The chart in Figure 3–7 on page 57 gives the sources and uses of some important vitamins.

Like vitamins, minerals help to keep your body functioning normally. Hemoglobin, the protein in red blood cells that carries oxygen, contains the mineral iron. Calcium, another important mineral, makes up a major part of teeth and bones. The sources and uses of some important minerals are listed in Figure 3–8.

3–1 (continued)

GUIDED PRACTICE

▶ *Laboratory Manual*

Skills Development

Skill: Making comparisons

At this point you may want to have students complete the Chapter 3 Laboratory Investigation in the *Laboratory Manual* called How Much Vitamin C Is in Fruit Juice? In this investigation students will use a starch and iodine standard to determine the amount of Vitamin C in a sample of fruit juice.

CONTENT DEVELOPMENT

Point out that animals will die from lack of water long before they will die

from lack of food. Most of the water lost from our bodies is replaced by drinking liquids. We do, however, obtain small quantities of water in two other ways. The foods we eat contain water, and water is released when carbohydrates are broken down to produce energy.

● ● ● ● **Integration** ● ● ● ●

Use Figure 3–9 and its caption to integrate the earth science concepts of ecology into your lesson.

INDEPENDENT PRACTICE

▶ *Product Testing Activity*

Have students perform the product test on orange juice from the Product Testing Activity worksheets. Ask students to relate this activity to different orange juices they have used.

REINFORCEMENT/RETEACHING

▶ *Activity Book*

Students who need practice in determining basic food and nutrient groups should complete the Chapter 3 activity

Water

Although you can survive many days without food, several days without water can be fatal. Why is water so important? There are several reasons. Most chemical reactions that take place in the body can do so only in the presence of water. Water carries nutrients and other substances to and from body organs through the bloodstream. Water also helps your body maintain its proper temperature, 37°C.

On the average, the human body is approximately 55 to 75 percent water. Under normal conditions, you need about 2.4 to 2.8 liters of water daily (that is about 10 to 12 8-ounce glasses). By drinking the proper amount of fluids (about 2 liters) and eating a balanced diet, you can provide your body with its much-needed supply of water.

Figure 3–9 *Water is essential for our survival. However, if people do not use existing water resources wisely, fertile land may soon become sandy desert.*

3–1 Section Review

1. What are nutrients? Describe the six types of nutrients.
2. What is a Calorie?
3. How do water-soluble and fat-soluble vitamins differ?
4. Why is water important to the body?

Critical Thinking—*Relating Concepts*
5. Explain how it is possible for a person to be overweight and suffer from improper nutrition at the same time.

called Classifying Foods. In the activity students will classify food into basic groups and identify the nutrient content(s).

INDEPENDENT PRACTICE

Section Review 3–1

1. Nutrients are the usable portions of food. Nutrients include proteins, carbohydrates, fats, vitamins, minerals, and water.
2. A Calorie is the measurement unit of the amount of energy that can be obtained from nutrients. It is also the amount of energy needed to raise the temperature of 1 kilogram of water by 1 degree Celsius.
3. Fat-soluble vitamins can be stored in fat tissue. Water-soluble vitamins cannot be stored in fat tissue and are constantly washed out of the body.
4. Water allows chemical reactions to occur, carries nutrients and other substances in the bloodstream, and helps to regulate body temperature.
5. Responses may vary but might suggest that the person's diet is high-calorie, high-fat food with low-nutrient density.

REINFORCEMENT/RETEACHING

Monitor students' responses to the Section Review questions. If students appear to have difficulty with any of the questions, review the appropriate material in the section.

CLOSURE

▶ *Review and Reinforcement Guide*
At this point have students complete Section 3–1 in the *Review and Reinforcement Guide.*

Integration
① Mathematics

PROBLEM SOLVING
READING FOOD LABELS

This feature enables students to relate the concept of nutrition to a real-life situation: reading food labels. Students should discover that reading ingredient lists and nutrition labels helps them become informed consumers. The answers to this Problem Solving feature are as follows:

1. 12 percent fat, 69 percent carbohydrate, 21 percent protein.

2. 21 percent fat, 61 percent carbohydrate, 19 percent protein.

3. Skim milk.

4. 17 g starch, 1 g sugars.

Integration: Use the Problem Solving feature to integrate mathematics concepts into your lesson.

PROBLEM ??? Solving

Reading Food Labels ①

Carmen has been asked by her teacher to determine the most nutritious breakfast cereal in her local market. Upon her arrival at the market, Carmen heads for the aisle containing the breakfast cereals and picks up the first cereal box. As a health-conscious and well-informed consumer, Carmen reads the list of ingredients and the nutrition labeling on the box of cereal. She knows that this information will help her compare similar foods on the basis of their share of nutrients to Calories.

Carmen knows that in order to burn up 1 gram of carbohydrate or protein, her body needs to use 4 Calories. For 1 gram of fat, her body needs to use 9 Calories. She realizes that it takes more than twice the number of Calories to burn up 1 gram of fat than it does to burn up 1 gram of carbohydrate or protein. That is one reason why Carmen tries to limit the amount of fats that she eats.

Carmen also knows that an ideal diet should get no more than 30 percent of its Calories from fats. Of the remaining Calories, 50 to 55 percent should come from carbohydrates and 15 to 20 percent from proteins. The carbohydrates should be in the form of starches rather than sugars.

Thanks to Carmen, you are on your way to becoming a more-informed consumer. Now look at a typical cereal box and determine if the dry cereal is high in nutrition and low in Calories.

1. To determine the percentage of fat Calories, multiply the grams of fat (in this case, 2) by 9 (the number of Calories

NUTRITION INFORMATION PER SERVING

SERVING SIZE .... 1 OUNCE (1¼ CUPS)
SERVINGS PER PACKAGE 15

	1 ounce cereal	plus ½ cup vitamin A & D fortified skim milk*
CALORIES	110	150
PROTEIN, g	4	8
CARBOHYDRATE, g	20	26
FAT, g	2	2
CHOLESTEROL, mg	0	0
SODIUM, mg	290	350
POTASSIUM, mg	105	310

PERCENTAGE OF U.S. RECOMMENDED DAILY ALLOWANCES (U.S. RDA)

PROTEIN	6	15
VITAMIN A	25	30
VITAMIN C	25	25
THIAMIN	25	30
RIBOFLAVIN	25	35
NIACIN	25	25
CALCIUM	4	20
IRON	45	45
VITAMIN D	10	25
VITAMIN B₆	25	25
FOLIC ACID	25	25
PHOSPHORUS	10	20
MAGNESIUM	10	15
ZINC	6	8
COPPER	6	6

*PLUS ½ CUP 2% MILK CONTAINS 170 CALORIES, 4 GRAMS FAT AND 10 MILLIGRAMS CHOLESTEROL. ALL OTHER NUTRIENTS REMAIN AS LISTED.

INGREDIENTS: WHOLE OAT FLOUR (INCLUDES THE OAT BRAN), WHEAT STARCH, SUGAR, SALT, CALCIUM CARBONATE, TRISODIUM PHOSPHATE.

VITAMINS AND MINERALS: VITAMIN C (SODIUM ASCORBATE), IRON (A MINERAL NUTRIENT), A B VITAMIN (NIACIN), VITAMIN A (PALMITATE), VITAMIN B₆ (PYRIDOXINE HYDROCHLORIDE), VITAMIN B₂ (RIBOFLAVIN), VITAMIN B₁ (THIAMIN MONONITRATE), A B VITAMIN (FOLIC ACID) AND VITAMIN D.

CARBOHYDRATE INFORMATION

	1 ounce	with ½ cup milk
COMPLEX CARBOHYDRATES, g	19	19
STARCH, g 17		
DIETARY FIBER, g 2*		
SUCROSE AND OTHER SUGARS, g	1	7
TOTAL CARBOHYDRATES, g	20	26

*1g SOLUBLE AND 1g INSOLUBLE FIBER

TEACHING STRATEGY 3–2

FOCUS/MOTIVATION

Pass a tray around the room containing small slices of raw potato. Ask volunteer students to take a slice of potato and chew it for a much longer length of time than they usually would before swallowing.

• **Did you notice anything happening to the taste of the potato as you chewed it for a long time?** (Answers may vary, but students should notice that the potato begins to taste sweeter.)

• **Why do you think the potato begins to taste sweeter?** (Accept all responses.)

CONTENT DEVELOPMENT

Explain to students that the main function of the digestive system is to break down food into simpler substances that can be transported by the blood to all parts of the body.

Point out that the slice of potato they chewed began to taste sweet because enzymes in the saliva had begun to break down starch in the potato into maltose, a kind of sugar. Usually, people do not experience potatoes as tasting sweet because they swallow the potatoes before they have a chance to experience the action of the enzymes.

Use the example of chewing the potato slices to illustrate that the digestive process consists of two basic parts: mechanical and chemical. The process of digestion begins with the mechanical part, when food enters the mouth and is bitten and chewed by the teeth. Reinforce the idea of mechanical digestion by asking the following question:

• **Biting into an apple and then chewing the piece that was bitten off is an exam-**

in 1 gram of fat). Then divide the result (18 Calories) by the total number of Calories (110). The resulting percentage of fat Calories is 16, which is to be expected, because grains, of which cereals are made, are low in fat.

2. To determine the percentage of carbohydrate Calories, multiply the grams of carbohydrate (20) by 4 (the number of Calories in 1 gram of carbohydrate). Then divide the result (80 Calories) by the total number of Calories (110). The resulting percentage of carbohydrate Calories is 73. This is normal for a cereal because it is high in carbohydrates and well above the 50 to 55 percent recommended as the maximum in a healthful diet.

3. To determine the percentage of protein Calories, multiply the grams of protein (4) by 4 (the number of Calories in 1 gram of protein). Then divide the result (16) by

the total number of Calories (110). The resulting percentage of protein Calories is 15, which is within the recommended 15 to 20 percent.

Now it is your turn to play consumer. You can use a calculator or computer to help you with your calculations.

1. What is the percentage of fat, carbohydrate, and protein Calories in the cereal to which one-half cup of skim milk has been added? (Refer to information that appears in the column headed Plus 1/2 cup skim milk.)

2. What is the percentage of fat, carbohydrate, and protein Calories in the cereal to which 2% milk has been added? (See information next to *.)

3. Based on your results, is it more healthful to use skim milk or 2% milk?

4. In the dry cereal, how many grams of carbohydrates are in the form of starch? In the form of sugars?

3-2 Digestion of Food

Most foods that you eat cannot be used immediately by your body. They must first be broken down into the usable forms you have just learned about. **Food must be broken down into nutrients by a process called digestion. The breaking down of food into simpler substances for use by the body is the work of the digestive system.** Once food has been digested, or broken down into nutrients, the nutrients are carried to all the cells of the body by the blood. There, in the cells, the nutrients can be used to provide energy and the raw materials for cell growth and repair. In the following sections, you will discover the path that food takes through the digestive system.

Guide for Reading

Focus on these questions as you read.

▶ What happens to food during the process of digestion?

▶ What are the parts of the digestive system?

MULTICULTURAL OPPORTUNITY 3-2

Have students research the work of the African-American food chemist Lloyd Augustus Hall (1894–1971). Hall was responsible for developing a new salt mixture of sodium nitrate and sodium nitrite for preserving meats. He also developed a procedure for sterilizing foods using ethylene oxide gas, which was subsequently applied to the sterilization of hospital supplies as well.

ESL STRATEGY 3-2

Give each student six small cards. Ask them to number and copy one of the following terms on each card:

1. Mouth   4. Liver
2. Esophagus   5. Pancreas
3. Stomach   6. Small intestine

Then have them write the correct phrase from the list below on the back of each card.

• Most digestion takes place here
• Epiglottis and windpipe
• Tube between mouth and stomach
• Taste bud
• Ptyalin
• Bile
• Digestion helper and insulin maker
• Digestion helper and largest organ
• Gastric juice—pepsin, hydrochloric acid, and mucus

Have students exchange cards and check for accuracy. Later, the cards can be used as individual study tools.

ple of mechanical digestion. **Can you name another example of mechanical digestion?** (Examples will vary.)

GUIDED PRACTICE

▶ *Laboratory Manual*

Skill: Making observations

At this point you may want to have students complete the Chapter 3 Laboratory Investigation in the *Laboratory Manual* called Observing the Digestion of Starches. In this investigation students will learn what happens to starch in the mouth.

ENRICHMENT

Most controls over body functions operate in response to an internal stimulus. In the digestive system, however, controls operate in response to an external stimulus—the amount and composition of food in the digestive tract.

INDEPENDENT PRACTICE

▶ *Activity Book*

Students who need practice on the concept of mechanical digestion should complete the chapter activity The Structure of Teeth. In this activity students will explore the four types of adult teeth in the upper and lower jaw.

ANNOTATION KEY

Answers

1 Mouth. (Interpreting diagrams)

2 Starch. (Applying concepts)

3 The front of the mouth. (Applying concepts)

Integration

1 Physical Science: Solubility. See *Chemistry of Matter,* Chapter 3.

BACKGROUND INFORMATION

THE SALIVARY GLANDS

The lining of the cheeks contains three pairs of salivary glands. The largest of these are the parotid glands, which are located in front of the ears. The submaxillary glands, which are found beneath the tongue, open into the floor of the mouth. The third pair of glands, the sublingual glands, are found in the front of the mouth below the tip of the tongue. They also open into the floor of the mouth.

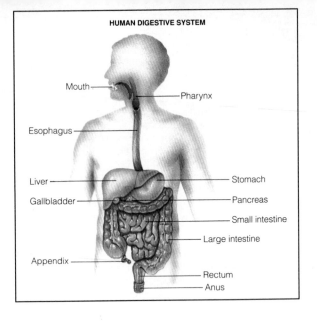

HUMAN DIGESTIVE SYSTEM
Mouth
Pharynx
Esophagus
Liver
Stomach
Gallbladder
Pancreas
Small intestine
Large intestine
Appendix
Rectum
Anus

Figure 3–10 *The breaking down of food into simpler substances that can be used by the body is the work of the digestive system. The digestive system consists of a number of different organs. Through which organ does food enter the digestive system?* 1

SIDE VIEW OF THE MOUTH
Incisor
Canine
Premolar
Molar
Tongue
Salivary glands

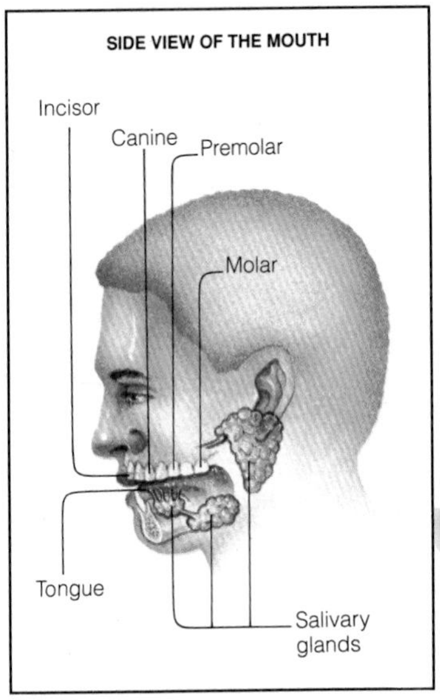

Figure 3–11 *Salivary glands, which are found in the mouth, produce saliva. Saliva contains the enzyme ptyalin. Which nutrient does ptyalin break down?* 2

The Mouth

Close your eyes and imagine your favorite food. Did your mouth water as you pictured something really delicious? Probably so. This response occurs because the mouth contains salivary (SAL-uh-vair-ee) glands. Salivary glands produce and release a liquid known as saliva (suh-LIGH-vuh). Seeing, smelling, or even thinking about food can increase the flow of saliva.

As you know from experience, saliva helps to moisten your food. But saliva has another important function. Saliva contains a chemical substance called **ptyalin** (TIGH-uh-lihn). Ptyalin breaks down some of the starches in food into sugars. You can actually detect this process by trying the following activity. Put a small piece of bread into your mouth and chew it for a few minutes. What happens? The bread begins to taste sweeter. Why? Bread is made mainly of starches, and starches are made of long chains of sugars. When ptyalin comes into contact with a starch, it begins to digest the starch, or break it down into sugars. The presence of these sugars makes the bread taste sweeter.

62 ■ H

3–2 (continued)

CONTENT DEVELOPMENT

Remind students that the digestive process consists of two basic parts—mechanical and chemical.

The process of digestion begins with the mechanical part, when food enters the mouth and is bitten and chewed by the teeth. The lips, cheeks, and tongue aid in mechanical digestion by working in a carefully coordinated manner to place food between the teeth for chewing.

The chemical part of digestion begins in the mouth as food is being chewed. Saliva contains the enzyme ptyalin, which works to break down some of the starches present in foods into sugars.

ENRICHMENT

Have interested students find out about some of the advances in dentistry that have taken place during the last 20 years. Students may wish to interview a dentist or visit a dental clinic or college of dentistry to learn how new technologies enable a dentist to improve and maintain the function and appearance of the teeth. Students may also wish to ask a dentist's opinion about the effectiveness of some relatively modern preventative measures such as fluoridated water and fluoride additives in toothpaste.

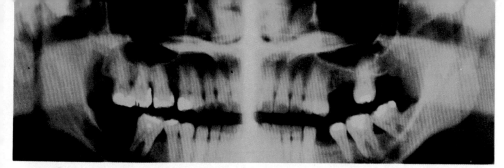

Figure 3–12 *The X-ray of the mouth shows the location of the four types of teeth: incisors, canines, premolars, and molars. The brighter areas in the teeth are the fillings. Where are the incisors located?* ③

Ptyalin belongs to a group of chemicals in your body known as **enzymes.** An enzyme helps to control a wide variety of chemical reactions, including the breaking down of foods into simpler substances. The digestion of foods by enzymes, such as ptyalin, is called chemical digestion. So although you may not have realized it, chemical digestion actually begins in your mouth!

Chemical digestion is not the only type of digestion that occurs in the mouth. Mechanical digestion, which is the physical action of breaking down food into smaller parts, also begins in the mouth. When you bite into your food, your incisors (ihn-SIGH-zerz), or front teeth, cut off a piece of the food. You then pull the food into your mouth with your lips and use your tongue to push it farther along into your mouth. Here the canines (KAY-nighnz), or eyeteeth, tear and shred the food while the flat-headed premolars and molars, or back teeth, grind and crush the food into small pieces.

Now that you have imagined your favorite food, think of the one you dislike most. The moment this food is in your mouth, something happens that makes you want to spit it out. If someone asked you why, you would probably say that the food tastes bad. Food tastes good or bad to you because there are taste buds on your tongue. Without taste buds, you would not be able to tell the difference between the food you dislike and the food you like.

Covering the surface of your tongue are small projections that give parts of the tongue a velvety

FIND OUT BY DOING

How Sweet It Is ①

1. Obtain two baby-food jars with lids. Label one jar A and the other B.

2. Fill each jar with equal amounts of water.

3. Place a whole sugar cube into jar A and a crushed sugar cube into jar B.

4. Place the lid on each jar and carefully shake each jar about five times.

5. Place the jars on a flat surface where they can remain undisturbed. Observe the rate of solution, or the time it takes for the sugar to dissolve completely, in each jar.

Which jar had the faster rate of solution? Can you think of any other factors that would affect the rate of solution? How would you test for these factors?

■ Relate the results of your investigation to the importance of mechanical digestion.

CONTENT DEVELOPMENT

Show students a model or a diagram of a set of human teeth. Point out the location of the four types of teeth: incisors, canines, premolars, and molars. The function of each type of tooth is different. The incisors bite, or cut off, pieces of food. The canines, or eyeteeth, tear and shred the food. The flat-headed premolars and molars crush and grind the food. Encourage students to use a mirror to identify these different types of teeth in their own mouths.

• **How does the shape of each type of tooth indicate its function?** (Canines and incisors are long, sharp, and pointed; molars and premolars are broader and flatter.)

• **Why do humans need to have different types of teeth?** (Because humans eat a variety of foods.)

• **Which teeth would we probably not need if we were herbivores, or plant-eaters? Why?** (We would probably not need the incisors and canines because we would not need to cut and tear meat.)

• **Suppose we were only carnivores, or meat-eaters. Would we still need molars and premolars? Explain your answer.** (Answers may vary. Possible answers include we might not need as many molars and premolars, but we would probably still need some of these teeth in order to grind the meat that we have cut with the incisors and canines.)

FACTS AND FIGURES

SALIVA

Saliva glands produce about 1.5 liters of saliva daily. Saliva is a mixture of water, mucin, and salivary amylase. About 98 percent of saliva is water. Mucin is a slippery substance that lubricates food, making it easier to swallow. Salivary amylase is a digestive enzyme that breaks down starches.

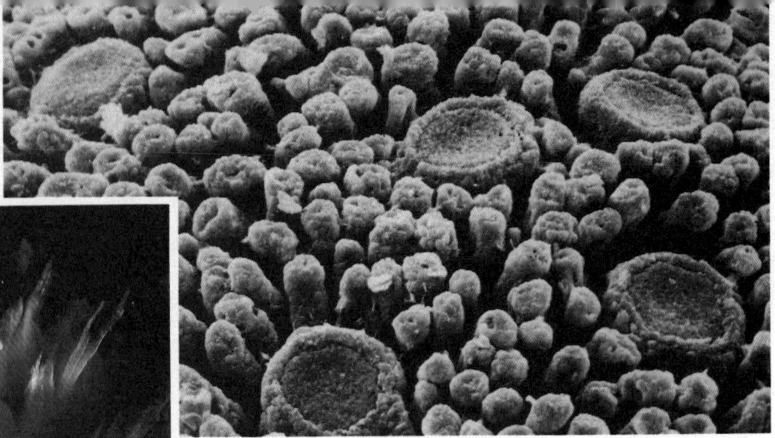

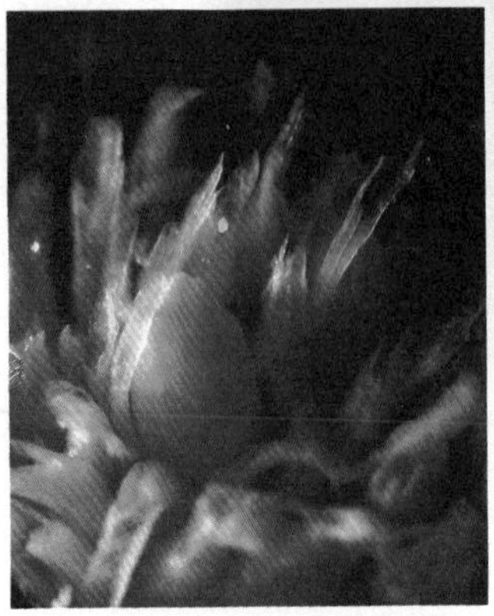

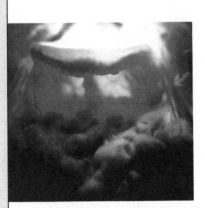

Figure 3–13 *Covering the tongue's surface are tiny projections that give it a velvety appearance (top). Located along the sides of these projections are the taste buds (left). The taste buds can detect four different kinds of tastes produced by the chemicals in food. What are these four tastes?* ❶

appearance. See Figure 3–13. Your taste buds are found along the sides of these projections. There are four types of taste buds, each of which reacts to a different group of chemicals in food. The reactions between taste buds and food chemicals produce four kinds of tastes: sweet, sour, bitter, and salty. The flavor of food, however, does not come from taste alone. Flavor is a mixture of taste, texture, and odor. Anyone who has ever had a stuffed nose caused by a cold knows how important the sense of smell is to the flavor of food.

What happens once you have finished chewing your food? You swallow it, of course! When you swallow, smooth muscles near the back of your throat begin to force the food downward. As you may recall from Chapter 2, smooth muscles are involuntary muscles. This means that they can contract without your actively causing them to. As you swallow, a small flap of tissue called the epiglottis (ehp-uh-GLAHT-ihs) automatically closes over your windpipe. The windpipe is the tube through which the air you breathe reaches your lungs. When the epiglottis closes over the windpipe, it prevents food or water from moving into the windpipe—or "down the wrong pipe," as we say. After swallowing, the epiglottis moves back into place to allow air into the windpipe.

Figure 3–14 *The epiglottis, which is a flap of tissue, folds over the windpipe to keep food or water from going "down the wrong pipe."*

64 ■ H

3–2 (continued)

INDEPENDENT PRACTICE

▶ *Activity Book*

Students who need practice on the concept of chemical digestion should complete the chapter activity What Color Is Your Cracker? In this activity students will explore the effect of saliva on starch, or crackers.

ENRICHMENT

All mammals that eat solid food use their teeth to cut and grind the food. Individually, each tooth is a wonder of biological design. Although teeth grow from the upper and lower jawbones, they are constructed from material that is much harder than ordinary bone. During chewing, the jaw muscles close the mouth with great force, pounding the teeth against the food and against one another with enough force to crack ordinary bones. To help in resisting this constant wear and tear, the crown, or top, of each tooth is covered by a layer of enamel, an extremely hard substance. Underneath the enamel is another hard material called dentin, which makes up the bulk of the tooth. The enamel and dentin have no nerve cells in them.

Each tooth is anchored by long, pointed roots that extend into the jawbone. A tough, fibrous periodontal membrane holds these roots in the jaw. The hollow center of the tooth, called the pulp cavity, contains the blood vessels and nerve cells that serve the tooth. If they are disturbed by heat, cold, or dental decay, these nerve cells send messages to the brain that signal "toothache."

CONTENT DEVELOPMENT

In most people, the tip of the tongue is most sensitive to sweet tastes, the sides are most sensitive to salty and sour tastes (with salty to the front of sour), and the back is most sensitive to bitter tastes.

The Esophagus

After you swallow, smooth muscles force the food into a tube called the **esophagus** (ih-SAHF-uh-guhs). The word esophagus comes from a Greek word that means to carry what is eaten. And that is exactly what this 25-centimeter-long tube does as it transports food down into the next organ of the digestive system.

The esophagus, like most of the organs in your digestive system, is lined with slippery mucus. The mucus helps food travel through the digestive system easily. The movement of food through your esophagus takes about seven seconds. However, mucus alone is not responsible for the speed of this trip. Waves of rhythmic muscular contractions, which begin as soon as food enters the esophagus, push food downward. These waves of contractions are called **peristalsis** (per-uh-STAHL-sihs). Peristalsis is so strong that it can force food through parts of your digestive system even if you are lying down. Because of peristalsis, a person can digest food even while floating upside down in the weightlessness of space.

FIND OUT BY DOING

Simulating Peristalsis

1. Obtain a 40-cm piece of clear plastic tubing.

2. Hold the tubing vertically and insert a small bead into the top opening of the tubing. The bead should fit snugly into the tubing.

3. Pinch the tubing above the bead so that the bead is pushed down along the length of the tubing.

How does this action compare with peristalsis?

■ What action would you be simulating if you were to pinch the tubing below the small bead?

FIND OUT BY DOING

SIMULATING PERISTALSIS

Discovery Learning

Skills: Making observations, relating concepts

Materials: clear plastic tubing, small bead

This activity will help students understand the process of peristalsis. The plastic tubing represents the portion of the digestive system through which food travels. The bead represents the food, and the pinching of the tube represents peristalsis. By pinching the tube below the bead, students will be simulating vomiting, or regurgitation.

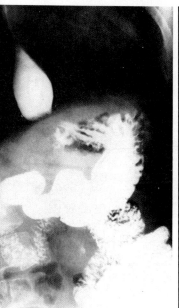
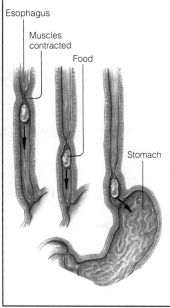

Esophagus

Muscles contracted

Food

Stomach

Figure 3–15 *Peristalsis is the waves of contractions that push food through parts of the digestive system. Use the diagram to identify the parts of the digestive system shown in the X-ray. Notice the vertebral column in the background.*

Have students examine Figure 3–13. Explain that these photographs of taste buds have been magnified many times. Information provided by the taste buds, the sense of smell, and the texture of the food all play a role in how food tastes.

GUIDED PRACTICE

Skills Development

Skill: Making observations

Prepare samples of the following for students to taste: salt water, sugar water, vinegar, and tonic water. Working in pairs, have students dip cotton swabs into each substance and touch their partner's tongue in various areas with the swab. Have students record whether or not the substance was tasted at each point and how strongly it was tasted. Then ask each pair to make a diagram of the tongue showing the areas where they think the tongue is most sensitive to sweet, sour, salty, and bitter tastes.

CONTENT DEVELOPMENT

Remind students that if they try and talk and eat at the same time, their epiglottis may not close properly. When that happens, they may feel that "something went down the wrong pipe," which is an appropriate description. The food slipped into the passageway leading to the lungs instead of the passageway leading to the stomach. Coughing usually clears the food out of the respiratory tract. Discuss with students other ways of helping a choking victim.

BACKGROUND INFORMATION

THE STOMACH

The stomach is made up of several layers of muscles. In the first muscle layer, the fibers run lengthwise. In the second muscle layer, the fibers are circular. In the third muscle layer, the fibers are diagonal.

Food stays in the stomach for two to six hours before entering the small intestine. Three factors determine how fast the stomach empties. First, a large meal tends to cause food to move out of the stomach faster than a small meal does. Second, foods that are high in fat content or high in acidity tend to make the stomach empty more slowly. The third factor that affects the stomach is a person's emotional state. Emotions such as fear and depression can trigger signals from the nervous system that slow down the emptying of the stomach. This is why a person who is depressed or anxious often finds that he or she has little appetite.

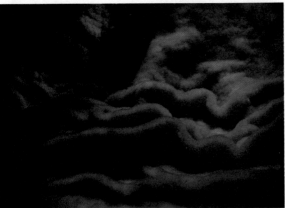

Figure 3–16 To protect the stomach from the effects of hydrochloric acid, tiny pits secrete a layer of mucus, which appears yellow in the photograph. The single red blood cell floating out of the pit is thought to be a sign that the stomach has been irritated by a substance such as alcohol.

The Stomach

After leaving the esophagus, the food enters a J-shaped organ called the **stomach.** Cells in the stomach wall release a fluid called gastric juice. Gastric juice contains the enzyme **pepsin,** hydrochloric acid, and thick, slippery mucus. If you were studying chemistry, you would learn that hydrochloric acid is a strong acid. This means that it is very reactive. In fact, the hydrochloric acid in your stomach is so reactive that if you could remove a drop of it and place it on a rug, it would burn a hole in the rug! The mucus, on the other hand, coats and protects the stomach wall. Can you see why such protection is necessary?

While food is in the stomach, it undergoes both mechanical digestion and chemical digestion. The contractions of the stomach muscles provide a kind of mechanical digestion as they churn the food and mix it with gastric juice. With the help of hydrochloric acid, pepsin breaks down some of the complex proteins in the food into simpler proteins. The action of pepsin on the proteins is a form of chemical digestion. Both of these types of digestion occur as peristalsis pushes the food toward the stomach's exit.

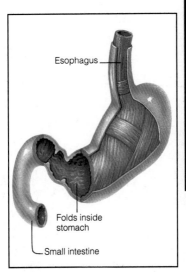

Esophagus

Folds inside stomach

Small intestine

Figure 3–17 The stomach wall consists of several layers of smooth muscles (left). When these muscles contract, food and gastric juice within the stomach are mixed together. Notice that the stomach's inner lining contains many folds (right). These folds will smooth out as the organ fills with food. What enzyme does gastric juice contain? ❶

3–2 (continued)

CONTENT DEVELOPMENT

Explain to students that when food enters the stomach, the stomach cells automatically release gastric juice. Gastric juice is made up of water, hydrochloric acid (HCl), an enzyme called pepsin, and mucus.

• **What is the function of the mucus?** (Mucus provides a coating for the stomach lining, which protects the stomach lining from being digested by the pepsin and hydrochloric acid.

• **What might occur if the mucus coating of the stomach lining is lacking?** (A peptic ulcer may result as hydrochloric acid and pepsin attack and break down the stomach lining.)

• **What kind of substances are broken down by the enzyme pepsin?** (Pepsin breaks down complex proteins into simpler proteins.)

• **Is the action of pepsin an example of chemical or mechanical digestion?** (Chemical digestion.)

• **Does any mechanical digestion occur in the stomach? Explain your answer.** (Yes. The food is mixed and broken up by muscle contractions, or peristalsis.)

● ● ● ● **Integration** ● ● ● ●

Use the discussion of hydrochloric acid to integrate the physical science concepts of acids and bases into your lesson.

ENRICHMENT

Tell students about the observations of the stomach made by a United States

The Small Intestine

The food moving out of your stomach is quite a bit different from the food that you placed in your mouth. After three to six hours in your stomach, muscle contractions and enzymes have changed the food into a soft, watery substance. In this form, the food is ready to move slowly into another organ of the digestive system—the **small intestine.** Although this organ is only 2.5 centimeters in diameter, it is more than 6 meters long. As in the esophagus and the stomach, food moves through the small intestine by peristalsis.

Although some chemical and mechanical digestion has already taken place in the mouth and the stomach, most digestion takes place in the small intestine. The cells lining the walls of the small intestine release an intestinal juice that contains several types of digestive enzymes.

Most chemical digestion that occurs in the small intestine takes place within the first 0.3 meter of this organ. Here, intestinal juice helps to break down food arriving from the stomach. This juice, however, does not work alone. It is helped by juices that are produced by two organs located near the small intestine. These organs are the **liver** and the **pancreas** (PAN-kree-uhs). Because food never actually passes

SOME DIGESTIVE ENZYMES

Digestive Juice	Digestive Enzyme	Works on	Changes It to
Saliva	Ptyalin	Starch	Complex sugars
Gastric	Pepsin	Protein	Simpler proteins
Pancreatic	Amylase Trypsin Lipase	Starch Proteins Fats	Complex sugars Simpler proteins Fatty acids and glycerol
Intestinal	Lactase, maltase, sucrase Peptidase Lipase	Complex sugars Simpler proteins Fats	Simple sugars Amino acids Fatty acids and glycerol

Figure 3–18 *According to this chart, which enzymes work on proteins? Which work on fats?* **②**

H ■ 67

FIND OUT BY DOING

Enzymes

Enzymes speed up the rate of certain body reactions that would otherwise occur very slowly. During these reactions, the enzymes are not used up or changed in any way. Using reference materials in the library, look up the meaning of "substrate" and the "lock-and-key hypothesis." Using posterboard and colored construction paper, make a labeled diagram of this hypothesis. Present the diagram to the class.

■ What is the relationship between an enzyme and a substrate?

By the time the patient Alexis St. Martin finally left for his home in Canada, Dr. Beaumont knew more than anyone else about digestion.

Army surgeon, Dr. William Beaumont, during the early 1800s. Dr. Beaumont had a young patient, Alexis St. Martin, who suffered from a gunshot wound to the stomach. The doctor was unable to close the wound, and the patient realized he would live, but with a 2-1/2-inch hole in his side that went clean through into his stomach. In time, a fold of stomach tissue grew down to keep St. Martin's meals where they belonged.

Dr. Beaumont used this opportunity to begin a series of studies on human digestion. For eight years, Dr. Beaumont subjected St. Martin's stomach to 238 trials. These trials included putting many different foods into the stomach on strings—the strings were pulled out later to observe how much of the food was digested.

Among other things, Beaumont confirmed that hydrochloric acid was a prime ingredient of gastric juice. He also identified another secretion that worked specifically on proteins. Later, that secretion was named pepsin.

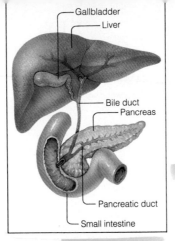

Figure 3–19 *The liver, pancreas, and gallbladder produce and store substances that are released into the small intestine to aid in the digestion of food.*

FIND OUT BY DOING

Do Oil and Water Mix?

1. Obtain two baby-food jars with lids. Place 5 mL of vegetable oil and 5 mL of water in each jar.

2. Cover both jars and gently shake them a few times. Then place the jars on a flat surface and observe what happens in each jar.

3. Remove the lid from one of the jars and add a few drops of liquid soap to the oil-and-water mixture. Repeat step 2.

Under what circumstances do oil and water mix?

■ How does the action of liquid soap resemble the action of bile?

through the liver and the pancreas, these organs are considered to be digestive helpers.

THE LIVER Located to the right of the stomach is the liver, the body's largest and heaviest organ. One of its many important functions is to aid digestion by producing a substance called bile. Once bile is produced in the liver, it moves into the gallbladder, where it is stored until needed.

As food moves into the small intestine from the stomach, the gallbladder releases bile through a duct (tubelike structure) into the small intestine. Because bile is not an enzyme, it does not chemically digest foods. It does, however, help to break up large fat particles into smaller ones in much the same way a detergent breaks up grease. These smaller fat particles can then be digested easily by enzymes in the small intestine.

THE PANCREAS The pancreas is a soft triangular organ located between the stomach and the small intestine. The pancreas produces a substance called pancreatic juice, which is a mixture of several enzymes. These enzymes move into the small intestine at the same time the bile does and help to break down proteins, starches, and fats.

The pancreas also produces a substance called insulin, which is important in controlling the body's use of sugar. You will read more about the pancreas and insulin in Chapter 6.

3–2 Section Review

1. Describe the process of digestion.
2. Compare mechanical and chemical digestion.
3. What is peristalsis? Why is it important?
4. Where does most of the digestion of food take place?
5. Why are the liver and the pancreas called digestive helpers rather than digestive organs?

Connection—*You and Your World*
6. Why is it important to chew your food thoroughly before swallowing it?

3-3 Absorption of Food

After a period of 3 to 5 hours, most of the food that is in the small intestine is digested. Proteins are broken down into individual amino acids. Carbohydrates (starches and sugars) are broken down into simple sugars. And fats are broken down into substances called fatty acids and glycerol. But before these nutrients can be used for energy, they must first be absorbed (taken in) by the bloodstream through the walls of the small intestine.

Absorption in the Small Intestine

The small intestine has an inner lining that looks something like wet velvet. This is because the inner lining of the small intestine is covered with millions of tiny fingerlike structures called **villi** (VIHL-igh; singular: villus, VIHL-uhs).

Digested food is absorbed through the villi into a network of blood vessels that carry the nutrients to all parts of the body. The presence of villi helps to increase the surface area of the small intestine, enabling more digested food to be absorbed faster than would be possible if the small intestine's walls were smooth. The villi contain tiny blood vessels that absorb and carry away the nutrients.

By the time the food is ready to leave the small intestine, it is basically free of nutrients, except for water. All the nutrients have been absorbed. What remains are undigested substances that include water and cellulose, a part of fruits and vegetables.

As the undigested food leaves the small intestine, it passes by a small finger-shaped organ called the appendix (uh-PEHN-diks). The appendix, which leads nowhere, has no known function. However, scientists suspect it may play a role in helping the body resist disease-causing bacteria and viruses. The only time that you may be aware of the appendix is when it becomes irritated, inflamed, or infected, causing appendicitis (uh-pehn-duh-SIGHT-ihs). The only cure for appendicitis is to remove the appendix by surgery as soon as possible.

Guide for Reading

Focus on this question as you read.

What is the process of absorption?

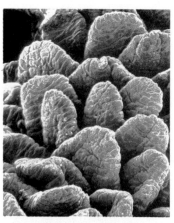

Figure 3–20 *These hills and ridges, which resemble part of a mountain range on the Earth's surface, are actually part of the small intestine. The tiny structures, called villi, line the inside of the small intestine. What is the function of the villi?* ①

3-3 Absorption of Food

MULTICULTURAL OPPORTUNITY 3-3

Have students research some common nutritional diseases. For example, the disease kwashiorkor is caused by a limitation of dietary protein and is found in tropical areas of America, Central and South Africa, and India. The name means "displaced child," because it occurs most often in children who are displaced from breast feeding by the arrival of a new sibling.

ESL STRATEGY 3-3

Give students a card to be added to the Digestive System "deck of cards" they made in ESL Strategy 3–2. This card should be labeled "7. Large intestine." The information below should be listed on the back of the card:

- Most water absorbed here
- Appendix attached
- Waste formed is stored in rectum
- Waste leaves through anus

Now continue to use the complete deck of cards as a study tool.

TEACHING STRATEGY 3-3

FOCUS/MOTIVATION

Distribute to the class several pieces of velvet. Explain that the velvet looks similar to the lining of the small intestine. Each tiny hairlike projection—about the size of a comma in the textbook—is called a villus (plural: villi). Because there are so many of these villi, the total surface area of the inside of the small intestine is larger than a volleyball court.

CONTENT DEVELOPMENT

Explain to students that once their food is digested, the nutrients must get to the individual body cells in order to be used for energy. The small intestine plays a double role: It is the primary organ of digestion, and it is also the site where digested nutrients are absorbed into the blood.

• **What is the purpose of the ridges and villi on the inner walls of the small intestine?** (They greatly increase the surface area over which the digested foods must travel, allowing the maximum amount of nutrients to be absorbed before they leave the small intestine.)

• **What would happen if the small intestine were just a straight tube?** (The food would pass through too quickly. Many of the digested nutrients would pass out of the body before they could be absorbed into the blood.)

Point out that the entire digestive process so far (from mouth to small intestine) has taken less than 12 hours.

Answers

① The large intestine received its name from its thickness, or circumference, not from its length. (Relating facts)

② The person must use more energy than is provided in the foods that he or she eats. (Applying concepts)

ECOLOGY NOTE

THE GREENHOUSE EFFECT

One of the byproducts of the digestive process is the gas methane. Cows, for example, produce a considerable amount of methane. Some scientists believe that large quantities of methane contribute directly to the greenhouse effect of our atmosphere. Have interested students research the effect of methane gas in our atmosphere.

3–3 (continued)

CONTENT DEVELOPMENT

Stress that once undigested food reaches the large intestine, it will remain there for several days. During this period, several processes are taking place. Helpful bacteria use the "leftovers" to make certain vitamins for use by your body. Water is absorbed from the remaining material to form feces. Feces are stored in the rectum until they are eliminated through the anus.

ENRICHMENT

▶ *Activity Book*

Students will be challenged by the Chapter 3 activity in the *Activity Book* called Digestive Trivia. In this activity students will use their knowledge of the digestive system to answer as many digestive-system trivia questions as possible.

Figure 3–21 *Notice the single layer of cells that cover each fingerlike villus in the photograph. The diagram shows what the inside of a villus looks like.*

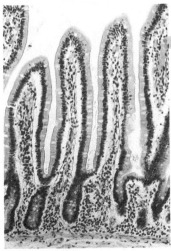

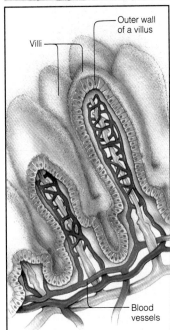

Villi — Outer wall of a villus

Blood vessels

70 ■ H

Absorption in the Large Intestine

After leaving the small intestine, the undigested food passes into the **large intestine.** The large intestine is shaped like a horseshoe that fits over the coils of the small intestine. The large intestine is about 6.5 centimeters in diameter but only about 1.5 meters long. How do you think the large intestine got its name? ①

After spending about 18 to 24 hours in the large intestine, most of the water that is contained in the undigested food is absorbed. At the same time, helpful bacteria living in the large intestine make certain vitamins, such as K and two B vitamins, that are needed by the body.

Materials that are not absorbed in the large intestine form a solid waste. This solid waste is made up of dead bacteria, some fat and protein, undigested food roughage, dried-out parts of digestive juices, mucus, and discarded intestinal cells. A short tube at the end of the large intestine called the **rectum** stores this waste. Solid wastes are eliminated from the body through an opening at the end of the rectum called the **anus.**

Figure 3–22 *The large intestine forms an upside-down horseshoe that fits over the small intestine (left). Lining the inside of the large intestine are many tunnels that contain mucus-making cells (right).*

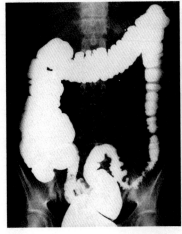
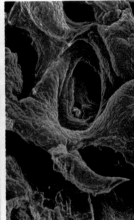

INDEPENDENT PRACTICE

▶ *Multimedia* ◀

You may want to show the video called Digestive System to reinforce the concepts of digestion. The video explores the structures of the digestive tract and their function, the movement of digested food, and how cells obtain and use nutrients produced by the digestion process. After viewing the video, have students work in groups to create a model of the digestive system. Models should be built using everyday classroom and laboratory objects.

Upon completion, models can be displayed and described by each group.

INDEPENDENT PRACTICE

Section Review 3–3

1. Absorption is the process by which digested food nutrients pass through the walls of the villi and enter the bloodstream.

2. In the small intestine, villi increase the surface area and increase the rate of nutrient absorption.

3–3 Section Review

1. Describe the process of absorption in the small intestine.
2. What is the function of the villi?
3. Describe the process of absorption in the large intestine.
4. What is the function of the rectum? The anus?

Critical Thinking—*Relating Facts*

5. Gallstones, which are crystals of minerals and salts that form in bile, sometimes block the entrance to the small intestine. What effect would this blockage have on the digestion of food?

3–4 Maintaining Good Health

As you have already learned, you can supply your body with the materials it needs for growth, repair, and energy by eating a balanced diet. **You can also keep your body healthy and running smoothly by controlling your weight and by getting proper amounts of exercise.**

Exercise

Activities such as swimming, jogging, bicycling, hiking, and walking briskly are good ways to exercise. Regular exercise helps to strengthen the heart. Exercise also results in firmer muscles, better posture, greater strength, increased endurance, and an improved sense of balance.

Weight Control

When a person eats more food than is needed, the body stores the excess energy in the form of fat. This fat is deposited mainly in a layer of tissue under the skin. In order to get rid of this stored fat, the person must use up more energy than is provided in the foods he or she eats. In this way, the body

Guide for Reading

Focus on this question as you read.

▶ *What are two important factors in maintaining good health?*

Figure 3–23 *When a person eats more food than is needed by the body, the body stores the excess food in the form of fat. This fat is deposited mainly in a layer of tissue under the skin. How can a person get rid of this stored fat?* ②

H ■ 71

3. In the large intestine, water and bile salts are absorbed, and bacteria produce vitamins B and K. Materials that are not absorbed form feces.
4. The rectum stores feces. The anus is the opening through which feces are eliminated from the body.
5. Gallstones blocking the entrance to the small intestine would result in intestinal blockage and a decrease or failure of nutrient absorption.

REINFORCEMENT/RETEACHING

Monitor students' responses to the Section Review questions. If students appear to have difficulty with any of the questions, review the appropriate material in the section.

CLOSURE

▶ *Review and Reinforcement Guide*

At this point have students complete Section 3–3 in the *Review and Reinforcement Guide.*

3–4 Maintaining Good Health

MULTICULTURAL OPPORTUNITY 3–4

The development of a national health insurance policy has been a topic of debate by the United States Congress for several years. Currently, infant mortality, as well as a wide range of diseases, is more common among the poor than among the rich. Access to medical care has decreased for many people and has become a cultural and financial issue. Divide your class into two groups and have them research, then present in debate fashion, the pros and cons of a national health insurance policy.

ESL STRATEGY 3–4

When discussing the importance that exercise plays in maintaining a healthy body, explain the American slang expression "couch potato." Working in cooperative groups, have students write a paragraph describing the habits of a couch potato. Then ask them to design a plan to help the couch potato become a healthier person. Suggest that different groups compare their plans.

TEACHING STRATEGY 3–4

FOCUS/MOTIVATION

Have students stand. Conduct some simple exercises with them such as running in place, jumping jacks, or stretching and bending exercises.
• **What physical activities do you enjoy?** (Accept all answers.)
• **How many of you feel that you get enough physical exercise?** (Accept all answers.)
• **Why is exercise important?** (Lead students to relate exercise to health.)

CONTENT DEVELOPMENT

Stress that getting the proper amount of exercise is important in maintaining a healthy body. Remind students that physical exercise should be done on a regular basis.

Some people exercise while wearing ankle weights. Have students collect as many of these weights as possible (from home, athletic team members, friends, and so on). Design an experiment that will determine the effect of wearing these weights on heart rate. Results of the experiment can be presented to the class. Students should attempt to relate the effect of wearing these weights to being several pounds overweight.

CAREERS

Nurse

Every student at one time or another makes a trip to the school **nurse.** The reason might be an aching tooth, a headache, a sore throat, or a gym injury. The visit also could be simply routine—a tuberculosis test or an eye exam.

In addition to schools, hospitals are among the many places that hire nurses. The services of nurses are also needed in doctors' offices, nursing homes, private homes, and in some industrial companies. The qualities needed for nursing are a desire to help others, good judgment, a sense of responsibility, a willingness to work hard, and an ability to work well with others.

If a career in nursing sounds interesting to you, you can learn more about it by writing to the American Nurses' Association, Inc., 2420 Pershing Road, Kansas City, MO 64108.

Figure 3–24 *In order to maintain good health, most people — including older people—need moderate exercise. What are some of the benefits of exercise?* ❶

will break down the stored fat to release the needed energy.

When a person is overweight, all the organs of the body, especially the heart, must work harder to bring materials to and remove wastes from the excess fat tissue. Some people who are overweight may choose to go on a weight-loss diet. It is important that the diet chosen is a balanced one—one that contains the proper amounts of nutrients needed by the body. Before starting any weight-loss diet, a person should go to a doctor. The doctor will give the person a complete checkup and discuss a sensible diet. Once a person loses the excess weight, he or she can maintain a steady weight by taking in only as many Calories in food as are used up.

3–4 Section Review

1. Explain how exercise and weight control contribute to good health.
2. List four activities that are good forms of exercise.
3. What must be included in any balanced diet?
4. How can you maintain a steady weight?

Connection—*You and Your World*
5. Imagine that you have put on a little weight. Design a balanced diet that will help you get rid of the weight.

3–4 (continued)

CONTENT DEVELOPMENT

Remind students that food is energy. When the energy equivalent of the food you eat exceeds the energy you expend, the body stores the excess energy as fat. In order to get rid of stored fat, you must use more energy than is provided in the meals you eat. Only then will your body break down the stored fat to release the additional energy that you need.

• **What two things can you do to get your body to use stored fat for energy?** (You can eat less—take in fewer Calories—or exercise more—use up a greater number of Calories. In either case, Calories used must be greater that Calories consumed.)

Point out that being overweight puts a strain on all body organs, especially the heart. If a person is overweight, participation in a sensible weight-loss program could lead to a healthier life.

• **What are some precautions one should take when choosing a weight-loss plan?** (A weight-loss diet should be a balanced diet that contains proper amounts of the six basic nutrient groups. Trendy diets should be analyzed carefully to determine whether or not they meet the basic requirements. A doctor should be consulted before a major weight-loss plan is undertaken. Prior to beginning a diet, a complete physical checkup is recommended.)

CONNECTIONS

What's Cooking? ❶

Recall the last time you cooked an egg or boiled some water. Did you use a gas stove or an electric stove? Or did you use a microwave oven? Whichever appliance you used, they had one thing in common: They are all sources of heat. Heat, which is a form of energy, cannot be seen. However, you can see the work that heat does by observing what happens to food when you cook it. In a way, cooking can be defined as the transfer of heat from its source to food. The various cooking methods, such as boiling, frying, and baking, bring about their effects by using different materials—water, oil, air—and different methods of *heat transfer*.

Heat is transferred by three methods: conduction, convection, and radiation. In conduction, heat is transferred through a material without carrying any of the material with it. For example, heat from a gas or an electric burner passes through a pan to the food inside it. In convection, heat is transferred as a liquid or a gas moves from a warm area to a cooler one. In a pan of cold water that has been placed on a hot burner, for example, the water nearer the burner will heat up and move to the top. This will cause the cooler water nearer the top of the pan to

sink. This process will continue until all the water reaches the same temperature.

Unlike the processes of conduction and convection, the process of radiation can occur through a vacuum. In radiation, waves of energy are used to heat materials. This energy is absorbed by the particles in the material, causing them to vibrate. In microwave ovens, for example, the microwaves produced by powerful electromagnetic (electric and magnetic) fields cause the water in food to vibrate. This action releases heat into the food. Because all of the energy is absorbed by the food and not wasted on heating the surrounding air or the oven itself, microwave cooking is quicker and more economical than other types of cooking methods.

CONNECTIONS
WHAT'S COOKING?

Students may not have previously connected the concept of nutrition and heat transfer through conduction, convection, and radiation. You may want to have students name several foods that are prepared by heat conduction, heat convection, and heat radiation. Interested students may want to design a meal that would be prepared using all three types of heat transfer.

If you are teaching thematically, you may want to use the Connections feature to reinforce the themes of energy, scale and structure, systems and interactions, and stability.

Integration: Use the Connections feature to integrate the physical science concepts of heat energy into your lesson.

ENRICHMENT

▶ *Activity Book*

Students will be challenged by the Chapter 3 activity in the *Activity Book* called Calculating Your Nutritional Budget. In this activity students will determine the nutritional value of foods.

INDEPENDENT PRACTICE

Section Review 3–4

1. Exercise helps to strengthen the heart, improve balance, firm muscles, strengthen the body, increase endurance, and improve posture. Weight control helps to maintain the body at its peak efficiency.
2. Answers will vary but may include jogging, running, hiking, and swimming.
3. Proper amounts of the four basic food groups.
4. Eat foods from all four basic food groups in moderation, get a reasonable amount of exercise, and take in only as many Calories as you burn.
5. Diets will vary; make sure each diet contains proper amounts of food from the four basic food groups.

REINFORCEMENT/RETEACHING

Review students' responses to the Section Review questions. Reteach any material that is still unclear, based on students' responses.

CLOSURE

▶ *Review and Reinforcement Guide*

Students may now complete Section 3–4 in the *Review and Reinforcement Guide*.

Laboratory Investigation

MEASURING CALORIES USED

BEFORE THE LAB

1. Gather all materials at least one day prior to the investigation. If a scale is not available at your school, you may need to bring one from home.
2. This laboratory investigation will require one and one-half days for completion.

PRE-LAB DISCUSSION

Have students read the complete laboratory procedure.

• **What is the purpose of this investigation?** (To find out how many Calories are burned in a 24-hour period.)

Have students examine the chart that shows the rates at which Calories are burned during various activities.

• **What do the numbers in the second column of this chart represent?** (The average calorie rate, or the number of Calories used per hour for each kilogram of body mass.)

• **Which activity burns the fewest number of Calories per hour?** (Sleeping.)

Have students suggest additional activities that could be included in the activity chart. Predict the average calorie rate for each of these additional activities.

• **If you know your mass in pounds, how can you convert pounds to kilograms?** (Divide the number of pounds by 2.2 pounds/kilogram.)

Explain to students that they are to keep a record of all their activities for the next 24 hours. Have each student copy the chart, adding a third column in which they will record the time spent in each category of activities. This column should be labeled Hours Spent.

While students are copying the chart, they can take turns using a scale to determine their body mass. The scale should be placed in a relatively private area of the room.

Laboratory Investigation

Measuring Calories Used

Problem

How many Calories do you use in 24 hours?

Materials *(per student)*

pencil and paper	scale

Procedure

1. Look over the chart of Calorie rates. It shows how various activities are related to the rates at which you burn Calories. The Calorie rate shown for each activity is actually the number of Calories used per hour for each kilogram of your body mass.
2. Using a scale, note your weight in pounds. Convert your weight into kilograms (2.2 lb = 1 kg). Record this number.
3. Classify all your activities for a given 24-hour period. Record the kind of activity, the Calorie rate, and the number of hours you were involved in that activity.

Activity	Average Calorie Rate
Sleeping	1.1
Awake but at rest (sitting, reading, or eating)	1.5
Very slight exercise (bathing, dressing)	3.1
Slight exercise (walking quickly)	4.4
Strenuous exercise (dancing)	7.5
Very strenuous exercise (running, swimming rapidly)	10.5

4. For each of your activities, multiply your weight by the Calorie rate shown in the chart. Then multiply the resulting number by the number of hours or fractions of hours you were involved in that activity. The result is the number of Calories you burned during that period of time. For example, if your weight is 50 kilograms and you exercised strenuously, perhaps by running, for half an hour, the Calories you burned during that activity would be equal to 50 x 10.5 X 0.5 = 262.5 Calories.
5. Add together all the Calories you burned in the entire 24-hour period.

Observations

How many Calories did you use in the 24-hour period?

Analysis and Conclusions

1. Explain why the values for the Calorie rates of various activities are approximate rather than exact.
2. What factors could affect the number of Calories a person used during exercise?
3. Why do young people need to consume more Calories than adults?
4. **On Your Own** Determine the number of Calories you use in a week. In a month.

Average Caloric Needs Chart		
	Age	Calories
Males	9–12	2400
	12–15	3000
Females	9–12	2200
	12–15	2500

TEACHING STRATEGY

1. Because the 24-hour recording period will end at the beginning of the class period, check to see that students have completed the entries for their charts. You may need to assist them in converting minutes to fractions of hours or common fractions to decimal fractions.
2. When the charts are completed, remind students of the conversion from pounds to kilograms. It may be helpful to work one or more sample calculations on the chalkboard. Assist anyone having difficulty with these conversions.

DISCOVERY STRATEGIES

Discuss how the investigation relates to the chapter by asking open questions similar to the following:

• **Is a person who consumes 1800 Calories per day and burns 1800 Calories per day considered to be healthy? Why or why not?** (Students should be able to cite many situations where this hypothetical person may not be healthy; for example, if the

Study Guide

Summarizing Key Concepts

3–1 The Importance of Food

▲ The six groups of nutrients are proteins, carbohydrates, fats, vitamins, minerals, and water.

3–2 Digestion of Food

▲ Digestion is the process of breaking down food into simple substances.

▲ The salivary glands release saliva, which contains the enzyme ptyalin. Ptyalin breaks down some starches into simple sugars.

▲ The changing of food into simple substances by the action of enzymes is called chemical digestion.

▲ Mechanical digestion occurs when food is broken down by chewing and by the churning movements of the digestive tract.

▲ After leaving the mouth, food enters the esophagus and is pushed downward into the stomach by peristalsis.

▲ The stomach releases gastric juice, which contains hydrochloric acid, mucus, and pepsin. Pepsin is an enzyme that breaks down proteins into amino acids.

▲ In the stomach, food undergoes both mechanical and chemical digestion.

▲ After leaving the stomach, food enters the small intestine, where it is acted upon by intestinal juice that digests proteins, starches, and fats.

▲ In the small intestine, bile, which is produced by the liver and stored in the gallbladder, aids in the digestion of fats .

▲ Pancreatic juice travels to the small intestine and digests proteins, starches, and fats.

3–3 Absorption of Food

▲ Nutrients are absorbed into the bloodstream through fingerlike structures called villi located on the inner lining of the small intestine.

▲ The large intestine absorbs most of the water from the undigested food.

▲ Undigested food substances are stored in the rectum and then eliminated from the body through the anus.

3–4 Maintaining Good Health

▲ A regular exercise program helps to strengthen the heart, develop better posture, firm up muscles, build a stronger body, and increase endurance.

Reviewing Key Terms

Define each term in a complete sentence.

3–1 The Importance of Food
nutrient
Calorie
protein
amino acid
carbohydrate

fat
vitamin
mineral

3–2 Digestion of Food
ptyalin
enzyme

esophagus
peristalsis
stomach
pepsin
small intestine
liver
pancreas

3–3 Absorption of Food
villus
large intestine
rectum
anus

ANALYSIS AND CONCLUSIONS

1. Each person's body chemistry is slightly different, so no exact rate per activity can be determined.

2. Answers may include the size of the person, how hard the person exercises, the temperature of the environment, and so on.

3. Young people are generally more active and need to consume more Calories, not only for basic metabolic functions, but also for growth.

4. Answers will vary, depending on the student.

GOING FURTHER: ENRICHMENT

Part 1

Have students use the chalkboard to record the number of Calories they burned in the 24-hour period. Results should be recorded separately for males and females. Have volunteers compute the average results for each of these two groups.

• **The average Calorie requirement for females is less than the average Calorie requirement for males. Why?** (On average, females weigh less than males do.)

Remind students that these numbers are averages and are not necessarily true for all individuals.

Part 2

Based on the Calorie needs as determined by this Laboratory Investigation, have students plan menus that provide the number of Calories roughly equivalent to their needs. Then have them analyze these menus in terms of the six basic nutrient groups.

1800 Calories consumed are not represented somewhat equally by the basic food groups—applying facts, relating information.)

• **As people get older, they tend to slow down. Do you think people need more, the same number, or fewer Calories, as they get older? Explain your reasoning.** (Lead students to reason that it depends on each person's activity level. Generally speaking, activities become less strenuous and less regular as a person grows older; in this case, Calorie intake should

decrease—relating facts, drawing conclusions.)

OBSERVATIONS

Answers will vary considerably, and students should be cautioned that each person burns a different number of Calories on any given day. The majority of students will burn between 1400 and 4000 Calories per day.

ALTERNATIVE ASSESSMENT

The *Prentice Hall Science* program includes a variety of testing components and methodologies. Aside from the Chapter Review questions, you may opt to use the Chapter Test or the Computer Test Bank Test in your *Test Book* for assessment of important facts and concepts. In addition, Performance-Based Tests are included in your *Test Book*. These Performance-Based Tests are designed to test science process skills, rather than factual content recall. Since they are not content dependent, Performance-Based Tests can be distributed after students complete a chapter or after they complete the entire textbook.

CONTENT REVIEW

Multiple Choice

1. a
2. a
3. c
4. b
5. d
6. d
7. b
8. b
9. c
10. d

True or False

1. T
2. T
3. F, carbohydrates
4. F, fat-soluble
5. F, Ptyalin
6. F, large intestine or rectum
7. T
8. T

Concept Mapping

Row 1: Provide Energy
Row 2: Fat
Row 3: Protein
Row 4: Water

CONCEPT MASTERY

1. The digestion of starch (bread) begins in the mouth, where ptyalin breaks down some of the starches into sugars. These sugars are further broken down by intestinal enzymes in the small intestine. Protein (milk) digestion begins in the stomach, where enzymes in gastric juice break complex proteins into simpler pro-

---

Content Review

Multiple Choice

Choose the letter of the answer that best completes each statement.

1. The nutrients that are used to build and repair body parts are
   a. proteins.   c. carbohydrates.
   b. minerals.   d. vitamins.
2. Which is not found in the mouth?
   a. pepsin   c. ptyalin
   b. saliva   d. taste buds.
3. The tube that connects the mouth and the stomach is the
   a. small intestine.   c. esophagus.
   b. pancreas.   d. epiglottis.
4. Gastric juice contains the enzyme
   a. bile.   c. ptyalin.
   b. pepsin.   d. mucus.
5. The digestion of proteins begins in the
   a. mouth.   c. small intestine.
   b. liver.   d. stomach.
6. In the digestive system, proteins are broken down into
   a. fatty acids.   c. simple sugars.
   b. glycerol.   d. amino acids.
7. The liver produces
   a. pepsin.   c. hydrochloric acid.
   b. bile.   d. ptyalin.
8. The fingerlike structures that form the inner lining of the small intestine are called
   a. cilia.   c. enzymes.
   b. villi.   d. nutrients.
9. Water is absorbed in the
   a. small intestine.   c. large intestine.
   b. pancreas.   d. liver.
10. Regular exercise helps a person have
    a. good posture.   c. a stronger heart.
    b. firm muscles.   d. all of these.

True or False

If the statement is true, write "true." If it is false, change the underlined word or words to make the statement true.

1. The nutrients that supply the greatest amount of energy are the <u>fats</u>.
2. A chemical that breaks down food into simple substances is called an <u>enzyme</u>.
3. Starches and sugars are examples of <u>proteins</u>.
4. Vitamin K is an example of a <u>water-soluble</u> vitamin.
5. <u>Pepsin</u> is the enzyme in saliva.
6. Undigested food substances are stored in the <u>epiglottis</u>.
7. The enzyme pepsin digests <u>proteins</u>.
8. The small, finger-shaped organ located where the small intestine and large intestine meet is the <u>appendix</u>.

Concept Mapping

Complete the following concept map for Section 3–1. Refer to pages H8–H9 to construct a concept map for the entire chapter.

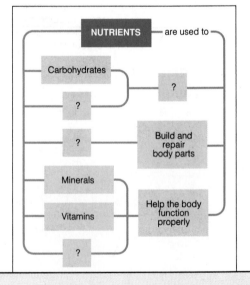

---

teins. Protein digestion is completed in the small intestine, where other enzymes break down simple proteins into amino acids. Fat (butter) digestion occurs in the small intestine, where intestinal and pancreatic enzymes break down fats into fatty acids and glycerol. Bile from the liver helps to digest fat by breaking up large fat molecules into smaller ones.

2. The digestive system, although inside the body, is also in a sense an open tube that passes through the body. Nutrients can be considered to enter the body when they are absorbed, by means of the villi, into the bloodstream.

3. Food does not pass through the appendix nor does the appendix produce any substance that aids in the digestion of food. Therefore, the removal of the appendix has no effect on the functioning of the digestive system.

4. The villi are hairlike projections that line the small intestine. They separate nutrients from undigested food and permit absorption of nutrients into the bloodstream.

5. The epiglottis is a small flap of tissue

Concept Mastery

Discuss each of the following in a brief paragraph.

1. If you were to eat a slice of bread (starch) with butter (fat) and drink a glass of milk (protein), what would happen to each of these foods during digestion?
2. Food does not really enter your body until it is absorbed into the blood. Explain why. *Hint:* Think of the digestive system as a tube passing through your body.
3. Appendicitis is usually treated by removing the appendix. Explain why this treatment does not interfere with the functioning of a person's digestive system.
4. Describe the structure of villi and their role in absorption.
5. Describe the location and function of the epiglottis.
6. Where does mechanical digestion occur? Chemical digestion?
7. Compare absorption in the small intestine with absorption in the large intestine.
8. Why can talking with food in your mouth be a dangerous thing to do?
9. Explain why vomiting can be considered reverse peristalsis.

Critical Thinking and Problem Solving

Use the skills you have developed in this chapter to answer each of the following.

1. **Making inferences** Suppose your doctor prescribed an antibiotic that killed all the bacteria in your body. What effect would this have on your digestive system?
2. **Making comparisons** Compare the human digestive system to an "assembly line in reverse."
3. **Making diagrams** Draw a diagram of the human digestive system and label all the organs. Use a red pencil to color the organs through which food passes. Use a blue pencil to color the organs through which food does not pass.
4. **Applying concepts** Fad diets have become popular in the United States. Some of these diets involve eating only a limited variety of food. Explain why some fad diets may be an unhealthy way to lose weight.
5. **Making comparisons** Compare the process of digestion to the process of absorption.
6. **Relating concepts** Following surgery, most patients are fed a glucose, or simple sugar, solution intravenously. Intravenously means into a vein. Why do you think this is done?
7. **Sequencing events** Trace the path of a piece of hamburger on a bun through the digestive system. Name each digestive organ and describe what happens in each organ.
8. **Using the writing process** Carbohydrate loading is a technique used by athletes to help them reach their peak of efficiency. To find out the benefits and potential problems of this practice, prepare a list of questions that you might ask a doctor and a coach during an interview on this subject.

product is constructed. In the digestive system, the entire finished product (food) is broken down into the raw materials from which it is made (nutrients).

3. Charts should reflect the data presented in the textbook.

4. Some fad diets may not provide all of the six nutrients (proteins, carbohydrates, fats, vitamins, minerals, and water) needed to achieve and maintain good health.

5. Digestion is the breaking down of food into simpler substances for use by the body. Absorption is the process during which these simpler substances, or nutrients, are taken into the bloodstream.

6. Glucose does not have to be digested. It is absorbed immediately by the bloodstream, and provides energy, or Calories.

7. The digestion of starch (bun) begins in the mouth, where ptyalin breaks down some of the starches into sugars. In the stomach, protein (hamburger) digestion begins: enzymes in gastric juices break down complex proteins into simple proteins. As the partially digested food enters the small intestine, intestinal juice containing enzymes that act on fats (in hamburger), proteins, starches, and sugars is secreted. Pancreatic juice, secreted by the pancreas, also breaks down the three types of foods. Bile, secreted by the liver, helps to break down large fat molecules into smaller ones. The absorption of the end products of digestion occurs in the small intestine. Undigested food is excreted through the large intestine.

8. Answers will vary.

that automatically closes over the trachea (windpipe) during swallowing.

6. Mechanical digestion occurs in the mouth and stomach. Chemical digestion occurs in the mouth, stomach, and small intestine.

7. In the small intestine, digested food is absorbed through the tiny fingerlike villi. In the large intestine, water is absorbed through the intestinal wall.

8. Talking with food in the mouth can lead to choking, or food entering the trachea (windpipe).

9. Waves of peristalsis reverse the direction of the movement of food, propelling it from the stomach into the esophagus and out the mouth.

CRITICAL THINKING AND PROBLEM SOLVING

1. Helpful bacteria in the large intestine would be killed. The body's supply of vitamins K and B would be temporarily depleted.

2. In an assembly line, raw materials are put together so that an entire finished

Chapter 4 CIRCULATORY SYSTEM

SECTION	LABORATORY INVESTIGATIONS AND DEMONSTRATIONS
4–1 The Body's Transportation System pages H80–H81	
4–2 Circulation in the Body pages H82–H88	**Student Edition** Measuring Your Pulse Rate, p. H102 **Laboratory Manual** Observing Blood Circulation Investigating the Heart **Teacher Edition** Listening to Heartbeats, p. H78d
4–3 Blood—The River of Life pages H88–H95	
4–4 Cardiovascular Diseases pages H96–H101	**Teacher Edition** Performing CPR, p. H78d
Chapter Review pages H102–H105	

*All materials in the Chapter Planning Guide Grid are available as part of the Prentice Hall Science Learning System.

OUTSIDE TEACHER RESOURCES

Books

Berger, Melvin. *The Artificial Heart,* New York: Watts.

Folkow, B., and E. Neil. *Circulation,* New York: Oxford University Press.

Harvey, W. *Circulation of the Blood,* New York: Dutton.

Tiger, Steven. *Heart Disease,* Englewood Cliffs, NJ: Julian Messner.

Audiovisuals

Blood: Composition and Functions, film or video, Coronet

Circulatory and Respiratory Systems, film or video, National Geographic

Heart and Circulation, film or video, Coronet

The Heart and Circulatory System, film or video, EBE

The Heart: An Inside Story, film or video, Coronet

Heart, Lungs, and Circulation, film or video, Coronet

The River of Life, video, EBE

OTHER ACTIVITIES	MULTIMEDIA

Activity Book
    Chapter Discovery: Simulating Blood Transfusions
Review and Reinforcement Guide
    Section 4–1
	Transparency Binder
	    Circulatory System
	English/Spanish Audiotapes
	    Section 4–1

Activity Book
    ACTIVITY: The Heartbeat
    ACTIVITY: Circulation Calculations
    ACTIVITY: Circulation Comparisons
Student Edition
    Find Out by Doing: Catch the Beat, p. H83.
    Find Out by Doing: Circulation, p. H86.
Review and Reinforcement Guide
    Section 4–2
	Video
	    Circulatory System
	Transparency Binder
	    The Heart
	English/Spanish Audiotapes
	    Section 4–2

Student Edition
    Find Out by Doing: Blood Donating Center, p. H93.
Review and Reinforcement Guide
    Section 4–3
	Courseware
	    Circulation System (Supplemental)
	English/Spanish Audiotapes
	    Section 4–3

Activity Book
    Surveying Risk Factors Related to Heart Disease
Student Edition
    Find Out by Calculating: Pumping Power, p. H97
    Find Out by Writing: Blood Pressure, p. H100.
Review and Reinforcement Guide
    Section 4–4
	English/Spanish Audiotapes
	    Section 4–4

Test Book
    Chapter Test
    Performance-Based Test
	Test Book
	    Computer Test Bank Test

Chapter 4   CIRCULATORY SYSTEM

CHAPTER OVERVIEW

The circulatory system delivers food and oxygen to body cells and carries carbon dioxide and other waste products away from body cells. The circulatory system is controlled by the heart, which pumps blood through arteries, veins, and capillaries.

Blood is a mixture of red blood cells, white blood cells, and platelets, immersed in a mixture called plasma. Blood is pumped from the heart to the lungs and back to the heart. At this point, the blood contains much oxygen. The blood then leaves the heart and travels through the arteries into the thin-walled capil-laries. The body cells receive oxygen and discard carbon dioxide through the capillary walls. The blood, being depleted of oxygen and loaded with carbon dioxide, then travels back to the heart through veins. The process of circulation never ceases.

Cardiovascular diseases affect millions of people throughout the world. The leading cause of death is coronary artery disease, a deterioration of the coronary arteries. Cardiovascular diseases are most often attributed to atherosclerosis and high blood pressure.

4–1 THE BODY'S TRANSPORTATION SYSTEM

THEMATIC FOCUS

The purpose of this section is to introduce students to the human body's transportation system for blood—the circulatory system. Students will learn that the circulatory system delivers food and oxygen to body cells and carries carbon dioxide and other waste products away from cells. The circulatory system also provides pathways for the body's defense systems against germs and other invading organisms. In addition, the circulatory system allows chemical messengers to travel from one portion of the body to another.

The themes that can be focused on in this section are stability and patterns of change.

*Stability: By delivering food and oxygen to body cells and carrying waste products from body cells, the circulatory system maintains homeostasis. The internal conditions of the circulatory system are constant, whereas the conditions outside it are frequently changing.

Patterns of change: The function of the circulatory system is to deliver food and oxygen to body cells and carry carbon dioxide and waste products from body cells. It also provides a network for both systems of defense and chemical messages.

PERFORMANCE OBJECTIVES 4–1

1. Describe the function of the circulatory system.

4–2 CIRCULATION IN THE BODY

THEMATIC FOCUS

The purpose of this section is to describe the structure and function of the heart, trace the flow of blood throughout the circulatory system, and describe the three types of blood vessels. Students will discover that the heart has four chambers, with each chamber having a different function. Arteries, veins, and capillaries are the various passageways through which blood can travel. Blood travels away from the heart in arteries and toward the heart in veins, except in the arteries and veins connecting the heart and lungs.

The themes that can be focused on in this section are scale and structure and unity and diversity.

*Scale and structure: The primary components of the circulatory system include the heart, blood, and blood vessels. The heart powers the system; the blood carries oxygen, food, and waste products; and the blood vessels provide the road network along which work can take place.

Unity and diversity: Although arteries, veins, and capillaries provide the paths along which work can occur, each has its own unique structure. Arteries must allow for the passage of a great volume of blood, and they are large and smooth on the inside. Veins are not as large as arteries and contain valves to help keep the blood moving in one direction. The capillaries are small and restrict the flow of blood to such a degree that nutrients, oxygen, carbon dioxide, and waste products can pass through capillary walls.

PERFORMANCE OBJECTIVES 4–2

1. Describe the structure and function of the three types of blood vessels.
2. List the four chambers of the heart.
3. Trace the path of blood through the circulatory system.

SCIENCE TERMS 4–2

atrium p. H83
ventricle p. H84
artery p. H85
capillary p. H87
vein p. H88

4–3 BLOOD—THE RIVER OF LIFE

THEMATIC FOCUS

The purpose of this section is to examine the primary components of blood and the structures of these components. Students will learn that the fluid portion of the blood is called plasma and that plasma contains three different types of blood cells: red blood cells, white blood cells, and platelets. Plasma is composed of about 90 percent water. Occupying about 45 percent of the plasma are the three types of blood cells. Red blood cells are the most numerous and contain a protein called hemoglobin. Hemoglobin binds oxygen molecules and distributes them throughout the body. It also carries some carbon dioxide wastes from body cells. White blood cells are larger and less numerous than red blood cells. White blood cells protect the body against attacks by invaders such as bacteria, viruses, and other foreign substances.

Platelets are more numerous than white blood cells but less numerous than red blood cells. When platelets come into contact with the torn edge of a blood vessel, they burst apart, releasing chemicals that begin a series of reactions that generate fibrin. Fibrin, which is composed of threadlike fibers, helps to trap blood cells and plasma across a wound, preventing further blood flow.

The themes that can be focused on in this section are systems and interactions and energy.

*Systems and interactions: The various blood cells in the circulatory system work together as a system, performing their duties. The interactions of these blood cells with the rest of the body help to keep the human body healthy and in peak operating condition.

*Energy: The red blood cells of the circulatory system provide the body with energy in the form of oxygen and various nutrients.

PERFORMANCE OBJECTIVES 4–3

1. **List the four components of human blood.**
2. **Describe the primary function of red blood cells, white blood cells, and platelets.**

SCIENCE TERMS 4–3

plasma p. H88
red blood cell p. H90
hemoglobin p. H91
white blood cell p. H91
platelet p. H92
fibrin p. H93

4–4 CARDIOVASCULAR DISEASES

THEMATIC FOCUS

The purpose of this section is to identify serious chronic diseases. Students will be introduced to two serious cardiovascular diseases: atherosclerosis and hypertension. Atherosclerosis, one of the most common cardiovascular diseases in the United States, is the thickening of the inner wall of an artery. Though some thickening of these walls occurs naturally as we age, we can expedite the process by consuming a diet rich in fats and cholesterol. Cholesterol is a substance that is necessary for hormone production and cell development, but too much of it in the bloodstream can cause clumping, or clogging, of arteries. Cholesterol is a "sticky" substance that can cling to and thicken arterial walls. Proper diet and exercise will decrease the likelihood of getting atherosclerosis.

Hypertension is another serious cardiovascular disease. Hypertension is a condition in which the blood pressure of the body is greater than normal for extended periods of time. Because people with hypertension often display no obvious symptoms, it is often called the "silent killer." Hypertension is a good reason why people should have their blood pressure checked on a regular basis.

The themes that can be focused on in this section are systems and interactions and stability.

*Systems and interactions: The circulatory system interacts with the body in many ways. It helps the individual parts of the body perform as a whole. We can help to keep the body interacting as a system by following a healthy diet and getting proper exercise. By doing these things, we also decrease the probability that we will be a victim of cardiovascular disease.

*Stability: The human body is an intricate system that tends to remain relatively stable and maintain homeostasis if its occupant does things that are beneficial, and not harmful, to it. Doing beneficial things for the human body tends to increase the prospects of a lengthy, healthy life.

PERFORMANCE OBJECTIVES 4–4

1. **Describe the different types of cardiovascular diseases.**
2. **Explain how different cardiovascular diseases relate to the circulatory system.**
3. **Explain some causes of cardiovascular disease.**
4. **Describe things that can be done to limit the likelihood, or severity, of cardiovascular diseases.**

SCIENCE TERMS 4–4

cardiovascular disease p. H96
artherosclerosis p. H96
hypertension p. H100

Discovery *Learning*

TEACHER DEMONSTRATIONS MODELING

Listening to Heartbeats

Obtain one or more stethoscopes and allow students to listen to the beat of their own heart.

• **What kinds of sounds does a beating heart make?** (The heartbeat has two phases, with each phase producing a different sound. The two phases are often said to sound like the syllables "lub" and "dub." They are repeated over and over again.)

Explain that these sounds are actually made when valves within the heart open and close.

Point out that the average adult heart beats approximately 70 times per minute.

Have students determine their own heartbeat rates.

• **What can a doctor learn about the functioning of your heart by listening to it with a stethoscope?** (Answers will vary. Rate and regulation of heartbeat can be determined. Irregularities, such as a heart murmur, can be detected.)

Performing CPR

Explain to students that CPR is an emergency procedure used to revive persons whose hearts have stopped beating. CPR stands for cardiopulmonary resuscitation. In CPR, the heart is squeezed between the rib cage and the spine. CPR should be used by a trained person in extreme emergencies when no pulse can be detected.

Using a dummy, demonstrate CPR for your students. An alternative is to invite a physical education instructor, or someone else who is certified in CPR, to conduct the demonstration for you.

CHAPTER 4
Circulatory System

INTEGRATING SCIENCE

This life science chapter provides you with numerous opportunities to integrate other areas of science, as well as other disciplines, into your curriculum. Blue numbered annotations on the student page and integration notes on the teacher wraparound pages alert you to areas of possible integration.

In this chapter you can integrate life science and cells (p. 81), physical science and electricity (pp. 83, 101), life science and biotechnology (p. 84), fine arts (p. 86), social studies (p. 93), language arts (pp. 93, 100), food science (p. 97), mathematics (pp. 97, 98), and physical science and fluid forces (p. 99).

SCIENCE, TECHNOLOGY, AND SOCIETY/COOPERATIVE LEARNING

Eggs, bacon, sweet roll, and milk; cheeseburger, fries, chocolate shake, ice cream, and cookies–great menus in the minds of some people. These menus, however, include more than twice the recommended amount of something that can kill people: cholesterol.

Many young people who hear adults talking about cholesterol levels do not think that cholesterol is something they have to worry about. But recent studies have shown that one third of American young people may be getting too much cholesterol in their diets. Too much cholesterol and saturated fat (which raises cholesterol levels) may lead to serious heart problems when young people grow older.

Cholesterol is a waxy, whitish substance found in animal tissues. It is used by the body to make various hormones, bile, vitamin D, and portions of cell membranes. Many people do not realize that the body, particularly the liver, can produce all the cholesterol it needs–we do not need to eat any cholesterol at all.

Foods containing cholesterol or saturated fat may taste great, but the cholesterol in them and the cholesterol produced by the body can combine to restrict blood flow in the arteries of the circulatory system. Restricted blood flow to the heart can lead to heart attacks, and restricted

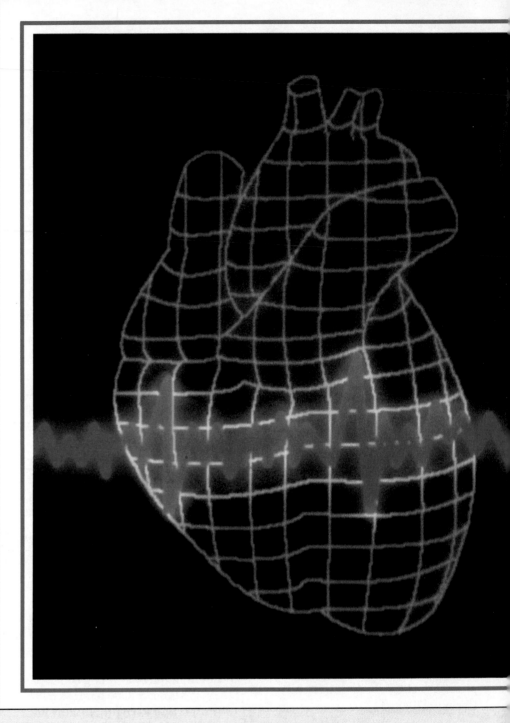

INTRODUCING CHAPTER 4

DISCOVERY LEARNING

▶ *Activity Book*

Begin your teaching of the chapter by using the Chapter 4 Discovery Activity, from the *Activity Book*. Using this activity, students will discover the conditions for transfusing blood between different blood groups.

USING THE TEXTBOOK

Have students observe the photograph on page H78.
• **Can you identify what is being shown in this photograph?** (Answers may vary. Lead students to understand that an electrocardiogram, or EKG, is superimposed on the computer graphic image of the heart.)
• **What is an electrocardiogram?** (It is a record of the electrical activities of the heart.)
• **Why do you think an electrocardiogram is useful in some medical instances?** (Lead

Circulatory System

Guide for Reading

After you read the following sections, you will be able to

4–1 The Body's Transportation System
- Identify the main function of the circulatory system.

4–2 Circulation in the Body
- Trace the path of blood through the body.
- Relate the structures of the heart and blood vessels to their functions.

4–3 Blood—The River of Life
- Compare the four main components of blood.
- Identify the two main human blood groups.

4–4 Cardiovascular Diseases
- Relate cardiovascular diseases to the circulatory system.

At 6:24 AM, the first call of the day came in. A 73-year-old man who lived 120 kilometers away was having severe chest pains. "Strap yourself in, we're taking off!" shouted the pilot to the chief flight nurse over the roar of the helicopter. The chief flight nurse is one of several highly trained members of Survival Flight, a special medical unit that comes to the aid of people who are having heart attacks.

By 8:12 AM, the nurse had given the patient an injection of a drug that dissolves blockages in the blood vessels near the heart. Such blockages can prevent the heart from receiving an adequate supply of blood. By 8:23 AM, the Survival Flight team was loading the patient onto the helicopter and preparing to rush him to a hospital.

The Survival Flight team's helicopter is equipped with a stretcher, medical instruments, and medicine. But the team's greatest strength is the knowledge possessed by its members. They all know how the heart works and what to do when something goes wrong. By reading the pages that follow, you too will discover some of this special knowledge.

Journal *Activity*

You and Your World In your journal, list all the activities that you do that affect your circulatory system. Then on a new page in your journal, make two columns with the headings Helpful and Harmful. Place the activities from your list in the appropriate column.

◀ *Superimposed on this computer graphic of the heart is a part of an electrocardiogram, or record of the electrical activities of the heart.*

H ■ 79

---

students to reason that it is sometimes difficult to determine the condition of an internal organ because the organ is not visible. An EKG provides a visible record of the performance of the heart at a particular time.)

• **What relationship does the heart have with the circulatory system of the human body?** (The heart provides the motion, or movement, of the circulatory system.)

Have students read the chapter introduction on page H79.

• **What is happening in this situation?** (Have students paraphrase the textbook information.)

• **Why do you think the use of helicopters has grown in medical emergencies?** (They are fast; cities are becoming more and more congested.)

• **What kinds of things do you think could lead to a heart blockage?** (Accept all logical answers. Remind students that questions such as these will be easier to answer after they have completed the chapter material.)

---

blood flow to the brain can lead to strokes. Although most young people are not in danger of having a heart attack or a stroke, deposits of cholesterol can be found in the arteries of people as young as ten years old. Studies also show that young people with high cholesterol levels tend to become adults with high cholesterol levels— a dangerous condition.

Young people can protect themselves from the hazards of too much cholesterol by exercising, not smoking, and eating a balanced diet of healthful foods. Wise food choices include cereal with low-fat milk instead of bacon, eggs, and a sweet roll; salad instead of cheeseburger, fries, and a shake; and fresh fruit instead of ice cream and cookies.

Cooperative learning: Using preassigned lab groups or randomly selected teams, have groups complete one of the following assignments:
• Have each group generate a one-day meal plan that is low in cholesterol, but which includes lunch at a fast-food restaurant or the school cafeteria.
• Write and perform a three-to-five minute skit designed to introduce fourth graders to cholesterol and to explain ways in which the children can prevent the early buildup of deposits in their arteries. The skits should not scare the children but rather present information in a factual and visually entertaining manner.

See Cooperative Learning in the *Teacher's Desk Reference.*

JOURNAL ACTIVITY

You may want to use the Journal Activity as the basis of a class discussion. As students discuss the various activities that affect the circulatory system, lead them to develop additional activities that could be used to substitute for the harmful activities on their lists. Students should be instructed to keep their Journal Activity in their portfolio.

4-1 The Body's Transportation System

4-1 The Body's Transportation System

The main task of the circulatory system in all organisms is transportation. **The circulatory system delivers food and oxygen to body cells and carries carbon dioxide and other waste products away from body cells.** The power behind this pickup-and-delivery system is the heart. The heart pumps blood to all parts of the body through a network of blood vessels. This network is so large that if it could be unraveled, it would wrap around the Earth more than twice!

As you may already know, oxygen combines with food inside your body cells to produce usable energy. Without energy, body cells would soon die. Thus, one of the most important jobs of the circulatory system is delivering oxygen to the cells. The cells

Figure 4-1 *The disk-shaped red objects in this photograph are red blood cells. Notice how densely packed the red blood cells are as they squeeze through the tiniest of blood vessels—the capillaries.*

CONTENT DEVELOPMENT

Point out that the heart is the pump that keeps blood moving through the body. Explain that the heart pump is the power behind the circulatory system. Tell students that the circulatory system delivers food and oxygen to body cells and carries carbon dioxide and other waste products away from body cells.

Have students observe Figure 4-2. Notice that the blood vessels form a network throughout the entire body.

Explain to students that their blood is not really blue. Blood carrying large quantities of oxygen and few waste products is bright red, whereas blood carrying little oxygen and many waste products is dark red.

Have students examine the blood vessels in their wrists or on the underside of their forearms. These veins appear blue because a yellow pigment in the skin makes the dark-red blood in the vessels look bluish.

that use the most oxygen—and the first to die without oxygen—are brain cells.

When cells combine oxygen and food to produce energy, they also produce a waste product called carbon dioxide. Removing carbon dioxide from cells is another important job of the circulatory system.

Still another important job of the circulatory system is to transport food to all body cells. At the same time, wastes produced by the cells are carried away by the blood. If the blood did not remove such wastes, the body would poison itself with its own waste products!

Sometimes the body comes under attack from microscopic organisms such as bacteria and viruses. At such times, another transporting function of the circulatory system comes into play: supplying the body with defenses against invaders. The defenses take the form of disease-fighting cells and chemicals. When invading organisms attack areas of the body, the circulatory system rushes the disease-fighting cells and chemicals to the area under attack.

Disease-fighting chemicals are not the only types of chemicals transported by the circulatory system. The circulatory system carries chemical messengers as well. Chemical messengers bring instructions from one part of the body to another. For example, a chemical messenger produced in the pancreas is carried by the blood to the liver. Its message is "Too much sugar in the blood. Remove some and store it."

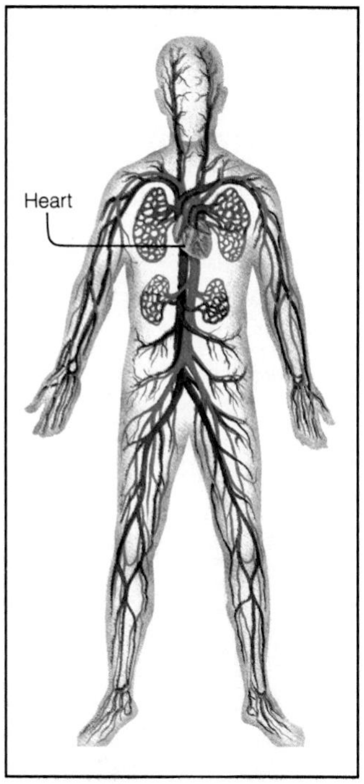

Figure 4–2 *The function of the circulatory system is to deliver food and oxygen to body cells and carry carbon dioxide and other waste products away from body cells. What organ pumps blood throughout the body?* **1**

4–1 Section Review

1. What are the functions of the circulatory system?
2. Why is it important that wastes produced by the cells are carried away by the blood?

Critical Thinking—*Making Calculations*
3. The heart of an average person pumps about 5 liters of blood per minute. How much blood is pumped out of the heart per hour? Per day? Per week?

H ■ 81

ANNOTATION KEY

Answers
1 Heart. (Interpreting diagrams)

Integration
1 Life Science: Cell Biology. See *Cells: Building Blocks of Life*, Chapter 3.

FACTS AND FIGURES
THE HEART

On the average, the heart pumps about 7600 liters, or 2000 gallons, of blood every day.

2. If blood did not carry away wastes, the body would poison itself with its own waste products.
3. 300 L per hour, 7200 L per day, 50,400 L per week.

REINFORCEMENT/RETEACHING

Monitor students' responses to the Section Review questions. If students appear to have difficulty with any of the questions, review the appropriate material in the section.

CLOSURE

▶ *Review and Reinforcement Guide*
At this point have students complete Section 4–1 in the *Review and Reinforcement Guide.*

● ● ● ● **Integration** ● ● ● ●
Use the discussion of cells and their function to integrate the life science concepts of cells into your lesson.

GUIDED PRACTICE
▶ *Multimedia* ◀
Skill Development
Skill: Interpreting graphics

Focus students' attention on the circulatory system by using the transparency in the *Transparency Binder* called Circulatory System.

• **What is the purpose of the system?** (To carry nutrients and oxygen to all cells and to carry wastes away from cells.)

INDEPENDENT PRACTICE
Section Review 4–1
1. The circulatory system transports food, oxygen, carbon dioxide, waste products, disease-fighting cells and chemicals, and chemical messengers.

H ■ 81

4-2 Circulation in the Body

MULTICULTURAL OPPORTUNITY 4-2

Have students research the work of Dr. Charles Richard Drew (1904–1950). Dr. Drew developed a procedure for long-term preservation of blood plasma. In 1950, Dr. Drew was killed in a car accident while traveling to a medical meeting at Tuskegee Institute. The irony was that he could have been saved if he had received an immediate blood transfusion—the nearest "whites-only" hospitals refused to admit him.

ESL STRATEGY 4-2

Enrich students' understanding of the word *chamber* by explaining that when it is used to describe a part of the body, it refers to an enclosed space (such as a room). Have students use simple sentences to state the number of chambers the heart contains, as well as what divides it into right and left sides.

Then ask students to explain the following:
1. Why blood cells in different circulatory system locations are different colors.
2. The similarities and differences of the three types of blood vessels.

Help students compare and contrast by suggesting that they use words such as *like, just as, too,* and *as well* when comparing, and that they use words such as *however, but, whereas,* and *on the other hand* when contrasting.

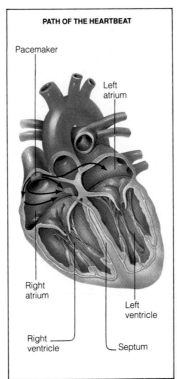

PATH OF THE HEARTBEAT

Pacemaker

Left atrium

Right atrium

Left ventricle

Right ventricle

Septum

Figure 4–3 *The heartbeat is controlled by an area of nerve tissue within the heart called the pacemaker. In the illustration, you can see the path a message from the pacemaker takes as it spreads through the heart. The photograph shows a network of nerves lining a section of a ventricle.*

82 ■ H

4-2 Circulation in the Body

In a way, the entire circulatory system is like a vast maze that starts at the heart. Unlike most mazes, however, this one always leads back to the place where it began. **In the circulatory system, blood moves from the heart to the lungs and back to the heart. Blood then travels to all the cells of the body and returns again to the heart.** In the next few pages, you will follow the blood on its journey through the circulatory maze. You will begin, of course, at the heart.

You may be surprised to learn that the heart is a muscle that rests only between beats. Even when you are asleep, about 5 liters of blood is pumped through your body every minute. During an average lifetime, the heart beats more than 2 billion times and pumps several hundred million liters of blood through the many thousands of kilometers of blood vessels in the body.

Not much larger than a fist, the heart is located slightly to the left of the center of your chest. If you place your fingers there and gently press down, you probably will be able to feel your heart beating. The heartbeat, or the heart's rhythm, is controlled by an area of nerve tissue within the heart. Because this

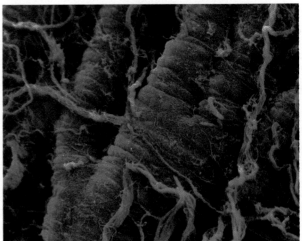

TEACHING STRATEGY 4-2

FOCUS/MOTIVATION

Have students make a fist.
• **Name an internal organ of your body that is about the size of your fist.** (Accept all reasonable answers. Lead students to answer heart.)

Tell students to place their fist slightly left of center on their chest.
• **Can you feel your heart beating?** (Most students will answer yes.)
• **Name several other locations on your body where you can feel your heartbeat.**

(Possible answers include underside of the wrist and either side of the throat.)
• **Tell one amazing fact about the human heart.** (List responses on the chalkboard. Possible responses: It is a muscle that needs no rest; it acts involuntarily, without signals from the brain; it pumps 5 liters of blood per minute; it beats more than 2 billion times during an average lifetime.)

CONTENT DEVELOPMENT

Review the functions of the circulatory system so far: (1) transportation of oxygen

to body cells, (2) transportation of food to body cells, (3) transportation of wastes away from body cells, (4) transportation of disease-fighting agents to needed areas, and (5) transportation of chemical messages from one part of the body to another.

Explain that in humans, as in all mammals, the heart has four chambers. Point out that a thick wall of tissue, called the septum, divides the right side of the heart from the left side. The upper chamber on the right side is called the right atrium (plural: atria). It acts as a collecting cham-

area regulates the heart's pace, or rate of beating, it is called the pacemaker. Located in the upper-right side of the heart, the pacemaker sends out signals to heart muscle, causing it to contract. For a variety of reasons, the body's pacemaker may fail to operate properly. If this happens, an artificial pacemaker, complete with a battery, can be inserted into the body or worn outside the body.

The Right Side of the Heart

Most people think of the heart as a single pump, but it is actually two pumps. One pump is located on the right side of the heart. The second pump is located on the left side of the heart. A thick wall of tissue called the septum separates the heart into a right side and a left side. Each side has two chambers. Your journey through the circulatory maze begins in the right upper chamber, called the right **atrium** (AY-tree-uhm; plural: atria). Figure 4–4 shows the location of the right atrium.

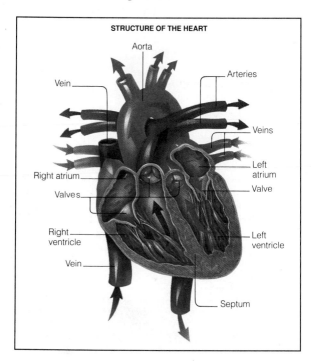

STRUCTURE OF THE HEART

- Aorta
- Vein
- Arteries
- Veins
- Left atrium
- Right atrium
- Valve
- Valves
- Left ventricle
- Right ventricle
- Vein
- Septum

Figure 4–4 *The heart is divided into a right side and a left side by a septum, or wall. Each side of the septum contains two chambers: an upper chamber and a lower chamber. The upper chambers are called atria, and the lower chambers are called ventricles. What is the function of the atria?* ❶

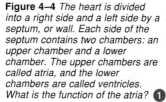

FIND OUT BY DOING

Catch the Beat

How does temperature affect heartbeat rate? Design an experiment to find the answer to this question by using the following materials:

Daphnia culture
2 glass depression slides
coverslip
microscope
stopwatch
ice cube

As you plan your experiment, keep in mind that it must contain only one variable. Remember to include a control.

■ What effect would warm (not hot) water have on the *Daphnia*'s heartbeat rate?

FIND OUT BY DOING

CATCH THE BEAT

Discovery Learning

Skills: Manipulative, making observations, inferring

Materials: **Daphnia** *culture, 2 glass depression slides, coverslip, microscope, stopwatch, ice cube*

Students are able to demonstrate and reinforce their understanding of the relationship between temperature and heartbeat rate through this activity. Experiments may differ but should include a control, a variable, and a determination of how temperature affects heartbeat rate.

Students should discover that decreasing temperature will result in a less-frequent heartbeat. Students also should be able to predict that warm water would cause an increase in the *Daphnia*'s heartbeat.

---

ber for blood returning from its trip through the body.
- **The atria act as a collection chamber for blood returning from its trip through the body. Do you think the blood returning to the atria is oxygen-enriched or oxygen-depleted. Why?** (The blood is oxygen-depleted because it has traveled through the body carrying oxygen to needed locations.)

The term *deoxygenated blood* is used to describe the blood that is oxygen-deficient, or returning to the atria.

● ● ● ● **Integration** ● ● ● ●

Use the discussion of the heart's pacemaker to integrate the physical science concepts of electricity into your lesson.

GUIDED PRACTICE

Skills Development

Skills: Making observations, drawing conclusions

At this point have students complete the in-text Chapter 4 Laboratory Investigation: Measuring Your Pulse Rate. In this investigation students will explore the effect of activity on pulse rate.

REINFORCEMENT/RETEACHING

▶ *Activity Book*

Students who need practice on the concept of the heart's relationship to the circulatory system should complete the chapter activity called The Heartbeat. In this activity students will construct a stethoscope and listen to another student's heartbeat.

Inside the right atrium, you find yourself swirling in a dark sea of blood. A great many red blood cells surround you. Red blood cells carry oxygen throughout the body. When the red blood cells join up with oxygen molecules, the blood turns bright red. Such blood is said to be oxygen-rich. The blood in which you are swimming in the right atrium, however, is dark red, not bright red at all. This can only mean that these red blood cells are not carrying much oxygen. Rather, they are carrying mostly the waste gas carbon dioxide. This blood, then, is oxygen-poor. And that makes sense. For the right atrium is a collecting chamber for blood returning from its trip through the body. Along the way, the red blood cells have dropped off most of their oxygen and picked up carbon dioxide.

Suddenly the blood begins to churn, and you feel yourself falling downward. You are about to enter the heart's right lower chamber, called the right **ventricle.** But before you do, you must pass through a small flap of tissue called a valve. The valve opens to allow blood to go from the upper chamber to the lower chamber. Then it closes immediately to prevent blood from backing up into the upper chamber.

You now find yourself in the right ventricle. Your stay here will be quite short. The ventricles, unlike the atria, are pumping chambers. Before you know it, you feel the power of a heartbeat as the ventricle contracts and blood is forced out of the heart through a large blood vessel.

To the Lungs and Back

Now your journey has really begun. Because you are surrounded by oxygen-poor blood, your first stop should be obvious. Do you know what it is? The right ventricle is pumping you toward the lungs. The trip to the lungs is a short one. In the lungs, the red blood cells drop off the waste gas carbon dioxide. As the carbon dioxide enters the lungs, it is immediately

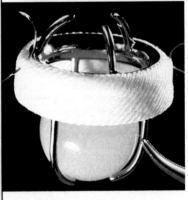

Figure 4–5 *Heart valves control the flow of blood through the heart. A heart valve called the bicuspid valve (top) is found between the left atrium and the left ventricle. Sometimes when a natural heart valve does not work properly, it must be replaced by an artificial heart valve (bottom).* ❶

84 ■ H

The walls of the ventricles are thick and muscular—they are pumping chambers.
• **What do you predict happens to blood in the lungs?** (Lead students to the response that two things happen in the lungs: The red blood cells drop off carbon dioxide so that it can be exhaled, and the red blood cells pick up oxygen.)
• **What happens to the color of the blood during this process?** (It changes from dark red to bright red.)

Now that oxygen has picked up blood in the lungs, the oxygenated blood needs to

be taken to the cells throughout the body.
• **Does oxygenated blood flow directly from the lungs to vessels throughout the body?** (No, it returns to the heart first.)
• **Why does oxygenated blood return to the heart?** (The heart is a powerful pump. Blood returns to the heart to be pumped throughout the body.)
• **To which chamber of the heart does blood from the lungs return?** (Left atrium.)

After passing through more valves, the blood then enters the left ventricle. Point out that the left ventricle works approxi-

exhaled (breathed out). At the same time, the red blood cells are busy picking up oxygen, which has been brought into the lungs as a result of inhaling (breathing in). What is the color of the blood now? ❶

As you leave the lungs, you might be expecting to travel with the oxygen-rich blood to all parts of the body. But to your surprise, you discover this is not the case. The oxygen-rich blood you are traveling in must first return to the heart so that it can be pumped throughout the body. Your next stop is the hollow chamber known as the left atrium.

The Left Side of the Heart

The left atrium, like the right atrium, is a collecting chamber for blood returning to the heart. The left atrium, however, collects oxygen-rich blood as it returns from the lungs. Once again, the blood quickly flows downward through a valve and enters the left ventricle.

The left ventricle has a lot more work to do than the right ventricle does. The right ventricle has to pump blood only a short distance to the lungs. But the left ventricle has to pump blood to every part of the body. In fact, the left side of the heart works about six times harder than the right side. That is why you feel your heartbeat on the left side of your chest.

Arteries: Pipelines From the Heart

As the left ventricle pumps the oxygen-rich blood out of the heart, the blood passes through the largest blood vessel in the body. This blood vessel is called the aorta (ay-OR-tuh). The aorta is an **artery,** or a blood vessel that carries blood away from the heart.

Soon after leaving the heart, the aorta branches into smaller arteries. Some of these smaller arteries return immediately to the heart, supplying the heart muscle with food and oxygen. Others branch again and again, like the branches of a tree. These branching arteries form a network that connects all parts of the body.

As you pass through the aorta and enter a smaller artery, you notice that the inner wall of the artery is

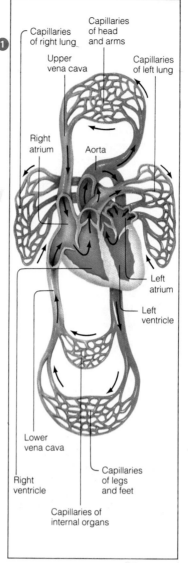

Figure 4–6 *Blood travels through the body in a continuous path. The path of oxygen-rich blood is shown in red, and the path of oxygen-poor blood is shown in blue.*

H ■ 85

FACTS AND FIGURES
HEARTBEATS

At birth, a human heart beats about 100 times per minute. This rate gradually decreases over time. The heart of a 6-year-old child beats about 100 times per minute, a 10-year-old's heart about 90 times per minute, and a 15-year-old's heart about 85 times per minute. Adult hearts beat about 60 to 80 times per minute.

---

mately six times harder than the right ventricle.
• **Why does the left ventricle work about six times harder than the right ventricle?** (The left ventricle pumps blood to the entire body. The right ventricle pumps blood only to the lungs, a relatively short distance.)

● ● ● ● **Integration** ● ● ● ●

Use Figure 4–5 and its caption to integrate concepts of biotechnology into your science lesson.

GUIDED PRACTICE
▶ *Laboratory Manual*
Skills Development
Skills: Making observations, interpreting diagrams

Students may now complete the Chapter 4 Laboratory Investigation in the *Laboratory Manual* called Investigating the Heart. In this investigation students will explore the heart in terms of its chambers, blood vessels, and the path of its blood.

INDEPENDENT PRACTICE
▶ *Activity Book*

Students who need practice on the concept of the capacity of the circulatory system should complete the chapter activity called Circulation Calculations. In this activity students will discover some interesting facts about the heart, blood, and circulatory system.

FIND OUT BY
DOING

Circulation

Human circulation is divided into two types of circulation: pulmonary circulation and systemic circulation.

Use reference books to find out the structures that are involved in each type of circulation. Draw a labeled diagram of the human circulatory system, using two different-colored pencils to illustrate the structures that make up each type of circulation.

■ Why do you think these two types of circulation are so named?

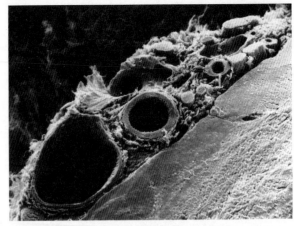

Figure 4–7 *This photograph shows that the wall of a small artery (right) is thicker than the wall of a medium-sized vein (left).*

quite smooth. The smooth inner wall allows blood to flow freely. Around the smooth inner wall is an elastic middle layer that is made mainly of smooth muscle tissue. Much of the flexibility of arteries comes from this elastic middle layer. The flow of blood in an artery is controlled by the contraction and relaxation of the smooth muscle tissue. As the artery contracts, large amounts of blood are sent to an area. When the artery relaxes, the amount of blood flowing to the area is lessened. The outer wall of the artery contains flexible connective tissue. Connective tissue allows arteries to stretch and return to normal size with each heartbeat.

Your trip continues as you travel to smaller branching arteries. Where you go from here depends on many factors. For example, if a meal has recently been eaten, much of the blood will be directed toward the intestines to pick up food. If the body is exercising, the blood supply to the muscles will probably be increased. If there are a great many wastes in the blood, you may be sent to the liver, where certain wastes are changed into substances that are not poisonous to the body. Or you may travel to one of the kidneys, where other wastes are removed from the blood. No matter where you are sent, however, one thing is sure. You will find the

hose in many ways. Arteries have three layers to their walls. The inner layer is smooth to allow blood to pass through freely. The middle layer is mainly made up of smooth muscle tissue. This muscle tissue expands and contracts to control the flow of blood to various parts of the body. The outer layer is like an elastic covering.

Stress that although arteries carry blood everywhere in the body, they cannot drop off or pick up any nutrients from body cells. The walls of arteries are simply too thick.

brain one of your primary destinations. For whether it is thinking very hard or not, the brain always gets priority over any other part of the body.

Capillaries: The Unseen Pipelines

The artery network carries blood all over the body. But arteries cannot drop off or pick up any materials from body cells. Can you think of a reason why not? *Hint:* Recall the description of the structure of an artery. The walls of arteries are too thick for oxygen and food to pass through. In order for the blood to do its main task—delivering and picking up materials—it must pass from the thick-walled arteries into very thin-walled blood vessels. Extremely thin-walled blood vessels are called **capillaries.**

You will probably have a hard time squeezing through the capillary in which you now find yourself. Don't feel bad. In most capillaries, there is only enough room for the red blood cells to pass through in single file. It is here in the capillaries that the basic work of the blood—giving up oxygen and taking on wastes—is carried out. Food and oxygen leak through the thin walls of the capillaries and enter the body cells. Wastes pass out of the body cells and enter the blood in the capillaries. Other materials transported by the blood can also leave and enter body cells at this time.

Figure 4–9 *Capillaries are so tiny that they permit only one red blood cell to squeeze through at a time. What is the function of a red blood cell?* ❸

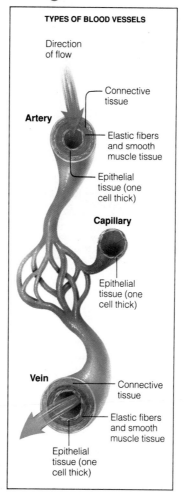

Figure 4–8 *The three types of blood vessels that make up the circulatory system are the arteries, capillaries, and veins. What is the function of each type of blood vessel?* ❶

TYPES OF BLOOD VESSELS

Direction of flow

Connective tissue

Artery

Elastic fibers and smooth muscle tissue

Epithelial tissue (one cell thick)

Capillary

Epithelial tissue (one cell thick)

Vein

Connective tissue

Elastic fibers and smooth muscle tissue

Epithelial tissue (one cell thick)

H ■ 87

FACTS AND FIGURES

KILOMETERS OF CAPILLARIES

Adding extra weight to your body can put an additional strain on your heart. It is estimated that each pound of fat requires 300 kilometers of capillaries to supply it.

INDEPENDENT PRACTICE

▶ *Multimedia* ◀

You may want to show the video called Circulatory System to reinforce the concepts of the circulation system. The video explores the structure of the heart, the relationship of the lymphatic system to the circulatory system, and the exchange of materials between the bloodstream and the body. After viewing the video, have groups of students design experiments using flexible plastic tubing and sphygmomanometers to demonstrate the concept of blood pressure and its relationship to the circulatory system.

Point out that arteries help to control the amount of blood that flows to different parts of the body. After eating, more blood is directed to the digestive system than to other parts of the body, such as the muscles and the brain. Although the brain always gets top priority, the blood supply (and food and oxygen supply) sent to the brain is somewhat reduced after eating. Therefore, you may feel drowsy.

CONTENT DEVELOPMENT

Point out that the body has millions of microscopic capillaries. These tiny capillaries connect the arteries and the veins. Capillaries branch off like small branches from the larger branches of trees. Stress that the principal function of blood circulation is carried out in the capillaries.

4-3 Blood—The River of Life

88 ■ H

MULTICULTURAL OPPORTUNITY 4-3

Have students research some blood diseases that have a cultural connection. For example, sickle cell anemia is much more common in the African-American culture than among other American cultures.

ESL STRATEGY 4-3

Introduce the word *role* as it pertains to work performed and have students write its definition in their ESL notebook. Ask students to substitute *role* for *job* or *function* when discussing the four main components of blood.

For extra practice, have volunteer students solve these mysteries:

What Am I?

1. I am the source of all red and most white blood cell production.

2. I am one of the three types of blood cells. I am not red or white. Actually, I have no color.

3. I am found in red blood cells, and I help to carry oxygen to all body cells and carbon dioxide back to the lungs.

4-2 (continued)

INDEPENDENT PRACTICE

Section Review 4-2

1. Blood leaves the right atrium and enters the right ventricle. The blood is then pumped to the lungs, where it picks up oxygen. The oxygenated blood returns to the heart and enters the left atrium. From there, it travels to the left ventricle and is pumped throughout the body. The blood eventually returns to the right atrium by way of veins.

2. Right and left atria, right and left ventricles.

3. Arteries, veins, and capillaries.

4. The thicker, more muscular walls are necessary because the ventricle pumps blood from the heart throughout the entire body.

5. Valves prevent blood from moving backward.

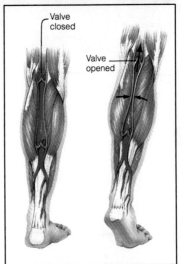

Figure 4-10 *Valves in the walls of veins prevent the backflow of blood and keep it moving in one direction—back to the heart. The contraction of nearby skeletal muscles such as those in the leg help the valves in performing this function.*

Guide for Reading

Focus on this question as you read.

▶ *What are the four main components of blood?*

REINFORCEMENT/RETEACHING

Review students' responses to the Section Review questions. Reteach any material that is still unclear, based on students' responses.

CLOSURE

▶ *Review and Reinforcement Guide*
Students may now complete Section 4-2 in the *Review and Reinforcement Guide*.

Veins: Pipelines to the Heart

Once the work of giving up oxygen and taking on wastes is completed in the capillaries, your trip through the circulatory maze is just about over. Because the blood has given up its oxygen, it is dark red again. The blood now starts back to the heart, trickling from the capillaries into blood vessels called **veins.** Veins carry blood back to the heart.

As you might expect, veins are much larger than capillaries. And unlike arteries, veins have thinner walls as well as tiny one-way valves. These valves help to keep the blood from flowing backward.

4-2 Section Review

1. Trace the path of blood through the circulatory system.
2. List the four chambers of the heart.
3. Describe the three types of blood vessels.
4. Explain why the walls of the ventricles are much thicker than the walls of the atria.

Critical Thinking—*Relating Facts*

5. Why is it important that veins contain valves?

4-3 Blood—The River of Life

If you were to look at blood under a microscope, you would see that it is made up of tiny particles floating in a fluid. This makes blood a fluid tissue—one of the body's two fluid tissues. Lymph (LIHMF) is the other. Recall from Chapter 1 that a tissue is a group of cells that work together for a specific function.

The fluid portion of the blood is called **plasma.** And the tiny particles floating in the plasma are different types of blood cells and cell fragments—three different types, to be exact. **The three different types of floating particles—red blood cells, white blood cells, and platelets—and the plasma in which they float, are the four main components of blood.**

TEACHING STRATEGY 4-3

FOCUS/MOTIVATION

Explain to students that the average person has about 6 liters of blood. Blood accounts for approximately 9 percent of a person's body weight.

Have each student determine how much his or her blood weighs. Blood weight is equal to the product of body weight and 9 percent, or 0.09.

Plasma

Plasma is a yellowish fluid that is about 90 percent water. The remaining 10 or so percent is made up of sugars, fats, salts, gases, and plasma proteins. The plasma proteins, which have a number of vital functions, are divided into three groups. One group of plasma proteins helps to regulate the amount of water entering and leaving the blood. The second group includes antibodies, which are special proteins

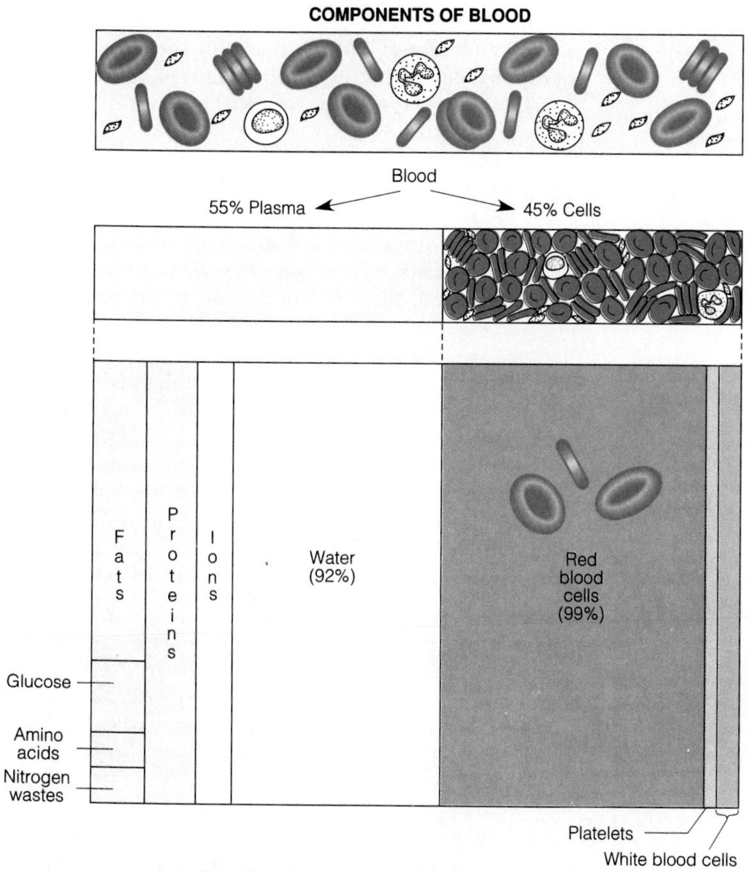

COMPONENTS OF BLOOD

Blood

55% Plasma ◄ ─────── ► 45% Cells

Fats

Proteins

Ions

Water (92%)

Red blood cells (99%)

Glucose

Amino acids

Nitrogen wastes

Platelets

White blood cells

Figure 4–11 *Blood is composed of a fluid portion called plasma and three different types of blood particles. Of what substance is plasma mainly composed?* ❶

BACKGROUND INFORMATION

A HEARTBEAT IS A WAVE OF CONTRACTIONS

The heart muscle does not contract in a single motion. The pumping of the heart is more efficient if the contraction moves in a wave. By squeezing from one end of a chamber to the other, blood can be pumped smoothly, much as toothpaste is squeezed from a tube.

CONTENT DEVELOPMENT

Point out that the fluid portion of the blood is called plasma. Floating in plasma are three different types of blood cells: red blood cells, white blood cells, and platelets. These three different types of blood cells, and the plasma they float in, make up the four main components of blood.

Also point out that blood is connective tissue. It does not stay in one place but connects different parts of the body, receiving and delivering various substances.

GUIDED PRACTICE

Skills Development

Skill: Making observations

Divide the class into teams of four to six students per team. Give each team a steel-wool pad. Have teams dip the steel-wool pad into water and set it in a dish for a day or two. Discuss the results.

• **What happened to the steel wool?** (The steel wool rusted and turned reddish brown.)

Have each group place the rusty steel wool into a beaker half-filled with water. Rinse the rusty pad in the water.

• **Why did the water turn reddish brown?** (The water coloring came from the iron, or steel.)

Point out that an iron pigment causes the blood to be red in our bodies as well. The iron pigment has a different shade of red (dark or bright) depending on the amount of oxygen in the blood.

MATHEMATICS

Have students work in groups. Provide them with the following information:

A cubic millimeter of blood contains about 5000 to 10,000 white blood cells, 300,000 to 400,000 platelets, and 4,200,000 (females) to 5,200,000 (males) red blood cells.

Encourage them to use additional information from the textbook, from their general knowledge of science, or from experiments to estimate the total number of blood cells in their body.

Have teams discuss and explain their results to the class.

Figure 4–12 *This photograph shows the three types of particles that make up blood. The red beret-shaped object is a red blood cell, the white fuzzy object is a white blood cell, and the yellow flattened object is a platelet. How do you think platelets got their name?* ❶

that help to fight off tiny invaders such as bacteria, viruses, and foreign substances. And the third group is responsible for blood clotting. The plasma also carries digested food, hormones (chemical messengers), and waste products.

Red Blood Cells

The most numerous cells in the blood are the **red blood cells.** Under a microscope, red blood cells look like round, flattened hats with thickened rims and flat centers—almost like tiny berets. The centers of these flexible red disks are so thin that they seem clear. This characteristic thinness enables red blood cells to bend at the center, a useful trick when trying to squeeze through a narrow capillary.

Red blood cells are produced in the bone marrow. A young red blood cell, like all living body cells, contains a nucleus. However, as the red blood cell matures, this nucleus grows smaller and smaller until it vanishes. Red blood cells pay a price for life

Figure 4–13 *In the bone marrow, a young red blood cell begins its life by filling up with hemoglobin and then getting rid of its nucleus (left). As the red blood cell moves into the bloodstream, it takes on its familiar disk shape (right).*

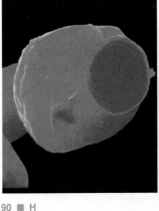

4–3 (continued)

CONTENT DEVELOPMENT

Have students observe Figure 4–13. Point out that these red blood cells have been magnified thousands of times.

• **What is the shape of a red blood cell?** (Accept all reasonable answers.)

Explain to students that the living part of blood contains three different kinds of cells. The most numerous cells are red blood cells. The red color is caused by

an iron-containing protein called hemoglobin. The function of hemoglobin is to bind to oxygen in the lungs and carry the oxygen to the body cells. The hemoglobin also helps to carry carbon dioxide back to the lungs.

Red blood cells have a life expectancy of about 120 days, or 4 months. One reason for this rather brief existence is that mature red blood cells lack nuclei. Like all cells, a nucleus is present when red blood cells are formed. The nucleus continues to grow smaller, however, as the cell grows.

When mature red blood cells are released into the bloodstream, they do not have a nucleus.

Point out that as red blood cells become old or damaged, they are removed from circulation in the liver and spleen. In fact, the spleen is sometimes called the cemetery of red blood cells. The liver removes the iron pigment (hemoglobin) from dead red blood cells. The hemoglobin is later transported to the bone marrow, where new red blood cells are manufactured.

without a nucleus. They are very delicate and have a life span of only 120 days. Red blood cells in your body are at this moment dying at a rate of about 2 million per second. Fortunately, new red blood cells are being formed in the bone marrow at the same rate. When a red blood cell wears out or is damaged, it is broken down in the liver and the spleen, an organ just to the left of the stomach. So many red blood cells are destroyed in the spleen each day that this organ has been called the "cemetery" of red blood cells.

Have you ever heard people complain that they have "iron-poor" blood? That phrase refers to a shortage of an iron-containing protein called **hemoglobin** (HEE-muh-gloh-bihn), which is found in red blood cells. In fact, it is the buildup of hemoglobin in the red blood cells that forces out the nucleus. As blood flows through the lungs, oxygen in the lungs binds to hemoglobin in the red blood cells. As blood is transported throughout the body, oxygen is delivered to all body cells. Hemoglobin also helps to carry some carbon dioxide wastes back to the lungs.

White Blood Cells

Outnumbered almost 500 to 1 by red blood cells, **white blood cells** make up in their size and life span what they lack in their numbers. White blood cells are larger than red blood cells—some are even twice the size of red blood cells. And although certain kinds of white blood cells live for only a few hours, most can last for months or even years!

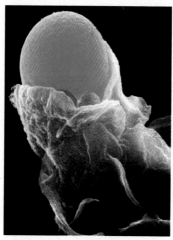

Figure 4–14 *A red blood cell will remain in the bloodstream for about 120 days, at which time the red blood cell will be digested by a white blood cell.*

Figure 4–15 *White blood cells are larger than red blood cells (left). The main function of white blood cells is to protect the body against attack by invaders such as bacteria, which are the two small rod-shaped structures in this photograph (right).*

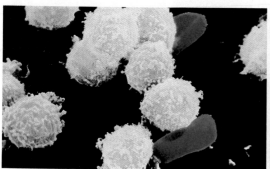

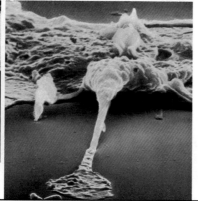

FACTS AND FIGURES
RED BLOOD CELLS

Red blood cells are extremely small. They are only about 7 microns in diameter. More than 3000 red blood cells could be placed side by side in the space of 2.52 centimeters.

CONTENT DEVELOPMENT

Tell students to think of white blood cells as their defense system—their own private army.

• **What does an army do?** (Lead students to suggest that an army protects against unwanted invaders.)

• **Do you think you have an army, or defense system, in your body?** (Accept all logical answers.)

• **What do you think this defense system might be?** (Accept all logical answers.)

Explain that white blood cells attack and kill invading organisms, such as bacteria and viruses. White blood cells are carried by the blood to the site of an invasion. They then move through the thin capillary walls and into or around body cells.

Like red blood cells, white blood cells are also made in the bone marrow. Unlike red blood cells, white blood cells are made in other parts of the body as well. Also unlike red blood cells, white blood cells have a nucleus; in fact, some white blood cells have several nuclei.

There are approximately 700 times as many red blood cells as white blood cells in the human body. Some white blood cells, however, are twice as large as red blood cells—and some can live for years.

• **If a doctor tells you that your white blood count is elevated or high, what might this mean?** (An elevated white blood count is often a sign of infectious disease. White blood cells are being produced by the body in great numbers to combat the infection.)

BLOOD CLOTTING
CHAIN REACTION

The actual reactions involved in blood clotting are extremely complicated. When a blood vessel is broken, the damaged tissue releases a protein factor known as thromboplastin. Thromboplastin helps to convert prothrombin into thrombin. Prothrombin is found in the blood plasma. Thrombin, which is formed from prothrombin, is an enzyme that converts still another plasma protein, fibrinogen, into fibrin. This threadlike chemical, fibrin, forms a sort of net over the cut to trap blood particles and plasma.

Like red blood cells, most white blood cells develop in the bone marrow. However, unlike red blood cells, white blood cells do not lose their nuclei when they mature. The main function of white blood cells is to protect the body against attack by tiny invaders such as bacteria, viruses, or other foreign substances. Quickly carried by blood to areas under seige, white blood cells can attack invaders in a variety of ways. Some white blood cells surround and digest the invaders. Others make antibodies. Still others produce special chemicals that help the body fight off disease. You will learn more about white blood cells and their role in protecting the body against invaders in Chapter 8.

Platelets

Have you ever wondered what happens inside a blood vessel when you cut yourself? Why doesn't all your blood ooze out of your body? The answer has to do with the third kind of blood particle, **platelets.** As soon as a blood vessel is cut, platelets begin to collect around the cut. When they touch the rough surface of the torn blood vessel, they burst apart, releasing chemicals that set off a series of reactions. One of these reactions produces a chemical called

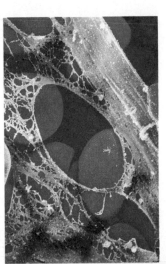
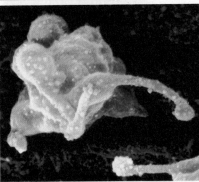
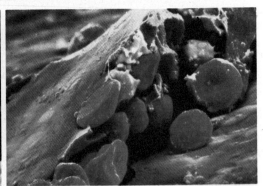

Figure 4–16 *When a blood vessel is punctured (bottom right), blood particles called platelets (bottom left) release chemicals that set off a series of reactions to help stop the flow of blood from the body. One of these reactions produces a threadlike chemical called fibrin that forms a net over the cut to trap blood particles and plasma (top).*

92 ■ H

4–3 (continued)

CONTENT DEVELOPMENT

Tell students that one of the protective mechanisms of the blood is the process of clotting.

• **Why do we call clotting a protective mechanism?** (Lead students to suggest that we would bleed to death from a small cut if blood did not clot.)

Have students observe Figure 4–16. Explain that a third kind of cell in whole

blood is the platelet. Platelets are tiny cells, actually bits of cells, that live for about 10 days. As soon as a blood vessel has been cut, platelets begin to collect around the cut. Platelets then release an enzyme that acts on other substances in the blood to create fibrin. Fibrin is a substance that causes the platelets to clump together. Fibrin causes tiny fibers to form. These fibers and the clumped platelets stop the flow of blood from the cut.

Draw the interconnecting threads of woven material on the chalkboard. Ex-

plain that the blood cells are trapped in the fibrin threads. Eventually, a clot builds up, trapped in the fibers. A scab is a blood clot that forms on the skin's surface.

GUIDED PRACTICE

Skills Development

Skill: Making observations

Divide students into groups of two to four students per group. Distribute a microscope and a prepared slide of human blood to each group. Have students ob-

fibrin (FIGH-brihn). Fibrin gets its name from the fact that it weaves tiny fibers across the cut in the blood vessel. These fibers act as a net to trap blood cells and plasma. See Figure 4–16.

Eventually, the plasma hardens and forms a clot. Although you may not realize it, you are probably quite familiar with blood clots and the clotting process. Anytime your body forms a scab in response to a cut or a scrape, you are experiencing the clotting process. A scab, you see, is a clot that forms on the surface of your skin.

Platelets are so named because they resemble tiny plates. Actually, platelets are not cells but rather fragments of cells. They have no nucleus or color. These fragments break away from large cells, which are produced in bone marrow, and enter the bloodstream. There they remain for no more than ten days. But in that short time, these cell fragments may save a life by helping to form leak-sealing clots!

Blood Groups

In the seventeenth century, the French scientist Jean-Baptiste Denis tried to transfer blood from lambs to humans. This process of transferring blood from one body to another is called a transfusion.

Were Denis's transfusions successful? No, they were not. But it was not until 300 years later that the American scientist Karl Landsteiner learned why Denis's transfusions failed. By mixing the plasma of one person with the red blood cells of another, Landsteiner discovered that in some cases the two blended smoothly. However, in other cases, the cells did not mix but instead clumped (stuck together). As you might expect, such clumping inside the body clogs the capillaries—a dangerous and sometimes deadly situation. Landsteiner found that the clue to the behavior was the way human red blood cells containing certain proteins on their outer coats reacted to plasma containing different proteins. These proteins in the plasma are called clumping chemicals. Lansteiner identified the proteins in the red blood cells as A and B, and those in the plasma as anti A and anti B. Anti A and anti B were so named because of their reactions against the presence of protein A and/or protein B.

FIND OUT BY **WRITING**

Blood Donating Center

Visit a local blood donating center. Interview a nurse or doctor to find out what techniques are used to screen potential donors. In a written report, include this information as well as what happens to the blood after it is donated.

H ■ 93

FIND OUT BY WRITING

BLOOD DONATING CENTER

Check each report for scientific accuracy and to determine whether students have correctly identified both the techniques that are used to screen potential blood donors and what happens to blood after donation. You may want to alert the language arts teacher of this assignment and have that teacher grade the reports as well.

Integration: Use the Find Out by Writing feature to integrate language arts into your science lesson.

---

serve the prepared slide under high magnification, then sketch and label the three types of cells they observed.
• **Which blood cells were the most abundant?** (Red blood cells.)
• **Which blood cells were the least abundant?** (White blood cells.)
• **Which blood cells were largest?** (White blood cells.)
• **Describe the general shape of red and white blood cells and platelets.** (Answers will vary.)

CONTENT DEVELOPMENT

Students might be surprised to learn that blood transfusions were tried as early as the seventeenth century. Jean-Baptiste Denis tried to transfer blood from lambs to humans. The process was not successful.
• **Why do you think the lambs' blood did not mix successfully with human blood?** (Lead students to realize that lambs' blood contains different proteins than human blood does.)

Tell students about another early researcher, Karl Landsteiner. Landsteiner classified blood into four groups, or types: A, B, AB, and O. Blood is typed according to the kind of proteins that are attached to the outer coat of the red blood cells. For example, people with type A blood have an A protein attached to the outer coat of each red blood cell.
• **What kind of protein is attached to the red blood cells of type B blood?** (Type B protein.)
• **What kind of protein is attached to the red blood cells of type AB blood?** (Both A and B proteins.)
• **What kind of protein is attached to the red blood cells of type O blood?** (Neither A nor B proteins.)

● ● ● ● Integration ● ● ● ●

Use the historical information in the textbook to integrate social studies into your science lesson.

ARTIFICIAL BLOOD

Can blood be manufactured from natural substances found on Earth? The answer is yes! Artificial blood is a synthetic compound containing the elements fluorine and carbon. Using reference materials, encourage students to find out about artificial blood. Volunteers can make an oral report to the class about their findings. Have students explain how artificial blood helps researchers understand more about the circulatory system and how artificial blood has been of direct benefit to some people.

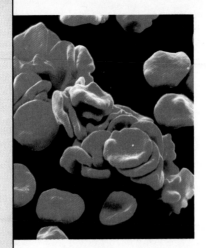

Figure 4–17 *When a person with group B blood receives a transfusion of, for example, group A blood, anti-A chemicals in the group B plasma recognize the group A red cells as foreign. As a result, the red blood cells from the group A blood will clump, or stick together, and possibly clog some of the body's important blood vessels.*

The presence or absence of protein A and/or protein B on the outer coat of every red blood cell in a person's blood determines the person's blood group. People with group A blood have red blood cells that contain protein A. People with group B blood have red blood cells that contain protein B. People with group AB blood have red blood cells that contain both proteins. And, as you might expect, people with group O blood have red blood cells that contain neither protein. On the basis of whether one or both of these proteins were present or absent in the blood, Landsteiner classified human blood into four basic groups, or types: A, B, AB, and O. He named this the ABO blood group.

Why are blood groups so important? Sometimes as a result of injury or illness a person loses quite a bit of blood and is too weak to produce more. In such instances, a blood transfusion is needed. But before a blood transfusion can be performed, blood from the donor (person giving blood) and the recipient (person receiving blood) must be tested to determine if the blood groups are compatible (similar to each other).

If blood groups that are not compatible are mixed, the red blood cells of the dissimilar blood group will clump together. Such clumps can cause fatal blockages in blood vessels. This is where the clumping chemicals (anti A and anti B) in the plasma come in. Refer to Figure 4–18 as you read about each blood group.

The plasma of people with group O blood, for example, contains both the anti-A and the anti-B chemical. The anti-A chemical causes red blood cells containing protein A to clump together, whereas the anti-B chemical causes red blood cells containing protein B to clump together. Thus people with group O blood can safely receive only group O blood. People with group A blood produce the anti-B chemical. The anti-B chemical causes red blood cells containing protein B to clump together. So people with group A blood can safely receive group A blood. The plasma of people with group AB blood does not contain either the anti-A or the anti-B chemical. Therefore, people with group AB blood can safely receive groups A, B, and O blood, as well as group AB blood.

4–3 (continued)

CONTENT DEVELOPMENT

Explain to students that blood may also produce chemicals against other blood proteins. For example, type B blood produces chemicals called anti A, which cause red blood cells with the A protein to clump together, or clot.

Have students examine Figure 4–18.

• **What kinds of chemicals are produced by type O blood?** (Type O blood produces anti-A and anti-B chemicals.)

• **If a transfusion of type A were given to a person with type O blood, what would happen?** (The A proteins in the blood would react with the anti-A chemicals. The blood would clot. The person might die.)

• **If you have type B blood, from whom can you safely receive a transfusion?** (From persons with type B or type O blood.)

• **If you have type O blood, from whom can you safely receive a transfusion?** (From person with type O blood.)

Explain that type O blood is sometimes called the universal donor.

• **Why do you think type O blood received the name "universal donor"?** (Because it can be given safely to all blood types. People with type O blood can safely donate blood to those with types A, B, AB, and O.)

• **Which blood type is called the universal recipient?** (Type AB, because it can safely receive all blood types without clumping or clotting occurring.)

CONTENT DEVELOPMENT

Karl Landsteiner, along with Alexander Wiener, discovered another group of proteins in human blood. These proteins are found also in the blood of rhesus monkeys.

ABO BLOOD SYSTEM			
Blood Group	**Proteins on Red Blood Cells**	**Clumping Chemicals in Plasma**	**Can Accept Transfusions from Group(s)**
A	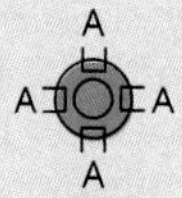	Anti B	A, O
B	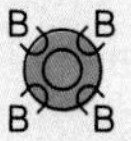	Anti A	B, O
AB	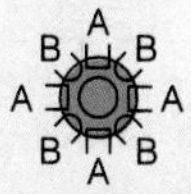	None	A, B, AB, O
O	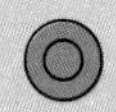	Anti A Anti B	O

Figure 4–18 *Each blood group is characterized by the protein on the red blood cells and the clumping chemical in the plasma. What protein does group AB blood have?* (1)

Several years after the discovery of the ABO blood group, Landsteiner and the American scientist Alexander Wiener discovered another group of about 18 proteins on the surface of human red blood cells. Because Landsteiner and Wiener first found this group of proteins in the rhesus monkey, they named the proteins the Rh blood group. You may be surprised to know that if a person has any one of the 18 Rh proteins, they are said to be Rh positive, or Rh^+. Those who do not have any of the Rh proteins in their blood are Rh negative, or Rh^-.

4–3 Section Review

1. List the four main components of whole blood.
2. What is plasma?
3. What is hemoglobin? What is its function?
4. Name, describe, and give the function of each of the three types of blood particles.

Critical Thinking—*Relating Facts*

5. Why do you think group O blood was once called the universal donor?

ANNOTATION KEY

Answers

(1) Proteins A and B. (Interpreting charts)

BACKGROUND INFORMATION

VELOCITY OF BLOOD FLOW

The velocity of blood flow in the human body is generalized in this way: When a continuous flow of blood moves through connected tubes (arteries, veins, and capillaries), the velocity of the flow decreases as some of the areas of the tubes increases. Stated another way, blood velocity is very great in the aorta. It progressively slows in the arteries and then in the veins, slowing markedly as it flows through the huge area of the capillaries. The significance of slow blood flow through the capillaries is very great: Blood flows through the capillaries so slowly that there is enough time for exchange of nutrients and waste products.

These proteins were named the Rh factor after the first two letters in *rhesus.*

Explain to students that people who have the Rh factor are said to be Rh positive. Those who do not are called Rh negative. If an Rh-negative person receives Rh-positive blood, clumping chemicals may form and cause a clotting reaction. Thus, the Rh factor is also an important consideration in transfusions.

INDEPENDENT PRACTICE

Section Review 4–3

1. Red blood cells, white blood cells, plasma, platelets.
2. Plasma is the liquid portion of blood.
3. Hemoglobin is an iron-containing protein. It transports oxygen to the body and carbon dioxide to the lungs.
4. Red blood cells are thin and numerous; they transport oxygen and carbon dioxide. White blood cells are larger and less numerous than red blood cells; they fight infection. Platelets are more numerous than white blood cells but less numerous than red blood cells; they help in blood clotting.
5. Group O blood could be given to any other blood type via transfusion.

REINFORCEMENT/RETEACHING

Monitor students' responses to the Section Review questions. If students appear to have difficulty with any of the questions, review the appropriate material in the section.

CLOSURE

▶ *Review and Reinforcement Guide*

At this point have students complete Section 4–3 in the *Review and Reinforcement Guide.*

4-4 Cardiovascular Diseases

MULTICULTURAL OPPORTUNITY 4-4

We often think about disease as being a factor of poverty, and many poor people are at risk of disease because of living conditions and lack of access to quality medical care. Some diseases, however, are diseases of the affluent. Hypertension and atherosclerosis are two examples of diseases that are more common among those who have high-pressure jobs and high-pressure lifestyles. Have students investigate other diseases that are connected to an individual's lifestyle.

ESL STRATEGY 4-4

To enrich students understanding of the word *cardiovascular*, explain that it is taken from a Greek word meaning "heart" and a Latin word that when referring to the heart means "a tube for circulating blood."

After discussing the role cholesterol plays in cardiovascular disease, have students collect as many labels of food products as possible that show cholesterol content. This will help them become aware of the variation in cholesterol levels that exist in everyday foods.

Guide for Reading

Focus on this question as you read.

▶ What are the effects of atherosclerosis and high blood pressure on the circulatory system?

4-4 Cardiovascular Diseases

Today, people are living longer than they have at any time in the past. But as people's life expectancies have increased, so have the numbers of people who suffer from chronic disorders. Chronic disorders, which are lingering (lasting) illnesses, are a major health problem in the United States. Usually developing over a long time, chronic disorders also last a long time. In terms of numbers of people affected, **cardiovascular** (kahr-dee-oh-VAS-kyoo-ler) **diseases** are the most serious chronic disorders. **Cardiovascular diseases, such as atherosclerosis** (ath-er-oh-skluh-ROH-sihs) **and high blood pressure, affect the heart and the blood vessels.**

Atherosclerosis

One of the most common cardiovascular diseases in the United States today is **atherosclerosis.** Atherosclerosis is the thickening of the inner wall of an artery. For this reason, atherosclerosis is sometimes known as hardening of the arteries. This thickening occurs as certain fatlike substances in the blood, such as cholesterol, slowly collect on the artery wall. Gradually, the inside of the artery becomes narrower and narrower. As a result, the normal movement of the blood through the artery is reduced or, in some cases, totally blocked.

Figure 4-19 *A high-fat diet has caused fat droplets, which are the large yellow objects in this photograph, to become deposited on the inside wall of an artery. As more of these fat droplets accumulate inside the artery, it becomes narrower, causing the cardiovascular disease known as atherosclerosis.*

TEACHING STRATEGY 4-4

FOCUS/MOTIVATION

Have students use colored paper and scissors to cut out a paper heart. The heart can be any color and size.

After students have finished, have them take several minutes to write as many reasons as they can think of for heart disease on their paper hearts. The paper hearts can then be passed to others, and a list of contributing factors of heart disease can be written on the chalkboard.

CONTENT DEVELOPMENT

Every time we eat, we provide our bodies with some of the nutrients we need for healthy bodies. At the same time, some things we eat can be harmful to the human body. Cholesterol is one substance in our diet that can be harmful if it is eaten in excessive amounts.

Cholesterol is a soft, fatlike substance found in our bloodstreams among fats called lipids. A major factor of heart disease and atherosclerosis is a high level of these fats (including cholesterol), or lipids, in the bloodstream.

Cholesterol is necessary for the production of certain hormones and the development of new cells. It is produced naturally by our bodies in the liver. Generally speaking, the liver produces sufficient quantities of cholesterol to maintain a healthy body. The problem is that we sometimes eat additional cholesterol in our diet, and this cholesterol combined with the cholesterol naturally produced in the liver adds up to too much cholesterol in the body.

Too much cholesterol and other fats in the bloodstream can affect the heart in a negative way. Cholesterol and fats tend

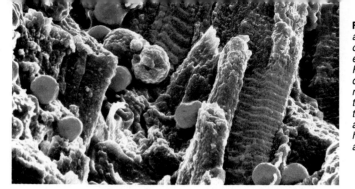

Figure 4–20 *A heart attack occurs when heart cells do not receive enough oxygen. Following a heart attack, dead muscle tissue replaces healthy muscle tissue. In this photograph, the dead muscle tissue appears brown, and the healthy muscle tissue appears red.*

If the flow of blood to a certain part of the body is reduced, the cells served by that blood may die. For example, if blood flow in the arteries of the heart is either partially or totally cut off, the heart cells will begin to die, and a heart attack may occur. If a blockage occurs in the arteries of the brain, a stroke may occur.

Atherosclerosis is often thought of as a chronic disorder affecting only older people. But it actually begins much earlier in life. By the age of 20, most people have some degree of atherosclerosis. For this reason, it is important to develop good eating habits and a proper exercise program to prevent atherosclerosis from becoming severe.

Many doctors suggest avoiding or limiting the intake of foods rich in fats and cholesterol. Such foods include red meats and dairy products. However, these foods are needed by the body in small amounts. So a person who wants to be sure that he or she gets these foods in their proper amounts should eat a sensibly balanced diet.

Even with proper diet and exercise, there is no guarantee that atherosclerosis and the problems associated with it can be avoided totally. Fortunately, more research and progress has occurred in the treatment of cardiovascular diseases than in any other area of medicine. For example, heart bypass operations have become commonplace. In this operation, a healthy blood vessel from the leg is removed and used to bypass damaged arteries serving the heart. In this way, blood flow to heart cells is increased.

FIND OUT BY CALCULATING

Pumping Power

If the heart of an average person pumps about 9000 liters of blood daily, how much blood will be pumped in an hour? In a year?

H ■ 97

to "stick" or build up on the walls of blood vessels. Point out that this buildup is similar to the buildup seen in old plumbing pipes. Plumbing pipes close over time, as do our blood vessels from cholesterol and fats. This narrowing of blood vessels, called atherosclerosis, prevents oxygen-carrying blood from reaching the heart. The result can be severe chest pain and eventually heart attack.

● ● ● ● **Integration** ● ● ● ●

Use the discussion of foods rich in fats and cholesterol to integrate food science concepts into your science lesson.

GUIDED PRACTICE

Skills Development

Skills: Relating concepts

Have students examine Figure 4–19. Explain that fatty substances in the blood, called lipids, usually travel through arteries without ever attaching to the side walls.

But these lipids, including cholesterol, can attach themselves to artery walls over time, and as the buildup thickens, the inside of the artery becomes smaller and smaller. This narrowing reduces the flow of blood and thus does not allow cells served by this blood to receive oxygen. When cells do not receive oxygen, they die.

Cardiovascular diseases affect the heart and blood vessels. *Cardio-* means "heart" and *vascular* means "vessels."

This feature enables students to relate the concept of heart attacks to cardiovascular diseases. Students should determine the following answers from this activity:

1. Answers may vary; possible answers include the data resembles a clock because the activity is focusing on time of day.
2. Approximately 700.
3. Greatest: 6 AM to 2 PM; least: 10 PM to midnight.
4. Morning.
• Answers will vary; answers should reflect a decision about the relationship of heart attacks to the time of day, then support that decision.

Integration: Use the Problem Solving feature to integrate mathematics concepts into your lesson.

PROBLEM ? ? ?
Solving

Are Heart Attacks Influenced by the Time of Day?

Whenever blood flow to the arteries of the heart is partially or totally cut off, the heart cells begin to die and a heart attack may occur. Does the time of day have an effect on the frequency of heart attacks? To help answer this question, researchers have interviewed people who have had heart attacks. Some of the data from these interviews are contained in the accompanying graph.

Analyzing Graphs

1. Why do you think the graph was drawn in this particular shape?

2. Approximately how many heart attack patients are represented in this study?

3. At which hour(s) of the day did the greatest number of heart attacks occur? The least number of heart attacks?

4. Did heart attacks tend to occur more often in the morning, afternoon, or evening?

■ Based on the data, do you think there is a relationship between time of day and frequency of heart attacks? Explain your answer.

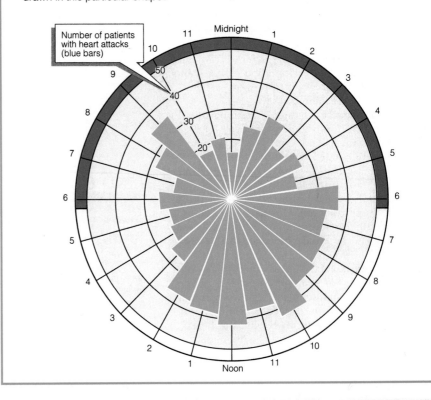

4–4 (continued)

CONTENT DEVELOPMENT

Hypertension, or high blood pressure, currently afflicts about 40 million Americans. It is interesting to note that hypertension is extremely rare in children, yet it is found in approximately 20 percent of the adult population over the age of 40.

Most physicians agree that factors in our lifestyles such as lack of exercise and poor diets, which cause clogging of our arteries, are prime causes of hypertension. Considering that clogging of arteries is directly attributed to diet, it can be said that diet is one of the primary causes of hypertension.

Hypertension is a serious problem because it is often associated with an increased risk of heart disease and an increased risk of fatal heart attacks and strokes. Hypertension is sometimes called the silent killer because its symptoms are not obvious.

In terms of diet, the causes of hypertension include excessive salt intake, excessive consumption of calories, and alcohol consumption. Obesity and smoking are also contributors. These factors, which are known to contribute to hypertension, should be reduced or eliminated from our diets and lifestyles to lessen the likelihood of hypertension.

● ● ● ● **Integration** ● ● ● ●

Use the discussion about water pressure to integrate the physical science concepts of fluid forces into your lesson.

Unfortunately, even after having a bypass operation, some people may still have heart attacks. Until recently, doctors did not completely understand why this happened. Now a group of doctors have proposed an explanation for these mysterious heart attacks. The doctors think that the heart arteries have a memory. That is, the arteries themselves try to recreate the type of blood flow that they were used to when they were clogged. Not all doctors are convinced that this theory is correct. However, they do believe that the arteries-with-a-memory theory may shed some light on what is happening.

Hypertension

If you have ever used a garden hose, you know that you can increase the water pressure inside the hose in two ways. The first way is to turn up the flow of water at the faucet. Because there is more water, the water flows out of the hose with more force. The second way is to decrease the size of the opening of the nozzle. In this case, the water pressure in the hose is a result of both the force of the water rushing through the hose and the resistance of the walls of the hose to the flow of water.

You can compare the flow of water in the garden hose to the flow of blood in the blood vessels. Just as the force of the water through the hose is controlled by how much you turn up the faucet, the force of the blood through the blood vessels is controlled by the pumping action of the heart. And because blood vessel walls are similar to the walls of a hose, any change in the diameter of the blood vessel walls causes a change in blood pressure. As you can see, blood pressure is produced by the force of blood through the blood vessels and the resistance of the blood vessel walls to the flow of blood.

In order to measure a person's blood pressure, an instrument called a sphygmomanometer (sfihg-moh-muh-NAHM-uht-er) is used. This instrument actually records two readings—the first when the heart contracts and the second when the heart relaxes. Using these two measurements, the blood pressure measurement is expressed as a fraction— for example, 120/80, which is read as "120 over 80." The first number (120) is the measurement of the

4–4 (continued)

CONTENT DEVELOPMENT

Remind students that a slight rise in blood pressure can be caused by excitement and/or exercise. But if blood pressure remains high for a long period of time, it is considered abnormal. This hypertension, or high blood pressure, can lead to blood vessel damage and other serious complications.

Also stress that high blood pressure usually has no symptoms or warning signs.

GUIDED PRACTICE

Skills Development

Skill: Applying concepts

Ask the following questions to reinforce the concepts of cardiovascular disease:

Figure 4–21 *Hypertension occurs when too much pressure builds up in the arteries. If this condition continues and goes untreated, damage to the walls of the arteries, to the heart, and to other organs may occur. What is another name for hypertension?* **1**

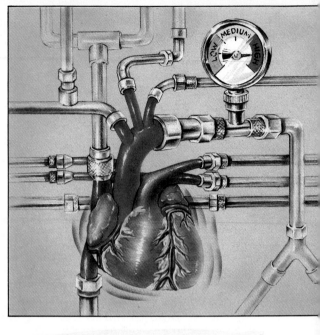

FIND OUT BY WRITING

Blood Pressure

1 Visit a library and look up information on what the two numbers of a blood pressure reading, such as 110/70, mean. In a written report, explain how a sphygmomanometer works. Explain what is meant by systole and diastole.

100 ■ H

---

blood pressure when the heart muscle contracts. The second number (80) is the measurement of the blood pressure when the heart muscle relaxes between beats. Why do you think the first number is larger than the second number? **2**

Normally, blood pressure rises and falls from day to day and hour to hour. Sometimes, however, blood pressure goes up and remains above the normal level. This condition is called **hypertension,** or high blood pressure. The increased pressure makes the heart work harder and may cause leaks to develop in the blood vessels.

Because people with hypertension often have no obvious symptoms to warn them, hypertension is often called the "silent killer." This is why it is important for a person to have his or her blood pressure checked at least once a year. If a person does have hypertension, a doctor may suggest a few changes in the person's lifestyle. These changes may include watching one's weight, reducing the amount of salt in the diet, eating more sensibly, and exercising regularly. In some cases, medicines may also be taken to lower the blood pressure.

• **How does diet contribute to increased cholesterol levels in the bloodstream?** (A diet that is high in fats will increase the level of fats, or cholesterol, in the bloodstream.)

• **How does a fatty diet contribute to hypertension, or high blood pressure?** (Cholesterol tends to clog, or clump, in the arteries, decreasing the effective capacity of that artery. This translates directly to higher blood pressure, or hypertension.)

• **Explain how cholesterol is both beneficial and harmful to the human body.** (The human body needs relatively small amounts of cholesterol to produce various hormones and to promote cell development. The cholesterol that is needed is produced by the liver. Excessive cholesterol in the bloodstream, resulting from a poor choice of diet, results in the clogging of arteries.)

• **Explain how obesity is harmful to the circulatory system.** (Answers will vary; students might suggest that the heart has

CONNECTIONS

It's All in a Heartbeat ❷

When you think of *electric currents* (flows of electric charges), electrical appliances and wall outlets probably come to mind. So it may surprise you to learn that your body produces electric currents as well.

The heart, for example, produces electric currents in order to function properly. These electric currents are so powerful that they can be picked up by an instrument called an electrocardiograph. An electrocardiograph is one of a doctor's most important tools in helping to diagnose heart disorders. It translates the electric currents produced by the beating of the heart muscle into wavy lines on paper or a TV-type screen. This record of wavy lines is called an electrocardiogram, and it is often abbreviated as ECG or EKG.

An ECG is made by attaching electrodes (strips of metal that conduct electric currents) to the skin of a patient's chest, arms, and legs. The electrodes pick up the electric currents produced by the heartbeat and send them to an amplifier inside the electrocardiograph. An amplifier is a device that increases the strength of the electric currents. The amplified currents then flow through a fine wire that is suspended in a magnetic field. As the electric currents react with the magnetic field, they move the wire.

The wire's motion is eventually recorded on a moving paper chart in the form of an ECG. A normal heartbeat produces an ECG with a specific pattern of waves; heart disorders change the pattern. By examining the change in pattern, a doctor can identify the type of heart disorder.

4–4 Section Review

1. What is a cardiovascular disease?
2. How do atherosclerosis and hypertension affect the circulatory system?

Connection—*Physical Education*
3. Predict two ways in which a regular exercise program could help a person with cardiovascular disease.

ANNOTATION KEY

Answers

❶ High blood pressure. (Applying definitions)

❷ Pressure during a contraction is greater than pressure during relaxation. (Relating concepts)

Integration

❶ Language Arts

❷ Physical Science: Electricity. See *Electricity and Magnetism,* Chapter 1.

CONNECTIONS

IT'S ALL IN A HEARTBEAT

Students will be interested to learn that the heart produces electric currents to function properly and that these currents can be "read" by an electrocardiograph machine. Many students may not have previously connected the relationship of electricity to the circulatory system, and you might want to discuss the scientific concepts in the article carefully to ensure that all students understand this relationship. Interested students may want to research heart pacemakers and report to the class.

If you are teaching thematically, you may want to use the Connections feature to reinforce the themes of energy, scale and structure, systems and interactions, and stability.

Integration: Use the Connections feature to integrate the physical science concepts of electricity into your lesson.

---

more work to do and must work harder because of the many extra kilometers of blood vessels.

• **Explain how lack of exercise is harmful to the human body.** (Answers will vary; students might suggest that the heart, being a muscle, will grow stronger through cardiovascular exercise and weaker through lack of exercise.

• **What are things you can do to decrease your risk of cardiovascular disease?** (Answers will vary; lead students toward the concept of a healthful lifestyle.)

INDEPENDENT PRACTICE

Section Review 4–4

1. Cardiovascular disease is a deterioration of the cardiovascular (heart and circulatory) system.

2. Atherosclerosis and hypertension make the function of the circulatory system and heart more difficult to complete.

3. Predictions will vary; check each prediction for scientific accuracy.

REINFORCEMENT/RETEACHING

Review students' responses to the Section Review questions. Reteach any material that is still unclear, based on students' responses.

CLOSURE

Review and Reinforcement Guide
Students may now complete Section 4–4 in the *Review and Reinforcement Guide.*

Laboratory Investigation

MEASURING YOUR PULSE RATE

BEFORE THE LAB

1. Discuss with the school nurse if any of your students has a heart problem.
2. Gather all materials at least one day prior to the investigation.

PRE-LAB DISCUSSION

Have students read the complete laboratory procedure.

Caution students who have had any kind of heart problem not to participate in the active portions of this investigation. These students can serve as monitors.

Discuss the terms *average* and *normal* with students. Make it very clear that many students will not necessarily fall within class averages but that their pulse rate is probably normal for them.

• **Does the fact that your pulse rate is not near an average indicate that you have a heart problem?** (Not necessarily.)

• **Under what conditions might someone with a pulse rate not near an average have a possible heart problem?** (Students whose pulse rate far exceeds 100 beats per minute probably should consult a physician.)

Discuss with students the idea that stress, even the stress associated with performing this experiment, may cause pulse rate to be elevated beyond its normal rate.

Laboratory Investigation

Measuring Your Pulse Rate

Problem

What are the effects of activity on pulse rate?

Materials *(per group)*

> clock or watch with a sweep second hand
> graph paper

Procedure

1. On a separate sheet of paper, construct a data table similar to the one shown here.
2. To locate your pulse, place the index and middle finger of one hand on your other wrist where it joins the base of your thumb. Move the two fingers slightly until you locate your pulse.
3. To determine your pulse rate, have one member of your group time you for 1 minute. During the 1 minute, count the number of beats in your pulse. Record this number in the data table.
4. Walk in place for 1 minute. Then take your pulse. Record the result.
5. Run in place for 1 minute. Again take your pulse. Record the result.
6. Sit down and rest for 1 minute. Take your pulse. Then take your pulse again after 3 minutes. Record the results in the data table.
7. Use the data to construct a bar graph that compares each activity and the pulse rate you determined.

Observations

1. What pulse rate did you record in step 3 of the Procedure? This is called your pulse rate at rest. How does your pulse rate at rest compare with those of the other members of your group? (Do not be alarmed if your pulse rate is somewhat different from those of other students. Individual pulse rates vary.)
2. What effect did walking have on your pulse rate? Running?
3. What effect did resting after running have on your pulse rate?

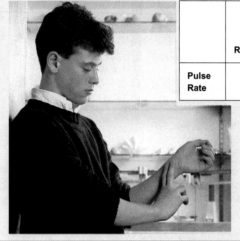

	Resting	Walking	Running	Resting After Exercise (1 min)	Resting After Exercise (3 min)
Pulse Rate					

Analysis and Conclusions

1. What conclusions can you draw from your data?
2. How is pulse rate related to heartbeat?
3. What happens to the blood supply to the muscles during exercise? How is this related to the change in pulse rate?

TEACHING STRATEGY

Circulate through the classroom, showing students how to find their pulse rate. Many students may need help in finding their pulse.

DISCOVERY STRATEGIES

Discuss how the investigation relates to the chapter by asking open questions similar to the following:

• **Are relatively minor fluctuations in pulse rate normal?** (Yes, depending on the activity—applying facts.)

• **Why does your pulse rate increase and your heart work harder when you exercise?** (During exercise, the oxygen requirements of your body increase. Oxygen must be transported to these active areas of the body, and the waste products created must be removed from the bloodstream—comparing, relating.)

• **How does exercise serve to strengthen the heart?** (Careful, controlled exercise strengthens the heart because the heart is a muscle, and muscles increase in

Study Guide

Summarizing Key Concepts

4–1 The Body's Transportation System

▲ The main task of the circulatory system is to transport materials through the body.

▲ Among the materials carried by the circulatory system are oxygen, carbon dioxide, food, wastes, disease-fighting cells, and chemical messengers.

4–2 Circulation in the Body

▲ Blood moves from the heart to the lungs and back to the heart. Then the blood travels to all the cells of the body and returns again to the heart.

▲ A wall of tissue called the septum divides the heart into a right and a left side.

▲ The two upper collecting chambers of the heart are called atria. The two lower pumping chambers of the heart are called ventricles. Valves between the atria and ventricles keep blood from flowing backward.

▲ Arteries carry blood away from the heart. Veins carry blood back to the heart. Capillaries connect the arteries and veins. Materials leave and enter the blood through the walls of the capillaries.

4–3 Blood—The River of Life

▲ The four main components of blood are plasma, red blood cells, white blood cells, and platelets.

▲ Plasma, which is mainly water, is the yellowish fluid portion of blood. Red blood cells, white blood cells, and platelets make up the solid portion of blood.

▲ Red blood cells contain hemoglobin, which binds to oxygen in the lungs and carries oxygen to body cells.

▲ White blood cells are part of the body's defense against invading bacteria, viruses, and other microscopic organisms.

▲ Platelets help form blood clots to stop the flow of blood when a blood vessel is cut.

▲ The two main blood group systems are the ABO blood group and the Rh blood group.

4–4 Cardiovascular Diseases

▲ The thickening of the inner lining of an artery is called atherosclerosis.

▲ Hypertension, or high blood pressure, makes the heart work harder and can cause damage to the blood vessels.

Reviewing Key Terms

Define each term in a complete sentence.

4–2 Circulation in the Body

atrium
ventricle
artery
capillary
vein

4–3 Blood—The River of Life

plasma
red blood cell

hemoglobin
white blood cell
platelet
fibrin

4–4 Cardiovascular Diseases

cardiovascular disease
atherosclerosis
hypertension

Part 1

Some students might like to repeat this activity at home with their family members. If so, have them compare their pulse rates to those of their family members. Pulse rate is considered a genetic characteristic in that a high pulse rate can be inherited.

Part 2

Interested students might like to research and write a report on pulse rates in mammals other than humans, such as dogs or cats.

Chapter Review

ALTERNATIVE ASSESSMENT

The *Prentice Hall Science* program includes a variety of testing components and methodologies. Aside from the Chapter Review questions, you may opt to use the Chapter Test or the Computer Test Bank Test in your *Test Book* for assessment of important facts and concepts. In addition, Performance-Based Tests are included in your *Test Book*. These Performance-Based Tests are designed to test science process skills, rather than factual content recall. Since they are not content dependent, Performance-Based Tests can be distributed after students complete a chapter or after they complete the entire textbook.

CONTENT REVIEW

Multiple Choice

1. b
2. a
3. c
4. d
5. b
6. d
7. d
8. a
9. a
10. c

strength through regular activity or exercise—inferring, applying.)

OBSERVATIONS

1. Pulse rate at rest is typically about 72 beats per minute but may vary widely from student to student.
2. Both running and walking should have increased pulse rate, with running causing a greater increase.
3. Resting should reduce the pulse rate back to or close to its normal rate, depending on the length of the rest period.

ANALYSIS AND CONCLUSIONS

1. Conclusions may vary but should indicate that activity increases pulse rate, and periods of rest or inactivity tend to minimize pulse rate.
2. The pulse is actually a way to measure the heartbeat because pulse rate and heartbeat are equal.
3. Blood supply to muscles increases during exercise. Because the heart must beat faster to provide an increased blood supply, pulse rate also increases during exercise.

True or False

1. T
2. F, right
3. T
4. T
5. T
6. T
7. F, fibrin

Concept Mapping

Row 1: Carries carbon dioxide to lungs

Row 2: Pumps

Row 3: Blood

CONCEPT MASTERY

1. Plasma: liquid portion of blood; red blood cells: transport oxygen and carry carbon dioxide; white blood cells: involved in fighting agents of infection; platelets: help in blood clotting.

2. Antigens or proteins on some blood cells become clumped if they interact with antibodies in the blood of people who have a different blood type than that of the donor. If a match is not performed, the patient usually survives after one transfusion. But this transfusion causes the body to produce many antibodies against the proteins in the donated blood, and the second transfusion can lead to death due to the clumping of red blood cells in the blood vessels.

3. Red blood cells are the most numerous of blood cells because they are needed to carry oxygen throughout the body.

4. Platelets aid blood clotting by collecting around a cut or an opening in a blood vessel. Platelets release an enzyme that causes fibrin to form. The fibrin fibers form a network across the cut. Blood cells and plasma become trapped, a clot forms, and bleeding stops.

5. A red blood cell leaves the right atrium and enters the right ventricle. It is then pumped to the lungs, where it picks up oxygen, then back to the left atrium of the heart. From there it goes to the left ventricle and is pumped throughout the body. The red blood cell eventually returns to the right atrium by way of veins.

6. Valves prevent blood from moving backward, controlling the direction of blood flow. Generally speaking, blood moving away from the heart is oxygen rich, and blood moving toward the heart is oxygen poor.

Content Review

Multiple Choice

Choose the letter of the answer that best completes each statement.

1. The two upper heart chambers are called
   a. ventricles.
   b. atria.
   c. septa.
   d. valves.

2. Oxygen-rich blood from the lungs enters the heart through the
   a. left atrium.
   b. right atrium.
   c. left ventricle.
   d. right ventricle.

3. From the right atrium, blood is pumped to the
   a. brain.
   b. lungs.
   c. right ventricle.
   d. capillary network.

4. The heart chamber that works hardest is the
   a. right atrium.
   b. right ventricle.
   c. left atrium.
   d. left ventricle.

5. The blood vessels that carry blood back to the heart are the
   a. arteries.
   b. veins.
   c. capillaries.
   d. ventricles.

6. The cells that contain hemoglobin are the
   a. plasma.
   b. platelets.
   c. white blood cells.
   d. red blood cells.

7. Red blood cells are produced in the
   a. heart.
   b. liver.
   c. spleen.
   d. bone marrow.

8. Platelets help the body to
   a. control bleeding.
   b. fight infection.
   c. carry oxygen.
   d. do all of these.

9. People with group AB blood have
   a. both A and B proteins.
   b. neither A nor B proteins.
   c. both anti-A and anti-B clumping chemicals.
   d. none of these.

10. Cholesterol is a fatlike substance associated with
    a. hemoglobin.
    b. fibrin.
    c. atherosclerosis.
    d. salt.

True or False

If the statement is true, write "true." If it is false, change the underlined word or words to make the statement true.

1. The two lower heart chambers are called <u>ventricles</u>.
2. Oxygen-poor blood enters the heart through the <u>left</u> atrium.
3. The <u>capillaries</u> are the thinnest blood vessels.
4. <u>Veins</u> are blood vessels that contain valves.
5. An iron-containing protein in red blood cells is <u>hemoglobin</u>.
6. The type of blood cell that fights infection is the <u>white blood cell</u>.
7. When you cut yourself, a net of <u>hemoglobin</u> threads forms over the area to stop the blood flow.

Concept Mapping

Complete the following concept map for Section 4–1. Refer to pages H8–H9 to construct a concept map for the entire chapter.

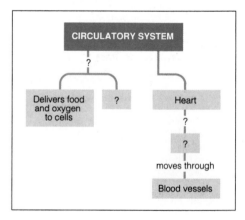

7. No, most arteries carry oxygenated blood, but arteries leading from the heart to the lungs do not. In the same way, veins usually carry deoxygenated blood, but veins leading from the heart to the lungs do not.

CRITICAL THINKING AND PROBLEM SOLVING

1. Blood leaves the right atrium and enters the right ventricle. The blood is then pumped to the lungs, then back to the left atrium of the heart. From there it goes to the left ventricle and is pumped throughout the body. The blood eventually returns to the right atrium by way of veins.

2. Columns should show that type O blood can be donated to all groups, type B blood to type B and AB groups, type A blood to type A and AB groups, and type AB blood only to type AB groups.

3. In the past, infectious diseases often killed many people before they became old enough to develop chronic disorders. Now that the human life span has increased, chronic disorders have become

Concept Mastery

Discuss each of the following in a brief paragraph.

1. List and describe the four components of blood.
2. Explain why blood must be matched before a blood transfusion.
3. Explain why red blood cells are the most numerous of the blood cells.
4. What role do platelets have in the body?
5. Describe the path a single red blood cell would take through the heart.
6. Explain why oxygen-rich and oxygen-poor blood never mix in human beings.
7. Do all arteries carry oxygen-rich blood? Do all veins carry oxygen-poor blood? Explain your answer.

Critical Thinking and Problem Solving

Use the skills you have developed in the chapter to answer each of the following.

1. **Sequencing events** Starting at the right atrium, trace the path of the blood through the body.
2. **Relating facts** On a separate sheet of paper, add another column to Figure 4–18. Call it Can Donate Blood to Group(s). Fill in this column.
3. **Making predictions** Explain why chronic disorders are more of a problem today than they were 200 years ago. Predict how great a problem they will be in the future.
4. **Applying concepts** To determine whether a person has an infection, doctors often do blood tests in which they count white blood cells. Explain why such a count is useful.
5. **Making generalizations** To determine whether a person has abnormally high blood pressure, at least three blood-pressure measurements should be taken on three separate days at three different times. Explain why this is so.
6. **Relating cause and effect** How are the structures of an artery, a vein, and a capillary adapted to their functions?
7. **Making inferences** An artificial heart actually replaces only the ventricles of a human heart. Suggest a reason why replacing the atria is not necessary.
8. **Analyzing data** Suppose you are a doctor and have two patients who are in need of a transfusion. Patient 1 has group A blood and Patient 2 has group O blood. Which ABO blood group would you determine safe to give to each of your patients?
9. **Using the writing process** Develop an advertising campaign in favor of the reduction of animal fat in the diet. Make it a full media blitz!

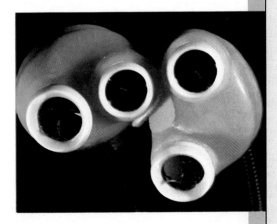

---

blood down so that transfer of nutrients, oxygen, and waste materials can occur.

7. The pumping portion of the heart that does most of the work is composed of the ventricles, which usually become worn or damaged during a heart attack. The atria are simple collecting stations and do not normally require replacement.

8. Patient 1 (blood type A) should receive type A or type O blood. Patient 2 (blood type O) should receive blood type O.

9. Campaigns will vary but should favor the reduction of animal fat in the diet.

KEEPING A PORTFOLIO

You might want to assign some of the Concept Mastery and Critical Thinking and Problem Solving questions as homework and have students include their responses to unassigned questions in their portfolio. Students should be encouraged to include both the question and the answer in their portfolio.

ISSUES IN SCIENCE

The following issue can be used as a springboard for discussion or given as a writing assignment:

More and more time and money are being spent in the area of heart-transplant research. Some people feel that the research time should be spent in other areas that would show success in a shorter amount of time. What is your opinion?

---

more prevalent. In the future, with an even longer expected life span, such disorders may become a more severe problem than they are today. Some students might point out, however, that such disorders might have cures in the future and thus actually become less of a problem.

4. When a person has an infection, the number of white blood cells in the blood increases to combat the infection. If a white blood cell count is higher than normal, the body may be in the process of fighting off an infection.

5. Blood pressure varies on a daily basis and may be higher than normal on a particular day. As a result, the average pressure taken on several days will be more accurate. The probability of getting a more accurate reading increases as the number of readings increases.

6. Blood is moving its fastest in arteries. Arteries have smooth inner walls and are generally flexible. Veins have thinner walls and are smaller than arteries; they contain valves to regulate blood flow direction. Capillaries are extremely small; they slow the

SECTION	LABORATORY INVESTIGATIONS AND DEMONSTRATIONS

5–1 The Respiratory System
pages H108–H117
	Student Edition
	   Measuring the Volume of Exhaled Air, p. H126
	Laboratory Manual
	   Investigating Breathing and Respiration
	   Investigating the Effect of Exercise on Respiration
	Teacher Edition
	   Why Do We Breathe?, p. H106d
	Teacher Edition
	   Inhale, Exhale, p. H106d

5–2 The Excretory System pages H118–H125	
Chapter Review pages H126–H129	

*All materials in the Chapter Planning Guide Grid are available as part of the Prentice Hall Science Learning System

OUTSIDE TEACHER RESOURCES

Books

The Kidneys: Balancing the Fluids, Torstar Books.

Kittredge, Mary. *The Respiratory System,* Chelsea House Publishers.

Lamberg, Lynne. *Skin Disorders,* Chelsea House Publishers.

Podolsky, Doug M. *Skin: The Human Fabric,* U.S. News Books.

Sebel, Peter. *Respiration: The Breath of Life,* Torstar Books.

Weibel, Ewald R. *The Pathway for Oxygen,* Harvard University Press.

Whipp, B. J., ed. *The Control of Breathing in Man,* University of Pennsylvania Press.

Audiovisuals

Circulatory and Respiratory Systems, film or video, National Geographic

The Lungs and Respiratory System, film or video, EBE

The Skin: Its Structure and Function, film or video, EBE

Work of the Kidneys, film or video, EBE

OTHER ACTIVITIES	MULTIMEDIA
Activity Book Chapter Discovery: Breathing and Exercise ACTIVITY: Measuring Pulse and Respiration Rates ACTIVITY: What's in the Air You Breathe? ACTIVITY: A Breathing Model ACTIVITY: Changes in Pitch **Student Edition** Find Out by Doing: What Is in Exhaled Air?, p. H109 **Review and Reinforcement Guide** Section 5–1	**Video** Respiratory System The Heart and the Lungs Play Ball **Courseware** Respiration System (Supplemental) **Transparency Binder** Respiratory System **English/Spanish Audiotapes** Section 5–1
Activity Book ACTIVITY: Keeping Cool **Student Edition** Find Out by Reading: Reading Poetry, p. H118 Find Out by Doing: Close At Hand, p. H122 **Review and Reinforcement Guide** Section 5–2	**Video** Excretory System **Courseware** Excretion System (Supplemental) **Transparency Binder** Urinary System **English/Spanish Audiotapes** Section 5–2
Test Book Chapter Test Performance-Based Test	**Test Book** Computer Test Bank Test

CHAPTER OVERVIEW

We need air to stay alive. Without air, the cells of our body would quickly die. The oxygen in the air supports the energy-releasing process that takes place in our cells. Cells burn the food they get from the blood and release the energy from the food. This energy-releasing process that is fueled by oxygen is called respiration. The respiratory system is the body system responsible for getting oxygen into the body and removing carbon dioxide and water from the body. The respiratory system consists of the nose, throat, larynx, trachea, bronchi, and lungs. In the lungs, round sacs called alveoli are the gateways for oxygen into the body. Through the thin walls of the alveoli, oxygen enters the bloodstream and is carried to cells throughout the body, and carbon dioxide leaves the bloodstream and returns through the respiratory system.

Other organs of the respiratory system include the larynx and the diaphragm. The larynx contains the vocal cords, which vibrate with the passing air and, with the mouth and tongue, produce sound or voice. The diaphragm helps the chest expand and contract, changing the air pressure and causing air to rush into and out of the lungs.

Because the lungs get rid of carbon dioxide and water, they are considered to be part of the excretory system, too. The organs of the excretory system are the lungs, the kidneys, the liver, and the skin. The kidneys filter wastes and poisons from the blood. The actual filtering takes place in the millions of nephrons, which allow nutrients, salts, and water to be reabsorbed into the blood and extract excess water, salts, and other wastes to be excreted from the body as urine. Urine moves from the kidneys through the ureters to the urinary bladder and eventually out through the urethra.

The liver, which also plays a role in the digestive system, filters excess amino acids from the blood as well as converts hemoglobin from worn-out red blood cells. The skin, which is made of two layers, the epidermis and the dermis, contains hair, nails, and sweat and oil glands. Sweat glands produce perspiration, which helps to regulate body temperature.

5–1 THE RESPIRATORY SYSTEM

THEMATIC FOCUS

The purpose of this section is to introduce students to the respiratory system. They will learn that the primary job of the respiratory system is to get oxygen into the body and remove carbon dioxide and water from the body. They will trace the path of air through the nose or mouth, down the throat, down the trachea, into the bronchi, through smaller and smaller branches of the bronchi, and into the alveoli of the lungs. Through the capillaries surrounding the alveoli, oxygen enters the blood, and carbon dioxide leaves the blood. Students will also learn about the larynx, or voice box, and about the diaphragm, which helps us breathe.

The themes that can be focused on in this section are energy, patterns of change, scale and structure, systems and interactions, and stability.

*Energy: Stress that the respiratory system provides the body cells with the oxygen that they need and that combines with food to produce energy and that it is this energy that keeps us alive.

Patterns of change: The respiratory system functions according to a set pattern to produce one particular change: the exchange of oxygen and carbon dioxide with the environment.

*Scale and structure: Point out to students that structure in the sense of organization plays a role in all systems. The respiratory system contains lungs, which are composed of structures called alveoli, in which the exchange of gases occurs.

*Systems and interactions: The respiratory system is a group of organs that work together for one purpose: to permit the exchange of gases between the body cells and the environment.

*Stability: All body systems work to maintain homeostasis; that is, to keep the body functioning at a constant level. The respiratory and excretory systems maintain homeostasis by delivering oxygen to the blood and by removing wastes from the blood.

PERFORMANCE OBJECTIVES 5–1

1. **Explain the major function of the respiratory system.**
2. **Name, in order, the respiratory structures through which air passes through breathing.**
3. **Describe the functions of the nose, epiglottis, larynx, and diaphragm.**

SCIENCE TERMS 5–1

respiration p. H109
nose p. H110
epiglottis p. H111
trachea p. H111
larynx p. H112
vocal cord p. H112
bronchus p. H113
lung p. H113
alveolus p. H114
diaphragm p. H115

5–2 THE EXCRETORY SYSTEM

THEMATIC FOCUS

The purpose of this section is to introduce students to the excretory system. They will learn that the lungs are part of the excretory system as well as the respiratory system and that the liver is part of the excretory system as well as the digestive system. They will trace the path of blood through the kidneys and find out what materials are reabsorbed and what materials are excreted. They will also trace the path of urine out of the body. The skin is presented as a major excretory organ that helps to rid the body of excess water, salts, and urea.

The themes that can be focused on in this section are energy, patterns of change, scale and structure, systems and interactions, and unity and diversity.

*Energy: Emphasize that the excretory system also contributes to the production of energy for the body by removing waste products from the cells.

Patterns of change: The excretory system functions according to a set pattern to produce one particular change: the removal of various waste products from the body into the environment.

*Scale and structure: Point out to students that the excretory system, as with all body systems, is composed of certain structures. The excretory system has the kidneys, which contain structures called nephrons. They remove wastes from the blood.

*Systems and interactions: The excretory system is a group of organs that work to achieve one goal: to remove wastes from the body.

Unity and diversity: Stress that although the structures of the respiratory and excretory systems are different, the two systems work together in transporting materials either to or from the blood.

PERFORMANCE OBJECTIVES 5–2

1. Explain why lungs are considered organs of both respiration and excretion.
2. List three other excretory organs and describe the function of each.
3. Trace the path of urine from the kidneys to the outside of the body.

SCIENCE TERMS 5–2

excretion p. H118
kidney p. H118
nephron p. H119
capsule p. H120
ureter p. H120
urinary bladder p. H121
urethra p. H121
liver p. H121
skin p. H122
epidermis p. H122
dermis p. H122

Discovery *Learning*

TEACHER DEMONSTRATIONS MODELING

Why Do We Breathe?

Show students pictures of several animals and ask them to describe the method of breathing used by each. Examples: fish—gills; insects—tracheae; spider—book lungs or tracheae; earthworms—skin; birds—lungs; mammals—lungs; frogs—skin and lungs.

Next, show pictures of an astronaut, a scuba diver, and a passenger in an airplane. (If pictures are not available, merely list these three types of individuals on the chalkboard.)
• **What do these individuals have in common?** (Many answers are possible. Emphasize that all three are in a foreign, or unnatural, environment. Their breathing must be aided by artificial means such as pressurized suits, oxygen tanks, pressurized cabins, and so on.)

Explain to students that the main function of the respiratory system in any animal, or in humans under any conditions, is to bring oxygen to the cells and to rid the body of carbon dioxide.
• **Why is oxygen necessary?** (Students should recall that oxygen is used in cellular respiration to break down food and release energy. Energy is required for all body activities.)
• **How is the waste carbon dioxide produced?** (Students should recall that carbon dioxide is produced as a result of cellular respiration.)

To indicate the presence of carbon dioxide in exhaled air, have a student blow through a straw into a glass of water to which the indicator bromthymol blue has been added.
• **What do you observe?** (The color changes from blue to greenish-yellow, indicating the presence of carbon dioxide.)

Explain to students that in Chapter 5 they will find out how the respiration system operates in bringing oxygen to the cells and in getting rid of carbon dioxide.

Inhale, Exhale

Select several students and measure their chest sizes after exhaling. Then measure their chest sizes once they have inhaled and not exhaled again.
• **Why does chest size increase during inhalation?** (To allow air to rush into the lungs.)
• **Why does the chest size decrease during exhalation?** (To allow air to rush out of the lungs.)

Ask students if they can relate what they know about changes in air pressure to the process of breathing.
• **What do you think happens to the air pressure inside the lungs when the chest expands?** (There would be more room in the lungs for air; because the air inside would spread out in the larger space, its pressure would decrease.)
• **So the air pressure in the lungs would be lower than the air pressure outside the body. What would happen then?** (The difference in pressure would cause air to rush into the lungs.)
• **What do you think happens to the air pressure in the lungs when the chest size decreases?** (Air would be pushed into a smaller space, and its pressure would increase.)
• **So now the air pressure in the lungs would be greater than the air pressure outside the body. What would happen then?** (The difference in pressure would cause air to rush out of the lungs.)

CHAPTER 5

Respiratory and Excretory Systems

INTEGRATING SCIENCE

This life science chapter provides you with numerous opportunities to integrate other areas of science, as well as other disciplines, into your curriculum. Blue numbered annotations on the student page and integration notes on the teacher wraparound pages alert you to areas of possible integration.

In this chapter you can integrate earth science and atmosphere (pp. 108, 125), life science and cell biology (p. 109), physical science and sound (p. 111), physical science and air pressure (p. 115), earth science and astronomy (p. 116), physical science and electricity (p. 117), and language arts (p. 118).

SCIENCE, TECHNOLOGY, AND SOCIETY/COOPERATIVE LEARNING

One of the greatest threats to a person's respiratory system is cigarette smoke. Particles from cigarette smoke can damage the lining of the system. For a while, the system is able to repair the damage and cleanse itself, but continued abuse can result in a variety of diseases: bronchitis, pneumonia, asthma, lung cancer, even heart disease. The dangers of cigarette smoke to smokers are obvious; they are inhaling chemicals, nicotine, tar, and carbon monoxide. But the nonsmoker is also at risk. A passive smoker is a person who breathes environmental cigarette smoke and is exposed to the same dangerous chemicals as a smoker.

Because research conducted by the U.S. Surgeon General, the National Research Council, the National Academy of Sciences, and the International Agency for Cancer Research has shown that cigarette smoke is dangerous to the general public, the Environmental Protection Agency (EPA) is considering labeling cigarette smoke as a pollutant. Passive smoking causes about 3800 lung cancer deaths every year. Cigarette smoke may soon join substances such as asbestos and benzene on lists of things dangerous to inhale. As an environmental pollutant, it would be subject to regulations affecting both the

INTRODUCING CHAPTER 5

DISCOVERY LEARNING

▶ *Activity Book*

Begin your teaching of the chapter by using the Chapter 5 Discovery Activity from the *Activity Book*. Using this activity, students will compare their breathing rate at rest to their breathing rate after exercise.

USING THE TEXTBOOK

Have students look at the photograph on page H106.
• **What do you predict is happening in the picture?** (Cyclists are having a race.)
• **How do you think the cyclists feel?** (Students might suggest that they could be hot, tired, sweating, or aching from all the effort pedaling.)
• **How do you feel when you do something as strenuous as bicycle racing?** (Lead students to the idea that they breathe harder, sweat more, need water, and so on.)

Respiratory *and* Excretory Systems

Guide for Reading

After you read the following sections, you will be able to

5–1 The Respiratory System

- Describe the structures of the respiratory system and give their functions.
- Explain how the lungs work.

5–2 The Excretory System

- Describe the structures of the excretory system and give their functions.

Watch a bicycle race on an autumn day and what do you see? You see cyclists pedaling hard and fast so that they can be the first to cross the finish line and win the race. What else do you notice about the cyclists? You probably see thin streams of sweat trickling down their faces and bodies. If you are close enough, you may see the quick, deep breaths that some cyclists take as they pedal. You may even see some cyclists drinking water from plastic bottles that are attached to their bicycles.

Why are the cyclists breathing so quickly and deeply? Where do the streams of sweat come from? What is the purpose of the water? In order to supply the cyclists with the energy they need to pedal their bicycles, the cells of their bodies must be provided with an enormous amount of oxygen. The oxygen must enter the cyclists' bodies, and an almost equal amount of wastes must be removed.

These vital functions are the tasks of two body systems: the respiratory system and the excretory system. Turn the page and begin to discover how these two systems perform their remarkable feats.

Journal *Activity*

> **You and Your World** Have you ever had a sore throat or laryngitis? What did you do to make yourself feel better? Draw a sketch of yourself showing how you felt while you had either of these conditions.

◀ *In order to pedal their bicycles hard and fast, these cyclists need an enormous amount of oxygen.*

work environment and all public places.

The tobacco industry feels that there is not enough scientific data to clearly identify cigarette smoke as an environmental pollutant and that the EPA is overzealous in its attempts to control public smoking. The industry also feels that labeling cigarette smoke as a pollutant would further persecute smokers and infringe on their personal freedoms protected by the Constitution. They also cite the negative impact that such a move would have on the economy: millions of tax dollars are collected every year from the sale of cigarettes.

Cooperative learning: Using preassigned or randomly selected groups, have groups complete one of these assignments:

- Conduct a survey on the issue of banning smoking in all public places as a health measure. Groups should determine the type of survey they want to use, identify the group of individuals they will survey (classmates, adults, teachers, and so on), and develop the survey (suggest a minimum number of survey items or questions).
- Produce an editorial page for the school newspaper that expresses an opinion on banning smoking in public places to reduce possible health hazards. The page should contain the following components:

   Background information (information about the respiratory system)

   Editorial cartoon (pro or con)

   Guest editorial in support of banning smoking in public

   Guest editorial opposing banning smoking in public

   See Cooperative Learning in the *Teacher's Desk Reference.*

JOURNAL ACTIVITY

You may want to use the Journal Activity as the basis for a class discussion. After students have finished drawing, ask volunteers to share their pictures with the class. Encourage them to describe how their throat felt and why the things they did—drinking cold liquids, for example—made their throat feel better. Point out that they will better understand why this is so after they complete the chapter. Students should be instructed to keep their Journal Activity in their portfolio.

Have students read the chapter introduction on page H107.

- **Do you know how exertion leads to hard breathing, sweating, and a need for water?** (Accept all answers that show students are aware of the connection between our need to take in oxygen and get rid of wastes.)

- **What is our respiratory system?** (Accept all logical answers; students might suggest that it has to do with how we breathe, or they might name parts such as nose or lungs.)

- **What is our excretory system?** (Accept all logical answers; students might suggest that it has to do with how we get rid of things our body doesn't need.)

- **How do you think hard exercise, like cycling, causes the respiratory and excretory systems to have to work harder?** (Students might say that the harder the body works or the more active it is, the more oxygen it must take in to supply energy, and, therefore, the more waste materials it has to get rid of.)

5–1 The Respiratory System

5–1 The Respiratory System

MULTICULTURAL OPPORTUNITY 5–1

What are the effects of living in a polluted environment? We often think of cities in the United States as having some of the most polluted air in the world. Encourage students to investigate pollution in other countries. Other industrialized countries (such as the former Soviet Union) also have serious air-pollution problems. Many of the developing countries cannot afford the expense of pollution-control devices and hence have high levels of pollution, even though their levels of industrialization may be lower than that of the United States.

ESL STRATEGY 5–1

As a group project, have students make a poster (or an individual illustration) labeling the structures of the respiratory system. This will serve as a visual aid for a shared oral presentation in which students explain the functions of the respiratory system.

Ask students to explain
1. What can cause them to hiccup.
2. Where the sound that is made when they hiccup comes from.

Tell them that the word in English is said to have originated as an imitation of the sound. Ask them what the word for *hiccup* is in their native language and have them share this information with the class.

Guide for Reading

Focus on these questions as you read.

▶ What is the function of the respiratory system?
▶ What path does air take through the respiratory system?

You cannot see, smell, or taste it. Yet it is as real as land or water. When it moves, you can feel it against your face. You can also see its effect in drifting clouds, quivering leaves, and pounding waves. It can turn windmills and blow sailboats across the sea. What is it?

If your answer is air, you are correct. Air is the mixture of gases that surrounds the Earth. The main gases that make up the air, or atmosphere, are nitrogen and oxygen. In fact, the atmosphere of the Earth is approximately 78 percent nitrogen and 21 percent oxygen. The remaining 1 percent is made of argon, carbon dioxide, water vapor (water in the form of an invisible gas), and trace gases—gases that are present in only very small amounts.

Humans, like all animals, need air to stay alive. You are breathing air right now. Every minute of the day you breathe in about 6 liters of air. Without this frequent intake of air, the cells in your body would soon die. Why? As you have just read, air contains the gas oxygen. It is oxygen that supports the energy-producing process that takes place in your cells. As a result of this process, your cells are able to perform all the various tasks that keep you alive. Try thinking of it this way. You know that a fire burns only if there is enough air—more specifically, enough oxygen in the air. Well, each body cell burns up the food it gets from the blood and releases the energy locked within the food only if it gets enough

Figure 5–1 *Like humans, plants, such as a heliconia, and animals, such as a barred leaf frog on the heliconia plant and a mountain gorilla, use the gases in the Earth's atmosphere to stay alive. What gases make up the Earth's atmosphere?* ❶

108 ■ H

TEACHING STRATEGY 5–1

FOCUS/MOTIVATION

Working with a partner, have each student count the number of breaths taken in 1 minute. (Breathing in and out counts as one cycle.)
• **How many breathing cycles occurred in 1 minute?** (Most will be in the range of 16 to 24 breaths per minute.)
• **What are factors that affect your rate of breathing?** (Physical activity, position, emotions, age, drugs, oxygen concentration, air temperature, air pressure, amount of

moisture in the air, carbon dioxide concentration, and so on.)

CONTENT DEVELOPMENT

• **Why is air important to us?** (We need air to stay alive.)
• **What does air contain that keeps us alive?** (Oxygen.)
• **Why do we need oxygen?** (Our body cells need oxygen in order to burn food from the blood and to release energy.)

• **What system is responsible for getting oxygen into our bodies?** (Respiratory system.)

● ● ● ● **Integration** ● ● ● ●

Use the discussion on the composition of Earth's atmosphere to integrate earth science concepts into your lesson.

Use the discussion on body cells and energy to integrate life science concepts of cell biology into your lesson.

oxissue. The energy-releasing process that is fueled by oxygen is called **respiration.** In addition to energy, carbon dioxide and water are produced during respiration.

As you may recall from Chapter 3, the digestive system breaks down food into small particles so that the food can get inside body cells. And as you learned in Chapter 4, the circulatory system transports oxygen and food to body cells via the blood. Now you will discover how oxygen combines with food in the cells to produce the body's much-needed energy and the waste products carbon dioxide and water vapor. **The body system that is responsible for performing the task of getting oxygen into the body and removing carbon dioxide and water from the body is the respiratory system.** Figure 5–2 is a diagram of the respiratory system. You may wish to refer to it as you follow the passage of air from the time it enters the respiratory system to the time it leaves.

The Nose and Throat

Even the purest country air contains dust particles and bacteria; city air contains these materials as well as soot and exhaust fumes. But whether you breathe city air or country air, the air must travel through the nose, trachea (TRAY-kee-uh), and bronchi (BRAHNG-kee) in the few short seconds in which it moves from the environment to your lungs.

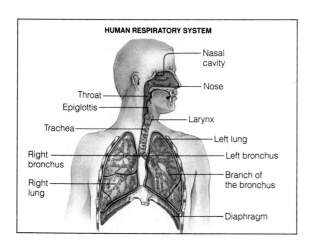

HUMAN RESPIRATORY SYSTEM

- Nasal cavity
- Nose
- Throat
- Epiglottis
- Larynx
- Trachea
- Left lung
- Right bronchus
- Left bronchus
- Right lung
- Branch of the bronchus
- Diaphragm

Figure 5–2 *The human respiratory system is composed of organs that work together to permit the exchange of oxygen and carbon dioxide with the environment. What is the name for the energy-releasing process that is fueled by oxygen?* ❷

PHASES OF RESPIRATION

Respiration in humans has several different phases:

1. Breathing is the movement of air into and out of the lungs.

2. External respiration is the exchange of oxygen and carbon dioxide between the air and the blood in the lungs.

3. Internal respiration is the exchange of oxygen and carbon dioxide between the blood and the body cells.

These stages of respiration are physical processes. They should not be confused with cellular respiration, which is a chemical process that occurs within cells. During cellular respiration, the oxygen is utilized to break down nutrients and to release energy.

5–1 (continued)

GUIDED PRACTICE

▶ *Laboratory Manual*

Skills Development

Skills: Making observations, recording data, comparing, applying concepts

You may want to have students complete the Chapter 5 Laboratory Investigation in the *Laboratory Manual* called Investigating the Effect of Exercise on Respiration. Students will discover the effect that exercise has on the amount of carbon dioxide produced.

CONTENT DEVELOPMENT

Explain that the next step in air's journey is the throat. Food travels down this same throat.

• **What directs food down the correct passage and not into the respiratory system?** (A small flap of tissue called the epiglottis acts as traffic director. When food is swallowed, the epiglottis closes over the

Figure 5–3 *When the spongy lungs are removed, the remaining parts of the respiratory system through which air passes resemble an upside-down tree.*

Figure 5–4 *A small piece of dirt that has invaded the body becomes trapped in the mucus and entangled in the cilia that line the bronchus.*

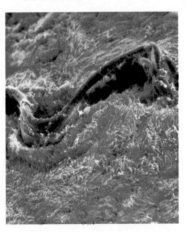

These structures are the channels through which air passes on its way to the lungs.

The air that you breathe usually enters the respiratory system through two openings in the **nose** called the nostrils. From there, the air flows into the nasal (pertaining to the nose) cavities, or two spaces in the nose. The cavities are separated by a wall of cartilage (flexible connective tissue) and bone. If the air is cold, as it may be in winter in certain locations, it is quickly heated by warm blood flowing through blood vessels in the lining of the nasal cavities. At the same time, slippery mucus in the nose moistens the air. This action keeps the delicate tissues of the respiratory system from drying out. In addition to moistening the air, the mucus traps unwanted dust particles and microscopic organisms such as bacteria and thereby cleanses the air.

It may surprise you to learn that the nose produces a fresh batch of mucus every 20 minutes or so. This amounts to about 0.9 liter of mucus per day. In order to get rid of the old mucus, billions of cilia (SIHL-ee-uh; singular: cilium), or tiny hairlike structures lining the nasal cavities, sweep the old mucus toward the esophagus and then into the stomach. The stomach, as you may recall from Chapter 3, gives off a digestive juice that contains hydrochloric acid. The hydrochloric acid destroys many of the bacteria that may have had the misfortune of becoming trapped in the mucus. Fortunately for you, some of the trapped particles never even make it past the nose. For one reason or another, they may begin to irritate the nasal cavities. Your body responds to this irritation by producing a little "explosion" to force the particles out. As you may already have guessed, this "explosion" is called a sneeze!

Because the nose warms, moistens, and filters the air coming into the body, it is healthier to take in air through the nose than through the mouth. However, if your nose is clogged because you have a cold, you have no other choice but to breathe through your mouth.

From the nose, the warmed, moistened, and filtered air moves into your throat, where it soon comes to a kind of fork in the road. One path leads to the digestive system. The other path leads deeper into the respiratory system. The structure that

---

opening to the windpipe so that food does not enter the respiratory system.)

• **Explain what is meant when someone says that "food went down the wrong pipe."** (You have only one pipe, or throat. What is really meant is that the epiglottis did not function properly. The food went down the windpipe, or trachea, instead of the esophagus.)

▶ *Multimedia* ◀

Use the transparency in the Transparency Binder called Respiratory System to help students follow the passage of air through the respiratory system.

FOCUS/MOTIVATION

Gently press on the front of your neck and run your finger up and down. You can feel the rings of cartilage in the trachea, or windpipe. You may also feel your Adam's apple, the cartilage that makes up the larynx, or voice box.

Ask students to swallow while holding their throat. Explain that when they swallow, breathing is stopped for a moment to

directs air down the respiratory path and food and water down the digestive path is the **epiglottis** (ehp-uh-GLAHT-ihs). As you may recall from Chapter 3, the epiglottis is a small flap of tissue that closes over the entrance to the rest of the respiratory system when you swallow. As a result, food and water are routed to the digestive system. When you breathe, the epiglottis opens, permitting air to enter the respiratory system.

The Trachea

Take a moment to gently run your finger up and down the front of your neck. Do you feel a bumpy tubelike structure? This tubelike structure is called the **trachea,** or windpipe. The bumps on the trachea are actually rings, or bands, of cartilage. The rings of cartilage make the trachea flexible enough so that you can bend your neck, yet rigid enough so that it keeps an open passageway for air. The rings of cartilage are held together by smooth muscle tissue. The smooth muscle tissue enables the diameter of the trachea to increase, thus allowing large amounts of air to move more easily along its path. Such action is especially helpful when you have to gulp down large amounts of air after doing some particularly strenuous work.

As the air moves down into the trachea, mucus along the inner lining traps dust particles and bacteria that have managed to get past the nose. These particles are swept out of the trachea and up to the mouth or nose by cilia that line the passageway.

Figure 5–5 *The larynx, which is located at the top of the trachea, contains the vocal cords (left). Notice that the vocal cords are made of two small folds of tissue that are stretched across the larynx (right). What is the function of the vocal cords?* ❶

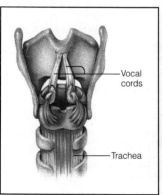
- Vocal cords
- Trachea

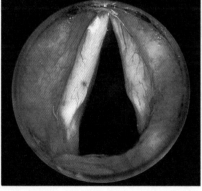

H ■ 111

ANNOTATION KEY

Answers
❶ To produce the voice. (Relating facts)

Integration
❶ Physical Science: Sound. See *Sound and Light,* Chapter 2.

BACKGROUND INFORMATION
RESPIRATORY SYSTEM OF BIRDS

Because air flows in and out of our lungs through the same passage, only about 10 percent of the air in our lungs is replaced with each breath. Birds have a system of air sacs that lighten their bodies and direct air through the lungs in a one-way pattern. This system allows air to flow through the lungs in one direction, ensuring that the lungs will have fresh, oxygen-rich air available at all times. The lungs of birds are one of the adaptations that makes them capable of the physical effort required for flying.

REINFORCEMENT/RETEACHING
▶ *Activity Book*

To help students understand about pollutants in the air, have them complete the chapter activity What's in the Air You Breathe? They will collect and examine various kinds of pollutants found in the air.

GUIDED PRACTICE
▶ *Laboratory Manual*

Skills Development
Skills: Making observations, comparing, applying concepts

Have students complete the Chapter 5 Laboratory Investigation in the *Laboratory Manual* called Investigating Breathing and Respiration. They will compare the processes of breathing and respiration.

let food go down the trachea. The movement students feel in their throats is actually the raising of the larynx under the epiglottis.

CONTENT DEVELOPMENT

Explain that the trachea is the second line of defense against dirt particles and bacteria. The trachea is lined with tiny hairs that trap the foreign particles that manage to get through the nose.
• **When the nose is irritated by foreign particles, what results?** (A sneeze.)

• **When the trachea is irritated by foreign particles, what results?** (A cough.)

Explain that sneezing and coughing are additional ways that your body attempts to remove foreign particles. Coughs may force air out of the trachea at speeds of up to 160 kilometers per hour.

● ● ● ● ● **Integration** ● ● ● ● ●

Use the photograph of the larynx and vocal cords to integrate the physical science concepts of sound into your lesson.

Sometimes, however, some of these particles may collect in the trachea, causing an irritation. This irritation triggers a response similar to a sneeze, or the tiny explosion that occurs in the nose. In the trachea, however, the explosion is called a cough. Air forced out of the trachea during a cough can sometimes reach speeds of up to 160 kilometers per hour!

Located at the top of the trachea is a box-shaped structure called the **larynx** (LAR-ihngks), or voice box. The larynx is made up of pieces of cartilage, one of which juts out from the neck rather noticeably. You know this piece of cartilage by the name Adam's apple. Everyone has an Adam's apple, although it tends to be more noticeable in males than in females. This is because the larynxes of males are generally larger, and also because males have less fat in their necks to hide the Adam's apple from view.

The structures in the larynx that are responsible for producing your voice are the **vocal cords.** The vocal cords are two small folds of tissue that are stretched across the larynx. These folds have a slit-like opening between them. When you talk, muscles in the larynx tighten, narrowing the opening. Then as air from your lungs rushes past the tightened vocal cords, it causes the vocal cords to vibrate. As they vibrate, they cause the air particles in the slit-like opening between them to vibrate. The result of this vibration is a sound: your voice.

The way that your vocal cords, muscles, and lungs work to produce sound is so well organized that you use them in combination without really thinking about it. You can prove this to yourself by trying the following activity. Speak in a high voice. Now speak in a low voice. Do you hear a difference? Do you know what you did to produce that difference? When you spoke in a high voice, you tightened your vocal cords, causing them to vibrate more rapidly and produce a higher sound. The reverse happened when you spoke in a low voice—you relaxed your vocal cords, causing them to vibrate more slowly and produce a lower sound.

The degree of highness or lowness of a sound is known as its pitch. The pitch of the human voice is determined by the size of the larynx and the length

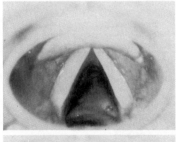

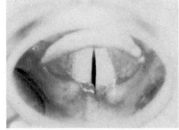

Figure 5–6 *These photographs show the vocal cords at work. When you breathe, the vocal cords move apart, allowing air to pass to and from the lungs (top). When you speak, the vocal cords move closer together (bottom).*

112 ■ H

rubber band to produce vibrations and, hence, sound.

• **What is the relationship between the tightness of the rubber band and the sound produced?** (The more tightly the rubber band is stretched, the higher the pitch of the sound.)

Explain to students that this is similar to the way the vocal cords work. The muscles attached to the vocal cords regulate the tautness of the vocal cords. The degree of tautness determines their rate of vibration and the pitch of the sounds pro-

duced. When the muscles pull tightly on the vocal cords, the vocal cord tissue vibrates rapidly and produces high-pitched sounds. When the muscles are more relaxed, the folds of tissue vibrate more slowly and produce low-pitched sounds.

ENRICHMENT

▶ *Activity Book*

Interested students can learn more about pitch and how it is produced by completing the chapter activity called Changes in Pitch.

of the vocal cords. Female voices are usually of a higher pitch than male voices because female vocal cords are shorter than male vocal cords. (The shorter the vocal cords, the more rapidly they vibrate and the higher the pitch of the sound they produce.) Actually, the vocal cords of males and females are about the same size until the teenage years. During that time, the larynxes of males begin to grow larger, causing their voices to become lower in pitch.

The vocal cords, muscles, and lungs are not alone in producing the sounds of your voice. They are helped by your lips, teeth, and tongue. In addition, vibrations of the walls in the nasal cavities give your voice its special quality. You may be more aware of the quality of your voice—or a change in the quality—when you have a cold and your nasal cavities are clogged. At such a time, your voice tends to sound different—a difference often described as nasal.

The Lungs

Having moved through the nose and the trachea, the incoming air is as clean, moist, and warm as it is going to get. Now the air reaches a place where the trachea branches into two tubes—the left and right **bronchi** (BRAHNG-kee; singular: bronchus). The left bronchus enters the left lung, and the right bronchus enters the right lung.

Once inside the **lungs,** which are the main organs of the respiratory system, the bronchi divide. They continue to divide again and again, becoming narrower each time, until they are tiny tubes the size of twigs. At the ends of these tiny tubes are hundreds of round sacs that resemble clusters of

Figure 5–7 *In order to sing effortlessly, opera singers draw in a full breath by expanding the lower ribs and lowering the diaphragm. When babies cry, they use their diaphragms the way opera singers do. What is the diaphragm?* ❶

H ■ 113

INTEGRATION
MEDICINE

As many as 10 million Americans, or 4 percent of the population, suffer from asthma. During an asthmatic attack, muscles surrounding the air passages that lead to the lungs contract. This contraction reduces the diameter of the bronchioles, which makes it difficult for large amounts of air to pass through.

Most asthma sufferers are treated with inhalers that spray drugs in the form of a mist to make breathing easier. With a few puffs of an inhaler, the muscles generally stop contracting, and the attack is under control. But the inhaler treats only the symptoms; it is not a cure. Worldwide, asthma is on the increase, for reasons that scientists have not yet figured out.

ENRICHMENT

• **Have you ever had laryngitis?** (Accept all answers.)

Explain that laryngitis occurs when the mucous membrane of the larynx becomes inflamed and swollen as a result of an infection or inhalation of irritating vapors. The swollen membranes prevent the vocal cords from vibrating as freely as before, and the voice may become hoarse—or "disappear."

• **Why is laryngitis a potentially dangerous condition?** (The swollen tissue could obstruct the airway and interfere with breathing.)

Explain that when this happens, it is necessary to insert a tube into the trachea through the nose, mouth, or a surgical opening in the trachea (tracheotomy).

Some people have had their larynxes removed due to cancer. They must learn to speak by a special method of "burping" air. Have interested students find out more about this technique. Other individuals who cannot speak in the usual way have developed sign languages. Interested students can learn the alphabet or certain expressions in sign language and teach them to the rest of the class.

CONTENT DEVELOPMENT
▶ *Multimedia* ◀

You may want to show the video The Heart and Lungs Play Ball before going on to the discussion of the lungs. The video will help students understand the lungs' role in the exchange of oxygen and carbon dioxide within the body. After students have viewed the video, ask them to draw their own diagram of the respiratory system showing the major organs they have studied.

WHO'S IN CHARGE?

The respiratory control center (medulla oblongata) is located at the base of the brain; it is regulated by the amount of carbon dioxide in the blood. If the carbon dioxide concentration is high, the respiratory center signals the diaphragm and rib muscles to increase the rate and/or depth of breathing. When carbon dioxide levels fall back to normal, the center signals for breathing to return to the normal rate.

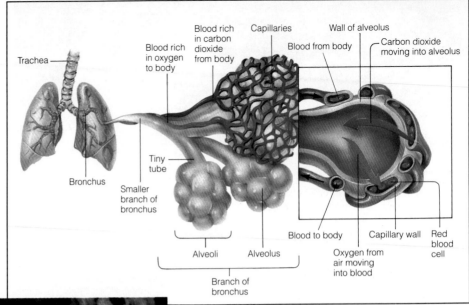

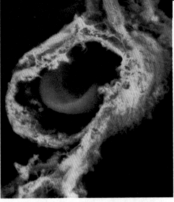

Figure 5–8 *Oxygen and carbon dioxide are exchanged between the blood in the capillaries and the air in the alveoli, or tiny air sacs. In the photograph, a single red blood cell squeezes through a capillary surrounding an alveolus that is less than 0.001 centimeter away.*

grapes. These round sacs are called **alveoli** (al-VEE-uh-ligh; singular: alveolus, al-VEE-uh-luhs). Alveoli are the gateways for oxygen into the body.

As you can see from Figure 5–8, each alveolus is surrounded by a network of tiny blood vessels called capillaries. It is here in the body's 600 million alveoli that the lungs perform their function—the exchange of oxygen and carbon dioxide in the blood. Let's take a closer look at this process.

When air enters the alveoli, oxygen in the air seeps through the thin walls of the tiny sacs into the surrounding capillaries. As blood slowly moves through the capillaries, it picks up the oxygen and carries it to cells throughout the body. When the oxygen-rich blood reaches the cells, it releases the oxygen. At the same time, the blood picks up the carbon dioxide produced by the cells during respiration and returns it to the alveoli.

Because air is rarely in the lungs for more than a few seconds, the exchange of gases (oxygen and carbon dioxide) must take place quickly. This is where the treelike structure of the respiratory system comes in. The branching structure enables more than 2400 kilometers of airways to fit into the small area called

---

5–1 (continued)

CONTENT DEVELOPMENT

Explain to students that the trachea branches into two tubes, or bronchi (singular: bronchus). The bronchi continue to branch into smaller and smaller tubes.
• **Why is this pattern of tubes in the lungs sometimes called the respiratory tree?** (The branching pattern resembles that of an upside-down tree.)

The smallest branches end in clusters of tiny sacs called alveoli (singular: alveolus). The alveoli make up most of the lung tissue and are the main organs of respiration. Each alveolus has thin walls and is surrounded by a network of capillaries. This arrangement makes gas exchange between the alveoli and the blood a relatively simple matter.

In the alveoli, the oxygen that is breathed in diffuses into the blood and is carried to the heart to be pumped throughout the body. In the meantime, carbon dioxide from the "used" blood diffuses into the alveoli to be exhaled.

INDEPENDENT PRACTICE

▶ *Activity Book*

Students who need practice with the structure and action of the respiratory system should complete the chapter activity called A Breathing Model.

GUIDED PRACTICE

Skills Development
Skills: Manipulative, recording data, comparing

At this point have students complete the in-text Laboratory Investigation: Measuring the Volume of Exhaled Air. Students compare average volumes of exhaled air before and after exercise.

FOCUS/MOTIVATION

Take a deep breath and watch your chest expand. Exhale and watch your chest shrink.
• **Does the air rushing into your chest make it expand? Or does your chest expand first, permitting air to rush into your lungs?** (The latter is true.)

the chest cavity. (If these airways were placed end to end, they would extend from Los Angeles, California, to Minneapolis, Minnesota.) As a result, a great deal of oxygen can seep out of the lungs, and an equal amount of carbon dioxide can seep back in in a very short time.

How You Breathe

On the average, you breathe in and out about 1 liter of air every 10 seconds. This rate, however, increases when you are playing or working hard—just as the cyclists that you read about at the beginning of this chapter were doing. Their breathing rates probably jumped to triple the normal breathing rate of 12 to 14 times a minute. Their depth of breathing increased, too.

When you are about to inhale, or breathe in, muscles attached to your ribs contract and lift the rib cage up and outward. At the same time, a dome-shaped muscle called the **diaphragm** (DIGH-uh-fram) contracts and flattens out. The actions of these muscles make your chest expand. The expansion of your chest results in more room in the lungs for air. So the same amount of air now occupies a larger space. This causes the pressure (a force that acts over a certain area) of air to decrease. As a result, the air pressure in your lungs becomes lower than the air pressure outside your body. The difference in pressure causes air to rush into your lungs.

When you exhale, or breathe out, the diaphragm relaxes and returns to its normal dome-shaped position. This action causes the space inside the chest to decrease. As it does, the air pressure in the chest cavity increases. This increase in pressure causes the lungs to get smaller, forcing air out of the lungs. And so you exhale.

Because the diaphragm is a skeletal muscle, its ability to contract and relax is under your control. (You may recall from Chapter 2 that skeletal muscle is called voluntary muscle.) Sometimes, however, the diaphragm contracts involuntarily. This usually occurs because the nerves (bundles of fibers that carry messages throughout the body) that control the diaphragm become irritated by eating too fast or by some other condition. Then, as you inhale air,

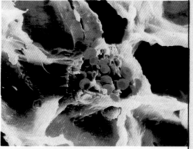
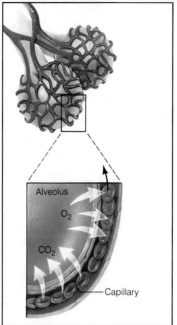

Figure 5–9 *Surrounding each alveolus is a network of capillaries. As blood flows through the capillaries, oxygen moves out of the alveolus into the blood. Carbon dioxide moves in the opposite direction—out of the blood into the alveolus. The photograph shows a section of a lung in which you can see a capillary containing red blood cells surrounded by alveoli.*

Alveolus
O_2
CO_2
Capillary

LIFE-SAVING TECHNIQUE

Sometimes a large piece of food gets stuck in the airway. The effects of this can be tragic. In the wrong place, the stuck food can shut off the flow of air completely. Victims are suddenly unable to breathe, speak, or call for help. They struggle, become unconscious, and may die from suffocation in a matter of minutes. For some years now, first-aid workers have used an effective technique to dislodge the food. In the Heimlich maneuver, the victim is grabbed around the waist from behind. Then the person attempting the maneuver forces his or her fists and forearms up against the bottom of the rib cage. This action compresses the lungs and usually exerts enough force to blast the food out of the airway with a stream of air.

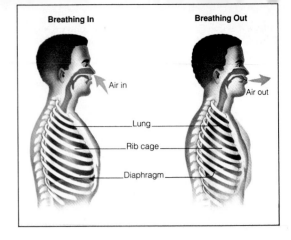

Figure 5–10 *When you breathe in, the muscles attached to your ribs contract and lift the rib cage up and outward, allowing more room in the lungs for air. When you breathe out, the muscles attached to your ribs relax and lower the rib cage, allowing less room in the lungs for air. What role does the diaphragm have in breathing?* ❶

Breathing In Breathing Out

Air in

Air out

Lung

Rib cage

Diaphragm

❶

Figure 5–11 *A swimmer has to gulp for air so that his lungs can deliver oxygen to every cell in his body quickly and frequently. On Jupiter, which has an atmosphere consisting of about 85 percent hydrogen and 15 percent helium, he would not be able to survive.*

the space between the vocal cords snaps shut with a clicking sound. You know this clicking sound as a hiccup!

You have probably had lots of experience with hiccups. And you have probably tried almost every remedy to get rid of them—from drinking a glass of water without stopping for air to holding your breath until they cease. These methods may help somewhat because they reduce the oxygen supply and increase the carbon dioxide level of your body. This condition can cause the involuntary contractions of the diaphragm muscle to stop, thereby bringing your hiccups to a much-welcomed end.

5–1 Section Review

1. What is the function of the respiratory system?
2. What is respiration?
3. What are the structures of the respiratory system? What is the function of each?
4. Explain how the exchange of oxygen and carbon dioxide occurs in the lungs.
5. How do you breathe?

Connection—*You and Your World*

6. When you have laryngitis, or an inflammation of the larynx, you have a hoarse voice, or no voice at all. How might cheering too enthusiastically at a football game cause laryngitis?

5–1 (continued)

CONTENT DEVELOPMENT

Point out to students that the diaphragm's movements happen automatically but that people can learn to control the muscle and thus regulate their breathing. Such control is important to actors and singers, who want to be able to project their voices, speak or sing at a certain volume, and always hit the right notes. Athletes practice deep breathing before they exercise to flush out carbon dioxide and take in more oxygen. Breathing exercises can help the body relax, clear the mind, and improve posture. Yoga, meditation, stress-reduction exercises, and even a natural child-birth method devel-

oped by Dr. Lamaze use controlled breathing techniques.

● ● ● ● **Integration** ● ● ● ●

Use the photograph of Jupiter's atmosphere to integrate astronomy into your lesson.

INDEPENDENT PRACTICE

Section Review 5–1

1. To get oxygen into the body and remove carbon dioxide and water from the body.

2. The energy-releasing process that is fueled by oxygen.

3. Nose—warms, moistens, and filters incoming air; throat—carries air; trachea—cleans and carries air; larynx and vocal cords—produce voice; bronchi—carry air into lungs; lungs and alveoli—exchange oxygen and carbon dioxide.

4. When air enters the alveoli in the lungs, the oxygen in the air seeps through the walls of the alveoli into the surrounding capillaries and hence into the blood, which carries it through the body. Carbon diox-

CONNECTIONS

How a Lie Detector Gives Its Verdict ②

You have probably seen television courtroom dramas in which the defendant was found guilty solely on the basis of the results of a lie detector test. While being entertained by the television program, you probably never thought that its story line had anything to do with your study of life science. How wrong you were! A lie detector, or polygraph, is an instrument that works on the following idea: People who tell a lie become nervous. Their nervousness increases their blood pressure, pulse and breathing rates, and makes them sweat.

Actually, the lie detector is a combination of three different instruments. The results of each instrument are recorded by a pen that makes ink lines on moving graph paper.

One of the instruments is called the *cardiosphygmometer.* It detects changes in blood pressure (pressure of blood in the arteries) and pulse rate (beating of the arteries caused by the pumping action of the heart). This information is picked up by a cufflike device that is placed over the upper arm. This device is similar to the one your doctor uses when checking your blood pressure.

The second instrument, called the *galvanometer,* monitors the flow of a tiny electric current (flow of charged particles) through the skin. When the skin is moist, as it is with perspiration, it will conduct the electric current better. Small electrodes are taped to the hand to record this activity.

The third instrument is called the *pneumogram,* which records breathing patterns. It consists of a rubber tube that is strapped across the chest. Within the tube are instruments that measure changes in breathing patterns.

One drawback to the use of lie detectors is that some people get so nervous about taking the test that they may appear to lie even though they are telling the truth. And in rare instances, some people may be able to control their emotions so well that they can lie without affecting the results of the test. Although lie detectors are seen in television dramas, their results are generally not considered admissible in real-life courtrooms.

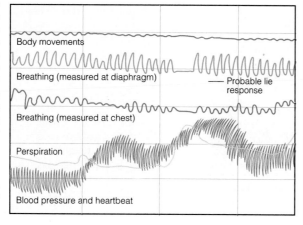

Body movements

Breathing (measured at diaphragm) — Probable lie response

Breathing (measured at chest)

Perspiration

Blood pressure and heartbeat

5-2 The Excretory System

Have students investigate the work of Dr. Samuel L. Kountz (1930–1981). The grandson of slaves, Dr. Kountz became a pioneer in organ transplants. During his career, he performed more than 500 kidney transplants. He was one of the first African-American students to enroll in the University of Arkansas Medical School. His work included the development of new techniques for organ preservation and for the prevention of organ rejection.

ESL STRATEGY 5-2

Have students look in their textbooks to find appropriate matching terms for the following definitions. Using these terms, they may enjoy playing Jeopardy: A student reads one of the definitions, and another student supplies the term that matches it.

• The respiratory system's main organs
• The excretory system's main organs and the body's filter
• The kidney's filtering factories
• Cup-shaped part of the nephron
• Liquid remaining in kidneys after reabsorption
• Tubes carrying urine to urinary bladder
• Small tube that releases urine from bladder

Guide for Reading

Focus on these questions as you read.

▶ What is the function of the excretory system?

▶ What are the four major organs of the excretory system?

FIND OUT BY READING

Reading Poetry

❶ The first line of John Donne's poem entitled "Meditation XVII" was quoted in this chapter. Find a copy of this poem in the library and read it. Is there another line in this poem that is familiar to you?

5-2 The Excretory System

When the sixteenth-century English poet John Donne wrote that "No man is an island, entire of itself," he was actually talking about the human mind and spirit. However, this phrase can also be used to describe the human body: No human body can function without help from its surroundings. For example, your body must obtain food, water, and oxygen from its surroundings and get rid of wastes that may poison you. In order to do this, three body systems work together to provide a pathway for materials to enter and leave the body.

You have already learned about two of these systems: the digestive system and the respiratory system. The digestive system is the pathway for food and water to enter the body. The respiratory system enables oxygen to enter and carbon dioxide and water vapor to leave the body. The third system is the excretory (EHKS-kruh-tor-ee) system. **The excretory system provides a way for various wastes to be removed from the body.** These wastes include excess water and salts, carbon dioxide, and urea (a nitrogen waste). The process by which these wastes are removed from the body is called **excretion.**

You have just read about one of the organs of the excretory system: the lungs. Because the lungs get rid of the wastes carbon dioxide and water vapor, they are members of the excretory system as well as the respiratory system. The remaining organs of the excretory system are the kidneys, the liver, and the skin.

The Kidneys

Have your ever made spaghetti? If so, you know that you have to use a strainer to separate the cooked spaghetti from the cooking water or else you will be eating soggy spaghetti! The strainer acts as a filter, separating one material (spaghetti) from the other (water). Like the spaghetti strainer, the **kidneys** act as the body's filter. In doing so, the kidneys filter wastes and poisons from the blood.

The kidneys, which are the main organs of the excretory system, are reddish brown in color and

---

TEACHING STRATEGY 5-2

FOCUS/MOTIVATION

You may have noticed that birds excrete uric acid "paste" rather than liquid urine.

• **Why do you think this is so?** (In order to fly efficiently, birds must have minimal weight. Water is very heavy. Storing enough water to flush out and dilute the water-soluble wastes of ammonia or urea would greatly increase a bird's weight.)

CONTENT DEVELOPMENT

Explain to students that the main job of the excretory system is to remove wastes from the body. We have just learned that the lungs remove some wastes.

• **What kind of wastes are removed by the lungs?** (Carbon dioxide and water.)

There are also other wastes that the body must remove. These include more water, salts, nitrogen-containing wastes, and certain poisons or drugs that are taken into the body.

Explain to students that most of the toxic wastes the body must get rid of were produced by the body during necessary cellular activities. If your excretory system did not function properly, your body would gradually poison itself. This buildup of poisons would lead to severe illness and death.

FOCUS/MOTIVATION

Ask students if they can answer this riddle:

shaped like kidney beans. There is one kidney on each side of the spinal column just above the waist. Although each kidney is not much bigger than an extra-large bar of soap, together they receive and filter almost 1 liter of blood per minute, pumped into them from the aorta (the body's largest artery).

The actual filtering process takes place within the kidney's millions of microscopic chemical-filtering factories called **nephrons** (NEHF-rahnz). As you can see from Figure 5–12, each nephron is made up of a complex network of tubes enclosed in an even more complex network of capillaries.

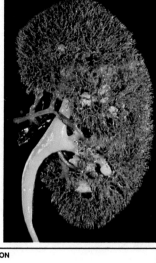

Figure 5–12 *The photograph shows the large number of blood vessels in a kidney. Some of the structures of a kidney as well as the structure of a microscopic nephron are shown in the illustrations.*

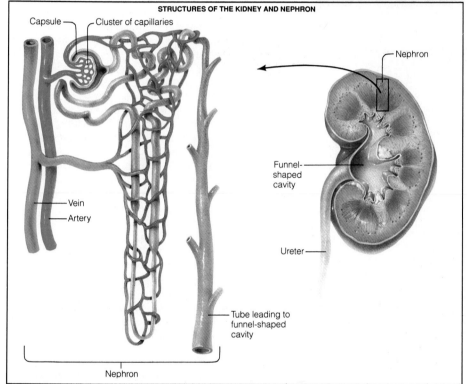

STRUCTURES OF THE KIDNEY AND NEPHRON

Capsule

Cluster of capillaries

Nephron

Vein

Artery

Funnel-shaped cavity

Ureter

Tube leading to funnel-shaped cavity

Nephron

H ■ 119

FIND OUT BY READING

READING POETRY

Skill: Reading comprehension

Have a volunteer read the poem aloud to the class. Point out that Donne's poetry, widely admired in his day and later ignored, was rediscovered with enthusiasm in the twentieth century. Students may recognize the line "And therefore never send to know for whom the bell tolls; It tolls for thee." Ernest Hemingway borrowed the phrase "for whom the bell tolls" to use as a title for a 1940 novel he wrote about the Spanish Civil War (1936–1939).

Integration: Use the Find Out by Reading activity to integrate language arts into your lesson.

FACTS AND FIGURES

NEPHRONS

The kidneys contain approximately 2 million nephrons. If the many tubules that make up one kidney were placed end to end, they would stretch for more than 280 kilometers. Each nephron is about 3 centimeters long, yet it is microscopic because the nephron is so narrow that it cannot be seen by the unaided eye.

• **What do you and the ocean have in common?** (Both contain large amounts of salt water.)

In addition to the removal of toxic wastes, an important job of the kidneys is to regulate the amount of salt found in body fluids.

• **How long do you think it takes the kidneys to process all the blood in your body?** (About 30 minutes.)

• **How much blood do you think is filtered through the kidneys every day?** (About 2000 liters.)

You can see that the kidneys are extremely vital organs for maintaining good health.

GUIDED PRACTICE

Skills Development

Skill: Interpreting illustrations

Have students study Figure 5–12. Notice that the kidney is divided into an inner section and an outer section. The outer section contains about a million microscopic units called nephrons. The illustration on the left shows the details of one nephron. Explain that each nephron acts as a filtering system.

Using Figure 5–12, have students follow the path of filtration as you describe the process. Blood is brought to the kidney by an artery. Once inside the kidney, the blood travels through smaller and smaller arteries until it reaches a cluster of capillaries. Here, various materials are filtered out of the blood.

HEALTH

Kidney stones are usually composed of uric acid, calcium oxalate, and calcium phosphate or magnesium phosphate. If these stones pass into the ureter, they may cause severe pain beginning in the region of the kidney and radiating into the abdomen, pelvis, and legs. Nausea and vomiting may also occur.

Patients suffering from kidney stones are instructed to drink large amounts of fluids in hopes that the stones will be flushed out in the urine. If this does not happen, doctors can use a laser or a lithotripter (a machine that projects shock waves through water) to break up the kidney stones.

HISTORICAL NOTE

ORGAN TRANSPLANT

The first organ to be transplanted in a human was a kidney. In 1954, the first kidney transplant was performed at Peter Bent Brigham Hospital in Boston.

5–2 (continued)

CONTENT DEVELOPMENT

• **What substances are included in those that are filtered out of the blood by the kidneys?** (Water, salts, digested food particles, and urea.)

• **Which of these substances does your body retain?** (Digested food and most of the water.)

• **Which of these substances does your body need to get rid of?** (Urea and some of the salts.)

The nitrogenous waste called urea, some salts, and some water are not reabsorbed by the blood. Instead, they form urine and pass into the cup-shaped part of the nephron called the capsule. The capsule leads to a complex set of tubes ending in a collecting tubule that leads to the ureter.

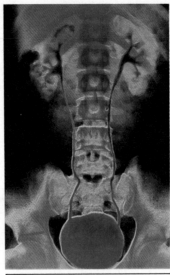

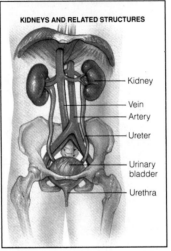

KIDNEYS AND RELATED STRUCTURES

- Kidney
- Vein
- Artery
- Ureter
- Urinary bladder
- Urethra

Figure 5–13 *The main organs of the excretory system are the two kidneys, which are the green bean-shaped organs in this color-enhanced X-ray. Use the illustration to locate the other excretory organs in the X-ray. What is the function of the kidneys?* **①**

As blood pours into the kidney through an artery, it travels through smaller and smaller arteries. Finally, it enters a bundle of capillaries. Here, materials such as water, salts, urea, and nutrients pass from the capillaries into a cup-shaped part of the nephron called the **capsule.** What remains in the capillaries are large particles such as proteins and blood cells. The capsule then carries the filtered material (water, salts, urea, and nutrients) to a tiny twisting tube. To picture this part of the nephron (the capsule and tiny tube), try the following: Clench one of your hands into a fist and then cup the other hand around your fist. Your clenched fist is the bundle of capillaries and your cupped hand is the capsule. The arm to which the cupped hand is attached is the tiny twisting tube.

As the filtered material moves through the tiny tube in the nephron, the nutrients, salts, and most of the water that passed through the capillaries are reabsorbed, or taken back, into the blood. If this reabsorption process did not take place, the body would soon lose most of the water, salts, and nutrients that it needs to survive.

The liquid that remains in the tiny tube after reabsorption has taken place is called urine. Urine is mostly water. The exact percentage of water in a person's urine varies depending on the person's health, what the person has been eating and drinking, and how much the person has been exercising. Generally, urine is about 96 percent water. The remaining 4 percent are wastes, such as urea and excess salts.

Suppose you drink a lot of liquid on a particular day. You will produce more urine than you normally would, and it will contain more water. If, on the other hand, you were to eat rather salty foods, you would produce less urine, and it would contain less water. So the amount of water or salts that you take into your body affects the amount of urine and the water content of the urine that is excreted. In this way, your kidneys control the amount of liquid in your body. Put another way, the amount of water that is excreted in your urine each day equals the amount of water that you take into your body each day.

From the kidneys, urine trickles down through two narrow tubes called **ureters** (yoo-REET-erz). The

---

Refer students to Figure 5–13. The ureter conducts the urine to the urinary bladder, where it is temporarily stored. Eventually, it passes out of the body through the urethra.

▶ *Multimedia* ◀

Use the transparency Urinary System in your *Transparency Binder* to help students understand how the urinary system functions.

REINFORCEMENT/RETEACHING

Have students use Figure 5–13 for the location of the kidneys in the body. Then have them locate their kidneys.

• **Where are your kidneys located?** (In the lower back region, near the spine.)

• **What shape are the kidneys?** (Accept all logical answers. If necessary, suggest they are shaped like beans.)

Pass around a few kidney beans for students to examine. Explain that these beans are appropriately named because they not

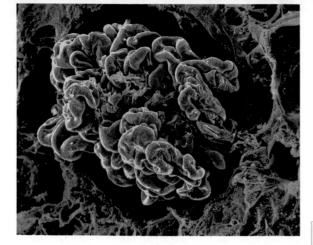

Figure 5–14 *The cluster, or bundle, of capillaries in the middle of this photograph carry waste-laden blood into the nephron. Here, wastes leave the blood through the walls of the capillaries and enter the nephron's cup-shaped capsule.*

ureters carry the urine to a muscular sac called the **urinary bladder.** The urinary bladder can store up to 470 milliliters of urine before releasing it from the body through a small tube called the **urethra** (yoo-REE-thruh).

Other Excretory Organs

In addition to the kidneys and the lungs, two other organs of the body play a major role in excretion. These organs are the liver and the skin.

THE LIVER You may recall from Chapter 3 that the **liver** plays a role in the digestion of foods. But did you also know that the liver helps to remove wastes from the body? The liver performs this function by filtering materials from the blood as the blood passes through the liver. One of the substances the liver removes from the blood is excess amino acids. You may recall from Chapter 3 that amino acids are the building blocks of protein. These amino acids are broken down in the liver to form urea, which, as you just learned, is a part of urine.

The liver also converts the hemoglobin from worn-out red blood cells into substances such as bile, which plays a role in the breakdown of fats. In addition, the liver cleanses the blood by removing and digesting most of the bacteria that enter from the large intestine.

only are shaped like the kidneys but are also a dark-red color like the kidneys.

FIND OUT BY DOING

CLOSE AT HAND

Discovery Learning

Skills: Manipulative, making observations, making references

Materials: hand lens, plastic glove, chalkboard, ink pad, index cards

In this activity students observe the epidermal layer of the skin through a hand lens. They should easily be able to identify the ridges on the skin and the openings to the sweat glands. When they put the glove on and take it off, they should observe moisture on the skin due to perspiration and condensation. They will observe the moisture on their hand when they press their hand against the chalkboard. They will find that all fingerprints are alike in that they are made of whorls and swirls. Some patterns may be very similar, especially to the unaided eye, but no two fingerprints are exactly alike.

FACTS AND FIGURES

KERATIN

Keratin, a tough protein substance, is found in the epidermis of the skin and is the main component of hair and nails.

Close at Hand

1. Using a hand lens, examine the skin on your hand.

2. Identify the epidermis and pores on the ridges of the skin.

3. Place a plastic glove on your hand and remove it after 5 minutes. Look at your hand. Describe what happened to your hand. If you placed your hand against a chalkboard and then quickly removed it, what would you see?

■ How does this activity illustrate a function of the skin?

4. Now place the tip of your right forefinger (finger nearest the thumb) on an ink pad. Move your finger from left to right with a slight rolling motion.

5. Immediately remove your finger from the ink pad and place it on an index card using the same rolling motion.

Compare your fingerprints with those of your classmates. Are they alike? How are they different? Do you notice any patterns that are similar in some of the fingerprints?

■ Are any two fingerprints ever exactly alike?

THE SKIN The remaining excretory organ is the **skin.** Are you surprised to learn that the skin is considered an organ? If so, you will be even more surprised to know that the skin is sometimes thought of as the largest organ of the human body. It covers an area of 1.5 to 2 square meters in an average person. This is about the size of a small area rug. It varies in thickness from under 0.5 millimeter on the eyelids to about 6 millimeters on the soles of the feet. The skin is made up of two main layers: the **epidermis** and the **dermis.** The word *-dermis* means skin. The prefix *epi-* indicates that the epidermis is on, or over, the dermis.

The top layer, or epidermis, contains mostly dead, flattened cells that are constantly shed from the body. If you have ever had a slight case of dandruff (flakes of skin from the scalp), then you have seen groups of these dead cells firsthand. If you are wondering why you still have skin even though its cells are constantly being shed from your body, wonder no more. The answer, you see, is that the innermost layer of the epidermis contains the living and active cells that produce more cells. As new cells are produced, they are pushed nearer the surface of the skin, where they become the outer layer of cells—soon to flatten and die.

Any experience you may have had accidentally jabbing your skin with a sharp object (such as a needle or a thorn) will tell you something else about the epidermis. Did you feel pain? Did you bleed? Probably not. The epidermis does not contain any nerves or blood vessels.

Unlike the epidermis, the dermis, or bottom layer of the skin, contains nerves and blood vessels. The dermis is also thicker than the epidermis. In addition, the upper part of the dermis contains small, fingerlike structures that are similar to the villi in the small intestine. Because the epidermis is built on top of these structures, it has an irregular outline that forms ridges. These ridges, in turn, form patterns on the fingertips, on the palms of the hands, and on the soles of the feet. On the fingertips, these patterns are more commonly known as fingerprints. Every human has a unique set of fingerprints. And although the fingerprints of identical twins are similar, no two fingertips are the same.

5–2 (continued)

FOCUS/MOTIVATION

If you have ever had a sunburn, you may have peeled off rather large pieces of your skin. This is the epidermis. Epidermal cells are continually being shed and replaced by new cells, which are produced in the dermis. The dermis is rich in blood vessels and connective tissue and contains small hairlike projections. Because the epidermis is built on top of these projections, your skin has ridges in it. These ridges form fingerprints, as well as the patterns on the palms of your hands and the soles of your feet.

CONTENT DEVELOPMENT

Have students examine Figure 5–15.

• **Name the various structures found in the skin.** (Hair, sweat glands, nerve fibers, fat cells, oil glands, blood vessels.)

Explain that hair, fingernails, and toenails are forms of dead skin cells.

• **What is the function of the sweat glands?** (They produce sweat, or perspiration, that helps the body get rid of excess water, salts, and wastes such as urea. Evaporation of perspiration also helps to cool the body.)

• **What do you think is the function of the oil glands?** (They produce oil to keep the hair soft and flexible and to keep the skin soft.)

• **What kinds of nerve receptors are found in the skin?** (Receptors for pain, pressure, heat, and cold.)

Summarize the four basic functions of the skin: (1) to protect the internal organs and to help protect against invasion by for-

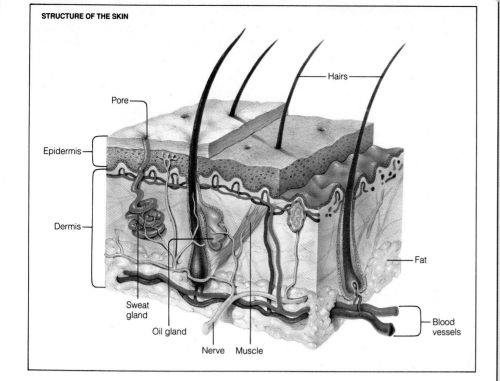

STRUCTURE OF THE SKIN

Hairs
Pore
Epidermis
Dermis
Sweat gland
Oil gland
Nerve   Muscle
Fat
Blood vessels

Thus fingerprints provide a foolproof way of identifying everyone, including those people who have lost their memories because of an injury or illness.

The skin also contains hair, nails, and sweat and oil glands. Hair and nails are formed from skin cells that first become filled with a tough, fiberlike protein

Figure 5–15 *The skin, which is the body's largest organ, is made of two main layers. The top layer is called the epidermis, and the bottom layer is called the dermis. In which layer of the skin would you find the blood vessels?* ❶

Figure 5–16 *A close-up of a fingertip (right) shows the pattern of ridges that form a fingerprint. An even closer view shows the individual ridges (left).*

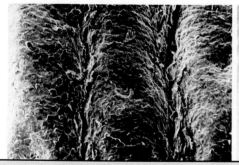

ANNOTATION KEY

Answers
❶ In the dermis. (Relating facts)

BACKGROUND INFORMATION

SKIN AND TEMPERATURE

The lungs help to remove some body heat, but the main regulator of body temperature is the skin. When the body becomes overheated, blood vessels in the skin dilate, allowing more blood to flow through them. Thus, more heat is brought to the surface of the body where it can be lost directly. Sweat glands also become more active, increasing the amount of perspiration. Evaporation of perspiration is a further cooling process.

The reverse happens when the body becomes cold. Blood vessels constrict, and sweat production decreases; both measures conserve body heat. The nervous system can also play a role in warming the body by signaling the muscles to contract, which causes the familiar signs of shivering and chattering of teeth.

eign substances; (2) to excrete excess water, salts, and urea; (3) to help regulate body temperature; and (4) to receive sensory information regarding temperature, pressure, and pain.

ENRICHMENT

▶ *Activity Book*

Students will be interested in investigating the effects of alcohol and water on skin temperature using the chapter activity Keeping Cool.

REINFORCEMENT/RETEACHING

Be certain that students understand the differences between the elimination of undigested food through the large intestine and excretion—the elimination of chemical wastes through the lungs, kidneys, skin, and liver. Wastes eliminated through the large intestine have been in contact only with the digestive tract; they were never absorbed into body cells. Chemical wastes, on the other hand, are produced as a result of various cellular activities.

INDEPENDENT PRACTICE

▶ *Multimedia* ◀

You may want to show the video called Excretory System at this point so that students can review how the kidneys, lungs, and skin extract wastes from the blood and eliminate them from the body. After students view the video, have them work in small groups to diagram feedback systems that regulate the action of the kidneys, lungs, and skin as excretory systems.

Figure 5–17 *Hair and nails are formed from skin cells that first become filled with a tough, fiberlike protein and then die. Nails grow at an average rate of 0.5 to 1.2 millimeters per day. Imagine how long it took for the man in the photograph to grow his nails!*

and then die. Sweat glands are coiled tubes that connect to pores, or openings, in the surface of the skin. Sweat glands help the body get rid of excess salts, urea, and about 0.5 liter of water every day. Together, these materials form a liquid called sweat, or perspiration.

Perspiration not only rids the body of wastes, it also helps to regulate body temperature. It does this by evaporating from body surfaces. Let's see how. When the temperature of your surroundings rises, or when you work really hard, you perspire more. As the sweat reaches the surface of the skin, it begins to evaporate, or change from a liquid to a gas. The process of evaporation requires heat. That heat comes from your body. Because the body loses heat, the evaporation of sweat is a cooling process—and your skin feels cool. During and after a strenuous activity, such as mowing the lawn or playing a game of soccer, you may sweat away up to 10 liters of liquid in a 24-hour period alone! However, as you may

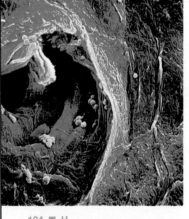

Figure 5–18 *One of the 3 million sweat glands contained in the skin of an adult is shown in this photograph. The tiny green round objects inside the sweat gland are bacteria. What is the function of the sweat glands?* ❶

PROBLEM ??? Solving

How Do I Explain This?

From what you have learned about the respiratory and excretory systems, try your hand at developing some explanations for the following situations.

Relating Concepts

1. A humidifier is a device that adds moisture to the surrounding air. A humidifier would be useful to have in a room or building during dry winter weather.

2. A dehumidifier removes moisture from the surrounding air. This device can make a person feel more comfortable during humid summer weather.

3. At higher altitudes, the air is less dense (packed closely together) than it is at lower altitudes. Mountain climbers and athletes who train at higher elevations often have difficulty breathing at these elevations. ❶

remember from the story at the beginning of this chapter, sweating makes you thirsty. You drink lots of water and thereby replenish the water lost by sweating.

5–2 Section Review

1. What is the function of the excretory system? What structures enable it to perform this function?
2. What is urea? How is it formed?
3. Name and describe the two layers of the skin.
4. Why do you sweat?

Critical Thinking—*Applying Concepts*

5. Suppose that it is a very hot day and you drink a lot of water. Would your urine contain more or less water than it would on a cooler day? Explain your answer.

PROBLEM SOLVING

HOW DO I EXPLAIN THAT?

This feature enables students to relate what they have learned about the respiratory and excretory systems to real-life situations.

1. Adding moisture to dry air would make breathing more comfortable because dry air can irritate nasal passages. Adding moisture to the air also slows evaporation of moisture from the skin, so people feel warmer at lower temperatures.

2. On hot, humid days, moisture does not evaporate easily from the skin. Reducing the moisture level in the air would help perspiration evaporate more easily. A person would feel cooler, even though the temperature was high.

3. The decrease in oxygen concentration and air pressure at higher altitudes makes breathing more difficult for people used to the higher pressure of oxygen at lower altitudes.

Integration: Use the Problem Solving feature to integrate earth science concepts about atmosphere into your lesson.

4. Sweat is part of a cooling process to help regulate body temperature. When your body temperature rises, you begin to sweat. When the sweat reaches the surface of the skin, it evaporates using the body's heat. Because the body loses heat, it feels cooler.

5. If you didn't drink enough water to replace the water you lost through perspiration, your urine would probably contain less water because the body would keep some water to make up for the amount lost through perspiration.

REINFORCEMENT/RETEACHING

Review students' responses to the Section Review questions. Reteach any material that is still unclear, based on students' responses.

CLOSURE

▶ *Review and Reinforcement Guide*

Students may now complete Section 5–2 in the *Review and Reinforcement Guide.*

Laboratory Investigation

MEASURING THE VOLUME OF EXHALED AIR

Laboratory Investigation

Measuring the Volume of Exhaled Air

BEFORE THE LAB

1. Gather all materials at least one day prior to conducting the lab. You should have one spirometer for each group of three or four students.

2. Have students read the laboratory procedure. Each student should prepare a data table for recording his or her results.

3. Divide the class into groups of three or four students, depending on the number of spirometers available.

PRE-LAB DISCUSSION

• **What is the purpose of this laboratory activity?** (To measure the volume of air that is normally exhaled.)

• **What is the name for the device that you will be using to measure the exhaled air?** (A spirometer.)

• **Why do you think vegetable coloring is added to the water?** (Colored water is easier to see; it is easier to read the volume in the graduated cylinder.)

• **Into which piece of tubing will you exhale?** (The shorter piece.)

• **Why should you cover the end of the rubber tubing with a paper towel before exhaling into it?** (For sanitary reasons; to provide protection against dirt, bacteria, and the like that may have accumulated on the rubber tubing.)

Demonstrate the exhaling procedure. Remind students to inhale and exhale normally.

• **What happens when you exhale into the tubing?** (The exhaled air pushes down on the water in the bottle. This causes some water to be pushed up the other

Problem

What is the volume of exhaled air?

Materials *(per group)*

glass-marking pencil	paper towel
spirometer	graduated cylinder
red vegetable coloring	

Procedure ⚠

1. Obtain a spirometer. A spirometer is an instrument that is used to measure the volume of air that the lungs can hold.
2. Fill the plastic bottle four-fifths full of water. Add several drops of vegetable coloring to the water. With the glass-marking pencil, mark the level of the water.
3. Reattach the rubber tubing as shown in the diagram.
4. Cover the lower part of the shorter length of rubber tubing with the paper towel by wrapping the towel around it. This is the part of the rubber tubing that you will need to place your mouth against. **Note:** *Your mouth should not come in contact with the rubber tubing itself, only with the paper towel.*
5. After inhaling normally, exhale normally into the shorter length of rubber tubing.
6. The exhaled air will cause an equal volume of water to move through the other length of tubing into the graduated cylinder. Record the volume of this water in milliliters in a data table.
7. Pour the colored water from the cylinder back into the plastic bottle.
8. Repeat steps 3 through 7 two more times. Record the results in your data table. Calculate the average of the three readings.

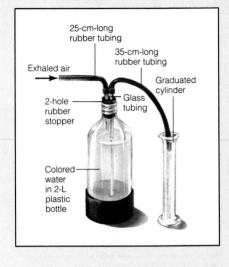

9. Run in place for 2 minutes and exhale into the rubber tubing. Record the volume of the water in the graduated cylinder.

10. Rest for a few minutes until your breathing returns to normal. Then repeat step 9 two more times and record the results. Calculate the average of the three readings.

Observations

How does your average volume of exhaled air before exercise compare to your average volume of exhaled air after exercise?

Analysis and Conclusions

1. Why is it important to measure the volume of exhaled air three times?
2. Explain how exercise affects the volume of exhaled air.
3. **On Your Own** Describe how you could determine the volume of air you exhale in a minute.

piece of tubing and collected in the graduated cylinder.)

• **How much water will be collected?** (An amount equal to the volume of air that was exhaled.)

Remind students of the correct way to read the volume of water in a graduated cylinder. (Read at eye level. Read the bottom of the curve, or meniscus.)

Demonstrate the proper way to replace the water in the plastic bottle. (Remove the rubber stopper only. None of the tubing needs to be altered.)

Have a student demonstrate running in place. Remind students to rest and allow their breathing to return to normal before repeating the running procedure. While one team member is resting, another can be running.

TEACHING STRATEGY

1. Stress cooperation among team members in timing, reading volumes, recording results, computing averages, and so on.

2. To guard against breakage of graduated cylinders, it is a good idea to have one

Study Guide

Summarizing Key Concepts

5–1 The Respiratory System

▲ Respiration is the combining of oxygen and food in the body to produce energy and the waste gases carbon dioxide and water vapor.

▲ The main task of the respiratory system is to get oxygen into the body and carbon dioxide out of the body.

▲ The respiratory system consists of the nose, throat, larynx, trachea, bronchi, and lungs. The bronchi divide into smaller tubes, which end inside the lungs in clusters of alveoli.

▲ The larynx, or voice box, contains the vocal cords. These structures are responsible for producing the human voice.

▲ The exchange of oxygen and carbon dioxide occurs in the alveoli, which are surrounded by a network of capillaries.

▲ Breathing consists of inhaling and exhaling. These motions are produced by movements of the diaphragm.

5–2 The Excretory System

▲ The excretory system is responsible for removing various wastes from the body.

▲ Excretion is the process by which wastes are removed.

▲ The principal organs of the excretory system are the kidneys.

▲ Each kidney contains millions of microscopic chemical filtration factories called nephrons.

▲ Within a nephron, substances such as nutrients, water, salt, and urea are filtered out of the blood. These substances pass into the cup-shaped part of the nephron called the capsule. Much of the water and nutrients is reabsorbed into the bloodstream. The liquid that remains in the tubes of the nephron is called urine.

▲ Urine travels from each kidney through a ureter to the urinary bladder. It then passes out of the body through the urethra.

▲ The liver removes excess amino acids from the blood and breaks them down into urea, which makes up urine. The liver also converts hemoglobin from worn-out red blood cells into bile.

▲ The skin has two main layers: the epidermis and the dermis. Sweat glands located in the dermis get rid of excess water, salt, and urea.

Reviewing Key Terms

Define each term in a complete sentence.

5–1 The Respiratory System
respiration
nose
epiglottis
trachea
larynx
vocal cord
bronchus
lung
alveolus
diaphragm

5–2 The Excretory System
excretion
kidney
nephron
capsule
ureter
urinary bladder
urethra
liver
skin
epidermis
dermis

• **Why would people's average volumes differ?** (Accept all logical answers, including differences in lung size because of sex and physical development—comparing, inferring, analyzing.)

OBSERVATIONS

For most students, exercise will increase the need for oxygen, and the body will comper.sate by inhaling and exhaling faster and deeper. Thus, the average amount of exhaled air should be greater after exercise.

ANALYSIS AND CONCLUSIONS

1. Three measurements will ensure more accurate data, as each exhalation may be slightly different from the next. Three trials will give a more accurate average.

2. Exercise increases the volume of exhaled air. This is due in part because exercise causes an increase in the amount of carbon dioxide wastes produced by the body, which, in turn, causes the body to exhale more deeply to eliminate this excess carbon dioxide.

3. Count the number of breaths normally taken per minute. Multiply the number of breaths per minute by the average volume of exhaled air before exercise. This would give the volume of air exhaled in a minute.

GOING FURTHER: ENRICHMENT

Part 1

Have students compare females' results with those for males. Using individual averages, calculate a class average for females and one for males. Does there appear to be a significant difference between the two? If so, what might account for this difference?

Part 2

Have students repeat the activity using a plastic bottle that has a volume of at least 7 liters and an equal-sized container to catch the displaced water. This time, instead of breathing normally, students should take very deep breaths and slowly expel all the air they can into the tubing. The volume of displaced water can be measured by pouring it into a graduated cylinder. This total volume approaches the maximum volume the lungs can hold, which is sometimes called vital capacity. Some students' vital capacity may be as great as 6 liters.

---

team member hold the graduated cylinder in place when another team member is exhaling into the spirometer.

3. You may need to assist some students in computing averages.

DISCOVERY STRATEGIES

Discuss how the investigation relates to the chapter ideas by asking open questions similar to the following:

• **Why is the exhaling procedure done three times?** (To obtain an average reading by having three numbers to add together and then divide by three; an average reading is generally more accurate than a single reading—relating, analyzing.)

• **How do you predict the volume of exhaled air after running will compare with the volume exhaled before running?** (Based on the chapter information, students should predict that the volume of exhaled air will be greater after exercise because exercise will increase the body's need for oxygen, which it will get by inhaling and exhaling more often—predicting, relating, analyzing.)

Chapter Review

ALTERNATIVE ASSESSMENT

The *Prentice Hall Science* program includes a variety of testing components and methodologies. Aside from the Chapter Review questions, you may opt to use the Chapter Test or the Computer Test Bank Test in your *Test Book* for assessment of important facts and concepts. In addition, Performance-Based Test are included in your *Test Book*. These Performance-Based Tests are designed to test science process skills, rather than factual content recall. Since they are not content dependent, Performance-Based Tests can be distributed after students complete a chapter or after they complete the entire textbook.

CONTENT REVIEW

Multiple Choice
1. b
2. c
3. b
4. d
5. a
6. c
7. d
8. b
9. a
10. a

True or False
1. T
2. F, mucus
3. F, epiglottis
4. T
5. T
6. F, urethra
7. T
8. T

Concept Mapping
Row 1: Nose
Row 2: Warms and moistens
Row 3: Larynx, Vocal cords
Row 4: Trachea, Alveoli

CONCEPT MASTERY

1. Breathing is the process of inhaling and exhaling air. Respiration is the process of combining oxygen with food to produce energy.
2. The kidneys help to keep water and waste levels in the body at a constant and safe level; keeping constant conditions in the body is part of homeostasis.

Content Review

Multiple Choice

Choose the letter of the answer that best completes each statement.

1. In the body cells, food and oxygen combine to produce energy during
   a. digestion.   c. circulation.
   b. respiration.   d. excretion.
2. The lungs, nose, and trachea are all part of the
   a. skeletal system.
   b. digestive system.
   c. respiratory system.
   d. circulatory system.
3. Air enters the body through the
   a. lungs.   c. larynx.
   b. nose.   d. trachea.
4. Another name for the windpipe is the
   a. alveolus.   c. epiglottis.
   b. larynx.   d. trachea.
5. The voice box is also known as the
   a. larynx.   c. trachea.
   b. windpipe.   d. alveolus.
6. The trachea divides into two tubes called
   a. alveoli.   c. bronchi.
   b. air sacs.   d. ureters.
7. The process by which wastes are removed from the body is called
   a. digestion.   c. circulation.
   b. respiration.   d. excretion.
8. The kidneys contain microscopic chemical filtration factories called
   a. alveoli.   c. bronchi.
   b. nephrons.   d. cilia.
9. Urine is stored in the
   a. urinary bladder.   c. alveolus.
   b. urethra.   d. kidneys.
10. The top layer of skin is the
    a. epidermis.   c. alveolus.
    b. dermis.   d. epiglottis.

True or False

If the statement is true, write "true." If it is false, change the underlined word or words to make the statement true.

1. The job of getting oxygen into the body and getting carbon dioxide out is the main task of the <u>respiratory</u> system.
2. Dust particles in the incoming air are filtered by <u>blood vessels</u> in the nose.
3. The flap of tissue that covers the trachea whenever food is swallowed is the <u>larynx</u>.
4. The clusters of air sacs in the lungs are called <u>alveoli</u>.
5. The organs that regulate the amount of liquid in the body are the <u>kidneys</u>.
6. The <u>ureter</u> is the tube through which urine leaves the body.
7. The <u>liver</u> converts hemoglobin into bile.
8. The <u>lungs</u> are excretory organs.

Concept Mapping

Complete the following concept map for Section 5–1. Refer to pages H8–H9 to construct a concept map for the entire chapter.

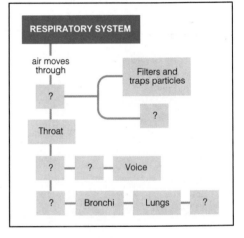

---

3. Rib muscles contract, pulling on the diaphragm muscle. As the diaphragm contracts and pulls down, the chest cavity enlarges. This causes a decrease in air pressure, which, in turn, causes air to rush into the lungs. The reverse occurs during exhalation.

4. The lungs help to remove carbon dioxide wastes and water. This is an excretory function. The lungs also take in oxygen from the air, which is a respiratory function.

5. The nephron is like a tiny filtering station, which allows important components of the blood such as food and water to be reabsorbed into the blood while waste products are concentrated in the nephron and eventually leave the kidney through the ureters.

6. The skin is an excretory organ because it releases various wastes such as excess water, salts, and some urea from the body.

7. The kidney removes wastes from the blood, much as a filter removes unwanted particles from air or water.

8. The liver is part of the digestive system because it produces bile, which helps to

Concept Mastery

Discuss each of the following in a brief paragraph.

1. What is the difference between respiration and breathing?
2. How do the kidneys help to maintain homeostasis?
3. What role do the rib muscles and diaphragm play in breathing?
4. Why are the lungs considered to be both respiratory and excretory organs?
5. Explain the structure and function of a nephron.
6. Why is the skin classified as an excretory organ?
7. How is the kidney similar to a filter?
8. Why is the liver considered to be part of the digestive system as well as part of the excretory system?
9. What changes occur in the lungs when you inhale? What changes occur in the lungs when you exhale?
10. Name and describe four organs of excretion.
11. Trace the path of excess water from the nephrons to the outside of the body.

Critical Thinking and Problem Solving

Use the skills you have developed in this chapter to answer each of the following.

1. **Making comparisons** How are respiration and the burning of fuel similar? How are they different?
2. **Relating concepts** Would urine contain more or less water on a hot day? Explain.
3. **Relating concepts** How do respiration and excretion relate to the process of homeostasis?
4. **Designing an experiment** Design an experiment to show that the lungs excrete water.
5. **Interpreting data** Use your knowledge of the respiratory system to interpret the data table. What are the differences between inhaled air and exhaled air? How do you account for these differences?

	Inhaled Air	Exhaled Air
Nitrogen	79%	79%
Oxygen	21%	16%
Carbon Dioxide	0.04%	4.00%

6. **Applying concepts** What do you think is the advantage of having two kidneys?
7. **Making comparisons** How are the substances in the capsule of the nephron different from those in the urine that leaves the kidneys?
8. **Relating cause and effect** Emphysema is a disease in which the alveoli are damaged. How would this affect a person's ability to breathe?
9. **Relating cause and effect** Explain what happens to your throat when you sleep with your mouth open, especially when your nose is clogged because of a cold.
10. **Using the writing process** A children's television studio wants to make a movie that explains the process of respiration to young students. You have been asked to write a script that describes the travels of oxygen and carbon dioxide through the human respiratory system. Write a brief outline of your script, including information about what happens in each part of the respiratory system.

---

break up fats from the foods we eat. The liver is also part of the excretory system because it filters materials such as excess amino acids and bacteria from the blood.

9. When you inhale, the chest cavity enlarges and causes air pressure in the lungs to decrease. This causes air to rush into the body. When you exhale, the chest cavity shrinks and causes air pressure to increase. This increased air pressure causes air to rush out of the body.

10. Lungs—excrete water and carbon dioxide; skin—excretes salts, water, and urea; kidney—excretes urine containing wastes, water, and salts; liver—helps to remove excess amino acids and stray bacteria from the blood.

11. Excess water passes from the nephron through the ureters to the urinary bladder. From the urinary bladder, urine passes out of the body through the urethra.

CRITICAL THINKING AND PROBLEM SOLVING

1. Both involve oxidation and the release of heat energy. Respiration is slow burning. Fuels burn rapidly.

2. The urine would contain less water because the body would retain more water to make up for water loss through perspiration.

3. Homeostasis is the ability to maintain constant conditions within the body. Excretion and respiration both help to keep the levels of oxygen, carbon dioxide, and various wastes at a constant and safe level.

4. Experiments should be logical and well thought out. Many students will realize that exhaling onto an object such as a mirror will show that water in the exhaled air condenses on the mirror. Most students will not be able to think of a control for this particular experiment.

5. Students should note from the chart that inhaled air contains more oxygen and less carbon dioxide than exhaled air does but that the nitrogen levels remain constant while inhaling and exhaling.

6. If one kidney is damaged or destroyed, the other kidney can continue to filter wastes and keep the person alive.

7. Blood passing into the nephron contains water, excess salts, and digested food. The food and some water, however, is reabsorbed into the blood so that the urine leaving the nephron contains only the remaining water and urea.

8. A person would have great difficulty breathing because the oxygen entering the lungs would not easily be able to pass through the damaged alveoli and enter the bloodstream. Although students may not be able to infer this, you may want to point out that emphysema makes people have more trouble exhaling than inhaling.

9. Your throat can become dry and sore because the incoming air has not been warmed, moistened, or cleaned of particles and bacteria as it would be if it had entered through the nose.

10. Students' outlines and information should be scientifically consistent with the chapter material.

KEEPING A PORTFOLIO

You might want to assign some of the Concept Mastery and Critical Thinking and Problem Solving questions as homework and have students include their responses to unassigned questions in their portfolio. Students should be encouraged to include both the question and the answer in their portfolio.

SECTION	LABORATORY INVESTIGATIONS AND DEMONSTRATIONS
6–1 The Nervous System pages H132–H137	**Laboratory Manual** Observing Human Reflexes **Teacher Edition** Modeling Nerve Cells, p. H130d
6–2 Divisions of the Nervous System pages H137–H144	**Laboratory Manual** Observing the Effect of Adrenalin on *Daphnia*
6–3 The Senses pages H144–H154	**Student Edition** Locating Touch Receptors, p. H162 **Teacher Edition** Maintaining Balance, p. H130d
6–4 The Endocrine System pages H155–H161	
Chapter Review pages H162–H165	

*All materials in the Chapter Planning Guide Grid are available as part of the Prentice Hall Science Learning System.

OUTSIDE TEACHER RESOURCES
Books
Ackerman, Diane. *A Natural History of the Senses,* Random House.

Asimov, I. *The Human Brain: Its Capabilities and Functions,* Houghton Mifflin.

Kashgarian, M., and G. N. Burrow. *Endocrine Glands,* Krieger.

Leibovic, K. N. *Nervous System Theory: An Introductory Study,* Academic Press.

Little, Marjorie. *The Endocrine System,* Chelsea House.

Silverstein, A., and V. B. Silverstein. *Endocrine System: Hormones in the Living World,* Prentice Hall.

Silverstein, A., and V. B. Silverstein. *Nervous System: The Inner Network,* Prentice Hall.

OTHER ACTIVITIES	MULTIMEDIA
Activity Book Chapter Discovery: Creating a Feedback Mechanism ACTIVITY: Determining Reaction Time **Student Edition** Find Out by Calculating: A Speedy Message, p. H133. Find Out by Doing: A Reflex Action, p. H137 **Review and Reinforcement Guide** Section 6–1	**Video** Nervous System **Courseware** Nervous System (Supplemental) **Transparency Binder** Three Types of Neurons **English/Spanish Audiotapes** Section 6–1
Student Edition Find Out by Doing: Fight or Flight?, p. H143. Find Out by Reading: A Master Sleuth, p. H144. **Review and Reinforcement Guide** Section 6–2	**Video** The Brain and Nervous System Think Science **English/Spanish Audiotapes** Section 6–2
Activity Book ACTIVITY: The Blind Spot ACTIVITY: The Senses of Taste and Smell ACTIVITY: Your Senses **Student Edition** Find Out by Doing: Reaction Time, p. H149. **Review and Reinforcement Guide** Section 6–3	**Interactive Videodisc** Invention: Mastering Sound **Transparency Binder** The Skin The Eye The Ear **English/Spanish Audiotapes** Section 6–3
Activity Book ACTIVITY: H.E.L.P. From Your Endocrine System ACTIVITY: Endocrine Riddles ACTIVITY: The Magic Square **Student Edition** Find Out by Writing: Bacterially Produced Hormones, p. H156. Find Out by Calculating: How Much Is Enough?, p. H160. **Review and Reinforcement Guide** Section 6–4	**Video** Endocrine System **English/Spanish Audiotapes** Section 6–4
Test Book Chapter Test Performance-Based Test	**Test Book** Computer Test Bank Test

Audiovisuals

The Brain, eight videocassettes, WNET/Thirteen

Endocrine Glands, film, Sterling

Endocrine Glands: How They Affect You, film, McGraw-Hill

The Hidden Universe: The Brain, film, McGraw-Hill

Hormones, filmstrip, Denoyer-Geppert

The Human Body: The Brain, film, Coronet

The Nervous System, filmstrip, Denoyer-Geppert

Chapter 6 NERVOUS AND ENDOCRINE SYSTEMS

CHAPTER OVERVIEW

The nervous and endocrine systems interact to control most of the body functions. Both systems are communication systems that receive and deliver messages throughout the body. The nervous system consists of the central nervous system and the peripheral nervous system. The central nervous system includes the brain and the spinal cord. The peripheral nervous system consists of all the other nerve cells in the body. The peripheral nervous system carries messages between the central nervous system and the rest of the body.

The endocrine system consists of the many major glands. Some of these glands are the hypothalamus, pituitary, thyroid, parathyroids, adrenals, pancreas, and the sex glands. In the endocrine system, glands produce chemical messengers called hormones that help to regulate certain body activities. Endocrine glands secrete hormones directly into the bloodstream.

6–1 THE NERVOUS SYSTEM
THEMATIC FOCUS

The purpose of this section is to introduce students to the nervous system. They will learn that this system controls most of the activities of the body.

Individual nerve cells are called neurons. All neurons have a cell body, a nucleus, and two kinds of fiberlike "arms" called axons and dendrites. Each fiberlike arm that carries messages toward the cell is called a dendrite. A single fiberlike arm that carries messages away from the cell is an axon.

The themes that can be focused on in this section are energy and patterns of change.

*Energy: The nervous and endocrine systems require the use of energy to control the activities of the body. Both electrical and chemical energy are involved in the movement of nerve impulses.

Patterns of change: When a nerve impulse is received in a sensory neuron, the impulse is sent to the spinal cord. The impulse is immediately transferred to a motor neuron, which may cause a reflex to occur.

PERFORMANCE OBJECTIVES 6–1
1. **Describe the function of the nervous system.**
2. **Compare the three types of neurons.**
3. **Identify the structures of the neuron.**

SCIENCE TERMS 6–1
stimulus p. H133
neuron p. H134
cell body p. H134
dendrite p. H134
axon p. H134
receptor p. H135
sensory neuron p. H135
interneuron p. H135
motor neuron p. H135
effector p. H135
nerve impulse p. H136
synapse p. H136

6–2 DIVISIONS OF THE NERVOUS SYSTEM
THEMATIC FOCUS

The purpose of this section is to show students the two parts of the nervous system: the central nervous system, which contains the brain and the spinal cord, and the peripheral nervous system, which is made up of a network of nerves and sense organs that connect the central nervous system to the rest of the body.

The themes that can be focused on in this section are systems and interactions and scale and structure.

*Systems and interactions: The two parts of the nervous system are the central nervous system and the peripheral nervous system. The central nervous system includes the brain and spinal cord. The peripheral nervous system includes all the nerves that connect the central nervous system to the rest of the body.

*Scale and structure: The three main parts of the brain are the cerebrum, the cerebellum, and the medulla. The cerebrum stores information. The cerebellum, or small cerebrum, is a coordinating center for all muscular activities. The medulla controls many of the automatic body processes.

PERFORMANCE OBJECTIVES 6–2
1. **List the structures and functions of the central nervous system.**
2. **Compare the functions of the three main parts of the brain.**
3. **List the structures and functions of the peripheral nervous system.**

SCIENCE TERMS 6–2
brain p. H139
spinal cord p. H139
cerebrum p. H139
cerebellum p. H141
medulla p. H141
reflex p. H142

6–3 THE SENSES
THEMATIC FOCUS

The purpose of this section is to introduce students to the special sense receptors that help them become aware of the external and internal environment. When the sense organ receptors are activated by a stimulus, they immediately send out an impulse to the central nervous system. The brain or spinal cord receives the impulse, interprets it, and sends back a response to the body.

The themes that can be focused on in this section are systems and interactions and unity and diversity.

*Systems and interactions: The five sense organs respond to light, sound, heat, pressure, and chemicals and detect changes in the position of the body.

Unity and diversity: The senses respond to an extremely wide range of different sources of information. Although the external environment of the body is constantly changing, the sense receptors help the body maintain a constant internal environment.

PERFORMANCE OBJECTIVES 6–3

1. List the five sense organs.
2. Describe the functions of the five sense organs.
3. Explain how the sense organs interact with the central nervous system.

SCIENCE TERMS 6–3

cornea p. H145
iris p. H146
pupil p. H146
lens p. H146
retina p. H147
eardrum p. H149
cochlea p. H150
semicircular canal p. H150

6–4 THE ENDOCRINE SYSTEM
THEMATIC FOCUS

The purpose of this section is to explain to students that the endocrine system is a system of glands that produce chemical messengers called hormones, which help to regulate certain body activities. The hormones produced by the glands move through the bloodstream and reach every cell of the body.

The themes that can be focused on in this section are unity and diversity and stability.

Unity and diversity: Although the nervous and endocrine systems both regulate activities in the body, they perform their functions in different ways. The nervous system sends its electrochemical signals

through neurons; the endocrine system sends its chemical messengers (hormones) through the blood.

*Stability: With the negative-feedback mechanism, the presence of an abnormally large amount of any hormone or other substance will trigger a gland to secrete a hormone to counterbalance or reduce it.

PERFORMANCE OBJECTIVES 6–4

1. Name the endocrine glands.
2. Describe the functions of the endocrine glands.
3. Explain how the endocrine system uses negative feedback.

SCIENCE TERMS 6–4

hormone p. H155
hypothalamus p. H156
pituitary p. H158
thymus p. H158
thyroid p. H158
parathyroid p. H159
adrenal p. H159
islets of Langerhans p. H160
ovary p. H160
testis p. H160
negative-feedback mechanism p. H161

Discovery *Learning*

TEACHER DEMONSTRATIONS MODELING

Modeling Nerve Cells

Obtain two 30-centimeter lengths of extension cord wire. Before the demonstration, fray one end of each piece of wire and spread out the tiny wires to look like dendrites.

Touch the frayed dendrite end of one wire to the cut end of the other wire. Tell students that with the ends together, an electrical impulse could travel from one wire to the other. Spread the two wires so that they are about a centimeter apart.

• **What would happen to an electrical impulse sent by the cut wire now?** (Accept all logical answers. The electrical impulse could not jump the gap.)

• **Why couldn't the impulse jump the gap?** (Accept all logical answers. Because the ends aren't connected together.)

• **If the ends are kept apart, what would have to happen to be able to send an impulse through the wire?** (Accept all logical answers.)

Maintaining Balance

Show the class a bottle half filled with colored water. Stopper the bottle and place it on a table.

• **What do you notice about the water?** (Accept all logical answers.)

• **What about the "balance" of the water and the bottle?** (Both the water and the bottle are balanced and level.)

Slowly turn the bottle to a 45-degree angle, with only one point of the bottle bottom resting on the desk.

• **What do you notice about the water now?** (The water is still level with the table.)

• **What about the "balance" of the water and the bottle now?** (The water is still level, but the bottle is unbalanced.)

• **What needs to be done to move the bottle to its level position?** (Accept all logical answers.)

• **How is the water helpful in putting the bottle into a level position?** (Water is always level or parallel to the floor.)

• **How is this model similar to the semicircular canals?** (Accept all logical answers.)

• **How is this model different from the semicircular canals?** (Accept all logical answers.)

CHAPTER 6

Nervous and Endocrine Systems

INTEGRATING SCIENCE

This life science chapter provides you with numerous opportunities to integrate other areas of science, as well as other disciplines, into your curriculum. Blue numbered annotations on the student page and integration notes on the teacher wraparound pages alert you to areas of possible integration.

In this chapter you can integrate mathematics (pp. 133, 160), physical science and electricity (p. 136), language arts (pp. 139, 144, 156), physical science and light (pp. 145, 148), physical science and sound (p. 150), physical science and computers (p. 154), and physical science and heat (p. 161).

SCIENCE, TECHNOLOGY, AND SOCIETY/COOPERATIVE LEARNING

Biometrics is a new area of technology that is making use of characteristics of the body in order to control access to sensitive information and facilities, to provide security in high-risk industries, and to prevent costly computer crime.

Biometric technology works by using computer microchips to pick up an individual's characteristics (eye patterns, fingerprints, signature dynamics, voice patterns) and then convert them into digital codes for comparison to data stored in the data bank. Once an individual's characteristics have been successfully matched to data in the data bank, access to information is allowed; if the match is not made or is questionable, identification is challenged, and access is denied.

One type of biometric technology uses the eye as the basis for controlling access. A person requesting access to either information or facilities looks into a retinal scanning machine. This machine reads the blood vessel pattern on the retina of the eye. There is no way to "fake out" the scanner! The machine cannot be tricked by a fake eye or by contact lenses. The accuracy of a scanner is one trillion to one when both eyes are scanned.

INTRODUCING CHAPTER 6

DISCOVERY LEARNING

▶ *Activity Book*

Begin your teaching of the chapter by using the Chapter 6 Discovery Activity from the *Activity Book*. Using this activity, students will create a model of the feedback mechanism used in the endocrine system.

USING THE TEXTBOOK

Have students observe the photograph and illustration on page H130.
• **What do you see in the picture?** (Accept all logical answers.)

Tell students to close their eyes and imagine that they are alone at home lying in bed. Tell them the wind is blowing, causing a slight whispering sound. A hazy light flitters occasionally on the walls. Tell them they fall asleep only to awaken abruptly, yet nothing in the room seems

Nervous and Endocrine Systems

Guide for Reading

After you read the following sections, you will be able to

6–1 The Nervous System
- Describe the functions of the nervous system.
- Identify the structures of a neuron.
- Describe a nerve impulse.

6–2 Divisions of the Nervous System
- List the structures of the central nervous system and give their functions.
- Describe the peripheral nervous system and its function.

6–3 The Senses
- Summarize the functions of five sense organs.

6–4 The Endocrine System
- List eight endocrine glands and give the function of each.
- Explain the negative-feedback mechanism.

It is one o'clock on a Sunday morning. Suddenly, you find yourself face to face with a horrible-looking creature. You let out a scream and wake yourself out of a deep sleep. As you become more awake, you realize that it was all just a dream. The creature was not real. But your reaction to confronting the creature certainly was! Your heart pounded thunderously in your chest. Your breathing rate almost doubled, and your body was covered with perspiration. Even though you now know it was only a dream, your whole body seemed ready to respond by running away from or fighting the terrible creature.

Unknown to you, your nervous system and endocrine system were at work. Together, they control your body's activities. Parts of your nervous system—the brain, nerves, and sense organs—obtain information from the outside world. In turn, they alert your endocrine system to flood your bloodstream with chemicals. The chemicals cannot tell whether or not the threat is real. But that really does not matter, because a day may come when, faced with real danger, you will be glad that these two systems are working automatically. To find out how the nervous and endocrine systems perform their jobs, in any kind of situation, turn the page.

Journal *Activity*

You and Your World Imagine that you have to do without one of your sense organs for a day. Which one would you choose to give up? In your journal, list five everyday tasks you would ordinarily do using this sense organ. Then describe how the absence of this sense organ would affect these tasks.

A young person having a scary dream

Future application of biometric technology similar to the retinal scanner may include driver's license identification; access control of expensive and/or dangerous equipment, store credit cards, and drugs; automatic banking transactions from remote sites; residential alarm systems; and even toys. Can you imagine toys that could be manipulated only by their owner? What was once science fiction technology seen only in movies is now a very real part of the ever-expanding security industry.

Cooperative learning: Using preassigned lab groups or randomly selected teams, have groups complete one of the following assignments:
- Invent a biometric device that could be used to check student attendance throughout the school day. Groups should illustrate their device and explain how it works.
- Write and perform a two-minute skit illustrating how biometric technology could affect some area of their lives in the year 2000. Areas you might suggest or assign to groups could include school, shopping, a visit to the doctor or dentist, work, and so forth.

See Cooperative Learning in the *Teacher's Desk Reference.*

JOURNAL ACTIVITY

You may want to use the Journal Activity as the basis of class discussion. Before students begin the activity, review the five senses: vision, hearing, smell, taste, and touch. Explain that the senses work together with the human nervous system to allow you to know what is going on around you. Students should be instructed to keep their Journal Activity in their portfolio.

---

to have changed. And whatever woke them does not seem to exist.

Tell them to imagine that they get out of bed and slowly walk into the next room. Point out that they find nothing in the next room. Tell them they walk into another room and before them stands the creature in the illustration.
- **How would you feel?** (Accept all logical answers.)
- **What would happen to your heartbeat?** (Accept all logical answers.)

- **What would happen to your breathing rate?** (Accept all logical answers.)

Point out that the body has a system that regulates the body activities when we face danger.

Have students read the chapter introduction on page H131.

Tell students that they should close their eyes and imagine that they are in a faraway, strange town. Tell them to imagine that they are strolling through a beautiful flower garden. Point out that near the end of the garden is a small vine-covered house.

- **How do you feel now?** (Accept all answers. Some students may feel they are in a pleasant situation, whereas others may be looking for the danger of the scene.)

Explain that they continue walking toward the house. As they approach, their best friend walks out.
- **How would you feel?** (Accept all logical answers. Lead students to say that they would feel happy or excited.)

Explain that the same systems that control the reactions to fear control the reactions to happiness and excitement.

6-1 The Nervous System

Figure 6-1 *The nervous system controls and monitors all body activities—from the most simple to the most complex.*

132 ■ H

6-1 The Nervous System

You look up at the clock and realize that you have been working on this one particular math problem for more than half an hour. "Why am I having such a hard time solving this problem?" you ask yourself. Soon your mind begins to wander. Your thoughts turn to the summertime when you will no longer worry about math problems. Suddenly, the solution comes to you! This example, which may sound familiar, shows one of the many remarkable and often mysterious ways in which your nervous system functions. **The nervous system receives and sends out information about activities within the body. It also monitors and responds to changes in the environment.**

The extraordinary amount of information that your body receives at any one time is flashed through your nervous system in the form of millions of messages. These messages bring news about what is happening inside and outside your body—about the itch on your nose, or the funny joke you heard, or the odor of sweet-potato pie. Almost immediately, your nervous system tells other parts of your body what to do—scratch the itch, laugh at the joke, eat the pie.

In the meantime, your nervous system monitors (checks on) your breathing, blood pressure, and body temperature—to name just a few of the processes it takes care of without your awareness. The simple act of noticing that the weather is getting cooler is an example of the way the nervous system

ment. One's environment is both internal and external. Thus, the nervous system coordinates responses to the outside world and also coordinates the different actions of the body. Some reactions to a stimulus are a matter of choice, or voluntary. Other reactions are automatic, or involuntary.

monitors what is happening around you. The way the nervous system responds to this change is to make you feel chilly so you put on warmer clothes.

By performing all its tasks, the nervous system keeps your body working properly despite the constant changes taking place around you. These changes, whether they happen all the time or once in a while, are called **stimuli** (singular: stimulus). To help you better understand what a stimulus is, imagine this situation. An insect zooms toward your eye. You quickly and automatically blink to avoid damage to your eye. In this case, the insect zooming toward you is the stimulus and the blinking of your eye is the response.

Although some responses to stimuli are involuntary (not under your control), such as blinking your eyes and sneezing, many responses of the nervous system are voluntary (under your control). For example, leaving a football game because it begins to rain (stimulus) is a voluntary reaction. It is a conscious choice that involves the feelings of the moment, the memory of what happened the last time you stayed out in the rain, and the ability to reason.

So you can see how important the nervous system is to you. From the instant you are born, the nervous system controls and interprets (makes sense of) all the activities going on within your body. Without your nervous system, you could not move, think, laugh, feel pain, or enjoy the taste of a wonderfully juicy taco.

Figure 6–2 *A nervous system enables organisms to respond to stimuli, or changes in the environment. In humans, the stimulus could be rain falling during a football game. The response could be opening umbrellas and donning rain gear, leaving the game, or both. In bears, a stimulus could be the sight of a salmon. What could the response be?* ❶

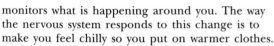

FIND OUT BY CALCULATING

A Speedy Message

Messages in the nervous system travel at a speed of 120 meters per second. How many seconds would it take a nerve message to travel 900 meters? 1440 meters? ❶

FIND OUT BY CALCULATING

A SPEEDY MESSAGE

Skills: Applying concepts, making calculations, calculator

This activity reveals the amazing speed at which nerve impulses are propagated. It also serves to reinforce mathematical skills. In each of the two problems, students are given the speed and the distance. The problems ask them to find the time.

Remind students of the formula

Speed × Time = Distance

The same formula can also be written in two other forms:

Distance ÷ Time = Speed
Distance ÷ Speed = Time

The third version of the formula is needed in this feature. The answers are 7.5 seconds and 12 seconds.

Integration: Use the Find Out by Calculating feature to integrate mathematics into your science lesson.

CONTENT DEVELOPMENT

Point out that many nervous system functions take place automatically, without conscious effort or awareness. We normally do not think about breathing, the beating of the heart, or the food passing through the digestive system.

GUIDED PRACTICE

Skills Development
Skill: Applying definitions

Have students make lists of involuntary and voluntary reactions. This may be done individually or as a small-group activity. Ask students to compare their lists.

GUIDED PRACTICE

▶ *Laboratory Manual*

Skills Development
Skills: Making observations, applying concepts, making inferences

At this point you may want to have students complete the Chapter 6 Laboratory Investigation in the *Laboratory Manual* called Observing Human Reflexes. In the investigation students will investigate different functions that the nervous system performs automatically.

ENRICHMENT

▶ *Activity Book*

Students will be challenged by the Chapter 6 activity in the *Activity Book* called Determining Reaction Time.

HISTORICAL NOTE
LUIGI GALVANI

Luigi Galvani (1737–1798) was an Italian physician, surgeon, and researcher in comparative anatomy. During some of his experiments, Galvani observed that a frog's leg contracted when touched by two different metals in a moist environment. His observation of this electrical activity caused him to conclude erroneously that animal tissues generate electricity.

Although Galvani's hypothesis was wrong, his observation stimulated research in electrotherapy and electric currents and led to the understanding we have today of the electrical nature of nerve impulses. Many electrical terms, such as *galvanometer*, are derived from Galvani's name.

6–1 (continued)

CONTENT DEVELOPMENT

Tell students that nerve cells have a very distinctive shape. Call their attention to Figure 6–3. A single nerve cell is called a neuron. It has a cell body, a nucleus, and two kinds of fiberlike arms—an axon and dendrites. Most neurons have many dendrites, which are short fibers that carry messages to the nerve cell. A single, longer axon carries messages away from the cell body.

▶ *Multimedia* ◀

Use the transparency in the *Transparency Binder* called Three Types of Neurons to help students understand the structure of the nervous system.

GUIDED PRACTICE

Skills Development

Skill: Interpreting illustrations

Have students locate the cell body in Figure 6–3.
• **What do you think the cell body does?** (Accept all answers.)

Point out that the cell body is the switchboard of the message-carrying neuron. Explain that all messages run into and out of the cell body.

Figure 6–3 *Use the diagram to identify the basic structures in these neurons from the spinal cord. What is the function of the cell body?* ❶

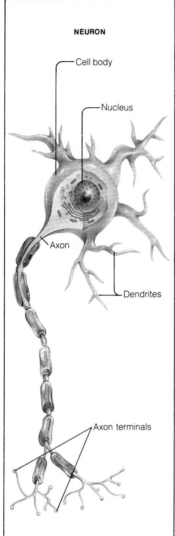

NEURON

- Cell body
- Nucleus
- Axon
- Dendrites
- Axon terminals

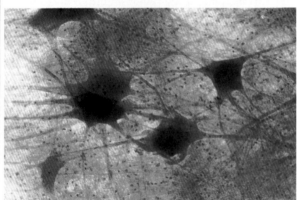

The nervous system is constantly alive with activity. It buzzes with messages that run to and from all parts of the body. Every second, hundreds of these messages make their journey through the body. The messages are carried by strings of one-of-a-kind cells called **neurons,** or nerve cells. Neurons are the basic units of structure and function in the nervous system. Neurons are unique because, unlike most other cells in the body, they can never be replaced. You need not worry about this, however. The number of neurons that you are born with is so large that you will have more than enough to last your entire lifetime.

Although neurons come in all shapes and sizes, they share certain basic characteristics, or features. You can see the features of a typical neuron in Figure 6–3. Notice that the largest part of the neuron is the **cell body.** The cell body contains the nucleus (a large dark structure), which controls all the activities of the cell.

You can think of the cell body as the switchboard of the message-carrying neuron. Running into this switchboard are one or more tiny, branching, threadlike structures called **dendrites.** The dendrites carry messages to the cell body of a neuron. A long tail-like fiber called an **axon** carries messages away from the cell body. Each neuron has only one axon, but the axon can be anywhere from 1 millimeter to more than 1 meter in length!

Have students locate the dendrites in the illustration.
• **What do you predict is the function of the dendrites?** (Accept all logical answers.)

Explain that the dendrites collect and carry messages from other neurons to the cell body. The dendrites are a one-way message system that carries messages to the cell body.

Have students locate the axon.
• **What do you predict the axon does?** (Accept all logical answers. By now, most students should respond that the axon carries messages away from the cell body.)

The axon is a slender extension of the neuron. Tell students that the axon is a one-way wire away from the cell body.

FOCUS/MOTIVATION

Place several common objects in a paper bag or a pillowcase. Have a student reach into the bag and feel the objects. The task is to identify one of the objects (without looking at it) and remove it from the sack.
• **Was the object correctly identified?** (Answers will vary.)

Notice in Figure 6–3 that the axon splits into many featherlike fibers at its far end. These fibers are called axon terminals (ends). Axon terminals pass on messages to the dendrites of other neurons. Axon terminals are usually found some distance from the cell body.

There are three types of neurons in your nervous system—sensory neurons, interneurons, and motor neurons. To find out the function of each neuron, try this activity: Press your finger against the edge of your desk. What happens? You feel the pressure of the desk pushing into your skin. You may even feel some discomfort or pain, if you press hard enough. Eventually, you remove your finger from this position.

How do neurons enable you to do all this? Special cells known as **receptors** receive information from your surroundings. In this activity the receptors are located in your finger. Messages travel from these receptors to your spinal cord and brain through **sensory neurons.** Your spinal cord and brain contain **interneurons.** Interneurons connect sensory neurons to **motor neurons.** It is through motor neurons that the messages from your brain and spinal cord are sent to a muscle cell or gland cell in your body. The muscle cell or gland cell that is stimulated by the motor neuron is called an **effector.**

Figure 6–4 *One of the body's billions of neurons can be seen in this photograph. The axon is the ropelike structure at the bottom of the photograph. What is the function of the axon?* 2

Figure 6–5 *There are three types of neurons in the nervous system: sensory neurons, interneurons, and motor neurons. What is an effector? A receptor?* 3

ANNOTATION KEY

Answers

1 The cell body controls all the activities of the neuron. It receives messages from the dendrites and sends messages to the axons. (Applying concepts)

2 The axon carries messages away from the cell body. (Applying concepts)

3 An effector is a cell that is stimulated by a motor neuron. A receptor is a cell that receives information from the surrounding environment and sends this information to the brain by way of the spinal cord. (Applying concepts)

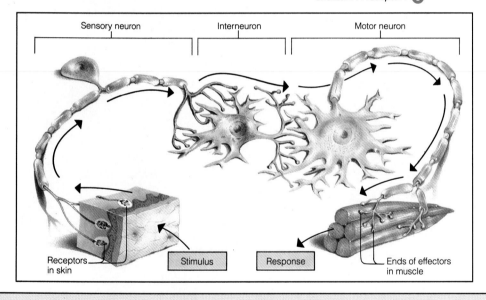

Sensory neuron | Interneuron | Motor neuron

Receptors in skin

Stimulus

Response

Ends of effectors in muscle

Repeat the procedure with several more students.
• **How were you able to identify the object?** (Accept all reasonable explanations.)

CONTENT DEVELOPMENT

Tell students that there are three main types of neurons in the human nervous system: sensory neurons, motor neurons, and interneurons.

Explain that a sensory neuron has special receptors that respond to stimuli.

Sensory neurons then send the messages to the central nervous system.
• **What receptors enabled you to identify the objects in the bag?** (Touch receptors in the hands, primarily in the fingertips.)
• **What receptors enabled the class to judge the correctness of your identification?** (Receptors in the eye.)

In both cases, sensory neurons carried the messages from the fingers or eyes to the brain. The brain then interpreted the messages and enabled you to identify the object.

Explain that the brain then instructed

the hand and arm muscles to grasp the identified object and remove it from the bag. The brain's instructions were carried to the muscles by a second kind of neuron, a motor neuron. The motor neurons carry messages away from the central nervous system to organs such as muscles.

Tell students that the connection between the sensory neuron and the motor neuron is called an interneuron. Interneurons are contained in the brain and spinal cord.
• **Why would you predict that this type of neuron would be called an interneuron?** (Accept all logical answers. Most students will say because it is connected to the sensory and motor neurons. The prefix *inter-* means "between.")

REINFORCEMENT/RETEACHING

▶ *Multimedia* ◀

An alternative way to help students understand the human nervous system is to have them use the video called Nervous System.

After students have seen the video, have them write a short report explaining how a stimulus is carried through the human nervous system. They should include a diagram similar to Figure 6–5 in their report.

FIND OUT BY DOING

A REFLEX ACTION

Discovery Learning

Skills: Applying concepts, making observations, relating concepts, making comparisons

Students should find that when the knee was struck at the kneecap, the lower leg jerked upward. This is known as the kneejerk reflex. Students should conclude that a reflex is automatic and does not require "thinking."

The nerve impulse traveled in the form of electrical and chemical signals from the receptor cells in the skin of the leg through sensory neurons to the interneuron cells in the spinal cord. In the spinal cord, the nerve impulse is relayed to interneurons, which then send impulses back to the motor neurons, instructing the muscles to contract.

Reflex actions occur more quickly than do responses that involve conscious choice.

6–1 (continued)

CONTENT DEVELOPMENT

Have students find the axon endings in the illustration in Figure 6–6. Explain that the axon endings are terminals where the electrical charge of the neuron is changed to a chemical signal. When the impulse reaches the end of the axon, there is a gap between the axon and the next dendrite. The gap between the axon of one neuron and the dendrite of the next neuron is called a synapse. The axon produces special chemicals that bridge the synapse to pass the impulse on to the dendrite of the next neuron.

The Nerve Impulse

You have just read that the path of a message, which is more accurately known as a **nerve impulse,** is basically from sensory neuron to interneuron to motor neuron. But how exactly does a message travel along a neuron? And how does it get from one neuron to another neuron? **When a nerve impulse travels along a neuron or from one neuron to another neuron, it does so in the form of electrical and chemical signals.**

① An electrical signal, which in simple terms is thought of as changing positive and negative charges, moves a nerve impulse along a neuron (or from one end of the neuron to the other). The nerve impulse enters the neuron through the dendrites and travels along the length of the axon. The speed at which a nerve impulse travels along a neuron can be as fast as 120 meters per second!

The way in which a nerve impulse travels from one neuron to another is a bit more complex. Do you know why? The reason is that the neurons do not touch one another. There is a tiny gap called a **synapse** (SIHN-aps) between the two neurons. Somehow, the nerve impulse must "jump" that gap. But how? Think of the synapse as a river that flows between a road on either bank. When a car gets to the

Figure 6–6 *The tiny gap between two neurons is called a synapse. The small reddish circles in the photograph are bubbles that contain chemicals which pour out of the axon terminal in one neuron, cross the synapse, and trigger a nerve impulse in the second neuron.*

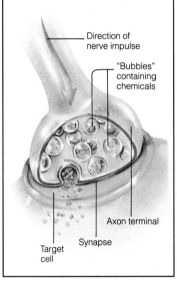

Direction of nerve impulse

"Bubbles" containing chemicals

Axon terminal

Synapse

Target cell

136 ■ H

● ● ● ● **Integration** ● ● ● ●

Use the discussion of the electrical signals in nerve impulses to integrate concepts of electricity into your lesson.

INDEPENDENT PRACTICE

Section Review 6–1

1. The nervous system receives and sends out information about activities within the body. It also monitors and responds to changes in both the external and internal environments.

2. A neuron is a nerve cell. It is composed of a cell body, branching structures called dendrites, and a long taillike structure called an axon.

3. Sensory neurons carry messages from receptors to the central nervous system. Motor neurons carry messages from the central nervous system to effectors. Interneurons connect sensory and motor neurons.

4. A nerve impulse is an electrical and chemical message carried throughout the body by nerve cells.

river, it crosses over by ferry. Then it drives right back onto the road and continues its journey.

Similarly, a nerve impulse is "ferried" across the synapse by a chemical signal. This chemical signal pours out of the ends of the neuron (axon terminals) as the nerve impulse nears the synapse. The electrical signal that brought the nerve impulse to this point shuts down, and the chemical signal takes the nerve impulse aboard, moving it across the synapse to the next neuron along its route. Then the chemical signal triggers the electrical signal again, and the whole process is repeated until the nerve impulse reaches its destination. You can appreciate how efficient this process is when you consider that for certain actions, this all happens in a matter of seconds!

6–1 Section Review

1. What are the functions of the nervous system?
2. What is a neuron? Describe its structure.
3. Identify the three types of neurons.
4. Describe a nerve impulse.

Critical Thinking—*Making Comparisons*
5. In the human nervous system, nerve impulses travel in only one direction along a neuron. How is this one-way traffic system better than a two-way traffic system along the same neuron?

FIND OUT BY DOING

A Reflex Action

1. Sit with your legs crossed so that one swings freely.

2. Using the side of your hand, gently strike your free-swinging leg just below your knee.

What happened when you struck that area? Describe in words or with a diagram the path the nerve impulse took as it traveled from your leg to the central nervous system and back to your leg.

■ What advantage does a reflex have over a response that involves a conscious choice?

6–2 Divisions of the Nervous System

In the previous section, you learned about the neuron as the basic unit of structure and function of the nervous system. You also gained some insight into the amazing job neurons do to keep you and your body in touch with the world inside and around you. Neurons, however, do not act alone. Instead, they are joined to form a complex communication network that makes up the human nervous

Guide for Reading

Focus on these questions as you read.

▶ *What are the two major parts of the human nervous system?*

▶ *What is the function and structure of each of the two major parts of the human nervous system?*

H ■ 137

6–2 Divisions of the Nervous System

MULTICULTURAL OPPORTUNITY 6–2

Some interesting research suggests that the different styles of music preferred by different cultures may be related to cerebral lateralization. For example, the atonality of Asian music and the structure of a European fugue are very different and may relate to a preference for the artistic side of the brain by one culture and the logical/mathematical orientation of another culture. Ask students to consider the merits of this hypothesis.

ESL STRATEGY 6–2

Have students match the terms in Column A with the definitions in Column B. A game of Jeopardy might be a way to check answers.

Column A
1. skull
2. cerebrum
3. cerebellum
4. left side of brain
5. right side of brain
6. spinal cord
7. reflex

Column B
a. bony covering encasing the brain
b. controls right side of body
c. simple response to stimulus
d. maintains balance
e. largest part of brain
f. controls artistic ability
g. connects brain with rest of nervous system
(**Answers:** 1. a, 2. e, 3. d, 4. b, 5. f, 6. g, 7. c)

5. Accept all logical responses. One possible response: If nerve impulses traveled in more than one direction, the dendrites and axons would be constantly stimulated, and the nervous system would not be able to tell the difference between incoming and outgoing impulses.

REINFORCEMENT/RETEACHING

Review students' responses to the Section Review questions. Reteach any material that is still unclear, based on students' responses.

CLOSURE

▶ *Review and Reinforcement Guide*
Have students complete Section 6–1 in the *Review and Reinforcement Guide*.

TEACHING STRATEGY 6–2

FOCUS/MOTIVATION

Ask students to stand. Have them attempt to rub their stomachs and pat their heads at the same time. Ask them to be

seated. Now ask them to list their ten favorite rock stars while they name all 50 states aloud.

Stop the activity after a minute or so. Explain to students that the nervous system cannot always handle the performance of several different actions at the same time. Many kinds of nervous system actions, however, do go on at the same time.

• **How many different kinds of nervous system messages are involved in watching television?** (Accept all reasonable answers.)

Even when you are asleep, 50,000,000 nerve messages a second are relayed back and forth between the brain and different parts of the body.

BACKGROUND INFORMATION

NERVE GAS

A weapon that has from time to time been used in warfare is poison gas, or nerve gas.

Normally, neurotransmitters released from one neuron bind to receptors on another neuron to produce a new nerve impulse. As soon as this occurs, enzymes on the cell membrane of the neuron quickly break down the neurotransmitters so that each release of neurotransmitter causes no more than one impulse.

Nerve gas inhibits the action of these enzymes, thus allowing the neurotransmitters to remain in the synapses almost indefinitely. As a result, continuous nerve impulses are produced, causing uncontrollable convulsions and muscular contractions. These reactions are so violent that the victim dies.

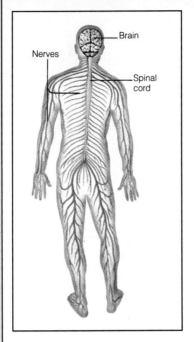

Figure 6–7 *The human nervous system is made up of the central nervous system and the peripheral nervous system. The central nervous system contains the brain and the spinal cord. The peripheral nervous system contains all the nerves that branch out from the central nervous system.*

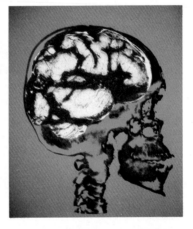

Figure 6–8 *This photograph is actually a combination of two photographs. One is an X-ray of a human skull. The other is of a human brain that has been properly positioned over the X-ray. What is the function of the skull?* ❶

system. The human nervous system is divided into two parts: the central nervous system and the peripheral nervous system.

All information about what is happening in the world inside or outside your body is brought to the central nervous system. **The central nervous system, which contains the brain and the spinal cord, is the control center of the body.**

The other part of the human nervous system is the peripheral (puh-RIHF-uh-ruhl) nervous system. **The peripheral nervous system consists of a network of nerves that branch out from the central nervous system and connect it to the organs of the body.** Put another way, the peripheral nervous system is made up of all the nerves that are found outside the central nervous system. In fact, the word peripheral means outer part.

The Central Nervous System

If you were asked to write a list of your ten favorite rock stars and at the same time name all fifty states aloud, you would probably say you were being asked to do the impossible. And you would be quite correct. It is obvious that the nervous system is not able to control certain functions at the same time it is busy controlling other functions. What is less obvious, however, is just how many functions the brain can control at one time! For example, even an action as simple as sitting quietly in a movie theater requires several mental operations.

Many kinds of impulses travel between your central nervous system and other parts of your body as you watch a movie. Some nerve impulses control the focus of your eyes and the amount of light that enters them. Other nerve impulses control your understanding of what you see and hear. At the same time, still other nerve impulses regulate a variety of body activities such as breathing and blood circulation. And all these impulses may be related to one another. For example, if you are frightened by a scene in the movie, your breathing and heart rates

---

6–2 (continued)

CONTENT DEVELOPMENT

Have students examine Figure 6–7. Point out that the human nervous system is divided into two parts: the central nervous system and the peripheral nervous system.

Explain that the peripheral nervous system is made up of the nerves and sense organs that connect the central nervous system with the rest of the body. A subsystem of the peripheral nervous system controls all involuntary body processes. It is called the autonomic nervous system.

• **What are some body processes that the autonomic nervous system controls?** (Possible answers are heartbeat, breathing, maintaining body temperature, feeling hunger, and so on.)
• **What structures make up the central nervous system?** (Brain and spinal cord.)
• **How many neurons do you think are in the human brain?** (Scientists estimate that more than 10 billion neurons make up the brain.)

Point out that the brain is the main control center for the human body—all

messages to the brain are transmitted and received through the spinal cord. Explain that the brain has a mass of about 1.4 kilograms. It is made of spongy nerve tissue and is surrounded by three membranes that nourish and protect the brain. Between the inner and middle membranes is a watery fluid on which the brain floats. This fluid cushions the brain against shock.

▶ *Multimedia* ◀

An alternative way to introduce students to the structure and functions of the brain is to have them use the video called The

will likely increase. If, on the other hand, you are bored, these rates may decrease. In fact, you might even fall asleep!

The activities that occur within the central nervous system are very complex. Interpreting the information that pours in from all parts of your body and issuing the appropriate commands to these very same parts are the responsibility of the two parts of the central nervous system: the **brain** and the **spinal cord.** The brain is the main control center of the central nervous system. It transmits and receives messages through the spinal cord. The spinal cord provides the link between the brain and the rest of the body.

THE BRAIN If you are a fan of the English author Agatha Christie, you may remember the words uttered by her fictional detective Hercule Poirot as he attempted to solve a mystery: "These little gray cells! It is up to them." Indeed, much of the human brain does appear to be gray as a result of the presence of the cell bodies of billions of neurons. Underneath the gray material is white material, which is made of bundles of axons.

Despite the presence of billions of neurons, the mass of the brain is only about 1.4 kilograms. As you might expect of such an important organ, the brain is very well protected. A bony covering called the skull encases the brain. (You may recall from Chapter 2 that the skull is part of the skeletal system.) The brain is also wrapped by three layers of connective tissue, which nourish and protect it. The inner layer clings to the surface of the brain and follows its many folds. Between the inner layer and the middle layer is a watery fluid. The brain is bathed in this fluid and is thus cushioned against sudden impact, such as when you bump heads with another person while playing soccer or when you take a nasty fall. The outer layer, which makes contact with the inside of the bony skull, is thicker and tougher than the other two layers.

Looking like an oversized walnut without a shell, the **cerebrum** (SER-uh-bruhm) is the largest and most noticeable part of the brain. As you can see from Figure 6–11 on page 140, the cerebrum is lined with deep, wrinkled grooves. These grooves greatly increase the surface area of the cerebrum, thus allowing more

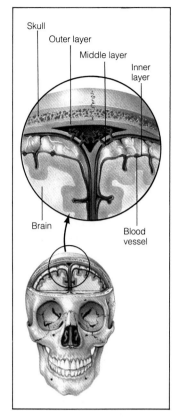

Figure 6–9 *The brain is wrapped by three layers of connective tissue, which nourish and protect it. Covering the brain and its three layers of connective tissue is a bony skull.*

H ■ 139

INTEGRATION
HEALTH

The stimulant caffeine—which is found in coffee, tea, chocolate, and cola drinks—affects several different parts of the brain, depending on how much caffeine is consumed. In low doses, caffeine stimulates the cerebral cortex, causing increased alertness and restlessness. In higher doses, caffeine affects the medulla oblongata and disrupts motor coordination as well as intellectual coherence.

FACTS AND FIGURES
THE BRAIN AND PAIN

Brain tissue has no nerve endings for sensing pain. This allows a surgeon to operate on the brain using only a local anesthetic for the surrounding tissue.

Brain and Nervous System Think Science.

After students have seen the video, have them write a short paragraph for each of the three parts of the brain. Each paragraph should describe the size, location, and structure, as well as a few functions controlled by that part of the brain.

● ● ● ● **Integration** ● ● ● ●

Use the discussion of the English mystery author Agatha Christie to integrate language arts into your lesson.

REINFORCEMENT/RETEACHING

Remind students that a nerve is a bundle of neurons, or nerve cells. Neurons have a cell body, nucleus, and two kinds of fiberlike arms. The neurons, like all cells, have one basic task to accomplish in the body. The task of the neurons is to carry messages throughout the body.

CONTENT DEVELOPMENT

Tell students that the first part of the brain they will study is called the cerebrum. Explain the most of the mental ac-

tivities that make humans different from other animals take place in the cerebrum. It is the information center, or thinking part, of the brain.

Explain that the cerebrum is the largest part of the brain, filling the entire upper part of the skull. It has lobes, or centers, that control intelligence, reasoning, consciousness, memory, imagination, and learning. The cerebrum also contains lobes that produce and direct voluntary activities such as shaking the hand or blinking an eye intentionally. This part of the brain receives and interprets signals from our senses such as hearing, sight, smell, taste, the feeling of pain, and many others.

INTEGRATION

DANCE THERAPY

Dance therapy is a form of psychiatric therapy that is practiced in many mental hospitals and mental health facilities. It is a system of treatment that uses movement to help heal the mentally ill. There is often marked improvement in a patient's mental condition as a result of learning certain movement skills and developing the capacity for expression through movement and dance.

Although this mind-body connection may seem mysterious at first glance, it is really quite logical if one looks at the workings of the cerebellum. The cerebellum is the area of the brain that must be activated if a person wishes to learn and perfect skills that require coordination and balance. But, because the cerebellum is not under conscious control, mastering dance movements must of necessity impinge on the patient's unconscious. Because most mental disturbances involve unconscious factors, dance therapy may be able to reach aspects of a patient's illness that would prove elusive to more verbal forms of therapy.

6–2 (continued)

GUIDED PRACTICE

Skills Development

Skill: Interpreting diagrams

Have students observe Figure 6–10. Read the caption and the accompanying text. Point out that three parts of the brain are labeled on the drawing: the cerebrum, the cerebellum, and the medulla.

• **Which brain part appears to be the largest?** (The cerebrum.)
• **What do you think the cerebrum does?** (Accept all answers.)
• **Which brain part appears to be the second largest?** (The cerebellum.)
• **What do you think the cerebellum does?** (Accept all answers.)
• **What is the function of the medulla?** (The medulla controls involuntary actions, such as heartbeat, breathing, and blood pressure.)

Point out that the cerebrum is composed of two halves. Explain that each

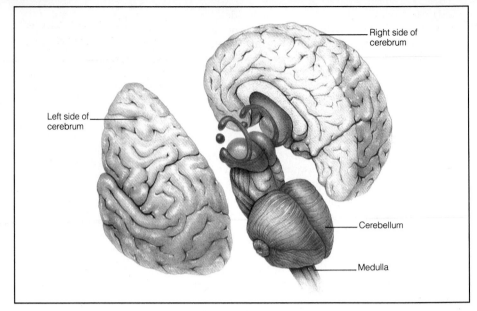

Figure 6–10 *The human brain consists of the cerebrum, cerebellum, and medulla. What is the function of each part?* ❶

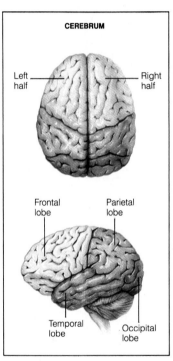

activities to occur there. You can appreciate how important this feature is when you consider that the cerebrum is the area where learning, intelligence, and judgment occur. Increased surface area means increased thinking ability. But this is not all the cerebrum does. It also controls all the voluntary (under your control) activities of the body. In addition, it shapes your attitudes, your emotions, and even your personality.

Another interesting feature of the cerebrum (which you may have noticed in Figure 6–11) is that it is divided into halves: a right half and a left half. Each half controls different kinds of mental activity. For example, the right half is associated with artistic ability and the left half is associated with mathematical ability. And each half controls the movement of and sends sensations to the side of the body opposite it. In other words, the right side of the brain

Figure 6–11 *The cerebrum is divided into two halves. Each half contains four lobes, or sections. What are the names of these lobes?* ❷

half controls movement and records sensations on the side of the body opposite it. Tell students that each half communicates its activities to the other half by a series of nerve paths running between the two halves.

FOCUS/MOTIVATION

Have students place their right hand on the top of the right side of their head. Have them place their left hand on the top of the left side. Remind students that the cerebrum is divided into two parts, the

right side and the left side.
• **Which side allowed you to put your right hand on the top of the right side of your head?** (The left side.)
• **Which side allowed you to put your left hand on the top of the left side of your head?** (The right side.)
• **Can you think of any reason why the brain seems to reverse the signals coming from the two sides of the body?** (Accept all responses.)

controls the left side of the body; the left side of the brain controls the right side of the body.

Below and to the rear of the cerebrum is the **cerebellum** (ser-uh-BEHL-uhm), the second largest part of the brain. The cerebellum's job is to coordinate the actions of the muscles and to maintain balance. As a result, your body is able to move smoothly and skillfully.

Below the cerebellum is the **medulla** (mih-DUHL-uh), which connects the brain to the spinal cord. The medulla controls involuntary actions, such as heartbeat, breathing, and blood pressure. Can you name some other types of involuntary actions? ❸

SPINAL CORD If you bend forward slightly and run your thumb down the center of your back, you can feel the vertebrae that make up your spinal column. As you may recall from Chapter 2, the vertebrae are a series of bones that protect the spinal cord. The spinal cord runs the entire length of the neck and back. It connects the brain with the rest of the nervous system through a series of 31 pairs of

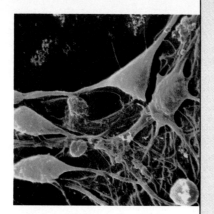

Figure 6–12 *Impulses are constantly traveling across neurons such as these located in the brain. To what part of the human nervous system does the brain belong?* ❹

Figure 6–13 *The brain directs and coordinates all the body's activities. What is the function of the cerebellum?* ❺

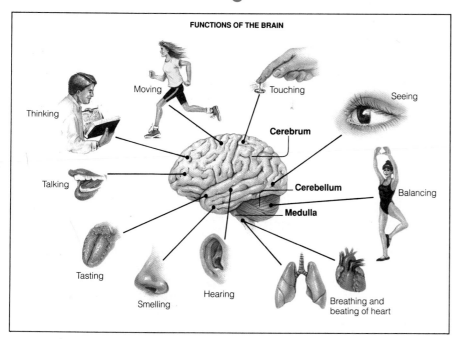

FUNCTIONS OF THE BRAIN

Thinking — Moving — Touching — Seeing — **Cerebrum** — **Cerebellum** — Balancing — **Medulla** — Talking — Tasting — Smelling — Hearing — Breathing and beating of heart

CONTENT DEVELOPMENT

The outer surface of the cerebrum is composed of cell bodies of neurons and is gray in color. It contains many grooves that increase its surface area. Increased surface area means increased thinking ability. Below the gray matter is the white matter, composed of the axons of neurons and fatty connective tissue.

ENRICHMENT

Give students a ball the size of a grapefruit, paper, and thin white glue. Have them make a papier-mâché cerebrum over the ball. Have them research and find where the lobes (frontal, temporal, parietal, and occipital) of the cerebrum are located and paint them different colors.

FOCUS/MOTIVATION

Have several students attempt to walk across the room carrying a book on their head. Explain that the cerebellum is important in controlling smooth muscular movements, balance, and posture.

CONTENT DEVELOPMENT

The second largest part of the brain is the cerebellum, which is found below and to the rear of the cerebrum. Cerebellum means "little cerebrum." It is a coordinating center for all muscular activities. The cerebellum adjusts the motor nerve impulses that begin in the cerebrum so that body movements are smooth rather than jerky. It also controls balance and posture.

Explain to students that bundles of nerves passing from the cerebrum and cerebellum form a thick stalk called the brain stem at the base of the brain. The lowest part of the brain stem is called the medulla. It controls many of the body's automatic processes such as breathing and heartbeat. Impulses from the medulla also control sneezing, coughing, swallowing, and blinking.

Have students discuss the word *peripheral*, which means pertaining to the outward boundary of something, the part away from the center or central region. Explain that the word *peripheral* comes from the Greek word *peripherein*, which means to carry around. Have students think of other words that have the same root, *peri-*, such as *perimeter* and *periscope*.

6–2 (continued)

FOCUS/MOTIVATION

Have students stand and bend forward slightly. Ask them to run a thumb down the center of their back and feel the vertebrae. Remind them that the vertebrae are part of the skeletal system. Then explain that the spinal cord runs through the vertebrae down the entire length of the neck and back.

CONTENT DEVELOPMENT

• **What is a vertebra?** (One of the bones in the backbone.)

Have students observe Figure 6–14. Point out that each vertebra has a large hole through which the spinal cord passes. Vertebrae also have smaller holes for the nerves that connect the spinal cord with other parts of the body.

• **What do the vertebrae do for the spinal cord?** (Protect it from injury.)

• **What does the spinal cord do for the central nervous system?** (Accept all logical answers. Students may say that it provides a way for messages to travel to and from the brain.)

FOCUS/MOTIVATION

Have two students volunteer to perform a simple activity that illustrates a reflex. Ask one student to hold a screen or clear plastic sheet in front of his or her face while the other student throws large paper wads at him or her. The class should observe what happens.

• **What do you observe?** (In most cases, the student will blink when the paper ball hits the screen.)

Explain to students that such an automatic reaction is called a reflex.

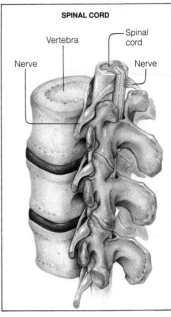

Figure 6–14 *The spinal cord, which provides the link between the brain and the rest of the body, is about 43 centimeters long and as flexible as a rubber hose. As the diagram shows, the spinal cord is protected by a series of bones called vertebrae that make up the vertebral column.*

SPINAL CORD

Vertebra
Spinal cord
Nerve
Nerve

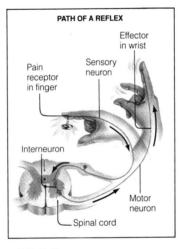

Figure 6–15 *If you touch a thumbtack, you will pull your finger away from it quickly. This reaction is an example of a reflex.*

PATH OF A REFLEX

Effector in wrist
Sensory neuron
Pain receptor in finger
Interneuron
Motor neuron
Spinal cord

142 ■ H

• **What function might blinking serve in this case?** (Blinking helps to protect the eye from injury. When objects touch the eyelashes or come close to the eyes, the eyes automatically blink shut so that the object does not come in contact with the surface of the eye.)

CONTENT DEVELOPMENT

• **Have you ever accidentally touched something that was very hot?** (Accept all answers.)

nerves. These nerves carry nerve impulses to and from the spinal cord.

Quite possibly, you are so interested in reading this chapter that you do not notice a fly circling in the air above your head. But if the fly happens to come close to your eyes, your eyes will automatically blink shut. Why?

A simple response to a stimulus (fly coming near your eyes) is called a **reflex.** In this example, the reflex begins as soon as the fly approaches your eyes. The fly's action sends a nerve impulse through the sensory neurons to the spinal cord. In the spinal cord, the nerve impulse is relayed to interneurons, which send the nerve impulse to motor neurons. The motor neurons stimulate the muscles (effectors) of the eyes, causing them to contract and so you blink.

Reflexes are not only lightning-fast reactions, they are also automatic. Their speed and automatic nature are possible because the nerve impulses travel only to the spinal cord, bypassing the brain. The brain does become aware of the event, however, but only after it has happened. So the instant after you

• **What happened?** (Accept all answers.)

• **What did you do?** (Accept all answers. Lead students to suggest they pulled their hand away.)

Point out that removing the hand from a hot surface is another example of a reflex action.

Tell students that a reflex action is the simplest type of action of the nervous system. Explain that reflexes can occur very quickly because the nerve impulses do not pass through the brain. The pathway of a reflex is as follows: sensory neuron in

blink, your brain knows that you blinked and why you blinked.

The Peripheral Nervous System

The peripheral nervous system is the link between the central nervous system (brain and spinal cord) and the rest of the body. The peripheral nervous system consists of pairs of nerves (43 to be exact) that arise from the brain and spinal cord and lead to organs throughout your body. Many of the nerves in the peripheral nervous system are under the direct control of your conscious mind. For example, when you "tell" your leg to move, a message travels from your brain to your spinal cord and through a peripheral nerve to your leg. There is one part of the peripheral nervous system, however, that is not under the direct control of your conscious mind. This part, called the autonomic (awt-uh-NAHM-ihk) nervous system, controls body activities that are involuntary—that is, body activities that happen automatically without your thinking about them. For example, contractions of the heart muscle and movement of smooth muscles surrounding the blood vessels and the organs of the digestive system are activities under the control of the autonomic nervous system.

The nerves of the autonomic nervous system can be divided into two groups that have opposite effects on the organs they control. One group of nerves triggers an action by an organ while the other group of nerves slows down or stops the action. Thus, the nerves of the autonomic nervous system work against each other to keep body activities in perfect balance.

FIND OUT BY DOING

Fight or Flight?

1. Working with a partner, determine your pulse rate (heartbeats per minute) and breathing rate (breaths per minute) while you are at rest. Record your data.

2. Now do ten jumping jacks. **CAUTION:** *If you have any respiratory illnesses, do not perform steps 2 and 3.*

3. After exercising, measure your pulse rate and breathing rate. Your partner can measure your pulse while you are counting your breaths. Record this "after exercise" data.

Describe any changes in pulse rate and breathing rate after exercising.

■ How do these changes compare with those that occur when you are faced with an emergency situation? What other body changes occur when you react to an emergency?

Part of Body Affected	Autonomic Nervous System Nerve Group That Triggers Action	Autonomic Nervous System Nerve Group That Slows Down Action
Pupil of eye	Widened	Narrowed
Liver	Sugar released	None
Urinary bladder muscle	Relaxed	Shortened
Muscle of heart	Increased rate and force	Slowed rate
Bronchi of lungs	Widened	Narrowed

Figure 6–16 *The nerves of the autonomic nervous system can be divided into two groups that have opposite effects on the organs they control.*

FIND OUT BY DOING

FIGHT OR FLIGHT?

Discovery Learning

Skills: Making comparisons, recording data, measuring, applying concepts, relating concepts

Materials: stopwatch or watch with second hand

All students should record an increase in heartbeat rate and breathing rate after exercise. These changes are similar to those that occur during an emergency situation in which the hormone adrenaline is released.

Some other body changes that occur during reactions to emergency situations are an increase in the release of glycogen by the liver, an increase in the rate of blood clotting, and constriction of blood vessels in the skin.

receptor → interneuron in spinal cord → motor neuron in effector.

REINFORCEMENT/RETEACHING

Have students make a list of other reflex actions and the stimuli that might cause the reaction. (Answers will vary. Examples: pulling your hand back from touching a hot object, knee jerk when knee is tapped with a blunt instrument, and so forth)

CONTENT DEVELOPMENT

Remind students that the central nervous system is made up of the brain and spinal cord. Tell students that the central nervous system can work properly only if connected to the rest of the body.

Point out that the peripheral nervous system connects the rest of the body with the central nervous system. Explain that the peripheral nervous system carries messages between the central nervous system and the rest of the body.

Explain that reflexes are automatic actions caused when a nerve in the peripheral nervous system is stimulated. The brain does not have to "think" for an automatic response. The automatic response is controlled by the autonomic nervous system at the spinal cord.

REINFORCEMENT/RETEACHING

Remind students that there are three different types of neurons: sensory neurons, motor neurons, and interneurons. Explain that these three types of neurons make up the peripheral nervous system.

GUIDED PRACTICE

▶ *Laboratory Manual*

Skills Development

Skills: Making observations, measuring, recording data, making inferences

At this point you may want to have students complete the Chapter 6 Laboratory Investigation in the *Laboratory Manual* called Observing the Effect of Adrenaline on *Daphnia.* In the investigation students will discover some involuntary reactions that occur when adrenaline is added to the environment of a water flea.

FIND OUT BY READING
A MASTER SLEUTH

Skill: Reading comprehension

Another well-known book by Agatha Christie is *The Murder of Roger Ackroyd*. Both this book and the one mentioned in the textbook feature her imaginary Belgian detective, Hercule Poirot. Poirot is almost as popular as his famous fictional successor Sherlock Holmes.

In a detective story, as in any story of ingenuity, the main interest is not in the character or in the setting but in a skillfully constructed plot. The reader is presented with a puzzling situation, and although clues are sometimes dropped as the story proceeds, the solution is not given until the end of the story. Edgar Allan Poe is often given credit for inventing the form of the detective story with stories such as "Murders in the Rue Morgue" and "The Purloined Letter."

Integration: Use the Find Out by Reading feature to integrate language arts into your science lesson.

FIND OUT BY READING

A Master Sleuth

If you truly enjoy a mystery, you may want to do some investigating on your own by reading some of Agatha Christie's books. The title of the book that was quoted on page 139 is *The Mysterious Affair at Styles*. If your local library does not have this particular work, ask your librarian for a list of some other Agatha Christie books.

Guide for Reading

Focus on these questions as you read.

▶ What are the five sense organs?
▶ What are the functions of the five sense organs?

For example, when you are frightened, nerves leading to organs such as the lungs and the heart are activated. This action causes your breathing rate and heartbeat to increase. Such an increase may be necessary if extra energy and strength are needed to deal with the frightening situation. But when the frightening situation is over, the other group of autonomic nerves bring your breathing rate and heartbeat back to normal.

6–2 Section Review

1. What are the two major parts of the human nervous system? What is the function of each?
2. Identify the three main parts of the brain and give their functions.
3. What is the function of the spinal cord?
4. Describe a reflex.

Critical Thinking—*Applying Concepts*
5. If a person's cerebellum is injured in an automobile accident, how might the person be affected?

6–3 The Senses

You know what is going on inside your body and in the world around you because of neurons known as receptors (neurons that respond to stimuli). Many of these receptors are found in your sense organs. Sense organs are structures that carry messages about your surroundings to the central nervous system. **Sense organs respond to light, sound, heat, pressure, and chemicals and also detect changes in the position of your body.** The eyes, ears, nose, tongue, and skin are examples of sense organs.

Most sense organs respond to stimuli from your body's external environment. Others keep track of the environment inside your body. Although you are not aware of it, your sense organs send messages to the central nervous system about almost everything—from body temperature to carbon dioxide and oxygen levels in your blood to the amount of light entering your eyes.

6–2 (continued)

GUIDED PRACTICE

Skills Development

Skill: Relating concepts

Relate the following situations to the class. Have students write possible automatic body reactions that might occur as a result of being in these situations:
1. A large dog is about to attack you.
2. You win a million dollars in a contest.
3. You are given a new car.
4. You read a frightening mystery story.

INDEPENDENT PRACTICE

Section Review 6–2

1. The central nervous system contains the brain and the spinal cord and is the control center of the body. The peripheral nervous system includes all the nerves that connect the central nervous system to other parts of the body.
2. The cerebrum permits thought, memory, speech, and the control of most voluntary muscle contractions and identifies information gathered by the senses. The

cerebellum controls balance and posture. The medulla controls automatic body processes.
3. The spinal cord contains nerve cells that carry messages to and from the brain.
4. A reflex is an automatic and extremely fast reaction to a stimulus.
5. Balance would be affected, and movements might appear jerky.

REINFORCEMENT/RETEACHING

Review students' responses to the Section Review questions. Reteach any ma-

Vision

Your eyes are one of your most wonderful possessions. They enable you to watch a beautiful sunset, pass a thread through the eye of a needle, and learn about a variety of topics by reading the printed word. They can focus on a speck of dust a few centimeters away or on a distant star many light-years away. Your eyes are your windows on the world.

Your eyes are designed to focus light rays (a form of energy you can see) to produce images of objects. But your eyes are useless without a brain to receive and interpret the messages that correspond to these images. What the brain does is receive the messages coming in through the eyes. These messages are then interpreted by the brain's visual center, located at the back of the brain. You will learn more about the brain's role in vision a little later in this section.

The eye is more correctly known as an eyeball—which is an appropriate name, as it is shaped like a ball. You may wish to refer to Figure 6–18 on page 146 as you read about the structures of the eyeball. The eyeball is slightly longer than it is wide. The eye is composed of three layers of tissue. The outer, protective layer is called the sclera (SKLEER-uh). The sclera is more commonly known as the "white" of the eye. In the center of the front of the eyeball, the sclera becomes transparent and colorless. This area of the sclera is called the **cornea.** The cornea is the part of the eye through which light enters. For this reason, the cornea is sometimes called "the window of the eye."

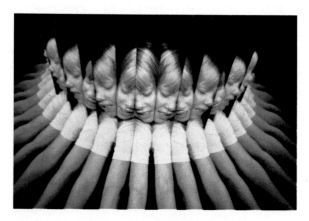

Figure 6–17 *Most sense organs respond to stimuli in the environment. But every now and then, sense organs can be fooled into sensing something that is not really as it should be. The optical illusion shown here, which is produced by mirrors, tricks the eyes into seeing many images of this young person.*

H ■ 145

6-3 The Senses

terial that is still unclear, based on students' responses.

When a person is said to have 20/20 vision, this means that he or she can see at a distance of 20 feet an object that a person with "normal" vision can see at 20 feet. People with 20/15 vision have better-than-normal vision. An object that a person with normal vision can see clearly at 15 feet can be seen clearly by someone with 20/15 vision at 20 feet. By the same token, people with 20/100 vision have poorer-than-normal vision. What a normal person sees at 100 feet, they must move up to 20 feet to see.

FACT AND FIGURES
EYEPRINTS?

Each person's retina has a unique pattern of blood vessels. Retina blood vessel patterns are as different in each person as fingerprints are.

6–3 (continued)

FOCUS/MOTIVATION

Have students examine Figure 6–18. Using the diagram in Figure 6–18, point out and read the names of the various parts of the eye. See if students can identify these eye structures in the photograph.

CONTENT DEVELOPMENT

Have students continue to use the diagram in Figure 6–18 as you discuss the various eye structures. Point out that three layers of tissue make up the eye.

The outside layer, called the sclera, surrounds the eye like the casing of a camera. The sclera is seen as the "white" of the eye.

At the center front of the eye, however, the sclera becomes transparent. This transparent tissue forms a protective shield called the cornea.

The middle layer of tissue that makes up the eye is called the choroid. The choroid layer contains blood vessels and the iris, or colored portion of the eye.

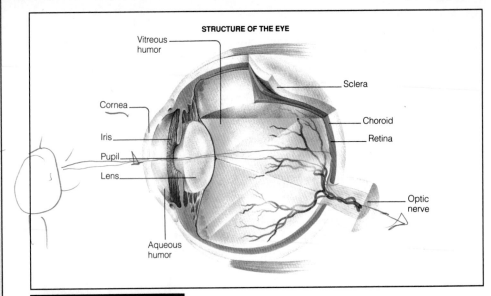

STRUCTURE OF THE EYE

- Vitreous humor
- Cornea
- Iris
- Pupil
- Lens
- Aqueous humor
- Sclera
- Choroid
- Retina
- Optic nerve

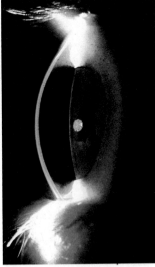

Figure 6–18 *What structures of the eye can you identify?* ❶

Just inside the cornea is a small chamber filled with a fluid called aqueous (AY-kwee-uhs) humor. At the back of this chamber is the circular colored portion of the eye called the **iris.** The iris is the part of the eye people refer to when they say a person's eyes are blue, brown, black, or hazel. The iris is part of the choroid (KOR-oid), or middle layer of the eye. Unlike the sclera and the cornea, the choroid contains blood vessels.

In the middle of the iris is a small opening called the **pupil.** The pupil is not a structure but an actual opening through which light enters the eye. The amount of light entering the pupil is controlled by the size of the opening. And the size of the opening is controlled by tiny muscles in the iris, which relax or contract to make the pupil larger or smaller. By observing the pupils of your eyes in a mirror as you vary the amount of light in the room, you can actually see the opening change size. Your pupils get larger in dim light and smaller in bright light. Why? Pupils get smaller in bright light to prevent light damage to the inside of the eye. They get larger in dim light to let in more light.

Just behind the iris is the **lens.** The lens focuses the light rays coming into the eye. Small muscles

146 ■ H

▶ *Multimedia* ◀

Use the Transparency in the *Transparency Binder* called The Eye as you teach the concepts in this section.

FOCUS/MOTIVATION

Divide students into groups of three or four. Have each member of the group look at the iris, pupil, and sclera of the other students.

• **What do you observe?** (The pupils of the eyes are black, the corneas are white, and the irises have many possible subtle colors.)

CONTENT DEVELOPMENT

Point out that the pupil is a circular opening in the iris. Because no light is coming from behind the lens, this opening appears black. The muscles in the iris relax or contract to make the pupil larger or smaller. This regulates the amount of light that enters the lens.

The internal part of the eye consists of the lens, retina, and vitreous humor. Explain that the lens focuses light on the back surface of the eye, an area known as

attached to the lens cause its shape to change constantly, depending on whether objects are close by or far away. When the muscles relax, the lens flattens out, enabling you to see distant objects more clearly. When the muscles contract (shorten), the lens returns to its normal shape, enabling you to see objects that are close by more clearly. Behind the lens is a large chamber that contains a transparent, jellylike fluid called vitreous (VIH-tree-uhs) humor. This fluid gives the eyeball its roundish shape.

The light that passes through the lens is focused on the back surface of the eye, which is known as the **retina** (REHT-'n-uh). The retina is the eye's inner layer of tissue. It contains more than 130 million light-sensitive receptors called rods and cones. Rods react to dim light but not to colors. Cones are responsible for color vision, but they stop working in dim light. This is the reason why colors seem to disappear at night, when you are seeing with only your rods.

Both rods and cones produce nerve impulses that travel from the retina along the optic nerve to the visual center of the brain. There the nerve impulses are interpreted by the brain. Because of the way the lens bends light rays as they enter the eye, the image that appears on the retina is upside down. The brain must automatically turn the image right side up—and do so quickly! The brain must also combine the two slightly different images provided by each eye into one three-dimensional image. This is a complex task, indeed, but your brain does it quickly and automatically almost every second of your waking day. Just imagine what it would be like living in a world in which everything was upside down!

Figure 6–19 *This image of a cat was produced by a silicon chip developed to imitate the light-sensitive cells in the retina. What are these light-sensitive cells called?* ❷

Figure 6–20 *The retina, which is the eye's inner layer of tissue, contains the light-sensitive cells called the rods and cones (right). The lens of the eye focuses light onto the retina. The upside-down image that you see in the photograph (left) was taken with a special camera that looked through the pupil of the eye.*

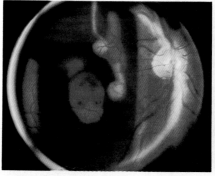 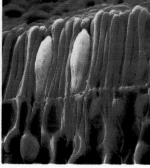

H ■ 147

BACKGROUND INFORMATION
COLORBLINDNESS

Most people can identify between 150 and 200 colors, but everyone does not see exactly the same colors, particularly if the person is colorblind.

Normal color vision is dependent on three types of cones. If any one type of cone is absent, the person will be colorblind for the color associated with that cone. Complete colorblindness is extremely rare, but red-green color blindness occurs in about 8 percent of the male population. A person with red-green colorblindness cannot distinguish red from green. In order to help these people see the proper lights at traffic signals, yellow has been added to the red light and blue to the green light.

Many animals are colorblind. Prairie dogs are colorblind to red and green, ants cannot see red, and owls are completely colorblind.

the retina. Unlike the lens of a camera, the lens of the eye actually changes shape when focusing.

GUIDED PRACTICE
Skills Development
Skill: Interpreting diagrams

• **In the diagram, what is located between the cornea and the lens?** (Aqueous humor.)

Explain that the aqueous humor is a watery fluid that protects and covers the lens.

• **What lies between the lens and the retina?** (Vitreous humor.)

Vitreous humor is more viscous than the watery aqueous humor. This fluid gives the eyeball its roundish shape.

CONTENT DEVELOPMENT

Explain that the impulses received by the retina pass through the optic nerve and travel to the brain to be interpreted. Because of the way the lens bends the light rays, the brain receives images from the retina upside down. It must automatically turn them right side up. The brain must also combine the two different images provided by the two eyes into a single three-dimensional image.

REINFORCEMENT/RETEACHING
▶ *Activity Book*

Students who need extra practice with the concepts of this section should be provided with the Chapter 6 activity called The Blind Spot.

PROBLEM SOLVING

I CAN SEE CLEARLY NOW

In nearsightedness (myopia), light coming from distant objects comes into focus in front of the retina. To correct this condition, a concave lens is placed in front of the eye. Parallel rays of light pass through the concave lens, are refracted, and diverge, or spread outward.

In farsightedness (hypermetropia), light rays are brought into focus behind the retina. To correct this condition, a convex lens is placed in front of the eye. Parallel rays of light pass through the convex lens, are refracted, and converge, or come together at a single point.

Nearsighted people see nearby objects clearly, but objects far away are blurry. Farsighted people see objects far away clearly, but nearby objects are blurry.

Bifocals have two types of lenses in them so that they can correct for both nearsightedness and farsightedness.

Integration: Use the Problem Solving feature to integrate concepts about light into your life science lesson.

6–3 (continued)

ENRICHMENT

Take a survey among students to determine how many are nearsighted, how many are farsighted, and how many have "normal" vision.

Explain that in nearsightedness, the eyeball is actually too long for the normal focusing power of the lens. Therefore, light rays from a distant object converge in front of the retina. This situation can be corrected with concave lenses. A concave lens diverges light rays slightly, and the image is moved back onto the retina.

The farsighted eye, on the other hand, is too short. For nearby objects, the lens cannot accommodate enough to keep images from falling beyond the retina. With the use of convex lenses, light rays converge and enable the eye's lens to focus in a normal manner.

I Can See Clearly Now

Look around at the students in your classroom. You will notice that some of them are wearing eyeglasses. Why do some people need glasses whereas others do not? The answer to this question has to do with the structure of the eyeball. Look at the diagrams of the eyeball shown here. Notice that when the eyeball looks at an object, the light rays from that object enter the eyeball and come to a focus point on the retina.

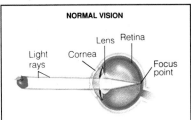

Sometimes, however, the light rays do not come to a focus point on the retina. When the eyeball is too long from front to back, the light rays come together at a point in front of the retina. The result is a blurred image of distant objects. This disorder is called nearsightedness. When the eyeball is too short from front to back, the light rays come together at a point behind the retina. The result is a blurred image of nearby objects. This disorder is called farsightedness.

To fix these disorders, eyeglasses containing corrective lenses are worn. Examine the path of the light rays through each of the two lenses below—a biconcave (sunken in at both surfaces) lens and a biconvex (arched at both surfaces) lens.

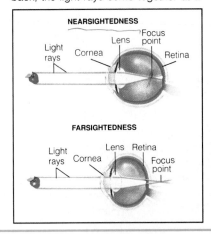

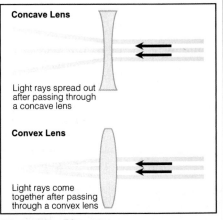

Interpreting Diagrams

1. Which type of lens corrects nearsightedness?

2. Which type of lens corrects farsightedness?

3. Why is nearsightedness an appropriate name for this disorder?

4. Why is farsightedness an appropriate name for this disorder?

5. What are bifocals?

FOCUS/MOTIVATION

• **How does a drum work to make sound?** (Lead students to realize that the drum must be hit to make sound. Hitting the drum sets up vibrations of the drumhead.)
• **What is the loudest sound you have ever heard?** (Accept all answers.)
• **What is the softest or quietest sound you have ever heard?** (Accept all answers.)

CONTENT DEVELOPMENT

Point out that sound is caused by air vibrating. Explain that hearing sound begins when the vibrating airwaves enter the external ear. The ear is like a skin-covered funnel. It gathers in the sound waves and passes them through the ear canal. The ear canal is a tubelike structure that is found between the external ear and the eardrum.

Hearing and Balance

When someone laughs or the telephone rings, the air around the source of the sound vibrates. These vibrations move through the air in waves. Hearing actually begins when some of the sound waves enter the external ear. If you look at Figure 6–21, you will see the external ear. This is the part of the ear with which you are probably most familiar. It is made mostly of cartilage covered with skin. You may recall from Chapter 2 that cartilage is strong enough to support weight, yet flexible enough to be bent and twisted. You can prove this to yourself by bending your external ear.

The funnellike shape of the external ear enables it to gather sound waves. These waves pass through the tubelike ear canal to the **eardrum.** The eardrum is a tightly stretched membrane that separates the ear canal from the middle ear. As sound waves

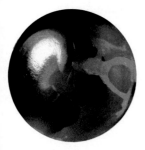

Figure 6–21 *Sound waves enter the ear and are changed into nerve impulses that are carried to the brain. The photograph of the middle ear shows the eardrum, which is colored yellow, and the three tiny bones known as the hammer, the anvil, and the stirrup.*

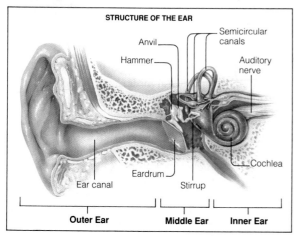

STRUCTURE OF THE EAR

Anvil
Hammer
Semicircular canals
Auditory nerve
Cochlea
Eardrum
Ear canal
Stirrup

Outer Ear | **Middle Ear** | **Inner Ear**

FIND OUT BY DOING

Reaction Time

1. Have a partner hold a ruler vertically above a table.

2. Without touching the ruler, position the zero mark between your thumb and forefinger.

3. Your partner should drop the ruler whenever he or she chooses. Moving only your thumb and forefinger, but not your hand, try to catch the ruler as soon as it falls.

4. Record the distance, in centimeters, that the ruler falls.

5. Repeat steps 1 through 4 four more times.

6. To obtain an average distance, add the five distances together and divide this sum by five. Record the average distance.

Why does measuring the distance that the ruler falls give a relative measure of reaction time, which is the length of time that passes between your seeing a change in your environment and your reacting to that change? Compare the reaction times of all your classmates. What can you conclude?

■ Design an experiment in which you determine the effect fatigue has on your reaction time.

ANNOTATION KEY

Integration

❶ Physical Science: Light. See *Sound and Light*, Chapter 4.

FIND OUT BY DOING
REACTION TIME

Discovery Learning

Skills: Making observations, measuring, making calculations, calculator, making inferences

Materials: ruler

Students should quickly determine that the farther the ruler falls, the longer the reaction time. This is only a relative measure of reaction time because students are measuring distance rather than the time itself. They will find that reaction times differ greatly among classmates.

In experiments to determine the effect of fatigue on reaction time, students should work in groups of three. One student drops the ruler, one catches it, and one records both the distances and the number of "drops" in a given time interval. Because fatigue is a phenomenon that occurs over time, experiments should include time as one of the variables and provide a way of measuring time. Reaction times will increase as the muscles become fatigued.

► *Multimedia* ◄

Use the transparency in the *Transparency Binder* called The Ear to help students understand the various structures in the ear.

GUIDED PRACTICE

Skills Development

Skill: Interpreting diagrams

Using Figure 6–21, have students locate the outer ear, ear canal, and eardrum. The sound waves "hit" the eardrum, setting up vibrations.

Vibrations enter the middle ear, which is composed of three small bones. Have students locate the hammer, anvil, and stirrup in Figure 6–21. Explain that the hammer, anvil, and stirrup are the smallest bones in the body.

CONTENT DEVELOPMENT

Explain that as the sound waves from the eardrum enter the middle ear, the hammer picks up the vibrations and passes the vibrations on to the anvil and finally to the stirrup. Point out that the stirrup vibrates against a membrane that separates the middle ear from the liquid-filled inner ear. Tell students that the vibrations travel into a spiraling tube called a cochlea. Explain that the cochlea contains nerve endings that react to the vibrations.

Point out that the neurons on the nerve endings send out impulses to the auditory nerve, which carries them to the brain for interpretation.

NOISE POLLUTION

There is evidence that exposure to loud noises, including loud rock music, is damaging to the hearing. In fact, the cochlear hair cells can be irreversibly damaged after just one exposure to a very loud noise. Workers in certain kinds of noisy factories and rock musicians are two groups of people who are especially susceptible to hearing impairment.

Loud and unpleasant noises are not an inevitable part of life. For example, steel-mesh blankets can be hung over a construction site to absorb the noise of the jackhammers, riveting, and other construction activities.

6–3 (continued)

FOCUS/MOTIVATION

Have students stand next to their desks. Tell them to stand on one foot without touching anything. Allow students time to lose their balance.

• **What happened to your balance after a period of time?** (We lost it.)

• **Why did you lose your balance?** (Accept all logical answers.)

• **Have you ever lost your balance doing normal activities?** (Accept all answers.)

CONTENT DEVELOPMENT

Explain that there are three curved tubes inside the inner ear. Each of these tubes is filled with a fluid. These fluid-filled tubes are responsible for our sense of balance. The tubes are called semicircular canals.

Have students look at Figure 6–22. Point out that as the fluid moves or shifts, it presses against tiny hairs on the inner surface of the curved tubes. Explain that when the hairs in the semicircular canals in the ear bend, a nerve impulse is sent to the cerebellum of the brain.

● ● ● ● **Integration** ● ● ● ●

Use the discussion of how vibrations are interpreted as sound to integrate physical science concepts of sound into your lesson.

Figure 6–22 *The semicircular canals are arranged at right angles to one another so that they can respond to up-and-down, side-to-side, and bending motions (top). Tiny grains commonly called hearing stones also play a part in maintaining balance (bottom). In what part of the ear are the semicircular canals located?* ❶

150 ■ H

---

strike the eardrum, it vibrates in much the same way that the surface of a drum vibrates when it is struck.

❶ Vibrations from the eardrum enter the middle ear, which is composed of the three smallest bones in the body—the hammer, anvil, and stirrup. The hammer, the first of these bones, picks up the vibrations from the eardrum and passes them along to the anvil and then to the stirrup. The stirrup vibrates against a thin membrane covering the opening into the fluid-filled inner ear.

Vibrations in the inner ear pass through the fluid and are channeled into a snail-shaped tube called the **cochlea** (KAHK-lee-uh). The cochlea contains nerves that are stimulated by the vibrations from a wide variety of sounds and range of loudness. The stimulated nerves produce nerve impulses that are carried from the cochlea to the brain by the auditory nerve. Once in the brain, these nerve impulses are interpreted, and you hear.

The ear not only enables you to hear, it also enables you to be aware of changes in movement and to keep your balance. The structures in the ear that are responsible for your sense of balance are the **semicircular canals** and the two tiny sacs behind them. The semicircular canals are three tiny canals located within your inner ear just above the cochlea. They are called semicircular because, as you can see from Figure 6–22, each makes a half circle (the prefix *semi-* means half).

The semicircular canals and the tiny sacs near them are filled with fluid and lined with tiny hairlike cells. These cells are embedded in a jellylike substance that contains tiny grains called hearing stones. When your head moves, the hearing stones roll back and forth, bending the hairlike cells. The hairlike cells respond by sending nerve impulses to the cerebellum of your brain. If your brain interprets these impulses to mean that your body is losing its balance, it will automatically signal some muscles to contract and others to relax until your balance is restored.

Even the most ordinary actions—such as walking, jogging, jumping, swimming, and skipping—require smooth coordination of muscles with the senses of vision, hearing, and balance. After much training

---

ENRICHMENT

▶ *Multimedia* ◀

In her book *A Natural History of the Senses*, Diane Ackerman writes, "Of all the senses, hearing most resembles a contraption some ingenious plumber has put together from spare parts." After students have used the Interactive Videodisc called Invention: Mastering Sound, have them try to improve on the human mechanism of hearing. Their "inventions" should be described both in text and with diagrams.

REINFORCEMENT/RETEACHING

Remind students that the cerebellum is responsible for the control of balance and posture. Point out that the cerebellum also adjusts motor impulses to make the body move smoothly. Tell students that the cerebellum coordinates muscle movement for balance, sight, touch, and any other eye-hand movement.

Figure 6–23 *The role of the ears in maintaining balance makes all sorts of activities possible.*

and practice, your brain can learn to quickly coordinate balance with eye and hand movements so that you can walk a tightrope as easily as you can lift a spoon to your mouth!

Smell and Taste

Unlike the senses of vision and hearing, the senses of smell and taste do not respond to physical stimuli such as light and sound vibrations. To what stimuli, then, do these senses respond? The following story—perhaps similar to an experience in your own kitchen—may provide the answer.

You are standing near the oven. Suddenly you smell the wonderful aroma of a chocolate cake. You cannot see a cake, so what tells you that there is one baking in the oven? Your sense of smell tells you, of course. Sense receptors in your nose react to invisible stimuli carried by the air from the oven to your nose. The invisible stimuli are chemicals that affect the smell receptors in your nose. So your sense of smell is a chemical sense. In turn, the smell receptors produce nerve impulses that are carried to the brain, where they are interpreted. As a result, you are not only able to smell a cake, but you are able to identify the smell as a chocolate cake!

Your sense of taste is also a chemical sense. In the case of taste, the chemicals are not carried through the air but in liquids in your mouth (solid foods mix with saliva to form liquids). The receptors for taste are located in the taste buds on your tongue. Although there are only four basic kinds of tastes—sweet, sour, bitter, and salty—there are at least 80 basic odors. Taken together, tastes and odors produce flavors. Thus your sense of smell must work

Figure 6–24 *You have no trouble in identifying the wonderful aroma of a chocolate cake thanks to the sense receptors in the nose.*

H ■ 151

optic N 147
auditory N 150

baking cookies, move through the air, the smell sense receptors are activated. The sense receptors then start the impulse moving to the brain. The brain interprets the impulse and identifies the odor to you from past experiences.

Point out that when we eat food, both taste and odor produce the flavor. The tongue's taste receptors are activated when a sweet, sour, salty, or bitter substance creates an impulse. The odor from the food activates the smell receptors.

INDEPENDENT PRACTICE

▶ *Activity Book*

You can provide further practice with the concepts of this section by having students use the Chapter 6 activity called The Senses of Taste and Smell.

CONTENT DEVELOPMENT

Point out that smell and taste senses are unusual because they do not respond to physical stimuli; instead, they respond to chemicals.

Explain that taste sense receptors also react to chemicals. The chemicals are not carried through the air but in liquids in the mouth. There are four kinds of receptors on the tongue. These taste receptors are sensitive to sweet, salty, sour, and bitter tastes.

FOCUS/MOTIVATION

Divide students into groups of three or four. Give each group five or more small bottles of substances unknown to them, such as ketchup, vinegar, egg white diluted with water, hand lotion, perfume, liquid detergent, shampoo, coffee, and/or tea. (**CAUTION:** *Do not give any strong substances that could cause injury to the delicate nasal membranes. Avoid strong acids, bases, bleach, ammonia, ether, and the like.*) Label the bottles A, B, C, and so on.

HAPTIC TOUCH

In the coin experiment described in the Focus/Motivation activity below, students will discover that it is easier to identify the coins by picking them up and handling them rather than just touching the tops of the coins with their index fingers.

The touch receptors are used only when the coins are touched by the index finger. When the coins are picked up and touched, they are actually being manipulated. Turning the coins and rolling them between the fingers is a process known as haptic touch. Manipulating the coins includes perceptions of pressure, movement, resistance, and position. This information enables the brain to create a three-dimensional picture of the object, which enables the student to identify the coins correctly.

6–4 (continued)

FOCUS/MOTIVATION

Divide students into groups of three or four. Give each group a paper cup containing a nickel, a dime, a quarter, and a penny. Instruct them to close their eyes, reach into the container, remove one coin, and attempt to identify it by holding it in their hand and touching it.

Now set the four coins on a flat surface. Using only the tip of the index finger, attempt to identify each of the coins. Do not pick up the coins.

• **Was it easier to identify the coins by picking them up and touching them or by touching their tops with your index finger?** (Picking them up and touching them.)

• **In which case are you actually using only touch receptors to identify the coins?** (When you touch them with the index finger.)

• **When you pick up the coins and hold them, what other receptors are you using?** (Manipulating the coins leads to perceptions of pressure, movement, resistance, and position. This enables the brain to develop a three-dimensional re-creation of the object, which permits an easier identification.)

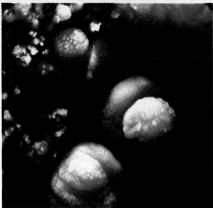
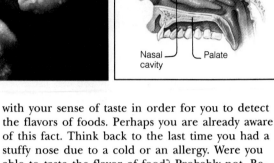

Figure 6–25 *Smell receptors in your nose (right) and taste receptors on your tongue (left) are responsible for identifying the flavors of foods. What are taste receptors called?* ❶

Figure 6–26 *The sense of touch, unlike the other senses, is not found in one particular place. All regions of the skin are sensitive to touch. For this reason, the sense of touch is one of the most important senses on which sightless people rely.*

with your sense of taste in order for you to detect the flavors of foods. Perhaps you are already aware of this fact. Think back to the last time you had a stuffy nose due to a cold or an allergy. Were you able to taste the flavor of food? Probably not. Because the smell receptors in your nose were covered by extra mucus, only your sense of taste was working—not your sense of smell. Without a combined effort, the food you ate had little, if any, flavor.

Touch

The sense of touch is not found in any one place. The sense of touch is found in all areas of the skin. For this reason, you can think of the skin as your largest sense organ!

Near the surface of the skin are touch receptors that allow you to feel the textures of objects. You do not need much force to produce nerve impulses in these receptors. Prove this to yourself by gently running your fingertips across a piece of wood so that you can feel the grain. You have stimulated these touch receptors. Located deeper within the skin are the receptors that sense pressure. The sense of pressure differs as much from the sense of touch as pressing your hand firmly against a piece of wood differs from feeling it with your fingertips.

Notice in Figure 6–27 that there are other types of sense receptors. These receptors respond to heat, cold, and pain. The receptors that respond to heat and cold are scattered directly below the surface of

▶ *Multimedia* ◀

Use the transparency in the *Transparency Binder* called The Skin as you explain the final concepts in this section.

CONTENT DEVELOPMENT

Point out that the sense of touch is actually several different senses. Near the surface of the skin are receptors that respond to heat, cold, pain, pressure, and touch.

Have students observe Figure 6–27. Point out that the touch receptor neurons lie just below the top layer of skin. Ex-

plain that when the skin comes in contact with a substance, one or more of the touch receptors are activated. The nerve impulse is carried through the peripheral nervous system to the brain. The brain interprets the impulses into feelings, sensations, and possible reactions.

Point out that this is extremely important in the case of pain.

• **Why is pain useful or important to your body's functioning?** (Nerves carry impulses of pain to the brain to alert the body that it may be in danger. This warn-

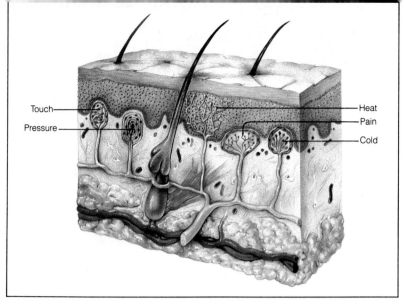

Touch
Pressure
Heat
Pain
Cold

Figure 6–27 *Human skin contains five types of sense receptors: pressure, touch, pain, heat, and cold.*

the skin. Pain receptors are found all over the skin. It should not surprise you to learn that pain receptors are important to the survival of your body, no matter how uncomfortable they may seem at times. Pain, you see, often alerts your body to the fact that it might be in some type of danger.

6–3 Section Review

1. What are the five basic senses? What organs are responsible for these senses?
2. Describe the structure of the eye. Identify the functions of the major structures.
3. Trace the path of sound from the external ear to the auditory nerve.
4. Explain the role of the ear in maintaining balance.
5. What are the four basic tastes?

Connection—*You and Your World*
6. Design an experiment to show that your sense of smell is important in determining the flavor of food.

INTEGRATION
LANGUAGE ARTS

Many expressions used in everyday speech make reference to the sense of touch. Examples include "rubbing someone the wrong way" and describing a person as "touchy," "thick-skinned," or a "soft touch."

the tongue, for taste; and the skin, for touch.

2. The eye contains three layers of tissue: the sclera, the choroid, and the retina. The sclera protects the inner layers, the blood vessels in the choroid provide nourishment, and the retina contains the light-sensitive cells.

3. Sound vibrations travel through the ear canal, strike the eardrum, are transmitted through the anvil, stirrup, and hammer to the cochlea, and pass through a liquid in the cochlea to stimulate the auditory nerves.

4. The semicircular canals contain a fluid that moves when the head and body move. As the fluid shifts, it bends tiny hairs. These hairs send nerve impulses to the brain so that the brain can signal you to catch your balance.

5. Sweet, sour, bitter and salty.

6. Answers will vary. Most students will suggest holding the nose to determine if smell affects our sense of taste.

REINFORCEMENT/RETEACHING

Review students' responses to the Section Review questions. Reteach any material that is still unclear, based on students' responses.

CLOSURE

▶ *Review and Reinforcement Guide*

Have students complete Section 6–3 in the *Review and Reinforcement Guide*.

ing of danger is a very important tool of survival.)

GUIDED PRACTICE

Skills Development

Skills: Making observations, recording data, making comparisons, making inferences

At this point you may wish to have students complete the in-text Chapter 6 Laboratory Investigation: Locating Touch Receptors. In the investigation students will

discover the location and quantity of the touch receptors.

ENRICHMENT

▶ *Activity Book*

Students who have mastered the concepts in this section will be challenged by the Chapter 6 activity called Your Senses.

INDEPENDENT PRACTICE

Section Review 6–3

1. The eyes are responsible for vision; the ears, for hearing; the nose, for smell;

Answers
① Hormones. (Applying concepts)

Integration
① Physical Science: Computers. See *Electricity and Magnetism*, Chapter 4.

CONNECTIONS

WITH OR WITHOUT PEPPERONI?

Explain that a robot is a computerized machine designed to perform various tasks that humans perform. So far, however, robots are quite limited in what they can do compared to what humans can do. One expert commented that making an "intelligent" robot is much harder than one might think; that what looks simple for a human to do is far from simple when one tries to program it into a robot's computer-brain.

Robots are already used for tasks that are repetitious, boring, or dangerous. Most likely, robots will be used even more widely in the future than they are today. In fact, there are now some inexpensive kits you can use to build a small robot.

If you are teaching thematically, you may want to use the Connections feature to reinforce the themes of patterns of change or systems and interactions.

Integration: Use the Connections feature to integrate computer science into your lesson.

CONNECTIONS

① With or Without Pepperoni?

Do not be too surprised if sometime soon you walk into a pizzeria and discover that the pizza you ordered is being whipped together by a voice-activated robot. As you may already know, robots are mechanical devices that do routine tasks. However, PizzaBot, as the pizza-making robot is called, is equipped with a little something extra—*artificial intelligence*. Artificial intelligence is a branch of *computer science* concerned with designing computer systems that perform tasks which seem to require intelligence. These tasks include reasoning, adapting to new situations, and learning new skills. When you recognize a face, learn a new language, or figure out the best way to arrive at a destination, you are performing such tasks.

Until recently, computers have only been able to follow instructions (a computer program). Now, however, scientists have developed computers that "think," or are able to perform complex

tasks such as diagnosing disease, locating minerals in the soil, and even making pizza! In order to "think," these computers need vast amounts of information. To make a pizza, a computer needs to recognize the sounds of a human voice as a pizza is ordered, to "decide" what possible pizza size and toppings it has just "heard," to repeat the order to confirm it (both aloud and on a screen), and then to follow the program for that pizza. The computer then processes these data one step at a time but extremely fast. (In contrast, your brain, with its billions of neurons, processes information along many pathways at the same time.)

As you can see, some of the applications of artificial intelligence are quite exciting, especially those in the field of *robotics*, or the study of robots. Just imagine the effects "thinking" robots such as PizzaBot could have on your life. The possibilities seem almost endless. In the not-too-distant future, you might even own a minirobot that would monitor your room, darting out every now and then to pick up the crumbs from your last snack! Seems impossible now, but who knows what will happen in the next few years. . . .

TEACHING STRATEGY 6–4

FOCUS/MOTIVATION

• **Would you get on a roller coaster? Why or why not?** (Accept all answers.)
• **If you have ridden on a roller coaster, how did you feel?** (Accept all answers.)
• **Why might some people feel excited on a roller coaster?** (Accept all answers.)
• **Why might some people feel tense on a roller coaster?** (Accept all answers.)
• **Why might some people get an upset stomach on a roller coaster?** (Accept all answers.)

CONTENT DEVELOPMENT

Point out that there are two special types of glands that produce chemicals to help regulate body activities—endocrine glands and exocrine glands.

Explain that glands in the endocrine system produce chemical messengers called hormones. These hormones work together with the nervous system to control body activites.

• **What do you think triggers the endocrine glands to produce hormones?** (Possible answers are fear, excitement, and various other emotions.)

Explain that these emotions are interpreted by the brain. The brain then sends messages through the nervous system to trigger the appropriate glands to release the needed hormones.

Point out that the endocrine glands also respond to stimuli from the internal chemical environment. For example, changes in the chemical makeup of the

6-4 The Endocrine System

It is late at night, and your room is dark. As you feel your way toward the light switch in the pitch-black room, something warm brushes against your leg. You let out a piercing shriek, or perhaps only a gasp. It is not until you realize it is the cat you have encountered that you breathe a sigh of relief. As your pounding heart begins to slow down and your stiffened muscles relax, you begin to feel calmer. Have you ever wondered what causes your body to react this way? As you read on, you will find the answer to this question.

Endocrine Glands

The reactions you have just read about are set in motion not only by your nervous system, but also by another system called the endocrine (EHN-doh-krihn) system. **The endocrine system is made of glands that produce chemical messengers called hormones. Hormones help to regulate certain body activities.** By turning on and turning off or speeding up and slowing down the activities of different organs and tissues, **hormones** (HOR-mohnz) do their job. Together, the nervous system and the endocrine system function to keep all the parts of the body running smoothly.

The rush of fear that you felt as you brushed against an unknown object in the dark is an example of how the nervous system and the endocrine system work together. Your senses reported all the necessary information about the event to your brain. Because your brain interpreted the information as a threat, it quickly sent nerve impulses through selected nerves. These nerves triggered certain glands of the endocrine system. The selected glands produced hormones, which traveled through the blood to their specific destinations.

In this particular example, the hormones that were produced caused an increase in your heartbeat, made your lungs work harder, and prepared your muscles for immediate action. In such a state, you were ready to fight or to flee. Put another way, you were ready to defend yourself or to run. Your body

Guide for Reading

Focus on these questions as you read.

▶ *What is the function of the endocrine system?*
▶ *How does the endocrine system keep the internal environment of the body stable?*

Figure 6–28 *The diagram shows some of the major glands of the endocrine system. What is the name of the chemicals produced by these glands?* ❶

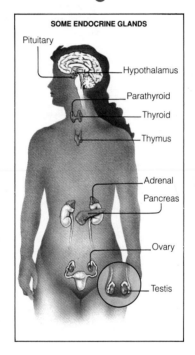

SOME ENDOCRINE GLANDS

- Pituitary
- Hypothalamus
- Parathyroid
- Thyroid
- Thymus
- Adrenal
- Pancreas
- Ovary
- Testis

H ■ 155

6-4 The Endocrine System

MULTICULTURAL OPPORTUNITY 6-4

You might wish to discuss with students the word origins for many of the endocrine systems. For example, by understanding the prefixes *endo-* (within) and *exo-* (without), students can better distinguish the endocrine and exocrine systems.

ESL STRATEGY 6-4

Ask students to complete the names of the eight glands listed below. Then have them match each numbered gland to a lettered description or function.

Glands
1. pi _____ _____ it _____ r _____
2. t _____ _____ m _____ s
3. a _____ _____ en _____ ls
4. p _____ n _____ r _____ _____ s
5. o _____ a _____ ies and
   t _____ st _____ s

Description
a. warn body of danger; produce adrenaline
b. controls blood pressure, growth, metabolism
c. regulates the immune system
d. controls blood's sugar level; produces insulin and glucagon
e. female and male reproductive organs; produce sex hormones

(**Answers:** a. 3, b. 1, c. 2, d. 4, e. 5)

---

blood may act as stimuli to endocrine organs to release hormones.

GUIDED PRACTICE

Skills Development

Skill: Interpreting diagrams

Have students read the names of the endocrine glands shown in Figure 6–28. Ask if they recognize any of the glands or know their functions.

Make a photocopy of Figure 6–28. Blank out the names of the glands. Re-produce copies of the unlabeled figure and have students write the name of each gland on their copy.

CONTENT DEVELOPMENT

Point out that the endocrine glands are ductless glands. Explain that ductless glands are glands that secrete directly into the bloodstream rather than moving their secretion through a tube or duct.

• **What is an advantage of using the circulatory system to deliver hormones?** (Because the circulatory system travels to all

parts of the body, the hormones can reach all the body cells and tissues.)

• **Why can endocrine glands be far away from the organ they control?** (The hormones from the endocrine glands are carried in the blood to all parts of the body. Thus, hormones can reach their target organs regardless of where they enter the bloodstream.)

Explain to students that body tissues can recognize the hormones that are made for them. They will accept certain hormones and reject others. Hormones do not affect tissues that are not in the target area.

Answers

❶ Thymosin is produced in the thymus. It regulates the development and function of the immune system (Interpreting charts)

Integration

❶ Language Arts

FIND OUT BY WRITING

BACTERIALLY PRODUCED HORMONES

Through this activity students will learn about the efforts of scientists to produce certain hormones, such as HGH, by means of bacterial genetic engineering. Encourage students to make use of recent issues of scientific periodicals in their research.

Integration: Use the Find Out by Writing feature to integrate language arts into your science lesson.

6–4 (continued)

FOCUS/MOTIVATION

Tell students to imagine that they have written a letter to their favorite musical group.

• **After you write the letter, what would you do with it?** (Most students will say they would mail the letter.)

• **After you mail it, what happens to the letter?** (Accept all logical answers. Lead students to realize that the letter is picked up by a postal worker, taken to the post office, and transferred to another post office, where another mail worker picks it up and delivers it to the musical group.)

Tell students to imagine that the musical group answered their letter.

• **What happened to their letter?** (Most students will say that the letter from the musical group traveled back through the same channels.)

FIND OUT BY WRITING

Bacterially Produced Hormones

❶ Scientists have developed certain bacteria that produce large amounts of some human hormones. Using reference material in the library, find out more information about the bacterially produced hormones. Use the information in a written report. Be sure to provide answers for the following questions: Which hormones are produced by bacteria? What is the function of the hormone? How are these hormones produced? Include labeled diagrams that show how the bacteria are made to produce these hormones.

remained prepared for any further trouble until your brain stopped sending out danger signals. Then the endocrine glands responded in turn, and your body calmed down.

Endocrine glands are not the only type of glands found in your body. You have another set of glands called exocrine (EHKS-oh-krihn) glands. Exocrine glands give off their chemicals through ducts, or tubes, into nearby organs. Unlike endocrine glands, exocrine glands do not produce hormones. They produce tears, sweat, oil, and digestive juices to name a few examples. Common exocrine glands include the salivary glands in the mouth and sweat glands in the skin.

The hormones secreted (given off) by the endocrine glands are delivered to their destinations through the circulatory system. Thus, endocrine glands do not need to be near the organs they control. No matter where hormones enter the bloodstream, they always find their way through the nearly 100,000 kilometers of blood vessels (that's almost two and a half times around the Earth!) to their intended target area. How is this possible? Body tissues have the ability to "recognize" the hormones that are made for them. Tissue cells are programmed to accept certain hormones and reject others. Hormones not meant for a particular type of tissue or organ will pass on until they come to their target tissue or organ.

Each of your body's eight endocrine glands releases a different set of hormones and thus controls different body processes. In the next few pages, you will read about these glands, their hormones, and the body activities they control. This information is summarized in Figure 6–29. How many of these glands and hormones sound familiar to you?

HYPOTHALAMUS The **hypothalamus** (high-poh-THAL-uh-muhs) produces hormones that help turn on and turn off the seven other endocrine glands in your body. The hypothalamus, which is a tiny gland located at the base of the brain, is the major link between the nervous system and the endocrine system. In fact, the hypothalamus is as much a part of one system as it is of the other. That is why the hypothalamus can be thought of as the way in which the brain and body "talk" to each other.

• **What function did the postal department have between you and the musical group?** (Accept all logical answers. Students are likely to suggest that the postal department was a messenger, transporter, communicator, and/or link between them and the musical group.)

▶ *Multimedia* ◀

An alternative way to introduce students to this section is to have them use the video called Endocrine System.

Before students watch the video, have them prepare a chart showing the eight endocrine glands listed in the illustration in Figure 6–28. The titles at the top of the chart should match those in Figure 6–29. As students watch the video, have them fill in missing information in their charts. When completed, have them compare the information they have learned with that given in Figure 6–29.

SOME ENDOCRINE GLANDS

Gland	Location	Hormone Produced	Functions
Hypothalamus	Base of brain	Regulatory factors	Regulates activities of other endocrine glands
Pituitary Front portion	Base of brain	Human growth hormone (HGH)	Stimulates body skeleton growth
		Gonadotropic hormone	Stimulates development of male and female sex organs
		Lactogenic hormone	Stimulates production of milk
		Thyrotropic hormone	Aids functioning of thyroid
		Adrenocorticotrophic hormone (ACTH)	Aids functioning of adrenals
Back portion		Oxytocin	Regulates blood pressure and stimulates smooth muscles; stimulates the birth process
		Vasopressin	Increases rate of water reabsorption in the kidneys
Thymus	Behind breastbone	Thymosin	Regulates development and function of immune system
Thyroid	Neck	Thyroxine	Increases rate of metabolism
		Calcitonin	Maintains the level of calcium and phosphorus in the blood
Parathyroids	Behind thyroid lobes	Parathyroid hormone	Regulates the level of calcium and phosphorus
Adrenals Inner tissue	Above kidneys	Adrenaline	Increases heart rate; elevates blood pressure; raises blood sugar; increases breathing rate; decreases digestive activity
Outer tissue		Mineralocorticoids	Maintains balance of salt and water in the kidneys
		Glucocorticoids— cortisone	Breaks down stored proteins to amino acids; aids in breakdown of fat tissue; promotes increase in blood sugar
		Sex hormones	Supplements sex hormones produced by sex glands; promotes development of sexual characteristics
Pancreas Islets of Langerhans	Abdomen, near stomach	Insulin	Enables liver to store sugar; regulates sugar breakdown in tissues; decreases blood sugar level
		Glucagon	Increases blood sugar level
Ovaries	Pelvic area	Estrogen	Produces female secondary sex characteristics
		Progesterone	Promotes growth of lining of uterus
Testes	Scrotum	Testosterone	Produces male secondary sex characteristics

Figure 6–29 *The location of some endocrine glands, the hormones they produce, and the functions they perform are shown in the chart. Where is thymosin produced? What is its function?* ❶

H ■ 157

HISTORICAL NOTE
HORMONES

The word *hormone* is derived from a Greek word meaning "to arouse to activity" or "to excite." The term was first used by British physiologist E. H. Starling in 1905 to describe substances secreted by the stomach in the digestive process. The next hormones to be studied were those produced by the thyroid gland; in particular, thyroxine.

The search to identify hormones remained a little-known part of scientific research until the discovery of insulin by Frederick Banting and Charles Best in 1921. The discovery of insulin revolutionized the treatment of diabetes and brought hormones to the attention of the general public.

REINFORCEMENT/RETEACHING

• **What does it mean when you say that a person "wears two different hats"?** (The expression refers to a person who has two different jobs or roles.)
• **Tell me about a person you know who "wears two different hats."** (Answers will vary. Some students may say that they wear two hats—as a student and a newspaper deliverer, for instance.)
• **Why would we be correct in saying that the hypothalamus wears two hats?** (The hypothalamus is part of the nervous system as well as part of the endocrine system.)

INDEPENDENT PRACTICE

▶ *Activity Book*

After students have studied the chart in Figure 6–29, have them use the Chapter 6 activity called The Magic Square.

ENRICHMENT

Tell students that involuntary actions such as heartbeat and body temperature are under the control of the hypothalamus. Although these actions are said to be involuntary, some people have learned to control them through training in yoga or biofeedback. Interested students may wish to learn about yoga and biofeedback.

REINFORCEMENT/RETEACHING

▶ *Activity Book*

Have students use the Chapter 6 activity called H.E.L.P. From Your Endocrine System to help them learn the names of the different endocrine glands.

CONTENT DEVELOPMENT

Tell students that there is a gland that is a link between the nervous system and the endocrine system. Write "Hypothalamus" on the chalkboard.

Explain that the hypothalamus gland is a small cluster of cells that lie beneath the brain. Messages that go to and from the brain may pass through the hypothalamus.

The hypothalamus gland works at two jobs. As an organ of the nervous system, it is the control station of body temperature, water balance, appetite, and sleep. As an organ of the endocrine system, it produces hormones that regulate other glands. The hypothalamus can "turn on" or "turn off" the other endocrine glands.

THE MASTER GLAND

For many years, the pituitary was dubbed the "master gland" because it was felt that almost all the other glands were controlled by hormones produced in the pituitary. Even though that term is occasionally still used, the pituitary is not the master gland. Almost all the secretions from the pituitary are triggered by secretions or nerve impulses arising in the hypothalamus. The hypothalamus is, in effect, the "master of the pituitary."

6–4 (continued)

FOCUS/MOTIVATION

• **What is the difference between a dwarf and a giant?** (A dwarf is a normally proportioned person who is abnormally small. A giant is a person who is abnormally tall.)

• **What do you think might cause a person to become a dwarf or a giant?** (Accept all logical answers.)

CONTENT DEVELOPMENT

Tell students that the hypothalamus often responds to messages and controls the activities of other endocrine glands through the pituitary gland. The pituitary gland lies just beneath the hypothalamus and is approximately in the center of the head. Although the pituitary gland is only about the size of a pea, it produces several important hormones. These hormones affect the body processes of growth, metabolism, sexual development, and reproduction.

GUIDED PRACTICE

Skills Development

Skill: Interpreting diagrams

Call students' attention to Figure 6–30.
• **Which is larger; the hypothalamus or the pituitary gland?** (Hypothalamus gland.)
• **What is the shape of the pituitary gland?** (It is rounded, or pea-shaped.)
• **How does the pituitary gland seem to be attached to the hypothalamus?** (By a stalk.)

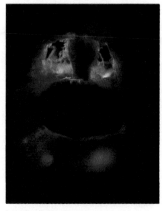

Figure 6–30 *The pituitary, which is found just under the hypothalamus, is located at the base of the brain in the center of the skull. The pea-shaped structure in the photograph is the pituitary, which is connected to the hypothalamus by a short stalk. What is the function of the pituitary?* ❶

Messages that travel to and from the brain go through the hypothalamus. So the hypothalamus "knows about" sensations you are aware of—a lovely sunset, a painful bee sting, or a pleasant smell. It also controls things you are not aware of—the level of hormones in the blood, the amount of nutrients in the body, or the internal temperature of the body.

PITUITARY The hypothalamus depends on another endocrine gland for information about the body. This gland is the **pituitary** (pih-TOO-uh-tair-ee). The hypothalamus "talks to" the pituitary—sometimes by means of nerve impulses and sometimes by way of hormones. In response to these stimuli from the hypothalamus, the pituitary produces its own hormones.

The pituitary, which is no larger than a pea, is found in the center of the skull right behind the bridge of the nose. The pituitary controls blood pressure, growth, metabolism (all the chemical and physical activities that go on inside the body), sexual development, and reproduction. For many years, the pituitary was called the "master gland" of the body. This was because the hormones the pituitary produces control many of the activities of other endocrine glands. When it was discovered that the pituitary itself was controlled by its own master—the hypothalamus—the nickname "master gland" gradually dropped out of use.

THYMUS Just behind the breastbone is another endocrine gland—the **thymus** (THIGH-muhs). Large in infancy, the thymus begins to get smaller as you grow. By the time you reach adulthood, the thymus has shrunk to about the size of your thumb. The thymus is responsible for the development of the immune system, which you will learn in Chapter 8 is your main defense against disease-causing organisms. During infancy, the thymus produces white blood cells that protect the body's tissues, triggering an immune response against invaders. Later, other organs in the body take over the thymus's job of producing these white blood cells.

THYROID Before the mid-1800s, doctors actually thought that another endocrine gland, the **thyroid,** which is located in the neck, lubricated and protected

Tell students that gigantism or dwarfism may occasionally be caused by an abnormal growth on the pituitary gland.

FOCUS/MOTIVATION

Have students observe Figure 6–31.
• **Where is the larynx located in the body?** (In front part of the neck.)
• **What is the common name of the larynx?** (Voice box.)
• **Where is the trachea located?** (In the front part of the neck, below the larynx.)

• **What is the common name of the trachea?** (Windpipe.)

Have students find and feel their larynx and trachea. Then have them talk or hum to feel the vibrations of the larynx.

CONTENT DEVELOPMENT

Tell students that the thyroid is a butterfly-shaped gland that straddles the trachea with "wings" on either side. Have them find the thyroid gland in Figure 6–31. Explain that the thyroid gland secretes two hormones: calcitonin and thyroxine. Cal-

the vocal cords. It was not until 1859 that the true function of the thyroid was discovered. That function is to control how quickly food is burned up in the body.

PARATHYROIDS Embedded in the thyroid are four tiny glands called the **parathyroids.** They release a hormone that controls the level of calcium in the blood. Calcium is a mineral that keeps your nerves and muscles working properly.

ADRENALS Of all the hormones in the body, adrenaline (uh-DREHN-uh-lihn) is perhaps one of the best understood by scientists. The effects of adrenaline are so dramatic and powerful that you can actually feel them as your heart rate increases and blood pulses through your blood vessels.

Adrenaline is part of the body's emergency action team. Whenever you are in a dangerous situation, such as the frightening dream you read about at the beginning of this section, your body reacts in a number of ways. Your first reaction is usually a nervous one—messages from your surroundings are sent to the brain, warning you of the danger. The brain shocks the body into action to avoid the threat. A rapid series of nerve impulses to the appropriate muscles makes you take whatever actions are necessary to ensure your safety. At the same time, the brain alerts the two **adrenals** to produce adrenaline. The word adrenal means above (*ad-*) the kidney (*-renal*). And that is exactly where each adrenal is located—atop each of the two kidneys.

PANCREAS Insulin, which is another hormone that scientists know a lot about, plays an important role in keeping the levels of sugar (glucose) in the bloodstream under control. It does this by helping body cells absorb the sugar and use it for energy. It also helps to change excess sugar into a substance called glycogen (GLIGH-kuh-juhn), which can be stored in the liver and the skeletal muscles until it is needed by the body. In this way, insulin prevents the level of sugar in the blood from rising too high. Without enough insulin, however, a person can develop diabetes mellitus (digh-uh-BEET-eez muh-LIGHT-uhs). Diabetes mellitus is a disorder in which the level of sugar in the blood is too high.

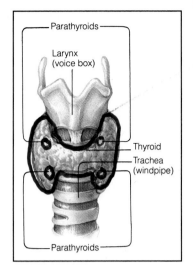

Figure 6–31 *The parathyroids are four tiny glands embedded in the thyroid, which is located in the neck. What hormone does the thyroid produce?* ❷

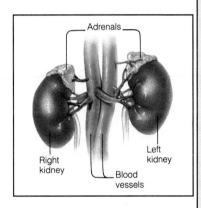

Figure 6–32 *Located atop each of the two kidneys is an adrenal gland. What is the function of the adrenal glands?* ❸

H ■ 159

increase the calcium level of the blood by releasing calcium from the bone tissue.

Explain that the glands that enable people to perform superhuman acts are the adrenal glands, located on top of each kidney. Have students locate these glands in Figure 6–32. The hormone, called adrenaline, that is released causes the heart to beat faster and steps up the rate of other body processes.

FOCUS/MOTIVATION

• **How many of you have heard of insulin?** (Acknowledge responses.)
• **What do you think insulin does for the body?** (Accept all logical answers. Many students will associate insulin with sugar intake and diabetes. Some students may not realize that insulin is produced by the body. They may know it only as a medicine taken by people with diabetes.)

Explain to students that insulin is a hormone produced by the pancreas.

INDEPENDENT PRACTICE

▶ *Activity Book*
Provide extra practice with the concepts of this section by having students use the Chapter 6 activity called Endocrine Riddles.

citonin regulates and controls the level of calcium and phosphorus in the body.
• **What are some important functions of the mineral calcium?** (Most students will probably know that calcium plays a role in maintaining healthy bones and teeth. It also plays a role in nerve functioning, muscle contraction, blood clotting, and stimulating other glands to produce hormones.)

ENRICHMENT

Explain that the thyroid gland uses iodine to produce its hormones. Point out

that the thyroid is the only body tissue that uses iodine. Point out that if the body has an iodine shortage, the thyroid will grow, causing the neck to swell. Explain that this growth is called a goiter. Point out that with the use of iodized salt, most diets have enough iodine.

CONTENT DEVELOPMENT

Have students locate in Figure 6–31 the four small glands embedded in the thyroid. Tell students that these parathyroid glands help the thyroid gland. They

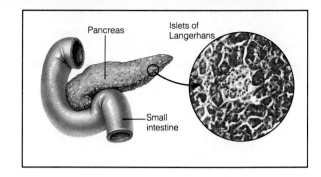

Figure 6–33 *The pancreas is located near the entrance to the small intestine. The pancreas contains small groups of cells called islets of Langerhans. What hormones are produced by the islets of Langerhans?* ❶

6–4 (continued)

ENRICHMENT

Explain to students that when glucagon has converted all the liver's supply of glycogen to glucose, other sources of sugar are needed. Therefore, glucagon then causes the breakdown of amino acids and fatty acids to glucose. In other words, when adequate carbohydrates are not available, body fat and proteins are broken down to provide the glucose necessary to meet the body's energy requirements.

CONTENT DEVELOPMENT

Call students' attention to Figure 6–33. Point out the islets of Langerhans. These groups of cells produce the two pancreatic hormones: insulin and glucagon. Point out that when the islets of Langerhans fail to produce enough insulin, the amount of glucose that can get to the body cells to be used for energy is greatly reduced. Instead, the glucose remains in the blood, and the

FIND OUT BY

CALCULATING

How Much Is Enough?

❶ The body cells are very sensitive to hormones. As little as 0.000001 milligram of a hormone per milliliter of blood can cause body cells to respond. How much of a hormone is needed to cause a response in 5000 mL of blood? In 10,000 mL?

Insulin is produced by a small group of cells called the **islets** (IGH-lihts) **of Langerhans** (LAHNG-er-hahns) within the pancreas. You may recall from Chapter 3 that the pancreas is also part of the digestive system, releasing enzymes into the small intestine. In addition to insulin, the islets of Langerhans produce another hormone called glucagon (GLOO-kuh-gahn). The effect of glucagon in the body is exactly opposite that of insulin. Glucagon increases the level of sugar in the blood by speeding up the conversion of glycogen to sugar in the liver.

Together, the effects of insulin and glucagon ensure that the level of sugar in the blood is always just right. If the level of sugar in the blood drops, the pancreas releases more glucagon to make up for the loss. If the level of sugar in the blood rises, the pancreas releases more insulin to get rid of the excess sugar.

OVARIES AND TESTES The **ovaries** (OH-vuh-reez) are the female reproductive glands, and the **testes** (tehs-teez; singular: testis, TEHS-tihs) are the male reproductive glands. The reproductive glands produce sex hormones that affect cells throughout the body. The ovaries and testes will be discussed in more detail in Chapter 7.

Negative-Feedback Mechanism

You can compare the way the endocrine system works to the way a thermostat in a heating and cooling system works. A thermostat is a device that controls the system in order to keep the temperature within certain limits. Suppose you set the thermostat in your classroom at 20°C. If the temperature of the room goes above 20°C, the thermostat turns on the

---

excess sugar is excreted in the urine. This condition is called diabetes mellitus.

FOCUS/MOTIVATION

Ask students if they have ever heard the word *feedback.*

• **Why would we use the word *feedback* when we are talking about the endocrine system?** (Accept all logical answers.)

Have one of the students look up *feedback* in the dictionary and read the definitions to the rest of the class. (Feedback—[1] the return to the input of a part of the

output of a machine, system, or process, [2] the partial reversion of the effects of a process to its source or to a preceding stage.)

● ● ● ● **Integration** ● ● ● ●

Use the discussion of the thermostat in an air conditioner to integrate concepts of heat into your lesson.

CONTENT DEVELOPMENT

Explain that the endocrine gland system works on a feedback system. Point out that the glands need to work with one an-

air conditioner. The cooling effect produced by the air conditioner brings the temperature of your classroom back down to 20°C. At this point, the thermostat turns the air conditioner off. If, on the other hand, the temperature of the room falls below 20°C, the thermostat turns on the heater rather than the air conditioner. The heater, which has a warming effect, stays on until the temperature again returns to 20°C. In this way, the thermostat controls the internal environment of your classroom. In a similar way, a **negative-feedback mechanism** automatically controls the levels of hormones in your body. **In a negative-feedback mechanism, the production of a hormone is controlled by the amount of another hormone in the blood, thereby keeping the body's internal environment stable.**

The actions of the pituitary and the thyroid are probably the best examples of the negative-feedback mechanism. The pituitary is very sensitive to the amount of thyroxine (thigh-RAHKS-een) in the blood. Thyroxine is the name of the hormone that is released by the thyroid. When the level of thyroxine in the blood drops too low, the pituitary releases its hormone, a hormone called thyroid-stimulating hormone, or TSH. This action causes the thyroid to make more thyroxine, thus restoring the level of thyroxine in the blood. When the amount of thyroxine in the blood is just right, the pituitary stops releasing TSH, and the thyroid stops producing thyroxine. In this way, the negative-feedback mechanism helps to keep the internal environment of the body stable.

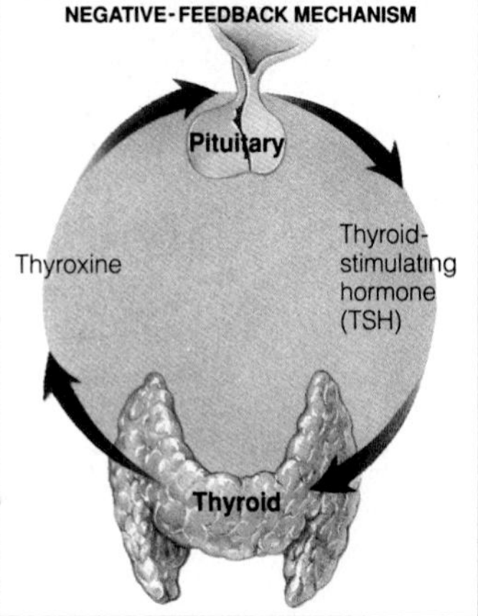

6–4 Section Review

1. What is the function of the endocrine system?
2. What is a hormone?
3. List eight endocrine glands in the body.
4. What is the negative-feedback mechanism?
5. Explain how the negative-feedback mechanism helps to maintain a state of balance within the body.

Critical Thinking—*Relating Facts*
6. If a person has diabetes mellitus, would his or her production of glucagon be increased or decreased? Explain your answer.

NEGATIVE-FEEDBACK MECHANISM

Pituitary

Thyroxine

Thyroid-stimulating hormone (TSH)

Thyroid

Figure 6–34 *The release of TSH into the bloodstream by the pituitary stimulates the production of thyroxine by the thyroid. When the level of thyroxine in the bloodstream increases, the pituitary reacts negatively by lowering the amount of TSH it releases. This is an example of a negative-feedback mechanism, which controls the levels of hormones in the blood.*

INDEPENDENT PRACTICE

Section Review 6–4
1. The endocrine system produces hormones that help to regulate some of the body's functions.
2. A hormone is a chemical messenger that travels through the blood and is secreted by an endocrine gland.
3. Pituitary, hypothalamus, parathyroids, thyroid, thymus, adrenals, pancreas, ovaries (female) or testes (male).
4. In the endocrine system, the production of one hormone is controlled by the concentration of another hormone. Examples of pairs of glands that are related in this way are the hypothalamus and the pituitary, and the thyroid and the pituitary.
5. Two glands that provide feedback to each other can be called Gland 1 and Gland 2. Gland 1 produces Hormone 1 and Gland 2 produces Hormone 2.

The mechanism is explained as follows: The increase of Hormone 1 stimulates Gland 2 to release Hormone 2, which slows or stops Gland 1 from producing Hormone 1.
6. The person has a decrease in the production of glucagon because blood-sugar levels are high. Glucagon in released only when blood-sugar levels are high.

REINFORCEMENT/RETEACHING

Review students' responses to the Section Review questions. Reteach any material that is still unclear, based on students' responses.

CLOSURE

▶ *Review and Reinforcement Guide*
Have students complete Section 6–4 in the *Review and Reinforcement Guide.*

other as a team to produce and regulate the amount of each hormone given to the body. Tell students that in the feedback mechanism of the endocrine system, the production of one hormone is controlled by the concentration of another hormone.

GUIDED PRACTICE

Skills Development

Skill: Interpreting illustrations

Have students refer to Figure 6–34 and read the caption.

• **Suppose that the pituitary gland kept producing the TSH thyroxine without stopping. What would happen to the thyroid gland?** (It would produce too much thyroxine.)
• **What prevents this overproduction of thyroxine from happening?** (When the level of thyroxine gets too high, it causes the pituitary gland to stop making TSH.)

Laboratory Investigation

LOCATING TOUCH RECEPTORS

BEFORE THE LAB

1. Gather all materials at least one day prior to the investigation. You should have enough supplies to meet your class needs, assuming two students per group.
2. It might be easier to cut the cardboard ahead of time into 6 × 10-cm pieces, using a paper cutter.
3. If necessary, review metric measuring skills using millimeters (mm) and centimeters (cm).
4. Divide the class into pairs.

PRE-LAB DISCUSSION

Have students read the complete laboratory procedure. Discuss the procedure by asking questions similar to the following:
• **What is the purpose of the laboratory investigation?** (To determine where touch receptors are located on the body.)
• **Why is it important not to apply pressure?** (To prevent the pins from breaking the skin.)
• **Why is the blindfold important?** (Accept all logical answers. Lead students to suggest that the blindfold keeps them from using their sense of sight.)
• **Why is it important to report what you actually feel?** (Accept all logical answers.)

Laboratory Investigation

Locating Touch Receptors

Problem

Where are the touch receptors located on the body?

Materials *(per pair of students)*

scissors	9 straight pins
metric ruler	piece of card-
blindfold	board (6 cm x 10 cm)

Procedure 🔲

1. Using the scissors, cut the piece of cardboard into five rectangles each measuring 6 cm x 2 cm.
2. Into one cardboard rectangle, insert two straight pins 5 mm apart. Into the second cardboard rectangle, insert two pins 1 cm apart. Insert two pins 2 cm apart into the third rectangle. Insert two pins 3 cm apart into the fourth rectangle. In the center of the remaining cardboard rectangle, insert one pin.
3. Construct a data table in which the pin positions on the cardboard appear across the top of the table.
4. Blindfold your partner.
5. Using the cardboard rectangle with the straight pins 5 mm apart, carefully touch the palm surface of your partner's fingertip, palm of the hand, back of the hand, back of the neck, and inside of the forearm. **CAUTION:** *Do not apply pressure when touching your partner's skin.* In the data table, list each of these body parts.

6. If your partner feels two points in any of the areas that you touch, place the number 2 in the appropriate place in the data table. If your partner feels only one point, place the number 1 in the data table.
7. Repeat steps 5 and 6 with the remaining cardboard rectangles.
8. Reverse roles with your partner and repeat the investigation.

Observations

On which part of the body did you feel the most sensation? The least?

Analysis and Conclusions

1. Which part of the body that you tested had the most touch receptors? The fewest? How do you know?
2. Rank the body parts in order from the most to the least sensitive.
3. What do the answers to questions 1 and 2 indicate about the distribution of touch receptors in the skin?
4. **On Your Own** Obtain a variety of objects. Blindfold your partner and hand one of the objects to your partner. Have your partner describe how the object feels. Your partner is not to name the object. Record the description along with the name of the object. Repeat the investigation for each object. Reverse roles and repeat the investigation. How well were you and your partner able to "observe" with the senses of touch?

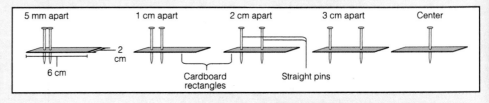

5 mm apart   1 cm apart   2 cm apart   3 cm apart   Center

2 cm   6 cm   Cardboard rectangles   Straight pins

TEACHING STRATEGY

1. Have teams follow the directions carefully as they work in the laboratory.
2. If necessary, assist students in setting up an appropriate data table.

DISCOVERY STRATEGIES

Discuss how the investigation relates to the chapter ideas by asking open questions similar to the following:
• **What types of cells are involved in the touch receptors in the skin?** (Nerve cells.)

• **How does the nervous system send the messages about the pins to the brain?** (Sensory nerves carry impulses from the touch receptors to the central nervous system.)

OBSERVATIONS

The most sensation is felt on the fingers, especially the fingertips. The least sensation is felt on the forearm.

Study Guide

Summarizing Key Concepts

6–1 The Nervous System

▲ The nervous system receives and sends out information about activities within the body and monitors and responds to changes in the environment.

▲ The basic unit of structure and function of the nervous system is the neuron, which is made up of the cell body, dendrites, an axon, and axon terminals.

▲ A nerve impulse sends messages in the form of electrical and chemical signals. The gap between neurons is called a synapse.

6–2 Divisions of the Nervous System

▲ The central nervous system is composed of the brain and the spinal cord. The brain is divided into three parts: the cerebrum, the cerebellum, and the medulla.

▲ The peripheral nervous system consists of all the nerves that connect to the central nervous system.

▲ The autonomic nervous system consists of two sets of nerves that have opposite effects on the organs they control.

6–3 The Senses

▲ Light entering the eye passes through the cornea, aqueous humor, lens, and vitreous humor to the retina. The optic nerve carries the impulses to the brain.

▲ Sound enters the ear as vibrations and strikes the eardrum, causing the hammer, anvil, and stirrup to vibrate. These vibrations finally reach the cochlea. The auditory nerve carries the impulses to the brain.

▲ Smell and taste are chemical senses.

▲ The skin contains receptors for touch, pressure, pain, heat, and cold.

6–4 The Endocrine System

▲ The endocrine system includes the hypothalamus, pituitary, thymus, thyroid, parathyroids, adrenals, pancreas, and ovaries or testes.

▲ In the feedback mechanism, the production of a hormone is controlled by the amount of another hormone in the blood, thereby keeping the body's internal environment stable.

Reviewing Key Terms

Define each term in a complete sentence.

6–1 The Nervous System
stimulus
neuron
cell body
dendrite
axon
receptor
sensory neuron
interneuron
motor neuron
effector
nerve impulse
synapse

6–2 Divisions of the Nervous System
brain
spinal cord
cerebrum
cerebellum
medulla
reflex

6–3 The Senses
cornea
iris
pupil
lens
retina
eardrum
cochlea
semicircular canal

6–4 The Endocrine System
hormone
hypothalamus
pituitary
thymus
thyroid
parathyroid
adrenal
islets of Langerhans
ovary
testis
negative-feedback mechanism

H ■ 163

Chapter Review

ALTERNATIVE ASSESSMENT

The *Prentice Hall Science* program includes a variety of testing components and methodologies. Aside from the Chapter Review questions, you may opt to use the Chapter Test or the Computer Test Bank Test in your *Test Book* for assessment of important facts and concepts. In addition, Performance-Based Tests are included in your *Test Book*. These Performance-Based Tests are designed to test science process skills, rather than factual content recall. Since they are not content dependent, Performance-Based Tests can be distributed after students complete a chapter or after they complete the entire textbook.

CONTENT REVIEW

Multiple Choice
1. b
2. a
3. c
4. c
5. d
6. b
7. a
8. b
9. a

True or False
1. F, cell body
2. F, adrenals
3. F, central
4. T
5. F, aqueous humor
6. T
7. F, sclera

Concept Mapping
Row 1: Performs four functions
Row 2: Sends out information,
   Monitors environmental changes,
   Responds to environmental changes
Row 3: Cell body, Axon terminals

CONCEPT MASTERY

1. A stimulus is anything in the internal or external environment that causes a reaction. Examples include a loud noise or a bright light.
2. Sensory nerves carry impulses from sense receptors to the central nervous system. Motor neurons carry impulses from the central nervous system to ef-

fectors. Interneurons connect sensory and motor neurons.
3. A receptor responds to stimuli such as smell or taste. An effector carries out the instructions of the central nervous system.
4. An impulse travels along an axon. As the nerve impulse reaches the synapse, a chemical is released from the axon. The chemical passes across the gap and triggers an impulse in a dendrite.
5. The lens focuses light rays that enter the eye onto the retinal wall.

6. Adrenaline increases heartbeat, breathing rate, and the ability to think and move quickly. Insulin affects glucose metabolism by lowering the blood glucose level.
7. The hypothalamus regulates the activities of other endocrine glands.
8. The feedback mechanism is the body's way of regulating the levels of hormones in the body. One example is the production of thyroxine in the thyroid.
9. Quick reflexes are an advantage for many reasons. Generally, they help to protect the body.

Chapter Review

Content Review

Multiple Choice

Choose the letter of the answer that best completes each statement.

1. A change in the environment is a(an)
   a. effector.   c. reflex.
   b. stimulus.   d. hormone.
2. The short fibers that carry messages from neurons toward the cell body are the
   a. dendrites.   c. synapses.
   b. axon terminals. d. axons.
3. The gap between two neurons is called the
   a. dendrite.   c. synapse.
   b. cell body.   d. axon.
4. The part of the brain that controls balance is the
   a. spinal cord.   c. cerebellum.
   b. cerebrum.   d. medulla.
5. Which endocrine gland provides a link between the nervous system and the endocrine system?
   a. pituitary   c. parathryoid
   b. adrenal   d. hypothalamus

6. The largest part of the brain is the
   a. spinal cord.   c. cerebellum.
   b. cerebrum.   d. medulla.
7. Which of the following is part of the central nervous system?
   a. medulla
   b. semicircular canals
   c. retina
   d. auditory nerve
8. The pancreas produces the hormones insulin and
   a. thyroxine.
   b. glucagon.
   c. human growth hormone.
   d. adrenaline.
9. The layer of the eye onto which an image is focused is the
   a. retina.   c. choroid.
   b. sclera.   d. cornea.

True or False

If the statement is true, write "true." If it is false, change the underlined word or words to make the statement true.

1. The part of the neuron that contains the nucleus is the <u>axon</u>.
2. The <u>pituitary</u> produces adrenaline.
3. The brain and the spinal cord make up the <u>peripheral</u> nervous system.
4. The reproductive glands are the ovaries and the <u>testes</u>.
5. The <u>retina</u> is the watery fluid between the cornea and the lens of the eye.
6. The <u>auditory nerve</u> carries impulses from the ear to the brain.
7. The outer layer of the eye is the <u>choroid</u>.

Concept Mapping

Complete the following concept map for Section 6–1. Refer to pages H8–H9 to construct a concept map for the entire chapter.

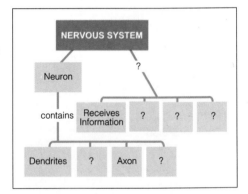

Concept Mastery

Discuss each of the following in a brief paragraph.

1. What is a stimulus? Give two examples.
2. What are the functions of the three types of neurons found in the nervous system?
3. Compare the functions of a receptor and an effector.
4. Explain how an impulse crosses a synapse.
5. Describe the role of the lens in vision.
6. Compare the effect of adrenaline and insulin on the body.
7. What is the function of the hypothalamus?
8. Explain what a negative-feedback mechanism is. Give an example.
9. Explain why it is an advantage to you that your reflexes respond quickly and automatically.
10. How does an endocrine gland differ from an exocrine gland?
11. How is the central nervous system protected?
12. Trace the path of light through the eye.
13. Trace the path of sound through the ear.

Critical Thinking and Problem Solving

Use the skills you have developed in this chapter to answer each of the following.

1. **Making comparisons** Compare the nervous system to a computer. How are they similar? Different?
2. **Applying concepts** Explain why many people become dizzy after spinning around for any length of time.
3. **Interpreting graphs** The accompanying graph shows the levels of sugar in the blood of two people during a five-hour period immediately after a typical meal. Which line represents an average person? Which line represents a person with diabetes mellitus? Explain your answers.

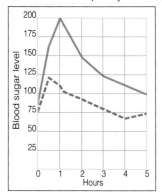

4. **Relating concepts** A routine examination by a doctor usually includes the knee-jerk test. What is the purpose of this test? What could the absence of a response indicate?
5. **Applying concepts** Explain why after entering a dark room, you are surprised to see how colorful the room is when the lights are turned on.
6. **Applying concepts** Sometimes as a result of a cold, the middle ear becomes filled with fluid. Why do you think this can cause a temporary loss of hearing?
7. **Making predictions** What might happen if the cornea becomes inflamed and as a result more fluid collects there?
8. **Using the writing process** Select a picture in a book or magazine. In a short essay, explain how what you see in the picture is influenced by your sense of touch, hearing, smell, or taste as well as your sense of vision.

---

is part of a living organism. Also, it can respond to a much wider variety of outside stimuli.

2. The fluids in the semicircular canals will sway back and forth during the spinning. A person will feel dizzy until the fluids in the canals stop swaying.

3. The dotted line represents the normal person, and the solid line represents the person with diabetes. The person with diabetes would have a high level of blood sugar for a longer period of time because too little insulin is produced.

4. The doctor is testing the autonomic nervous system. A lack of such a reflex could mean damage to the nerves leading to the leg.

5. The rods in the retina react to dim light and work well in a dark room, but they do not perceive color. When the lights go on, the cones are also activated; cones do perceive color.

6. When the ear is filled with fluid, the vibrations that are transmitted through the ear may be blocked or inhibited. As a result, hearing will be impaired.

7. Fluid accumulation in the cornea would increase its water content, which would tend to decrease its transparency and interfere with normal vision.

8. Answers will vary. Make sure students accurately describe the functioning of the sense organs.

KEEPING A PORTFOLIO

You might want to assign some of the Concept Mastery and Critical Thinking and Problem Solving questions as homework and have students include their responses to unassigned questions in their portfolio. Students should be encouraged to include both the question and the answer in their portfolio.

ISSUES IN SCIENCE

The following issue can be used as a springboard for discussion or given as a writing assignment:

It has been said that the brains of girls and those of boys are different. What is your opinion? What evidence (not opinion) can you use to support your opinion?

---

10. Endocrine glands are ductless, releasing hormones directly into the bloodstream. Exocrine glands release their hormones through ducts that connect them to nearby organs.

11. The skull protects the brain, and the vertebrae protect the spinal cord.

12. Light entering the eye passes through the cornea, pupil, aqueous humor, lens, and vitreous humor and forms an image on the retina at the back of the eye.

13. Sound waves pass down the ear canal to the eardrum, causing it to vibrate. The vibrations are then transmitted to the oval window. This causes hair cells in the cochlea to move back and forth, which stimulate the auditory nerve.

CRITICAL THINKING AND PROBLEM SOLVING

1. Both the nervous system and a computer have mechanisms to receive and send out information. Most computers also have a monitoring function to alert users to potential problems. The nervous system differs from a computer in that it

SECTION	LABORATORY INVESTIGATIONS AND DEMONSTRATIONS
7–1 The Reproductive System pages H168–176	**Teacher Edition** Comparing Mammal Babies, p. H166d Observing Chicken Eggs, p. H166d
7–2 Stages of Development pages H177–H185	**Student Edition** How Many Offspring?, p. H186 **Laboratory Manual** Observing the Development of Frog Eggs
Chapter Review pages H186–H189	

*All materials in the Chapter Planning Guide Grid are available as part of the Prentice Hall Science Learning System.

OUTSIDE TEACHER RESOURCES

Books

Grabowski, C. *Human Reproduction and Development,* Saunders.

Kitzinger, Sheila, and Lennard Nilson. *Being Born,* Putnam Publishing Group.

Nourse, Alan E. *Menstruation,* Watts.

Rugh, R., and L. Shettles. *From Conception to Birth,* Harper & Row.

Audiovisuals

Birth: How Life Begins, film or video, EBE

Human Reproduction, film or video, EBE

Life Before Birth, film or video, Media Guild

Reproductive Systems, film or video, National Geographic

Stages of Life: Reproduction, Growth, and Change, Human Body Series, Part III, filmstrip with cassettes, National Geographic

OTHER ACTIVITIES	MULTIMEDIA
Activity Book Chapter Discovery: Baby in the Making ACTIVITY: Male or Female? **Review and Reinforcement Guide** Section 7–1	**Transparency Binder** Male Reproductive System Female Reproductive System **Courseware** Laws of Genetics (Supplemental) Reproductive System (Supplemental) **English/Spanish Audiotapes** Section 7–1 **Video** Reproductive Systems
Activity Book ACTIVITY: Name It! ACTIVITY: Stages of Human Development **Student Edition** Find Out by Writing: The Developing Embryo, p. H177 Find Out by Doing: Multiple Births, p. H180 Find Out by Writing: You Only Look as Old as You Feel, p. H184 **Review and Reinforcement Guide** Section 7–2	**English/Spanish Audiotapes** Section 7–2
Test Book Chapter Test Performance-Based Test	**Test Book** Computer Test Bank Test

CHAPTER OVERVIEW

Reproduction is essential for the continuation of a species. Humans and many other organisms reproduce sexually by the joining of the male's sperm cell with a female's egg cell. This two-parent system of reproduction produces variety in offspring that allows for adaptation to an ever-changing environment.

In addition to producing the sex cells, the male and female reproductive systems produce several hormones. These hormones influence the development of secondary sex characteristics, including the growth of facial hair and the deepening of the voice in males and the growth of breasts and the widening of hips in females. In females, hormones also regulate the menstrual cycle.

Humans progress through various stages of development both before birth and after birth. The prenatal stages include formation of the zygote, embryo, and fetus. Human development after birth includes the periods of infancy, childhood, adolescence, and adulthood. Each stage is marked by characteristic patterns of development. Adolescence is the period of development in which the human matures sexually.

7–1 THE REPRODUCTIVE SYSTEM
THEMATIC FOCUS

The purpose of this section is to introduce the male and female reproductive systems. Students will identify the organs of the reproductive systems and the functions of the systems. Students identify the testes as the male's primary reproductive organs and the ovaries as the female's primary reproductive organs. The systems produce, store, and release specialized cells known as gametes. The fusion of male and female gametes produces a fertilized egg, or zygote, that eventually gives rise to all cells of the human body. The section ends with the discussion of the menstrual cycle in the female and its purpose, which is to prepare the body for carrying a fertilized egg.

The themes that can be focused on in this section are energy, evolution, systems and interactions, and unity and diversity. All these themes, as they relate to the reproductive systems, are interconnected by the commonality that all humans result from the reproductive process.

*Energy: The processes of reproduction and development require the use of energy for the production of new cells. The male reproductive system produces sperm that can be joined with eggs from the female reproductive system. The division of cells in the fertilized eggs eventually results in a human baby. Energy for the process is provided by nourishment taking place through the placenta.

Evolution: Without the capacity to reproduce, the human species would become extinct. The reproductive systems and the process of reproduction ensure the survival of the human species. The reproductive system is not essential to the survival of an individual within a species but is essential for the survival of the species itself.

*Systems and interactions: The function of the male and female reproductive systems is to produce sex cells that are needed for reproduction and to produce hormones that regulate certain body activities. Within the female system, a series of complex interactions prepare for the development of a fertilized egg. Within the male system, interactions result in the development of sperm that can fertilize the eggs of the female. The interaction of the male and female systems can result in the development of a new human.

Unity and diversity: The male and female reproductive systems differ in structure and function, but they each produce sex cells that are needed for reproduction as well as hormones that are needed for the proper functioning of the body. The systems are complementary—one cannot result in reproduction without the other. A major purpose of both systems is to ensure the continuation of the human species through the reproductive process.

PERFORMANCE OBJECTIVES 7–1

1. Name the structures of the male reproductive system and of the female reproductive system.
2. Compare the primary structures and functions of the male reproductive system and the female reproductive system.
3. Explain why human sperm and egg cells carry only 23 chromosomes.
4. Describe the stages in the menstrual cycle.

SCIENCE TERMS 7–1

sperm p. H169
egg p. H169
fertilization p. H169
testis p. H171
ovary p. H172
Fallopian tube p. H172
uterus p. H172
menstrual cycle p. H174
ovulation p. H175

7–2 STAGES OF DEVELOPMENT
THEMATIC FOCUS

The purpose of this section is to introduce the stages of human development. The primary focus of the lesson is on the stages of development of the unborn child and the stages following birth, which include infancy, childhood, adolescence, and adulthood. Students investigate characteristics common to each stage of development and recognize that although the rate of development varies in individuals, all individuals experience the same stages of development.

The themes that can be focused on in this section are patterns of change, scale and structure, systems and interactions, and stability. All these themes as they relate to human development express the similarities and differences among individuals.

Patterns of change: The major emphasis of this section is on the stages of development through which humans pass. The stages are the same for all humans, and the patterns of change that result are common to all humans. From the moment of fertilization, the human undergoes a series of changes that continue throughout the lifetime. From growth to aging, the process of life is a continual series of changes that follow the same pattern in all individuals.

*Scale and structure: The structure and function of the human reproductive systems make possible the development of new humans. Through the joining of microscopic gametes, a series of cell divisions begin that result in the formation of a new human. The general reproductive-related structures and characteristics are common to all members of a sex in the species.

*Systems and interactions: Following reproduction, a series of interactions between mother and the unborn child begins in which the mother's systems meet the child's need for nourishment, respiration, and excretion. Throughout life, the body's systems work together to enable an individual to grow and develop into adulthood. The interactions of most systems are critical to an individual's survival; however, the interactions of the reproductive systems are critical to the species' survival.

*Stability: The hormones produced by the male and female reproductive systems maintain a chemical stability within the body. Throughout life, the hormones are produced in males; however, in females, at menopause the female hormones are no longer produced. Some women undergo a variety of symptoms until their bodies adjust to chemical changes caused by the lack of the hormones. Hormonal treatment often reduces these symptoms.

PERFORMANCE OBJECTIVES 7–2

1. Define zygote, pregnancy, embryo, and fetus.
2. Explain how a fetus obtains food and oxygen and gets rid of wastes.
3. Identify the stages of development following birth.
4. Compare and contrast infancy with childhood and adolescence with adulthood.

SCIENCE TERMS 7–2

zygote p. H177
embryo p. H177
amniotic sac p. H177
placenta p. H177
fetus p. H178
umbilical cord p. H178
infancy p. H181
childhood p. H182
adolescence p. H182
puberty p. H183
adulthood p. H183

Discovery *Learning*

TEACHER DEMONSTRATIONS MODELING

Comparing Mammal Babies

Show students photographs or 35-mm slides of the young of a variety of mammals, including humans. Explain that students should study the similarities and differences in the individuals as they view the photographs or slides.
• **What characteristics do these young mammals have in common?** (A variety of answers are possible, including the following: feed on mother's milk, are quite helpless, are smaller than adults, look different from adults.)

Focus students' attention on the dependency of the young. They cannot feed or defend themselves. They are nurtured and protected by their parents or by older members of the species. They look different, and many species give off a special odor to ensure that other members will recognize their helplessness.

• **How old is a puppy when it is able to leave its mother?** (Most puppies can be weaned at about 8 weeks. They are considered to be puppies until reaching puberty—at about 7 months of age. A female dog often has puppies of her own when she is 1 year old.)

Discuss these stages of development for other animals, such as cats, horses, and monkeys.
• **How old are humans when they are "on their own"?** (Most babies are weaned from the bottle or breast at 9 to 15 months. Humans reach puberty around 12 to 13 years of age. Many adolescents do not leave home and become independent of their parents until after age 18.)

Explain to students that of all animals, humans are the slowest to reach physical maturity.
• **Why do you think the human species has developed such a long childhood compared with that of other animals?** (Nearly all human behavior is learned rather than inherited. Humans are much less creatures of instinct than are other animals. A long childhood gives humans time to acquire the mass of information and skills without which they could not survive as adults.)

Observing Chicken Eggs

Obtain a fertilized chicken egg that is 7 to 10 days old. Carefully remove a portion of the shell so that students can observe the development of the embryo. Point out the amniotic sac that surrounds the developing chick embryo. The yolk sac provides nourishment to the chick, whereas a human embryo obtains its nourishment from the food the mother eats. Because the chicken egg is no longer connected to the mother, it must carry its own food supply. There is a yolk sac present in humans, but it does not function in feeding. It does form cells, however, that will become part of the embryo's reproductive organs. Students can also observe developing structures in the embryo, such as head, eyes, and heart.

If incubated chicken eggs are not available, show students prepared slides of the stages of development in a chicken.

CHAPTER 7
Reproduction and Development

INTEGRATING SCIENCE

This life science chapter provides you with numerous opportunities to integrate other areas of science, as well as other disciplines, into your curriculum. Blue numbered annotations on the student page and integration notes on the teacher wraparound pages alert you to areas of possible integration.

In this chapter you can integrate life science and heredity (p. 169), life science and cells (p. 170), language arts (p. 174), fine arts (p. 177), physical science and sound (p. 180), and physical science and electricity (p. 185).

SCIENCE, TECHNOLOGY, AND SOCIETY/COOPERATIVE LEARNING

Because of infertility, many couples wanting children have turned to newly developed and refined reproductive technologies, such as artificial insemination and in-vitro fertilization. Today, about 2000 babies are born each year as a result of artificial insemination. Semen used in the technique may be from the husband or from a donor. Using the technique of in-vitro fertilization, doctors are able to help women conceive who cannot ovulate or who have some type of blockage of the Fallopian tubes. In in-vitro fertilization, doctors surgically remove eggs from the ovaries and place them in a dish with sperm so that fertilization takes place. After several days, developing embryos are injected into the woman's uterus.

Some couples have turned to surrogate parenting as a way to have a baby. A surrogate mother bears a child for another woman, usually for a monetary fee. The child that the surrogate bears can be produced by in-vitro fertilization of eggs and sperm from the couple; by artificial insemination, in which the sperm used to fertilize the surrogate mother's egg is donated by the couple; or by in-vitro fertilization, in which the sperm and the egg are from other donors.

These techniques have enabled childless couples to have children. At the same time, the reproductive techniques and

INTRODUCING CHAPTER 7

DISCOVERY LEARNING

▶ *Activity Book*

Begin your teaching of the chapter by using the Chapter 7 Discovery Activity from the *Activity Book*. Using this activity, students will discover characteristics of embryonic and fetal development in the unborn child.

Have students look at the chapter-opening picture.
• **What do you see in this picture?** (Many different babies.)
• **In what way are all these babies alike?** (Answers may include shared physical characteristics such as number of arms, legs, fingers, and so forth, level of dependency, and type of dress.)
• **How are they different?** (Possible responses include the color of hair, eyes,

Reproduction and Development

Guide for Reading

After you read the following sections, you will be able to

7–1 The Reproductive System

- Identify the function and importance of the reproductive system.
- Define fertilization.
- Compare the functions and structures of the male and female reproductive systems.

7–2 Stages of Development

- Describe the changes that occur between fertilization and birth.
- Describe the process of birth.
- List and describe the stages of development after birth.

Almost everyone loves babies—all kinds of babies: animal babies (bunnies, kittens, and puppies, to name just a few) and human babies. Babies can be one of the funniest and most appealing subjects of photography. Just look at the photograph on the opposite page!

One of the many common characteristics of all newborn human babies is their total helplessness. They cannot sit up, move from one place to another, feed themselves, or talk in a language understood by other people. Their basic means of communicating hunger, discomfort, unhappiness, or pain is by crying. With proper care and training, however, babies gradually learn to do some things for themselves. And they eventually become children, adolescents, and then adults.

At this point, you may be asking yourself this question: What changes take place as a baby develops and grows into a full-sized adult? As you read this chapter you will find the answer to this question as well as the answers to others. And you will also discover that human development is an exciting, ongoing process.

Journal *Activity*

You and Your World Place photographs of yourself as an infant, toddler, or young child in your journal. Below each photograph, describe what you were doing when the photograph was taken and what you remember about it. What physical and social changes have you undergone since the photographs were taken?

◄ *These human babies—products of reproduction—guarantee the survival of the human species.*

H ■ 167

and skin, the amount of hair, and the type of sleeper worn.)

Have students read the text on page H167. Ask students to consider what stages of development a child goes through in the first year of life. (Most babies learn to hold up their head, roll over, sit up, say a few words, and crawl in their first year of life.)

Then ask students if they think babies can communicate and how. (Most students will agree that babies communicate through sounds, such as crying, giggling, and gurgling, and through facial and body movements, such as smiling and reaching out.)

Explain that in this chapter, students will study the human reproductive system and the growth and development of human beings from unborn child through adulthood.

• **Why is the process of reproduction important to the human species?** (It ensures the continuation of the human species.)

• **When do you think people become physically adult?** (When the body is completely matured and growth has ceased.)

strategies have raised serious legal, ethical, and social issues. The issues and concerns raised will not be easy to resolve, but the techniques are helping infertile couples have children.

Cooperative learning: Using preassigned lab groups or randomly selected teams, have groups complete one of the following assignments:

• One of the most difficult cases involving reproductive technologies occurred in Australia in 1983. Elsa and Mario Rios died in a plane crash, leaving behind a million-dollar estate and two frozen embryos. Before the couple died, eggs from Maria had been fertilized by an anonymous donor's sperm. Ask each group to consider what should be done with the frozen embryos. Should the embryos be used by other couples? If one of the embryos was implanted into another woman, should the child inherit the estate?

• Groups should consider themselves members of a task force of medical personnel making recommendations to the United States Congress about laws needed to prevent abuses of reproductive technologies.

See Cooperative Learning in the *Teacher's Desk Reference.*

JOURNAL ACTIVITY

You may want to use the Journal Activity as the basis of a class discussion. As students discuss their own physical, emotional, and intellectual development, emphasize that they have made extraordinary advances—from being totally dependent to being prepared to take on greater responsibilities—since they were born. Also emphasize the differences in the rates of growth and development. Have students place their Journal Activity in their portfolio.

7–1 The Reproductive System

MULTICULTURAL OPPORTUNITY 7–1

Have students research the life of Ernest Everett Just (1883–1941). A distinguished African-American scientist, Just pioneered work in egg fertilization during his 20 years at the Marine Biology Laboratory in Cape Cod, Massachusetts.

ESL STRATEGY 7–1

The Intruder: Have students circle the word that does not belong in each group and then write definitions for the words not circled.
1. testes, ovaries, sperm, testosterone
2. ovaries, sperm, ova, estrogen
3. uretha, penis, estrogen, semen
4. uterus, cervix, scrotum, vagina

Guide for Reading
Focus on these questions as you read.
▶ *What is the importance of reproduction?*
▶ *What are the structures of the male and female reproductive systems?*

7–1 The Reproductive System

In the previous chapters of this textbook, you learned about the human body systems that are vital to the survival of the individual. Without the proper functioning of these systems, humans would no doubt be unable to live healthy, normal lives. The loss of the digestive system, nervous system, or circulatory system would be fatal (deadly) in humans. Can you explain why? ❶

There is one body system, however, that is not essential to the survival of the individual. In fact, humans can survive quite well without the functioning of this system. What this system is important to is the survival of the human species—that is, the continuation on Earth of people just like you. Have you figured out what this system is?

The body system is the reproductive system, which contains special structures that enable reproduction to take place. Reproduction is the process through which living things produce new individuals of the same kind. Thus the reproductive system ensures the continuation of the species. Without it, a species will cease to exist. Do you know the scientific word that means a species no longer exists on Earth? ❷

Figure 7–1 *The process of reproduction results in new individuals of the same kind. Without reproduction, humans, hippopotamuses, and, for that matter, all species of living things would cease to exist.*

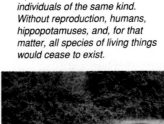

TEACHING STRATEGY 7–1

FOCUS/MOTIVATION

Have students observe the photographs of the sperm and egg on page H169.
• **Can you tell from these pictures which is larger—the sperm or the egg?** (No.)
• **Which do you think is larger?** (Help students understand that the egg is significantly larger than the sperm.)
• **Why do you think the egg is so much larger?** (The egg must provide food—energy—for the early growth and divisions of the fertilized egg.)
• **How is the shape of the sperm well adapted to its function?** (The elongated tail of the sperm helps it swim like a tadpole on its journey to unite with the egg.)

CONTENT DEVELOPMENT

Help students understand that the reproductive system is not essential to the survival of an individual, but it is essential to the survival of a species.

• **Why is a system of reproduction important to a species?** (Reproduction enables a species to perpetuate itself.)
• **What would happen to a species if all its members could not reproduce?** (The species would die out and become extinct.)
• **What would happen to an individual that could not reproduce?** (That individual could not bear offspring but could survive as an individual.)
• **What would happen to an individual if the individual's circulatory system shut**

In humans, the reproductive system produces, stores, nourishes, and releases specialized cells known as sex cells. From the union of these sex cells will come a new individual—the next generation. How does the reproductive system function? How does the extraordinary process of reproduction take place? And how do single cells become complete humans millions and millions of times every year? ❸

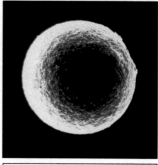

Sexual Development

Does it surprise you to learn that you began life as one single cell? Well, that's just how you started. This single cell was produced by the joining of two other cells. These two other cells are specialized cells known as sex cells. Sex cells are unlike any other cells that make up your body. Biologists call the sex cells gametes (GAM-eets). There are two kinds of sex cells (or gametes)—a male sex cell and a female sex cell. The male sex cell is called the **sperm.** The female sex cell is called the **egg,** or ovum (OH-vuhm; plural: ova, OH-vuh). The joining of a sperm nucleus and an egg nucleus is called **fertilization.** Recall that the nucleus of a cell contains the genetic material. Fertilization is the process by which organisms produce more of their own kind. The result of fertilization is a fertilized egg—one single cell from which come all the trillions of cells in a human body!

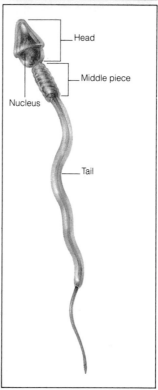

Head

Middle piece

Nucleus

Tail

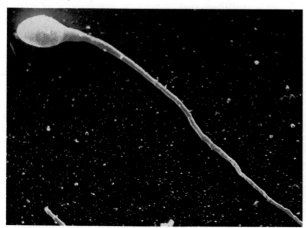

Figure 7–2 *The tadpole-shaped sperm, which consists of a head, a middle piece, and a tail, is the male sex cell. The ball-shaped egg is the female sex cell. What is the name of the process in which the nuclei of these two sex cells join?* ❹

H ■ 169

FACTS AND FIGURES

COMPARING SIZES

A human sperm is incredibly small. It is one ten-thousandth the size of the human egg, which is about the size of a grain of sand.

down? (The individual could not survive without an operating circulatory system.)
• **What would happen to a species if the circulatory system of one individual shut down?** (The species would be unaffected as long as there were other members of the species that could reproduce.)
• **How do the roles of the reproductive system and the circulatory system differ in terms of their effect on individuals? On a species?** (The reproductive system is not essential to the survival of an individual. It is, however, essential to the survival of a species. The circulatory system is essential to the survival of an individual. A species is not affected by the failure of one individual's circulatory system.)

Explain to students that fertilization is the first stage in the beginning of a new human. Fertilization is the joining of a sperm cell with an egg cell.
• **Where is genetic material contained in each cell?** (In the nucleus.)
• **Why is genetic material important?** (It determines the inherited characteristics of the individual.)

● ● ● ● **Integration** ● ● ● ●
Use the discussion of fertilization to integrate life science concepts of heredity into your lesson.

ENRICHMENT
Ask students if they know any myths about the origin of babies. Examples include the stork delivering babies and finding babies in the cabbage patch. Ask students to research information about the myths.

The presence or absence of testosterone, not estrogen, seems to be the determining factor in the matter of male and female development. One possible explanation is that the human embryo develops within the uterus of the mother. As a result, whether it is male or female, the embryo lives in an environment permeated with estrogen. A small amount of extra estrogen produced by the embryonic ovaries would not make much difference. Therefore, during the sixth and seventh week of development, the signal to the embryonic tissues comes in the form of testosterone. If it is present, the male pattern develops. If it is absent, the female pattern develops.

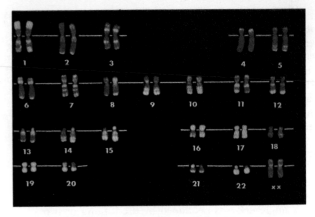

Figure 7–3 *Chromosomes are thick rodlike structures that are responsible for passing on inherited characteristics. The photograph shows the size, number, and pairs of chromosomes for a human body cell. How many chromosomes are in each human body cell?* ❶

Both the sperm and the egg contain thick, rodlike structures called chromosomes (KROH-muh-sohmz). Chromosomes are responsible for passing on inherited characteristics such as skin, eye, and hair color from one generation of cells to the next. With the exception of the sex cells (sperm and egg), every cell in the human body contains 46 chromosomes. The sex cells contain only half this number, or 23 chromosomes. As a result of the joining of sperm (23 chromosomes) and egg (23 chromosomes) nuclei during fertilization, the nucleus of a fertilized egg contains 46 chromosomes—the normal number of chromosomes for all body cells. Within these 46 chromosomes is all the information needed to produce a complete new human—you!

If it surprised you to learn that humans begin life as a single cell, then the following fact will probably surprise you just as much, if not more. For the first 6 weeks after fertilization, male and female fertilized eggs (now called embryos) are identical in appearance. Then, during the seventh week of development, major changes occur. If the fertilized egg is a male, certain hormones are produced that cause the development of the male reproductive organs. If the fertilized egg is a female, certain other hormones are produced that cause the development of the female reproductive organs. (Hormones, you will recall from Chapter 6, are chemical messengers

7–1 (continued)

CONTENT DEVELOPMENT

• **How many chromosomes does a sperm cell have?** (23.)

• **How many chromosomes does an egg cell have?** (23.)

• **Why do you think each sperm cell and egg cell contains only 23 chromosomes rather than the 46 chromosomes found in all other body cells?** (If the sperm and egg cell each contained 46 chromosomes, the new

individual would be composed of cells with 92 chromosomes! The chromosome number in sex cells is reduced to one half the number of the other cells. The process that reduced the number of chromosomes in sex cells is known as meiosis. When fertilization occurs, the regular number of chromosomes is restored.)

● ● ● ● **Integration** ● ● ● ●

Use the discussion of chromosomes to integrate life science concepts of cells into your lesson.

that regulate certain activities of the body.) Thus the male and female reproductive organs develop from exactly the same tissues in a fertilized egg.

After birth and for the next 10 to 15 years, the hormones specific to the male and those specific to the female continue to influence the development of their respective reproductive organs. Accompanying this development is the appearance of certain sex characteristics such as growth of facial hair in males and broadening of the hips in females. You will read more about this process in the next section. At the end of this process, the male and female reproductive organs are fully developed and functional.

The Male Reproductive System

The primary male reproductive organs are the **testes** (TEHS-teez; singular: testis, TEHS-tihs). The testes are oval-shaped organs found inside an external pouch (sac) of skin called the scrotum (SKROHT-uhm). The major role of the testes is to produce sperm. The fact that the testes remain in the scrotum outside the body is very important to the development of sperm. The external temperature is

Figure 7–4 *In the male reproductive system, sperm and the hormone testosterone are produced within two oval-shaped organs called the testes. Sperm travel from the testes through tubes to the urethra. What is the function of testosterone?* ❷

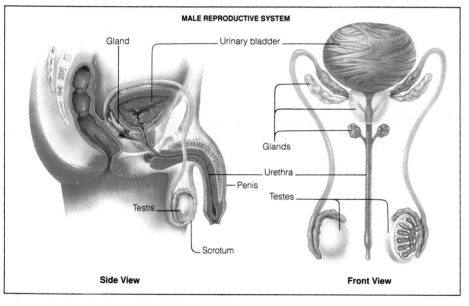

MALE REPRODUCTIVE SYSTEM

Gland
Urinary bladder
Glands
Urethra
Penis
Testis
Testes
Scrotum

Side View　　　　**Front View**

H ■ 171

BACKGROUND INFORMATION
CELLS IN THE TESTES

Three kinds of cells are found in the testes. Spermatogonia are the cells capable of developing into sperm. Sertoli cells wrap themselves around groups of developing sperm cells. They seem to assist in sperm development and transfer nutrients to the developing sperm. The third type of cell is known as the interstitial cell. The interstitial cells produce the male sex hormones.

about 1° to 3°C lower than the internal temperature of the body (37°C). Sperm development in the testes requires a lower temperature.

The testes are actually clusters of hundreds of tiny tightly coiled tubes. It is in these tubes that sperm are produced. Developed sperm travel from the tubes through several other structures to the urethra (yoo-REE-thruh). The urethra is a larger tube that leads to the outside of the body through the penis. During their passage to the urethra, sperm mix with a fluid produced by glands in the area. The combination of this fluid and sperm is known as semen (SEE-mehn). The number of sperm present in just a few drops of semen is astonishing. Between 100 and 200 million sperm are present in 1 milliliter of semen—about 5 million sperm per drop!

If you look at Figure 7–2 on page 169, you can see that a sperm cell consists of three parts: a head, a middle piece, and a tail. The head contains the nucleus, or control center of the cell. Energy-releasing cell structures pack the middle piece. And the tail propels the sperm cell forward.

In addition to producing sperm, the testes produce a hormone called testosterone (tehs-TAHS-ter-ohn). Testosterone is responsible for a number of male characteristics: the growth of facial and body hair, broadening of the chest and shoulders, and deepening of the voice.

The Female Reproductive System

Unlike the male reproductive system, all parts of the female reproductive system are within the female's body. The primary female reproductive organs are the **ovaries** (OH-vuh-reez). The ovaries are located at about hip level, one on each side of a female's body. The major role of the ovaries is to produce eggs, or ova. Located near each ovary, but not directly connected to it, is a **Fallopian** (fuh-LOH-pee-uhn) **tube**, or oviduct. From the ovary, an egg enters a Fallopian tube and travels slowly through it. At the opposite end of a Fallopian tube, an egg enters a hollow muscular organ called the **uterus** (YOOT-er-uhs), or womb. The uterus, which is shaped like an upside-down pear, is the organ in

---

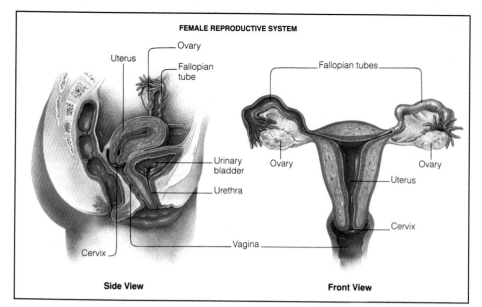

FEMALE REPRODUCTIVE SYSTEM

Side View

Front View

Figure 7–5 *In the female reproductive system, the ovaries produce eggs and hormones. From an ovary, an egg travels through a Fallopian tube to the uterus. What is another name for a Fallopian tube? For the uterus?* ❶

which a fertilized egg develops. The lower end of the uterus narrows into an area called the cervix (SER-vihks). The cervix opens into a wider channel called the vagina (vuh-JIGH-nuh), or birth canal. The vagina is the passageway through which a baby passes during the birth process.

Compared to a sperm cell, an egg cell is enormous. It is one of the largest cells in the body. It is so large, in fact, that it can be seen with the unaided eye. Its size is often compared to that of a grain of sand.

It is interesting to note that whereas a male continually produces sperm cells, a female is born with all the eggs she will ever have. A female will not produce any new eggs in her lifetime. The average number of undeveloped eggs a female has in her ovaries is about 400,000. Only about 500 of these, however, will actually leave the ovaries and journey to the uterus.

Like the testes, the ovaries produce hormones. One of these hormones is called estrogen (EHS-truh-juhn). Estrogen triggers the development of a number of female characteristics: broadening of the hips, enlargement of the breasts, and maturation (aging) of egg cells in the ovaries.

H ■ 173

BACKGROUND INFORMATION

OVUM

During meiosis, an immature ovum splits in half. Each half has 23 chromosomes. One half, however, takes more nutrients from the immature ovum. The unequal sharing of nutrients is important. The half with the most nutrients forms into a mature ovum. The other half attaches itself to the mature ovum as a polar body. After the mature ovum is released from the ovaries, it will travel about 10 days before it reaches the uterus. If the mature ovum is fertilized in the Fallopian tube, it will have to provide nutrients to the embryo until the embryo is implanted in the uterus.

• **How does an ovum get from the ovaries to the uterus?** (It travels through the Fallopian tube.)

• **Are the Fallopian tubes connected to the ovaries?** (No, but they have openings surrounding the ovaries.)

• **What is another name for the vagina?** (The birth canal.)

• **Why is this an appropriate name?** (The vagina, or birth canal, is the passageway through which the baby passes during the birth process.)

• **What role does the uterus play in the reproductive system?** (The uterus is the place where the developing fetus grows and is nourished before birth.)

CONTENT DEVELOPMENT

Explain that the ovaries usually produce only one egg per month. Fertilization of the egg normally takes place in one of the Fallopian tubes, and the fertilized egg travels slowly to the uterus. The uterus is usually about the size of a fist. During pregnancy, it stretches to accommodate the growing fetus. The outer wall of the uterus has thick muscle tissue that contracts in the birth process to expel the baby from the uterus. The lower end of the uterus forms a narrow section called the cervix, or neck of the uterus. The cervix opens into the vagina, which leads to the outside of the body.

MENARCHE

Menarche is a girl's first menstrual period. It does not always coincide with the first ovulation. The first ovulation may occur before menarche or years after it. Following menarche for the next one or two years, menstruation is often irregular. Ovulation on a regular basis usually occurs about a year after menarche. It may be signaled by more regular periods and premenstrual signs such as tenderness of the breasts.

FACTS AND FIGURES

FALLOPIAN TUBES

Each Fallopian tube is about 11 centimeters long.

The Menstrual Cycle

The monthly cycle of change that occurs in the female reproductive system is called the **menstrual** (MEHN-struhl) **cycle**. The menstrual cycle has an average length of about 28 days, or almost a month. In fact, the word menstrual comes from the Latin word *mensis*, meaning month. The menstrual cycle involves the interaction of the reproductive system and the endocrine system. It is controlled by hormones operating on a negative-feedback mechanism. Do you remember how such a mechanism works? If you do not, you may want to review Section 6–4 in the previous chapter.

Although the menstrual cycle affects the entire body of a female, it has two basic purposes: (1) the development and release of an egg for fertilization and (2) the preparation of the uterus to receive a fertilized egg. The menstrual cycle consists of a complex series of events that occur in a periodic fashion. It is not necessary for you to know about these events in detail. What you should understand and appreciate is the purpose of the menstrual cycle and some of its basic characteristics.

As you just learned, unlike male sex cells, female sex cells are formed in the ovaries at birth. Each sex cell, or egg, is held within a little pocket of cells called a follicle (FAHL-ih-kuhl). By the time a female

Figure 7–6 *During ovulation, an egg bursts from a follicle (right). The egg is then swept into the feathery tunnel-shaped opening of a Fallopian tube (left). What organ does an egg enter after it leaves a Fallopian tube?*

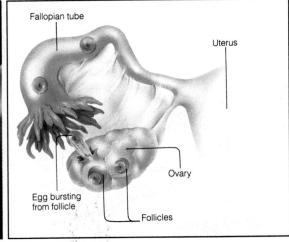

174 ■ H

7–1 (continued)

CONTENT DEVELOPMENT

Emphasize that the whole purpose of the menstrual cycle is to release a mature egg and to prepare the body to nourish and protect that egg if it is fertilized. The entire menstrual cycle consists of four phases. In one phase, called the follicle phase, an egg is ripened in the ovaries. In the next phase, ovulation, the ripened egg is released into a Fallopian tube,

where it could be fertilized by sperm. Following ovulation, the egg continues to move toward the uterus, and the luteal phase begins. In this phase, the hormone progesterone is released, which further prepares the body for pregnancy. If an egg is not fertilized, the egg and the lining prepared to shelter the fertilized egg pass from the uterus during menstruation. During menstruation, the cycle begins anew as another egg ripens. If the egg is fertilized, however, the luteal phase

continues so that the developing embryo can be nourished and protected.

●　●　●　● **Integration** ●　●　●　●

Use the discussion of the Latin root of the word *menstrual* to integrate language arts into your lesson.

REINFORCEMENT/RETEACHING

To ensure that students understand the menstrual cycle, you may want to use the illustration of the female reproductive system on page H173 as you explain the

is ready to begin the menstrual cycle, there may be nearly half a million follicles in the ovaries. Only a few follicles, however, release ripened (mature) eggs.

If an egg does ripen, increased hormone levels cause the follicle to burst through the side of the ovary, releasing the egg. This process is called **ovulation** (ahv-yoo-LAY-shuhn). The egg is then swept into the feathery funnel-shaped opening of a Fallopian tube. Pushed along by microscopic cilia lining the walls, the egg is moved through the Fallopian tube toward the uterus.

If sperm are present in the Fallopian tube when the egg arrives, the egg can be fertilized. Although hundreds of millions of sperm are released by the male, only relatively few—perhaps 10,000 to 100,000—enter the proper Fallopian tube (the Fallopian tube containing the egg). Of these sperm, barely 1000 make it to the egg. Nevertheless, only 1 sperm is needed for fertilization.

The changes occurring in the ovary are not the only changes taking place during the menstrual cycle. In preparation for the arrival of a fertilized egg, the lining of the uterus is thickening, and the blood

Figure 7–7 *Although hundreds of millions of sperm are released by the male (top left), very few sperm enter the proper Fallopian tube (top right). The proper Fallopian tube is the one that contains the egg (bottom left). Of all the sperm that make it to the egg (bottom right), only one is needed to fertilize it.*

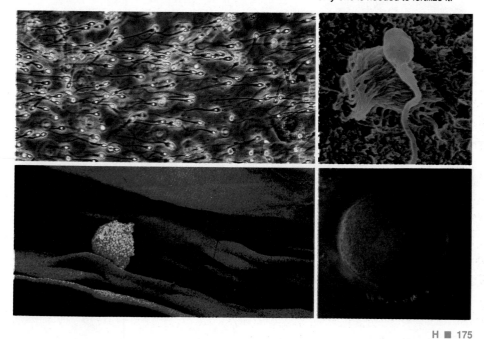

BACKGROUND INFORMATION
PMS

A phenomenon associated with the menstrual cycle is premenstrual syndrome, or PMS. About two weeks to a few days before menstruation begins, many women suffer from PMS. Symptoms may include wide mood swings, headaches, aching joints, weight gain, and tender breasts. The severity of the symptoms varies from woman to woman and from menstrual cycle to menstrual cycle. Although the cause of PMS is still unknown, scientists strongly suspect that a hormonal imbalance is the source of the condition. Some scientists have claimed success in treating the syndrome with progesterone injections before menstruation begins. Others recommend the use of diuretics and high-energy meals.

process. Have students identify the organs through which the ovum passes during the cycle. Make sure students understand the purpose and function of the organs during the menstrual cycle.

ENRICHMENT

Although many sperm may try to fertilize the egg, only one will be successful. The sperm releases an enzyme that slices through the exterior of the egg, creating an entry point for the sperm. As the sperm enters the egg, its tail disintegrates, and only its head and middle part penetrate the egg. The egg's surface quickly changes to prevent other sperm from entering. It discharges enzymes that dislodge sperm bound to its surface and prevents others from binding to it. The nuclei of the egg and the sperm join, and their chromosomes pair off. The fertilized egg can then begin to develop.

ANNOTATION KEY

Answers

1 The extra blood and tissue in the thickened lining of the uterus pass from the body. At the same time, the cycle begins again as a new egg ripens in the ovaries. (Relating facts)

Integration

1 Fine Arts

FIND OUT BY WRITING

THE DEVELOPING EMBRYO

Material: posterboard

This activity will enable students to gain an appreciation for the complexity of human development. You may wish to emphasize that the first trimester is the most important in terms of embryonic development.

Encourage students to incorporate illustrations as well as words into their charts. Suggest that students organize the information on paper before they begin their posterboard chart.

Integration: Use the Find Out by Writing activity to integrate fine arts into your science lesson.

7–1 (continued)

INDEPENDENT PRACTICE

Section Review 7–1

1. In the male, the testes, which are located in the scrotum, produce sperm and the hormone testosterone. The glands secrete a fluid that mixes with the sperm to form semen. Semen is released through the uretha in the penis. In the female, the ovaries produce eggs and hormones. The egg is released into a Fallopian tube, where it can be fertilized. If it is not fertilized, the egg and extra blood and tissues pass out of the body through the vagina. If the egg is fertilized, it grows and develops in the uterus. The baby passes through the vagina when it is born.

2. The joining of a sperm nucleus and an egg nucleus.

3. The menstrual cycle is the process by which the body prepares for carrying a baby. The ovaries prepare a ripe egg and release hormones. The egg is released into a Fallopian tube during ovulation. The egg moves into the uterus, where it is implanted if it is fertilized. An unfertilized egg and extra blood and tissue pass out of the body through the vagina during menstruation.

4. The mucus helps the egg move more easily through the Fallopian tube and provides an environment in which the sperm and egg can be united.

REINFORCEMENT/RETEACHING

Monitor students' responses to the Section Review questions. If students seem to have difficulty with any of the concepts, review the appropriate material.

Figure 7–8 *The monthly cycle of change that occurs in the female reproductive system is called the menstrual cycle. It consists of a complex series of events that occur in a periodic fashion. What events take place during menstruation?* **1**

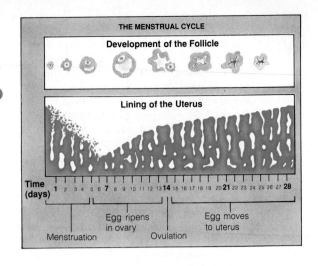

supply to the tissues is increasing. If a fertilized egg reaches the lining, it implants (inserts) itself there, divides and grows, and eventually develops into a new human.

If the egg is not fertilized, it and the lining of the uterus will begin to break down. When this happens, the extra blood and tissue in the thickened lining of the uterus pass out of the body through the vagina. This process is called menstruation (mehn-STRAY-shuhn). On the average, menstruation lasts 5 days. At the same time menstruation is occurring, a new egg is maturing in its follicle in the ovary, and the changing levels of hormones are causing the cycle to begin anew.

7–1 Section Review

1. What are the structures and functions of the male and female reproductive systems?
2. What is fertilization?
3. Describe the menstrual cycle.

Critical Thinking—*Relating Facts*

4. A Fallopian tube is lined with mucus. How does this contribute to the function of the tube?

7–2 Stages of Development

You have just read that an egg can be fertilized only during ovulation and for several days after. Ovulation usually occurs about 14 days after the start of menstruation. If the egg is fertilized, the remarkable process of human development begins. In the course of this process, a single cell no larger than the period at the end of this sentence will undergo a series of divisions that will result in the formation of a new human. Approximately 9 months after fertilization, a baby will be born. As you well know, this is only the beginning of a lifetime of developmental changes.

Humans go through various stages of development before and after birth. **Before birth, a single human cell develops into an embryo and then a fetus. After birth, humans pass through the stages of infancy, childhood, adolescence, and adulthood.**

Development Before Birth

As the fertilized egg, now called a **zygote** (ZIGH-goht), begins its 4-day trip through the Fallopian tube to the uterus, it begins to divide. From one cell it becomes two, then four, then eight, and so on. At this point, the cells resemble a hollow ball. During this early stage of development, and for the next 8 weeks or so, the developing human is called an **embryo** (EHM-bree-oh).

Soon after the embryo enters the uterus, it attaches itself to the wall and begins to grow inward. As it does so, several membranes form around it. One of those membranes develops into a fluid-filled sac called the **amniotic** (am-nee-AHT-ihk) **sac**. The amniotic sac cushions and protects the developing baby. Another membrane forms the **placenta** (pluh-SEHN-tuh). The placenta is made partly from tissue that develops from the embryo and partly from tissue that makes up the wall of the uterus.

The placenta provides a connection between developing embryo and mother. The developing embryo needs a supply of oxygen and food. It also needs a way of getting rid of wastes. You may think that the embryo's needs could be met if the blood supply of mother and embryo were joined. But such

FIND OUT BY
WRITING

The Developing Embryo

The first trimester, or 3 months, of a pregnancy is the most important in the development of a baby. Use reference materials in the library to find out about the changes that occur in the developing baby during the first trimester. On posterboard, construct a chart in which you describe these changes on a weekly basis for the first 12 weeks of a typical pregnancy.

H ■ 177

THE WORLD'S FIRST TEST-TUBE BABY

On July 25, 1978, history was made when the first human baby conceived outside the mother's body was born. The successful birth was the result of the work of two British doctors, Patrick Steptoe and Robert Edwards. They fertilized an egg from the mother with sperm from the father in a laboratory dish, or *in vitro*, which means "outside the body." The newly forming embryo was then implanted in the mother's uterus. This procedure gave couples who were having difficulty conceiving children hope that they, too, could become parents.

FACTS AND FIGURES

GIFT AND ZIFT

Through two relatively new laboratory procedures, successful pregnancies have resulted. GIFT, short for gamete intra-Fallopian transfer, is one of these procedures. Gametes—sperm and eggs—are inserted into a Fallopian tube, where fertilization takes place. If fertilization results, the zygote enters the uterus naturally by flowing down the Fallopian tube, where it implants itself. ZIFT, or zygote intra-Fallopian transfer, is basically the same procedure, but fertilized zygotes, rather than gametes, are inserted in the Fallopian tubes. GIFT and ZIFT can have as high as a 50-percent success rate. A healthy couple trying to have a baby naturally experiences only a 25-percent success rate.

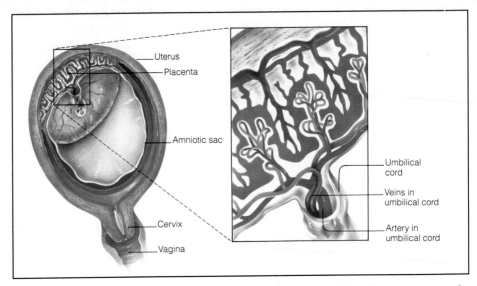

Figure 7–9 *The placenta provides a connection between the mother and the developing baby. Through blood vessels in the umbilical cord, food and oxygen from the mother and wastes from the developing baby are exchanged. What is the function of the amniotic sac?* ❶

an arrangement would also allow diseases to spread from mother to embryo and would cause other problems related to the mixing of different blood types.

Actually, the blood of mother and embryo flow past each other, but they do not mix. They are separated by a thin membrane that acts as a barrier. Across this thin barrier, food, oxygen, and wastes are exchanged. Thus the placenta becomes the embryo's organ of nourishment, respiration, and excretion. The placenta also permits harmful substances such as alcohol, chemicals in tobacco smoke, and drugs to pass from the mother to the developing baby. For this reason, it is important that pregnant women not drink alcohol, smoke tobacco, or take any type of drug without a doctor's approval.

After eight weeks of development, the embryo is about the size of a walnut. Now called a **fetus** (FEET-uhs), it begins to take on a more babylike appearance. By the end of 3 months, it has the main internal organs, dark eye patches, and fingers and toes. During this time, a structure known as the **umbilical** (uhm-BIHL-ih-kuhl) **cord** forms. The umbilical cord, which contains two arteries and one vein, connects the fetus to the placenta. The large size of the fetus's head—about half the total size—indicates

---

7–2 (continued)

INDEPENDENT PRACTICE

▶ *Activity Book*

Students can use the chapter activity called Stages of Human Development to trace the development of the fertilized egg into a newborn baby. In the activity students sequence the stages of development from fertilization to birth.

CONTENT DEVELOPMENT

Students may be surprised to learn that an unborn baby is quite active. Fetuses make faces, swim, drink amniotic fluid, move their arms and legs, turn somersaults, sleep, turn their heads in response to sound, and suck their thumbs. In fact, some babies are born with thumb calluses from too much thumb-sucking in the womb.

GUIDED PRACTICE

▶ *Laboratory Manual*

Skills Development

Skills: Observing, interpreting data, drawing conclusions, making inferences

At this point you may want students to complete the Chapter 7 Laboratory Investigation called Observing the Development of Frog Eggs in the *Laboratory Manual.* In the investigation students observe developing frog eggs and note the

the rapid brain development that is taking place. At this point, the fetus is about 9 centimeters long and has a mass of about 15 grams.

During the fourth, fifth, and sixth months, the tissues of the fetus continue to become more specialized. A skeleton begins to form, a heartbeat can be heard with a stethoscope, and a layer of soft hair grows over the skin. The mass of the fetus is now about 700 grams.

The final 3 months prepare the fetus for a completely independent existence. The lungs and other organs undergo a series of changes that prepare them for life outside the mother. The mass of the fetus quadruples. A baby is about to be born. The entire time period between the fertilization of an egg and the birth of a baby is known as pregnancy. An average full-term pregnancy is about 9 months.

In recent years, medical technology has made it possible to detect, and in some cases treat, fetal disorders. Such advances have opened up a new frontier in medicine: diagnosing and treating babies before they are born! In one technique, a small amount of the amniotic fluid in which a fetus floats is removed through a hollow needle. The amniotic fluid, which contains cells from the fetus, is then studied to determine the health of the fetus. If there are problems that can be corrected, doctors are now able to inject medication through the hollow needle into the fetus. In a recent medical breakthrough, doctors have safely given blood transfusions to babies still in the uterus. This amazing feat was performed

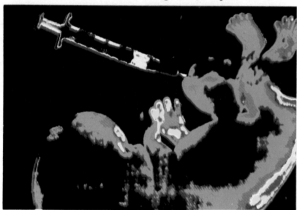

Figure 7–10 *In this photograph you can see a needle removing a small amount of fluid from the amniotic sac. This sac contains cells from the fetus that will be examined to determine the health of the fetus.*

H ■ 179

BACKGROUND INFORMATION

ALCOHOL USE DURING PREGNANCY

Alcohol consumed by the mother can have a great effect on the developing baby. Excessive use of alcohol can lead to a condition called fetal alcohol syndrome, or FAS. FAS results in growth retardation before and after birth. FAS babies are subject to such abnormalities as defective limbs and heart defects. FAS children exhibit such facial characteristics as short and upturned noses and flat upper jaws. They may also exhibit behavioral problems and can have impaired speech and impaired fine motor skills. FAS children also may be mentally retarded. The mortality rate for babies with FAS is higher than that for normal babies. Research indicates that four or five drinks a day during pregnancy can result in children with FAS. Research also shows that even moderate use of alcohol can result in abnormalities. As a result, researchers agree that there is no safe level of alcohol consumption for pregnant women. The United States has enacted a law that requires warning labels on containers of alcohol to alert pregnant women to the possible dangers of alcohol use on their developing babies.

impact of water temperature on that development. Point out that in the early stages of the development of vertebrate embryos, the embryos are nearly identical.

• **How can the study of frog eggs help you understand the development of human eggs?** (Accept all logical answers. Point out that at the earliest stages, the development of human eggs and frog eggs is similar. By viewing what happens to the frog eggs, students can better understand very early human development.)

• **In the investigation, you see how an out-** side factor affects the development of frog eggs. Can outside factors affect the development of human embryos? (Students should recognize that outside factors, including such harmful substances as alcohol, cigarettes, and drugs, do have an impact on a human embryo.)

CONTENT DEVELOPMENT

Emphasize the importance of the placenta to the developing embryo and fetus. The placenta is the means of nourishment, respiration, and excretion. Remind stu- dents that an individual can die if the digestive, respiratory, and excretory systems fail. Explain that if the placenta fails, the developing baby can die. One very serious condition for the developing child is placenta abruption—the tearing of the placenta from the uterine wall. If the placenta becomes completely detached, the result could be fatal for the developing baby.

• **Why can placenta abruption result in fetal death?** (The developing baby loses its source of nutriton, excretion, and respiration.)

FIND OUT BY DOING

MULTIPLE BIRTHS

Discovery Learning

Skills: Researching information, applying information, making and using diagrams

In this activity students investigate multiple births. They gather information about the frequency of births that result in fraternal and identical twins as well as identical triplets.

Students should note that fraternal twins result from the fertilization of two separate eggs and may be different sexes. Identical twins result from the division of a single egg and are always the same sex and resemble each other closely. Identical triplets result from a three-way division of a single egg, whereas fraternal triplets result from the fertilization of three eggs or of two eggs with one egg dividing into two separate embryos.

7–2 (continued)

CONTENT DEVELOPMENT

Explain to students that sound waves are used to help evaluate a pregnancy and the state of the fetus. Using technology known as ultrasound, or sonogram, doctors can examine the status of a fetus with no known risk to the unborn child. Ultrasound is used to detect fetal abnormalities, the presence of more than one fetus, the size and rate of growth of the fetus, fetal motion, and also in connection with amniocentesis. It has proven to be an effective diagnostic tool for doctors.

● ● ● ● **Integration** ● ● ● ●

Use the information about the use of sound waves during prenatal treatment to

---

FIND OUT BY DOING

Multiple Births

A multiple birth occurs when two or more children are born at one time to one mother. Using reference materials in the library, look up information on twins. In a written report, describe how twins develop. You might wish to use diagrams in your explanation.

■ What is the difference in origin and appearance between identical and fraternal twins?

■ How do identical triplets develop?

■ How do fraternal triplets develop?

Figure 7–11 *After about 9 months of growth and development inside the uterus, a baby is born. This baby is only minutes old. What are the names of the three stages in the birth process?* ❶

---

with the help of sound waves, which produce an image on a television screen similar to the one shown in Figure 7–10 on page 179.

Birth

After about 9 months of development and growth inside the uterus, the fetus is ready to be born. Strong muscular contractions of the uterus begin to push the baby through the cervix into the vagina. These contractions are called labor. Labor is the first stage in the birth process. As labor progresses, the contractions of the uterus become stronger and occur more frequently. Finally, the baby—who is still connected to the placenta by the umbilical cord—is pushed out of the mother (usually head first). This stage, known as delivery, is the second stage in the birth process. Delivery usually takes less time than labor does. For example, labor may last anywhere from 2 to 20 hours or more; delivery may take from several minutes to a few hours. Within a few seconds of delivery, a baby may begin to cough or cry. This action helps to rid its lungs of fluid with which they have been filled, as well as to expand and fill its lungs with air.

Shortly after delivery, the third stage in the birth process begins. The umbilical cord, which is still attached to the placenta, is tied and then cut about 5 centimeters from the baby's abdomen. This procedure does not cause the baby any pain. A few minutes later, another set of contractions pushes the placenta and other membranes from the uterus. This is appropriately called afterbirth. Within 7 to 10

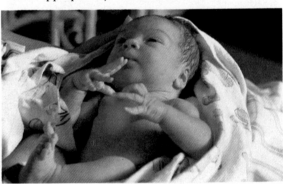

---

integrate physical science concepts of sound into your science lesson.

GUIDED PRACTICE

Skills Development

Skills: Making and interpreting graphs, making comparisons, classifying, hypothesizing

Explain that the gestation period for humans is about 280 days.

• **Is the gestation period the same for all species of animals? Explain.** (Most stu-

dents will agree that gestation periods vary from species to species. Help students relate gestation period to life span and age at puberty.)

At this point you may want students to complete the in-text Laboratory Investigation called How Many Offspring? In the investigation students will compare the human gestation period to those of other mammals.

days, the remaining part of the umbilical cord dries up and falls off the baby's abdomen, leaving a scar. This scar is known as the navel. Do you know a more common name for the navel? **2**

Development After Birth

The human body does not grow at a constant rate. The most rapid growth occurs before birth, when in the space of 9 months the fetus increases its mass about 2.4 billion times! After birth, there are two growth spurts (sudden increases in height and mass). These growth spurts occur in the first 2 years of life and again at the beginning of adolescence.

You may be surprised to learn that as you grow from infancy to adulthood, the number of bones in your body decreases. The 350 or so bones you were born with gradually fuse (come together) into the approximately 206 bones you will have in your skeleton as an adult. (Some simple arithmetic should tell you that is about 144 fewer bones.) The actual number of bones in a person's body varies because some people may have an extra pair of ribs or they may have fewer vertebrae in their spine.

INFANCY Have you ever watched a 6-month-old baby for a few minutes? Its actions, or responses, are simple. It can suck its thumb, grasp objects, yawn, stretch, blink, and sneeze. When lying in bed, the infant often curls up in a position much like the one it had in the uterus.

One of the most obvious changes during **infancy,** which extends from 1 month to about 2 years of age, is a rapid increase in size. The head of a young

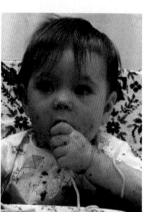

Figure 7–12 *During infancy, which extends from about 1 month to 2 years, mental and muscular skills begin to develop. What skills are illustrated by the 5-month-old (left), the 1-year-old (top), and the 1½-year-old (right)?* **3**

H ■ 181

BACKGROUND INFORMATION

LAMAZE METHOD

In recent years, more and more women have turned to natural-childbirth methods for delivering their babies. Natural childbirth means many things to many different people. Most agree that natural childbirth is birth with as few artificial procedures—such as the use of drugs—as possible. A widely popular method of childbirth education is the Lamaze method. In this method, the expectant mother and a labor coach work together to achieve a "mind over matter" approach to labor. The mother is trained to perform breathing exercises, to block out pain by focusing on an object, and in other methods of concentration to help her relax during labor and to reduce labor pains. Even with this method, complications may occur, and the mother may require medication or surgery to deliver the baby.

REINFORCEMENT/RETEACHING

▶ *Activity Book*

To reinforce the concept that the male, female, and young of a species are identified by different names, have students complete the chapter activity called Name It! In the activity students will identify the names of the various members of different species. Before assigning the activity, ask these questions:

• **What do we call a human male?** (Man.)

• **What do we call a human female?** (Woman.)

• **What do we call the offspring of humans?** (Baby, child, boy, girl.)

You may want students to work with partners to complete this activity. Encourage students to use reference materials to help them identify any names if necessary.

ENRICHMENT

Have students work in groups to create time lines for human development. Suggest that students start their time lines for a human before birth and then develop it through late adulthood. For each stage in development, have students identify a number of characteristics associated with that stage of development. Have students present their time lines to the class and display them on classroom walls.

In many cultures and religions, traditional celebrations mark the transition from childhood to adulthood. The traditional celebrations of the transitions are called "rites of passage." For example, a 13-year-old Jewish boy is initiated into the faith as an adult responsible for his moral and religious duties in a ceremony called bar mitzvah. The equivalent ceremony for girls is called bat mitzvah. In Mexican tradition, a girl celebrates her transition from childhood to adulthood on her fifteenth birthday in a gala celebration known as Quinceanera. Ask students to choose a culture and determine if that culture has a traditional rite of passage marking the transition between childhood and adulthood.

BACKGROUND INFORMATION
PUBERTY

Public-health scientists have long noted that the onset of puberty is extremely variable. Some girls will enter puberty when they are 9 years old, whereas others wait until 14 or even later. Boys are at least as variable. Careful studies of human sexual development show that the age at which puberty starts generally has no significance in later life. You might assure students that if their own experience was earlier or later than the norm, they have nothing to worry about.

Figure 7–13 *Childhood begins around the age of 2 years and continues until the age of 13 years. In addition to understanding and speaking a language, children can be taught to read before they attend school (top). Children also learn to interact socially with others, as these 8- to 11-year-olds are doing (bottom).*

baby is rather large compared to the rest of its body. Actually, a baby's head makes up about one fourth of its body length. As an infant gets older, the head grows more slowly—and the body, legs, and arms begin to catch up.

Mental and muscular skills begin to develop in a fairly predictable order. The exact ages at which they occur, however, vary from baby to baby. A newborn infant cannot lift its head. But after about 3 months, it can hold its head up and can also reach for objects. Within the next 2 months, the infant can grasp objects. At about 7 months, most infants are able to move around by crawling. Somewhere between 10 and 14 months, most infants begin to walk by themselves.

CHILDHOOD Infancy ends and **childhood** begins around the age of 2 years. Childhood continues until the age of 13 years. During childhood, mental abilities increase and memory is strengthened. Muscular skills develop. With practice, a small child becomes better at walking, holding a knife and fork, writing with a pencil, and playing sports. Over a period of several years, baby teeth are lost and replaced by permanent teeth.

During childhood, young children develop language skills. As you probably already know, all babies make babbling sounds. However, as a child becomes aware of itself and others, these sounds are shaped into language. Language skills come from observing and imitating others. At first, a child uses only one word at a time. For example, the child might say "ball." Soon after that, the child uses an action word and produces a two-word sentence, perhaps "Hit ball." By the age of 4 or 5, the child is able to speak in adultlike conversation.

In addition to understanding and speaking a language, children can be taught to read and solve problems even before they attend school. During childhood, children learn a great deal about their environment. They also learn to behave in socially appropriate ways.

ADOLESCENCE In many cultures, **adolescence** is thought of as a passage from childhood to adulthood. The word adolescence comes from a Latin word meaning to grow up. Adolescence begins

---

7–2 (continued)

FOCUS/MOTIVATION

Explain to students that learning to articulate certain sounds follows a fixed sequence of events.
• **Which of these sounds do you think a child learns first—m, s, or t?** (M is one of the first sounds a child can make.)
• **Arrange these sounds in the order in which you think a child learns to pronounce them—f, j, b, t, s.** (According to linguistic experts, the correct order is f (3 years), b (4 years), s (4 1/2 years), t (6 years), and j (7 years). Remind students that these are

the "usual" ages at which a child can clearly pronounce these specific sounds, and actual ability may vary from individual to individual. The order, however, is generally the same for all children.)

CONTENT DEVELOPMENT

• **What does the word *adolescence* mean?** (The word comes from a Latin word meaning "growing up." It is the period between childhood and adulthood.)

• **When does adolescence begin?** (When one is about 13 years old. Puberty marks the beginning of adolescence.)

Explain to students that puberty is the time when the sex organs develop rapidly, when girls begin to menstruate, and when sperm production begins in boys. Secondary sex characteristics, such as growth of body and facial hair in boys and breast development in girls, develop. A growth spurt also occurs during adolescence. This sudden increase in height and weight generally occurs earli-

Figure 7–14 *In many cultures, adolescence is seen as a passage from childhood to adulthood. In this ceremony, a 14-year-old Apache girl is sprinkled with cattail pollen by members of her tribe to signify this passage. In Austin, Texas, teenagers socialize at a dance.*

at **puberty** (PYOO-ber-tee) and continues through the teenage years to the age of 20. During puberty, the sex organs develop rapidly. Menstruation begins in females and the production of sperm begins in males. In addition, a growth spurt occurs. In females, this rapid growth occurs between the ages of 10 and 16. During these years, females may grow about 15 centimeters in height and gain about 16 kilograms or more in mass. In males, the growth spurt occurs between the ages of 11 and 17. During this time, males may grow about 20 centimeters in height and gain about 20 kilograms in mass.

ADULTHOOD   At about the age of 20, **adulthood** begins. All body systems, including the reproductive system, have become fully matured, and a person's full height has been reached. As a human passes from infancy through adulthood, fat beneath the skin keeps moving farther and farther away from the surface. The round, padded, button-nosed face of a baby is slowly replaced by the leaner, more defined face of an adult. The nose and the ears continue to grow and take on more individual shapes.

After about 30 years, a process known as aging begins. This process becomes more noticeable between the ages of 40 and 65. During this time, the skin loses some of its elasticity (capacity to return to its original shape), the eyes lose their ability to focus on close objects, the hair sometimes loses its coloring, and muscle strength decreases. During this period, females go through a physical change known as

ECOLOGY NOTE
LOVE CANAL

Love Canal, a neighborhood in Niagara Falls, New York, was the site of an environmental disaster caused by the dumping of toxic industrial wastes. The abandoned canal in the area was used as a dumping site for chemical wastes. After the site was covered over, houses were built there. In 1978, officials detected leakage of the toxic chemicals. The residents also showed a high incidence of chromosomal damage. Most people believed the damage was caused by the long-term exposure to the chemicals. The neighborhood was abandoned, and its residents resettled in other areas. The Love Canal disaster demonstrates the impact hazardous wastes can have on the growth and development of humans. Ask students to consider how hazardous wastes can be disposed of without endangering human life.

---

er in females (10 to 16 years old) than in males (11 to 17 years old).
• **At what age do you think you become an adult?** (Answers will vary.)

GUIDED PRACTICE

Skills Development

Skills: Researching information, making and using charts

Point out that there is no set age at which one becomes an adult. Legally, one may be regarded as an adult at different ages, and this may vary from state to state. Ask students to find out at what age your state or the national government considers a person old enough to drive a car, vote, get married, drop out of school, obtain a work permit, no longer be treated as a juvenile in court, join the armed forces, and so forth. Have students record the information on a data chart.

CONTENT DEVELOPMENT

Explain to students that biologically speaking, one becomes an adult when all body systems have become fully matured and full height has been reached. This normally occurs at about age 20.
• **When does the process of aging begin?** (At about 30 years old.)
• **What are some physical signs of aging?** (Hair turns gray or is lost, skin loses its elasticity [wrinkles] muscle strength decreases, menopause, farsightedness.)

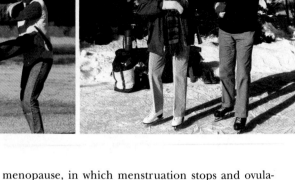

**FIND OUT BY
WRITING**

**YOU ONLY LOOK
AS OLD AS YOU FEEL**

Before students begin their research or their interviews, help them create an outline for the report they will write. Explain that they should address the definition of geriatrics, physical characteristics of aging and problems associated with them, as well as common diseases of the elderly. Students might work in teams to conduct research and interviews and to write their research paper.

**BACKGROUND
INFORMATION**

AARP

In 1958, the American Association of Retired People, or AARP, was founded. Today the organization is 30-million-members strong and is the largest private non-profit organization in the world. The main purpose of AARP is to address the needs of older people. The organization provides a variety of educational and community services, including social programs, volunteer programs, and education programs for its members. It also offers such benefits as group health insurance. AARP is a powerful lobbying group in the nation's capital. It tries to influence legislators to pass laws that protect the interests of senior citizens.

Figure 7–15 *By the time people reach adulthood, all their body systems have become fully matured.*

menopause, in which menstruation stops and ovulation no longer occurs. Males do not go through similar changes in their reproductive processes. In fact, males continue to produce sperm throughout their lives. However, the number of sperm they produce decreases as they age.

After age 65, the aging process continues, often leading to less efficient heart and lung action. But the effects of aging can be slowed down or somewhat reversed if people follow sensible diets and good exercise plans throughout their lives.

**FIND OUT BY
WRITING**

You Only Look as Old as You Feel

Use reference materials in the library to find out about gerontology, or the study of aging. You may wish to interview a doctor who specializes in geriatrics, or the branch of medicine involving diseases of old age. Here are some questions that you should ask: What are the most common diseases of old age? What can a person do to lessen the chances of getting these diseases?

7–2 Section Review

1. What stages of development does a human go through before birth?
2. What stages of development does a human go through after birth?
3. What is a developing baby called during the first 8 weeks of development? After the first 8 weeks?
4. What is the function of the amniotic sac? The placenta?
5. What is puberty?

Connection—*Medicine*
6. Why is it important for pregnant women to have good health practices?

7–2 (continued)

CONTENT DEVELOPMENT

Point out to students that menopause refers to the time in females when ovulation no longer occurs and menstruation stops. Therefore, a female no longer can become pregnant. Menopause generally occurs during a woman's late forties and early fifties. Point out that among mammals, only human females undergo menopause.

ENRICHMENT

Explain that through medical and technological achievements, doctors have been able to reverse the effects of menopause, and through treatment, women who have experienced menopause can once again bear children. In 1991, a 52-year-old woman became pregnant after reversal of menopause and the use of in-vitro fertilization. Ask students to consider what problems the mother and child may face before birth and after birth as the child grows.

INDEPENDENT PRACTICE

Section Review 7–2

1. After fertilization, the zygote travels to the uterus and becomes implanted. It is called an embryo for the next 8 weeks or so. During this stage, the embryo grows to about the size of a walnut. After 8 weeks, the embryo becomes a fetus, which develops babylike features and gains weight. Between 3 and 6 months, the fetus forms a skeleton and develops a heartbeat. In the final 3 months, the fetus is prepared for

CONNECTIONS

Electronic Reproduction ❶

Have you ever wondered what it would be like to have several exact copies of yourself? One could go to class and do homework. One could do chores at home. One could spend the day playing—or perhaps you would let the real you do that. Well, dream on. By now, you know how complex the process of human reproduction really is and that there is only one "you" in the world. There will never be another.

Fortunately, the same is not true for photographs, illustrations, or the printed word. For today, modern photocopying machines can print out exact copies at the rate of hundreds per minute. Hundreds of copies per minute—now that's reproduction!

You might be surprised to learn that photocopying machines do not use ink. They rely instead on *electricity*, or the flow of charged particles called electrons. Inside the photocopy machine is a circular drum. The drum is charged with static electricity and is coated with a material that conducts electricity when exposed to light.

Let's say you want to make a copy of a page of this textbook. When you place the sheet of paper you want to copy on the machine, light shines onto it. The blank parts of the paper reflect the light and the light strikes the circular drum. Wherever the light strikes, the charge on the drum is removed. The dark parts of the paper (either words or visuals) do not reflect the light onto the drum. So the drum has parts that are charged and parts that have had the charge removed. When, in the next step, a liquid known as toner is introduced onto the drum, the toner is attracted to the charged parts only. The parts of the drum that are not charged do not attract toner. In seconds, the toner is laid down and an image is created on the photocopying machine paper.

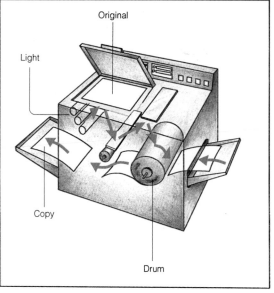

Original

Light

Copy

Drum

CONNECTIONS

ELECTRONIC REPRODUCTION

Students will be fascinated with the description of photocopiers and the comparison to human reproduction. You might ask students to explain how the results of human reproduction and photocopying differ. (Photocopiers provide an exact duplicate. Human reproduction results in a unique individual.) If you have a photocopying machine in the school, you might demonstrate its operation and describe its parts to the students.

If you are teaching thematically, you may want to use the Connections feature to reinforce the themes of energy, stability, and systems and interactions.

Integration: Use the Connections feature to integrate the physical science concept of electricity into your lesson.

---

independent life outside the mother as organs undergo a series of changes.
2. Infancy: Mental and muscular skills develop, increase in size; childhood: mental abilities increase, more muscular skills develop; adolescence: sex organs develop during puberty, growth spurt; adulthood: all body systems matured, aging begins after about 30 years.
3. Embryo; fetus.
4. To cushion and protect the developing baby; to provide nourishment, respiration, and means of eliminating wastes.

5. Puberty is the stage at which the sex organs and secondary sex characteristics develop.
6. The health practices of the mother directly affect the developing baby. To avoid possible damage to the developing baby, the mother must follow good health practices.

REINFORCEMENT/RETEACHING

Monitor students' responses to the Section Review questions. Review material based on students' responses to the questions.

CLOSURE

▶ *Review and Reinforcement Guide*
At this point have students complete Section 7–2 in the *Review and Reinforcement Guide*.

Laboratory Investigation

HOW MANY OFFSPRING?

BEFORE THE LAB

1. Be certain that you have an ample supply of graph paper and colored pencils, crayons, or magic markers for the investigation.
2. You may want to have resource books available in which students can locate information on gestation period, offspring, puberty, and life span for other animals.

PRE-LAB DISCUSSION

Have students read the complete laboratory procedure. Discuss the procedure by asking questions similar to the following:

• **What is the purpose of this laboratory investigation?** (To compare the length of gestation, number of offspring per birth, age of puberty, and life span of various mammals.)

• **Which of the animals listed has the shortest period of gestation?** (The opossum.)

• **Which of the mammals listed has the earliest age of puberty?** (The house mouse.)

• **Which of the mammals listed has the longest life span?** (The human.)

• **What would you suggest for the title of the first graph?** (Answers might include "The Gestation Periods of Mammals.")

• **In addition to the title, what other words should be shown on this graph?** (The axes should be labeled—for example, the horizontal axis might be labeled Type of mammal and include the names of the mammals; the vertical axis might be labeled Gestation period in days and include a range of numbers.)

TEACHING STRATEGY

1. Guide students through the procedure for setting up the first graph. You may want to have a sample graph (partially completed) on the chalkboard or on an overhead transparency.
2. Because the second graph will be easier to construct, encourage students to complete it on their own.

Laboratory Investigation

How Many Offspring?

Problem

How do the length of gestation, number of offspring per birth, age of puberty, and life span of various mammals compare?

Materials (per group)

> graph paper
> colored pencils

Procedure

1. Study the chart, which shows the length of gestation (pregnancy), the average number of offspring per birth, the average age of puberty, and the average life span of certain mammals.
2. Construct a bar graph that shows the length of gestation for each mammal.
3. Construct another bar graph that shows the average number of offspring of each mammal.
4. Construct a third bar graph that shows the life span of each mammal. Color the portion of the bar that shows the length of childhood, or time from birth to puberty.

Observations

1. Which of the mammals has the longest gestation period?
2. Which mammal has the largest number of offspring per birth?
3. Which of the mammals has the shortest life span?
4. Which mammal takes longer to reach puberty than Rhesus monkeys?

Analysis and Conclusions

1. What general conclusions can you draw after studying the graphs you have made?
2. If a mouse produces five litters per year, how many mice does the average female mouse produce in a lifetime?
3. Of all the mammals listed, which care for their young for the longest period of time after birth? Why do you think this is the case?
4. **On Your Own** Gather the same kinds of data for five additional mammals. Add these data to your existing graphs. How do the five new mammals compare with those provided in this investigation?

Mammal	Gestation Period (days)	Number of Offspring per Birth	Age at Puberty	Life Span (years)
Opossum	12	13	8 months	2
House mouse	20	6	2 months	3
Rabbit	30	4	4 months	5
Dog	61	7	7 months	15
Lion	108	3	2 years	23
Rhesus monkey	175	1	3 years	20
Human	280	1	13 years	74
Horse	330	1	1.5 years	25

DISCOVERY STRATEGIES

Discuss how the investigation relates to the chapter ideas by asking open questions similar to the following:

• **The opossum is a marsupial. Do you think this accounts for its short period of gestation?** (Accept all logical answers. Although the young of the opossum are born very small and immature, they remain in the mother's pouch until they are able to get about on their own—applying information, inferring.)

• **Why do you think some mammals bear only one offspring per birth?** (Accept all logical answers. Point out that the size of the infant at birth and the secondary sex characteristics of the mother are factors—inferring, relating information.)

• **Agree or disagree with this statement: The shorter the life span, the shorter the gestation period in mammals.** (Accept all answers. There does seem to be some correlation between gestation period and life span. Many mammals with shorter life spans seem to have shorter gestation

Summarizing Key Concepts

7–1 The Reproductive System

▲ The joining of a sperm, or male sex cell, and an egg, or female sex cell, is known as fertilization.

▲ Each sperm and egg contains 23 chromosomes, which pass on inherited characteristics from one generation of cells to the next.

▲ The male reproductive system includes two testes, which produce sperm and a hormone called testosterone. The female reproductive system includes two ovaries, which produce eggs and hormones.

▲ Located near each ovary is a Fallopian tube that leads to a hollow, muscular uterus. At the lower end of the uterus is a narrow cervix, which opens into the vagina, or birth canal.

▲ The monthly cycle of change that occurs in the female reproductive system is called the menstrual cycle.

▲ During the menstrual cycle, ovulation, or the release of an egg from an ovary, occurs. The lining of the uterus also thickens in preparation for the attachment of a fertilized egg. If fertilization does not take place, the egg and thickened lining of the uterus break down and pass out of the body. This process is called menstruation. If sperm are present in the Fallopian tube at the time of ovulation, an egg may become fertilized.

7–2 Stages of Development

▲ A fertilized egg is called a zygote. A zygote undergoes a series of divisions, forming a ball-shaped structure of many cells.

▲ During the first 8 weeks of its development, the developing human is called an embryo. It is surrounded and protected by several membranes. One of these membranes, called the placenta, provides the embryo with food and oxygen and eliminates its wastes. Another membrane forms around the fluid-filled amniotic sac, which cushions and protects the embryo.

▲ The umbilical cord, which contains blood vessels, connects the embryo to the placenta.

▲ During the birth process, the fetus and placenta pass out of the uterus through the cervix into the vagina.

▲ Humans pass through various stages of development during their lives. These stages are infancy, childhood, adolescence, and adulthood. Adolescence begins at puberty, when the sex organs develop rapidly.

Reviewing Key Terms

Define each term in a complete sentence.

7–1 The Reproductive System
sperm
egg
fertilization
testis
ovary
Fallopian tube
uterus
menstrual cycle
ovulation

7–2 Stages of Development
zygote
embryo
amniotic sac
placenta
fetus
umbilical cord
infancy
childhood
adolescence
puberty
adulthood

Part 1

If an animal were continuously pregnant and could bear young throughout its life span, what would be the maximum number of offspring that could be produced by a single female of each of the mammals listed. What conditions exist that normally reduce this potential number of offspring?

Part 2

A. Collect information on number of eggs laid and on life spans for various reptiles, amphibians, birds, or fishes. Which group of vertebrates seems to have the longest life spans? Why do amphibians and fishes lay larger numbers of eggs than birds and reptiles do?

B. Using a long piece of adding machine tape or shelf paper, construct a time line of average life spans for all the animals for which the class has collected data. Display the time line on a wall of the classroom.

Chapter Review

ALTERNATIVE ASSESSMENT

The *Prentice Hall Science* program includes a variety of testing components and methodologies. Aside from the Chapter Review questions, you may opt to use the Chapter Test or the Computer Test Bank Test in your *Test Book* for assessment of important facts and concepts. In addition, Performance-Based Tests are included in your *Test Book*. These Performance-Based Tests are designed to test science process skills, rather than factual content recall. Since they are not content dependent, Performance-Based Tests can be distributed after students complete a chapter or after they complete the entire textbook.

periods, but the generalization does not hold true for all mammals—generalizing, drawing conclusions.)

OBSERVATIONS

1. The horse
2. The opossum
3. The opossum
4. The human

ANALYSIS AND CONCLUSIONS

1. Generally, the longer the gestation period, the lower the number of offspring per birth. In some cases, the longer the life span, the longer the gestation period.
2. 90 offspring.
3. Humans, because they take the longest amount of time to reach puberty and need to be cared for longer.
4. Students should use reference resources to identify needed data for the additional mammals and then compare the information with their original data.

CONTENT REVIEW

Multiple Choice

1. c
2. a
3. d
4. b
5. b
6. b
7. a
8. b
9. c
10. c

True or False

1. T
2. T
3. F, Fallopian tubes
4. T
5. F, vagina
6. F, umbilical cord
7. F, a child

Concept Mapping

Row 1: Male
Row 2: Ovaries
Row 3: Testosterone, Sperm; Egg

CONCEPT MASTERY

1. A mature egg ripens and is released into a Fallopian tube during the process of ovulation. If the egg is not fertilized, the lining of the uterus, which has become thicker in preparation for fertilization, will break down. The blood and tissue from the thickened lining will pass out of the body through the vagina in a process known as menstruation. Menstruation usually lasts about 5 days. At the same time that menstruation is occurring, a new egg is maturing in the ovary so that the cycle may begin again.

2. The placenta provides the means of nourishment, respiration, and excretion for the fetus.

3. A zygote results from the penetration of a sperm into an egg within a Fallopian tube.

4. After about 9 months of development in the uterus, a baby is ready to be born. Birth begins with strong muscular contractions of the uterus. The contractions help to push the baby out of the uterus through the vagina. Eventually, the baby is forced out of the mother. Finally, the umbilical cord, which connected the baby to the placenta, is cut.

5. Doctors use both amniocentesis and sound waves to study fetuses inside the womb. Amniocentesis involves drawing off a small amount of amniotic fluid and studying the DNA for signs of inherited problems. Sound waves produce a moving image of the fetus on a television screen.

6. Infancy: mental and muscular skills develop, increase in size; childhood: mental abilities increase, more muscular skills develop; adolescence: sex organs develop during puberty, growth spurt; adulthood: all body systems matured, aging begins after about 30 years.

7. The process ensures the survival of the species.

Content Review

Multiple Choice

Choose the letter of the answer that best completes each statement.

1. What is the female sex cell called?
   a. testis   c. egg
   b. sperm   d. ovary

2. Sperm are produced in male sex organs called
   a. testes.   c. scrotums.
   b. ovaries.   d. urethras.

3. Sperm leave the male's body through the
   a. testes.   c. vagina.
   b. scrotum.   d. penis.

4. Eggs are produced in the
   a. scrotum.   c. cervix.
   b. ovaries.   d. Fallopian tubes.

5. A structure made up of tissues from both the embryo and the uterus is the
   a. ovum.   c. cervix.
   b. placenta.   d. fetus.

6. Another name for the womb is the
   a. Fallopian tube.   c. vagina.
   b. uterus.   d. scrotum.

7. The release of an egg from the ovary is known as
   a. ovulation.   c. menstruation.
   b. fertilization.   d. urination.

8. The structure in which a fertilized egg first divides is the
   a. ovary.   c. uterus.
   b. Fallopian tube.   d. vagina.

9. Sex organs develop rapidly during
   a. infancy.   c. puberty.
   b. childhood.   d. adulthood.

10. Adulthood begins at about the age of
    a. 13 years.   c. 20 years.
    b. 1 year.   d. 30 years.

True or False

If the statement is true, write "true." If it is false, change the underlined word or words to make the statement true.

1. The joining of a sperm and an egg is called <u>fertilization</u>.
2. The testes are found inside a sac called the <u>scrotum</u>.
3. To reach the uterus, an egg travels through the <u>cervix</u>.
4. An egg can be fertilized only while it is in a <u>Fallopian tube</u>.
5. If an egg is not fertilized, the lining of the uterus leaves the body through the <u>urethra</u>.
6. The structure that connects the embryo to the placenta is the <u>uterus</u>.
7. At 2 years of age, a person is considered to be an <u>infant</u>.

Concept Mapping

Complete the following concept map for Section 7–1. Refer to pages H8–H9 to construct a concept map for the entire chapter.

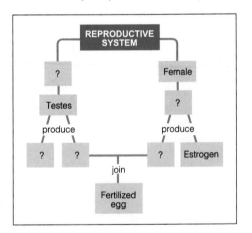

CRITICAL THINKING AND PROBLEM SOLVING

1. Both growth before birth and growth during adolescence occurs rapidly. Growth before birth, however, is much more rapid than growth during adolescence.

2. While in the womb, a developing baby depends on its mother for both food and oxygen. Even though mother and baby have separate circulatory systems, whatever the mother takes into her body can be transported through the placenta to

Concept Mastery

Discuss each of the following in a brief paragraph.

1. What changes occur in the female reproductive system during the menstrual cycle?
2. Describe how a fetus receives food and oxygen and how it gets rid of wastes.
3. How does a zygote form?
4. Describe the birth process.
5. Describe one method that is used by doctors to study babies while they are in the uterus.
6. Summarize the four stages of human development after birth.
7. Why is the process of reproduction so important?

Critical Thinking and Problem Solving

Use the skills you have developed in this chapter to answer each of the following.

1. **Making comparisons** In what way is development during adolescence similar to development before birth?
2. **Relating cause and effect** Why is it dangerous for pregnant women to smoke, drink, or use drugs not prescribed by a doctor?
3. **Relating facts** Why do you think the first stage in the birth process is called labor?
4. **Making inferences** The word adolescence means to grow up. Why is adolescence a good name for the teenage years of life?
5. **Applying concepts** Explain why a proper diet and an adequate amount of exercise can lessen the effects of aging.
6. **Drawing conclusions** Why do broken bones heal more rapidly in young children than in elderly people?
7. **Making comparisons** In what way is amniotic fluid similar to the shock absorbers of a car?
8. **Making predictions** Explain how a child's environment can affect its development.
9. **Relating facts** Explain how the shape of a sperm helps it function.
10. **Relating concepts** Why do you think a 1- to 2-year-old child is called a toddler?

11. **Making graphs** Use the information in the table to construct a graph. What conclusions can you draw from the graph?

Age Group in Years	Average Height in Centimeters	
	Female	Male
At birth	50	51
2	87	88
4	103	104
6	117	118
8	128	128
10	139	139
12	152	149
14	160	162
16	163	172
18	163	174

12. **Using the writing process** Develop an advertising campaign highlighting the dangers of alcohol and drug use during pregnancy.

anist if given piano lessons and exposure to music and musicians throughout childhood.

9. Tail helps it swim. Small size enables it to move more rapidly than if it were large.

10. *Toddle* means "walking slowly and unsteadily." Because a 1- to 2-year-old child is just learning to walk, he or she is unsteady, hence the name toddler.

11. From their graphs, students should be able to conclude that males tend to be larger than females, that growth tends to slow in females at an earlier age than in males, and that the largest growth spurt in both males and females occurs between the ages of 2 and 4.

12. Campaigns will vary in terms of emphasis and media but should concentrate on the harmful effects of alcohol and drug use on both the parent and the developing baby.

KEEPING A PORTFOLIO

You might want to assign some of the Concept Mastery and Critical Thinking and Problem Solving questions as homework and have students include their responses to unassigned questions in their portfolio. Students should be encouraged to include both the question and the answer in their portfolio.

ISSUES IN SCIENCE

The following issue can be used as a springboard for class debate or given as a writing assignment:

Imagine that a new wonder drug called "Forever Young" has been produced. It delays the aging process and lengthens life expectancy to 200 years. The drug has no known side effects. Would you be in favor of making such a drug available to the general population? What if it worked only for females or only for males? What if it worked only if taken before the age of 12? What if only a limited supply of the drug were available?

the developing baby.

3. The body of the mother must work very hard to help the baby move from the uterus to the outside world.

4. Adolescence is the period in a person's life in which he or she usually grows up, or begins to assume more responsibilities.

5. If a person takes proper care of his or her body throughout life by exercising and eating correctly, he or she is less likely to develop chronic diseases associated with aging.

6. Because they are in the process of growing, children will experience quicker healing of bones. In addition, the bones of elderly people tend to become brittle and so heal very slowly.

7. Just as the shock absorbers of a car cushion the car against jolts and bumps, amniotic fluid cushions a fetus in its mother's womb.

8. Answers will vary. One example is that a child may become obese if he or she grows up in a family that consistently overeats. Or a child may become a pi-

Chapter 8 IMMUNE SYSTEM

SECTION	LABORATORY INVESTIGATIONS AND DEMONSTRATIONS
8–1 Body Defenses pages H192–H197	**Laboratory Manual** A Model for Disease Transmission **Teacher Edition** What's in Air?, p. H190d
8–2 Immunity pages H197–H202	
8–3 Diseases pages H203–H209	**Student Edition** Observing the Action of Alcohol on Microorganisms, p. H210 **Laboratory Manual** Relating Chronic Disorders and Nutrition **Teacher Edition** Trends in Death Rates, p. H190d
Chapter Review pages H210–H213	

*All materials in the Chapter Planning Guide Grid are available as part of the Prentice Hall Science Learning System.

OUTSIDE TEACHER RESOURCES

Books

Clarke, Loren K., and Malcolm Potts. *The AIDS Reader,* Branden.

Edelson, Edward. *The Immune System,* Chelsea House Publishers.

Fine, Judylaine. *Afraid to Ask,* Lothrop, Lee & Shepard.

Metos, Thomas H. *Communicable Diseases,* Franklin Watts.

Nilsson, Lennart. *The Body Victorious,* Delacorte Press.

Nourse, Alan E. *Your Immune System,* Franklin Watts.

Silverstein, Alvin, and Virginia B. Silverstein. *The Sugar Disease: Diabetes,* Lippincott.

Stedman, Nancy. *The Common Cold and Influenza,* Julian Messner.

Audiovisuals

AIDS: Everything You Should Know, film or video, AIMS Media

Allergies: Nothing to Sneeze At, video or two sound filmstrips, American School Publishers

Bacteria and Health, film or video, AIMS Media

The Immune System, two sound filmstrips, American School Publishers

OTHER ACTIVITIES	MULTIMEDIA
Activity Book 　Chapter Discovery: Antigens and Antibodies 　ACTIVITY: Animal Disease Carriers **Student Edition** 　Find Out by Writing: Antiseptics and Disinfectants, p. H194 **Review and Reinforcement Guide** 　Section 8–1	**Courseware** 　Body Defenses (Supplemental) **English/Spanish Audiotapes** 　Section 8–1
Activity Book 　ACTIVITY: AIDS. 　ACTIVITY: The Distribution of Disease **Student Edition** 　Find Out by Writing: Vaccines, p. H198 　Find Out by Doing: How Antibodies Work, p. H199 **Review and Reinforcement Guide** 　Section 8–2	**English/Spanish Audiotapes** 　Section 8–2
Activity Book 　ACTIVITY: Call on the Experts in Infectious Diseases 　ACTIVITY: Complete-A-Disease 　ACTIVITY: Chronic Disorders **Review and Reinforcement Guide** 　Section 8–3	**Courseware** 　Agents of Infection (Supplemental) **English/Spanish Audiotapes** 　Section 8–3
Test Book 　Chapter Test 　Performance-Based Tests	**Test Book** 　Computer Test Bank Test

Infectious Disease: Causes and Defenses, three
　sound filmstrips or three videocassettes,
　EBE
Your Immune System, filmstrips with
　cassettes, National Geographic

Chapter 8 IMMUNE SYSTEM

CHAPTER OVERVIEW

The immune system is the body's defense against disease-causing organisms. It can recognize and destroy invaders without hurting the body's tissues. The body has three lines of defense. The first line includes the skin, the mucus and cilia in the respiratory tract, and the saliva in the mouth.

The second line of defense is the inflammatory response. When organisms attack body cells, the body increases the blood supply to the area, causing white blood cells to attack the organisms and destroy them. The body also uses interferon, a substance that "interferes" with the reproduction of viruses.

Antibodies are the third line of defense. They are proteins produced by the immune system in response to particular organisms, or antigens. Special white blood cells called T-cells alert other special cells called B-cells to start producing the appropriate antibodies. If the antibody has been produced before, it can quickly be produced again, but if the invader is a new antigen, it can take a while for the antibodies to be produced.

In active immunity, the needed antibodies are produced by the person's body, either naturally or through vaccination—a deliberate introduction of the antigen to stimulate the body's immune system. In passive immunity, the antibodies are produced in another person's body or in an animal's body. Immune disorders include allergies, which occur when the immune system becomes overly sensitive to foreign substances, and AIDS, which is caused by a virus that cripples the immune system, leaving the body vulnerable to disease-causing organisms.

Infectious diseases are caused by bacteria, viruses, protozoans, and fungi. We usually call these microorganisms germs. Infectious diseases can be transmitted, or spread, usually through contact with a sick person. Infectious diseases include colds, flu, measles, mumps, tuberculosis, gonorrhea, syphilis, Lyme disease, Rocky Mountain spotted fever, rabies, hepatitis, cholera, typhoid, mononucleosis, and tetanus. Noninfectious diseases are not caused by microorganisms. Today, they include some of our most deadly diseases, such as cardiovascular diseases, cancer, and diabetes mellitus.

8–1 BODY DEFENSES
THEMATIC FOCUS

The purpose of this section is to introduce students to the body's three lines of defense against disease-causing organisms. Students will learn that the first line includes the skin, mucous membranes, and cilia. These form a barrier between the body and its surroundings. Students will then be introduced to the immune system, which consists of special cells and tissues that help to resist invading organisms once they enter the body. The second line of defense, the white blood cells, attack and attempt to destroy all invaders. The third line, the antibodies, fight specific invaders, or antigens.

The themes that can be focused on in this section are energy, scale and structure, systems and interactions, and unity and diversity.

*Energy: Point out to students that in order for the body's immune system to work to defend the body against disease-causing organisms, the body must have a sufficient supply of energy to fuel the activities of its cells.

*Scale and structure: Discuss the idea that the body's three lines of defense against disease are (1) the skin, mucus, and cilia; (2) special white blood cells; and (3) antibodies. Point out that the first and second lines of defense are general, whereas the third line is specific.

*Systems and interactions: Stress that the body's three lines of defense—the immune system and the structures that help it—protect the body by attacking and destroying organisms that may harm it.

Unity and diversity: Empahsize that although the structures that make up the body's lines of defense are different, they all work together for a common goal: to protect the body against invaders.

PERFORMANCE OBJECTIVES 8–1
1. **Describe the function of the body's immune system.**
2. **Explain how the body's three lines of defense fight disease-causing organisms.**

SCIENCE TERMS 8–1
inflammatory response p. H195
interferon p. H195
antibody p. H195
antigen p. H195

8–2 IMMUNITY
THEMATIC FOCUS

The purpose of this section is to introduce students to the concept of immunity, or the body's resistance to disease. They will learn about active immunity, in which the body produces its own antibodies. Active immunity includes the process of vaccination. The antigens in the vaccines are weakened or chemically developed. When injected into the body, the body develops antibodies against the disease, just as it would if it had gotten the disease naturally. Students will learn that passive immunity occurs when the antibodies come from some source other than the person's body. They will discover that the immune system can malfunction by becoming overly sensitive to foreign substances, as in the case of allergies, or by being fooled and then destroyed by invaders, as in the case of AIDS.

The themes that can be focused on in this section are systems and interactions, unity and diversity, and stability.

*Systems and interactions: The process of vaccination was developed to take advantage of the way the body produces antibodies. Deliberately introducing the antigen causes the body to respond by producing antibodies, just as it would if the antigen had occurred naturally.

Unity and diversity: Point out that there are two types of immunity: active and passive. In active immunity, the person's own immune system produces antibodies in response to the presence of an antigen. In passive immunity, the person gets antibodies from another source.

*Stability: Stress that the body's immune system—that is, its ability to develop and maintain immunity—helps to maintain homeostasis by destroying foreign invaders.

PERFORMANCE OBJECTIVES 8–2
1. Compare active and passive immunity.
2. Describe how a vaccine prevents disease.

SCIENCE TERMS 8–2
immunity p. H197
active immunity p. H198
vaccination p. H198
passive immunity p. H199
allergy p. H200
AIDS p. H201

8–3 DISEASES
THEMATIC FOCUS

The purpose of this section is to compare infectious and noninfectious diseases. Students will learn that infectious diseases are caused by microorganisms such as bacteria and viruses. They will find out how viruses and bacteria attack body cells. Infectious diseases can be transmitted from person to person through coughing or sneezing; contact with a diseased person or animal; or contaminated food, water, or objects. Students will discover that noninfectious diseases are not caused by microorganisms, and because of vaccines and other medications that deal with infectious diseases, noninfectious diseases are becoming the major cause of death. Two of the most serious of these diseases are cancer and dia-

betes mellitus. Students will learn about the causes and treatments of these two diseases.

The themes that can be focused on in this section are patterns of change and unity and diversity.

Patterns of change: It is important to note that modern medicine has been successful in combating infectious diseases with vaccines and drugs, thereby prolonging people's lives. Now people suffer more from noninfectious diseases, with cardiovascular diseases and cancer being the two leading causes of death.

Unity and diversity: Point out that although there are many infectious diseases with different symptoms, causes, and ways of spreading, all infectious diseases are caused by microorganisms and can be transmitted or spread through the population.

PERFORMANCE OBJECTIVES 8–3
1. Compare infectious and noninfectious diseases.
2. List examples of infectious diseases and discuss what causes them and how they spread.
3. Explain the causes and treatments of two noninfectious diseases.

SCIENCE TERMS 8–3
infectious disease p. H203
noninfectious disease p. H206
cancer p. H206
diabetes mellitus p. H208

Discovery Learning

TEACHER DEMONSTRATIONS MODELING

What's in Air?
Put a stopper in a clear glass bottle. Show the bottle to the class.
• **What do you observe in the bottle?** (Accept all logical answers. Most students are likely to say "nothing.")
Remove the stopper and then replace it.
• **What is in the bottle now?** (Accept all logical answers. Most students are likely to say "air from the room.")

• **What is in the air in the bottle?** (Accept all logical answers.)
Remind students that although air is invisible, it carries many tiny particles, such as dust, pollen grains, and many microorganisms.
• **What might happen if the air in this bottle were emptied into a hospital operating room?** (Accept all logical answers.)

Trends in Death Rates
Display a graph showing the changes in death rates from diseases. Such a graph may be obtained from encyclopedias, health service publications, and textbooks. Alternatively, you may wish to construct a hypothetical graph that shows that the death rate from infectious diseases has dropped gradually during this century, whereas the death rate from noninfectious diseases such as cancer is gradually increasing.
• **What is the title of this graph?** (Answers will vary, depending on the graph.)
• **What happens to the death rate from infectious diseases as you go from 1900 to the present?** (Decreases.)
• **What happens to the death rate from noninfectious diseases?** (Increases.)
• **What are some examples of noninfectious diseases?** (Accept all logical answers.)
Explain that noninfectious diseases, unlike infectious diseases, cannot be transmitted from one individual to another. Point out that noninfectious diseases are generally lingering and longer lasting than infectious diseases.
• **Why has the death rate from noninfectious diseases increased?** (Accept all logical answers. Lead students to suggest that people are living longer because of advances in medical treatment and that noninfectious diseases are often associated with aging.)

CHAPTER 8
Immune System

INTEGRATING SCIENCE

This life science chapter provides you with numerous opportunities to integrate other areas of science, as well as other disciplines, into your curriculum. Blue numbered annotations on the student page and integration notes on the teacher wraparound pages alert you to areas of possible integration.

In this chapter you can integrate language arts (pp. 194, 198), life science and monerans (p. 196), life science and microbiology (p. 203), life science and cell biology (p. 206), and life science and ecology (p. 209).

SCIENCE, TECHNOLOGY, AND SOCIETY/COOPERATIVE LEARNING

AIDS, a disease unknown until the 1980s, has become one of the deadliest diseases in human history. As researchers determine the genetic structure and the method of attack of the HIV virus, they hope to produce an effective vaccine against AIDS and to identify strategies for treating this deadly disease.

Because of the unique characteristics of the AIDS virus, scientists were not sure that the human immune system—even with the help of a vaccine—could successfully defend itself against the disease. People infected with the HIV virus did produce antibodies; nevertheless, they almost all became sick. Now scientists optimistically predict the development of an AIDS vaccine by the year 2000. These predictions are based on results from tests in which animals were protected from infection by viral relatives of the HIV virus. Scientists have identified parts of the HIV virus that are common to most strains and that could be used to produce an immune response.

Scientists are looking at several different AIDS vaccine strategies. One approach would use inoculation with killed AIDS virus. Using killed virus would eliminate the risk of infection, but the presence of all parts of the virus should stimulate the immune system to produce antibodies. The drawback is that the killed virus may not produce a full range of immune

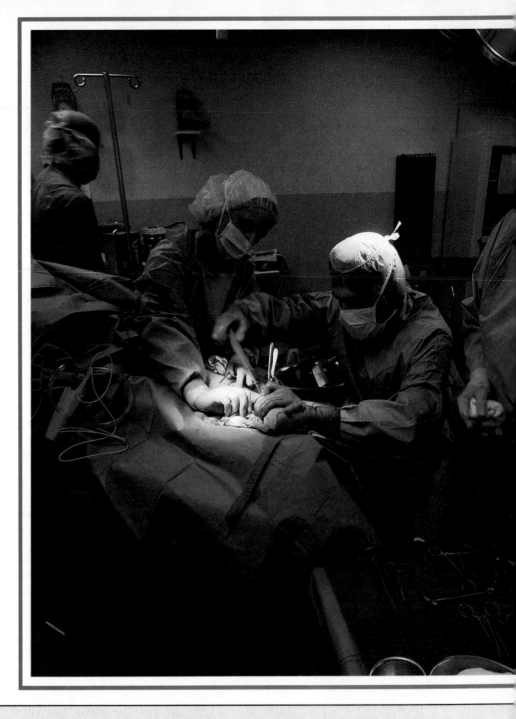

INTRODUCING CHAPTER 8

DISCOVERY LEARNING
▶ *Activity Book*
Begin teaching the chapter by using the Chapter 8 Discovery Activity from the *Activity Book*. Using this activity, students will learn about the relationship between antigens and antibodies.

USING THE TEXTBOOK

Have students look at the photograph on page H190.
• **What is happening in the picture?** (Surgeons are operating on a patient.)
• **How can you tell that these people are in an operating room?** (Students might suggest that they see medical instruments, the people are wearing masks and gowns, and so forth.)

Immune System

Guide for Reading

After you read the following sections, you will be able to

8–1 Body Defenses
- Describe the function of the immune system.
- Describe the body's three lines of defense against invading organisms.
- Define antibody and antigen.

8–2 Immunity
- Define immunity.
- Compare active and passive immunity.
- Describe how vaccines work.

8–3 Diseases
- Define disease.
- Describe how diseases spread.
- List some examples of infectious and noninfectious diseases.

The scene: a dimly lit room. Occupying the middle of the room is a rectangular table covered with large soiled cloths. A patient ready for surgery lies on the table. The operation is about to begin.

But wait! Why is the patient lying on dirty cloths? Why are the surgeons wiping their hands (and on soiled cloths!) instead of washing them? Is this a scene from a horror movie?

What you are reading about actually occurred in hospital operating rooms before the middle of the 1800s. Fortunately, such scenes no longer take place. And we have the work of the English surgeon Joseph Lister to thank for that! In 1865, Lister demonstrated that microorganisms were the cause of many deaths after surgery. Thus Lister reasoned that if the microorganisms could be kept away from surgical wounds many more patients would survive surgery.

Today, surgeons wash thoroughly before an operation and wear surgical gowns, masks, and gloves. And operating rooms are kept spotlessly clean and free of germs. As you read the pages that follow, you will learn some interesting things about microorganisms and disease. And you may even make a discovery as important as Lister's!

Journal *Activity*

You and Your World Have you ever had a sore throat? How about an upset stomach? A fever? How did you feel? What did you do? In your journal, explore your thoughts and feelings during these times.

◀ *Today, operations are performed in spotlessly clean operating rooms by surgical teams wearing gowns, gloves, and masks.*

H ■ 191

- **Why are the doctors wearing masks and gowns?** (Accept all logical answers. Students will probably suggest that the masks and gowns are for reasons of cleanliness.)
- **Why would doctors worry about cleanliness during an operation?** (Accept all logical answers. Lead students to the idea that doctors don't want germs to enter the patient's body during the operation.)

Have students read the chapter introduction on page H191.

- **Were you surprised to find out that a connection was made between microorganisms (germs) and disease only about 150 years ago?** (Encourage students to offer their opinions.)
- **How do you think Lister made the connection between microorganisms and infections?** (Accept all logical answers. Suggest that students consider the scientific method as a clue.)

---

responses because some immune activity occurs in response to cells infected with the virus.

The use of a weakened virus as a vaccine is common with many other types of diseases. The weakened virus cannot cause serious disease but does cause a full-scale response from the immune system. This strategy is considered much too risky for the AIDS virus because even the weakened virus may alter itself into a potentially lethal form.

A third strategy involves the injection of only a portion of the AIDS virus as a vaccine. Using either protein from the coat of the virus or proteins found inside the AIDS virus could result in the production of antibodies that would attack the entire virus. There would be no risk of infection because the protein coat does not contain the RNA required for viral replication. Genetic engineering techniques could provide large quantities of both the protein coat and interior proteins for use as a vaccine.

Cooperative learning: Using preassigned or randomly selected groups, have them complete one of these assignments:
- Brainstorm ways in which AIDS has affected our society socially, politically, and economically. Compare the impact on society of other diseases, such as bubonic plague, with that of AIDS.
- Consider the following scenario: Researchers have announced the development and successful testing of an AIDS vaccine. This vaccine would provide active immunity, but the length of immunity and the frequency of booster shots are unknown. Legislators are debating this question. Should the AIDS vaccine be required for every American? Groups should compose a letter to their congressional representative that states their position on this issue.

See Cooperative Learning in the *Teacher's Desk Reference.*

JOURNAL ACTIVITY

You may want to use the Journal Activity as the basis for a class discussion. Encourage students to share their journal entries with the class and compare their thoughts and feelings during illnesses. Students should be instructed to keep their Journal Activity in their portfolio.

8-1 Body Defenses

MULTICULTURAL
OPPORTUNITY 8-1

To better help students understand the immune system, you might make an analogy between the body's immunity from disease and our attempts to protect ourselves from crime. What are some of our defenses? For example, we live in houses that can be secured with locks (perhaps analogous to the skin), and our cities are patrolled by police (similar to white blood cells).

ESL STRATEGY 8-1

Ask students to remember when they have had a cut or a scrape, a bad cold, or a stomach virus. Have them describe the injury or illness and explain how the three lines of defense of their body's immune system went to work to help fight the infection.

When discussing active immunity, explain to students who may be newcomers to this country that their defense systems will require time to adjust to microorganisms that may be foreign to them. Therefore, all the vaccinations they must endure are doubly important to ensure a healthy start in their new homeland.

TEACHING STRATEGY 8-1

FOCUS/MOTIVATION

Have students look at Figure 8-2. Point out that the green objects are bacteria on the surface of the skin.
• **What do you predict normally happens to bacteria on the skin surface?** (Accept all logical answers.)
• **If there were an open cut on the skin, what do you predict the bacteria would do?** (Most students will say enter the body through the cut area.)
• **How would you predict the skin helps keep bacteria out of the body?** (Accept all logical answers.)

CONTENT DEVELOPMENT

Point out that the skin is the "first line" of defense against bacteria entering the

Guide for Reading

Focus on these questions as you read.
▶ *What is the function of the immune system?*
▶ *What are the body's three lines of defense against invading organisms?*

Figure 8–1 *Every minute of every day fierce battles are fought within your body. The invaders in these battles—such as influenza viruses (left) and the flatworm that causes the disease known as schistosomiasis (right)—are incredibly tiny. What body system defends against disease-causing organisms?* ❶

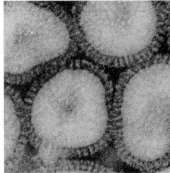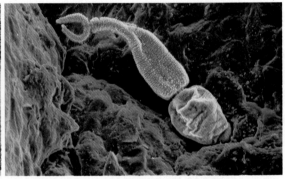

192 ■ H

8-1 Body Defenses

Considering the number of entries that invaders can successfully make into the body, it is amazing that a disease rarely occurs. Amazing, but no accident. Almost every human has a body system that works 24 hours a day all over the body to ensure its health. This body system is the immune system. **The immune system is the body's defense against disease-causing organisms.** The immune system not only repels disease-causing organisms, it also "keeps house" inside the body. It does this by removing dead or damaged cells and by looking for and destroying cells that do not function as they should.

The immune system has the remarkable ability to distinguish friend from foe. It identifies and destroys invaders and, at the same time, recognizes the body's own tissues. How does the immune system do all this? If you continue reading, you will find the answer.

The Body's First Line of Defense

Your body has certain important structures that help the immune system, although they are not actually part of it. Most invaders must first encounter these structures. These structures make up your body's first line of defense, forming a barrier between the body and its surroundings. The skin and the substances it produces, as well as protective reflexes such as sneezing and coughing, make up the first line of defense.

---

body. Explain that normally when bacteria lay on the skin surface, they are washed off with soap and water.

Point out that most bacteria cannot enter the body through the skin. Remind students that both viruses and bacteria can enter the body by droplets in the air.
• **What defense do you think the body has against breathing in bacteria?** (Accept all logical answers.)

Explain that mucous membranes and cilia are also part of the first line of defense against bacteria that are in the form

of droplets in the air. The nose, mouth, and respiratory system are lined with a sticky substance called mucus. Point out that mucus helps to trap organisms such as bacteria and prevents them from traveling farther into the body.

Explain that there are also tiny hairs in the nose, throat, and airways to the lungs that prevent bacteria, dirt, and any excess mucus from getting into the breathing tubes and lungs. These tiny hairs are called cilia.

As you may recall from Chapter 5, the skin forms a protective covering over most of the body. This extraordinary organ has the ability to produce new cells and repair itself. Despite its daily dose of ripping, scratching, burning, and exposure to harsh chemicals and weather, the skin still performs admirably. It continues to produce new cells in its outer layer (epidermis) and repair tears in its inner layer (dermis). When cuts occur in the skin, however, they provide a means of entry for disease-causing organisms. What results is an infection, or a successful invasion into the body by disease-causing organisms.

Not all disease-causing organisms enter the body through the skin, however. Some are inhaled from the air. In much the same way as the skin defends the entire body against invaders, mucus (MYOO-kuhs) and cilia (SIHL-ee-uh) defend the respiratory system against airborne organisms. Mucus is a sticky substance that coats the membranes of the nose, trachea, and bronchi (parts of the respiratory system). As organisms enter these structures along with incoming air, they are trapped by the mucus and are thus prevented from traveling any farther into the body. In addition to mucus, the membranes are lined with tiny hairlike structures called cilia. The cilia, acting like brooms, sweep bacteria, dirt, and excess mucus out of the air passages at an amazing rate—about 2.5 centimeters a minute! These unwanted materials are carried to the throat, where they can be coughed out or swallowed.

Sometimes disease-causing organisms enter the body through the mouth, rather than through the skin or the nose. Here they mix with saliva, which is loaded with invader-killing chemicals. Most invaders do not survive the action of these chemicals. Those that do soon find themselves encountering a powerful acid in the stomach. This acid is so strong that it destroys the invaders. The dead invaders are eliminated from the body along with the body's other wastes.

Figure 8–3 *As disease-causing organisms invade the body through the respiratory system, they are trapped by excess mucus that coats the membranes of the bronchus (top). The membranes are also lined with hairlike cilia that sweep the organisms out of the respiratory system (bottom).*

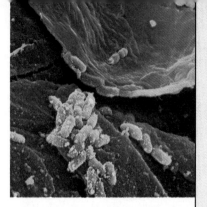

Figure 8–2 *The green objects in this photograph of the surface of the skin are bacteria. The skin is one of the body's first lines of defense against invading organisms.*

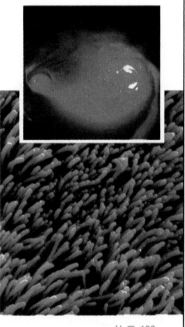

H ■ 193

HISTORICAL NOTE
THE SPREAD OF DISEASE

Prior to the discovery of microorganisms and their role in spreading disease, people believed that disease was spread by magic, evil spirits, or miasmas—supposedly poisonous vapors that arose from swamps. People got sick, it was thought, because they were cursed or had bad luck. The work of French chemist Louis Pasteur and German bacteriologist Robert Koch in the mid-nineteenth century established the germ theory of infectious disease: Diseases are caused by microorganisms, certain microorganisms cause certain diseases, and killing those microorganisms stops the spread of disease.

Pasteur's and Koch's discoveries inspired Joseph Lister, an English surgeon, who concluded that bacteria were responsible for the post-surgical infections that killed 50 percent of all surgical patients. He introduced antiseptic surgery in 1865 by using carbolic acid to sterilize surgical cuts and instruments. Later, antiseptic surgery, in which doctors focused on getting rid of the germs that were already present, gave way to aseptic surgery, in which doctors concentrate on keeping germs away in the first place by thorough washing and the use of gloves, gowns, and masks.

---

*Antiseptics
and Disinfectants*

Find out the following information about antiseptics and disinfectants by using reference materials in the library. What is the function of these substances? How do they help to control disease? What are three examples of each substance? Arrange this information in the form of a written report. Include the work of Joseph Lister and any other scientists who contributed to the discovery of these substances.

The Body's Second Line of Defense

If the first line of defense fails and disease-causing organisms enter the body, the second line of defense goes into action. When disease-causing organisms such as bacteria enter through a cut in the skin, they immediately try to attack body cells. The body, however, is quick to respond by increasing the blood supply to the affected area. This action causes white blood cells, which constantly patrol the blood and defend the body against disease-causing organisms, to leave the blood vessels and move into nearby tissues. Once inside, some of the white blood cells—the tiny ones—attack the invading organisms and then gobble them up.

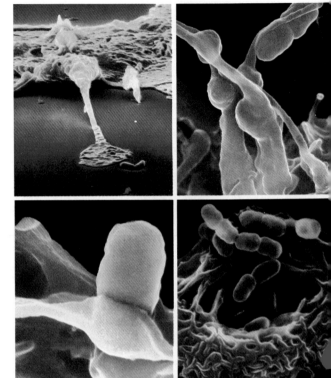

Figure 8–4 *White blood cells make up the body's second line of defense. This sequence of photographs shows what happens when a white blood cell encounters bacteria. The white blood cell first reaches out toward two bacterial cells (top left). Extensions from the white blood cell trap the bacteria (top right). Chemicals produced by the white blood cells begin to digest one of the bacterial cells (bottom left). Eventually, the bacteria will be digested and the material of which they are made will be absorbed by the white blood cells (bottom right).*

194 ■ H

8–1 (continued)

CONTENT DEVELOPMENT

Tell students that if the first line of defense fails to stop a bacterium or a virus from entering the body, a second line of defense starts. Explain that the second line of defense is part of the immune system.

Point out that the immune system consists of special cells and tissues that help to fight invading organisms after they have entered the body.

• **What is immunity?** (The ability to fight off disease.)

GUIDED PRACTICE

Skills Development

Skill: Interpreting illustrations

Have students look at Figure 8–4. Point out that the white shape at the top of the first photograph is a white blood cell. The green rods are bacteria. Have students focus on the top-right photograph showing the white blood cell trapping the bacteria.

• **What does the white blood cell appear to be doing?** (Accept all logical answers.

Lead students to suggest that the white blood cell is "gathering" in the bacteria.)

Have students look at the bottom-left photograph.

• **What appears to be happening to the bacteria in this photograph?** (Most students will say that the bacteria are being "swallowed up" by the white blood cell.)

• **What do you predict the white blood cell will do with the bacteria now?** (Accept all logical answers. Lead students to suggest that the white blood cell will kill the bacteria.)

Soon after, the tiny white blood cells are joined by reinforcements—larger white blood cells. The larger white blood cells, which are similar to the heavy artillery used by an attacking army, destroy almost all bacteria they attack. In time, the area resembles a battlefield. Dead bacteria and the dead and wounded white blood cells are everywhere. Taken together, these events form the body's second line of defense—the **inflammatory** (ihn-FLAM-uh-tor-ee) **response.** Sometimes an infection (a successful invasion into the body by disease-causing organisms) causes a red, swollen area to develop just below the skin's surface. If you were to touch the infected area, you would discover that it is hotter than the surrounding skin area. For this reason, the area is said to be inflamed, which actually means "on fire."

In addition to the inflammatory response, the body has another second line of defense called **interferon.** Interferon is a substance produced by body cells when they are attacked by viruses. Interferon "interferes" with the reproduction of new viruses. As a result, the rate at which body cells are infected is slowed down. Other lines of defense have the time to move in and destroy the viruses.

The Third Line of Defense

Although most disease-causing invaders are stopped by the body's first and second lines of defense, a few invaders are able to make it past them. If this happens, it is time for the body's third line of defense—the **antibodies**—to go to work. Antibodies are proteins produced by the immune system. Some antibodies are attached to certain kinds of white blood cells. Others are found floating freely in the blood. But regardless of their type, all antibodies are responsible for destroying harmful invaders.

Unlike the body's first two lines of defense, which you just read about, antibodies are very specific—they attack only a particular kind of invader. Thus, they can be thought of as the body's guided missiles, zeroing in on and destroying a particular target. The invading organism or substance that triggers the action of an antibody is called an **antigen.** The word antigen is derived from the term *anti*body *gene*rator, which means producer of antibodies.

Figure 8–5 *Although having a fever is no fun, there is a good reason for it. A fever, if mild and short-lived, helps the body fight disease-causing organisms.*

H ■ 195

BACKGROUND INFORMATION
INFLAMMATION

The inflammatory response is a series of interrelated events that destroy invading disease-causing microorganisms and restore tissues and cell conditions to normal. The events that characterize inflammation are summarized below:

1. In damaged or invaded tissues, capillaries dilate and become more permeable, causing the skin to become warm and red.

2. Seepage from blood vessels causes swelling.

3. Seepage also brings in infection-fighting proteins.

4. White blood cells are drawn by the release of chemicals.

5. White blood cells engulf and destroy microorganisms.

6. Tissues are repaired by such mechanisms as clotting.

Have students look at the bottom-right photograph. Point out that the chemicals inside the white blood cell will break down and destroy the bacteria.

FOCUS/MOTIVATION

Tell students to imagine that they have a cut on their knee or a sprained ankle.
• **What does the area around the injury look like?** (Red and swollen.)
• **How does it feel?** (It is generally tender and hot to the touch; it hurts.)

CONTENT DEVELOPMENT

Explain to students that when bacteria invade the body and attack its cells, the body responds quickly. An increased blood supply is sent to the infected area, causing it to appear red and swollen. This is called the inflammatory response; that is, the body produces an inflammation. The increase in blood supply causes an increase in body temperature, or fever. Fever actually helps your body fight disease-causing organisms by slowing down or killing bacteria. It is also a signal that disease-causing organisms are at work in the body; it provides a warning that something is wrong.

ENRICHMENT

▶ *Activity Book*

Students will be challenged by investigating the animals that carry infectious diseases. Have them complete the chapter activity called Animal Disease Carriers.

BACKGROUND INFORMATION

ANTIBODIES AND ORGAN TRANSPLANTS

Antibodies are produced in response to organ transplants from other individuals. The transplanted organ represents a foreign invader; the body's natural reaction is to try to destroy it. Patients who receive transplants are generally given drugs and/or radiation to help prevent rejection. Unfortunately, these treatments also hinder the immune system from destroying other invaders. Thus, the body's resistance to other diseases is lowered, and the patient may die from a complication such as pneumonia.

8–1 (continued)

CONTENT DEVELOPMENT

Point out that because skin, cilia, mucous membranes, and white blood cells attack any incoming organism, they are called nonspecific lines of defense. Explain that once in a while an invader is too tough for the white blood cells to conquer. Then a specific attacker called an antibody is needed. Antibodies are the body's third line of defense. They are specialized proteins developed by certain white blood cells, and they constitute a specific line of defense. Different antibodies are produced in response to different invaders, called antigens. Each antibody will attack only one kind of antigen. For

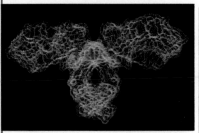

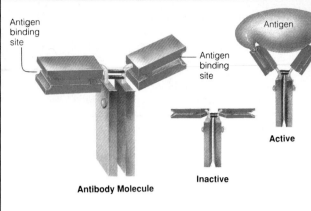

Figure 8–6 *Antibodies, such as the one in the computer-generated photograph, are proteins produced by the immune system. As the diagram illustrates, an antibody particle has two identical antigen-binding sites. What happens to the shape of an antibody particle when it encounters its specific antigen?* 1️⃣

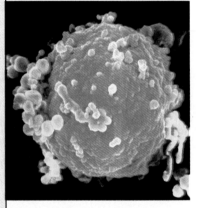

196 ■ H

What does an antibody look like? If you look at Figure 8–6, you can get a pretty good idea. Notice that the shape of an antibody is much like the letter T. When an antibody encounters its specific antigen, it changes shape—converting from a T shape to a Y shape. This action activates the antibody so that the two arms of the Y attach and bind to the antigen. In this way, an antibody prevents invaders such as viruses from attaching to cells.

When antibodies attach to surfaces of antigens such as bacteria, fungi, and protozoans, they slow down these organisms so that they can be gobbled up by white blood cells. Some antibodies may even destroy invaders by blasting a hole in the outer covering of the invaders' cells.

How does the immune system produce specific antibodies? How do the antibodies bind to antigens? The answers involve special white blood cells called T-cells and B-cells. (The T in T-cells stands for thymus, which is where T-cells originate; the B in B-cells refers to the bone marrow, which is where B-cells mature.) The function of T-cells is to alert B-cells to produce antibodies. If this is the first time the body is invaded by a particular antigen, it may take the B-cells a longer time to produce antibodies. During

Figure 8–7 *This photograph shows a B-cell covered with bacteria. B-cells produce antibodies that attack particular kinds of invaders. What are these invaders called?* 2️⃣

example, antibody A attacks only antigen A; antibody B attacks only antigen B.

White blood cells can attack invading microorganisms very quickly. It takes time, however, for the body to produce antibodies. T-cells have to detect the presence of the invader and then alert B-cells to produce the appropriate antibodies. Thus, a person may be sick for a time before the antibodies can destroy the invaders.

● ● ● ● **Integration** ● ● ● ●

Use the photograph of the B-cell covered with bacteria to integrate concepts about monerans into your lesson.

INDEPENDENT PRACTICE

Section Review 8–1

1. The immune system repels disease-causing organisms, removes dead or damaged cells, and destroys malfunctioning cells.
2. First line-skin, mucus, cilia, saliva, coughing, sneezing; second line—in-

this time, the person is experiencing the symptoms, or physical signs, of the disease. In other words, the person feels sick. Eventually, the B-cells begin to produce antibodies. The antibodies then join with the invading antigens much as the pieces of a jigsaw puzzle join together. Once joined to the invaders, the antibodies are able to destroy them. It is important to note that an antibody is specific for a certain antigen, and thus is not effective against any other antigens.

8-1 Section Review

1. What is the function of the immune system?
2. What are the body's three lines of defense against invading organisms?
3. What roles do B-cells and T-cells play in the immune system?

Critical Thinking—*Relating Concepts*

4. Explain why it is an advantage that the immune system produces antibodies specific for certain antigens rather than antibodies that work against any and all antigens.

8-2 Immunity

As you have just read, it takes time for your immune system to produce antibodies the first time a particular antigen enters your body. While your body is waiting for the immune system to make antibodies, you will, unfortunately, become ill. However, the next time the same antigen invades your body, your immune system will be ready for it. Your B-cells and T-cells, which are now familiar with the antigen, will be ready and waiting. In fact, they will produce antibodies so quickly that the disease will never even get a chance to develop. And what is more important, you will now have an **immunity** (ihm-MYOON-ih-tee) to that antigen. **Immunity is the resistance to a disease-causing organism or a harmful substance. There are two basic types of immunity: active immunity and passive immunity.**

Guide for Reading

Focus on these questions as you read.

▶ What is immunity, and what is the difference between the two types of immunity?

▶ How do vaccines work?

flammatory response and interferon; third line—antibodies.

3. They are both special white blood cells. The T-cells alert the B-cells to produce antibodies.

4. Because the antibodies are designed specifically to destroy certain antigens, they will seek out only those dangerous invaders and not other, perhaps harmless or even helpful, substances.

REINFORCEMENT/RETEACHING

Monitor students' responses to the Section Review questions. If students appear to have difficulty understanding any of the concepts, review this material with them.

CLOSURE

▶ *Review and Reinforcement Guide*

At this point have students complete Section 8–1 in the *Review and Reinforcement Guide.*

MULTICULTURAL OPPORTUNITY 8-2

There is a concern that there will be a rise in infant mortality because many poor people do not have their children immunized because of the expense. Some cities are establishing clinics or free immunization programs. Have students contact the local health department to determine how your community promotes health by encouraging immunization. What are the regulations about school attendance and immunization in your community?

ESL STRATEGY 8-2

Have students match the terms with their definitions.

Active immunity	Immunity
Vaccination	Passive immunity
Sabin vaccine	Booster shot

• Helps the body develop antibodies to fight polio virus
• Body makes its own antibodies to fight an antigen
• Resistance to a disease-causing organism or harmful substance
• Weakened antigens help to develop antibodies
• Given to help body continue producing antibodies
• Transfer of antibodies from one person or animal to another

Ask students to name some diseases that happen when the immune system's defense "forgets" who the enemy is and attacks itself. Have them consult the school nurse or go to the school library to find out more about these illnesses. Ask them to report their findings to the class either orally or in writing.

FIND OUT BY WRITING

Vaccines

Using reference materials found in the library, make a list of five diseases that have been treated and controlled by the use of vaccines. What symptoms did these diseases produce? How and when was each vaccine developed?

Figure 8–8 *There are two types of immunity: active and passive. This young boy is receiving a vaccine. Vaccines are made from disease-causing organisms that have been killed or weakened in a laboratory. Which type of immunity do you develop as a result of having a disease or receiving a vaccine?* ❶

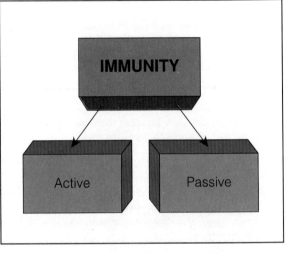

198 ■ H

Active Immunity

Suppose you come into contact with an antigen. Your immune system responds by producing antibodies against the invader. Because your own immune system is responding to the presence of an antigen, this type of immunity is called **active immunity**. The word active means you are doing the action. In this case, you are making the antibodies.

In order to gain active immunity, one of two things must occur—either you come down with the disease or you receive a **vaccination** (vak-sih-NAY-shuhn) for the disease. A vaccination is the process by which antigens are deliberately introduced into a person's body to stimulate the immune system. The antigens are usually developed from disease-causing organisms that have been killed or weakened in a laboratory. Now called a vaccine (vak-SEEN), the antigens alert the body's white blood cells to produce antibodies. Most vaccines are introduced into the body by an injection through the skin. You probably experienced this firsthand when you received your measles vaccination. Some other vaccines, such as the Sabin polio vaccine, are taken into the body through the mouth. In general, vaccines will not usually cause the symptoms of a disease to occur.

How long does active immunity last? There is no set answer to this question because the length of immunity to a disease (actually to the antigen that causes the disease) varies with the type of antigen. For example, an immunity to the common cold lasts only a few weeks, whereas an immunity to the chicken pox lasts for a person's lifetime. Even after receiving a vaccination, the body sometimes has to be reminded how to produce antibodies. In such a case, a booster shot has to be given. A booster shot, as its name implies, boosts (increases) the production of antibodies in the body. Diseases that require the use of booster shots include measles, German measles, poliomyelitis, mumps, whooping cough, diphtheria, and tetanus.

Passive Immunity

The way in which you receive **passive immunity**, the second type of immunity, is to get the antibodies from a source other than yourself. In other words, you are not actually producing the antibodies that protect you—another organism is. (You are not active; you are passive.) For example, passive immunity can be acquired by the transfer of antibodies from a mother to her unborn baby across the placenta. Following the baby's birth, the antibodies give protection to the baby during its first few months. Eventually, however, the mother's antibodies become ineffective, and the baby must rely on its own immune system to protect itself from disease.

A person can receive passive immunity in another way. If an animal such as a horse is vaccinated, its immune system will respond by producing antibodies. The antibodies can be removed from the animal and injected into a person's bloodstream. Unfortunately, this method gives the body only temporary immunity. Soon after these antibodies do their job (which is only about a few weeks), they are eliminated from the body.

Immune Disorders

As you have just read, the function of the immune system is to defend the body against invaders. Sometimes, however, the immune system

FIND OUT BY DOING

How Antibodies Work

1. On a sheet of white paper, trace two adjacent pieces of a jigsaw puzzle.

2. With scissors, cut out the drawings. **CAUTION:** *Be careful when using scissors.*

3. Repeat steps 1 and 2 using two other sets of adjacent pieces of the puzzle.

4. Mix up the six puzzle pieces. Place them on a flat surface. Label three pieces Antibody A, Antibody B, and Antibody C. Label the remaining puzzle pieces Antigen A, Antigen B, and Antigen C.

5. Now try to fit the matching pieces of the puzzle together.

Prepare a chart that shows which antibody fits together with which antigen. How are antibodies and antigens like the pieces of a puzzle?

■ Why do you think it is important that each antibody attaches to a specific antigen?

H ■ 199

ANNOTATION KEY

Answers
❶ Active. (Relating definitions)

Integration
❶ Language Arts

FIND OUT BY DOING

HOW ANTIBODIES WORK

Discovery Learning

Skills: Making a model, comparing, hypothesizing, relating

Materials: scissors

Students should discover that antibodies are very specific; that is, they join only with certain antigens, like the pieces in a puzzle. At this point you may want to introduce the concept of the lock-and-key hypothesis. Like the key for a lock, each antibody can attach itself to and destroy only one kind of antigen. This makes antibodies very efficient weapons.

Which kind of immunity are they? (Active, because in each case, the body is stimulated to produce the needed antibodies.)

• **What is passive immunity?** (Antibodies that come from some source other than your body.)

• **What would be examples of passive immunity?** (Antibodies that an unborn baby gets from its mother; antibodies taken from the blood of a human donor who has already had the disease and built up antibodies against it; antibodies from animals who are given the disease and develop antibodies against it.)

INDEPENDENT PRACTICE

▶ *Activity Book*

Students can find out about the prevalence of different diseases in different parts of the world by completing the chapter activity The Distribution of Disease.

the body is ready to produce them again on short notice if the same kind of invader returns.)

• **What is a booster shot?** (As the name implies, this kind of shot boosts the level of antibodies in the blood. It reminds the body how to produce that particular kind of antibody.)

Explain to students that some of the newer vaccines do not contain viruses at all. Artificial vaccines have been developed using chemicals that resemble viruses. They work in the same way as the older vaccines—by stimulating the production of antibodies.

GUIDED PRACTICE

Skills Development

Skill: Interpreting illustrations

Have students look at Figure 8–8.

• **The diagram shows that there are two kinds of immunity. What are they?** (Active and passive.)

• **We have talked about getting immunity by catching a disease or by being vaccinated.**

HOW DO THEY KNOW?

Cells have many different proteins in their plasma membranes. In human body cells, these proteins include markers that project from the cell's surface and label the cell as "self." Such proteins are called MHC markers, which is short for major histocompatibility complex. Cells in the immune system leave cells with MHC markers alone; they know that these are the "good guys."

If cells from another human enter the body—as happens in an organ transplant—the MHC self-markers for this other human are recognized by the immune system of the recipient as foreign. That is why transplanted tissue is so often rejected.

When cells engulf foreign substances, they display the invader's antigens along with their own MHC markers. A combination of antigen and self-MHC markers stimulates the immune system to launch a full-scale attack.

Figure 8–9 *Allergies result when the immune system is overly sensitive to certain substances called allergens. Examples of allergens are dust, which contains dust mites (top left); feathers (top right); pet hairs (bottom left); and pollen (bottom right).*

becomes overly sensitive to foreign substances or overdoes it by attacking its own tissues. In some instances, the immune system may be fooled by invaders that hide within its cells. Whatever the cause of the malfunction, the outcome is usually serious, as you will now discover.

ALLERGIES Achoo! Achoo! And so it begins. Another attack of hay fever. As you may already know, hay fever is neither a fever nor is it caused by hay. Hay fever is an **allergy** that is caused by ragweed pollen. An allergy results when the immune system is overly sensitive to certain substances called allergens (AL-er-jehnz). Allergens may be in the form of dust, feathers, animal hairs, pollens, or foods.

When an allergen such as pollen enters the body, the immune system reacts by producing antibodies. Unlike the antibodies that help to fight infection,

---

8–2 (continued)

FOCUS/MOTIVATION

Show the class a pepper shaker filled with powdered black pepper.
• **What would happen if you breathed some black pepper into your nose?** (Accept all logical answers. Most students will respond that they would sneeze.)
• **What is the cause?** (Breathing black pepper.)
• **What is the automatic body reaction?** (Sneezing.)
• **Why do you think the body reacted?** (Accept all logical answers.)
• **What things are you allergic to?** (Accept all logical answers.)
• **What is an allergy?** (Accept all logical answers.)

CONTENT DEVELOPMENT

Point out that many people suffer from allergies. Explain that a person can become allergic to almost anything at any time. Tell students that any allergy can occur when the body becomes sensitive to certain substances called allergens. Allergens can be airborne and enter the body through dust particles, feathers, pollen from various plants, animal hair or dander (minute scales from hair, feathers, or skin).

Some people have allergies to certain foods or drugs. Tell students that allergens can enter the body when a person comes in contact with various substances. Many of the allergenic foods, drugs, and substances are normal things that we have around the house—such as shampoo or soap, aspirin, toothpaste, strawberries, eggs, milk, nuts, and so forth.

CONTENT DEVELOPMENT

Point out to students that although there is no cure for an allergy, there are

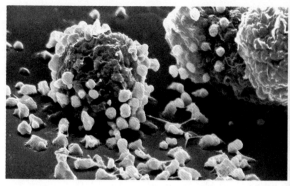

Figure 8–10 *The large round objects in this photograph are white blood cells that are found in the lining of the nose, eyes, and throat. When allergens attach themselves to white blood cells, the white blood cells explode, releasing tiny structures that contain histamines. For those who suffer from hayfever, a bubble helmet with hose and filter may be the last resort.*

the antibodies that are produced by allergens release histamines (HIHS-tuh-meenz). Histamines are chemicals that are responsible for the symptoms of the allergy—that is, the itchy, watery eyes; the runny nose; the tickly throat; and the sneezing.

Although no complete cure for an allergy exists, people may be able to avoid allergy attacks by avoiding the allergen that causes them. This may involve removing from their diet the foods that contain the allergen or finding a new home for their pet. But if parting with a favorite food or a beloved pet is simply out of the question, then some relief may be obtained from antihistamines. As the name implies, antihistamines work against the effects of histamines.

AIDS *Acquired Immune Deficiency Syndrome,* or **AIDS,** is a very serious disease caused by a virus that hides out in healthy body cells. The virus, first discovered in 1984, is named *human immunodeficiency virus,* or HIV. When HIV enters the body, it attacks helper T-cells. This action prevents helper T-cells from carrying out their regular job—to activate the immune system when a threat arises. Once inside a helper T-cell, HIV reproduces and thereby destroys the T-cell. Although the body produces antibodies against HIV, the virus evades them by growing within the cells that make up the immune system. HIV slowly destroys most of the helper T-cells.

The destruction of helper T-cells leaves the body practically undefended. As a result, disease-causing invaders that would normally be destroyed by a healthy immune system grow and multiply. It is the

VIOLENT ALLERGIC REACTIONS

In a few individuals, secretions caused by allergic reactions are so extreme that they can be life-threatening. Air passages leading to the lungs undergo massive constriction. Capillaries become so permeable that plasma escapes rapidly, and plummeting blood pressure may lead to circulatory shock. An example of this type of reaction occurs in people who are hypersensitive to bee or wasp venom. Such individuals can die within minutes of a single sting.

It is possible to prevent some violent allergic reactions when the allergy-producing substance has been identified by laboratory tests. The allergy sufferer is given large injections of antigen to stimulate the production of IgG antibodies, or "blocking antibodies." Circulating IgG antibodies will bind with the allergy-producing substance and mask its identity before it can be attacked by the immune system.

pleted the section on AIDS to see what information they can add or change.

INDEPENDENT PRACTICE

▶ *Activity Book*

To encourage students to learn about AIDS, have them complete the chapter activity AIDS, in which they compile recent information on the disease.

CONTENT DEVELOPMENT

Remind students that AIDS stands for Acquired Immune Deficiency Syndrome. The AIDS virus attacks the body's immune system and reduces its ability to fight other infections. Thus, people who have AIDS can easily get diseases such as certain pneumonias and cancers that the immune system would normally prevent. It is the repeated and uncontrollable infections that weaken and eventually kill people with AIDS.

various medications people can take to relieve the symptoms. Explain that the best relief is to stay away from whatever causes the allergic reaction.

When that is not possible, as in the case of air dust, there are injections that can be given to help counteract the allergy. These injections work similarly to the vaccines. The injection is usually a minute dose of the allergen. The body's immune system produces antibodies to fight the allergen.

GUIDED PRACTICE

Skills Development
Skill: Relating facts

Before beginning the section on AIDS, find out how much factual information students know about this disease. Ask them to write answers to a series of questions: What causes AIDS? How does it affect the body? How does it spread? How can it be prevented? Tell students to keep these questions and answers and to review their answers when they have com-

Figure 8–11 *The virus that causes AIDS— seen as tiny blue dots in this photograph—has infected a T-cell. What is the function of a T-cell?* ❶

Figure 8–12 *Pamphlets such as these inform people about AIDS: what it is and how it is spread. What is the name of the virus that causes AIDS?* ❷

repeated attacks of disease that weaken and eventually kill people with AIDS.

How is AIDS spread? Contrary to popular belief, AIDS can be spread only if there is direct contact with the blood and/or body secretions of an infected person. Because HIV has been found in semen and vaginal secretions, it can be spread through sexual contact. In fact, recent data point to an alarming increase in AIDS among sexually active teenagers. Contaminated blood can also spread HIV from one person to another. Prior to 1985, this made blood transfusions a possible source of HIV transmission. Since 1985, however, mandatory screening of all blood donations for HIV has been in effect. AIDS can also be spread by the sharing of needles among intravenous (directly into a vein) drug users. Even unborn babies can be victims of AIDS, as HIV can also travel across the placenta from mother to unborn child.

Is there a cure for AIDS? Unfortunately, there is none at this time. However, there are several drugs that appear effective in slowing down the growth of the virus, thereby allowing AIDS patients to live longer. It is hoped that a drug to cure this terrible disease will be developed soon. In the meantime, there is only one way to prevent AIDS—avoid exposure to HIV, or the virus that causes AIDS.

8–2 Section Review

1. What is immunity? Compare active immunity and passive immunity.
2. How do vaccines work?
3. What is an allergy? An allergen?
4. What is AIDS? What causes it? How does AIDS affect the immune system?

Critical Thinking—*You and Your World*
5. After receiving a vaccine, you may develop mild symptoms of the disease. Explain why this might happen.

8-3 Diseases

You may not realize it, but few people go through life without getting some type of disease. Even the healthiest person has probably come down with the common cold at one time or another. Now that you have an understanding of how the body defends and protects itself, let's see just what it is up against. In the next few pages, you will read about the causes and symptoms of several diseases.

Infectious Disease

Many diseases are caused by tiny living things such as bacteria, viruses, protozoans, and fungi that invade the body. These living things are commonly called germs. Scientists, however, call them microorganisms. **Diseases that are transmitted among people by disease-causing microorganisms are called infectious** (ihn-FEHK-shuhs) **diseases.** There are three ways by which an **infectious disease** can be transmitted, or spread. They are by people, by animals, and by nonliving things. Sometimes, an infectious disease becomes very contagious (catching) and sweeps through an area. This condition is called an epidemic.

Many common infectious diseases are spread as a result of close contact with a sick person. Such contact often takes place through coughing or sneezing. A cough or a sneeze expels droplets of moisture that may contain disease-causing microorganisms. You

Guide for Reading

Focus on these questions as you read.

▶ What are some examples of infectious diseases, and how are they spread?

▶ What are some examples of noninfectious diseases?

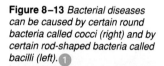

Figure 8–13 *Bacterial diseases can be caused by certain round bacteria called cocci (right) and by certain rod-shaped bacteria called bacilli (left).* ①

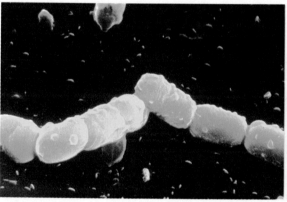
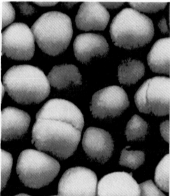

H ■ 203

---

stances. These substances are called allergens. They can be dust, feathers, animal hairs, pollens, or foods.

4. AIDS, or Acquired Immune Deficiency Syndrome, is a disease caused by a virus that attacks, hides in, and destroys helper T-cells. Because helper T-cells signal the presence of disease-causing organisms, the immune system is crippled, and diseases that normally would be destroyed are free to attack the body.

5. Even though the antigens are weakened, they could still cause symptoms of the disease before the body is able to produce antibodies.

REINFORCEMENT/RETEACHING

Review students' responses to the Section Review questions. Reteach any material that is still unclear, based on students' responses.

CLOSURE

▶ *Review and Reinforcement Guide*
Students may now complete Section 8–2 in the *Review and Reinforcement Guide.*

8-3 Diseases

MULTICULTURAL OPPORTUNITY 8-3

Have students investigate some diseases that are endemic to developing countries of the world. What local conditions (for example, poor sanitation, poor quality of water) promote the spread of disease?

ESL STRATEGY 8-3

Ask students to prepare a brief oral report about either cancer or diabetes mellitus, explaining what kind of disease it is, what causes it, what its symptoms are, and what some of the available treatments are. Suggest that students who are learning English work with English-speaking tutors. It may be helpful to start by writing down some of the essential information and presenting it to the tutor.

TEACHING STRATEGY 8–3

FOCUS/MOTIVATION

• **How many of you have ever had a cold? Flu? Measles? Mumps? Chicken pox?** (Acknowledge the number of raised hands.)
• **Name at least one way in which all these diseases are alike.** (They are all infectious, or communicable, diseases. They are all contagious diseases. They are all caused by viruses.)

CONTENT DEVELOPMENT

• **What is an infectious disease?** (One that is caused by a harmful organism such as a virus, bacterium, protozoan, or fungus.)

Explain to students that they act as host for a number of microorganisms, many of which are not harmful. In fact, they may even be helpful, such as those microorganisms that help to digest the food you eat.

● ● ● ● **Integration** ● ● ● ●

Use the photographs of the bacteria to integrate microbiology into your lesson.

LYME DISEASE VS. DEER

Lyme disease, which was discovered in the 1970s, begins with a rash and can lead to rheumatoid arthritis. The disease is transmitted by the bite of a deer tick. As the name indicates, the deer tick lives on deer. All but seven states have reported cases of Lyme disease. Currently, there are about 5000 cases every year. The disease has continued to spread as infected deer ticks increase in number and range every year. The main reason for the spread is the explosion in the deer population, from just under 300,000 in 1900 to 15 million in 1990. Attempts to control ticks by capturing deer and dusting them with insecticide have failed, and some communities have begun to kill deer. But 90 to 95 percent of the deer population would have to be killed to effectively destroy the ticks. This possible course of action has brought opposition from animal-protection groups.

Figure 8–14 *Many infectious diseases are spread by the cough of a sick person (left), by infected animals such as mosquitoes (center), and by contaminated water (right).*

Figure 8–15 *Animals are also responsible for the spread of disease. The female deer tick can carry the microorganism that causes Lyme disease. What is another disease that is spread by the bite of a tick?* ❶

204 ■ H

may be surprised to learn that a sneeze may contain as many as 5000 droplets and that these droplets may travel as far as 3.7 meters (almost the entire length of a small room)! If you are standing near a person who coughs or sneezes, you will probably breathe in these droplets—and the disease-causing microorganisms along with them. Diseases that are spread mainly through coughing and sneezing include colds, flu, measles, mumps, and tuberculosis.

Some infectious diseases are transmitted when a healthy person comes into direct contact with a person who has the disease. Such is the case for gonorrhea and syphilis, which are examples of sexually transmitted diseases, or STDs.

Animals can spread infectious diseases, too. Ticks, which are cousins of the spider, are responsible for spreading Lyme disease (named after the town in Connecticut where it was first observed) and Rocky Mountain spotted fever (named after the region in the United States where it was first discovered). Some other types of animals that are responsible for spreading disease are mammals and birds. Rabies, a serious disease that affects the nervous system, is transmitted by the bite of an infected mammal such as a raccoon or a squirrel.

Living things are not the only transmitters of disease. Contaminated (dirty) food or water can also spread infectious diseases. Food contaminated with certain bacteria, for example, can cause food poisoning. And in areas that have poor sanitation, diseases such as hepatitis, cholera (KAHL-er-uh), and typhoid (TIGH-foid) fever are fairly common.

DISEASES CAUSED BY VIRUSES Your head aches, your nose is runny, and your eyes are watery. You also have a slight cough. But do not be alarmed. More than likely, you are suffering from the common cold.

The common cold is caused by perhaps one of the smallest disease-causing organisms—a virus. A virus is a tiny particle that can invade living cells. When a virus invades the body, it quickly enters a body cell. Once inside the cell, the virus takes control of all the activities of the cell. Not only does the virus use up the cell's food supply, it also uses the cell's reproductive machinery to make more viruses. In time, the cell—now full of viruses—bursts open, releasing more viruses that are free to invade more body cells. Viruses cause many infectious diseases, including measles, chicken pox, influenza, and mononucleosis.

DISEASES CAUSED BY BACTERIA If you are like most people, you probably think that all bacteria (one-celled microscopic organisms) are harmful and cause disease in humans. Then perhaps this fact will surprise you: Most bacteria are harmless to humans! Those bacteria that do produce diseases do so in a variety of ways. Some bacteria infect the tissues of the body directly. For example, the bacterium that causes tuberculosis grows in the tissues of the lungs. As the bacterium multiplies, it kills surrounding cells, causing difficulty and pain in breathing.

Other bacteria cause disease by producing toxins, or poisons. One such bacterium causes tetanus. The tetanus bacterium lives in dust and dirt and enters the body through breaks in the skin. Once inside the body, the tetanus bacterium begins to produce a toxin that affects muscles far from the wound. Because the toxin causes violent contractions of the jaw muscles, which make it hard for an infected person to open his or her mouth, tetanus is commonly called lockjaw.

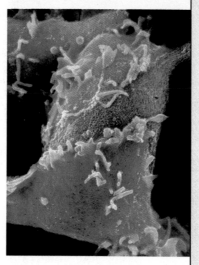

Figure 8–16 *This photograph shows how viruses—seen as tiny blue dots—are released by an infected human cell when it ruptures.*

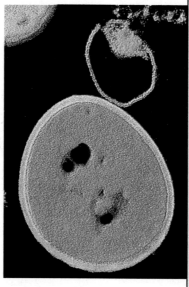

Figure 8–17 *The round objects in this photograph are bacterial cells. The bacterial cell at the top of the photograph has burst because of the addition of an antibiotic. An antibiotic is a substance produced by living organisms such as fungi that weakens or kills bacteria.*

HISTORICAL NOTE
POLIO

Poliomyelitis (polio) is an acute infection of the central nervous system, sometimes resulting in paralysis. The disease was once known as infantile paralysis because its victims were often children. Polio is caused by a virus that enters the system through the nose or mouth and attacks the nerves controlling the muscles. In bulbar polio, breathing and swallowing are affected.

In the early 1950s, outbreaks of polio increased dramatically in the United States. Many parents were as frightened of the polio virus then as they are afraid of the AIDS virus today. No cure for polio was known. No vaccines to protect against the disease were available.

Fortunately, in 1953, Jonas Salk developed a vaccine consisting of killed polio viruses that were injected into the body. The Sabin vaccine, which is given through the mouth, was developed several years later. It consists of live but weakened viruses. Although there is still no known cure for polio, these vaccines have brought the disease under control.

once a virus is free to move about the body, it invades other cells.

CONTENT DEVELOPMENT

Point out that disease-causing bacteria invade the body by two different methods. Most bacteria attack the body cells directly. Some bacteria produce a poison called a toxin. Explain that scientists have developed antitoxins to act against some of these toxins. For example, an antitoxin has been developed to counteract the toxin produced by the tetanus-causing

bacterium. In order to be effective, however, it must be administered soon after exposure to the deadly bacteria.

GUIDED PRACTICE

Skills Development
Skill: Relating concepts

Divide students into groups of four or five. Assign each group one of the viral or bacterial diseases mentioned in the textbook. Have students research and report

on the symptoms of each disease and the recommended medication.

INDEPENDENT PRACTICE

▶ *Activity Book*

Students will learn more about infectious diseases by completing the chapter activity Call on the Experts in Infectious Diseases.

REINFORCEMENT/RETEACHING

▶ *Activity Book*

Students who need practice with identifying infectious diseases should complete the chapter activity called Complete-a-Disease.

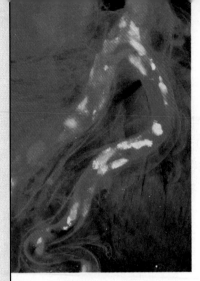

Figure 8–18 *The yellow-colored material in these arteries of the heart is a buildup of fatty substances. Such substances block the flow of blood to the heart muscle. What are the diseases that affect the heart and blood vessels called?* ❶

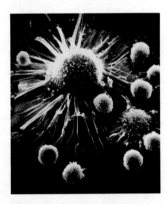

Figure 8–19 *Notice the crablike growth of the large cancer cell. The round objects are T-cells that have surrounded the cancer cell and are preparing to attack and destroy it.*

206 ■ H

Noninfectious Diseases

Diseases that are not caused by microorganisms are called noninfectious diseases. There are many causes of **noninfectious diseases**. Some noninfectious diseases are caused by substances that harm or irritate the body. Others come from not eating a balanced diet. Still others are produced when the immune system fails to function properly. Worry and tension can also cause illness.

Because modern medicine has found more and more ways to combat many infectious diseases through the use of drugs and vaccines, people have begun to live longer. And as people's life spans have increased, so have the number of people who suffer from noninfectious diseases.

Some of the more serious noninfectious diseases are cancer, diabetes mellitus (digh-uh-BEET-eez muh-LIGHT-uhs), and cardiovascular diseases. You will now read about two noninfectious diseases—cancer and diabetes mellitus. Cardiovascular diseases, or diseases that affect the heart and blood vessels, were discussed in Chapter 4.

CANCER The noninfectious disease that is second only to cardiovascular diseases in causing death is **cancer**. Cancer is a disease in which cells multiply ❶ uncontrollably, destroying healthy tissue. Cancer is a unique disease because the cells that cause it are not foreign to the body. Rather, they are the body's own cells. This fact has made cancer difficult to understand and treat.

Cancer develops when something goes wrong with the controls that regulate cell growth. A single cell or a group of cells begin to grow and divide uncontrollably, often resulting in the formation of a tumor. A tumor is a mass of tissue. Some tumors are benign (bih-NIGHN), or not cancerous. A benign tumor does not spread to surrounding healthy tissue or to other parts of the body. Cancerous tumors, on the other hand, are malignant (muh-LIHG-nehnt). Malignant tumors invade and eventually destroy surrounding tissue. In some cases, cells from a malignant tumor break away and are carried by the blood to other parts of the body.

The cells often form tumors. Most tumors are harmless, or benign. If a tumor is called malignant, it is cancerous and therefore life-threatening. Tell students that cancer cells rob healthy cells of food and space. They invade neighboring tissue, crowd it out, take its nourishment, and then destroy it. If a cancer cell breaks away from the original growth, it can spread by traveling through the bloodstream to other parts of the body.

Point out that the sooner cancer is detected, the better the possibility of a complete cure. The location and stage of development of the cancer tumor are also factors in determining the life-threatening possibilities of the cancerous growth.

● ● ● ● **Integration** ● ● ● ●

Use the discussion about cancer to integrate cell biology into your lesson.

Although the basic cause of cancer is not known, scientists believe that it develops because of repeated and prolonged contact with carcinogens (kahr-SIHN-uh-juhnz), or cancer-causing substances. In a few cases, scientists have found certain cancer-causing hereditary material (genes) in viruses. The hereditary material in the viruses transforms normal, healthy cells into cancer cells. Scientists also suspect that people may inherit a tendency to develop certain types of cancer. This does not mean, however, that such people will get cancer.

The most important weapon in the fight against cancer is early detection. If a cancer is detected early on, the chances of successfully treating it are quite good. Doctors mainly use three methods to treat cancer: surgery, radiation therapy, and drug therapy. These methods may be used alone or in combination with one another.

Doctors tend to use surgery to remove malignant tumors that are localized, or are not capable of spreading. In radiation therapy, radiation (energy in the form of rays) is used to destroy cancer cells. Drug therapy, or chemotherapy, is the use of specific chemicals against cancer cells. Like radiation, these chemicals not only destroy cancer cells, but they also can injure normal cells. These injuries may account for undesirable side effects, such as nausea and high blood pressure, that often accompany such treatment.

Recently, scientists have been experimenting with drugs that can strengthen the body's immune system against cancer cells. These drugs, called monoclonal (mahn-oh-KLOH-nuhl) antibodies, are produced by joining cancer cells with antibody-producing white blood cells. Monoclonal antibodies have already

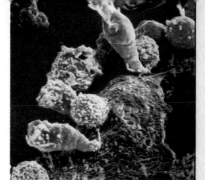
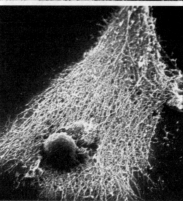

Figure 8–20 *Normally round killer T-cells become elongated when they are active, such as when they are destroying a cancer cell (top). All that remains of a cancer cell that has been attacked by a T-cell is its fibrous skeleton (bottom). What is cancer?* ❷

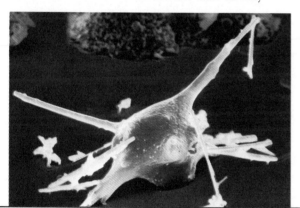

Figure 8–21 *Some chemicals, such as asbestos, are carcinogenic, or cancer-causing. The asbestos fibers visible in this photograph are being engulfed by a white blood cell.*

H ■ 207

INTEGRATION

HEALTH

The most common cancers in the United States are skin cancers. Overexposure to the sun is the major cause of skin cancers. Ultraviolet radiation from sunlight can damage skin-cell DNA, producing mutations. These mutations can cause cancer. UV radiation may also break down the body's immune system, making it less able to fight the growth of cancer cells.

Have students discuss questions such as the following:

• **How can you enjoy yourself at the beach and still protect yourself from overexposure to the sun's UV rays?** (Wear a sunscreen that blocks UV rays; wear protective clothing; avoid the hottest part of the day; and so forth.)

working on new methods to help the immune system, including monoclonal antibodies. It is hoped that these antibodies will attack only cancer cells in the body.

GUIDED PRACTICE

▶ *Laboratory Manual*

Skills Development

Skills: Making calculations, recording data, applying concepts

Students may now complete the Chapter 8 Laboratory Investigation in the *Laboratory Manual* called Relating Chronic Disorders and Nutrition. They will find out what is involved in planning nutritionally balanced menus.

GUIDED PRACTICE

Skills Development

Skill: Relating facts

Point out that cancer is believed to develop because of repeated and prolonged contact with a group of substances called carcinogens. Have students research some of the better-known carcinogens, such as tobacco, drugs, air or water pollution, radiation, and chemicals such as pesticides, plastics, and asbestos. Have them report their findings to the class.

CONTENT DEVELOPMENT

Explain to students that sometimes lasers are used in cancer surgery. They are beams of light that can cut or kill body tissue. Lasers allow the surgeon to "pinpoint" the surgery, thus destroying fewer healthy cells. Point out that new chemicals are always being introduced to help with the treatment of cancer. Often after surgery, medications are used to kill cancer cells that might have been missed by the surgery. Explain that scientists are

INSULIN

The principal discoverer of insulin was Frederick Grant Banting. He and three others, J.J.R. Macleod, C. H. Best, and J. B. Collip, worked together at the University of Toronto to isolate the hormone. It took them only 8 months. The discovery of insulin revolutionized the treatment of diabetes mellitus. Insulin was first used on human patients in 1922. Banting and Macleod won the Nobel prize for medicine in 1923 for their discovery. They shared the prize money with their fellow workers, Best and Collip. Until 1978, insulin came mostly from the pancreases of hogs and cattle. In that year, insulin was genetically engineered and produced.

8–3 (continued)

FOCUS/MOTIVATION

Point to the picture on page H208. Discuss what the football player is doing. Conclude that he is doing a very strenuous activity.

• **What changes occur in the body as a person exercises?** (Accept all logical answers.)

Explain that strenuous exercise causes the body to burn sugar faster. Usually the body is able to counteract this situation by releasing more sugar into the bloodstream. But people with diabetes must regulate the amount of sugar in their blood through medication or diet.

CONTENT DEVELOPMENT

Explain that insulin reduces the level of sugar in the bloodstream by helping body cells absorb the sugar. (Specifically, insulin attaches to special sites on the cell membranes of target cells. This makes the cell membrane more permeable to glucose.)

• **When does your body produce more insulin: before or after you eat?** (After.)

• **Why do you need insulin after you eat?** (Because sugar from the digested food enters the blood, increasing the blood-sugar levels.)

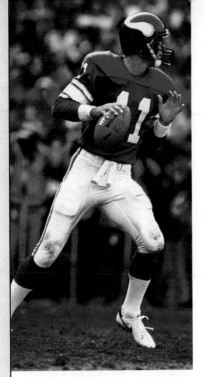

Figure 8–22 *With proper treatment and diet control, people who have diabetes can exercise and participate in sports. Wade Wilson of the Minnesota Vikings is a perfect example. What is diabetes mellitus?* ❶

proven to be effective against certain types of flu virus and a type of hepatitis virus. It is hoped that monoclonal antibodies will play an important role in the fight against cancer.

DIABETES MELLITUS Loss of weight, excess urine production, weakness, and extreme hunger and thirst are all symptoms of a serious disease known as **diabetes mellitus.** Diabetes mellitus occurs because the body either secretes (releases) too little insulin or is not able to use the insulin that it does secrete.

As you may recall from Chapter 6, insulin is a hormone that is produced by the islets of Langerhans (clusters of cells in the pancreas). The job of insulin is to reduce the level of sugar (glucose) in the blood by helping the body cells absorb sugar and use it for energy. Without insulin, sugar cannot be absorbed into body cells and energy cannot be produced. This condition causes the body to look elsewhere for its energy. And, unfortunately, the body looks to its own tissues for "food." As a result, a person begins to show the symptoms of diabetes (weight loss, weakness, and extreme hunger).

There are two types of diabetes mellitus. Juvenile-onset diabetes, as its name implies, most commonly develops in people under the age of 25. In this type of diabetes, there is little or no secretion of insulin. The treatment for this type of diabetes includes daily insulin injections and strict diet control. Adult-onset diabetes, on the other hand, develops in people over the age of 25. Although most people with adult-onset diabetes produce normal amounts of insulin, for some unknown reason their body cells cannot use the insulin to absorb the much-needed sugar. Adult-onset diabetes can often be controlled by diet.

8–3 Section Review

1. What is an infectious disease? A noninfectious disease? Give two examples of each.
2. How are infectious diseases spread?

Critical Thinking—*Applying Facts*

3. It's a fact: There is no single cure for the common cold. Why do you think this is so?

• **What happens if the body doesn't produce enough insulin, as in juvenile-onset diabetes?** (Sugar cannot be absorbed properly.)

• **What happens if the body cells cannot respond to insulin, as in adult-onset diabetes?** (Sugar is not absorbed.)

• **Why do cells need sugar?** (For energy.)

• **What happens to cells that do not get sugar?** (They cannot produce energy; they starve and eventually die.)

• **Why do people with severe untreated diabetes lose weight rapidly?** (They are starv-

ing because their cells cannot absorb and use sugar.)

GUIDED PRACTICE

Skills Development

Skill: Applying concepts

After discussing the importance of diet in controlling diabetes, have students develop lists of foods they think should be eaten or avoided by a person with diabetes. Discuss the lists, encouraging stu-

CONNECTIONS

A Cure for Us or Yews? ❶

Recently, doctors announced the discovery of a new cancer drug capable of melting away tumors that have resisted all other treatment. Unfortunately, very few people will receive this drug, which is known as taxol. Why? The answer lies in its source—the Pacific yew tree.

When it became clear that taxol has great potential in the fight against cancer, certain people became alarmed about what effect this would have on the Pacific yew trees. They started asking how many Pacific yews there were and what was going to happen to them. These people are concerned about *ecology*. Ecology is the study of the relationships and interactions of living things with one another and with their environment. As one ecology activist said of the Pacific yews, "Our concern is that there will not be any left the way we are approaching this."

In the past, Pacific yews were seen as commercially unimportant. So they were treated as weeds and were cut down and burned. As a result, the population of Pacific yews, which are found in forests in the Pacific Northwest, dwindled. Of the remaining Pacific yews, most are far too small to be used for making taxol. The height at which a Pacific yew is harvested for taxol is about 9 meters (or the distance needed to make a first down in football). It takes 100 years for

a yew to grow that tall! In addition, it takes six 100-year-old Pacific yews to treat one cancer patient!

To further complicate the situation, Pacific yews are found in areas where logging is prohibited in order to protect the habitat of the spotted owl. The spotted owl is an endangered species. But if the yews continue to be harvested for taxol, they, too, may become an endangered species. So what can be done? Does a decision have to be made as to which is more important—cancer treatment or ecology? Most ecology activists believe that if people are careful, the yew can be preserved even as the maximum number of trees are harvested for taxol. What do you think?

dents to give reasons why they included certain foods on their lists.

INDEPENDENT PRACTICE

▶ *Activity Book*

Students who need practice with the concept of noninfectious diseases should complete the chapter activity called Chronic Disorders.

ENRICHMENT

Have interested students investigate what is currently being done to find a cure for juvenile-onset diabetes. Ask them to present their findings to the class.

INDEPENDENT PRACTICE

Section Review 8–3

1. A disease transmitted among people by disease-causing microorganisms, such as flu and measles; a disease not caused by microorganisms, such as cancer and diabetes. Examples will vary.

2. By people through droplets in the air or direct contact, by animals, by food or water.

3. Colds are caused by viruses, and there are many different viruses. It would be difficult to find a cure that would work against them all.

REINFORCEMENT/RETEACHING

Monitor students' responses to the Section Review questions. If students appear to have difficulty with any of the questions, review the appropriate material in the section.

CLOSURE

▶ *Review and Reinforcement Guide*

At this point have students complete Section 8–3 in the *Review and Reinforcement Guide.*

Laboratory Investigation

OBSERVING THE ACTION OF ALCOHOL ON MICROORGANISMS

BEFORE THE LAB

1. Gather all materials at least one day prior to the activity. You should have enough supplies to meet your class needs, assuming six students per group.
2. Sterilize and prepare the petri dishes with agar, or obtain classroom sets of sterilized petri dishes and agar from a biological supply company.
3. Use isopropyl alcohol from a pharmacy.
4. The paper clips, thumbtacks, and pennies should be used. If they are new, have students handle and touch them before the lab starts to make sure they have been in contact with common organisms.

PRE-LAB DISCUSSION

Have students read the complete laboratory procedure. Discuss the activity and safety procedures by asking questions similar to the following:

• **What is the purpose of the laboratory activity?** (To determine the effect of alcohol on the growth of organisms.)
• **Why is it important to keep the lids on the petri dishes while labeling?** (Accept all logical answers. To prevent organisms from entering the sterile agar.)
• **What is the experimental variable in this setup?** (The dish that contains materials soaked in alcohol.)
• **What is the control in this setup?** (The dish that contains materials not soaked in alcohol.)
• **Why is it important that all starting pennies, thumbtacks, and paper clips have been touched and contain common organisms?** (Accept all logical answers. Without starting organisms, they could not grow or be affected by the alcohol.)

• **Why is it important to open the covers only for a very short time?** (Accept all logical answers. Lead students to suggest that is important to avoid contamination from the many organisms in the air.)
• **What do you predict will happen in the experimental setup? In the control setup?** (Accept all logical answers.)
• **Why do you predict this will happen?** (Accept all logical answers.)

Laboratory Investigation

Observing the Action of Alcohol on Microorganisms

Problem

What effect does alcohol have on the growth of organisms?

Materials (per group)

glass-marking pencil	alcohol
2 paper clips	100-mL beaker
2 thumbtacks	transparent tape
2 pennies	graduated cylinder
	forceps
2 petri dishes with sterile nutrient agar	

Procedure 🧪 📦

1. Obtain two petri dishes containing sterile nutrient agar.
2. Using a glass-marking pencil, label the lid of the first dish Soaked in Alcohol. Label the lid of the second dish Not Soaked in Alcohol. Write your name and today's date on each lid. **Note:** *Be sure to keep the dishes covered while labeling them.*
3. Using a graduated cylinder, carefully pour 50 mL of alcohol into a beaker.
4. Place a paper clip, a thumbtack, and a penny into the alcohol in the beaker. Keep these objects in the alcohol for 10 minutes.
5. Slightly raise the cover of the dish marked Not Soaked in Alcohol. **Note:** *Do not completely remove the cover from the dish.* Using clean forceps, place the other paper clip, thumbtack, and penny into the dish. Cover the dish immediately.
6. Again using clean forceps, remove the paper clip, thumbtack, and penny from the alcohol in the beaker. Slightly raise the cover of the dish marked Soaked in Alcohol and place these objects into it.

7. Tape both dishes closed and put them in a place where they will remain undisturbed for 1 week.
8. After 1 week, examine the dishes. Make a sketch of what you see.
9. Follow your teacher's instructions for the proper disposal of all materials.

Observations

What did you observe in each dish after 1 week?

Analysis and Conclusions

1. What effect did alcohol have on the growth of organisms?
2. Why did you use forceps, rather than your fingers, to place the objects in the dishes?
3. Why did you have to close the petri dishes immediately after adding the objects?
4. Explain why doctors soak their instruments in alcohol.

Summarizing Key Concepts

8–1 Body Defenses

▲ The immune system is the body's defense against disease-causing organisms.

▲ The body's first line of defense consists of the skin, mucus, and cilia.

▲ The body's second line of defense is the inflammatory response.

▲ The body's third line of defense consists of antibodies. Antibodies are produced by special white blood cells called B-cells. B-cells are alerted to produce antibodies by T-cells when there is an antigen in the body.

8–2 Immunity

▲ Immunity is the resistance to a disease-causing organism or a harmful substance. There are two types of immunity: active and passive.

▲ Active immunity results when a person's own immune system responds to an antigen by producing antibodies. To have active immunity, a person must get the disease or receive a vaccination. Passive immmunity results when antibodies are produced from a source other than oneself.

▲ An allergy occurs when the immune system is overly sensitive to certain substances called allergens.

▲ AIDS is a disease caused by a virus called HIV. HIV destroys helper T-cells, which ordinarily activate the immune system when a threat arises.

8–3 Diseases

▲ Diseases that are transmitted among people by disease-causing microorganisms are called infectious diseases. Some infectious diseases are caused by viruses and bacteria.

▲ Diseases that are not caused by microorganisms are called noninfectious diseases. Cancer, diabetes mellitus, and cardiovascular diseases are examples of noninfectious diseases.

▲ Cancer is a disease in which cells multiply uncontrollably, destroying healthy tissue.

▲ In diabetes mellitus, the body either secretes too little insulin or is not able to use the insulin that it does secrete.

Reviewing Key Terms

Define each term in a complete sentence.

8–1 Body Defenses
inflammatory response
interferon
antibody
antigen

8–2 Immunity
immunity
active immunity
vaccination

passive immunity
allergy
AIDS

8–3 Diseases
infectious disease
noninfectious disease
cancer
diabetes mellitus

may be surprised that some organisms may grow even after the materials were disinfected with alcohol—observing, relating.)
• **Were the results similar to your prediction? Why or why not?** (Accept all logical answers—predicting, analyzing.)

OBSERVATIONS

All dishes will contain circular colonies growing around the objects, but dishes marked Not Soaked in Alcohol will have far more colonies than dishes marked Soaked in Alcohol.

ANALYSIS AND CONCLUSIONS

1. It killed off or stopped the growth of most microorganisms.
2. Fingers may have transferred microorganisms from the hand to the dish.
3. To keep out any microorganisms from the air.
4. To kill certain microorganisms on their instruments that could cause infection in a patient.

GOING FURTHER: ENRICHMENT

Part 1
Have students test common household disinfectants such as mouthwashes, detergents, and cleaning materials.

Part 2
Encourage students to do library research to find more in-depth specific information about disinfectants and the growth of organisms.

Chapter Review

ALTERNATIVE ASSESSMENT

The *Prentice Hall Science* program includes a variety of testing components and methodologies. Aside from the Chapter Review questions, you may opt to use the Chapter Test or the Computer Test Bank Test in your *Test Book* for assessment of important facts and concepts. In addition, Performance-Based Tests are included in your *Test Book*. These Performance-Based Tests are designed to test science process skills, rather than factual content recall. Since they are not content dependent, Performance-Based Tests can be distributed after students complete a chapter or after they complete the entire textbook.

TEACHING STRATEGY

1. Suggest to the teams that two members may want to work together on each petri dish.
2. Have extra petri dishes with agar on hand in case a team needs to replace a dish.
3. Have the teams follow the directions carefully as they work in the laboratory.

DISCOVERY STRATEGIES

Discuss how the investigation relates to the chapter ideas by asking open questions similar to the following:
• **What did you find out?** (Accept all answers. Teams are likely to share a wide variety of information—relating, analyzing.)
• **What happened in the control setup?** (Accept all logical answers—observing, relating.)
• **Were the results similar to your prediction? Why or why not?** (Accept all logical answers—predicting, analyzing.)
• **What happened in the experimental setup?** (Accept all logical answers. Students

CONTENT REVIEW

Multiple Choice

1. c
2. a
3. a
4. a
5. d
6. d
7. c
8. a
9. a
10. d

True or False

1. F, skin, mucus, and cilia
2. F, interferon
3. T
4. F, B-cells
5. T
6. T
7. T

Concept Mapping

Row 1: First line, Third line
Row 2: Mucus, Cilia, Interferon
Row 4: Antibodies

CONCEPT MASTERY

1. The skin acts as a protective covering and prevents some microorganisms from entering the body.

2. Once an antigen or organism invades the body, special white blood cells called T-cells and B-cells spring into action. T-cells alert B-cells to produce antibodies. If the body has never been invaded by this kind of antigen before, the B-cells will take a while to produce antibodies.

3. Through contact with an infected person or animal or through food or water.

4. A benign tumor is a harmless tumor, and when removed surgically, it will not usually grow back. A malignant tumor, on the other hand, is life-threatening and cancerous.

5. Radiation therapy, chemotherapy, surgery.

6. Monoclonal antibodies are developed by joining cancer cells with antibody-producing white blood cells. The monoclonal antibodies will seek out cancer cells and kill them.

7. When dust enters the person's body, an allergic reaction may occur, and histamines are released. Histamines are the chemicals that are responsible for the symptoms that go along with allergies.

8. An antibody is produced to attack a specific antigen. When it meets that antigen, it changes from a T shape to a Y shape, and the two arms of the Y attach and bind to the antigen. The antibody can prevent the antigen from attaching to body cells, or slow the antigen down so that it can be gobbled up by white blood cells, or even blast a hole in the antigen's cell walls.

9. AIDS destroys the helper T-cells, thus crippling the body's immune system and making the body vulnerable to disease-causing organisms. Repeated attacks of disease weaken and eventually kill people with AIDS. The HIV virus that causes AIDS is spread through contact with the blood and body secretions of an infected person; that is, through sexual contact, contaminated blood, or sharing needles for intravenous drugs. The only way to prevent AIDS at the present time is to avoid exposure to HIV.

CRITICAL THINKING AND PROBLEM SOLVING

1. The first time that you got the mumps your body produced antibodies against the mumps viruses. These antibodies will

---

Content Review

Multiple Choice

Choose the letter of the answer that best completes each statement.

1. What is the body's second line of defense?
   a. skin
   b. antibodies
   c. inflammatory response
   d. cilia

2. Proteins that are produced by the immune system in response to disease-causing invaders are called
   a. antibodies.
   b. antigens.
   c. allergens.
   d. vaccines.

3. The resistance to a disease-causing invader is called
   a. immunity.
   b. vaccination.
   c. interferon.
   d. antigen.

4. A vaccination produces
   a. active immunity.
   b. passive immunity.
   c. no immunity.
   d. both active and passive immunity.

5. An example of an allergy is
   a. rabies.
   b. diabetes mellitus.
   c. tetanus.
   d. hay fever.

6. Which disease is caused by HIV?
   a. rabies
   b. cancer
   c. hay fever
   d. AIDS

7. Which is an example of an infectious disease?
   a. cancer
   b. diabetes mellitus
   c. measles
   d. allergy

8. Tumors that are not cancerous are said to be
   a. benign.
   b. infectious.
   c. malignant.
   d. contagious.

9. Another name for a cancer-causing substance is a(an)
   a. carcinogen.
   b. allergen.
   c. interferon.
   d. vaccination.

10. Which disease results from the secretion of too little insulin?
   a. measles
   b. cancer
   c. AIDS
   d. diabetes mellitus

True or False

If the statement is true, write "true." If it is false, change the underlined word or words to make the statement true.

1. The body's first line of defense against invaders is the <u>inflammatory response</u>.
2. An <u>allergen</u> is a substance that is produced by body cells when they are attacked by viruses.
3. Antibodies are produced to fight <u>antigens</u>.
4. <u>T-cells</u> produce antibodies.
5. A vaccine usually contains dead or weakened <u>antigens</u>.
6. <u>Cancer</u> is a disease in which cells multiply uncontrollably
7. Cancer and diabetes mellitus are examples of <u>noninfectious diseases</u>.

Concept Mapping

Complete the following concept map for Section 8–1. Refer to pages H8–H9 to construct a concept map for the entire chapter.

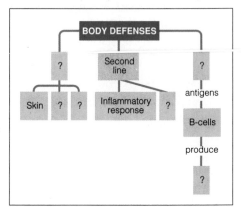

Concept Mastery

Discuss each of the following in a brief paragraph.

1. Explain how the skin functions as the body's first line of defense.
2. Explain how antibodies are produced.
3. Describe three methods by which infectious diseases are spread.
4. What is a benign tumor? A malignant tumor?
5. What are three methods that are used for treating cancer?
6. What are monoclonal antibodies? How are they produced?
7. Describe what happens in the body of a person who has an allergy to dust.
8. How do antibodies fight antigens in the body?
9. What effect does AIDS have on the body? How is AIDS prevented?

Critical Thinking and Problem Solving

Use the skills you have developed in this chapter to answer each of the following.

1. **Relating concepts** Why do you get mumps only once?
2. **Relating facts** Why should you clean and bandage all cuts?
3. **Applying concepts** Explain why you should not go to school with the flu.
4. **Interpreting diagrams** The chart shows the occurrence and survival rates of some cancers in the United States. Which type of cancer has the worst survival rate? The best? Why do you think the five-year survival rates increased between 1960 and 1963 and between 1977 and 1983?

5. **Applying concepts** Explain why it is important for you to know what vaccines you have been given and when they were given.
6. **Making predictions** Suppose your cilia were destroyed. How would this affect your body?
7. **Recognizing fact and opinion** Are colds caught by sitting in a draft? Explain your answer.
8. **Applying concepts** Suppose a person was born without a working immune system. What are some of the precautions that would have to be taken so that the person could survive?
9. **Relating concepts** The Black Death, or bubonic plague, swept through England in the seventeenth century killing thousands of people. This disease is spread by fleas infected with plague microorganisms. These fleas transmit the plague microorganisms to humans by biting them. Explain why the Black Death is not a problem today.
10. **Using the writing process** In the United States, the incidence of sexually transmitted diseases is on the rise. Prepare an advertising campaign in which you alert people to the serious medical problems of these diseases.

FIVE-YEAR SURVIVAL RATES		
Site of Cancer	1960–63	1977–83
Digestive tract		
Stomach	9.5%	16.0%
Colon and rectum	36.0%	46.0%
Respiratory tract		
Lung and bronchus	6.5%	12.0%
Urinary tract		
Kidney and other urinary structures	37.5%	51.0%
Reproductive system		
Breast	54.0%	68.0%
Ovary	32.0%	38.0%
Testis	63.0%	74.5%
Prostate gland	42.5%	63.0%
Skin	60.0%	79.0%

---

destroy any further invasion by the mumps viruses. You now have active immunity to the mumps.

2. By cleaning and bandaging all cuts, you kill and keep out most bacteria that can cause an infection.

3. The flu, or influenza, is an infectious disease and can be transmitted to others. Also, it is important to rest when you have the flu.

4. Respiratory tract; skin; probably due to promotion of early detection and treatment and to improved methods of treatment.

5. It is important to know what vaccines you have been given so that you know what types of diseases you are immune to. It is important to know when the vaccines were given because the immunity could be limited and you may need a booster shot.

6. The destruction of all the cilia in the respiratory system will make you more apt to get respiratory infections. The cilia act like little brushes that sweep particles up and out of the respiratory system. Without the cilia, these particles, including disease-causing organisms, would invade the respiratory system.

7. Colds are caused by viruses, not by drafts. Sitting in drafts may lower your resistance to the cold virus, making you more apt to catch a cold.

8. The person would have to live in an environment that is totally free of any and all disease-causing organisms. The person may have to live in a type of "bubble" that contains filtered air. In addition, all surfaces would have to be disinfected, and there would probably be no direct contact with other people.

9. Improved living conditions, including modern methods of sanitation, have reduced the opportunities for fleas and humans to come in contact with each other.

10. Students' campaigns should be scientifically consistent with the information presented in the textbook. Encourage them to be creative in their approach. Remind them to think of advertising that made an impact on them.

KEEPING A PORTFOLIO

You might want to assign some of the Concept Mastery and Critical Thinking and Problem Solving questions as homework and have students include their responses to unassigned questions in their portfolio. Students should be encouraged to include both the question and the answer in their portfolio.

ISSUES IN SCIENCE

The following issue can be used as a springboard for discussion or given as writing assignment:

Many Third World countries still suffer from epidemics of diseases that rarely occur in the United States. Many citizens of these countries do not have access to the vaccines that are commonplace in this country. Should the United States donate vaccines and money for their dissemination to people in developing nations.

Chapter 9 ALCOHOL, TOBACCO, AND DRUGS

SECTION	LABORATORY INVESTIGATIONS AND DEMONSTRATIONS

9–1 What Are Drugs?
pages H216–H219
	Teacher Edition
	    Simulating the Effects of Drugs, p. H214d
	    Examining Drug and Alcohol Advertisements, p. H214d

9–2 Alcohol pages H219–H223	

9–3 Tobacco
pages H223–H225
	Student Edition
	    Analyzing Smoking Advertisements, p. H232
	Laboratory Manual
	    Effects of Alcohol and Tobacco on Seed Germination

9–4 Commonly Abused Drugs pages H226–H231	
Chapter Review pages H232–H235	

*All materials in the Chapter Planning Guide Grid are available as part of the Prentice Hall Science Learning System.

OUTSIDE TEACHER RESOURCES

Books

Fishman, Ross. *Alcohol and Alcoholism,* Chelsea House Publishers.

Gano, Lila, *Smoking,* Lucent Books.

Giles, H. G., and B. M. Kapur. *Alcohol and the Identification of Alcoholics,* Lexington Books.

Goodwin, Donald W. *Alcoholism: The Facts,* Oxford University Press.

Hughes, Barbara. *Drug-related Diseases,* Franklin Watts.

Julien, Robert. *Drugs and the Body,* W. H. Freeman.

Lang, Alan R. *Alcohol: Teenage Drinking,* Chelsea House Publishers.

Zaridze, B., and R. Petro, eds. *Tobacco: A Major International Health Hazard,* Oxford University Press.

Zonderman, Jon, and Laurel Shader. *Drugs and Disease,* Chelsea House Publishers.

Audiovisuals

All My Tomorrows, film or video, Coronet

Drug Abuse: Sorting It Out, film or video, EBE

Drugs, Alcohol, and Tobacco, three sound filmstrips or videocassettes, EBE

Drugs and How They Affect You, filmstrip with cassettes, National Geographic

Straight Talk About Alcohol, filmstrip with cassettes, National Geographic

Tattle, video, Media Guild

OTHER ACTIVITIES	MULTIMEDIA
Activity Book Chapter Discovery: Looking at Drugs ACTIVITY: Symptoms of Abuse **Student Edition** Find Out by Writing: What Are Generic Drugs?, p. H216 Find Out by Doing: Drugs and *Daphnia*, p. H218 **Review and Reinforcement Guide** Section 9–1	**Video/Videodisc** America Hurts: The Drug Epidemic (Supplemental) **English/Spanish Audiotapes** Section 9–1
Activity Book ACTIVITY: Effects of Alcohol ACTIVITY: Teenagers and Alcoholism **Student Edition** Find Out by Writing: What Is DWI?, p. H220. **Review and Reinforcement Guide** Section 9–2	**Video/Videodisc** You Can Say No to a Drink or a Drug (Supplemental) **English/Spanish Audiotapes** Section 9–2
Student Edition Find Out by Doing: Up in Smoke, p. H224. Find Out by Calculating: Cigarette Smoking, P. H225. **Review and Reinforcement Guide** Section 9–3	**English/Spanish Audiotapes** Section 9–3
Review and Reinforcement Guide Section 9–4	**English/Spanish Audiotapes** Section 9–4
Test Book Chapter Test Performance-Based Test	**Test Book** Computer Test Bank Test

CHAPTER OVERVIEW

A drug is any substance that causes a change in the body in some way. Many helpful drugs are legal and are used to treat disease and infection. Others are powerful and dangerous and illegal to use. Any drug, if used improperly, is potentially harmful. Drugs vary widely in the ways that they affect the body. Among the most powerful drugs are those that affect the nervous system and change behavior.

Drug abuse is the use of any drug in a way that would not be medically recommended. This abuse or misuse may involve either legal or illegal drugs. Legal drugs that are commonly misused or abused include prescription stimulants and depressants, over-the-counter drugs, alcohol, tobacco, and caffeine. Commonly abused or misused illegal drugs include marijuana, hallucinogens, and opiates.

Drug abuse or misuse can cause physical and psychological dependence. A misuser or abuser also develops an increased tolerance for the drug, requiring more and more quantities of the drug to achieve the desired effect. Withdrawal from a drug can be difficult and may require medical attention. Drug abuse and misuse also cause physical damage.

9–1 WHAT ARE DRUGS?
THEMATIC FOCUS

The purpose of this section is to introduce the terms *drug abuse* and *drug misuse* and to identify the dangers associated with drug abuse. A drug is any substance that has an effect on the body. Both legal and illegal substances fit this definition—even aspirin and caffeine. Drugs that are used to treat medical conditions are called medicines. Medicines can be generally placed into two groups—prescription drugs and over-the-counter drugs.

Drug abuse and drug misuse can lead to physical and psychological dependence, increased tolerance levels, and withdrawal difficulties.

The themes that can be focused on in this section are systems and interactions and patterns of change.

*Systems and interactions: Each drug has a particular effect on the body. Stress to students that the effect of a drug on a person varies from one person to another. Drug misuse and abuse are dangerous in many ways. One danger arises from the variability of a drug's effect on different people.

Patterns of change: The various systems in the human body that combine to support life are changed by the presence of drugs. These changes can be internal, such as changes in brain activity, or external, such as behavioral changes. These changes can also create a physical and/or psychological dependence on drugs.

PERFORMANCE OBJECTIVES 9–1
1. Explain the difference between drug abuse and drug misuse.
2. Describe the effects that drugs have on the body.
3. Compare physical dependence to psychological dependence.

SCIENCE TERMS 9–1
drug p. H216
drug abuse p. H217
tolerance p. H217
psychological dependence p. H218
physical dependence P. H218
withdrawal p. H218

9–2 ALCOHOL
THEMATIC FOCUS

The purpose of this section is to introduce alcohol, the oldest drug known to human culture. Alcohol affects several body systems, but the most immediate effect is that of a depressant on the nervous system. High concentrations of alcohol are toxic. One danger of alcohol—aside from its physical damage—is its cultural acceptance, which has led to its widespread abuse. If a person cannot function properly without satisfying the need for alcohol, that person has an alcohol-abuse problem. People who have become addicted to alcohol suffer from a disease called alcoholism.

The themes that can be focused on in this section are energy and stability.

*Energy: Alcohol has several effects on the body, with its most immediate effect being on the brain. Alcohol affects the brain psychologically, in terms of how you think, and physically, in terms of how you behave. Alcohol is a depressant that slows down, or decreases, the activities of the nervous system.

*Stability: The internal environment of the body is stable, and alcohol causes a change in this stable, internal environment. The change caused by alcohol can be both predictable and unpredictable.

PERFORMANCE OBJECTIVES 9–2
1. Describe the effect of alcohol abuse on the body.
2. Predict the dangers of driving while intoxicated.

SCIENCE TERMS 9–2
depressant p. H220
alcoholism p. H221

9–3 TOBACCO
THEMATIC FOCUS

The purpose of this section is to discuss the dangers of tobacco. Tobacco contains many substances that affect the body. Nicotine, carbon monoxide, and tar are some substances that have been implicated as the causes of many medical problems associated with smoking tobacco. The use of tobacco is one of the leading causes of premature death in this country. Lung cancer, heart disease, bronchitis, and emphysema are some of the diseases associated with tobacco use. There is much evidence to indicate that tobacco smoke also affects nonsmokers.

The themes that can be focused on in this section are systems and interactions and patterns of change.

*Systems and interactions: Tobacco has an effect on various body systems. Smoking irritates the respiratory system, increases heartbeat, lowers skin temperature, constricts or narrows blood vessels, and increases blood pressure.

Patterns of change: Tobacco is a drug that causes changes in the body. Use of tobacco can result in lung cancer, heart disease, bronchitis, and emphysema. The damage caused by smoking is not limited only to smokers; nonsmokers are also affected by smoke.

PERFORMANCE OBJECTIVES 9–3

1. Describe the effects of tobacco on the body.
2. Compare the various components of cigarette smoke.

9–4 COMMONLY ABUSED DRUGS

THEMATIC FOCUS

The purpose of this section is to introduce various categories of drugs and describe their effects.

Drugs that are inhaled to get a desired effect are called inhalants. Because inhalants are able to enter the bloodstream directly through the lungs, they affect the body quickly. Typical inhalants include various glues, nitrous oxide, and amyl and butyl nitrate. Inhalants damage the kidneys, lungs, liver, and brain, and an abuser often has nausea, dizziness, loss of coordination, blurred vision, and/or a headache after the effect has worn off.

The most widely abused illegal drug is marijuana. The active ingredient in all forms of marijuana is THC. Smoking or ingesting this chemical can produce a feeling of disorientation. There is evidence that smoking marijuana is harmful to the lungs and can cause physical and psychological problems.

Hallucinogens, such as LSD or PCP, can affect a user's view of reality. High doses of hallucinogens can cause seizures and heart attacks and can induce violent behavior.

Stimulants are drugs that speed up, or increase, the actions of the nervous system. The most powerful stimulants are a group of drugs called amphetamines. Heavy users cannot function without stimulants in their body. Depressants, on the other hand, decrease, or reduce, the rate of nervous system function. The most commonly used and abused depressants are barbiturates. Abusers of depressants who try to quit often find themselves with serious medical problems and may need professional help to stop.

Cocaine is smoked, sniffed, or injected directly into the nervous system. Cocaine causes the brain to release a chemical called dopamine. Psychological dependence on cocaine can be a particularly difficult habit to break. A potent and dangerous form of cocaine that can become addictive after only a few doses is crack.

Some of the most powerful known drugs are opiates. Opium, morphine, and heroin are all examples of this type of drug.

The themes that can be focused on in this section are energy and stability.

*Energy: Certain drugs such as stimulants increase the activity of the nervous system. Other drugs decrease the activity of the nervous system. Both an increase or a decrease of nervous system activity is directly related to the increase or decrease of the body's activity.

*Stability: Regardless of the type of drug used, it will have some effect on the body. The longer a drug is used, the more serious the complications that will develop from its use.

PERFORMANCE OBJECTIVES 9–4

1. Identify some commonly abused drugs.
2. Describe the effect various drugs have on the body.
3. Compare depressants to amphetamines.

SCIENCE TERMS 9–4

inhalant p. H226
stimulant P. H228
marijuana p. H229
hallucinogen p. H230
opiate p. H230

Discovery *Learning*

TEACHER DEMONSTRATIONS MODELING

Simulating the Effects of Drugs

Obtain a stopwatch prior to the demonstration. Ask for a volunteer to write his or her name on the chalkboard using his or her dominant hand. Use the stopwatch to note how long it takes. Then have the student repeat the task using his or her other hand. Note how long this trial takes. Compare the two times. Repeat the activity with other volunteers.

• **With which hand is the task performed the fastest?** (With the dominant hand.)
• **Why is this so?** (Writing is a normal action of the dominant hand.)

Tell students that their ability to perform the task with their recessive hand is similar to the reaction of a person under the influence of marijuana or alcohol. Both these drugs slow down the actions of the central nervous system. In a similar manner, the poor coordination of their recessive hand slowed down their ability to perform this simple task.

Examining Drug and Alcohol Advertisements

Use magazines to obtain advertisements for over-the-counter drugs and alcohol products.
• **What do these advertisements seem to have in common?** (Accept all logical responses. Students should observe that in many instances, advertisers try to make the products appear desirable and/or effective.)
• **What techniques do advertisers use to sell more products?** (Accept all logical responses.)
• **Have you or another family member ever bought a product because of an advertisement you saw?** (Answers will vary.)
• **What part of the advertisement made you or your family member buy this product?** (Accept all responses.)

Tell students that advertisers spend millions of dollars every year to promote the sale of drug, tobacco, and alcohol products. In this chapter they will study the various effects of drugs.

Alcohol, Tobacco, and Drugs

INTEGRATING SCIENCE

This life science chapter provides you with numerous opportunities to integrate other areas of science, as well as other disciplines, into your curriculum. Blue numbered annotations on the student page and integration notes on the teacher wraparound pages alert you to areas of possible integration.

In this chapter you can integrate language arts (pp. 216, 220), social studies (pp. 217, 219), physical science and electricity (p. 222), physical science and chemistry (p. 223), mathematics (p. 225), and life science and zoology (p. 228).

SCIENCE, TECHNOLOGY, AND SOCIETY/COOPERATIVE LEARNING

Society has become more and more conscious of the harmful effects of cigarette smoking and cigarette smoke since 1964. That year, the Surgeon General of the United States issued the first report on the dangers of smoking. In 1971, the United States Congress banned tobacco advertisements from radio and television in an effort to lessen the exposure of young people to the use of tobacco. Efforts by tobacco manufacturers to promote their products did not stop in 1971. They shifted their advertising dollars to print media and billboards and greatly increased the amount of money they spent on the sponsorship of major athletic events.

Many people feel that because sports are so popular among young people, sporting events sponsored by tobacco companies encourage and glamorize the use of tobacco products—behavior known to be life-threatening. Recently, Health and Human Services Secretary Louis Sullivan asked fans, event promoters, and sports arenas to boycott sporting events sponsored by tobacco companies. He also suggested that athletes refuse prize and sponsorship money from these companies.

Tobacco companies have responded to this latest challenge by reminding Secretary Sullivan that the sale and use of tobacco products in this country is legal

"Before I'll ride with a drunk, I'll drive myself." —*Stevie Wonder*

Driving after drinking, or riding with a driver who's been drinking, is a big mistake. Anyone can see that.

INTRODUCING CHAPTER 9

DISCOVERY LEARNING

▶ *Activity Book*

Begin teaching the chapter by using the Chapter 9 Discovery Activity from the *Activity Book*. Using this activity, students will examine the various kinds of information related by the labels on prescription drugs, over-the-counter drugs, alcoholic beverages, and soft drinks.

USING THE TEXTBOOK

Have students examine the picture on page H214.

• **Do you think the picture encourages drinking and driving or discourages drinking and driving?** (The picture discourages drinking and driving.)

• **Why do you think Stevie Wonder was chosen for this advertisement?** (Answers may vary. Lead students to understand that Stevie Wonder is blind.)

• **Do you think the picture relates an**

Alcohol, Tobacco, and Drugs

Guide for Reading

After you read the following sections, you will be able to

9–1 What Are Drugs?
- Define the word drug.
- Describe the effects of drug abuse.

9–2 Alcohol
- Describe the effects of alcohol abuse.

9–3 Tobacco
- Relate cigarette smoking to certain diseases.

9–4 Commonly Abused Drugs
- Describe the effects of smoking marijuana.
- Classify inhalants, depressants, stimulants, hallucinogens, and opiates.

Only one more kilometer to go and you will have reached your goal! You and your friends are running a marathon to raise money for SADD, or *S*tudents *A*gainst *D*runk *D*riving. You are running to gain support for your battle against a dangerous combination—alcohol and driving. Alcohol-related accidents are the greatest health hazard facing teenagers today.

What effect does alcohol have on the body? Why do people use alcohol? Why do they abuse it? What are the long-term effects of heavy drinking? Is alcoholism a disease? Is there a cure for it? As you read the pages that follow you will find the answers to these questions. And you will learn that alcohol is not the only substance that threatens the health and safety of teenagers and adults. Tobacco and other drugs have profound effects on the body. Read on and get wise!

Journal *Activity*

You and Your World A friend of yours is thinking of smoking cigarettes. In your journal, write a letter to your friend explaining that tobacco use is harmful. Then, after you have completed the chapter, reread your letter.

◄ *Posters such as this alert people to the dangers of drunk driving.*

---

and that they have a right to promote and sell their products.

Cooperative learning: Using preassigned groups or randomly selected teams, have groups complete one of the following assignments:
- Select and watch a sporting event during the weekend. (You may want to allow students to select a partner in order to complete this assignment.) While watching the event, teams are to identify the sponsors of the event by listing the companies that are advertising their products during commercial breaks, in or around the stadium, or on the equipment of the participants, and so forth. Encourage teams to observe the different types of promotions that companies may be using. When the event has finished, have teams analyze their data and report to the class.
- Assign one of the following roles: fans, athletes, stadium owners, or tobacco companies. Each group should prepare a position statement on the issue of tobacco companies sponsoring sporting events. Allow each group to present its position to the class.

See Cooperative Learning in the *Teacher's Desk Reference.*

JOURNAL ACTIVITY

You may want to use the Journal Activity as the basis of a class discussion. Have students create a letter that cites both general and specific examples of damage that can be caused by smoking. Also, have students include other examples of harm caused by smoking, such as secondhand smoke. Point out that the damage caused by smoking and the use of other drugs will be explored in this chapter. Students should be instructed to keep their Journal Activity in their portfolio.

---

effective message? (Most students will respond yes.)
- **Why do you think the picture is effective?** (Answers may vary. Lead students to infer that Stevie Wonder, a blind person, is claiming to be a better driver than someone who is drunk.)

Have students read the chapter introduction on page H215. Then have them suggest answers to these questions:
- **What effect does alcohol have on the body?** (Answers might include alcohol decreases coordination and motor skills.)

- **Why do people use alcohol?** (Answers might include peer pressure.)
- **What do you think the punishment should be for a person convicted of drinking and driving?** (Answers will vary.)
- **Do you think strict punishments will stop people from driving while drunk, or will some just do it anyway? Why do you think so?** (Answers will vary.)

9-1 What Are Drugs?

MULTICULTURAL OPPORTUNITY 9-1

Many local police departments have representatives who will talk to the class about drug use in your community. Investigate the possibility of inviting a police officer from your community to give students a local perspective on the drug-abuse problem.

ESL STRATEGY 9-1

Have students answer the following questions:
1. Which of these two descriptions is an example of drug abuse? Which is not?
• A person deliberately taking drugs for purposes other than medical reasons.
• A person taking drugs that were prescribed for someone else.
2. What are the dangers associated with each of these scenarios?

Guide for Reading

Focus on these questions as you read.
▶ *What is a drug?*
▶ *What are some dangers of drug misuse and abuse?*

Figure 9–1 *Drugs come in many shapes and sizes. Some are legal; some are not. What is a drug?* ❶

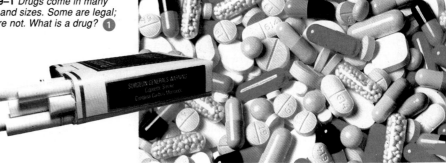

F<small>IND</small> OUT BY

❶ *What Are Generic Drugs?*

Today there is a great deal of talk about generic drugs. Using reference books and materials in the library, find out what the term generic drug means. What are the advantages of generic drugs? What are the possible disadvantages?

9-1 What Are Drugs?

Drugs! You probably hear and see that word a lot today—on radio, television, billboards, and in newspaper articles and advertisements. What is a drug, and why are drugs drawing so much attention? **A drug is any substance that has an effect on the body.** Many substances fit this definition—even aspirin, which is used to reduce pain. Drugs that are used to treat medical conditions are called medicines. Aspirin is a medicine. There are two groups of medicines: prescription drugs and over-the-counter drugs.

Prescription drugs usually are strong drugs that are safe to use only under the supervision of a doctor. Prescription drugs are used to treat diseases or to control conditions such as high blood pressure and pneumonia. Over-the-counter drugs, on the other hand, do not need a doctor's prescription and may be purchased by anyone. Aspirin and cold tablets are examples of over-the-counter drugs.

Drug Misuse and Drug Abuse

When you use a prescription drug exactly as it is prescribed or take an over-the-counter drug according to its directions, you are engaging in drug use. Some people, however, use prescription or over-the-counter drugs incorrectly. Usually these people do so because they are misinformed. The improper use of drugs is called drug misuse.

TEACHING STRATEGY 9-1

FOCUS/MOTIVATION

Obtain a variety of empty over-the-counter drug containers. Also, try to represent some of the over-the-counter drugs that most students may have had contact with, such as aspirin, cough medicine, antacids, and cold tablets. In addition, obtain an empty cigarette pack, an empty beer can, a tea bag, and an empty coffee can. Display these items to students.
• **Describe these things.** (Students should identify each item displayed.)

• **How could these items be grouped or classified?** (Answers should include grouping the aspirin, cough medicine, antacid, and cold tablets together as medicines; grouping the tea bag and coffee together as morning beverages.)
• **How are each of these items used?** (Answers will vary.)
Tell students that each item displayed represents a type of drug. Explain that in this chapter they will learn about drugs and the effects that particular drugs have on the body.

CONTENT DEVELOPMENT

Emphasize that a drug is any substance that has an effect on the body.
• **What is an over-the-counter drug?** (Any drug that can be purchased without a doctor's prescription.)
• **What is a prescription drug?** (A drug that can be purchased only with a doctor's prescription.)
• **Why do you suppose some drugs can be obtained only with a doctor's prescription?** (The side effects of these drugs can

Some people misuse drugs by taking more than the amount a doctor prescribes. They mistakenly believe that such action will speed their recovery from an illness. Other people take more of the drug because they have missed a dose. This action is particularly dangerous because it could cause an overdose. An overdose can cause a serious reaction to a drug, which can sometimes result in death.

When people deliberately misuse drugs for purposes other than medical ones, they are taking part in **drug abuse**. Some drugs prescribed by doctors are abused. Other drugs that are abused are illegal drugs. Drug abuse is extremely dangerous. Do you know why? As you have just read, drugs are substances that have an effect on the body. Drugs can produce powerful changes in your body.

Why do people use drugs? There are many answers to this question. Some seek to "escape" life's problems; others to intensify life's pleasures. Some take drugs because their friends do; others because their friends do not. Some people abuse drugs to feel grown up; others to feel young again. The list is as endless as the range of human emotions. Unfortunately, the desired effects are often followed by harmful and unpleasant side effects.

Dangers of Drug Abuse

People of all ages abuse drugs. Some know that they are abusing drugs; others do not. And still others deny their abuse. The 18- to 25-year-old age group has the highest percentage of drug abuse.

Drug abuse is dangerous for a number of reasons. When you take a drug, for example, the internal functioning of your body changes immediately. Over time, your body also changes its response to the drug. These responses can produce some serious side effects. Let's examine some of these serious and sometimes fatal side effects.

TOLERANCE When a drug is used or abused regularly, the body may develop a **tolerance** to it. Tolerance causes the body to need increasingly larger amounts of the drug to get the same effect that was originally produced. This is exactly what happens to people who abuse drugs. They soon discover that they must take more of the drug each time in order

Figure 9-2 *This clay tablet contains the world's oldest known prescriptions, dating back to about 2000 BC. The prescriptions show the medicinal use of plants.*

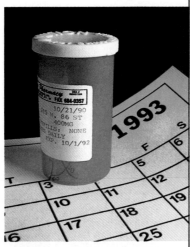

Figure 9-3 *Notice the expiration date on this container of pills. Using a medicine after its prescription has expired is an example of drug misuse. What is a prescription drug?* ❷

H ■ 217

H ■ 217

FIND OUT BY DOING

DRUGS AND *DAPHNIA*

Discovery Learning

Skills: Making comparisons, relating concepts

Materials: Daphnia culture, depression slide, microscope, coverslip, dropper, cola with caffeine

In this activity students will discover the effect of cola on the heart rate of a *Daphnia,* or water flea. Students should determine that a drop of cola increased the heart rate of the *Daphnia* and infer that the increased rate is due to a substance in the cola. Students should conclude that caffeine in the cola increases the *Daphnia*'s heart rate.

9–1 (continued)

INDEPENDENT PRACTICE

Section Review 9–1

1. A drug is any substance that has an effect on the body; prescription drugs usually are strong drugs that are safe to use only with the supervision of a doctor; over-the-counter drugs do not require a doctor's prescription and can be used by anyone.
2. Drug misuse is the improper use of a drug. Drug abuse occurs when drugs are deliberately misused for purposes other than medical purposes.
3. Psychological dependence is an emotional need for a drug; physical depen-

Drugs and Daphnia

1. With your teacher's help, place a *Daphnia* (water flea) in the depression on a depression slide.

2. Cover the slide with a coverslip and place the slide under a microscope.

3. Use the low-power objective to observe the *Daphnia*. You should be able to clearly see the *Daphnia*'s heart beating.

4. Calculate the average heart rate per minute of the *Daphnia.*

5. Remove the coverslip and with a dropper, place one drop of cola in the depression. Replace the coverslip and observe the *Daphnia* again.

6. Calculate the average heart rate per minute again.

Was there a difference in heart rate after the cola was added? If there was a difference, what may have caused it?

■ What does this investigation tell you about cola?

to get the same feeling they did in the beginning. Tolerance can cause people to take too much of a drug—a problem that can lead to overdose and even death.

DEPENDENCE Some drugs produce a dependence, or a state in which a person becomes unable to control drug use. Dependence can be psychological (sigh-kuh-LAHJ-ih-kuhl), physical, or both. In all cases, dependence changes the way the body functions, and it can seriously damage a person's health.

Psychological dependence is a strong desire or need to continue using a drug. When people become psychologically dependent on a drug, they link the drug with specific feelings or moods. When the drug's effect wears off, so does the feeling.

Drug abusers who are psychologically dependent on a drug often believe they can stop using the drug if they want to. Unfortunately, stopping drug abuse once a person is psychologically dependent is not easy and may require a doctor's care.

Physical dependence occurs when the body becomes used to a drug and needs the drug to function normally. This type of dependence generally takes time to develop and usually occurs as tolerance builds. Physical dependence is sometimes referred to as an addiction.

WITHDRAWAL A person who is physically dependent on a drug such as heroin needs to take the drug at least three to four times a day. Miss a dose and the body begins to react: The nose runs, the eyes tear. Miss several doses and the body reacts more violently: chills, fever, vomiting, cramps, headaches, and body aches. In time, the muscles begin to jerk wildly, kicking out of control. This is the beginning of **withdrawal**, or stopping the use of a drug.

Figure 9–4 *In this anti-crack wall mural, an artist describes his attitude toward drug abuse. These children express their views during an anti-drug rally. What types of dependence can result from drug abuse?* **1**

218 ■ H

dence means that the body cannot function properly without a drug.
4. Answers will vary; responses might include drugs can harm the human body.

REINFORCEMENT/RETEACHING

Monitor students' responses to the Section Review questions. If students appear to have difficulty with any of the questions, review the appropriate material in the section.

CLOSURE

▶ *Review and Reinforcement Guide*

At this point have students complete Section 9–1 in the *Review and Reinforcement Guide.*

TEACHING STRATEGY 9–2

FOCUS/MOTIVATION

Have students brainstorm and suggest ten different ways a drunk driver could cause an accident. Use a volunteer to

Although it takes a few days, the most painful symptoms of heroin withdrawal pass. However, heroin abusers are never entirely free of their need for the drug. In fact, far too many heroin abusers who have "kicked the habit" return to the drug again unless they receive medical, psychological, and social help.

9–1 Section Review

1. What is a drug? Compare prescription and over-the-counter drugs.
2. What is drug misuse? Drug abuse?
3. Compare psychological and physical dependence.

Critical Thinking—*You and Your World*
4. How might you convince someone not to use drugs?

Figure 9–5 *People take drugs for many reasons. One reason is to escape from personal problems.*

9–2 Alcohol

Alcohol is a drug. In fact, alcohol is the oldest drug known to humans. Egyptian wall writings, which are among the oldest forms of written communication, show pictures of people drinking wine. It was not until the Egyptian writing symbols were decoded, however, that the meaning of some of the wall paintings was revealed. Their message warned of the dangers of alcohol abuse. **The abuse of alcohol can lead to the destruction of liver and brain cells, and it can cause both physical and psychological dependence.**

How Alcohol Affects the Body

Unlike food, alcohol does not have to be digested. Some alcohol, in fact, is absorbed directly through the wall of the stomach into the bloodstream. If the stomach is empty, the alcohol is absorbed quickly, causing its effects to be felt almost immediately. If the stomach contains food, the alcohol is absorbed more slowly. Upon leaving the

Guide for Reading

Focus on this question as you read.

▶ *What effects does alcohol have on the body?*

Figure 9–6 *This Egyptian wall painting, painted thousands of years ago, shows how grapes were gathered to make wine.*

H ■ 219

9–2 Alcohol

somewhat limited—only small amounts of alcohol can be converted at a time. For this reason, most of the alcohol remains unchanged in the bloodstream.

Alcohol in the bloodstream depresses, or slows down, the actions of the nervous system. Although alcohol sometimes appears to act as a stimulant, it actually depresses parts of the brain that control behavior and inhibitions.

● ● ● ● **Integration** ● ● ● ●

Use the photograph of the Egyptian wall painting to integrate social studies concepts into your science lesson.

INDEPENDENT PRACTICE

▶ *Activity Book*

Students who need practice on the concept of the effect of alcohol on the human body should complete the chapter activity Effects of Alcohol. In this activity students will explore the effect of alcohol on reaction time and judgment.

record suggestions on the chalkboard. (Responses might include poor judgment, reduced reaction time, double vision.)

Have students decide which of the suggestions on the chalkboard are an immediate reaction of the body to the presence of alcohol and which are long-term reactions of the body to the presence of alcohol.

Inform students that they will now study the immediate and long-term effects of alcohol abuse.

CONTENT DEVELOPMENT

Explain to students that alcohol is unlike food in that it does not have to be digested—it is absorbed directly through the wall of the stomach into the bloodstream. After absorption, alcohol travels to, and has an effect on, all parts of the body.

Alcohol in the bloodstream is changed into carbon dioxide and water as it passes through the liver. Stress that the capacity of the liver to perform this role is

FIND OUT BY
WRITING

WHAT IS DWI?

Check charts to determine whether students have displayed the data from each state correctly. Also, check to determine that students have correctly identified the states that allow the highest and the lowest levels of blood alcohol.

Integration: Use the Find Out by Writing feature to integrate language arts concepts into your science lesson.

FACTS AND FIGURES

CALORIES AND ALCOHOL

Alcohol contains many calories but has little food value. The calories are, in a sense, wasted calories. For this reason, most weight-loss diets severely restrict or eliminate the use of alcohol during the weight-loss period.

FIND OUT BY
WRITING

What Is DWI?

1 DWI, or driving while intoxicated, is against the law in every state. However, the amount of alcohol in the blood, or BAC, that determines whether a person is legally drunk differs in many states. Using reference materials in your library, find out the BAC at which a person is considered legally drunk in each state. Arrange this information in the form of a chart. Which states have the highest BAC to be considered legally drunk? The lowest?

Figure 9–7 *As this diagram illustrates, alcohol can cause harmful effects throughout the body. What effect does alcohol have on the brain?* **1**

stomach, the alcohol enters the small intestine, where more of it is absorbed.

After the alcohol is absorbed, it travels through the blood to all parts of the body. As the alcohol in the blood passes through the liver, it is changed into carbon dioxide and water. Carbon dioxide and some water are released from the body by way of the lungs. Most of the water, however, passes out of the body as perspiration and urine.

Because the liver can convert only a small amount of alcohol at a time into carbon dioxide and water, much of the alcohol remains unchanged in the blood. When the alcohol reaches the brain, it acts as a **depressant**. A depressant is a substance that slows down the actions of the central nervous system (brain and spinal cord). Perhaps this seems confusing to you if you have noticed that people who drink do not seem to be depressed at all. Rather, they seem quite energetic.

The reason for this false sense of energy is that alcohol initially affects the part of the brain that controls judgment and self-control. At the same time, alcohol makes people become more relaxed and unafraid. The net result is that the controls people put on their emotions are reduced, causing them to behave in ways they would never normally consider. Thus, people may seem quite stimulated during this time.

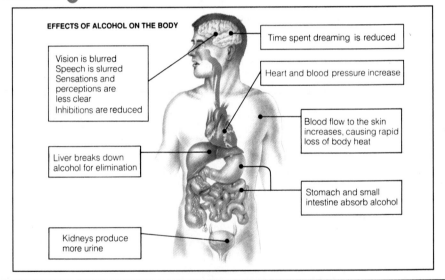

EFFECTS OF ALCOHOL ON THE BODY

Time spent dreaming is reduced

Vision is blurred
Speech is slurred
Sensations and perceptions are less clear
Inhibitions are reduced

Heart and blood pressure increase

Blood flow to the skin increases, causing rapid loss of body heat

Liver breaks down alcohol for elimination

Stomach and small intestine absorb alcohol

Kidneys produce more urine

9–2 (continued)

ENRICHMENT

▶ *Activity Book*

Students will be challenged by the Chapter 9 activity in the *Activity Book* called Teenagers and Alcoholism. In this activity students will quantitatively explore the role of teenagers and alcohol.

CONTENT DEVELOPMENT

Sometimes students have a difficult time understanding how a depressant can make a person feel "high." Explain that this feeling is a kind of euphoria because nothing is bothering the person; the nervous system

is so depressed that it does not "recognize" whatever problems or worries exist. People begin to suffer the side effects of alcohol some time before they reach the legal level of drunkenness. Depending on the individual person and other factors, between the levels 0.01 and 0.04, drinkers may feel dizzy; may say or do things that are uncharacteristic of them; may appear flushed because of the increased rate of blood circulation; and may begin to lose their coordination, making them more prone to accidents. Between the levels 0.05 and 0.09,

drinkers cannot think clearly or make wise decisions, their behavior may be uncharacteristic of them, and their loss of coordination is more obvious. Around 0.10, most senses and balance are impaired. About 0.30, vomiting and/or coma may occur. At 0.40 and beyond, drinkers are endangering their lives from alcohol poisoning. Other symptoms are pointed out in Figure 9–8. Remind students again that individual reactions to alcohol vary considerably because of a number of factors.

Figure 9–8 *Blood alcohol concentration, or BAC, is a measure of the amount of alcohol in the bloodstream per 100 mL of blood. The BAC is expressed as a percentage. The higher the BAC, the more powerful the effect of alcohol on the brain. What type of behavior occurs if the BAC is 0.1 percent?* ❷

ALCOHOL'S EFFECTS ON THE BRAIN

BAC	Part of Brain Affected	Behavior
0.05%		Lack of judgment; lack of inhibition
0.1%		Reduced reaction time; difficulty in walking and driving
0.2%		Saddened, weeping, abnormal behavior
0.3%		Double vision; inadequate hearing
0.45%		Unconscious
0.65%		Death

But if people continue to drink, the alcohol in their blood begins to affect other areas of the brain. Soon the areas that control speech and muscle coordination are affected. A person may slur words and have trouble walking. More alcohol can lead to a state of total confusion as more of the brain is affected. Often a person loses consciousness. Sometimes the areas of the brain controlling breathing and heartbeat are affected. Such an overdose of alcohol is life threatening.

Alcohol and Health

For most people, the moderate use of alcohol does not result in health problems. Drinking large amounts of alcohol on a daily basis, however, can cause health problems. Prolonged alcohol abuse may cause mental disturbances, such as blackouts and hallucinations (seeing or hearing things that are not really there). It can also damage the linings of the stomach and small intestine. The risk of cancer of the mouth, esophagus, throat, and larynx is increased among alcohol abusers. Continued use of alcohol also causes cirrhosis (suh-ROH-sihs) of the liver. Cirrhosis is a disease in which liver cells and the connective tissue that hold the cells together are damaged by the heavy intake of alcohol. The damaged liver cells and connective tissue form scar tissue, which interferes with the liver's ability to perform its normal functions. Figure 9–9 shows the difference in appearance between a normal liver and a liver with cirrhosis. Cirrhosis is responsible for about 13,000 deaths in America every year.

The abuse of alcohol can lead to **alcoholism**. Alcoholism is an incurable disease in which a person is physically and psychologically dependent on alcohol. A person who has the disease is called an alcoholic. An alcoholic needs both medical and psychological help. The aid of organizations such as Alcoholics Anonymous is also important in helping alcoholics

Figure 9–9 *Long-term alcohol use destroys liver cells. Notice the differences in appearance of a normal liver (left), one that has some fatty deposits due to alcohol abuse (center), and one that is consumed by cirrhosis (right).*

H ■ 221

FACTS AND FIGURES

ALCOHOL-RELATED DEATHS

Aside from more than 25,000 highway deaths every year, drinking is involved in about one third of all suicides, one half of all murders, and about one fourth of all other accidents and fires. The result—about 200,000 alcohol-related deaths a year.

ENRICHMENT

Many good films and cassettes are available that document the facts of living with alcoholic family members. If students have not had this experience, it may be difficult for them to comprehend it. If they have had the experience, they usually prefer not to talk about it. A film or a speaker may be the best way to impress students with the scope of alcoholism and the problems that it causes. Alcoholics can refuse to recognize their problems, and sometimes their families become part of the coverup.

Another subject that you may want to discuss because some students may fear it is the idea that the children of alcoholics have a genetic predisposition toward alcoholism. Stress to students that a genetic predisposition does not mean that they will become alcoholics. It simply means that they may have to be more careful than others are. A similar analogy is that children of overweight parents may have to be more careful about their weight than other people are, but they do not all become obese.

You might ask interested students to find out about the Alcoholics Anonymous and family support groups in your community. Ask them to find out when and where these groups meet and how someone could become a participant if he or she wishes to do so. This information can be presented to the class.

ANNOTATION KEY

Answers
❶ Accept all reasonable responses. (Applying concepts)

Integration
❶ Physical Science: Electricity. See *Electricity and Magnetism*, Chapter 1.
❷ Physical Science: Chemistry. See *Chemistry of Matter*, Chapter 3.

CONNECTIONS
"BAD BREATH?"

Students may be familiar with or have heard of a breath analyzer. But many students may not have realized that these breath analyzers, or field-sobriety units, use electricity to help determine the amount of alcohol present in an exhaled breath. Discuss with students the scientific concepts involved in these analyzers. Interested students might consider researching other tests that are used when drivers are suspected of being under the influence of alcohol.

If you are teaching thematically, you may want to use the Connections feature to reinforce the themes of energy, scale and structure, systems and interactions, and stability.

Integration: Use the Connections feature to integrate physical science concepts of electricity into your life science lesson.

overcome their problems. There are even organizations for the relatives of the 10 million or more alcoholics in this country. One, called Alateen, is for the children of people who have an alcohol problem.

Knowing about the damage that alcohol does to the body and the brain, one would think alcohol abusers would stop drinking. Unfortunately, withdrawal from alcohol can be very difficult. Like other drug abusers, alcoholics may suffer from withdrawal symptoms when they try to stop drinking. About one fourth of the alcoholics in the United States experience hallucinations during withdrawal.

CONNECTIONS

"Bad Breath?" ❶

You have probably seen television programs in which a person suspected of driving while intoxicated is stopped by police and asked to exhale into a breath analyzer. A breath analyzer is a device that determines the amount of alcohol in the body.

The first breath analyzer, which consisted of an inflatable balloon, was developed in the late 1930s by the American doctor Rolla N. Hager who called it a "Drunkometer." Today, most breath analyzers in use are electronic. That is, they are powered by *electric currents* (flow of charged particles). About the size of a television remote-control device, an electronic breath analyzer contains a fuel cell that works like a battery. A person exhales into the breath analyzer, and the air is pulled into the fuel cell through a valve. There the air comes in contact with a small strip of positively charged platinum. This strip is in contact with a disk containing sulfuric acid. The platinum changes any alcohol that might be present to acetic acid. When this happens, particles of platinum lose electrons and an

electric current is set up in the disk. The electric current then flows from the positively charged platinum particles to the negatively charged particles on the other side of the disk.

The more alcohol the breath contains, the stronger the electric current. A weak electric current or no electric current produces a green light, indicating that a person's breath contains little or no alcohol. A stronger current produces an amber light, showing that a person's breath contains some alcohol. A very strong electric current produces a red light, meaning that a person's breath contains a lot of alcohol. In the case of either an amber light or a red light, a person has failed the breath test. The person needs to be tested further to determine exactly how much alcohol the body contains.

9–2 (continued)

INDEPENDENT PRACTICE

Section Review 9–2
1. Alcohol affects both brain cells and liver cells and causes both physical and psychological dependence.
2. Alcoholism is the disease of alcohol abuse. Alcoholism occurs when drinking large amounts of alcohol becomes a habit.
3. Drinking impairs judgment, reduces reaction time, and deteriorates motor

skills, making the operation of a motor vehicle dangerous and unsafe.

REINFORCEMENT/RETEACHING

Review students' responses to the Section Review questions. Reteach any material that is still unclear, based on students' responses.

CLOSURE

▶ *Review and Reinforcement Guide*
Students may now complete Section 9–2 in the *Review and Reinforcement Guide.*

TEACHING STRATEGY 9–3

FOCUS/MOTIVATION

Have students examine Figure 9–11. Ask students to describe the photographs.
• **What has damaged the smoker's respiratory system?** (The tars and poisons found in cigarette smoke.)

An alternative is to perform any of several simple demonstrations illustrating the residue left by cigarette smoke. If you want to make a more elaborate demon-

9–3 Tobacco

In 1988, the Surgeon General (chief medical officer in the United States Public Health Service) warned that the nicotine in tobacco products is as addictive (habit-forming) as the illegal drugs heroin and cocaine. This report was the fifth on the effects of smoking tobacco to come from the Surgeon General's office. The first report, which was issued in 1964, declared that cigarette smoking causes lung cancer, heart disease, and respiratory illnesses. In 1972, the Surgeon General issued the first report to suggest that secondhand (passive) smoke is a danger to nonsmokers. A 1978 report warned pregnant women that smoking could affect the health of their unborn children. This report also stated that smoking could prevent the body from absorbing certain important nutrients. In 1982, cigarette smoking was named as the single most preventable cause of death in the United States. Four years later, another report published the results of studies linking secondhand smoke to lung cancer and respiratory diseases in nonsmokers. Despite all these warnings, our nation still has millions of tobacco smokers!

Guide for Reading

Focus on this question as you read.

▶ *What effects does tobacco have on the body?*

Some Harmful Chemicals in Tobacco Smoke

acetaldehyde
acetone
acetonitrile
acrolein
acrylonitrile
ammonia
aniline
benzene
benzopyrene
2,3 butadione
butylamine
carbon monoxide
dimethylamine
dimethylnitrosamine
ethylamine
formaldehyde
hydrocyanic acid
hydrogen cyanide
hydrogen sulfide
methacrolein
methyl alcohol
methylamine
methylfuran
methylnaphthalene
nicotine
nitric oxide
nitrogen dioxide
phenol
pyridine
toluene

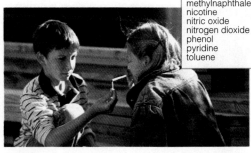

Figure 9–10 *Smoking at any age is dangerous. In addition to the harmful substances listed in the chart, about 4000 other substances are inhaled when smoking cigarettes. Why do people smoke cigarettes?* ❶

H ■ 223

FIND OUT BY DOING

Up in Smoke

1. Place a few pieces of tobacco in a test tube. Using some cotton, loosely plug up the mouth of the test tube.

2. With your teacher's permission, use a Bunsen burner to heat the test tube until the tobacco burns completely. **CAUTION:** *Be very careful when working with a Bunsen burner.*

3. Allow the test tube to cool before removing the cotton plug.

Describe the appearance of the cotton plug before and after the investigation. Which substance in tobacco smoke was collected in the cotton?

■ Design an investigation in which you determine whether a brand of cigarettes that is advertised as low in tar really is.

Figure 9–11 *There is a significant difference between the walls of the bronchus of a nonsmoker (right) and those of a smoker (left). This difference can often be fatal. The large grayish-green objects are cancer cells.*

Effects of Tobacco

Why is smoking so dangerous? When a cigarette burns, about 4000 substances are produced. Many of these substances are harmful. Some of these substances are listed in Figure 9–10. Although 10 percent of cigarette smoke is water, 60 percent is made of poisonous substances such as nicotine and carbon monoxide. Nicotine, as you have just read, is an addictive drug. Once in the body, nicotine causes the heart to beat faster, skin temperature to drop, and blood pressure to rise. Carbon monoxide is a poisonous gas often found in polluted air. Yet even the most polluted air on the most polluted day in history does not contain anywhere near the concentration of carbon monoxide that cigarette smoke does!

The remaining 30 percent of cigarette smoke consists of tars. Tars are probably the most dangerous part of cigarette smoke. As smoke travels to the lungs, the tars irritate and damage the entire respiratory system. Unfortunately, this damage is particularly serious in the developing lungs of teenagers.

Tobacco and Disease

Cigarette smoking causes damage to both the respiratory system and the circulatory system. Long-term smoking can lead to lung diseases such as bronchitis (brahng-KIGH-tihs) and emphysema (ehm-fuh-SEE-muh). These diseases are often life threatening. In addition, a heavy smoker has a twenty-times-greater chance of getting lung cancer than a nonsmoker has.

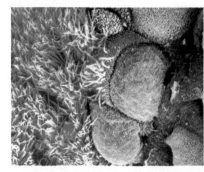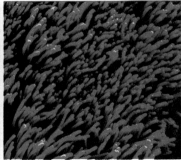

In addition to lung irritation, smoking also increases heartbeat, lowers skin temperature, and causes blood vessels to constrict, or narrow. Constriction of blood vessels increases blood pressure and makes the heart work harder. Heavy smokers are twice as likely to develop some forms of heart disease than are nonsmokers.

The Surgeon General's 1982 report not only named cigarette smoking as the single most preventable cause of death in the United States, it also contained a long list of cancers associated with smoking. In addition to lung cancer, the report named cancer of the bladder, mouth, esophagus, pancreas, and larynx. In fact, at least one third of all cancer deaths may be caused by smoking.

Not everyone who experiences the harmful effects of cigarette smoking has chosen to smoke. Many people are passive, or involuntary, smokers. A passive smoker is one who breathes in air containing the smoke from other people's cigars, pipes, or cigarettes. If one or both of your parents smoke, you probably have been a passive smoker all your life. As you may already know, passive smoking can be extremely unpleasant. It can cause your eyes to burn, itch, and water, and it can irritate your nose and throat.

What is even more important, however, is that passive smoking is harmful to your health. Recent research shows that nonsmokers who have worked closely with smokers for many years suffer a decrease in the functioning of the lungs. Other studies show that infants under the age of one year whose mothers smoke have twice as many lung infections as infants of nonsmoking mothers.

9-3 Section Review

1. What effects does tobacco smoking have on the body?
2. What is nicotine? Tar?

Critical Thinking—*You and Your World*

3. What factors do you think influence someone to use tobacco?

THIS IS A

SMOKE-FREE BUILDING

Figure 9–12 *Because passive smoking is harmful, some companies have made their buildings totally smoke free.*

FIND OUT BY CALCULATING

Cigarette Smoking

In 1980, there were 54 million smokers in the United States. If these people smoked 630 billion cigarettes each year, approximately how many cigarettes did each person smoke in a year? In a month? ①

FIND OUT BY CALCULATING
CIGARETTE SMOKING

Skills: Making computations, calculator

This activity helps to make students aware of the enormous quantity of cigarettes smoked by Americans every year. Students should determine that each person smokes approximately 11,667 cigarettes per year, or approximately 972 cigarettes per month.

Integration: Use the Find Out by Calculating feature to integrate mathematics into your science curriculum.

increases heart rate, increases blood pressure, and decreases skin temperature; tar is a substance that irritates and damages the entire respiratory system.
3. Answers will vary. Responses might include peer pressure.

REINFORCEMENT/RETEACHING

Monitor students' responses to the Section Review questions. If students appear to have difficulty with any of the questions, review the appropriate material in the section.

CLOSURE

▶ *Review and Reinforcement Guide*

At this point have students complete Section 9–3 in the *Review and Reinforcement Guide.*

GUIDED PRACTICE

▶ *Laboratory Manual*

Skill: Applying concepts

At this point you may want to have students complete the Chapter 9 Laboratory Investigation in the *Laboratory Manual* called Effects of Tobacco and Alcohol on Seed Germination. In this investigation students will explore the effect that alcohol and tobacco smoke have on the germination rate of mustard seeds.

ENRICHMENT

Have interested students create posters to place in various elementary schools in your district. Each poster should be designed to convey an antismoking message.

INDEPENDENT PRACTICE

Section Review 9–3

1. Cigarette smoking causes damage to both the respiratory and the circulatory systems.
2. Nicotine is an addictive substance that

9-4 Commonly Abused Drugs

MULTICULTURAL OPPORTUNITY 9-4

Invite a physician from the community to discuss the physiological effects of various classes of drugs. If you have a class that is composed predominantly of one minority group, it would provide an effective role model to invite a physician from the local community who is also a member of that minority group.

ESL STRATEGY 9-4

Write the groups of words below on the chalkboard. Have volunteers circle the word or words, if any, that do not belong in each group and then name and define each group of drugs.

1. paint thinner, nitrous oxide, codeine, glue
2. cocaine, barbiturates, amphetamines, crack
3. barbiturates, caffeine, tranquilizers, nail polish remover
4. mescaline, PCP ("angel dust"), paregoric, LSD
5. morphine, butyl oxide, opium, heroin

TEACHING STRATEGY 9-4

FOCUS/MOTIVATION

Give every student five small pieces of paper (use scratch paper, if you have it, to avoid waste). Ask students to write words representing five things that are important to them—family, girlfriend or boyfriend, home, car, money, and so on. Ask students to wad up the papers and collect them in a wastebasket. A person who is dependent on drugs (including alcohol) will literally do what students have just done figuratively. Ask students to discuss the following questions:

• **How does it feel to think about throwing away all these things?** (Answers will vary.)
• **How do you think a drug abuser feels about throwing away all these things?** (Answers will vary.)

Figure 9–13 *Because products such as paint thinner give off dangerous fumes, their labels contain warnings for their use in well-ventilated rooms.*

9-4 Commonly Abused Drugs

As you have already learned, drugs are substances that have an effect on the body. The specific effects differ with the type of drug. Some drugs affect the circulatory system, whereas others affect the respiratory system. The most powerful drugs, however, are those that affect the nervous system and change the user's behavior.

For the most part, drugs that affect the nervous system are the drugs that are most commonly abused. **Some commonly abused drugs include inhalants, depressants, stimulants, hallucinogens** (huh-LOO-sih-nuh-jehnz)**, and opiates** (OH-pee-ihtz)**.** In this section you will learn about the effects these drugs have on the body.

Inhalants

Drugs that are inhaled to get a desired effect are called **inhalants.** Because inhalants are able to enter the bloodstream directly through the lungs, they affect the body quickly.

Typically, people abuse inhalants to get a brief feeling of excitement. One such example of inhalant abuse is glue sniffing. After the effects of inhaling the fumes have worn off, the abuser often has nausea, dizziness, loss of coordination, blurred vision, and a headache. Some inhalants do permanent damage to the brain, liver, kidneys, and lungs. Continued abuse can lead to unconsciousness and even death.

Other examples of inhalants include nitrous oxide, amyl nitrite (AM-ihl NIGH-tright), and butyl (BYOO-tihl) nitrite. Nitrous oxide, which is more commonly known as "laughing gas," is used by dentists as a painkiller because it causes the body to relax. Long-term abuse of nitrous oxide can cause psychological dependence and can damage the kidneys, liver, and bone marrow. Both amyl nitrite and butyl nitrite cause relaxation, light-headedness, and a burst of energy. As with nitrous oxide, abuse of these drugs can cause psychological dependence and certain circulatory problems.

CONTENT DEVELOPMENT

Stress with students that commonly abused drugs are grouped as inhalants, depressants, stimulants, hallucinogens, and opiates.

Write the word *inhalant* on the chalkboard. Have the class discuss the meaning of the word; then have a volunteer write the definition for this term on the board. Remind students that inhalants are drugs that are inhaled. Point out that inhalants are drugs that generate relatively immediate effects because they enter the bloodstream directly through the lungs.

Typical substances used as inhalants include glue, nitrous oxide, amyl nitrate, and butyl nitrate. Emphasize that the use of inhalants includes several serious side effects as well as organ damage.

• **What are the serious side effects of the use of inhalants?** (The serious side effects often include nausea, dizziness, loss of coordination, blurred vision, headache, and psychological dependence.)

COMMONLY ABUSED DRUGS

Type of Drug	Examples	Basic Action on Central Nervous System	Psychological Dependence	Physical Dependence	Withdrawal Symptoms	Development of Tolerance
Opiates and related drugs	Heroin Demerol Methadone	Depressant	Yes, strong	Yes, very fast development	Severe but rarely life-threatening	Yes
Barbiturates	Phenobarbital Nembutal Seconal	Depressant	Yes	Yes	Severe, life-threatening	Yes
Tranquilizers (minor)	Valium Miltown Librium	Depressant	Yes	Yes	Yes	Yes
Alcohol	Beer Wines Liquors Whiskey	Depressant	Yes	Yes	Severe, life-threatening	Yes, more in some people than in others
Cocaine	As a powder Crack	Stimulant	Yes, strong	Yes	Yes	Possible
Cannabis	Marijuana Hashish	Ordinarily a depressant	Yes, moderate	Probably not	Probably none	Possible
Amphetamines	Benzedrine Dexedrine Methedrine	Stimulant	Yes	Possible	Possible	Yes, strong
Hallucinogens	LSD Mescaline Psilocybin	Stimulant	Yes	No	None	Yes, fast
Nicotine	In tobacco of cigarettes, cigars; also in pipe tobacco, chewing tobacco	Stimulant	Yes, strong	Yes	Yes	Yes
Inhalants	Nitrous oxide Amyl nitrite Butyl nitrite	Depressant	Yes	No	None	No

Figure 9–14 *This chart lists some of the commonly abused drugs. What type of drug is nicotine?* ❶

Depressants

Earlier you read that alcohol is a depressant. Depressants slow down or decrease the actions of the nervous system. Two other commonly abused depressants are the powerful barbiturates (bahr-BIHCH-er-ihts) and the weaker tranquilizers (TRAN-kwihl-ighz-erz). Usually, these drugs are taken in pill form.

Because depressants calm the body and can bring on sleep, doctors once prescribed them for people who had sleeping problems or suffered from

H ■ 227

BACKGROUND INFORMATION
THE EFFECTS OF DRUGS

Different people react differently to the same drug. Factors that contribute to the effect of a drug include the strength of the drug; the duration of its use; the time involved; the presence or absence of food or other drugs; and the size, health, and tolerance of the individual.

After sufficient time, have volunteers relate the specific examples from each group to the remainder of the class.

CONTENT DEVELOPMENT

Remind students that one danger of barbiturate use is addiction in a relatively short period of time. Another danger of barbiturate abuse is that withdrawal of barbiturates from the body can result in serious medical problems. The withdrawal from most other abused drugs results in less serious medical problems that may not require immediate medical attention. Barbiturate withdrawal requires medical attention.

• **What organs of the human body can be harmed by the use of inhalants?** (Kidneys, liver, and bone marrow.)
• **Can organ damage from the use of inhalants occur from just one use?** (Lead students to relate that the use of any drug risks organ damage.)

GUIDED PRACTICE

Skills Development
Skill: Relating cause and effect

Point out that the group of drugs known as depressants slow down, or depress, the nervous system. Divide students into groups of four to six students per group. Have groups think about and discuss the way heavy barbiturate use would affect a person's lifestyle. Have each group generate specific examples.

CRACK COCAINE

Crack is a yellow powdery form of cocaine. It is often prepared by mixing cocaine with chemicals, boiling it down to a paste, and letting it harden. The crack can then be smoked. When it is smoked, crack makes crackling sounds; hence, its name. Crack users generally experience a high soon after smoking crack. This high is accompanied by a surge of power and joy that makes the user feel euphoric.

Figure 9–15 *When people take drugs such as barbiturates in combination with alcohol, the results are often fatal. Why?* **①**

Figure 9–16 *Under the influence of amphetamines, an orb-weaver spider weaves an irregular web. What type of drug is an amphetamine?* **②**

nervousness. But depressants, particularly barbiturates, cause both physical and psychological dependence. Withdrawal from barbiturate abuse is especially severe and can result in death if done without medical care. And because a tolerance to depressants builds up quickly, a person must continue to take more and more of the drug. This can lead to an overdose, which can lead to death. When barbiturates are used with alcohol, the results are often fatal because the nervous system can become so slowed down that even breathing stops.

Stimulants

While depressants decrease the activities of the nervous system, **stimulants** increase these activities. Caffeine, a drug in coffee, is a stimulant. However, caffeine is a mild stimulant. Far more powerful stimulants make up a class of drugs called amphetamines (am-FEHT-uh-meenz).

Today, the legal use of amphetamines is limited. Yet many people abuse amphetamines illegally. They seek the extra pep an amphetamine pill may bring. Long-term amphetamine abuse, however, can lead to serious psychological and physical problems. Perhaps no side effects are more dramatic than the feelings of dread and suspicion that go hand in hand with amphetamine abuse.

A stimulant that has been increasingly abused in recent years is cocaine. Cocaine comes from the leaves of coca plants that grow in South America. Cocaine may be injected by needle but is usually inhaled as a powder through the nose. In time, the lining of the nose becomes irritated from the powder. If abuse continues, it is not uncommon for cocaine to burn a hole through the walls of the nose.

Psychological dependence from cocaine abuse is so powerful that the drug is difficult to give up. Long-term cocaine abuse can lead to the same mental problems as those of amphetamine abuse.

Within the last 10 years, a very dangerous form of cocaine known as crack has become popular. Unlike cocaine, crack is smoked. Once in the body, crack travels quickly to the brain, where it produces an intense high. This high, however, wears off quickly, leaving the user in need of another dose. Crack is

---

9–4 (continued)

CONTENT DEVELOPMENT

Amphetamines, or stimulants, increase the activities of the nervous system.

• **Why do you think stimulants have been used for many years as diet pills?** (Responses might include they speed up the activity of the nervous system and burn up food and calories more quickly.)

• **Do you think amphetamines have any effect on the aging process?** (Answers will vary.)

• **If yes, why?** (Every body system is overstimulated and affected by amphetamines. It is like being very excited all the time, which is really exhausting and taxing to the body.)

● ● ● ● **Integration** ● ● ● ●

Use the photographs of the orb-weaver spider to integrate zoology into your science lesson.

GUIDED PRACTICE

Skills Development

Skill: Making observations

Emphasize the idea that drugs influence the behavior of a person. Drugs also influence the behavior of animals. Have students examine Figure 9–16.

• **Describe what you see.** (A spider in its web.)

• **How do spiders know how to build a web?** (The ability to spin a web is instinctive.)

• **Can you think of any other instinctive behaviors of a particular animal?** (Answers will vary.)

Tell students that animals influenced by drugs are unable to follow their instincts. The same is true for human beings.

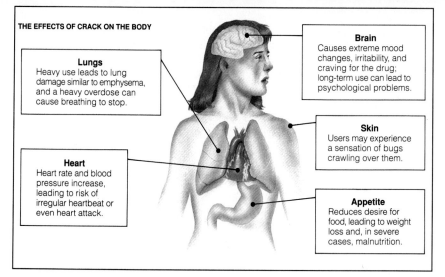

THE EFFECTS OF CRACK ON THE BODY

Lungs
Heavy use leads to lung damage similar to emphysema, and a heavy overdose can cause breathing to stop.

Brain
Causes extreme mood changes, irritability, and craving for the drug; long-term use can lead to psychological problems.

Skin
Users may experience a sensation of bugs crawling over them.

Heart
Heart rate and blood pressure increase, leading to risk of irregular heartbeat or even heart attack.

Appetite
Reduces desire for food, leading to weight loss and, in severe cases, malnutrition.

Figure 9–17 *Crack is an extremely powerful form of cocaine. What effects does crack have on the brain?* 3

among the most addictive drugs known. A crack user can become hooked on the drug in only a few weeks. Figure 9–17 shows some effects that crack has on the body.

Marijuana

Another drug that is usually smoked is **marijuana**. Marijuana is an illegal drug made from the flowers and leaves of the Indian hemp plant. The effects of marijuana are due mainly to a chemical in the plant known as THC. The THC in marijuana affects different people in different ways. And the effects are often hard to describe once they have passed.

Some users of marijuana report a sense of well-being, or a feeling of being able to think clearly. Others say that they become suspicious of people and cannot keep their thoughts from racing. For many, marijuana distorts the sense of time. A few seconds may seem like an hour, or several hours may race by like seconds.

Research findings now point to a variety of possible health problems caused by marijuana. Like alcohol, marijuana slows reaction time and is the direct cause of many highway accidents. Marijuana seems to have an effect on short-term memory. Heavy users

Figure 9–18 *Marijuana is an illegal drug made from the flowers and leaves of the Indian hemp plant. What chemical in marijuana is responsible for its effects?* 4

H ■ 229

CONTENT DEVELOPMENT

Point out that the most commonly abused drug is marijuana. It is commonly called grass or pot. The active ingredient in all forms of marijuana is THC. Smoking or ingesting this chemical can produce a temporary feeling of euphoria and disorientation. Short-term use of marijuana is harmful to the lungs. Long-term use can cause more serious physical and psychological problems.

Also, point out that cocaine is another illegal drug that was actually used during the nineteenth century as a painkiller during surgery. A potent, relatively inexpensive, and dangerous form of cocaine that becomes addictive after only a few doses is crack. Crack interferes with proper heart function and can cause a heart attack. Crack also damages the lungs and can cause respiration to stop.

THE POPPY PLANT

The poppy plant requires certain climate conditions for growth. Have students research places where the poppy plant grows naturally and then determine the way in which poppy plants have affected the countries in which they grow.

CAREERS

Emergency Medical Technician

A call reporting a traffic accident caused by a drunk driver comes into the dispatcher. A team of four people jumps into an ambulance and heads out. The team consists of a driver, a "navigator" who directs and guides the driver to the emergency quickly and safely, and two EMTs, or **emergency medical technicians**. Emergency medical technicians are specially trained to provide on-the-scene care and treatment for accident victims.

To learn more about this exciting career, write to the National Association of Emergency Medical Technicians, 9140 Ward Park, Kansas City, MO 64114.

often have trouble concentrating. And there can be no doubt that marijuana irritates the lungs and leads to some respiratory damage. It may surprise you to learn that smoking marijuana harms the lungs more than smoking tobacco does. Long-term abuse of marijuana produces psychological dependence but does not seem to lead to physical dependence. Withdrawal symptoms usually do not occur, but heavy users may suffer sleep difficulties and anxiety.

Hallucinogens

All **hallucinogens** are illegal. Hallucinogens are drugs that alter a user's view of reality. Abusers of hallucinogens cannot tell what is real and what is not. They may also experience memory loss and personality changes, and they may not be able to perform normal activities.

The strongest hallucinogen is LSD. The effects of LSD are unpredictable—it can either stimulate or depress the body. Abusers commonly see colorful pictures. A person may report seeing sound and hearing color. Solid walls may move in waves. Not all hallucinations are pleasant, however. Some people experience nightmarelike "bad trips" in which all sense of reality is lost. Fears are heightened, and a feeling of dread overcomes the user. During this time, accidental deaths and even suicide are not uncommon. A small percentage of abusers do not recover from an LSD experience for months and have to be hospitalized.

The hallucinogen called PCP or "angel dust" was originally developed as an anesthetic (painkilling substance) for animals. PCP may be smoked, injected, sniffed, or eaten. PCP can act as a stimulant, depressant, or hallucinogen. PCP abusers often engage in violent acts and some have even committed suicide.

Opiates

Some of the most powerful drugs known are the **opiates**, or painkilling drugs. Opiates, which are produced from the liquid sap of the opium poppy plant, include opium, morphine, codeine, paregoric (par-uh-GOR-ihk), and heroin. With the exception of

---

9–4 (continued)

CONTENT DEVELOPMENT

Historically, opiates are an interesting group of drugs. You might ask interested students to research the use of opiates in other countries and other cultures. They might wish to include the medical uses of opiates.

A public health official could speak to the class or give you some information about heroin users, their general health concerns, and the types of treatment available, including information about methadone and its successes and problems.

REINFORCEMENT/RETEACHING

Ask students to decide whether the following statements are true or false.
1. A cigarette is an example of a drug. (True.)
2. Taking one aspirin per month is considered drug misuse. (False.)
3. Once a person has developed a tolerance to a drug, that person requires less of the drug. (False.)
4. People can develop a psychological dependence on tobacco. (True.)

5. Cigarette smoking can lead to cirrhosis of the liver. (False.)
6. Alcohol enters the blood almost immediately after it is drunk. (True.)
7. Cocaine acts as a stimulant to the brain. (True.)
8. PCP is a depressant. (False.)
9. Heroin is not physically addictive. (False.)
10. It is not possible to abuse prescription drugs. (False.)
11. Alcohol is a stimulant. (False.)
12. A smoker has a much greater chance

Figure 9–19 *A close-up of a ripe poppy pod shows some of the opium-containing juice oozing out (left). The roundish yellow structure in the middle of the poppy flower is the pod (right).*

heroin and opium, all opiates can legally be used under a doctor's supervision.

In addition to causing a strong physical and psychological dependence, there are other dangers of opiate abuse. The most obvious to nonabusers is the antisocial behavior of people who have a strong need for the drug heroin but no money with which to buy it illegally. Such abusers become trapped in a world from which they cannot escape without help. And the longer they use heroin, the longer they are likely to suffer the dangers of its abuse. For example, most abusers risk an overdose. And overdoses often lead to death. In addition, life-threatening diseases such as AIDS and hepatitis can be transmitted by sharing needles. In their weakened condition, heroin abusers are no match for such serious diseases.

9–4 Section Review

1. Compare the effects a depressant and a stimulant have on the body.
2. Describe the effect hallucinogens have on the body.

Critical Thinking—*You and Your World*

3. You are at a party where drugs are being used. What should you do?

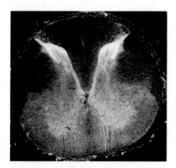

Figure 9–20 *The bright spots in this cross section of the spinal cord are opiate receptors. Opiate receptors are those areas where opiates attach to nerve cells.*

H ■ 231

of getting lung cancer than a nonsmoker. (True.)

13. Caffeine is a drug. (True.)

Laboratory Investigation

ANALYZING SMOKING ADVERTISEMENTS

BEFORE THE LAB

1. Gather a wide assortment of magazines. Be sure there are at least three magazines for each group of students. (Perhaps the magazines could be obtained from the school library because they will not be destroyed.)

2. Preview the magazines to be certain they are suitable for this lab. Be alert for inappropriate pictures and cartoons and other objectionable matter.

PRE-LAB DISCUSSION

Have students read the complete laboratory procedure.

• **Why do tobacco companies produce cigarettes?** (A logical response is to make money.)

• **Do you predict that a magazine would generally contain more advertisements encouraging smoking or more advertisements discouraging smoking?** (A logical response is more advertisements encouraging smoking.)

• **Why?** (A possible response might be that tobacco manufacturers spend, and have access to, more money than do antismoking campaigns.)

• **Because the use of tobacco is unhealthy, do you think our government would be correct or incorrect to try and limit its use? Explain your reasoning.** (Answers and explanations will vary.)

TEACHING STRATEGY

1. If students have difficulty determining the theme of an advertisement, allow them sufficient time to discuss and agree on the theme of a particular advertisement.

2. Advertisements typically target a certain group of people. Have students interested in advertising research the word *demographics* and then report their findings to the class.

DISCOVERY STRATEGIES

Discuss how the investigation relates to the chapter by asking open questions similar to the following:

• **Cigarettes and other tobacco products were once advertised on television commercials. Why do you think these commercials are no longer allowed?** (A logical response would be that the use of tobacco is unhealthy—analyzing, generalizing.)

• **Certain restrictions exist about the advertising of alcoholic beverages on television. One restriction does not allow an actor or actress to be shown actually drinking the alcoholic beverage. Why do you think this is so?** (Answers will vary—analyzing, generalizing.)

Laboratory Investigation

Analyzing Smoking Advertisements

Problem

How are advertisements used to convince people to smoke or not to smoke?

Materials (per group)

> magazines
> paper

Procedure

1. Choose two or three different types of magazines. Glance through the magazines to find advertisements for and against cigarette smoking.

2. On a sheet of paper, make a chart like the one shown. Then, for each advertisement you found, fill in the information in the chart. In the last column, record the technique that the advertisement uses to attract the public to smoke or not to smoke. Examples of themes used to attract people to smoke are "Beautiful women smoke brand X"; "Successful people smoke brand Y"; "Brand Z tastes better." Examples of themes used to stop people from smoking are "Smoking is dangerous to your health"; "Smart people do not smoke"; "If you cared about yourself or your family, you would not smoke."

Observations

1. Were there more advertisements for or against smoking?

2. Which advertising themes were used most often? Least often?

Analysis and Conclusions

1. Which advertisements appealed to you personally? Why?

2. In general, how are the advertising themes that are used related to the type of magazine in which the advertisements appear?

3. **On Your Own** Repeat the procedure, but this time look for advertisements for and against drinking alcohol. Compare the way in which drinking alcohol is advertised to the way in which smoking cigarettes is advertised.

Magazine	Advertisements for Smoking (specify brand)	Advertisements Against Smoking (specify advertisement)	Theme

OBSERVATIONS

1. Answers will vary, but generally speaking, a publication will contain more prosmoking than antismoking advertisements.

2. Answers will vary, but in general, smoking advertisements depict attractive men and women engaged in sports or other forms of exercise. It is likely that the theme used least often is that smoking is harmful.

Study Guide

Summarizing Key Concepts

9–1 What Are Drugs?

▲ A drug is any substance that has an effect on the body.

▲ Tolerance, dependence, and withdrawal are serious dangers of drug abuse.

▲ Tolerance causes the body to need increasingly larger amounts of the drug to get the same effect originally produced.

▲ Psychological dependence is a strong desire or need to continue using a drug. Physical dependence, or addiction, occurs when the body becomes used to a drug and needs it to function normally.

▲ Withdrawal is stopping the use of a drug.

9–2 Alcohol

▲ The abuse of alcohol can lead to destruction of liver and brain cells and can cause both physical and psychological dependence.

▲ In the brain, alcohol acts as a depressant and slows down the actions of the central nervous system.

▲ Treatment for alcoholism includes medical and psychological help.

9–3 Tobacco

▲ Cigarette smoking causes damage to both the respiratory system and the circulatory system.

▲ Cigarette smoke contains poisonous substances such as nicotine, carbon dioxide, and tars.

▲ Cigarette smoking is the most important cause of lung cancer. Cigarette smoking irritates the lining of the nose, throat, and mouth; increases heartbeat; lowers skin temperature; and constricts blood vessels.

▲ Passive smokers are those people who breathe in air containing smoke from other people's cigars, cigarettes, and pipes.

9–4 Commonly Abused Drugs

▲ Some commonly abused drugs include inhalants, depressants, stimulants, hallucinogens, and opiates.

▲ Inhalants are drugs that are inhaled to get a desired effect.

▲ Depressants are drugs that decrease the actions of the nervous system.

▲ Stimulants speed up the actions of the nervous system.

▲ The effects of marijuana are due mainly to a chemical called THC. Like alcohol, marijuana slows down reaction time.

▲ Hallucinogens are drugs that produce hallucinations.

▲ Opiates, which are produced from the opium poppy, are used as painkillers.

Reviewing Key Terms

Define each term in a complete sentence.

9–1 What Are Drugs?
drug
drug abuse
tolerance
psychological depen-
dence
physical dependence
withdrawal

9–2 Alcohol
depressant
alcoholism

9–4 Commonly Abused Drugs
inhalant
stimulant

marijuana
hallucinogen
opiate

H ■ 233

ANALYSIS AND CONCLUSIONS

1. Answers will vary. Encourage students to analyze the reasons for their responses and the ways the advertisements seem to encourage them to smoke.

2. In general, advertisements are designed to appeal to the type of person who reads the particular magazine in which the advertisement is found.

3. Have students construct charts like the one they used for the smoking advertisements. After they have collected information about drinking advertisements, have them answer the same questions about the number of advertisements for and against, advertising themes used most and least often, personal appeal of advertisements, and relationship between advertising theme and type of magazine. Students will probably find that there are many similarities in the ways alcohol and cigarettes are advertised.

Chapter Review

ALTERNATIVE ASSESSMENT

The *Prentice Hall Science* program includes a variety of testing components and methodologies. Aside from the Chapter Review questions, you may opt to use the Chapter Test or the Computer Test Bank Test in your *Test Book* for assessment of important facts and concepts. In addition, Performance-Based Tests are included in your *Test Book*. These Performance-Based Tests are designed to test science process skills, rather than factual content recall. Since they are not content dependent, Performance-Based Tests can be distributed after students complete a chapter or after they complete the entire textbook.

CONTENT REVIEW

Multiple Choice

1. d
2. a
3. d
4. c
5. a
6. c
7. d
8. c
9. a
10. b

True or False

1. T
2. T
3. T
4. F, liver
5. F, carbon monoxide
6. F, Alcohol
7. F, hallucinogens

Concept Mapping:

Row 1: Drug abuse
Row 2: Dependence, Withdrawal
Row 3: Psychological

CONCEPT MASTERY

1. Any substance that affects the body and is taken in excess and/or in a way doctors would not approve of is considered a drug that is being abused.

2. Even though a person stops abusing a drug, there is always the danger that he or she may return to abusing the drug in the future. For this reason, it is often said that no one is ever cured of a drug dependence.

Content Review

Multiple Choice

Choose the letter of the answer that best completes each statement.

1. Which requires no prescription?
   a. barbiturate   c. amphetamine
   b. tranquilizer   d. aspirin
2. Which is not an example of drug misuse?
   a. buying an over-the-counter drug
   b. taking an illegal drug
   c. taking more of a drug than the amount prescribed by a doctor
   d. taking a drug prescribed for someone else
3. Alcohol acts as a(an)
   a. stimulant.   c. hallucinogen.
   b. opiate.   d. depressant.
4. Alcohol mainly affects the
   a. heart.   c. brain.
   b. muscles.   d. stomach.
5. Which system does bronchitis, a disorder aggravated by smoking, affect?
   a. respiratory   c. digestive
   b. circulatory   d. nervous

6. An addictive drug found in tobacco products is
   a. tar.   c. nicotine.
   b. THC.   d. heroin.
7. An example of an inhalant is
   a. THC.
   b. a barbiturate.
   c. codeine.
   d. nitrous oxide.
8. Barbiturates are
   a. opiates.
   b. hallucinogens.
   c. depressants.
   d. stimulants.
9. Crack is classified as a(an)
   a. stimulant.   c. depressant.
   b. opiate.   d. hallucinogen.
10. Heroin is a(an)
   a. stimulant.   c. depressant.
   b. opiate.   d. hallucinogen.

True or False

If the statement is true, write "true." If it is false, change the underlined word or words to make the statement true.

1. The deliberate misuse of drugs for uses other than medical ones is known as <u>drug abuse</u>.
2. <u>Physical dependence</u> is also known as addiction.
3. The abuse of alcohol can lead to <u>alcoholism</u>.
4. Cirrhosis affects the <u>lungs</u>.
5. The most dangerous part of cigarette smoke is <u>carbon dioxide</u>.
6. <u>Amphetamines</u> and barbiturates are examples of depressants.
7. LSD belongs to a group of drugs known as <u>opiates</u>.

Concept Mapping

Complete the following concept map for Section 9–1. Refer to pages H8–H9 to construct a concept map for the entire chapter.

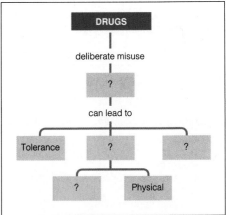

3. Alcohol is considered a depressant because it slows down, or depresses, the brain and the nervous system.

4. Dependence occurs when the body is physically dependent on a drug and cannot function properly without it. Withdrawal occurs when a person who is physically dependent stops using a drug and the body reacts to the lack of a drug on which it has become physically dependent. Tolerance occurs when a person must take more and more of a drug to achieve the desired effect.

5. Students should use the information in Figure 9–14 to create their lists and descriptions.

6. An alcoholic is physically and psychologically dependent on alcohol. An occasional drinker is not.

7. Cigarette smoke contains nicotine, carbon monoxide, and tars, which cause damage to both the respiratory and the circulatory systems.

8. Lung cancer, heart disease, emphysema, and bronchitis.

Concept Mastery

Discuss each of the following in a brief paragraph.

1. Explain how any drug can be abused.
2. It has been said that no one is ever cured of drug dependence. Explain why.
3. Why is alcohol considered a depressant?
4. What are dependence, withdrawal, and tolerance?
5. List the six commonly abused drugs. Describe the effect each has on the body.
6. How does an alcoholic differ from those who drink occasionally?
7. Describe the substances in cigarette smoke and their effects on the body.
8. List and describe some of the disorders that can result from smoking.
9. Compare psychological dependence and physical dependence.

Critical Thinking and Problem Solving

Use the skills you have developed in this chapter to answer each of the following.

1. **Applying facts** What precautions would you take when working with paint thinner?
2. **Applying concepts** Explain why heroin abusers need medical help while they are going through withdrawal.
3. **Relating facts** Almost 30 percent of the people in the United States smoke. Explain why people smoke even when they know the dangers.
4. **Making comparisons** Compare cocaine and crack.
5. **Relating cause and effect** How is cigarette smoke related to respiratory and circulatory problems?
6. **Relating concepts** Cigarette smoke is harmful to nonsmokers as well as to smokers. Explain this statement.
7. **Expressing an opinion** What are some ways in which people who abuse drugs can be discouraged from doing so?
8. **Applying concepts** Explain the meaning of this old Japanese proverb: "First the man takes a drink, then the drink takes a drink, then the drink takes the man!"
9. **Making inferences** In what ways are drug abuse and criminal acts related?
10. **Using the writing process** Imagine you are a parent. Write a letter to your child in which you try to discourage your child from experimenting with drugs.

CLAIRE VERONICA BROOME: DISEASE DETECTIVE

Background Information

Dr. Claire Broome received her MD degree from Harvard Medical School in 1975. She completed her internship and residency in internal medicine at the University of California, San Francisco. Prior to accepting the position of Chief of the Meningitis and Special Pathogens Branch at the Centers for Disease Control (CDC), she served as a fellow in the Infectious Diseases Unit of Massachusetts General in Boston.

Claire Broome's specialty is infectious disease epidemiology. Epidemiology is the study of the distribution and control of infectious diseases. At CDC, Dr. Broome has worked on public health programs for controlling bacteria-caused diseases, especially pneumonia and meningitis. An interesting area of her work has involved evaluating the effectiveness of various prevention strategies. She has developed innovative methods of evaluation for cases where randomized controlled trials are not feasible. Dr. Broome has also been involved in research and publications dealing with Legionnaire's disease and toxic-shock syndrome.

GAZETTE

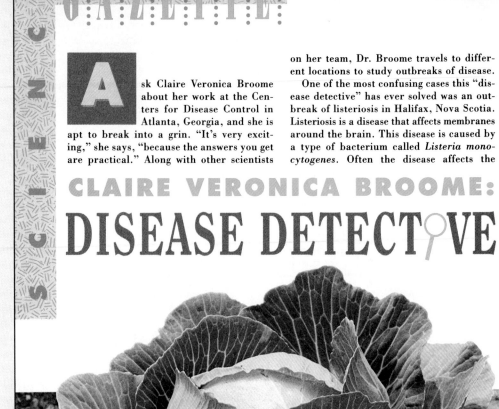

CLAIRE VERONICA BROOME: DISEASE DETECTIVE

Ask Claire Veronica Broome about her work at the Centers for Disease Control in Atlanta, Georgia, and she is apt to break into a grin. "It's very exciting," she says, "because the answers you get are practical." Along with other scientists on her team, Dr. Broome travels to different locations to study outbreaks of disease.

One of the most confusing cases this "disease detective" has ever solved was an outbreak of listeriosis in Halifax, Nova Scotia. Listeriosis is a disease that affects membranes around the brain. This disease is caused by a type of bacterium called *Listeria monocytogenes*. Often the disease affects the

---

TEACHING STRATEGY: ADVENTURE

FOCUS/MOTIVATION

Imagine the following scenario. In a period of three days, 53 cases of a rare disease called mysteriosis have occurred in your hometown. Victims of mysteriosis suffer from severe headaches, dizziness, and temporary loss of memory. Six of the hospitalized patients have slipped into comas, and two others have died.

Your job is to find out what is causing this disease.

• As a disease detective, how would you go about your search for the cause of the epidemic of mysteriosis that has swept your community? (Accept all reasonable answers. Suggestions should focus on determining the cause of the disease as well as the method(s) by which the disease was transmitted. Possible suggestions include analyzing the body fluids of the victims for the presence of unusual chemicals or microorganisms and collecting data on the victims for comparison studies. Data should focus on events in the victims' lives for a few days or weeks prior to the onset of the disease—places visited, foods eaten, people contacted, and so on.)

Point out to students that there are really two puzzles to solve: what is causing the disease as well as where and how the victims came into contact with the disease-causing agent.

elderly. However, it can infect an infant before it is born. In fact, it was an epidemic of listeriosis in newborn infants that brought this case to Dr. Broome's attention.

Before going to Halifax, Dr. Broome gathered as much data on listeriosis as possible. She discovered that the bacteria that cause listeriosis were identified as a cause of human disease in 1929. At that time, it was learned that the bacteria live in soil and can infect animals. But as late as the 1980s, no one was certain how the bacteria are transmitted to unborn humans.

When Claire Broome and her team of researchers arrived in Halifax, they set to work reviewing hospital records and talking to physicians about past occurrences of listeriosis. Soon, they discovered the hospital in Halifax was experiencing an epidemic.

Dr. Broome compared two groups of people. The mothers of infants born with listeriosis made up one group. Mothers who gave birth to healthy babies made up the second group. People in both groups were interviewed. Dr. Broome collected data that covered several months of the new mothers' lives before they gave birth. Dr. Broome soon noticed a definite trend. The women with sick babies had eaten more cheeses than the women with healthy babies. Could the cheese have been contaminated by the bacteria that made the babies ill?

During her research, Dr. Broome became aware of another case of listeriosis. This case occurred in a Halifax man who had not spent time in a hospital. After examining the contents of the man's refrigerator, Dr. Broome added coleslaw to her list of possible transmitters of listeriosis. She reasoned that coleslaw is made from uncooked cabbage and cabbage grows in soil—a place in which listeria bacteria had already been discovered. Careful chemical analysis revealed that listeria bacteria were present in the coleslaw found in the sick man's refrigerator.

Dr. Broome and her team traced some of the contaminated coleslaw to a cabbage farm.

▲ In her laboratory, Dr. Broome uses a computer to analyze data about epidemics.

They found that the farmer used sheep manure to fertilize the cabbage. When the sheep were tested, they were also found to contain the listeria bacteria.

Now it was time for Dr. Broome to interview the mothers of the sick babies again. Not surprisingly, she found that many of them had eaten coleslaw during the time they were carrying their child. Later, Dr. Broome discovered that the bacteria that causes listeriosis can also live in milk and milk products, including cheese.

What made the packaged coleslaw and the milk products a good environment for bacteria to live in? Actually, it was the refrigerator in which these foods were stored that contributed to this disease outbreak. Refrigerators are used to keep foods from spoiling quickly. However, *Listeria monocytogenes* can survive, and even multiply, in cold temperatures. Even under proper storage conditions, the coleslaw and the cheese contained enough bacteria to make people ill.

The mystery of the Halifax listeriosis outbreak was solved. This case was closed. Dr. Broome returned to her office in Atlanta, but she barely had time to unpack before she was off to discover the cause of another "mystery" disease.

GAZETTE ■ 237

Additional Questions and Topic Suggestions.

1. How do you think the bacterium *Listeria monocytogenes* got its name? (The bacterium was probably named in honor of Sir Joseph Lister, who was one of the first surgeons to use antiseptics to cleanse his surgical instruments and operating rooms. Lister recognized the connection between unsanitary conditions and the spread of bacteria.)

2. Find out about outbreaks of Legionnaire's disease that occurred in the United States in the 1970s. What is the cause of this disease? How was it transmitted in these epidemics?

Critical Thinking Questions

1. Mayonnaise has sometimes been suspected as a transmitter of bacteria that cause food poisoning. Why did Dr. Broome suspect that the cabbage rather than the mayonnaise was the transmitter of *Listeria* bacteria? (Her knowledge that the *Listeria* bacteria lived in soil and could infect animals aided her in tracing the coleslaw to the source of contamination—infected sheep whose manure was used as fertilizer for growing cabbage.)

2. Why is it so important to determine the cause of a disease? (Knowing the cause of a disease is important in at least two ways. It helps doctors determine the best course of treatment for those already stricken. It also suggests possibilities as to how and where the disease may be transmitted. This information is helpful in preventing further outbreaks of a disease and is essential in controlling an epidemic of the disease.)

CONTENT DEVELOPMENT

Explain to students that Dr. Claire Broome is a real-life "disease detective," or epidemiologist. Write the word *epidemiologist* on the chalkboard and define it as one who studies the distribution and control of infectious diseases.

• **Can you think of a more familiar word that is related to the word *epidemiologist*?** (Students will probably be familiar with the word *epidemic*, the rapid spreading of a disease, which causes many people to have the disease.)

Have students read this Adventure in Science to find out about an epidemic case that Dr. Broome solved.

• **What is the name of the disease involved in this case? What bacterium causes it?** (The disease is listeriosis. It is caused by the bacterium *Listeria monocytogenes*.)

• **Who were the victims of listeriosis in the Halifax case?** (Most of the victims were newborn babies.)

• **How did Dr. Broome go about solving this puzzling case?** (Help students trace the series of steps that Claire Broome followed.)

INDEPENDENT PRACTICE

▶ *Activity Book*

After students have read the Science Gazette article, you may want to hand out the reading skills worksheet based on the article in the *Activity Book*.

ISSUES IN SCIENCE

ARE AMERICANS OVEREXERCISING?

Background Information

The issue of overexercising centers around two major concerns: the damage and possible death that can result when stress is placed on the cardiovascular system and injuries that can result when stress is placed on the muscular and skeletal systems. For the average population—that is, those persons with no history of heart disease—the second concern is by far the greater. In fact, it is often because of the desire to improve the condition of one's heart and lungs that a person undertakes a serious exercise program.

Scientists have found that a physically active person generally has a slower heart rate at a given level of exercise than a person who is not physically active. A slower heart rate is desirable because it enables the heart muscle to have more time to rest between beats. As a result, the person with a slower heart rate can exercise harder for a longer time without feeling tired. One good way to achieve a slower heart rate is through aerobic exercises, which include running, walking, swimming, and aerobic dancing.

The "fitness craze" that reached such popularity in the 1970s evolved out of scientific findings regarding the benefits of aerobic exercise. People all over the country began running, jogging, and participating in aerobic exercise classes. An important part of the aerobic ritual often included taking one's pulse at regular intervals to determine whether a desirable pulse rate had been reached.

★ ARE AMERICANS ★ OVEREXERCISING?

One summer day in 1984, 13-year-old Rory Bentley left his home for his daily 6-mile jog through Carlisle, Massachusetts. On this particular day, however, Rory never made it back home. After jogging, he collapsed and died on the sidewalk in front of his house. Although he was only 13 and a veteran of many races, Rory died from heart failure.

Less than two months before Rory died, a motorcyclist found the body of a man lying on a country road in Vermont. The dead man was identified as James Fixx, the 52-year-old author of *The Complete Book of Running*. Fixx died of a heart attack during one of his daily 20-mile jogs.

Deaths such as these have led Americans to question the value of vigorous exercise, and running in particular. Soon after these incidents occurred, many magazines began publishing articles warning runners of the dangers of too much exercise. Doctors, medical writers, athletic directors, and others have recently expressed doubt over whether exercise is always good and whether more exercise is always better. In fact, doctors recently have reported many more patients with exercise-related injuries. For example, shin splints, a condition in which the shin tendons peel away from the bone, have become much more common since the exercise boom began. One cause of shin splints is running on hard surfaces.

Even grade school and high school athletics may be getting out of hand. Some scientists point out that young people can suffer serious long-term effects from too much exercise. For example, overdoing running or other sports can stunt growth by damaging the flexible tissue that surrounds the bones.

Adults, too, can be victims of serious problems caused by exercise, doctors say. Among the most serious to female runners is the loss of calcium in the body. This loss can eventually damage the spine and other bones. Muscles and tendons can also be damaged—sometimes causing lasting joint problems.

Nutrition experts have discovered a rise in what they call "eating disorders" among amateur runners and others who exercise a great deal. Such people tend to undereat out of fear that they'll lose their trim, athletic look. In doing so, they deprive their bodies of essential proteins, vitamins, and minerals. In the most serious cases, heart muscles are weakened and fatal heart attacks can occur.

RUNNERS, RUNNERS EVERYWHERE

Despite the recent warnings, however, there appears to be little decrease in the popularity of exercise. The jogging craze began in the mid-1970s, and there seems to be no shortage of runners today. There's hardly a place where runners are not a common sight. A few years ago, a 1-mile run by an amateur runner was considered special. But today's runners regularly run 3, 5, or more miles.

But running is just one part of the exercise boom. People exercise in their homes, their offices, and in their health clubs or gyms. These people learn their exercises from

▶ **Off and running—toward better health or serious injury?**

TEACHING STRATEGY: ISSUE

FOCUS/MOTIVATION

Begin by asking students the following questions. Record their responses on the chalkboard.
- **How many times a week do you exercise?**
- **For how long do you exercise?**
- **What type of exercise do you do?**
- **Why do you exercise?**

- **Would you prefer to exercise more or less than you do now?**
- **Have you ever been injured as a result of exercise?**
- **Do the adults in your family exercise?**
- **How often? For how long? What types of exercise do they do? Have they ever been injured as a result of exercise?**

CONTENT DEVELOPMENT

Discuss the benefits of exercise. Emphasize that a person who exercises regularly will tend to have a slower heart rate,

firmer muscles, more endurance, better posture, and better balance than a person who does not exercise. In addition, people who exercise often claim that they feel better, get sick less often, and sleep better than they did before they started to exercise.

Point out that in the 1970s, many people took up running, jogging, and other aerobic activities. The main reason for this sudden interest in exercise was a desire to improve the condition of the heart and lungs. Soon, however, other motivations began to appear. Running became

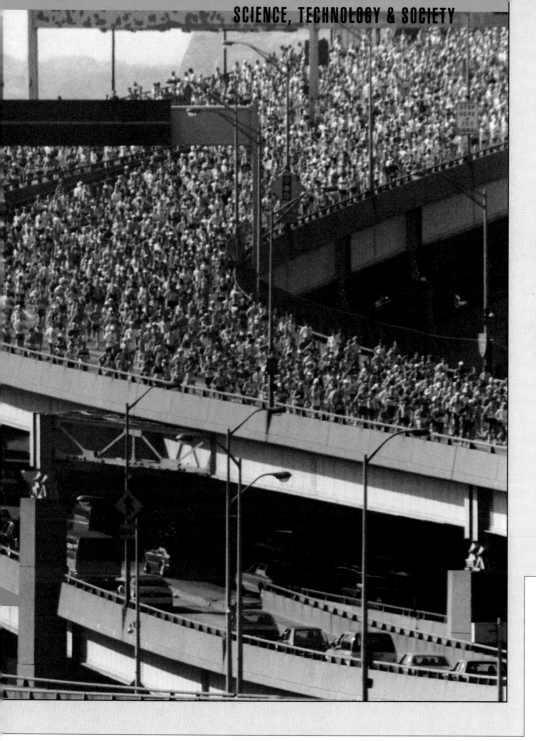

Coupled with the focus on cardiovascular improvement were the claims of scientists, doctors, and popular "gurus" about the psychological benefits of exercise. Many people began to experience a "runner's high," which scientists attribute to the production of endorphins—pleasure-producing chemicals—in the brain.

Additional Questions and Topic Suggestions

1. Contact the emergency room of your local hospital. Find out how many cases of injuries or heart failure related to exercise have been treated in the past month. You may also wish to interview local doctors and ask the same question.

2. Go to a bookstore and note how many books are available on running and other forms of aerobic exercise. Flip through each book and report on how the books reflect or do not reflect the concerns raised in this article.

3. Get together with several classmates and discuss the following statement: "People are not injuring themselves because they are running but because they are trying to conform to some kind of external standard. They think they have to run as far and as often, be as thin, and look as young as the person pictured on the cover of a fitness magazine." (Accept all answers.)

disease dying from exercise are extremely small.

A more common concern is the possibility of injury from exercise.

• How might a person become injured from too much exercise? (Accept all logical answers. Possible injuries include shin splints, torn cartilage, sprains or falls suffered when one is overtired, and so on.)

Emphasize the idea that injuries cannot always be attributed to "too much" exercise.

• Do you think some of the injuries caused by so-called overexercising could have been prevented even if the people involved had exercised the same amount? How? (Accept all answers. It is possible that some injuries are the result of poor warm-up habits, inappropriate shoes or other equipment, and poor exercise techniques. In addition, people may be exercising when they have not had enough sleep or when they are in poor health.)

fashionable—the "in" thing to do. Books began to appear that stressed the idea that one could lose weight by exercising. The American preoccupation with thinness and looking young fit in easily with the new exercise craze. As can happen with any fad, some people went too far and began to overdo exercise, or at least to overdo it in terms of their own physical condition.

• Which type of person do you think is more likely to overdo exercise: the one who exercises for better health or the one who exercises to lose weight or to be "in fashion"? (Accept all answers.)

• Do you think that there are "right" reasons and "wrong" reasons for exercising? (Accept all answers.)

Point out that this article reflects two different concerns about too much exercise. One concern is the possibility of death from overexercising. Although cases of heart attacks or heart failure during exercise have received a lot of publicity, experts admit that the chances of a person with no family or personal history of heart

Class Debate

Have students work in small groups. Challenge each group to imagine that they are members of a round-table discussion on a public-television station. The topic of the discussion is "Are Americans Overexercising?" Each group should present a discussion in which members of the group represent the following people: an aerobic dance instructor; a doctor of sports medicine; a psychologist; and an amateur runner who has just won the Boston Marathon.

▲ **More and more men and women of all ages are exercising in their homes, offices, and gyms. Should everyone do this? And how much exercise is good for a person? Scientists, sports health experts, and doctors have different opinions.**

a variety of books, records, videocassettes, TV programs, and magazine articles. Not only are more people exercising, but there has been an increase in the amount of exercising that individuals do.

THE BIG QUESTION

Should exercise be avoided? To begin with, there is strong evidence that people who exercise regularly are much less likely to have heart attacks, develop high blood pressure, and suffer from diseases related to old age. One study of nearly 17,000 Harvard University graduates showed that there were twice as many heart attacks among those who did *not* exercise as there were among those who exercised regularly. Another study of about 6000 men and women aged 20 to 65 who exercised showed fewer people with high blood pressure. Some of the researchers said that regular exercise also helped rid the body and mind of stress and anxiety, which can cause health and psychological problems.

Those who favor regular exercise and see running as a definite health benefit are not stopped by "horror stories" such as the sudden deaths of Rory Bentley and James Fixx. They argue that carelessness and not the ex-

ercise itself is to blame in most cases of injury or death. People with a family history of heart disease should be careful not to overdo their exercise and, in fact, should exercise only under a doctor's care. When that is done, exercise is healthy.

SOME TIPS ON EXERCISING

People should warm up before strong exercise, avoid overdoing exercise, and cool down slowly afterward. People should also eat the proper foods, wear correct shoes, and learn the rules of the sport they are playing.

Picking the right exercise and the right amount of it for you is the key rule. "We think that people need a prescription for exercise just as they need a prescription for a drug," said a sports health expert. "While there is a sport for everyone, not everyone can play each and every sport."

Studies indicate that even if exercise does have some risks and drawbacks, lack of exercise is even worse. Statistics seem to show that more Americans die from sitting around than from running around. But are too many Americans running around too much, too far, and too often? What do you think?

ISSUE (continued)

GUIDED PRACTICE

Skills Development

Skills: Drawing conclusions, making inferences

1. What types of personal problems might a person have who tends to overexercise? Do you think there is such a thing as an "exercise-aholic"? (Accept all answers. Guide students to recognize that overdo-

ing anything is usually a symptom of other problems in a person's life.)

2. Do you think a school's physical education curriculum should include instruction on how to exercise sensibly? Explain your answer. (Accept all answers.)

3. Express your opinion of the following statement: "People overreact when a story such as the death of running advocate Jim Fixx hits the newspapers. Yet nobody writes about the thousands of people whose health has been improved by regular exercise."

INDEPENDENT PRACTICE

▶ *Activity Book*

After students have read the Science Gazette article, you may want to hand out the reading skills worksheet based on the article in the *Activity Book*.

THE BIONIC BOY

FROM: Dr. R. K. Smith, Moon Base Alpha,
Crater Village (6M14Y14)
TO: Evelyn Washington, Futura Center,
Dakotas (1/ZM-43BY)
DATE: 06/14/2071

Dear Evelyn:

Thank you so much for your last interspace message. Both your Aunt Mary and I are thrilled that you want to be a doctor of medicine. It is an ancient and wonderful profession. We are also pleased because you will be the fourth doctor in our family. It's a tradition that goes back over one hundred and fifty years! I recall my father telling me that our family helped develop the first vaccines against cancer in the early 1990s!

You asked what it was like "being a doctor in the old days." The year I started treating people, 2006, seems like yesterday. I was a new physician then, and I wanted to set up a small-town practice. The town I chose, Chesterville, was so old-fashioned that it still had push-button telephones.

Chesterville turned out to be a good choice. Beth and Mike played on the same spaceball team as many of the children I treated, and Aunt Mary was a Scoutmaster. I still

GAZETTE ■ 241

Background Information

From false teeth to wooden legs, artificial body parts have been used by people for hundreds, probably thousands, of years. Many of these devices were crude, ill-fitting, and limited in their usefulness. A new technology has begun to change that, however, as the joining of medicine and engineering has opened up a new field called bioengineering.

Bioengineering began during World War II with the invention of the first artificial kidney—the dialysis machine. An obvious limitation of the dialysis machine is that it is external to the patient; the patient must be "hooked up" to it. During the 1940s and 1950s, bioengineers worked to develop smaller and lighter artificial devices that could be implanted. During the past several decades, medical technology has taken advantage of advances in microsurgery, microelectronics, and biochemistry to produce a wide variety of prosthetic parts that can be inserted into the body. The body parts that are now available include artificial joints for the knee, shoulder, elbow, hip, and wrist; limbs made from surgical steel, special alloys, and plastics; synthetic blood vessels and heart valves; artificial lenses for the eyes; and artificial skin. Artificial organs that are still in the experimental stages includes lungs, eyes, ears, and hearts.

The field of bioengineering has expanded so rapidly that research has been split into four areas of specialization: motion, speech and hearing, vision, and artificial internal organs. Of the four areas, devices involving motion are the most effective. Today, the replacement of a hip or finger joint is a fairly commonplace operation.

TEACHING STRATEGY: FUTURE

FOCUS/MOTIVATION

Have students observe the picture of Tommy on this article's first page.
• **What is happening to the boy in this picture?** (He is falling or being thrown through a glass window.)
• **What types of injuries do you think he might receive as a result of this accident?** (Accept all answers.)

• **What types of medical treatment exist for such injuries?** (Accept all answers.)

Additional Questions and Topic Suggestions.

1. Discuss the advantages of artificial organs over transplanted organs. (Most obvious is the reduced risk of rejection. Other advantages include that artificial organs can be tailored to perfectly fit a given person's body and that artificial organs are "new" and would not be prone to deterioration or disease in the same way as human organs are.)

2. Find out about the first artificial organ, the dialysis machine, which was invented in the 1940s.

3. What was the purpose of the pea-sized computer implanted in Tommy's arm? (To relay nerve impulses between arm muscles and the brain.)

smile when I think back to how excited the kids were when we took them to the first Undersea Colony in the Atlantic Ocean.

But what I remember most clearly was a terrible accident. A group of children were on their way home from the learning center. As they were crossing the main intersection on the moving sidewalk, an old gravity-car lost its automatic steering. A crash occurred, and Tommy, a boy of only 14, was thrown through a plate-glass window. Tommy suffered terrible damage to his muscles and skin, and his lungs were destroyed as well. Fortunately, by then—the early part of the twenty-first century—we had learned how to replace all destroyed body parts with artificial parts. Since you want to be a doctor, Evelyn, I thought I'd tell you a little more about how we performed surgery on Tommy.

It might be interesting if I told you a little about artificial body parts. During an important period of research, 1960 to 1990, scientists tried to perfect transplant techniques. That is, they would take organs from one person and put them into the body of another person to help that person live. By the time I was born in 1976, doctors had learned how to transplant skin, hearts, livers, lungs, kidneys, and bone tissue.

Unfortunately, in most cases, the organs would not live in the new body for very long—even with the use of special drugs.

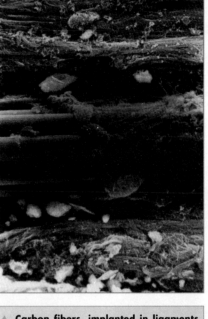

▲ Carbon fibers, implanted in ligaments, strengthen injured limbs and become part of the living system.

The reasons are complicated, and you will learn about them in time. However, the main reason has to do with the fact that the body "thinks" that living tissues, cells, or organs not of its own making must be destroyed. Even though a transplanted human heart, for example, may work perfectly, the body will use all its defenses to destroy it.

So, as early as 1950, scientists began to experiment with special metals, plastics, and filters that could be used to replace real body parts. I think I know what you must be thinking. Why wouldn't the body try to destroy these artificial hearts, livers, and lungs? The simplest answer is that the body doesn't "think" the plastic part is dangerous.

By 1965, doctors were using metal and plastic parts to replace hip and finger joints. With further research, they learned to build organs that could work just like the real thing for short periods of time. A few years after I was born, the first artificial heart was put inside a man. It worked for only a few weeks. Now, of course, the heart transplant lasts indefinitely! But the big news toward the end of the twentieth century was the making of artificial parts that would, in time, become living parts. The body's own cells would slowly grow around it and in it until it was alive!

Now back to Tommy. After he was brought into our emergency center, our examination showed that his lungs were damaged beyond

---

FUTURE (continued)

CONTENT DEVELOPMENT

Point out that injuries from accidents can result in damage to limbs and vital organs. One way that such injuries can be treated is with the use of artificial body parts.

Some artificial body parts are probably familiar to students. They may know people who have false teeth, artificial hip joints, or prosthetic hands or legs. At the present time, artificial joints are among the most effective artificial body parts. Scientists are working to develop artificial lungs, hearts, eyes, and ears, as well as vastly improved artificial limbs.

Discuss the types of materials used to construct Tommy's artificial body parts. Of particular interest is the special "glue" used to hook up the lungs and attach the arm muscle to the bones. This glue is similar to the artificial skin that is currently being used to treat burn victims. As with the glue, cells grow over and around the skin. Eventually, the artificial skin becomes part of the body's tissue.

Emphasize that one of the main problems with artificial body parts is the possibility of rejection. The human body has a defense system that rejects anything not of its own making. Scientists have discovered that most likely to be rejected are organic materials, which is why organ transplants have not been completely successful. Much

repair. Also, the muscles in his left arm were destroyed, and he had several broken bones.

A set of artificial lungs was hooked up to Tommy's windpipe, or trachea. The hookup was done with a special "glue." The amazing thing about this glue was that the cells of the body grew over and around it, making new tissue. In a few months, this body glue actually became part of the body's tissue.

The artificial lungs looked a lot like large, gray sponges. When we attached these artificial organs to the chest wall, they moved in and out with the diaphragm and chest muscles, just like real lungs. As you know, our lungs are needed to help us take in oxygen and get rid of carbon dioxide. Real lungs work because tiny blood vessels, or capillaries, surround the air sacs, or alveoli, of the lung and carry gases back and forth. Our artificial lungs were made so that Tommy's own capillaries would grow into the channels in the spongy material.

▼ Artificial lungs would be made of spongy material so they could move as a person breathes.

As I mentioned before, a great deal of the boy's arm muscle was destroyed during the accident by glass. We had to rebuild his arm using a new substance called Bionic Jelly. This jelly was made from plastic fibers that could be molded into any shape we wanted. The jelly could get bigger and smaller just like real muscle when the arm moved. We glued the ends of the fake muscle to the bones of the arm using our special glue. Then we hooked up the nerve endings to a pea-sized computer in the jelly itself. The arm looked and worked like the real thing.

Why do I remember Tommy? Because it was just so amazing to me, as a young doctor, to see how far science had come.

Now, at the age of 95, I look back at our achievements with pride. Science is wonderful, and I am glad you want to take part in it. I hope to be at your medical school graduation, which should be on my 110th birthday!

Love,
Uncle Bill

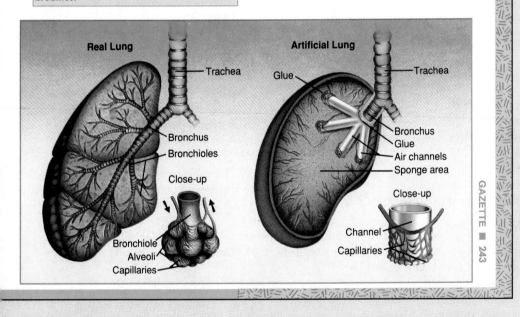

Real Lung
— Trachea
— Bronchus
— Bronchioles
Close-up
Bronchiole
Alveoli
Capillaries

Artificial Lung
Glue —
— Trachea
— Bronchus
— Glue
— Air channels
— Sponge area
Close-up
Channel
Capillaries

GAZETTE ■ 243

less likely to be rejected are materials that scientists refer to as "biologically inert." Such materials include steels and plastics.

ENRICHMENT

Have students contact local hospitals to find out what artificial body parts are currently being used to treat patients. You may wish to arrange a field trip to a hospital's physical therapy or orthopedic department, where students can learn in detail about artificial joints and limbs. If a nearby hospital has a special burn unit, students may be able to find out how artificial skin is used.

CONTENT DEVELOPMENT

Students may enjoy making a list on the chalkboard of all the futuristic items mentioned in this article. They can begin by noting the return address of Uncle Bill, who lives in a space colony on the moon. Other interesting items of the future include cancer vaccines; the existence of undersea colonies; moving sidewalks; cars with automatic steering; the replacement of all destroyed body parts with artificial body parts; and people who talk about living to be 110 years old.

INDEPENDENT PRACTICE

▶ *Activity Book*

After students have read the Science Gazette article, you may want to hand out the reading skills worksheet based on the article in the *Activity Book.*

For Further Reading

If you have been intrigued by the concepts examined in this textbook, you may also be interested in the ways fellow thinkers—novelists, poets, essayists, as well as scientists—have imaginatively explored the same ideas.

Chapter 1: The Human Body

Asimov, Isaac. *Fantastic Voyage.* New York: Bantam.
Platt, Kin. *The Boy Who Could Make Himself Disappear.* New York: Dell.
Swift, Jonathan. *Gulliver's Travels.* New York: Penguin Books.

Chapter 2: Skeletal and Muscular Systems

Blume, Judy. *Deenie.* New York: Bradbury Press.
Savitz, Harriet May. *Run, Don't Walk.* New York: Signet Vista Books.

Chapter 3: Digestive System

Atwood, Margaret. *The Edible Woman.* New York: Warner Books.
Dacquino, V. T. *Kiss the Candy Days Goodbye.* New York: Delacorte Press.
Levenkron, Steven. *The Best Little Girl in the World.* New York: Warner Books.
Silone, Ignazio. *Bread and Wine.* New York: Atheneum.

Chapter 4: Circulatory System

Arnold, Elliott. *Blood Brother.* Lincoln, NE: University of Nevada Press.
McCullers, Carson. *The Heart Is a Lonely Hunter.* Boston: Houghton.
Paterson, Katherine. *Jacob Have I Loved.* New York: Crowell.

Chapter 5: Respiratory and Excretory Systems

Myers, Walter Dean. *Hoops.* New York: Delacorte Press.
Winthrop, Elizabeth. *Marathon Miranda.* New York: Holiday House.

Chapter 6: Nervous and Endocrine Systems

Keller, Helen. *The Story of My Life.* New York: Watermill Press.

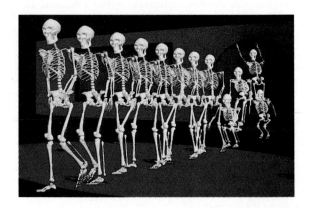

Pomerance, Bernard. *The Elephant Man.* New York: Grove-Weidenfeld.
Young, Helen. *What Difference Does It Make, Danny?* New York: Andre Deutsch.

Chapter 7: Reproduction and Development

Eyerly, Jeanette. *He's My Baby Now.* New York: J. B. Lippincott Co.
Zindel, Paul. *The Girl Who Wanted a Boy.* New York: Bantam Books.

Chapter 8: Immune System

Crichton, Michael. *Five Patients: The Hospital Explained.* New York: Avon Books.
Gunther, John. *Death Be Not Proud.* New York: Harper and Row.
Hoffman, Alice. *At Risk.* London: MacMillan.
Lipsyte, Robert. *The Contender.* New York: Harper.

Chapter 9: Alcohol, Tobacco, and Drugs

Abbey, Nancy and Ellen Wagman. *Say No to Alcohol.* Santa Cruz, CA: Network Publications.
Anonymous. *Go Ask Alice.* Englewood Cliffs, NJ: Prentice Hall.
Newman, Susan. *It Won't Happen to Me: True Stories of Teen Alcohol & Drug Abuse.* New York: Putnam.
Scott, Sharon. *How to Say No and Keep Your Friends, Peer Pressure Reversal.* Amherst, MA: Human Resource Development Press.
Ward, Brian. *Smoking and Health.* New York: Watts.

Appendix A

The metric system of measurement is used by scientists throughout the world. It is based on units of ten. Each unit is ten times larger or ten times smaller than the next unit. The most commonly used units of the metric system are given below. After you have finished reading about the metric system, try to put it to use. How tall are you in metrics? What is your mass? What is your normal body temperature in degrees Celsius?

Commonly Used Metric Units

Length   The distance from one point to another

meter (m)	A meter is slightly longer than a yard.
	1 meter = 1000 millimeters (mm)
	1 meter = 100 centimeters (cm)
	1000 meters = 1 kilometer (km)

Volume   The amount of space an object takes up

liter (L)	A liter is slightly more than a quart.
	1 liter = 1000 milliliters (mL)

Mass   The amount of matter in an object

gram (g)	A gram has a mass equal to about one paper clip.
	1000 grams = 1 kilogram (kg)

Temperature   The measure of hotness or coldness

degrees	0°C = freezing point of water
Celsius (°C)	100°C = boiling point of water

Metric–English Equivalents

2.54 centimeters (cm) = 1 inch (in.)
1 meter (m) = 39.37 inches (in.)
1 kilometer (km) = 0.62 miles (mi)
1 liter (L) = 1.06 quarts (qt)
250 milliliters (mL) = 1 cup (c)
1 kilogram (kg) = 2.2 pounds (lb)
28.3 grams (g) = 1 ounce (oz)
°C = 5/9 x (°F – 32)

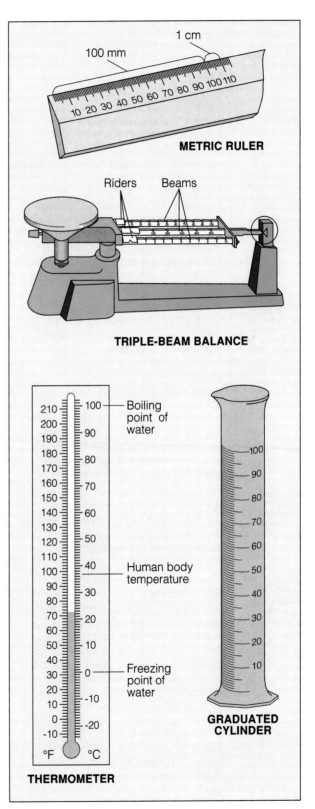

METRIC RULER

Riders   Beams

TRIPLE-BEAM BALANCE

Boiling point of water

Human body temperature

Freezing point of water

THERMOMETER

GRADUATED CYLINDER

Glassware Safety

1. Whenever you see this symbol, you will know that you are working with glassware that can easily be broken. Take particular care to handle such glassware safely. And never use broken or chipped glassware.
2. Never heat glassware that is not thoroughly dry. Never pick up any glassware unless you are sure it is not hot. If it is hot, use heat-resistant gloves.
3. Always clean glassware thoroughly before putting it away.

Fire Safety

1. Whenever you see this symbol, you will know that you are working with fire. Never use any source of fire without wearing safety goggles.
2. Never heat anything—particularly chemicals—unless instructed to do so.
3. Never heat anything in a closed container.
4. Never reach across a flame.
5. Always use a clamp, tongs, or heat-resistant gloves to handle hot objects.
6. Always maintain a clean work area, particularly when using a flame.

Heat Safety

Whenever you see this symbol, you will know that you should put on heat-resistant gloves to avoid burning your hands.

Chemical Safety

1. Whenever you see this symbol, you will know that you are working with chemicals that could be hazardous.
2. Never smell any chemical directly from its container. Always use your hand to waft some of the odors from the top of the container toward your nose—and only when instructed to do so.
3. Never mix chemicals unless instructed to do so.
4. Never touch or taste any chemical unless instructed to do so.
5. Keep all lids closed when chemicals are not in use. Dispose of all chemicals as instructed by your teacher.

6. Immediately rinse with water any chemicals, particularly acids, that get on your skin and clothes. Then notify your teacher.

Eye and Face Safety

1. Whenever you see this symbol, you will know that you are performing an experiment in which you must take precautions to protect your eyes and face by wearing safety goggles.
2. When you are heating a test tube or bottle, always point it away from you and others. Chemicals can splash or boil out of a heated test tube.

Sharp Instrument Safety

1. Whenever you see this symbol, you will know that you are working with a sharp instrument.
2. Always use single-edged razors; double-edged razors are too dangerous.
3. Handle any sharp instrument with extreme care. Never cut any material toward you; always cut away from you.
4. Immediately notify your teacher if your skin is cut.

Electrical Safety

1. Whenever you see this symbol, you will know that you are using electricity in the laboratory.
2. Never use long extension cords to plug in any electrical device. Do not plug too many appliances into one socket or you may overload the socket and cause a fire.
3. Never touch an electrical appliance or outlet with wet hands.

Animal Safety

1. Whenever you see this symbol, you will know that you are working with live animals.
2. Do not cause pain, discomfort, or injury to an animal.
3. Follow your teacher's directions when handling animals. Wash your hands thoroughly after handling animals or their cages.

One of the first things a scientist learns is that working in the laboratory can be an exciting experience. But the laboratory can also be quite dangerous if proper safety rules are not followed at all times. To prepare yourself for a safe year in the laboratory, read over the following safety rules. Then read them a second time. Make sure you understand each rule. If you do not, ask your teacher to explain any rules you are unsure of.

Dress Code

1. Many materials in the laboratory can cause eye injury. To protect yourself from possible injury, wear safety goggles whenever you are working with chemicals, burners, or any substance that might get into your eyes. Never wear contact lenses in the laboratory.

2. Wear a laboratory apron or coat whenever you are working with chemicals or heated substances.

3. Tie back long hair to keep it away from any chemicals, burners and candles, or other laboratory equipment.

4. Remove or tie back any article of clothing or jewelry that can hang down and touch chemicals and flames.

General Safety Rules

5. Read all directions for an experiment several times. Follow the directions exactly as they are written. If you are in doubt about any part of the experiment, ask your teacher for assistance.

6. Never perform activities that are not authorized by your teacher. Obtain permission before "experimenting" on your own.

7. Never handle any equipment unless you have specific permission.

8. Take extreme care not to spill any material in the laboratory. If a spill occurs, immediately ask your teacher about the proper cleanup procedure. Never simply pour chemicals or other substances into the sink or trash container.

9. Never eat in the laboratory.

10. Wash your hands before and after each experiment.

First Aid

11. Immediately report all accidents, no matter how minor, to your teacher.

12. Learn what to do in case of specific accidents, such as getting acid in your eyes or on your skin. (Rinse acids from your body with lots of water.)

13. Become aware of the location of the first-aid kit. But your teacher should administer any required first aid due to injury. Or your teacher may send you to the school nurse or call a physician.

14. Know where and how to report an accident or fire. Find out the location of the fire extinguisher, phone, and fire alarm. Keep a list of important phone numbers—such as the fire department and the school nurse—near the phone. Immediately report any fires to your teacher.

Heating and Fire Safety

15. Again, never use a heat source, such as a candle or burner, without wearing safety goggles.

16. Never heat a chemical you are not instructed to heat. A chemical that is harmless when cool may be dangerous when heated.

17. Maintain a clean work area and keep all materials away from flames.

18. Never reach across a flame.

19. Make sure you know how to light a Bunsen burner. (Your teacher will demonstrate the proper procedure for lighting a burner.) If the flame leaps out of a burner toward you, immediately turn off the gas. Do not touch the burner. It may be hot. And never leave a lighted burner unattended!

20. When heating a test tube or bottle, always point it away from you and others. Chemicals can splash or boil out of a heated test tube.

21. Never heat a liquid in a closed container. The expanding gases produced may blow the container apart, injuring you or others.

22. Before picking up a container that has been heated, first hold the back of your hand near it. If you can feel the heat on the back of your hand, the container may be too hot to handle. Use a clamp or tongs when handling hot containers.

Using Chemicals Safely

23. Never mix chemicals for the "fun of it." You might produce a dangerous, possibly explosive substance.

24. Never touch, taste, or smell a chemical unless you are instructed by your teacher to do so. Many chemicals are poisonous. If you are instructed to note the fumes in an experiment, gently wave your hand over the opening of a container and direct the fumes toward your nose. Do not inhale the fumes directly from the container.

25. Use only those chemicals needed in the activity. Keep all lids closed when a chemical is not being used. Notify your teacher whenever chemicals are spilled.

26. Dispose of all chemicals as instructed by your teacher. To avoid contamination, never return chemicals to their original containers.

27. Be extra careful when working with acids or bases. Pour such chemicals over the sink, not over your workbench.

28. When diluting an acid, pour the acid into water. Never pour water into an acid.

29. Immediately rinse with water any acids that get on your skin or clothing. Then notify your teacher of any acid spill.

Using Glassware Safely

30. Never force glass tubing into a rubber stopper. A turning motion and lubricant will be helpful when inserting glass tubing into rubber stoppers or rubber tubing. Your teacher will demonstrate the proper way to insert glass tubing.

31. Never heat glassware that is not thoroughly dry. Use a wire screen to protect glassware from any flame.

32. Keep in mind that hot glassware will not appear hot. Never pick up glassware without first checking to see if it is hot. See #22.

33. If you are instructed to cut glass tubing, fire-polish the ends immediately to remove sharp edges.

34. Never use broken or chipped glassware. If glassware breaks, notify your teacher and dispose of the glassware in the proper trash container.

35. Never eat or drink from laboratory glassware. Thoroughly clean glassware before putting it away.

Using Sharp Instruments

36. Handle scalpels or razor blades with extreme care. Never cut material toward you; cut away from you.

37. Immediately notify your teacher if you cut your skin when working in the laboratory.

Animal Safety

38. No experiments that will cause pain, discomfort, or harm to mammals, birds, reptiles, fishes, and amphibians should be done in the classroom or at home.

39. Animals should be handled only if necessary. If an animal is excited or frightened, pregnant, feeding, or with its young, special handling is required.

40. Your teacher will instruct you as to how to handle each animal species that may be brought into the classroom.

41. Clean your hands thoroughly after handling animals or the cage containing animals.

End-of-Experiment Rules

42. After an experiment has been completed, clean up your work area and return all equipment to its proper place.

43. Wash your hands after every experiment.

44. Turn off all burners before leaving the laboratory. Check that the gas line leading to the burner is off as well.

Glossary

Pronunciation Key

When difficult names or terms first appear in the text, they are respelled to aid pronunciation. A syllable in SMALL CAPITAL LETTERS receives the most stress. The key below lists the letters used for respelling. It includes examples of words using each sound and shows how the words would be respelled.

Symbol	Example	Respelling
a	hat	(hat)
ay	pay, late	(pay), (layt)
ah	star, hot	(stahr), (haht)
ai	air, dare	(air), (dair)
aw	law, all	(law), (awl)
eh	met	(meht)
ee	bee, eat	(bee), (eet)
er	learn, sir, fur	(lern), (ser), (fer)
ih	fit	(fiht)
igh	mile, sigh	(mighl), (sigh)
oh	no	(noh)
oi	soil, boy	(soil), (boi)
oo	root, tule	(root), (rool)
or	born, door	(born), (dor)
ow	plow, out	(plow), (owt)

Symbol	Example	Respelling
u	put, book	(put), (buk)
uh	fun	(fuhn)
yoo	few, use	(fyoo), (yooz)
ch	chill, reach	(chihl), (reech)
g	go, dig	(goh), (dihg)
j	jet, gently, bridge	(jeht), (JEHNT-lee), (brihj)
k	kite, cup	(kight), (kuhp)
ks	mix	(mihks)
kw	quick	(kwihk)
ng	bring	(brihng)
s	say, cent	(say), (sehnt)
sh	she, crash	(shee), (krash)
th	three	(three)
y	yet, onion	(yeht), (UHN-yuhn)
z	zip, always	(zihp), (AWL-wayz)
zh	treasure	(TREH-zher)

active immunity: immunity in which a person's own immune system responds to the presence of an antigen

adolescence: stage of development that begins at age 13 and ends at age 20

adrenal: endocrine gland on top of each kidney that produces the hormone adrenaline

adulthood: stage of development that begins at age 20 and lasts the rest of a person's life

AIDS: Acquired Immune Deficiency Syndrome; disease in which certain cells of the immune system are killed by a virus called HIV

alcoholism: incurable disease in which a person is physically and psychologically dependent on alcohol

allergy: reaction that occurs when the body is overly sensitive to certain substances called allergens

alveolus (al-VEE-uh-luhs): grapelike clusters of round sacs in the lungs; site of gas exchange

amino acid: building block of protein

amniotic (am-nee-AHT-ihk) **sac:** fluid-filled sac that cushions and protects the developing baby

antibody: protein produced by the immune system in response to an antigen

antigen: invading organism or substance that triggers the action of an antibody

anus: opening at the end of the rectum through which solid wastes are eliminated

artery: blood vessel that carries blood away from the heart

atherosclerosis (ath-er-oh-skluh-ROH-sihs): thickening of the inner wall of an artery

atrium (AY-tree-uhm): upper heart chamber

axon: taillike fiber that carries messages away from the cell body

bone: structure that makes up the body's skeleton

brain: main control center of the central nervous system

bronchus (BRAHNG-kuhs): tube that branches off from the trachea and enters the lung

Calorie: amount of energy needed to raise the temperature of 1 kilogram of water by 1 degree Celsius

cancer: noninfectious disease in which the body's own cells multiply uncontrollably

capillary: tiny, thin-walled blood vessel that connects an artery to a vein

capsule: cup-shaped part of the nephron

carbohydrate: energy-rich nutrient found in foods such as vegetables and grain products

cardiac muscle: muscle tissue found only in the heart

cardiovascular (kahr-dee-oh-VAS-kyoo-ler) **disease:** disease that affects the heart and blood vessels

cartilage: dense, fibrous, flexible connective tissue

cell: building block of living things

cell body: largest part of the neuron, which contains the nucleus

cerebellum (ser-uh-BEHL-uhm): part of the brain that controls balance and coordinates muscle activity

cerebrum (SER-uh-bruhm): largest part of the brain; controls the senses, thought, and conscious activity

childhood: stage of development that begins at about 2 years of age and continues until the age of 13

cochlea (KAHK-lee-uh): snail-shaped tube in the inner ear from which nerve impulses are carried to the brain

cornea: transparent protective covering of the eye

dendrite: threadlike structure in the neuron that carries messages to the cell body

depressant: substance that slows down the actions of the brain and spinal cord

dermis: bottom layer of the skin

diabetes mellitus (digh-uh-BEET-eez muh-LIGHT-uhs): noninfectious disease in which the body either secretes too little insulin or is not able to use the insulin that is does secrete

diaphragm (DIGH-uh-fram): dome-shaped muscle that aids in breathing

disease: sickness or illness

dislocation: injury in which a bone is forced out of its joint

drug: substance that has an effect on the body

drug abuse: deliberate misuse of a drug for a use other than a medical one

eardrum: membrane in the ear that vibrates when struck by sound waves

effector: muscle cell or gland cell that is stimulated by a motor neuron

egg: female sex cell; ovum

embryo (EHM-bree-oh): developing baby from the second to the eighth week of development

enzyme: chemical substance that helps control chemical reactions

epidermis: top layer of the skin

epiglottis (ehp-uh-GLAHT-ihs): small flap of tissue that closes over the trachea (windpipe)

esophagus (ih-SAHF-uh-guhs): tube that carries food to the stomach

excretion: process by which wastes are removed from the body

Fallopian (fuh-LOH-pee-uhn) **tube:** structure through which an egg travels from the ovary to the uterus; oviduct

fat: nutrient that supplies the body with energy and also helps support and cushion the vital organs in the body

fertilization: process by which a sperm nucleus and an egg nucleus join

fetus (FEET-uhs): developing baby from the eighth week to birth

fibrin (FIGH-brihn): chemical that forms a net across cut in a blood vessel to trap blood cells and plasma

fracture: break in a bone

hallucinogen (huh-LOO-sih-nuh-jehn): illegal drug that alters an abuser's view of reality

hemoglobin (HEE-muh-gloh-bihn): iron-containing protein found in red blood cells

homeostasis (hoh-mee-oh-STAY-sihs): process by which the delicate balance between the activities occurring inside the body and those occurring outside is maintained

hormone (HOR-mohn): chemical messenger produced by an endocrine gland

hypertension: high blood pressure

hypothalamus (high-poh-THAL-uh-muhs): endocrine gland at base of brain that provides a link between the nervous system and the endocrine system

immunity (im-MYOON-ih-tee): resistance to a disease-causing organism or a harmful substance

infancy: stage of development that lasts from 1 month to about 2 years of age

infectious (ihn-FEHK-shuhs) **disease:** disease transmitted by disease-causing microorganisms

inflammatory (ihn-FLAM-uh-tor-ee) **response:** body's second line of defense against invading organisms, in which fluid and white blood cells leak from blood vessels into tissues

inhalant: drug that is inhaled

interferon: substance produced by body cells when they are attacked by viruses

interneuron: type of neuron that connects sensory and motor neurons

iris: circular, colored portion of the eye

islets (IGH-lihts) **of Langerhans** (LAHNG-er-hahns): small group of cells in the pancreas that produce the hormones insulin and glucagon

joint: place where two bones meet

kidney: main excretory organ

large intestine: organ in the digestive system in which water is absorbed and undigested food is stored

larynx (LAR-ihngks): voice box; organ that contains the vocal cords

lens: part of the eye that focuses light rays coming into the eye

ligament: connective tissue that holds bones together

liver: organ that produces bile

lung: main respiratory organ

marijuana: illegal drug that is made from the leaves and flowers of the Indian hemp plant

marrow: soft material found within bone

medulla (mih-DUHL-uh): part of the brain that controls involuntary actions

menstrual (MEHN-struhl) **cycle:** monthly cycle of change that occurs in the female reproductive system

mineral: nutrient that helps maintain the normal functioning of the body

motor neuron: type of neuron that carries messages from the brain and spinal cord to an effector

negative-feedback mechanism: mechanism by which the production of a hormone is controlled by the amount of another hormone

nephron (NEHF-rahn): microscopic chemical filtering factory in the kidneys

nerve impulse: electrical and chemical signals that travel across a neuron

neuron: nerve cell

noninfectious disease: disease not caused by disease-causing microorganisms

nose: organ through which air enters the respiratory system

nutrient (NOO-tree-ehnt): usable portion of food

opiate: pain-killing drug produced from the opium poppy

organ: group of different tissues that have a specific job

organ system: group of organs that work together to perform a specific job

ovary (OH-vuh-ree): endocrine gland that produces female hormones; female sex gland

ovulation (ahv-yoo-LAY-shuhn): process by which the follicle in the ovary releases the egg

pancreas (PAN-kree-uhs): organ that produces pancreatic juice and insulin

parathyroid: endocrine gland embedded in the thyroid that produces a hormone which controls the level of calcium in the blood

passive immunity: immunity that is gotten from another source

pepsin: enzyme produced by the stomach that digests proteins

peristalsis (per-uh-STAHL-sihs): waves of muscular contractions that move food through the digestive system

physical dependence: effect of drug abuse that occurs when the body becomes used to a drug and needs it to function normally

pituitary (pih-TOO-uh-ter-ee): endocrine gland located below the hypothalamus that controls many body processes

placenta (pluh-SEHN-tuh): structure through which a developing baby receives food and oxygen from its mother

plasma: fluid portion of the blood

platelet: cell fragment that aids in blood clotting

protein: nutrient that is used to build and repair body parts; made of amino acids

psychological (SIGH-kuh-lahj-ih-kuhl) **dependence:** effect of drug abuse in which a person has a strong desire or need to continue using a drug

ptyalin (TIGH-uh-lihn): enzyme in saliva that breaks down some starches into sugars

puberty (PYOO-ber-tee): beginning of adolescence

pupil: small opening in the middle of the eye

receptor: special cell that receives information from its surroundings

rectum: end of the large intestine

red blood cell: cell that carries oxygen throughout the body

reflex: simple response to a stimulus

respiration: energy-releasing process that is fueled by oxygen

retina (REHT-'n-uh): inner layer of the eye on which an image is focused; contains the light-sensitive rods and cones

rheumatoid (ROO-muh-toid) **arthritis:** disabling disease that affects the skin, lungs, and joints

semicircular canal: tiny canal in inner ear that is responsible for the sense of balance

sensory neuron: type of neuron that carries messages from the receptors to the brain or spinal cord

skeletal muscle: muscle tissue that is attached to bone and moves the skeleton

skin: outer covering of the body

small intestine: digestive organ in which most digestion takes place

smooth muscle: muscle tissue responsible for involuntary movement

sperm: male sex cell

spinal cord: provides the link between the brain and the rest of the body

sprain: injury in which ligaments are torn or stretched

stimulant: substance that speeds up the actions of the brain and spinal cord

stimulus: change in the environment

stomach: J-shaped digestive organ that connects the esophagus to the small intestine

synapse (SIHN-aps): tiny gap between two neurons

tendon: connective tissue that attaches bone to muscle

testis (TEHS-tihs): endocrine gland that produces male hormones; male sex gland

thymus (THIGH-muhs): endocrine gland that is responsible for the development of the immune system

thyroid: endocrine gland located in the neck that produces a hormone which controls how quickly food is burned up

tissue: group of similar cells that perform the same function

tolerance: effect of drug abuse in which the body needs increasingly larger amounts of the drug to get the same effect that was originally produced

trachea: windpipe; carries air from the nose to the lungs

umbilical (uhm-BIHL-ih-kuhl) **cord:** cordlike structure that connects the fetus to the placenta

ureter (yoo-REET-er): tube that carries urine from a kidney to the urinary bladder

urethra (yoo-REE-thruh): tube through which urine leaves the body

urinary bladder: muscular sac that stores urine

uterus (YOOT-er-uhs): pear-shaped organ in which a fertilized egg develops into a child; womb

vaccination (vak-sih-NAY-shuhn): process by which an antigen is deliberately introduced to stimulate the immune system

vein: blood vessel that carries blood to the heart

ventricle: lower heart chamber

villus (VIHL-uhs): fingerlike structure that lines the small intestine through which food is absorbed into the bloodstream

vitamin: nutrient that helps regulate growth and normal body functioning

vocal cord: fold of tissue stretched across the larynx that vibrates with the movement of air to form sounds

white blood cell: cell that defends the body against invading organisms

withdrawal: stopping the use of a drug

zygote (ZIGH-goht): fertilized egg

Index

ABO blood group, H94
Absorbing cells, H17–18
Absorption of food
  large intestine, H70
  small intestine, H69
Active immunity, H198–199
  vaccination, H198–199
Adam's apple, H112
Adolescence, H182–183
  growth during, H183
  puberty, H183
Adrenal gland, H157, H159
Adrenaline, H159
Adulthood, H183–184
  aging in, H183–184
Adult-onset diabetes, H208
Afterbirth, H180–181
Aging, H183–184
AIDS, H201–202
  and HIV infection, H201–202
  transmission of, H202
Alateen, H222
Alcohol
  alcoholism, H221–222
  breath analysis, H222
  as depressant, H220
  effects on body, H219–221
  health problems from, H221
Alcoholics Anonymous, H221–222
Allergies, H200–201
  and antibodies, H201
  histamines, H201
  treatment for, H201
Alveoli, H114
Amino acids, H54
  essential amino acids, H54
  and liver, H121
Amphetamines, H228
Amyl nitrite, H226
Animals, and transmission of disease,
  H204
Antibodies, H195–197
  and allergies, H201
  antigens, H195, H196
  function of, H89–90
  and passive immunity, H199
  production of, H196–197
  shape of, H196
Antigens, H195–196
Anus, H70
Aorta, H85–86
Appendix, H69
  appendicitis, H69
Arteries, H85–87
  aorta, H85–86
  and blood flow, H85
  function of, H85
Artificial intelligence, H154
Artificial joints, H44
Assembly cells, H18
Atherosclerosis, H96–99
  and bypass surgery, H97, H99
  cause of, H96
  and diet, H97
  effects of, H97
Atrium, H83–84

Autonomic nervous system, H143–144
  functions of, H143
  types of nerves of, H143–144
Axon, H134–135

Bacterial disease, H205
  tetanus, H205
Balance, and ear, H150–151
Ball-and-socket joint, H35–36
Barbiturates, H227–228
B-cells, H196–197
Bile, H121
  and digestion, H68
Birth process, H180–181
  afterbirth, H180–181
  labor, H180
Blood
  circulation of, H82–88
  components of, H88
  as connective tissue, H19
  plasma, H89–90
  platelets, H92–93
  red blood cells, H90–91
  white blood cells, H91–92
Blood clotting, H90
  and platelets, H93
Blood groups, H93–95
  ABO blood group, H94
  discovery of, H93
  importance of, H94
  and proteins in blood, H93–94
  Rh blood group, H95
  and transfusions, H94
Blood pressure
  hypertension, H100
  instrument for measurement of, H99
  nature of, H99
Blood vessels, H80
Bones, H30, H32–34
  composition of, H33–34
  as connective tissue, H19
  development of, H32
  dislocation, H43–44
  fractures, H43
  functions of, H31
  marrow, H34
  spongy bone, H34
  treatment of bone injuries, H44
Brain, H139–141
  cerebellum, H141
  cerebrum, H139–141
  medulla, H141
  protection of, H139
Breath analysis, alcohol, H222
Breathing
  diaphragm, H115–116
  measurement of exhaled air, H126
  process of, H115–116
  See also Respiratory system.
Bronchi, H113
Bronchitis, H224
Butyl nitrite, H226
Bypass surgery, and atherosclerosis,
  H97, H99

Calcium, H58
Calories, H53–54
Cancer, H206–208
  cause of, H207
  development of, H206
  early detection of, H207
  treatments for, H207–208
Capillaries, H87
  function of, H87
Capsule, kidneys, H120
Carbohydrates, H55–56
  starches, H55
  sugars, H55–56
Carbon dioxide, and respiration,
  H84–85, H114–115
Cardiac muscle, H40
Cardiosphygmometer, H117
Cardiovascular disease
  atherosclerosis, H96–99
  hypertension, H99–100
Cartilage
  and bone development, H32
  functions of, H32
Cell body, H134
Cells, H16–18
Central nervous system, H138–143
  brain, H139–141
  spinal cord, H141–142
Cerebellum, H141
Cerebrum, H139–141
Cervix, H173
Chemical messengers, H90
  and circulatory system, H81
  See also Hormones.
Chemotherapy, cancer treatment,
  H207
Chicken pox, H205
Childhood, growth during, H182
Cholera, H204
Chromosomes, and inherited traits,
  H170
Cigarette smoking. See Tobacco.
Cilia, and protection from disease,
  H193
Circulatory system
  arteries, H85–87
  blood vessels, H80
  capillaries, H87
  and chemical messengers, H81
  and cigarette smoking, H224–225
  and disease-fighting cells, H81
  functions of, H80–81
  heart, H80, H82–85
  and hormones, H156
  movement of blood in, H82–88
  and oxygen transport, H80–81
  veins, H88
Cirrhosis, H221
Cocaine, H228
Cochlea, H150
Codeine, H230
Colds, H204–205
Complete proteins, H54
Cones, in retina, H147

Connective tissue, H19
Cornea, H145–146
Crack, H228–229

Dendrites, neurons, H134
Denis, Jean-Baptiste, H93
Dependence, physical and
   psychological, H218
Depressants, H227–228
   alcohol as, H220
   types of, H227–228
Dermis, H122, H193
Developmental stages
   adolescence, H182–183
   adulthood, H183–184
   after birth, 180–181
   childhood, H182
   infancy, H181–182
   prenatal development, H177–180
Diabetes mellitus, H159, H208
Diaphragm, and respiration, H115–116
Diet, and atherosclerosis, H97
Digestive system
   absorption of food, H69–70
   esophagus, H65
   function of, H61
   and liver, H68
   mouth, H62–64
   and pancreas, H68
   small intestine, H67–68
   stomach, H66
Disease
   infectious disease, H203–206
   noninfectious disease, H206–208
Dislocation, of bones, H43–44
Driving while intoxicated (DWI), H220
Drug abuse, H217–219
   and dependence, H218
   depressants, H227–228
   hallucinogens, H230
   inhalants, H226
   marijuana, H229–230
   most commonly abused drugs, chart
      of, H227
   opiates, H230–231
   stimulants, H228–229
   and tolerance, H217–218
   and withdrawal, H218–219
Drugs
   definition of, H216
   drug misuse, H216–217
   over-the-counter drugs, H216
   prescription drugs, H216

Ear
   and balance, H150–151
   cochlea, H150
   eardrum, H149–150
   semicircular canals, H150
Ecology, H209
Effectors, H135, H142
Egg, human
   fertilization of, H169
   as zygote, H177
Electrical current
   and bone growth, H45
   to heal fractures, H44
   of heart, H101
   osteoporosis treatment, 45
Electrocardiogram (ECG), H101
Embryo, H170

Emphysema, H224
Endocrine glands, H155–160
   adrenal gland, H159
   glands/hormones, chart of, H157
   hormones, H155–156
   hypothalamus, H156, H158
   ovaries, H160
   pancreas, H159–160
   parathyroid glands, H159
   pituitary gland, H158
   testes, H160
   thymus, H158
   thyroid gland, H158–159
Endocrine system
   endocrine glands, H155–160
   negative-feedback mechanism,
      H160–161
Enzymes
   function of, H18, H67
   of mouth, H62–63, H67
   of pancreas, H67
   of small intestine, H67
   of stomach, H66, H67
   types of digestive enzymes, H67
Epidemics, H203
Epidermis, H122, H193
Epiglottis, H111
   and swallowing, H64
Esophagus, H65
Estrogen, H173
Excretion, definition of, H118
Excretory system
   function of, H118
   kidneys, H118–121
   liver, H121
   skin, H122–125
Exercise, and health, H71
Exocrine glands, H156
Eye, H145–147
   cornea, H145–146
   eyeball, H145
   iris, H146
   lens, H146–147
   pupil, H146
   retina, H147
   sclera, H145

Fallopian tubes, H172
Farsightedness, H148
Fat
   and body weight, H71–72
   as connective tissue, H19
Fats, dietary, H56
   digestion of, H68
   oils as, H56
   sources of, H56
Fat-soluble vitamins, H57
Female reproductive system, H172–176
   cervix, H173
   eggs, H173
   Fallopian tubes, H172
   menstrual cycle, H174–176
   ovaries, H172
   uterus, H172–173
   vagina, H173
Femur, composition of, H33–34
Fertilization of egg
   and menstrual cycle, H175–176
   process of, H169
Fetus, H178–179
Fingerprints, H122–123

Food
   absorption of food, H69–70
   calories, H53–54
   and digestion, H61
   importance of, H52–53
   information from food labels,
      H60–61
   nutrients, H53, H54–59
   See also Digestive system.
Food poisoning, H204
Fractures, H43
   treatment of, H44

Gallbladder, and bile, H68
Galvanometer, H117
Gas exchange, in lungs, H114–115
Glands
   endocrine glands, H155–160
   exocrine glands, H156
Glucagon, H160
Glucose, H159
Glue sniffing, H226
Glycogen, H159

Hair, H123
Hallucinogens, H230
   LSD, H230
   PCP, H230
Health
   and exercise, H71
   and weight control, H71–72
Hearing, H149–151
   process of, H149–150
   See also Ear.
Heart, H80, H82–85
   aorta, H85–86
   circulation of blood, H84–86
   and electrocardiogram (ECG),
      H101
   heartbeat, H82–83
   left atrium, H85
   left ventricle, H85
   muscle tissue, H19
   as organ, H21
   pacemaker, H83
   right atrium, H83–84
   right ventricle, H84
   size of, H82
Heat transfer, methods of, H73
Hemoglobin, H58, H121
   and red blood cells, H91
Hepatitis, H204
Heroin, H230
Hinge joint, H36
Histamines, H201
HIV infection, and AIDS,
   H201–202
Homeostasis, definition of, H15
Hormones, H155–156
   and circulatory system, H156
   functions of, H155
   and negative feedback, H161
   produced by bacteria, H156
   and sexual development, H171
Human body
   homeostasis, H15
   levels of organization, H15–21
Hydrochloric acid, and digestion, H66
Hypertension, H99–100
   treatment of, H100
Hypothalamus, H156, H158

Immune disorders
  AIDS, H201–202
  allergies, H200–201
Immune system
  antibodies, H195–197
  first line of defense, H192–193
  functions of, H192
  inflammatory response, H195
  second line of defense, H194–195
  third line of defense, H195–197
  and thymus, H157
Immunity
  active immunity, H198–199
  definition of, H197
  passive immunity, H199
Incomplete proteins, H54
Infancy, H181–183
Infectious disease, H203–206
  bacterial disease, H205
  definition of, H203
  epidemics, H203
  transmission of, H203–204
  viral diseases, H205
Inflammatory response, H195
  and white blood cells, H195
Influenza, H205
Inhalants, H226
Inherited traits, and chromosomes,
  H170
Insulin, H68, H159–160
  and diabetes mellitus, H208
  functions of, H159–160
  production of, H160
Interferon, and viral infection, H195
Interneurons, H135
Iris, H146
Iron, and hemoglobin, H91
Islets of Langerhans, H160

Joints, H34–36
  artificial joints, H44
  ball-and-socket joint, H35–36
  functions of, H35
  hinge joint, H36
  pivot joint, H35
Juvenile-onset diabetes, H208

Kidneys, H118–121
  capsule, H120
  filtering process in, H119–120
  functions of, H118
  nephrons, H119–120
  and urine, H120–121

Labor, birth process, H180
Landsteiner, Karl, H93–94
Language development, H182
Large intestine
  absorption of food, H70
  and digestion, H70
Larynx, H112
Lens, of eye, H146–147
Levels of organization, H15–21
  cells, H16–18
  organs, H21
  organ systems, H21
  tissues, H18–20
Lie detector, H117
Ligaments, H30
  sprains, H43
Lister, Joseph, H191

Liver
  and digestion, H68
  and excretory function, H121
Living things, H15–16
Lockjaw, H205
LSD, H230
Lungs, H113–115
  alveoli, H114
  bronchi, H113
  and circulation of blood, H84–85
  gas exchange in, H114–115
Lyme disease, H204

Male reproductive system, H171–172
  sperm, H172
  testes, H171–172
Marijuana, H229–230
Marrow
  bones, H34
  and red blood cells, H90
  and white blood cells, H92
Measles, H205
Medulla, H141
Menopause, H184
Menstrual cycle, H174–176
  and fertilization of egg, H175–176
  menstruation, H176
  ovulation, H175
  purposes of, H174
Menstruation, H176, H183
Minerals, H57–58
  functions of, H58
  types of, H58
Monoclonal antibodies, in cancer
  treatment, H207–208
Mononucleosis, H205
Morphine, H230
Motor neurons, H135
Mouth, H62–64
  and digestion, H62–64
  enzymes of, H67
  and protection from disease, H193
  saliva, H62–63
  swallowing, H64
  teeth, H63
  tongue, H63–64
Mucus, and protection from disease,
  H193
Multicellular organisms, H15–16
Muscle cells, H18
Muscles
  cardiac muscle, H40
  contraction of, H41–42
  skeletal muscle, H38–39
  smooth muscle, H39–40
  types of injuries to, H43–44
Muscle tissue, H19

Nails, H123
Nearsightedness, H148
Negative-feedback mechanism, of
  endocrine system, H160–161
Nephrons, H119–120
Nerve impulse, H136–137
  chemical signals for, H137
  path of, H136
  synapse, H136–137
Nerve tissue, H19
Nervous system
  central nervous system, H138–143
  functions of, H132–133

nerve impulse, H136–137
neurons, H134–135
peripheral nervous system,
  H143–144
Neurons, H134–135
  characteristics of, H134–135
  interneurons, H135
  motor neurons, H135
  sensory neurons, H135
Nitrous oxide, H226
Noninfectious disease, H206–208
  cancer, H206–208
  causes of, H206
  diabetes mellitus, H208
Nose
  and respiration, H110
  and smell, H151
  and taste, H152
Nutrients, H53, H54–59
  carbohydrates, H55–56
  fats, H56
  minerals, H57–58
  proteins, H54
  vitamins, H57
  water, H59

Oils, as fat, H56
Opiates, H230–231
Opium, H230
Organs, H21
Organ systems, H21
  types of, H22
Osteoporosis, treatment with electrical
  current, H45
Ovaries, H160, H172
  hormones of, H157, H173
Over-the-counter drugs, H216
Ovulation, H175
Oxygen
  oxygenation of blood, H84–85
  and respiration, H114–115
  transport and circulatory system,
    H80–81

Pacemaker, heart, H83
Pacific yew trees, cancer treatment
  from, H209
Pancreas, H159–160
  cells of, H18
  and digestion, H68
  enzymes of, H67
  hormones of, H157
  insulin, H68, H159–160
  islets of Langerhans, H160
  pancreatic juice, H68
Parathyroid glands, H159
  function of, H159
  hormones of, H157
Paregoric, H230
Passive immunity, H199
  and antibodies, H199
  methods of, H199
Passive smoking, H225
PCP, H230
Pepsin, and digestion, H66
Peripheral nervous system, H143–144
Peristalsis, esophagus, H65
Perspiration, H124–125
Photocopying machines, H185
Physical dependence, H218
Pituitary gland, H157, H158

Pivot joint, H35
Placenta, H177–178
Plasma, H89–90
Plastics, for artificial body parts, H23
Platelets, H92–93
Pneumogram, H117
Prenatal development, H177–180
Prescription drugs, H216
Proteins, H54
Psychological dependence, H218
Ptyalin, and digestion, H62–63
Puberty, H183
Pulse rate, measurement of, H102
Pupil, of eye, H146

Rabies, H204
Radiation therapy, in cancer treatment, H207
Reaction time, measurement of, H149
Receptors, H135
Rectum, H70
Red blood cells, H90–91
Reflexes, H142
Reproduction, fertilization of egg, H169
Reproductive glands, H160
Reproductive system
    female reproductive system, H172–176
    function of, H169
    glands of, H160
    male reproductive system, H171–172
    sexual development, H169–171
Respiration, process of, H108–109, H115–116
Respiratory system
    and cigarette smoking, H224–225
    function of, H109
    lungs, H113–115
    nose, H110
    protection from disease, H193
    throat, H110–111
    trachea, H111–113
Retina, H147
    rods and cones, H147
Rh blood group, H95
Rocky Mountain spotted fever, H204
Rods, in retina, H147

Saliva
    and digestion, H62–63
    and protection from disease, H193
Salivary glands, H156
Sclera, H145
Semen, H172
Semicircular canals, H150
Sense receptors, H151, H152
Senses
    functions of, H144
    hearing, H149–151
    smell, H151
    taste, H151–152
    touch, H152–153
    vision, H145–148
Sensory neurons, H135
Sexual development, H169–171
    and hormones, H171
Sexually transmitted disease, H203
    See also AIDS.

Skeletal muscle, H38–39
    actions of, H40–42
Skeletal system
    bones, H32–34
    functions of, H30–31
    joints, H34–36
    parts of, H31
    types of injuries to, H43–44
Skin
    dermis, H122
    epidermis, H122
    as epithelial tissue, H20
    excretory function, H124–125
    perspiration, H124–125
    protection from disease, H193
    sweat and oil glands, H123–124
Small intestine, H67
    absorption of food, H69
    cells of, H17–18
    and digestion, H67–68
    enzymes of, H67
    villi, H69
Smell, sense of, H151
Smooth muscles, H39–40
    and swallowing, H64, H65
Sperm
    fertilization of egg, H169, H175
    parts of, H172
    production of, H172
Sphygmomanometer, H99–100
Spinal cord, H141–142
Spleen, and red blood cells, H91
Spongy bone, H34
Sprains, H43
Starches, H55
Stimulants, H228–229
Stimulus, H133, H142
Stomach, H66–67
Sugar, H55–56
    and insulin, H159–160
    sources of, H55
Surgery, in cancer treatment, H207
Swallowing
    process of, H64
    and smooth muscles, H64, H65
Sweat glands, H123, 124, H156
Synapse, H136–137

Taste
    sense of, H151–152
    taste buds, H64
    types of tastes, H64
Taxol, H209
T-cells, H196
    and HIV infection, H201
Teeth, and digestion, H63
Tendons, H30
    sprains, H43
Testes, H157, H160, H171–172
Testosterone, H172
Tetanus, H205
Thermogram, H13
Thirst, H125
Throat
    epiglottis, H111
    and respiration, H110–111
Thymus, H157, H158
Thyroid gland, H157–159
Thyroid-stimulating hormone, H161
Thyroxine, H161
Tissues, H18–20

connective tissue, H19
    definition of, H18
    epithelial tissue, H20
    muscle tissue, H19
    nerve tissue, H19
Tobacco
    effects on body, H224
    health problems from, H224–225
    passive smoking, H225
    Surgeon General reports, H223, 225
Tolerance, and drug abuse, H217–218
Tongue, and taste, H63–64
Touch, H152–153
Trachea, H111–113
Tranquilizers, H227
Transfusions
    and blood groups, H94
    to fetus, H179–180
Typhoid, H204

Umbilical cord, and prenatal development, H178–179
Unicellular organisms, H15
Ureters, H120–121
Urethra, H121
Urinary bladder, H121
Urine, passage in body, H120–121
Uterus, H172–173

Vaccination, H198–199
    booster shots, H199
Vagina, H173
Vegetarians, H54
Veins, H88
Ventricle
    left, H85
    right, H84
Vertebrae, H31
Vertebral column, H31
Villi, in small intestine, H69
Viral infection, H205
    and interferon, H195
Vision, H145–148
    farsightedness, H148
    nearsightedness, H148
    role of brain in, H145, H147
    See also Eye.
Vitamins, H57
    fat-soluble vitamins, H57
    vitamin deficiency disease, H58
    water-soluble vitamins, H57–58
Vitreous humor, H147
Vocal cords, H112–113
Voice production, H112–113

Water, H59
Water-soluble vitamins, H57–58
Weight control, and health, H71–72
Weiner, Alexander, H95
White blood cells, H91–92
    B-cells, H196–197
    function of, H92
    and inflammatory response, H195
    production of, H92
    T-cells, H196
Windpipe, and swallowing, H64
    See also Trachea.
Withdrawal, and drug abuse, H218–219

Zygote, H177

Credits

Cover Background: Ken Karp
Photo Research: Natalie Goldstein
Contributing Artists: Warren Budd Assoc., Ltd.; Fran Milner; Function Thru Form
Photographs: **4** left: Calvin Larsen/Photo Researchers, Inc.; right: Mary Kate Denny/Photoedit; **5** left: Lee Wardle/Sports File; center: Obremski/Image Bank; right: Dan McCoy/Rainbow; **6** top: Bill Longcore/Photo Researchers, Inc.; center: A. Upitis/Image Bank; bottom left: Granger Collection; bottom right: USDA; **7** top: Stuart Franklin/Sygma; center: Art Siegel; bottom: David Madison/Duomo Photography, Inc.; **8** top: Lefever/Grushow/Grant Heilman Photography; center: Index Stock Photography, Inc.; bottom: Rex Joseph; **10** top: David Madison Photography; bottom: Chris Jones/Stock Market; **11** David Madison/Duomo Photography, Inc.; **12** and **13** Dr. R. P. Clark & M. Goff/Science Photo Library/Photo Researchers, Inc.; **14** Richard Hutchings/Photoedit; **16** left: M. P. Kahl/DRK Photo; right: David Phillips/Visuals Unlimited; **17** top: Dwight Kuhn Photography; bottom: Michael Webb/Visuals Unlimited; **18** Alfred Pasieka/Science Photo Library/Photo Researchers, Inc.; **19** Veronika Burmeister/Visuals Unlimited; **20** top left: Bruce Iverson/Visuals Unlimited; top right: Cabisco/Visuals Unlimited; center: Robert E. Daemmrich/Tony Stone Worldwide/Chicago Ltd.; bottom left: Dwight Kuhn Photography; bottom right: Don Fawcett/Visuals Unlimited; **23** top left, right, and bottom left: Dan McCoy/Rainbow; **27** Tony Duffy/Allsport; **28** and **29** Leonard Kamsler; **30** Seltzer/OSU/Dan McCoy/Rainbow; **31** Tom McHugh/Photo Researchers, Inc.; **32** Biophoto Associates/Photo Researchers, Inc.; **33** Prof. Aaron Polliack/Science Photo Library/Photo Researchers, Inc.; **34** From TISSUES AND ORGANS: A TEXT-ATLAS OF SCANNING ELECTRON MICROSCOPY by Richard G. Kessel and Randy H. Kardon. Copyright © 1979 by W. H. Freeman and Company. Reprinted by permission.; **35** top left: © Lennart Nilsson, BEHOLD MAN, Little, Brown and Company; top right: © Lennart Nilsson, THE INCREDIBLE MACHINE, National Geographic Society; bottom: Dan McCoy/Rainbow; **36** Tim Davis/David Madison Photography; **38** top left: Dwight Kuhn Photography; bottom left: Steven J. Krasemann/DRK Photo; bottom right: Brooks Dodge/Sports File; **40** left: Eric Grave/Photo Researchers, Inc.; center: Triarch/Visuals Unlimited; right: Michael Abbey/Photo Researchers, Inc.; **41** Ken Karp; **43** Bruce Curtis/Peter Arnold, Inc.; **44** left: Photo Researchers, Inc.; right: Princess Margaret Rose Orthopaedic Hospital/Science Photo Library/Photo Researchers, Inc.; **45** right and bottom: © Lennart Nilsson, THE INCREDIBLE MACHINE, National Geographic Society; **49** left and right: Biophoto Associates/Science Source/Photo Researchers, Inc.; **50** and **51** NASA; **52** top and bottom: USDA; **53** top left: Tony Freeman/Photoedit; top right: Myrleen Ferguson/Photoedit; bottom left: David Young-Wolff/Photoedit; bottom right: Don & Pat Valenti/F/Stop Pictures, Inc.; **54** CNRI/Science Photo Library/Photo Researchers, Inc.; **56** top left: L. Morris/Photoquest, Inc.; top right: Wolfgang Kaehler; bottom: Kristen Brochmann/Fundamental Photographs; **59** left: Guido Alberto Rossi/Image Bank; right: A. Upitis/Image Bank; **63** Howard Sochurek Inc.; **64** top left and bottom: © Lennart Nilsson, BEHOLD MAN, Little, Brown and Company; top right: Omikron/Science Source/Photo Researchers, Inc.; **65** L. V. Bergman & Associates; **66** top and bottom: Lennart Nilsson, THE INCREDIBLE MACHINE, National Geographic Society, © Boehringer Ingelheim International GmbH; **69** © Lennart Nilsson, THE INCREDIBLE MACHINE, National Geographic Society; **70** top and bottom left: L. V. Bergman & Associates; bottom right: © Lennart Nilsson, THE INCREDIBLE MACHINE, National Geographic Society; **71** John McGrail; **72** top: Tony Duffy/Allsport; bottom: Robert Rathe/Folio, Inc.; **73** Derik Murray/Image Bank; **77** Nancy Coplon; **78** and **79** David Wagner/Phototake; **80** CNRI/Science Photo Library/Photo Researchers, Inc.; **82** Lennart Nilsson, THE INCREDIBLE MACHINE, National Geographic Society, © Boehringer Ingelheim Internationl GmbH; **84** top: Philippe Plailly/Science Photo Library/Photo Researchers, Inc.; bottom: VU/SIU/Visuals Unlimited; **86** R. G Kessel and R. H. Kardon; **87** © Lennart Nilsson, BEHOLD MAN, Little, Brown and Company; **90** top: NIBSC/Science Photo Library/Photo Researchers, Inc.; bottom left: Lennart Nilsson, THE INCREDIBLE MACHINE, National Geographic Society, © Boehringer Ingelheim International GmbH; bottom right: Bill Longcore/Photo Researchers, Inc.; **91** top: © Lennart Nilsson, THE INCREDIBLE MACHINE, National Geographic Society; bottom left: CNRI/Science Photo Library/Photo Researchers, Inc.; bottom right: Lennart Nilsson, THE INCREDIBLE MACHINE, National Geographic Society, © Boehringer Ingelheim International GmbH; **92** Lennart Nilsson, THE INCREDIBLE MACHINE, National Geographic Society, © Boehringer Ingelheim International GmbH; **94** © Lennart Nilsson, THE INCREDIBLE MACHINE, National Geographic Society; **96** and **97** Lennart Nilsson, THE INCREDIBLE MACHINE, National Geographic Society, © Boehringer Ingelheim International GmbH; **99** Alexander Tsiaras/Science Source/Photo Researchers, Inc.; **101** Simon Fraser, Hexham General/Science Photo Library/Photo Researchers, Inc.; **102** Ken Karp; **105** Dan McCoy/Rainbow; **106** and **107** Tim Davis/Duomo Photography, Inc.; **108** left: Michael Fogden/DRK Photo; right: Peter Veit/DRK Photo; **110** top: Art Siegel; bottom: Lennart Nilsson, THE INCREDIBLE MACHINE, National Geographic Society, © Boehringer Ingelheim International GmbH; **111** Chet Childs/Tony Stone Worldwide/Chicago Ltd.; **112** top and bottom: Dr. G. Paul Moore; **113** left: Jack Vartoogian; right: Myrleen Ferguson/Photoedit; **114** © Lennart Nilsson, THE INCREDIBLE MACHINE, National Geographic Society; **115** CNRI/Science Photo Library/Photo Researchers, Inc.; **116** top: Paul J. Sutton/Duomo Photography, Inc.; bottom: NASA; **119** L. V. Bergman & Associates; **120** CNRI/Science Photo Library/Photo Researchers, Inc.; **121** top: © Lennart Nilsson, THE INCREDIBLE MACHINE, National Geographic Society; bottom: David York/Medichrome/The Stock Shop; **123** left: Veronika Burmeister/Visuals Unlimited; right: Obremski/Image Bank; **124** top left: P. Bartholomew/Gamma-Liaison, Inc; top right: Biophoto/Photo Researchers, Inc.; bottom: © Lennart Nilsson, BEHOLD MAN, Little, Brown and Company; **125** Eric Reynolds/Adventure Photo; **130** and **131** Alan Goldsmith/Stock Market; **132** top: David Madison/Duomo Photography, Inc.; bottom left: Mary Kate Denny/Photoedit; bottom right: Bob Daemmrich Photography; **133** left: Johnny Johnson/DRK Photo; right: Bob Daemmrich/The Image Works; **134** Michael Abbey/Photo Researchers, Inc.; **135** © Lennart Nilsson, THE INCREDIBLE MACHINE, National Geographic Society; **136** CNRI/Science Photo Library/Photo Researchers, Inc.; **138** Bill Longcore/Photo Researchers, Inc.; **141** CNRI/Science Photo Library/Photo Researchers, Inc.; **142** © Lennart Nilsson, THE INCREDIBLE MACHINE, National Geographic Society; **145** left: Randy Trine/DRK Photo; right: Andrew McClenaghan/Science Photo Library/Photo Researchers, Inc.; **146** © Lennart Nilsson, BEHOLD MAN, Little, Brown and Company; **147** top: Jesse Simmons Photo; bottom left: © Lennart Nilsson, BEHOLD MAN, Little, Brown and Company; bottom right: © Lennart Nilsson, THE INCREDIBLE MACHINE, National Geographic Society; **149** © Lennart Nilsson, BEHOLD MAN, Little, Brown and Company; **150** top: © Lennart Nilsson, BEHOLD MAN, Little, Brown and Company; bottom: © Lennart Nilsson, THE INCREDIBLE MACHINE, National Geographic Society; **151** top left: John Zoiner/Stock Boston, Inc.; top right: Hank Morgan/Rainbow; bottom: Garry Gay/Image Bank; **152** top: © Lennart Nilsson, BEHOLD MAN, Little, Brown and Company; bottom: Nathan Benn/Woodfin Camp & Associates; **154** top: Synaptek Scientific Products, Inc./Science Photo Library/Photo Researchers, Inc.; bottom: © 1991 Bill Redic; **158** © Lennart Nilsson, THE INCREDIBLE MACHINE, National Geographic Society; **160** Martin M. Rotker; **166** and **167** Michael Tcherevkoff/Image Bank; **168** left: Animals Animals Stock/Animals Animals/Earth Scenes; right: David W. Hamilton/Image Bank; **169** top: John Giannicchi/Science Source/Photo Researchers, Inc.; bottom: Dr. G. Schatten/Science Photo Library/Photo Researchers, Inc.; **170** Dr. Ram Verna/Phototake; **172** Bob Daemmrich/The Image Works; **174** © Lennart Nilsson, THE INCREDIBLE MACHINE, National Geographic Society; **175** top left: © Lennart Nilsson, A CHILD IS BORN, Dell Publishing Company; top right: © Lennart Nilsson, BEHOLD MAN, Little, Brown and Company; bottom left and bottom right: © Lennart Nilsson, THE INCREDIBLE MACHINE, National Geographic Society; **179** Howard Sochurek Inc.; **180** Mickey Pfleger; **181** left: Niki Mareschal/Image Bank; center: Richard Hutchings/Photo Researchers, Inc.; right: Edward Lettau/FPG International; **182** top: Bob Daemmrich Photography; bottom: W. Rosin Malecki/Photoedit; **183** Bill Hess/National Geographic Magazine; right: Bob Daemmrich Photography; **184** left: Janeart Ltd./Image Bank; right: Don Hamerman/Folio, Inc.; **185** Karen Leeds/Stock Market; **190** and **191** Larry Mulvehill/Photo Researchers, Inc.; **192** left: K. G. Murti/Visuals Unlimited; right: © Lennart Nilsson, National Geographic Society; **193** top: © Lennart Nilsson, THE INCREDIBLE MACHINE, National Geographic Society; center and bottom: Lennart Nilsson, THE INCREDIBLE MACHINE, National Geographic Society © Boehringer Ingelheim International GmbH; **194** Lennart Nilsson, THE INCREDIBLE MACHINE, National Geographic Society, © Boehringer Ingelheim International GmbH; **195** Gabe Palmer/Stock Market; **196** top: E. D. Getzoff, J. A. Tainer, A. J. Olson of the Scripps Research Institute; bottom: Lennart Nilsson, National Geographic Society, © Boehringer Ingelheim International GmbH; **198** Bob Daemmrich/The Image Works; **200** top left: Manfred Kage/Peter Arnold, Inc.; top right: Robert Dudzic/F/Stop Pictures, Inc.; bottom left: Dick Canby/DRK Photo; bottom right: Dr. Jeremy Burgess/Science Photo Library/Photo Researchers, Inc.; **201** left: Lennart Nilsson, National Geographic Society, © Boehringer Ingelheim International GmbH; right: Stuart Franklin/Sygma; **202** top: Lennart Nilsson, National Geographic Society, © Boehringer Ingelheim International GmbH; bottom: Susan Van Etten/Photoedit; **203** left and right: CNRI/Science Photo Library/Photo Researchers, Inc.; **204** top left: Don Smetzer/Tony Stone Worldwide/Chicago Ltd.; top center: © Lennart Nilsson, THE INCREDIBLE MACHINE, National Geographic Society; top right: G. I. Bernard/Animals Animals/Earth Scenes; bottom: Dr. Willy Burgdorfer/Rocky Mountain Laboratories; **205** top: Lennart Nilsson, National Geographic Society, © Boehringer Ingelheim International GmbH; bottom: CNRI/Science Photo Library/Photo Researchers, Inc.; **206** top: © Lou Lainey/1984 Discover Publications; bottom: Lennart Nilsson, National Geographic Society, © Boehringer Ingelheim International GmbH; **207** Lennart Nilsson, National Geographic Society, © Boehringer Ingelheim International GmbH; **208** Lee Wardle/Sports File; **209** Tom & Pat Leeson/Photo Researchers, Inc.; **214** and **215** Bobby Holland/Reader's Digest Foundation; **216** left: Michael P. Gadomski/Photo Researchers, Inc.; right: Benn Mitchell/Image Bank; **217** top: The University Museum, University of Pennsylvania; bottom: Ken Karp; **218** left: Tony Savino/Sipa Press; right: Bruce Delis/Gamma-Liaison, Inc; **219** top: Richard Hutchings/Photo Researchers, Inc.; bottom: Granger Collection; **221** A. Glauberman/Science Source/Photo Researchers, Inc.; **222** Stacy Pick/Stock Boston, Inc.; **223** Richard Hutchings/Photo Researchers, Inc.; **224** Lennart Nilsson, THE INCREDIBLE MACHINE, National Geographic Society, © Boehringer Ingelheim International GmbH; **225** Calvin Larsen/Photo Researchers, Inc.; **226** Ken Karp; **228** top: Ken Karp; center: Edward S. Ross/Phototake; bottom: Howard Sochurek Inc.; **229** Fred Lombardi/Photo Researchers, Inc.; **230** David Alan Harvey/Woodfin Camp & Associates; **231** top left: Walter H. Hodge/Peter Arnold, Inc.; top right: Michael Hardy/Woodfin Camp & Associates; bottom: National Institutes of Health; **235** Wesley Bocxe/Photo Researchers, Inc.; **236** Grant Heilman/Grant Heilman Photography; **237** Centers for Disease Control; **239** UPI/Bettmann; **240** Charles Gupton/Stock Boston, Inc.; **242** Dr. Jack Ricci, Department of Orthopaedic Research, New Jersey Medical School; **244** Seltzer/OSU/Dan McCoy/Rainbow; **248** Dick Canby/DRK Photo; **253** Dwight Kuhn Photography